In memory of Philip W. Love,
father, reader and storyteller,
and fascinated observer of human events.

McDONALD'S

John F. Love

McDONALD'S

BEHIND
THE
ARCHES

Revised Edition

BANTAM BOOKS
NEW YORK · TORONTO · LONDON · SYDNEY · AUCKLAND

MCDONALD'S: BEHIND THE ARCHES
A Bantam Book

PUBLISHING HISTORY

Bantam hardcover edition/November 1986
Bantam revised trade paperback edition/August 1995

All photographs courtesy of McDonald's Corporation.

Book design by Barbara N. Cohen.

Library of Congress Cataloging-in-Publication Data

Love, John F.
 McDonald's : behind the arches / John F. Love. — Rev. ed.
   p.   cm.
 Includes index.
 ISBN 0-553-34759-4
 1. McDonald's Corporation.   2. Kroc, Ray, 1902–
 3. Restaurateurs—United States—Biography.   I. Title.
 TX945.5.M33L68   1995
 338.7′616479573—dc20   *95-11540*
                                                 CIP

ISBN 0-553-34759-4

Published simultaneously in the United States and Canada

Bantam Books are published by Bantam Books, a division of Bantam Doubleday Dell Publishing Group, Inc. Its trademark, consisting of the words "Bantam Books" and the portrayal of a rooster, is Registered in U.S. Patent and Trademark Office and in other countries. Marca Registrada. Bantam Books, 1540 Broad-way, New York, New York 10036.

PRINTED IN THE UNITED STATES OF AMERICA
BVG   0 9 8 7 6 5 4 3 2

Acknowledgments

This is not a corporate book, not the type of history that companies commission to commemorate some milestone. I am an independent journalist, and McDonald's Corporation had no editorial control over this work.

However, I could never have revealed the secrets of success of one of America's most visible but least understood corporations without obtaining its cooperation in the reporting process.

Rarely has a company revealed so much about itself to an outsider. That is particularly surprising for McDonald's, traditionally one of America's most secretive companies. Yet, when it comes to this book, no question went unanswered; no source was inaccessible. It has taken four and a half years and interviews with more than three hundred people inside and outside of McDonald's to complete the book, but this close-up view of McDonald's was only feasible because the company was willing to subject itself to such intensive scrutiny. I have Senior Chairman Fred Turner to thank for that.

I am also thankful to the many people who agreed to be interviewed and to share their personal experiences. The McDonald's System—its corporate executives, its franchisees, and its suppliers—is too broad and diverse to be explained merely through interviews with top executives. Thus this book tells the personal stories of dozens of individuals who are closely associated with the McDonald's System and who give us their unique perspectives on it.

Given the detailed reporting required, I could never have completed a project such as this without some special assistance from a number of people inside McDonald's. I benefited enormously from research provided by Ken Props, the eighty-three-year-old director of licensing. Ken is a walking encyclopedia on McDonald's, and I was fortunate that he was an open book to me—each week sending me additional historical data. My special thanks also to Helen Farrell and Gloria Nelson, who gathered and verified hundreds of facts, making this a more complete and current work. Interviewing so many sources would also have been a much more difficult task were it not for the assistance of Merne Bremner and Jan Woody, who located sources, helped arrange interviews, and opened doors to contacts who otherwise would not have been as receptive. Finally, I am indebted to Chuck Rubner of McDonald's, who coordinated the search for historical photographs.

This final version of the McDonald's history has been favorably influenced by Ann Poe, who read the initial manuscript and suggested revisions. Ann's enthusiasm for the McDonald's story gave me a boost at a critical point—when the first draft is done and the author is drained. She helped me see how much better the story would read if the first draft were trimmed considerably. However, I only listened to Ann's advice because I saw her commitment to the quality of the book.

But the greatest commitment came from my wife, JoAnn, who was told nearly five years ago that this would be a one-year project. As I held two jobs for nearly the next five years, JoAnn raised our children with too little help from me. She also supported me whenever the project got more involved—and more frustrating. More important, she prodded me to do what all journalists must do, however reluctantly, with a great story—finish it.

JOHN LOVE
November 1986

Contents

Foreword
THE UNKNOWN MCDONALD'S

Just outside Senior Chairman Fred Turner's former office on the eighth floor of McDonald's Plaza in Oak Brook, Illinois, the suburb west of Chicago where McDonald's Corporation is headquartered, there used to be a small circular conference room called the "war room." It was where top management meetings were held, and if the name seems pretentious, it depicts with remarkable accuracy how seriously this company plays the hamburger game.

There is little else pretentious about it. Like everything at McDonald's, the war room is strictly functional, even egalitarian. It has little more than a large circular table where corporate managers face one another as equals and freely debate policies. There is no mahogany furniture, no high-back leather chairs, and no expensive wood paneling. The room is devoid of any trappings that might be expected in the inner sanctum of an organization with annual worldwide sales of $24 billion and climbing.

Even the telephone is a Bell misfit, with one of those numbers that gets more than its share of misdialed calls. On one such occasion, Turner himself interrupts a meeting to take the call. "Hello, McDonald's," he answers. The caller is confused, and Turner clarifies: "No, you've called McDonald's Corporation." The caller still does not understand, and Turner persists with a final clarification: "We're the hamburger people."

Forget that the caller unwittingly has the chairman of the world's largest food service company on the line. The real puzzle is that he needs an explanation of what McDonald's is. This is the system that spends more than $1 billion a year promoting the most advertised

brand in the world. Its advertising spokesman—a clown named Ronald
—is as well recognized by American youngsters as Santa Claus. It has
more retail outlets than any other merchant in the United States. How
can anyone have trouble linking McDonald's to the "hamburger people"?

The caller can be forgiven. This type of call has been made to the
war room dozens of times before. More important, the hesitancy to link
the McDonald's hamburger to a major corporation is commonplace.
McDonald's is now perhaps the world's most recognized retail trademark, but the organization behind it is one of America's least understood corporations. The marketing image is fabled. The corporate
reality is unknown.

There are some good reasons for that. One is certainly the way the
company is covered by the press. While McDonald's is now America's
fourth largest retailer, the press is fascinated mostly with the company's
glossy exterior. When McDonald's opened its eight thousandth restaurant or served its fifty billionth hamburger—both of which it did in
1984—it made big news. But the strategies McDonald's uses to dominate the $200 billion food service industry in the United States never
get such attention.

Such trivial coverage cannot be attributed entirely to the fourth
estate. McDonald's itself has had a hand in promoting the lighter aspects of its business. From the beginning, it encouraged press reports
that focused on hamburger sales volumes. The McDonald brothers
started it in 1950 when they flashed their sales in neon on the sign in
front of their California drive-in. It read: "Over 1 million sold." Since
then, McDonald's has churned out numbers revealing how many times
the hamburgers it has sold would stretch to the moon and how many
times the Mississippi River bed could be filled by the ketchup it has
dispensed.

When McDonald's wasn't promoting such statistics, it was presenting itself through romantic, but often superficial, tales of its colorful and legendary founder, Ray A. Kroc. The story of McDonald's
became the story of its founder. In many minds, Kroc so embodied
his company's success that the corporate McDonald's lacked an
identity of its own. Indeed, McDonald's seems to prefer corporate
anonymity. Though anxious to promote its marketing image, McDonald's is secretive when it comes to its internal workings. Its executives eschew participation in trade shows, just as the company refuses
to join industry associations. And over the years, McDonald's corpo-

rate managers have been hesitant to grant interviews to the business press.

There is yet another reason why the inside of McDonald's remains a mystery. It is simply that the chain's exterior is now such a common feature of the American lifestyle that the organization behind it is taken for granted. Fully 96 percent of American consumers have eaten at one of its restaurants in the last year. Slightly more than half of the U.S. population lives within a three-minute drive to a McDonald's unit. In a typical television market, its brand is promoted through thirty television and radio advertising spots aired each day. It is as if McDonald's retail presence is so expected that its corporate presence and power go unnoticed. McDonald's is the closest thing America has to a retailing utility.

It is such an integral part of American culture that the competitive and economic significance of its more than 14,000 restaurants worldwide is rarely measured in a meaningful way. Everyone knows McDonald's is big, but very few know just how significant its impact on American business really is. A casual observer knows from reading the sign under the Golden Arches that McDonald's has served more than 100 billion hamburgers. But in an industry that has nearly 200,000 separate restaurant companies, how many would even guess that McDonald's captures 14 percent of all restaurant visits in the United States —one out of every six—and commands a 6.6 percent share of all dollars Americans spend on eating out? How many would know that it controls 18.3 percent of the $72 billion fast-food market in the United States—more than the next three chains combined? How many would suspect that McDonald's sells 34 percent of all hamburgers sold by commercial restaurants and 26 percent of all french fries? Those are figures that astound even George Rice, whose GDR/Crest Enterprises compiles such market share information. Says Rice, "Our first reaction to figures like that is to say, 'This does not compute.'"

Control of such market share has given McDonald's an impact on the food processing system in the United States that food processors themselves do not fully comprehend. With its staggering hamburger sales, McDonald's is the country's largest purchaser of beef. The chain serves up so many french fries that each year it purchases 5 percent of the entire U.S. potato crop harvested for food, and 2 percent of all the chicken. Because of those volumes and because of its insistence on product quality and consistency, McDonald's has wrought revolutionary changes in meat and potato processing.

It has such enormous purchasing power that the successful introduction of a new product into its system changes eating habits of most
Americans and in the process creates fortunes for certain food processors and growers. When the chain introduced the Egg McMuffin as the
first item on its breakfast menu in the early 1970s, English muffins were
big sellers only in certain regions of the country. By popularizing the
muffin nationwide, McDonald's helped create a major market segment
that has since grown twice as fast as the baking industry as a whole. Its
novel Chicken McNuggets had much the same type of impact when
they were introduced in 1982. Now, chicken nuggets are widely duplicated, and McDonald's—the hamburger king—has become the second largest purveyor of chicken (behind Kentucky Fried Chicken).

McDonald's impact is also evident in the competitive positions of
major companies in the food processing business. Consider the impact
on the soft drink business alone: McDonald's stores account for 5
percent of all Coca-Cola sold in the United States—whether through
fountains or in bottles and cans. And if McDonald's shifted to Pepsi-
Cola as the required cola for its stores, the Coke brand's eight percent-
age-point lead over the Pepsi brand would nearly be cut in half, and
Coke's better than two-to-one lead in fountain syrups would nearly be
eliminated.

McDonald's economic power as it relates to nonfood industries is
even less understood. It is likely that most real estate experts do not
realize that McDonald's in 1982 surpassed Sears as the world's largest
owner of retail real estate. In fact, it is the company's control of real
estate that explains why McDonald's profits so handsomely from its
industry-leading food volumes. Were it not for its real estate connection, McDonald's would never have become the financial powerhouse
of the food service business, one that has enjoyed an average return on
equity of 25.2 percent and an annual earnings growth of 24.1 percent
since becoming a public company in 1965. Yet, its financial performance is now so expected and predictable that its growth no longer
excites industry watchers. Perhaps only those who still hold the Mc-
Donald's stock they bought when the company went public two decades ago fully appreciate the chain's growth. Their initial investment
of $2,250 for 100 shares has grown through eleven stock splits and one
stock dividend to 37,180 shares worth more than $1 million on June 30,
1994.

But it is in the area of manpower that McDonald's influence on the
American economy is perhaps most overlooked. With more than

500,000 people on the payroll at any one time, the McDonald's System is easily one of the largest employers in the United States. Because the chain trains so many high school students for their first jobs, most of its workers quickly advance to higher-paying jobs, which explains why McDonald's turnover rate at the restaurant level has historically run better than 100 percent per year. But it also explains how McDonald's in its first thirty-seven years has employed about eight million American workers now in other jobs—fully 12.5 percent of the American work force has worked for McDonald's. One out of every fifteen American workers got his or her first job from McDonald's. And while most of those now work elsewhere, it was at McDonald's where they first learned about work routines, job discipline, and organizational teamwork. McDonald's by now has replaced the U.S. Army as the nation's largest job training organization.

Merely explaining the economic impact of McDonald's, however, does not begin to reveal the unknown McDonald's. It is the character of McDonald's—the people who run it and the way they operate—that is its most intriguing unknown. That is where the image of McDonald's conflicts so sharply with reality. Here is the most successful service company in a nation increasingly dependent on service industries, and we really do not know its secrets of success.

Those are buried under layers of often misleading images. By some accounts, the secrets of McDonald's are almost completely contained in Kroc's entrepreneurial spirit. However, while Kroc's contributions to the food service business were monumental, the Ray Kroc legend does not do justice to Kroc's genius. Kroc has long been portrayed as the dreamer who conceived of a whole new form of food service. Others have pictured him as a marketing maven who figured out how to sell hamburgers to the masses. Kroc is sometimes seen as the disciplinarian who treated his franchisees almost like children, regimenting them to conform to his rules. Above all, he is remembered as an omnipotent corporate founder, the font of all corporate wisdom. The perception is understandable. Even today, Ray Kroc's disciples in McDonald's are legion. Their reverence to his principles has no bounds.

Yet, when it comes to isolating the reasons for McDonald's success, the founder's legend misses the target. Kroc was a dreamer, but he did not dream up the fast-food invention and was not the first to discover the McDonald brothers who did. Nor was Kroc primarily a marketing expert. Every food product he thought of introducing—and the list is long—bombed in the marketplace. And while the founder was known for dressing down franchisees who permitted litter in their parking lots or who kept hamburgers in the serving bin too long, his creativity in franchising was not found in his regimentation of franchisees.

Few people outside McDonald's understand that Ray Kroc's brilliance is found in the way he selected and motivated his managers, his franchisees, and his suppliers. He had a knack for bringing out the best in people who worked with him. To be sure, Kroc's success with McDonald's is a story of his own entrepreneurship. But it is more. He succeeded on a grand scale because he had the wisdom and the courage to rely on hundreds of other entrepreneurs.

Kroc traveled light-years ahead of other franchisers of his day, but not by disciplining franchisees. Instead, he used franchising to unleash the power of operators who have an ownership stake in their businesses. Though he demanded adherence to strict operating standards, he also freed franchisees to market their service as they saw fit, and he motivated them by giving them an opportunity—unheard of in franchising—to become rich before he became rich. He made them fiercely competitive by creating the food service industry's most efficient supply system, a testimony to his own expertise in perfecting operating details. And because this supply system was built by relying exclusively on fledgling vendors of food and equipment, it became as entrepreneurial—and as loyal to McDonald's—as Kroc's franchisees were. All three elements of the McDonald's System—franchisees, corporate managers, and suppliers—represent more than 3,700 independent companies, and Kroc skillfully bonded them into one family with a common purpose.

But Kroc's management talents are best reflected in the type of organization he built to bring together all the elements of his system. Kroc was often considered the archetypical corporate founder who dominated his subordinates. In fact, he constructed a corporation of natively intelligent, fanatically aggressive, and extremely divergent personalities. The striking uniformity of McDonald's 14,000 restaurants creates the impression of a corporation with a centralized bureaucracy. Viewed from the outside, it is easy to assume that McDonald's is run by Ray Kroc clones.

Those on the inside know different. Kroc built franchising's most talented service organization not by dictating to his managers but by giving them enormous decision-making authority. From the beginning, his management team consisted of extremely diverse individuals, not the type of managers who typically survive in corporate bureaucracies. These were not organization persons, they were Kroc's version of corporate entrepreneurs.

Decisions at McDonald's have always been the product of individual initiative. Ideas are never homogenized by committees. New directions are the result of a continuous trial-and-error process, and new ideas spring from all corners of the system. The key ingredient in Kroc's management formula is a willingness to risk failure and to admit mistakes. James Kuhn, a former vice president and a twenty-year veteran of McDonald's, graphically described the disparity between the image and the reality of McDonald's management: "We have a public image of being slick, professional, and knowledgeable marketers who also happen to be plastic and shallow. In fact, we are a bunch of motivated people who shoot off a lot of cannons, and they don't all land on target. We've made a lot of mistakes, but it is the mistakes that make our success, because we have learned from them. We are impulsive, we try to move faster than we can, but we are also masters at cleaning up our own messes."

The fundamental secret to McDonald's success is the way it achieves uniformity and allegiance to an operating regimen without sacrificing the strengths of American individualism and diversity. McDonald's manages to mix conformity with creativity.

The dichotomy is evident in the way the three elements of the McDonald's System—its franchisees, managers, and suppliers—relate to one another. All are entrepreneurs in their own right. None is the other's master. Ray Kroc's greatest accomplishment is that he found a way to make them mesh in an extremely productive manner. It is unfortunate that the very hero worship that surrounds Kroc as the founder of McDonald's depicts him inaccurately as the wellspring of all of its attributes. The unknown McDonald's is not the expression of a single man. Indeed, it is not even a single company. It is a federation of hundreds of independent entities connected by an intricate web of partnerships.

The participants of the system have common economic incentives and a common standard of quality, service, and cleanliness. But nothing else about them is the same. Nor is there any structure to their relationship. "You never know who is really in charge of anything at McDonald's," observes Ted Perlman, a longtime supplier. "There is no organization chart there." That lack of structure can be traced to Kroc, who had a habit of picking new ideas from anyone who offered them. What counted was not where the idea came from but whether it worked. And because the system still places such a premium on individual performance, McDonald's remains surprisingly entrepreneurial despite its formidable size.

While individuals within the system are driven by entrepreneurial self-interest, selfish interests never prevail. The entities in McDonald's are so diverse and power is so fragmented that the system has no master. A large part of the real strength of McDonald's can be attributed to the fact that the relationship between the corporation's managers, its 3,500 franchisees, and the system's 500-plus suppliers is one based on a concept of checks and balances. The meticulous store inspections the company uses to enforce operating disciplines are well known. What is not known is the power franchisees have in checking the excesses of corporate managers. Supplier relationships are built on similar principles: Vendors are not outsiders but part of the family, every bit as responsible for preserving McDonald's quality as franchisees and managers are.

The history of the McDonald's System is the story of an organization that learned how to harness the power of entrepreneurs—not several but hundreds of them. It is run by decisions and policies considered to be for the common good. But the definition of *common good* is not set by a chief executive or by a management committee. Rather, it is the product of the interaction between all the players. Ray Kroc's genius was building a system that requires all of its members to follow corporate-like rules but at the same time rewards them for expressing their individual creativity. In essence, the history of McDonald's is a case study on managing entrepreneurs in a corporate setting.

At a time when some American corporations are looking to emulate their foreign rivals, the story of McDonald's reminds us that businesses can still succeed—beyond their creator's wildest dreams—by relying on typically American traits. This is not merely a corporate history, because McDonald's is not strictly a corporate success story. Rather it is the story of the company that changed the eating habits of Americans, that revolutionized the food service and processing industries of the United States, and that legitimized the now widespread practice of franchising. It is the story of the unknown McDonald's, America's first modern entrepreneurial success—a system that bridges the gap between entrepreneurs and corporations.

Chapter 1

YES, THERE IS A McDONALD

"Over the years, I have received letters and phone calls from television stations, radio stations, authors, reporters, et cetera, and they all told me the same story. It seems that if they contact your company in Oak Brook regarding my present address, they have been told that the company has no idea where I live or if I am even alive. On several occasions they have been told that there really was *never a McDonald.* They were told McDonald's was only a fictitious name that was chosen because it was easy to remember."

Richard J. McDonald wrote this in a letter shortly after McDonald's announced that it would close the McDonald's unit that Ray Kroc had built in 1955 in Des Plaines, a suburb northwest of Chicago. The announcement drew protests from local history buffs who proposed converting the store into a museum (which McDonald's did), and newspapers around the country carried the story of the closing of the "original" McDonald's. If those stories mentioned the McDonald brothers at all, it was only by way of explaining the common notion that Kroc had gotten little more from them than their name. Kroc, everyone accepted, built the first McDonald's.

Somehow, the two brothers whose name adorns 14,000 McDonald's restaurants have been all but washed out of the McDonald's legend. In an age of mass media, the first one to mass market a new product is credited as its inventor. So, it is not surprising that Kroc, who founded the company that took the fast-food concept to the masses, is celebrated as the creator of the self-service, quick-service restaurant. It is not surprising, but it is not accurate.

Ray Kroc did not invent fast food. He did not invent the self-service restaurant. And *his* first McDonald's restaurant was not *the* first McDonald's. The credit for those firsts properly belongs to the brothers McDonald, Richard and his older brother Maurice, more intimately known as Dick and Mac. They were inventors who had the vision but lacked the drive and organizational skills needed to capitalize on their invention. How they discovered the fast-food concept provides fascinating insight on the process of invention. How they failed to develop it is the key to understanding what Ray Kroc brought to the party.

The McDonald brothers were not restaurant men by training or background, and in the tradition-bound food service business, that may have been something of a prerequisite to igniting a revolution in the trade. Restaurants are typically family businesses, and industry traditions are passed down through families established in the business.

The brothers were not bound by such traditions. They were not long out of high school when they left their native New Hampshire and moved to California in 1930 in search of a new opportunity—anything that promised a better fate than had befallen their father. A foreman in a shoe factory, the Depression had taken away the only job he ever had. The shoe factories and cotton mills of New Hampshire were closing, and California offered a fresh start in new trades.

Not surprisingly, the McDonalds looked for the obvious opportunity first—in Hollywood. They landed jobs pushing sets around for Hollywood movies, primarily one-reelers of slapstick comedian Ben Turpin. Intrigued with the potential of a brand-new industry, the brothers opened a movie theater in Glendale. But in four years of operation, they never made enough money to pay the $100 monthly rent on the theater, and only regular concessions from the landlord kept them in business. But the brothers never ceased looking for better entry-level business opportunities, and they found it in the form of a new service that was taking California by storm—the drive-in restaurant.

The year was 1937, and already Californians were beginning to develop their extraordinary dependence on the automobile. Some independent operators in southern California were just beginning to capitalize on the trend by building restaurants that catered to the drive-in customer. The idea was not completely novel. As early as the 1920s, some restaurants in the East had developed a so-called curb service, where waitresses delivered sandwiches and drinks to customers parked on the street in front of the restaurant. But by the mid-1930s,

California operators took the idea one step further. Instead of treating it as a sideline, they made the motorized trade the central feature of their business. Large and accessible parking lots replaced the tiny curb service area, and full-time carhops were hired to serve customers in their automobiles.

By most accounts, the first carhop drive-in, called the Pig Stand, opened in 1932 on the corner of Sunset and Vermont in Hollywood. As its name implies, it specialized in barbecued pork sandwiches. It was quickly followed by larger drive-ins, such as Carpenter's, generally considered the first of many drive-in chains to take root in Los Angeles. Founded by Charles and Harry Carpenter in the mid-1930s, it catered exclusively to customers in cars. The Carpenters even produced training films for carhops. At about the same time, Sydney Hoedemaker, a well-known Los Angeles restaurateur, opened his Herbert's drive-ins, adding credibility to the new segment of the restaurant business otherwise populated by maverick operators who had no previous experience in food service.

In just a few years, California became a land of carhop drive-ins, and the new breed of restaurateurs who ran them quickly became the industry's most innovative operators. They experimented with everything. In their drive to speed up service, nothing was sacrosanct. Carhops on foot led to carhops on roller skates. Soon customers were placing their orders using novel speaker phones located at each parking stall.

The drive-ins were also experimenting with new and different food products tailored for their carryout trade. When members of a local band that routinely ate a midnight snack at Bob Wian's drive-in in Glendale complained about their steady diet of hamburgers, Wian concocted a sandwich that looked more like a meal—two hamburger patties topped with "the works" and served on a triple-decker bun. It was so good that Wian put it on his menu; and before he knew it, traffic was jammed around his Bob's Pantry drive-in as customers lined up to try the sandwich, which had become a local sensation. In 1937, Wian decided to rename his drive-in after the new product—Bob's, Home of the Big Boy. Within a few years, Wian had built a small California chain of drive-ins around his Big Boy sandwich, and by the early 1940s he was using it as a vehicle to export California's carhop drive-in phenomenon throughout the United States. Fully a decade before fast-food franchising developed, Wian began selling Big Boy franchises to Gene

Kilburg and Ben Marcus (Marc's) in Milwaukee, Dave Frisch in Cincinnati, the Elias brothers in Detroit, and Alex Schoenbaum (Shoney's) in Nashville as well as to a half dozen other drive-in operators.

Thus, when the McDonald brothers opened their tiny drive-in just east of Pasadena in 1937, they stumbled onto the cutting edge of the food service business and into the company of operators who were fascinated with speed of service and carryout service and who were only a few years away from franchising. Though clearly in the carhop drive-in family, the first McDonald's was a modest effort, even by drive-in standards. While Dick and Mac cooked the hot dogs (not hamburgers), mixed the shakes, and waited on customers seated on a dozen canopy-covered stools, three carhops served patrons parked in the lot.

This led to the much grander drive-in that the McDonalds opened in 1940 at Fourteenth and E streets in San Bernardino, about fifty miles east of Los Angeles. An erstwhile orange grove capital and onetime center of Seventh Day Adventism, San Bernardino in the 1940s was becoming a working-class boomtown, and one of the chief beneficiaries was the McDonald's drive-in.

No one would have suspected from looking at it that this would be the birthplace of a new generation of restaurants. With just six hundred square feet of space, it was a fraction of the size of the more fashionable drive-ins in Los Angeles. It had a strange shape for a restaurant—octagonal—and the slightly slanted, roof-to-counter windows that ran around the front half of the building violated a basic rule of restaurant design by exposing the entire kitchen to the public. There was no inside seating, but several stools were placed on the outside along the side counter. The exterior walls below the counter were made of stainless steel.

But it was nothing if not an attention-getter, and by the mid-1940s it was the town's number one teenage hangout. A staff of twenty carhops served the 125 cars crowded into the lot on weekend evenings. The brothers' twenty-five-item menu featured beef and pork sandwiches and ribs that were cooked in a barbecue pit stocked with hickory chips that the McDonalds had delivered from Arkansas. If the drive-in looked strange by food service standards, its cash register spoke a language all restaurateurs understood: annual sales regularly topped $200,000.

Their tiny drive-in had catapulted the McDonalds into the ranks of San Bernardino's newly rich. Each year the brothers split $50,000 in profits, and they suddenly found themselves on a social par with the local establishment—the Guthrie family, which published the *Daily Sun;* the Stater brothers, who ran the largest supermarket chain; and the Harrises, who owned the big department store. They even moved into one of the city's largest houses, a $90,000, twenty-five-room mansion atop a hill just northeast of town.

Despite their new wealth, the brothers remained uncomplicated men with simple pursuits. Their leisure activities seldom ranged beyond dining out or catching the local boxing matches. Since both men refused to fly, they rarely traveled far from home. They prided themselves on being the first in town to purchase the new-model Cadillacs, and each year the local dealer waited eagerly to take their old cars in trade. Selling a used Cadillac with five thousand miles on it was the closest thing there was in the car business to coining money.

By 1948, the McDonalds had achieved greater wealth than they had dreamed was possible a decade earlier when they built a tiny hamburger stand with borrowed lumber. They had but one problem. Recalls Dick McDonald: "We just became bored. The money was coming in, and there wasn't much for us to do."

But the McDonald brothers were beginning to feel some competitive pressure. When they had opened at Fourteenth and E streets, theirs was the only drive-in in town, but by 1948 there were imitators. That alone would not have been troublesome had the market for the conventional drive-in continued to broaden beyond high schoolers. Unfortunately, it did not. The moment carhop drive-ins became teenage meccas, they turned off a much broader family market. Competition for such a limited customer base became destructive, and though the McDonald's operation was still the market leader, the brothers nonetheless felt the pinch.

More important, Dick and Mac discovered that the drive-in concept they had helped to pioneer had serious economic flaws. Drive-ins had become identified as a source of low-priced food and yet were burdened by an increasingly high-cost, labor-intensive format. They were being clobbered by turnover rates in their work force. They found themselves competing with the newer drive-ins for carhops almost as much as they were for customers. And if they didn't lose them to competitors, they lost them to higher-paying jobs in other industries that were fueling California's booming economy. Thanks in part to their teenage clientele, the turnover of eating utensils was as bad as the turnover of carhops. Paying the tab to replace stolen or broken flatware ran counter to their New England thrift ethic. The brothers longed for a less complicated operation without the annoyances of unreliable carhops and the leather-jacketed customers they attracted.

Bothered by such trends, the brothers nearly decided to sell their drive-in and open a different hamburger restaurant in one of the new strip shopping centers that would soon spread throughout America's burgeoning suburbs. There, the brothers could be free of the problems of carhops and all the other headaches of drive-ins. The new restaurant was to be called The Dimer, because everything on its limited menu of mostly soft drinks, french fries, and hamburgers would sell for either one dime or two. The McDonalds even planned to polish dimes every morning and give them out as change. "We thought that every time someone pulled a shiny dime from their pocket, they'd think of The Dimer," McDonald recalls.

But just before they were about to execute their plan, the brothers reacted to the risks inherent in a venture that took them beyond their relatively limited expertise. Their only experience with food service was with drive-ins, and with drive-ins they would stay. Still, they did something that very few owners of small businesses dare to do once they have become established—they decided to revamp entirely their existing operation. By studying their sales receipts for the previous three years, they found that fully 80 percent of their business was generated by hamburgers. They could no longer justify the attention they lavished on their barbeque pit, not to mention the money they spent on newspaper and radio ads to plug their barbecued fare. "The more we hammered away at the barbeque business, the more hamburgers we sold," Dick recalls.

The discovery led to a complete overhaul of the McDonald's drive-in—and the beginning of a revolution in food service. Like other drive-in operators, the McDonalds had been grappling with ways to increase volume by improving speed. Now they decided to make speed the essence of their business. "Our whole concept was based on speed, lower prices, and volume," says McDonald. "We were going after big, big volumes by lowering prices and by having the customer serve himself. My God, the carhops were slow. We'd say to ourselves that there had to be a faster way. The cars were jamming up the lot. Customers weren't demanding it, but our intuition told us that they would like speed. Everything was moving faster. The supermarkets and dime stores had already converted to self-service, and it was obvious the future of drive-ins was self-service."

The brothers responded to their "intuition" by closing their lucrative business for three months in the fall of 1948. Their twenty carhops were fired, and the two service windows where the carhops filled their orders were changed to service windows where customers could place their own orders. The kitchen was rearranged to facilitate speed and volume production. The only grill, a standard three-footer, was replaced by two six-foot grills that the brothers had custom designed by a Los Angeles kitchen equipment supplier. Paper bags, wrappers, and cups replaced the china and flatware, which eliminated the need for the dishwasher. And the menu was slashed from twenty-five items to just nine: a hamburger, a cheeseburger, three soft drink flavors in one twelve-ounce size, milk, coffee, potato chips, and a slice of pie. The size of the hamburger was cut from eight to the pound to ten to the pound, but the price was slashed even more—from a competitive 30 cents to an unheard-of 15 cents. The brothers refused to let even the choice of condiments impede their fast-food format. All hamburgers were prepared with ketchup, mustard, onions, and two pickles. Any order deviating from that was penalized by a delay in service. That not only allowed the McDonalds to streamline their production techniques, it opened the way for preparing food in advance of the order. That was a major break from conventional food service practices, but the brothers believed it was vital to their concept of volume through speed. "If we gave people a choice," explains McDonald, "there would be chaos."

When the McDonalds reopened the drive-in in December, they installed a sign featuring a miniature animated chef named Speedee, but their new "Speedee Service System" did not come close to producing the volume increases the brothers were counting on. In fact, their business fell to 20 percent the preconversion level. "The carhops we fired would come in and heckle us about getting their uniforms ready," McDonald recalls. "Even the old customers would ask us when we were going back to the old system."

The brothers decided to hang on, and their patience was amply rewarded. Within six months, their drive-in business began recovering, partly from the addition of milk shakes and french fried potatoes. But the real recovery was provided by the new type of customers the drive-in began attracting. With the carhops gone, McDonald's lost a good bit of its teenage appeal. But it also lost its image as a hangout, which gave it newfound appeal to a much bigger segment: families. Working-class families could finally afford to feed their kids restaurant food. Since the octagonal building was all window from the roof to the counter, the food preparation system itself became an attraction. Kids were fascinated by their first glimpse of a commercial kitchen. The "fishbowl" design, as McDonald's later dubbed it, was also a selling tool to convince a skeptical adult market that lower prices did not translate into lower quality. "We were selling a 15-cent hamburger, and at first customers naturally thought that was cheap in more ways than one," McDonald explains. "But when they saw our kitchen, it opened their eyes. There was a spotless grill and all that shining stainless steel, and they could see that our hamburger was the nicest meat you could find."

Nevertheless, it was clear from the start that the new format had a special appeal to the children. Art Bender, the first counterman in the remodeled store, recalls that the very first fast-food customer was a nine-year-old girl who bought a bag of hamburgers to take home for dinner. The first purchase was prophetic, and in time the kids came in droves to the one restaurant where they could place their own orders. "The kids loved coming to the counter," Bender observes. "They would come with two bits in their fists and order a hamburger and a Coke. They could still see Mama in the car, but they also could feel independent. Pretty soon, it sinks in that this is great for the business; this is important."

The importance of it lay in the potential for attracting adults by appealing to kids. That was not lost on the McDonalds. Immediately, the brothers adapted their marketing to their new market. Advertising highlighted the family appeal of McDonald's, and promotions featured giveaways to children. At the same time, McDonald's countermen were carefully instructed to be extra attentive to young customers.

In little more than a year, McDonald's drive-in regained all the business it had lost following the conversion. But the extraordinary volumes the brothers wanted did not come until Dick and Mac began doing to the antiquated restaurant trade what Henry Ford had done to machine assembly. In an industry that prided itself on extremely personalized procedures, the brothers began replacing timeworn food preparation techniques with assembly line procedures. Perhaps without realizing it, they were ushering in a new era of food service automation. Indeed, the brothers became enamored of any technical improvement that could speed up the work and keep their twelve-man crew—crammed into a twelve-by-sixteen-foot kitchen—working like a crack drill team.

The brothers had defined a totally new food service concept, but to make it work they realized they badly needed unique kitchen tools. Since the kitchen equipment of the day was not designed for their assembly line production, the McDonalds began inventing the first implements of the fast-food industry. For example, Dick McDonald designed a portable stainless steel lazy Susan that could hold twenty-four hamburger buns. In a staging area away from the grill, the buns were "dressed" with condiments by two crewmen as the lazy Susan rotated. Attached to a mobile platform, the lazy Susan was then rolled to the grill, loaded with hamburgers, and rolled back to an area where the burgers could be wrapped.

To produce their new kitchen instruments, the McDonalds relied on a local craftsman who had no experience in food service equipment—a "handicap" that produced a fresh perspective. In fact, Ed Toman was anything but a sophisticated kitchen equipment supplier. His tiny machine shop was constructed of sheet metal siding in 1908, and in the oppressive heat of San Bernardino's summers the temperatures inside reached a stifling 115 degrees. But it was there that Toman worked, often until midnight, designing the first tools of the fast-food trade. Aside from having designed a widely used machine for grinding orange peels into marmalade, Toman's exposure to food processing was nil. Yet, his work for the brothers suggests that lack of experience in serving traditional restaurants was helpful in understanding the needs of such a novel operation as McDonald's.

Some of Toman's fast-food equipment was mundane, such as the larger and more rigid spatulas that replaced the thinner conventional products, which were ill suited for volume production. Other Toman designs were ingenious. To automate the hamburger dressing process, Toman developed a hand-held stainless pump dispenser that required but one squeeze on a trigger to squirt the required amount of ketchup and mustard evenly onto the bun. Unfortunately, Toman never patented this device. He sold $500,000 worth of the dispensers to early fast-food operators, but he obviously missed a much bigger market: A variation of the device is still standard equipment in all 14,000 McDonald's as well as in most other fast-food hamburger chains.

Customized equipment was not the McDonald brothers' only secret to speeding up food service. Rigid operating procedures were adopted to eliminate the principal obstacle to fast-food service—the human element. Before fast food, commercial cooking was considered a personal art, and the resulting service varied widely in quality and speed. But the brothers' concept of a limited menu allowed them to break down food preparation into simple, repetitive tasks that could be learned quickly even by those stepping into a commercial kitchen for the first time. As the McDonalds refined their production techniques, the members of their kitchen crew became specialists. Typically, there were three "grill men," who did nothing but grill hamburgers; two "shake men," who did nothing but make milk shakes; two "fry men," who specialized in making french fries; two "dressers," who dressed and wrapped the hamburgers; and three "countermen," who did nothing but fill orders at the two customer windows.

Even those tasks were broken down into detailed procedures designed to save time. Specific rules were developed for calling out hamburger orders to the grill men and for filling and packaging orders speedily. The restaurant's shake department was equipped with four Multimixers; as many as eighty milk shakes were prepared in advance and stored in a refrigerated holding cabinet. As the predictability of high volume became more apparent, the McDonald brothers began a practice that further distinguished their new fast-food operation from all other restaurants. To fill orders in thirty seconds or less, even during the peak periods, the McDonald's crew began cooking and packaging food products in anticipation of orders rather than in response to them. That, in turn, led to standards for when to discard cooked products that had been sitting too long.

The procedures were so detailed and the jobs so specialized that the McDonald's operation benefited not only from higher production speeds but from the same labor-saving advantages that Henry Ford had discovered when he introduced modern assembly line techniques to manufacturing. The brothers could now employ untrained cooks at a lower wage and with minimal training, they could turn out products faster and with better quality control than even the best short-order cooks are capable of. Even the hiring practices of the newly converted McDonald's began to project a no-nonsense assembly line atmosphere that was clearly lacking at other drive-ins. Perhaps as an overreaction to the brothers' frustrations with carhops and the crowds they attracted, the new McDonald's restaurant employed only men.

Within a year of reopening their San Bernardino drive-in, the McDonald brothers' fascination with speed had converted their hamburger stand into a small assembly plant. They had so refined their production techniques that they had discovered a unique restaurant format. The keys were self-service, paper service, and quick service, and there was nothing in the food service business that remotely resembled it.

Years before, others had created restaurants with limited menus and low-cost hamburgers. Indeed, the nation's first hamburger chain was founded in 1921, when E. W. (Billy) Ingram began serving up a 5-cent, steam-fried, onion-laden burger in a restaurant he grandiosely called White Castle, in an attempt to give the product a touch of elegance it otherwise lacked. Several years later, Ingram had an eleven-state operation, and White Castle's success had spawned such regal look-alikes as White Tower and Royal Castle.

Ingram's business had some of the trappings of fast food. Almost from the beginning, White Castle encouraged devotees of its 5-cent hamburger to "buy 'em by the sack," and the tiny burgers (eighteen to the pound) were often consumed in such gluttonous quantities that they became known as "sliders" for their reputed laxative effect. But the White Castle system was originally not designed for high-speed self-service. The chain's small stores typically included counter seating. White Castles also featured flatware service, and most units were staffed by only one or two short-order cooks who did everything from flipping burgers to ringing up sales.

The McDonald brothers had clearly developed a vastly different system, tailor-made for a postwar America that was faster paced, more mobile, and more oriented to conveniences and instant gratification. The brothers were plugging into the same trends that were replacing corner grocery stores with supermarkets and giving rise to discounting in nonfood retailing.

But nowhere was the popularity of self-service more strikingly evident than at the McDonald's drive-in at Fourteenth and E streets. With lines 20 or more deep winding out from each of the two serving windows during peak periods, the drive-in produced annual sales of $277,000 during 1951, nearly 40 percent above the preconversion rate. As it turned out, that was only the beginning. By the mid-1950s, the mechanized McDonald's hamburger stand was hitting annual revenues of $350,000, and the brothers were splitting net profits of about $100,000. During the lunch and dinner hours, it was not unusual for 150 customers to crowd around the tiny hamburger stand. Such impressive volumes and profits would have been respectable even for large carhop drive-ins with seating, but it was a stunning achievement for an operation with one-third the capital investment, one-third the labor, and a product that sold for just 15 cents. The conversion of McDonald's from a standard drive-in to a fast-food factory had produced a runaway success.

On the edge of the desert fifty miles east of Los Angeles, San Bernardino is anything but a crossroads for the restaurant industry. Yet, the word of the fast-food breakthrough there had spread quickly around the trade. While legend suggests that Ray Kroc was the first to discover the brothers cloistered away at their high-volume drive-in, the fact is that by the time Kroc met the brothers in July 1954, McDonald's drive-in had already become something of a mecca for scores of opportunists from all over the country. When *American Restaurant Magazine* ran a cover story in July 1952 on the phenomenal success of the McDonald's concept, the brothers were flooded with letters and telephone inquiries, as many as three hundred a month by Dick McDonald's count. "Drive-in operators and restaurant owners who were having the same problems we were having wanted to know if they could come out and copy the operation and if we had any plans they could buy," McDonald recalls. "So many people were coming to see us that Mac and I were spending most of our time just talking to them. We knew then we had to have a franchise agent."

It is also part of the myth that Kroc suggested the franchising concept to the McDonalds. In fact, the brothers began licensing their Speedee Service System on their own about two years before they met Kroc. They even ran a full-page ad in a trade magazine seeking franchisees. It took about a minute to read the copy, and a come-on headline read: "This may be the most important 60 seconds of your life."

Neil Fox, an independent gasoline retailer, became their first licensee in 1952, and the brothers decided to make his drive-in in Phoenix a prototype for the chain they now wanted to build. They hired a local architect, Stanley Meston, to design the new store. It would be more than twice the size of the octagonal structure at Fourteenth and E streets, but it was not its dimensions that made the Phoenix store a standout. The brothers wanted an attention-grabbing design, and what Meston produced delivered that in spades: a gleaming—and more than a bit gaudy—red-and-white tiled rectangular building with a roof that slanted downward sharply from the front to the rear. Like the original, the front half of the building was constructed of glass from counter to roof. Nothing inside the kitchen was hidden from the customer's view.

While Meston did not know it, his circuslike design was to become a classic period piece of 1950s architecture, a symbol of the youthful, experimental, and burgeoning fast-food business. But the most noticeable feature of the new building was not Meston's idea. In fact, it was initially rejected by him. McDonald recalls: "I was drawing some sketches late one evening in an effort to give the new building some height, because it looked too flat. I drew one big arch that ran parallel with the building, from side to side, and that looked kind of funny. So then I drew two arches running the other way." Delighted with his rough sketch, McDonald showed them to his friend Meston, who agreed with everything, save those "terrible" arches. If the arches stayed, Meston told McDonald, the brothers would have to find a new architect. McDonald, however, had no intention of yielding. "The arches were the whole damned thing," he recalls. "Without them it was just another rectangular building."

But, to appease the only architect he knew, McDonald told Meston to proceed with the archless design, and when those drawings were in hand he went elsewhere to add the finishing touch he wanted. That led McDonald to George Dexter, a sign maker who had none of the architect's qualms about the arches. Since Dexter ran a neon sign company, it was no surprise when he came up with bright yellow arches that could be seen from blocks away. Originally, McDonald had thought of using the arches as a structural support for the building, and if an architect had designed them, that might have been all they were. But when the job went to a sign maker, Dick McDonald's "golden arches" became easily the most prominent feature of the new drive-in —and a new symbol for the McDonald's System.

The McDonald brothers showed similar inventiveness when they designed the kitchen for the new building. It was more than twice the size of the one in San Bernardino, and the brothers wanted to be certain that its design accommodated their well-defined production system. They had a brainstorm. They drew the outline of the new kitchen on their home tennis court, and after closing one night at Fourteenth and E, they invited the night crew over to go through all the hamburger assembly motions. As the crew members moved around the court making imaginary hamburgers, shakes, and fries, the brothers followed them, marking in red chalk exactly where all the kitchen equipment should be placed. By 3:00 A.M., the tennis court markup was completed; and for a fraction of the cost of conventional design work, the brothers had a detailed kitchen layout. But the draftsman they hired to record the layout on paper decided it was too late to begin work. He promised to get a fresh start the next morning, but by then a rare change in San Bernardino's arid climate nullified the work of the night before. "It was the damnedest cloudburst you ever saw," McDonald recalls. "There was nothing but red streaks all over the tennis court."

If the brothers were perfecting the design of the new drive-in, their program to license the Speedee Service System was a long way from perfection. Fox, whose Phoenix store opened in 1953, was provided the plans for the new building, a one-week loan of Art Bender, and a basic description of the Speedee Service System—all for a one-time franchise fee of $1,000. After that, the first McDonald's franchisee was on his own, financially and operationally. The McDonalds had no continuing revenue, and thus no economic incentive to help ensure their franchisee's success, and the franchisee was not required to follow any of their procedures. The brothers' licensing program amounted to little more than a rent-a-name scheme.

With all the attention the brothers were getting, they might have made fast money selling such a franchise. Yet, they showed little enthusiasm for pursuing franchising's big payoff, and their licensing program did not show the same dedication as their store operations displayed. Indeed, they seemed to have little appreciation for the power of their own reputation. When Neil Fox applied for the first franchise, they assumed he wanted to call his Phoenix store Fox's, but Fox surprised them. He wanted to call it McDonald's instead. "What the hell for?" Dick McDonald asked Fox. " 'McDonald's' means nothing in Phoenix." In addition, the brothers feared that if the Phoenix McDonald's were not run as well as the San Bernadino store, their own business might be adversely affected. Still, they conceded to Fox's marketing desires, and McDonald's—the hamburger chain—was born.

Given such conservatism, it is no mystery why the McDonalds' franchising program was a bust. In their first two years of licensing before their historic meeting with Ray Kroc, the brothers sold just fifteen franchises, ten of which became operating McDonald's units. Even those were sold with little effort. The brothers were getting so many inquiries that they rarely had to look for prospects. Yet, they showed neither the skill nor the desire to persuade would-be franchisees to part with their money. They turned down one investor willing to pay $15,000 for six franchises in Sacramento. Their reason: they had just accepted $2,500 for a single franchisee in the California capital earlier that day. When Harriett Charlson, a middle-aged schoolteacher, came looking for a franchise, the brothers tried to dissuade her. "Why don't you open up a little dress shop," Dick McDonald advised. McDonald was certain that his nonselling tactics had worked, but two days later Charlson was back on his doorstep—with a $2,500 check. She bought the franchise and operated the store in Alhambra for sixteen years before selling the franchise and property to McDonald's in 1969 for $180,000. Years later, McDonald would concede that he was "a lousy franchise salesman."

Indeed, the McDonalds turned down a golden opportunity to expand their system with the powerful financial backing of their dairy supplier, Carnation Corporation, which was looking for outlets that consumed its frozen milk shake mix the way the brothers' store did. A Carnation representative approached them with the idea of his company building a chain of McDonald's drive-ins in partnership with the brothers. Carnation, the executive said, would bankroll the construction of the first units in San Francisco and expand the chain down the California coast, and presumably eastward after that. But Mac came to Dick at the time of the Carnation offer and described a scenario neither brother wanted. "We are going to be on the road all the time, in motels, looking for locations, finding managers," he told Dick. "I can see just one hell of a headache if we go into that type of chain."

The brothers turned down the offer, revealing in the process that their only "problem" in expanding beyond San Bernardino was that they were content with the way things were. Contentment of that sort is not the stuff from which business empires are made. "We couldn't spend all the money we were making," McDonald recalls. "We were taking it easier and having a lot of fun doing what we wanted to do. I had always wanted financial independence, and now I had it."

In short, the brothers did not succeed on their own in building a national chain because they were not consumed with the idea of it. Neither one wanted to travel. Both were happy splitting the $100,000 per year they were making in San Bernardino. Making any more, they thought, only meant income tax headaches. Neither brother had children and thus no one to whom to leave a big estate. "We'd be leaving it to a church or something," says McDonald, "and we didn't go to church."

By late 1953, the brothers' franchising effort was such a dismal failure that the original McDonald's System was nearly lost in the chaotic scramble by dozens of other independents to market a dizzying array of fast-food formats—all lacking the discipline of a franchising system. Earlier that year, the McDonalds had finally gotten themselves a franchise agent, William Tansey, who for a few months sold several franchises before giving up the job because of a heart ailment. But the franchises Tansey sold were no different from the ones the McDonalds had sold on their own. Franchisees were buying only the blueprints to the red-and-white tile building, the right to use the arches, a fifteen-page operating manual describing the Speedee Service System, and the McDonald's name. Each franchisee also received one week of training at the McDonald's in San Bernardino. After that, they were free to operate as they wished, and most did. They sold their hamburgers at different prices. Some added new items to the menu. Others added more serving windows. One licensee even decided to bring the golden arches to a point and rename his drive-in. He called it Peaks.

Lack of product uniformity was not the only result of the McDonalds' failure to supervise their franchisees. Few of their licensees operated their restaurants with the personal care and attention to detail that the McDonalds exhibited. For example, none of the licensed operators kept their units as clean as the one in San Bernardino, where windows were washed daily, floors were mopped continually, and cleaning towels were always at the ready. Not surprisingly, sales at the franchised stores did not begin to approach those at the brothers' drive-in.

Essentially, the problem was that both the brothers and their licensees were looking at franchising as a way of making easy money. Most of the franchisees were investors, absentee owners who used hired managers to run their drive-ins. For their part, the McDonalds saw franchising as a way of making money without building an organization to supervise the quality of the franchised operations. That was not unusual. No one before them had viewed franchising in any other light.

Thanks to a poorly conceived franchising scheme, the McDonalds were belatedly realizing that an original idea that is not promoted and controlled by its creator will soon be stolen. In the early 1950s, the brothers' fast-food concept was being copied by independent operators more successfully than it was being franchised by the McDonalds. Indeed, the brothers were so generous in providing visitors at their store with information about their production procedures, their equipment, and their suppliers, that no one really needed a franchise to learn the McDonalds' secrets.

The first of the plagiarized units opened in 1952, and within two years the California market had become the cradle of a fledgling fast-food business. Dozens of self-serve drive-ins, all featuring a limited menu of 15- to 19-cent burgers, 10-cent french fries, and 15- to 20-cent shakes were in business, and all of them could trace their origins to a single prototype—the McDonald's store at Fourteenth and E streets. "There was a fraternity of us, and every one of us saw the McDonald's in San Bernardino and basically copied it after the boys [the McDonald brothers] gave us a tour," recalls James A. Collins, chairman of Collins Foods International, who by 1986 was the largest Kentucky Fried Chicken franchisee and the operator of Sizzler Restaurants.

Collins first heard about the McDonald's drive-in in 1952, just before putting the finishing touches on a Culver City coffee shop he had planned to open. A California Edison representative checking on the utilities connection for the coffee shop persuaded Collins to take a four-hour trip with him to San Bernardino to see a brand-new restaurant format before he got committed to an old one. Collins arrived at Fourteenth and E streets just before the lunch-hour traffic swamped McDonald's. "I have never seen anything as breathtaking since then," Collins recalls. "There was a line of people halfway out to the curb and the parking lot was full. There was just nothing else like it. They had two hamburger lines, and they were handling people every ten seconds. I tore up my coffee shop plans and entered the hamburger business, and except for the fact that I sold hamburgers for nineteen cents, everything else was the same as McDonald's."

Collins's reaction was by no means unusual. He opened his Hamburger Handout store in Culver City in September 1952, but not before he got his fast-food training from Ken McConnell, who had opened his Ken's Drive-In in Long Beach the previous June, also copying the McDonald's operation. A month later, Mel Hall opened Mel's in Pomona, another copy. "We became good friends, and we all took our lessons from the McDonald brothers," Collins remembers.

The lessons were provided by surprisingly candid instructors. Before opening the Hamburger Handout, Collins met with the McDonald brothers and got a tour of their kitchen. The brothers told him where they got their big grills, how they organized their assembly production, how they prepared shakes and fries, and even where they purchased their automatic condiment dispenser. It was the type of information franchisees pay for, but the McDonald brothers were giving it away. Dick McDonald reasons: "The store was all glass, and we were in a fishbowl. We couldn't conceal what we were doing. So, we would talk to anyone who had questions. They would come in with paper and pens and copy the layout, and my brother and I would laugh."

The humor did not last, because the brothers wound up putting more competitors in business than they did franchisees. In fact, those who took informal instruction from the McDonald brothers were themselves passing on the new fast-food concept to other entrepreneurs, and by 1954 the revolution the brothers had started in California was spreading eastward. Collins himself began collecting $100 a day training independents brought to him by Carnation, which was helping operators get into the quick-service hamburger business to get their dairy trade. In all, Collins trained ten operators who started their own McDonald's-like chains in such widely scattered markets as San Francisco, Seattle, and Austin.

Some of Collins's trainees would later develop their own sizable chains. One was Henry's, a drive-in chain operated by the Chicago-based Bressler Ice Cream Company, which was one of the early leaders in fast food. Another operator inspired by one of the early copiers of McDonald's in San Bernardino was Dee Anderson, who sold his forty-four-store fast-food chain in Salt Lake City to Hardee's Food Systems in 1983. Anderson had caught the fast-food fever rather unexpectedly in the early 1950s when he saw Ken's Drive-In, the McDonald's look-alike in Long Beach. In fact, Anderson, who ran stool-and-counter hamburger shops in Salt Lake City, was planning to leave the restaurant trade and was visiting California to look at real estate investments. But when he took one look at the McDonald's clone in Long Beach, he told his wife that he was going back to Salt Lake City to build a unit just like it. "I thought you were leaving the restaurant business," his wife declared. Anderson replied: "I just got back in it."

Even some of their steady customers began copying the brothers' fast-food concept. Glen Bell, a telephone repairman, was a regular patron of the McDonald's drive-in in San Bernardino before its conversion to fast food. When he saw the business that the brothers were doing in the remodeled unit, he persuaded home builder Neal Baker, a close friend, to build him a self-service restaurant. After erecting Bell's first unit, Baker decided to start his own San Bernardino chain of fast-food outlets. Still others followed Bell and Baker, and soon the rush to imitate the McDonald brothers' bonanza was converting San Bernardino into a fast-food haven. However, it was Bell who became the most celebrated of the local McDonald's copiers when he extended the fast-food concept into the ethnic market with a Mexican restaurant chain bearing his name: Taco Bell.

Yet, the stampede into fast food in California had not produced anything close to a dominant chain by the mid-1950s. Clearly, the McDonald brothers themselves were going nowhere with their franchising attempts. While their informal instruction had spawned scores of competitors, virtually all were young, thinly capitalized independents who lacked the resources or experience to build a national chain. Furthermore, the rush into the new market tended to prevent any of the new competitors from hitting a bonanza in fast food. To be sure, some of the early copiers had made more money than they had dreamed was possible from a hamburger stand. In his first year with Hamburger Handout, the then twenty-six-year-old Collins grossed $420,000 and took home $80,000. But as other independents flooded into the new fast-food market, the individual store volumes took a dive. For example, none of Collins's three additional Hamburger Handouts did as well as the first.

Searching for a competitive difference, most of the newcomers began experimenting with all forms of variation on the McDonald's theme, so much so that the concept itself began to lose its identity. The fast-food industry in California was mutating into a confusing competitive strain of independent operators, most of whom did not come close to matching the quality, cleanliness, productivity—and profitability— of the original McDonald's.

However, the failure of the McDonald brothers—or anyone else— to seize the obvious opportunity to take a fast-food hamburger chain nationwide only meant that the opportunity was still there for someone to exploit. That someone walked into the picture in the summer of 1954 in the form of a food service equipment salesman by the name of Ray A. Kroc. Kroc held the national marketing rights to the five-spindle Multimixers that the brothers used to make their milk shakes, and from his West Coast sales representative, William Jamison, Kroc had been getting a blow-by-blow account of the McDonald brothers' progress for more than a year. In fact, Kroc even carried a feature on McDonald's in the newsletter he had distributed to his sales reps and dealers in late 1953.

While the McDonalds were not close to being Kroc's largest account, they had become his most intriguing one. It was common for drugstore fountains to have only one Multimixer, and even the large operations required no more than two. By comparison, the McDonald's drive-in kept three or four in use at any one time. By 1954, the brothers had purchased about ten of the machines, including replacements and spares, and Kroc was beside himself. What in the world could one hamburger stand be doing with ten Multimixers? He could not contain his curiosity any longer—he had to see for himself. On his next sales trip to the West Coast, Kroc called Dick McDonald and arranged a personal visit to the San Bernardino store.

By the time Ray Kroc laid eyes on it, the tiny hamburger stand at Fourteenth and E streets had already become legend in California and was being widely duplicated there. It had been featured on the cover of a national trade magazine, and it had captivated hundreds of prospective operators and investors from around the country. None of that diminished Kroc's sense of personal discovery. He had parked his rental car in the McDonald's lot a full hour before noon, but already lines were forming at the two front windows, where the main orders were filled, and at the side window, where orders for french fries were handled separately.

Kroc had seen scores of new hot dog, hamburger, and milk shake formats before, and at first glance this one did not appear stunningly different. While Kroc would later view pictures of the new Golden Arches design, the brothers had not yet converted their store to the new look when Kroc paid his visit in July 1954. (When they did convert one year later, they marked the occasion with their typical promotional flair—a grand opening featuring ten huge spotlights that lit up the San Bernardino sky more brightly than anything before. They attracted so many curious spectators that traffic into town was jammed for miles. Unfortunately, they attracted an even bigger swarm of insects, and the brothers were forced to close early.)

But if Kroc had to be content to look at the old octagonal building on his first McDonald's visit, that mattered little. It was not the shape of things that caught his eye but the speed of them. By noon, the tiny parking lot was filled with 150 customers, and the McDonald's crew was in high gear. Ray Kroc had never before seen anything that came close to matching the speed of an operation that filled orders in fifteen seconds. "I've never waited in line for a hamburger in my whole life," Kroc blurted, hoping to provoke conversation from customers. Soon he was overwhelmed with testimonials on the quality and price of the food, on the service, and on the cleanliness of the kitchen. But it was the orders that the customers were placing that positively excited him: easily one in three included milk shakes made on *his* Multimixers.

Someone at Carnation had figured out that the McDonalds were selling 20,000 shakes a month, and while Kroc had not heard the figure, he nevertheless recognized other signs of the enormous dimensions of the brothers' milk shake business. The McDonalds were making milk shakes so fast that they had Ed Toman cut a couple of inches off the spindles on Kroc's Multimixer so that they could mix shakes right in the twelve-ounce paper cup, not in the sixteen-ounce stainless steel mixers the soda fountains used. Kroc's company marketed a two-inch stainless rim to accommodate cup mixing, but the brothers had no time to wash the rims.

Kroc watched the store through the lunch-hour rush, and when it was over he had the answer to the Multimixer riddle he had come to San Bernardino to solve. He was bubbling over with enthusiasm as he walked inside to introduce himself to two of his best customers. "My God, I've been standing out there looking at it but I can't believe it," he told the brothers. Dick and Mac assured him that his reaction was normal—and as typical as that day's business. "When will this die down?" Kroc asked. "Sometime late tonight," Dick replied. "Some way," Kroc declared, "I've got to become involved in this."

Chapter 2
THE SALESMAN

Before his fast-food company had been in operation for three decades, Ray A. Kroc had become an American business legend. He was immortalized as the founder of a major new industry. His accomplishments in food service were likened to those of John D. Rockefeller in oil refining, Andrew Carnegie in steel manufacturing, and Henry Ford in automotive assembly. He was seen as one of America's most enterprising capitalists, a rugged individualist who took his biggest gamble —and collected his biggest payoff—just thirteen years before he could begin collecting on his social security.

The problem with such instant legends is that they often miss the essence of the man. They even distort reality, and in Kroc's case the distortions are substantial. Many traits that were crucial to his success have been overlooked by simplistic accounts of his "overnight" fortune. He has been described as a visionary who invented a totally new form of food service geared to the faster-paced lifestyles he foresaw. Yet, by the time he had discovered McDonald's and fast food, dozens of others had made the same discovery. Some suggest that Kroc was simply a dreamer who got lucky and was carried to riches on the wave of social change that swept this country in the 1950s and 1960s. Yet, so many others who tried to ride the fast-food wave were engulfed by it. Still others conclude that Kroc was a modern-day corporate builder. In fact, Kroc could not care less about professional managers and corporate bureaucracies.

In one word, Ray Kroc was a salesman. He was the kind of man who was prized in business during the formative years of American corporations. Up until the go-go era of the late 1960s, salesmen dominated the executive suites. Anyone with an eye on the corporate presidency had little chance of getting there without first rising through the ranks of the sales department. That was before the Harvard Business School established the MBA as a prerequisite for senior management. It was before excessive government regulation increased the corporate profile of accountants and lawyers. It was before the Wall Street analysts began worshiping the financial strategists and before technology elevated the corporate technocrats.

Indeed, the fundamental talents of the salesman have nearly disappeared from top management in recent years, surfacing occasionally in such celebrated cases as the rescue of Chrysler Corporation by the nation's preeminent auto salesman, Lee Iacocca. The salesman's devotion to the basics may be sorely missed in American businesses today, but when Ray Kroc was preparing for his career with McDonald's, his were the talents that ruled economic enterprise.

His skills were not picked up in the classroom; Kroc dropped out of high school after his sophomore year. He was an activist, not a scholar. When he was still in high school, he opened his own music store to put his considerable talents as a piano player to commercial use. When World War I started, he got the fever to go overseas, and he lied about his age to become a Red Cross ambulance driver at age fifteen, working in the same company as another now famous underaged driver—Walt Disney. Curiously, the two would develop remarkably similar business empires—both dedicated to perfection in their operations and a youthful spirit in their marketing. Though each admired the other, they were character opposites. Kroc was open and outgoing; Disney was so much the reverse that the men in his ambulance company voted him least likely to succeed. "He was always drawing pictures while the rest of us were chasing girls," Kroc would recall half a century later. "Therein lies a lesson, because his drawings have gone on forever—and most of those girls are dead now."

After the war, Kroc mixed professional piano playing with selling. He was hired as a salesman for the Lily Cup Company in 1922, and sold paper cups by day while playing piano for a local radio station by night. Still searching for his niche, he took a leave from Lily in the mid-1920s and drove to Florida to peddle real estate. But when the Great Florida Land Boom busted in 1926, leaving Kroc stranded fifteen hundred miles from home, he fell back on his talent as a piano player. He was only twenty-five when he returned to Chicago, having concluded that he had no desire for the life of an itinerant musician and that his future lay in sharpening his other natural gift—selling. When Kroc returned to his job with Lily, he found himself on the ground floor of a completely new and fast-growing segment of the food service industry, one built around the idea of selling carryout foods.

Kroc spent nearly the next twenty-five years selling new retailing concepts to a food service industry full of hidebound traditionalists. He had never run a restaurant, never served a hamburger, and never sold a milk shake, but by the end of that period he knew more about the trend toward convenience foods than did most food service professionals. So, when he saw the McDonald's drive-in in San Bernardino in 1954, he was no outsider looking in. Unlike the dozens of young entrepreneurs attracted to fast food in the 1950s solely because of its newness, Kroc knew from years of experience exactly how important the brothers' discovery was. "When I met the McDonald brothers, I was ready for the opportunity," Kroc explained. "By then, I had enough experience in food and beverage that I could tell a real idea from a counterfeit."

Kroc could see the trends in a market because he had developed the salesman's most important asset—a knack for putting himself in the position of his customers and for addressing their needs and interests, not his own. He started selling paper cups to street vendors who used them to dispense Italian ice, but when Lily merged with Tulip Cup in 1929, it gave Kroc a much broader line of products. He quickly progressed to such larger commercial accounts as baseball parks, drugstore chains, and the commissaries in Chicago's biggest plants. In each case, Kroc made a practice of analyzing the customer's operations and suggesting changes that would improve them, and in the process increase his sales of cups.

His suggestions were not always warmly received. Such was certainly the case at Wrigley Field, one of Kroc's most valued accounts. With baseball attendance soaring, the ballparks easily could have been serviced by order takers, but Kroc never took selling so passively. An inveterate baseball fan, he would hang out at Wrigley Field watching the Cubs and thinking of cups—dreaming up promotions that would boost attendance further and move his cups faster. Repeatedly, he brought his ideas to Bill Veeck, a youthful operations manager in the Wrigley organization. Veeck would later make his name in baseball with his own offbeat promotions, but he resented Kroc's interference. "What the hell do you know about my business," Veeck would snap at Kroc. "Stick to selling paper cups."

But it was a sales promotion suggestion that gave Kroc a new appreciation for the appeal of convenient food service. The break-through came when Kroc persuaded Walgreen Drugs, the Midwest's largest drugstore chain, to launch carryout food service, a totally new concept. The drug chains and other luncheon counters resisted using paper cups because they believed that replacing glasses with dispos-able cups only raised their supply costs without increasing their sales. Kroc was convinced that the carryout food service would solve that problem, and he proposed it to Walgreen's.

The chain's lunch counters could each serve one hundred people an hour, and although they were packed at lunchtime, Kroc believed Walgreen was missing a golden opportunity. "There could be another hundred people at each of your stores who might want to buy lunch but either they can't get a seat or can't get away from work," Kroc told Walgreen's purchasing manager. He rejected the idea, but Kroc kept proposing it until the manager agreed to test the carryout service at one store. The experiment was an instant winner, and Walgreen's quickly expanded carryout service to all its stores. Within months, the chain was one of Lily-Tulip's largest accounts, and Kroc was one of the company's star salesmen.

Kroc's sales success was also driven by his appreciation of techni-cal improvements. He was by no means a technician himself, but he was fascinated with the innovations of those who were. This was ac-companied by a remarkably keen eye for inefficiency and an intense interest in making things work better. Kroc's relentless pursuit of inno-vations that might improve his cup business eventually led him to the product he thought would be his big score—the Multimixer.

While at Lily-Tulip, Kroc had made a good business selling cups to so-called dairy bars, a fixture throughout the Midwest during the days of Prohibition and just afterward. One of his dairy bar clients was Ralph Sullivan, a dairy producer who mixed stabilizers, corn syrup, and vanilla flavoring into milk to invent the first ice milk product Kroc had seen that was suitable for use in milk shakes. Instead of making a shake with the standard eight ounces of milk and two scoops of ice cream, Sullivan made a shake consisting of equal amounts of milk and his new ice milk mix. The result, Kroc recalls, "was a colder and more viscous drink that people preferred to the thin, semicool, conventional milk shake. It was more refreshing and it would wear better because it produced less of a bloated feeling."

Sullivan's dairy bar in Battle Creek, Michigan, was doing land office business during the Depression selling a sixteen-ounce shake for only a dime, a price directly related to its lower-cost ingredients. Looking to increase his cup sales, Kroc took the idea to Earl Prince, who ran a chain of ice cream stands in Chicago. Prince was content selling only ice cream, but when Kroc persuaded him to see Sullivan's operation, he changed his mind and decided to introduce the new milk shake at his ice cream parlors. Soon Kroc was selling five million cups a year to Prince, who started looking for a way to speed up the production of his 12-cent milk shakes.

A mechanical engineer, Prince developed by the late 1930s a new mixing machine that used one large motor to drive five separate spindles, a vast improvement over the single-spindle mixers that were standard in the soda fountains. He called it the Multimixer, and Ray Kroc was fascinated by it. He seized on the invention as a tool he could use to greatly increase milk shake production at the soda fountains, his prime cup customers. But to Kroc's utter amazement, Lily-Tulip turned down the opportunity to distribute Prince's machine, and Kroc was suddenly at a major fork in the road. At age thirty-seven, he decided the time was finally right to do what he had always wanted—go into business for himself. He obtained from Prince the exclusive marketing rights for the new Multimixer, while Sterling Manufacturing Company, a sheet metal company, got the manufacturing rights.

It was 1939 when Kroc set up his Malt-A-Mixer Co., Inc. (later renamed Prince Castle Sales Division) and began capitalizing on the Multimixer's obvious appeal to the soda fountain chains. He also began cultivating less obvious prospects by relying on what was by now a proven technique: finding a way to increase their business by using his product. He tried replacing the single-spindle mixers in taverns and restaurants by suggesting new mixed drinks that would improve their beverage profit margins while at the same time creating a demand for a more efficient mixer. Among the new drinks Kroc concocted and promoted in his regular newsletters he mailed to his Multimixer sales reps were the Delacato (brandy, Kahlúa, and ice cream) and the Dusty Road (cherry herring, orange curaçao, and lime juice). Even to the soda fountains, Kroc promoted the Multimixer not only for making malts but for mixing new drinks such as limeades and orangeades, which carried higher margins thanks to lower-cost ingredients.

But Kroc had no sooner built national sales momentum for the Multimixer than his company was nearly put out of business. Two years after Prince Castle Sales was formed, the country entered a world war, and a wartime embargo on the domestic use of copper wiped out the supply of electric motors that powered the Multimixer. Kroc was living the salesman's worst nightmare: he had created demand but had no product to satisfy it.

The young entrepreneur was suddenly scrambling to save his company. Others might have quit and sought the security of a former employer, but Kroc showed the flexibility that would later become one of his company's trademarks. "I just had to finagle around for something else," Kroc recalled years later.

He was looking for a product that would benefit from the wartime market instead of being victimized by it. His "finagling" put him in contact with Harry Burke, son of the founder of Good Humor, the ice cream vending company. Burke had just developed a new product that could be added to ice milk to give it the sweeter taste and thicker consistency of ice cream without requiring sugar, which was so tightly rationed that it all but stopped the production of ice cream. Burke's product consisted of corn syrup and a secret stabilizer. When dairies added it to ice milk, they got a product that tasted enough like ice cream to rescue the soda fountains that were deprived of their key beverages—malts and milk shakes.

When Kroc saw Burke's Shake-A-Plenty and Malt-A-Plenty additive products, he knew he had found what he needed to help his young Prince Castle Sales survive the war. Kroc became the national marketing agent for the two additive products, but he had no illusions about their long-term viability. "They were just war babies," he recalled.

Still, the experience taught Kroc a critical lesson. A company, he realized, must be ready to react quickly to unforeseen changes in its market, even when they require a completely new course. When the war was over, the market changed radically again, and Kroc responded. Electric motors and ice cream were available once more, and Kroc immediately turned to the task of reviving the Multimixer business and capitalizing on the postwar boom he was certain would develop.

For the Multimixer at least, it did. Sales soon soared to nine thousand units per year. Prince Castle had three full-time salesmen (including Kroc), eight sales representatives around the country, and three clerks who handled the flood of direct-mail orders. Kroc was making $25,000 a year, an impressive income in the late 1940s. He had become a member of Rolling Green Country Club in Arlington Heights, a suburb northwest of Chicago. He even had time for a couple of rounds of golf a week, including one on Wednesday, when he took off from work at noon. For the first time in his life, Kroc—now a veteran salesman—was on easy street, and the Multimixer had all the makings of a product he could retire on.

That contentment did not last long. By the early 1950s, annual sales of the Multimixer plummeted to two thousand units. Kroc was forced to trim his staff to himself, another salesman, his secretary, and one clerk. All but one of the sales reps were terminated. What had seemed such a solid business opportunity a couple of years before was suddenly coming unglued.

Part of Multimixer's demise was competition. When Kroc's product was introduced, it took market share away from market leader Hamilton Beach, which sold only a single-spindle mixer. But in the late 1940s Hamilton Beach responded with a three-spindle device that was cheaper and more compact than Prince Castle's five-spindle unit. Within a few years, Beach regained its hegemony in the mixer market.

However, Kroc's instincts as a merchandiser told him that the real enemy was not Hamilton Beach but the market itself. The exodus from the old inner-city neighborhoods to the expansive suburbs was killing the corner drugstore soda fountains that had dominated the retail ice cream trade since Kroc had entered the market in the 1920s. When the business was transplanted to the suburbs, it took a different form—cones and sundaes made from premixed soft ice cream dispensed from special machines. During the decade after World War II, the hottest and most lucrative franchise operations in the country belonged to the biggest two names in soft-serve ice cream: market leader Dairy Queen and arch rival Tastee-Freez.

In moving to the suburbs, the two chains realized that retailing there required a different format. Residential areas were planned on a larger scale with tract housing, and commercial properties were more centralized along busy thoroughfares. Roads in the suburbs were far better than those in the city, and suburban residents thought nothing of driving two or three miles to stores that city residents walked to. Neighborhood retailing was giving way to the strip retail centers. The new soft-serve ice cream stands—with parking lots for fifteen or more cars and quick window service—were designed to serve a motorized suburban clientele. They provided a clear sign to Kroc that when broader food service operations moved to the suburbs, they, too, would have to be structured along the drive-in patterns of Dairy Queen and Tastee-Freez.

Kroc immediately sought Multimixer business from the Dairy Queen and Tastee-Freez operators who were replacing his soda fountain clients. Unfortunately, the soft-serve vendors were not nearly as interested in making milk shakes, because their profits were so high from the cones and sundaes they made simply by opening the spigot on their soft-serve machines. While Kroc was gaining valuable insight on the new food service trends, the death of the soda fountains was having a devastating impact on his Multimixer trade. The fountains had accounted for two-thirds of his business, and Multimixer sales to the soft-serve operators did not come close to filling the void.

Ray Kroc was scrambling for his economic life once more. Though he was at a point in life when most men think of slowing down, Kroc amazingly had lost none of his enthusiasm for the sales challenge. With his organization nearly wiped out, he took on the task of selling the Multimixer with renewed vigor. When the largest restaurant equipment wholesaler in Denver called him hinting that he had a major order of Multimixers, Kroc hopped aboard the Burlington Zephyr that afternoon and rode the train all night to show up at the wholesaler's office the next morning. After he made the last leg of the trip—up four flights of stairs with a heavy display case in hand—Kroc was told that the wholesaler was interested in ordering only two machines for display purposes. Refusing to accept the fact that he had traveled a thousand miles for a $300 order, Kroc grabbed a cab and asked the driver if he knew which drugstores in town did the biggest business in milk shakes. He spent the rest of the day cabbing it from one soda fountain operator to another, offering each a free thirty-day trial of a Multimixer. He sold ten machines. A week later, the wholesaler wrote Prince Castle to explain why he was not making an order under the "commitment we had given to your man": the customers to whom he intended to sell Multimixers had just purchased them from someone else.

Kroc's primary response to Multimixer's shrinking market was to broaden his company's product line. He pressed Sterling, the maker of the Multimixer, to develop new food service products, but what resulted were ancillary items, not the lifesaving products Kroc wanted. For example, Prince Castle Sales soon began marketing a square ice cream scooper that required less effort to scoop ice cream and produced a more controlled serving that reduced waste. Unfortunately, a cube of ice cream required more effort to eat. According to Al Steiner, the president of Prince Castle in 1986: "It dispensed ice cream in a shape that was not meant for humankind because it was impossible to keep it on your plate."

Convinced that the food service business could no longer support his company, Kroc desperately looked for an opportunity on the outside. One of his former Prince Castle salesmen came up with a kitchen table and bench set that he called Fold-A-Nook, which folded up and out of sight into a cabinet. When Kroc saw it, he thought it might be a revolutionary furniture piece—and a savior for Prince Castle. Louis Martino, the husband of Kroc's secretary, June, became interested in the unit, and he and a friend constructed a small building in Addison, Illinois, in which to manufacture it. Kroc agreed to market the new product nationally, and Martino made a production prototype of Fold-A-Nook to show him. But at the last minute Kroc abruptly decided against the venture. "Ray had to have something to sell," Martino recalls. "But when he looked at the prototype, something inside of him told him this wasn't it."

After closing Fold-A-Nook in early 1954, Kroc decided to work harder at finding a new market for his Multimixer, and the first order of business was to find out why two brothers in California were buying so many Multimixers for their one small drive-in. Kroc had just received yet another order from the McDonald brothers for two more units— their ninth and tenth. "What are they doing with them?" Kroc asked Jamison, his West Coast salesman. "Well, Ray, they use them all," Jamison replied.

Kroc also realized that the McDonald's drive-in at San Bernardino had sparked a number of imitators because he was getting calls from new hamburger drive-in operators asking for the same Multimixer that the McDonald brothers used. Though they may not have known it, the McDonalds were becoming the Multimixer's best promoters, and Kroc had to find out why. When he saw the San Bernardino McDonald's he knew. He also saw the potential of the new fast-food format, even more clearly than did the McDonald brothers themselves. Kroc had experienced firsthand the market shifts that were creating an enormous opportunity for a new, convenient food service catering to automobile-oriented suburban families. The very trends creating that opportunity were killing the soda fountains and his Multimixer business.

The closest thing to a rescue for Multimixer had come from conventional drive-in operators. They were doing a big business with milk shakes, and Kroc was selling his machine to most of them. But, like the

McDonald brothers, he knew all the problems of the conventional carhop drive-ins that were severely limiting their appeal. Because the early drive-ins offered both inside seating and car service, they required a capital investment of about $300,000. In the mid-1950s that was a substantial investment for an independent operator, and that alone restricted the franchising opportunity for the big drive-ins. Kroc knew that Dairy Queen and Tastee-Freez were attracting thousands of independents with a store that cost only $30,000 to build.

From his dealings with the carhop drive-ins, however, Kroc knew that they had far more serious weaknesses than their capital restrictions. They were saddled with a bad image. In many drive-ins, if the carhops were not having sexual encounters with the fry cooks, they were with the customers. The unsavory reputation of the drive-ins created expansion problems even for chain operations that were trying to legitimize this new food service. When Bob Wian opened one of his first franchised Big Boy outlets in Dallas, he had to fly in twenty carhops from California, because the image problem had kept him from recruiting locally the type of help he wanted. Wian countered the image of the drive-in as a sex playground by enforcing tough rules. Recalls one of his early operations managers: "You'd get fired faster if you messed around with a carhop than if you messed around with the cash register."

Kroc realized that as a result of such problems, conventional drive-ins were not attracting the major market in the suburbs—the young families contributing most to the postwar baby boom. He knew the soft-serve chains were capitalizing on that market but with a very limited product line. Because of weaknesses in their franchising systems and limitations in their facilities, most of the soft-serve operators had gone after only the ice cream trade of the drugstore soda fountains and had left the convenience food segment untouched.

Thus, when Kroc saw his first McDonald's, he realized that it filled a huge void in the food service market. A McDonald's could be opened for only $75,000, including building and land, which made it perfect for franchising. Without carhops, it could be aimed squarely at the family market that the McDonald brothers had captured. And it sold more milk shakes than any soda fountain operator ever dreamed of making.

Kroc immediately saw the potential for expanding McDonald's nationwide. Unlike the homebound McDonalds, he had traveled extensively, and he could envision hundreds of large and small markets where a McDonald's could be located. He knew the existing food service businesses and understood how a McDonald's unit could be a formidable competitor.

By contrast, the McDonald brothers were parochial. Neal Baker, whose San Bernardino–based fast-food chain was one of many California imitations of the first McDonald's, believes that alone explains why the McDonalds needed a Ray Kroc. Baker himself seldom traveled, and like the McDonalds, he thought mainly in terms of a local market. "We couldn't see the forest for the trees," says Baker. "Ray Kroc was always traveling, and when he thought of McDonald's, he thought big. He had seen cities all over the country, and he could just picture a McDonald's in every one of them."

On his first visit to the McDonald's in San Bernardino, Kroc had learned that the McDonald brothers were looking for another franchising agent to replace Bill Tansey. He returned to Chicago after getting a promise from Dick and Mac to notify him of their choice of an agent so that he could work out a sales agreement to supply Multimixers to the McDonald's franchisees.

However, after pondering the McDonald's opportunity for a week, Kroc's thinking changed radically. He called Dick McDonald. "Have you found a franchising agent yet?" he inquired. "No, Ray, not yet," was McDonald's response. "Well then," asked Kroc, "what about me?"

The next day, Kroc was on a flight to the West Coast, this time to negotiate a contract with the brothers that would give him exclusive rights to franchise the McDonald's System nationally. While Dick and Mac welcomed having a man of Kroc's experience to take over the franchising task, they insisted on setting all the conditions, the most important of which were the franchising fees. "Don't charge too much for the franchise," Dick McDonald advised. In fact, the terms the McDonald brothers demanded made certain that Kroc would sell perhaps the most economical—and unprofitable—franchise in the food service business. The brothers held the franchise fee to $950, and they required that Kroc charge each franchisee a service fee of only 1.9 percent of a store's sales. Of that, Kroc's company could retain only 1.4 percent to cover its costs of servicing the store. The rest—0.5 percent of all McDonald's sales—was to go to the McDonald brothers for the use of their name and fast-food system.

Had Kroc been more financially oriented, he might have realized just how one-sided that deal was. Had the McDonald brothers understood that there was more to franchising than selling their name and providing a skimpy operating manual, they would have realized that there was no way Kroc could properly service his franchisees and still make a profit. That Kroc accepted the deal was the surest evidence of his desperation. "I went along with it because the Multimixer business was so bad, and I had to get into something that had a future," Kroc recalled.

He also went along because his initial goal was not making money on franchising but on selling Multimixers to his franchisees. With the prospect of hundreds of McDonald's around the country, Kroc saw a way to reverse the decline in Multimixer sales. But, he recalled years later, even on the plane trip back home after signing the master franchising contract, he concluded that the Multimixer could not be the heart of the new business. While the high-volume San Bernardino operation used as many as four Multimixers at once, most McDonald's operators would not require more than two. Even the store that Kroc planned to build as a showcase in Des Plaines, Illinois, would use only two Multimixers. Indeed, Kroc could sell hundreds of McDonald's franchises in a single year, and his company still could not sustain itself by selling each a pair of $150 milk shake mixers. "I started thinking about McDonald's more realistically," Kroc remembered. "When my franchisees bought a Multimixer, it would last them for ten years, whereas the hamburger business had sales every day, every day."

Kroc's decision to focus on hamburgers was validated by Multimixer's sales record. Even with patronage from McDonald's operators, by the mid-1960s Kroc's Prince Castle Sales was still selling only two thousand of the machines a year—the same level as a decade before, and about one-quarter of the sales volume of Multimixer's best years. Then in 1965, McDonald's discontinued use of the Multimixers and shifted to direct-draw milk shake machines similar to those that the chain uses today.

Kroc's background as a salesman in the food service industry had given him the vision to see the opportunity in fast food. But it also gave him the tools to capitalize on it. When Kroc, on March 2, 1955, formed his new franchising company, McDonald's System, Inc. (the name was changed to McDonald's Corporation in 1960), his initial strategies were clearly those of an experienced food service salesman. Chief among those was Kroc's decision not to deviate from the basic format the McDonald brothers had developed. While his company made major operational changes to improve efficiency and encourage systemwide consistency, those changes were refinements and not fundamental alterations of what the McDonald brothers had invented.

Such an inclination was natural for a salesman who got more satisfaction from selling an existing product than from inventing a new one. Yet, it was an inclination many others who ventured into fast food did not have. Most of those who entered the business by copying an existing fast-food format eventually were tempted to add their signature to it, creating a new format they could call their own. The temptation was understandable: the field was in its infancy and there were no recognized experts. Who was to say that the McDonald brothers had invented the best fast-food system or even one worth franchising nationally without substantial modification?

Indeed, before Kroc, most of those who were lured into fast food after seeing the brothers' San Bernardino store were not so enamored of their concept that they resisted toying with it. They copied only what they perceived were the essentials, and modified everything else to create what they hoped was a better system, one that carried *their* name. Typically, they failed to perceive all of the essentials, and their operations were seldom as good or as profitable. The mistake was repeated often in the development of fast food, and the worst offenders were the more experienced food service operators who entered the new market late and who were convinced that they knew more than the upstart fast-food pioneers.

Perhaps because he was *only* a salesman, not a veteran food service operator, Kroc saw the trap. Like the others who copied the McDonalds, Kroc could simply have copied their concept and franchised his version of it without cutting them in on 0.5 percent of the gross. Though some believe that he chose otherwise to get a more marketable name than "Kroc's," that explanation is superficial. Kroc provided a more complete explanation two decades ago when he was asked at a management class at Dartmouth College why he had franchised the McDonald's System instead of "stealing" it. Kroc replied that if he had done the latter, he would have "paid in an intangible way a hell of a lot to find out all the mistakes that they [the McDonald brothers] had made years before. I didn't want to go through those mistakes. When something works and is proven, you have a big head start."

Yet, when it came to franchising the McDonald's System, Kroc concluded that the methods others had used—including the brothers themselves—did not work. He was convinced that a totally new approach to franchising had to be tried. That, too, was a product of his equipment sales experience. The most critical lessons of his years selling Multimixers were probably those he picked up watching the mounting troubles of the very first food service franchisers, many of whom, such as Dairy Queen and Tastee-Freez, were his customers. Kroc was a fascinated observer of these franchising pioneers. What fascinated him most was how they had taken such a short-term, easy-money approach to their business by stacking the deck so much in their favor and against their partners, the franchisees.

Don Conley, the first franchising vice president for McDonald's and before that a sales manager for a company that sold fudge warmers to the same accounts that Kroc sold Multimixers, recalls how Kroc would excoriate the franchisers they saw at restaurant trade shows. "He would talk about what asses these guys were," Conley says, "how they were taking all the money at the expense of the franchisees. They were always more concerned about what they were going to get than about what their franchisees were going to get, and it blinded them to other aspects of the business. Ray's theory was totally opposite. He thought that if franchisers made their franchisees successful, they would automatically be successful. His new idea was to provide the franchisees with enough services to be successful."

Essentially, the approach Kroc took in franchising was the same as he took in selling food service supplies: his success was based on finding a way to make his customers successful with his product. As simple as it sounds, it was a revolutionary idea in the rapidly expanding food franchising business, and Kroc's notion of a fair and balanced franchise partnership is without question his greatest legacy.

In all other food franchising schemes, franchisers made their profits before their franchisees did, either by selling franchise territories to investors for huge up-front fees or by supplying franchisees with food, paper, and equipment—typically at markups that were higher than they would pay on the open market. By comparison, everything in Kroc's franchising plan was designed to encourage the success of his franchisees first, and on that McDonald's itself would prosper. Kroc instinctively knew that making an easy killing at the expense of his franchisees would not produce anything that would last. McDonald's was in business to satisfy the retail consumer, but as a veteran salesman Kroc knew he was also in business to serve his franchisees and build loyalty with them. They were his customers, too, and if they failed, he failed.

The fact that so many entrepreneurs were willing to join in partnership with Kroc during the lean early years of McDonald's reveals the most powerful aspect of Kroc's salesmanship—his belief in what he was selling and his ability to communicate it. To be sure, Kroc's salesmanship was to be put to its severest test, because the idea of a national hamburger chain selling a product for only 15 cents was more than unorthodox. It was considered unworkable by most food service professionals.

But if he had done nothing else, Kroc had mastered the art of selling, and no small part of that involved a natural gift for communication. Kroc was an engaging and articulate conversationalist, and whenever he stepped up to a microphone he worked magic. McDonald's Senior Chairman Fred Turner recalls how effortlessly Kroc could deliver a stirring speech: "Ray was the best extemporaneous speaker I ever heard. He would walk up to a podium with a piece of paper with three words on it. He would talk for ten minutes, look down and get a word, and go off on another subject."

When Kroc put those speaking skills to work in a personal presentation, he could sell almost anything, even an idea as unproven as fast food. To those who heard it, Kroc's sales pitch for McDonald's was riveting, and few were unmoved by it. "When Ray talked about McDonald's, he could touch people, move them," Turner observes. "He was human, warm, had a good sense of humor, but he would also get to the gut issues. He would have his rallying points, such as quality and cleanliness, but he could humanize them, personalize them. Quality was not a subjective thing; it was real. When he talked about the bun and how you toast it, you could see the bun. By the time he got through talking about buns, you were hungry."

Kroc had to make his sales pitch to four critical audiences—his prospective suppliers, his young managers, his company's first lenders, and his franchisees. In the end, Kroc built McDonald's by persuading all four to cast their lots with him and take the same substantial risks on a new idea as he was taking. While Kroc had a better than average fast-food format and an extremely attractive franchising plan, his success at persuading his four audiences rests largely in the way he sold his system, not in the system itself.

His sales method combined an appealing personal style with a surprisingly open and honest approach. Kroc was a man with few personal secrets and was almost embarrassingly open about his personal finances—what he earned, what he paid for his house, what he owed. That candor carried over into his business. Kroc's descriptions of the prospects of a McDonald's franchise were not filled with the glowing promises that were commonly made by franchisers in the 1950s. They were, instead, reasoned, hard hitting, and real.

From the beginning, Kroc's operators provided him with detailed reports on sales and costs, and those financial details were freely provided to prospective franchisees. When those prospects asked Kroc how much money they would make in a McDonald's unit, he provided them with samples of profit and loss statements, but he was careful to warn new franchisees that there was no guarantee their stores would do the same. "The hardest question I faced was when a fellow would ask, 'How much money do I pay myself in salary?' " Kroc recalled. "I'd say, 'Nothing. When you need twenty-five or fifty dollars, take it out. That's what you live on. At the end of the year, whatever money you have in the business is the money you make.' I couldn't tell them a salary to pay themselves because I didn't know what it would be."

Kroc expected the same open relationship with his suppliers. Their costs and prices would be fully disclosed so that the franchisees would know that his company was not benefiting from any kickbacks. To Kroc, complete honesty was essential in selling something as nebulous as a franchise. "When you sell something like that, anyone can say you are a con man," Kroc said. "But if they figure you are honest, then that's something different. I think most franchisees thought I was being honest with them."

Kroc's candid sales approach was reinforced by his disarming capacity for dealing with hundreds of people on an extremely personal basis. Even when he was in his seventies and the McDonald's System encompassed thousands of outlets, Kroc would astonish franchisees whom he had not seen in years by remembering details about them that had surfaced in casual conversation years before. "From the moment he met someone," Turner observes, "Ray was entering notes in his mental book on them—what they liked to eat and drink, what music they liked, and what kind of ties they wore. He never forgot those details, and years later he would pull them out of the book and use them. It never failed to impress people."

Simply put, Kroc charmed people into McDonald's, and the ultimate source of that charm was Kroc's unshakable belief in the future of the fast-food concept he had discovered on the fringe of the Mojave Desert. When the early suppliers who extended his franchisees credit, or the licensees who took second mortgages on their homes to get a

McDonald's, or the managers who gave up traditional career paths are asked why they linked their destinies to a fifty-two-year-old salesman who was questioning all the rules of the food service business, they reply with unanimity that they were caught off guard by Kroc's enthusiasm for McDonald's. When Jack Smith popped into McDonald's headquarters office in 1958 to satisfy his curiosity about the new fast-food franchise operation that was sprouting up in his hometown of Chicago, he was introduced immediately to Kroc, who showed Smith profit-and-loss statements with 20 percent bottom lines and told him how his background as a clothing store manager was "perfect" for a McDonald's franchise. "I thought at first that I was in the hands of a con man, and I started thinking about making a graceful exit," recalls Smith, an eight-store franchisee in Mobile, Alabama. "I knew that nothing legal in retailing made that type of return. But when I looked in his blue eyes, they showed a sincere and credible man. I had looked into Henry's [another 15-cent-hamburger chain starting in Chicago at the same time as McDonald's], and I had run into a blowhard who told me how they were going to make it big. Ray was not a blowhard, not an exaggerator. You felt a charisma, a glow about his down-to-earth enthusiasm. When I left his office, I thought that even if I never went back to McDonald's, my life had been enriched."

Kroc's enthusiasm for McDonald's no doubt sprang from his chief trait as a salesman—eternal optimism. Kroc never doubted the future of what he was selling, and he seemed undaunted by current failures. Even when his Multimixer business was falling apart in early 1952, Kroc was writing uplifting newsletters to his dealers, noting in one 1953 newsletter that "new fields must be tackled and new and better sales gimmicks constantly tested by any sales team that is worth being on." He concluded the message with one of a dozen positive-thinking "Krocisms" that still adorn McDonald's corporate offices and affect the outlook of the managers in them: "No one knows all the answers to increased sales. If you did, you would be ripe and when you ripen, you rot."

Though Kroc had turned fifty-two years old a few months before he incorporated McDonald's System, he had yet to ripen. He possessed the energy and stamina of a man in his thirties. Don Conley, Kroc's first licensing manager, recalls how he and Kroc would leave the McDonald's office at five minutes to six just in time to double-time it four blocks to catch the six-o'clock train at the Northwestern station. As they boarded the train, Conley could never understand why he, a man in his thirties, was gasping for breath when his boss, nearly twenty years his senior, was not.

Despite the fact that he was at an age when most achievers think of savoring their success, Kroc was ready to put his bountiful energies behind his newest venture. He knew he would become totally preoccupied with a new business, working again seventy hours a week as he had as a youth. He knew that meant cutting back on other passions such as golf. (Kroc later admitted that McDonald's added ten strokes to his handicap.) He knew also that he would have to make a considerable financial sacrifice at a period in his life when most people begin thinking of financial security. Kroc was not entering McDonald's as a wealthy man. His income from Multimixer had been cut in half, to $12,000 a year. He would live off that income for the next eight years and would not collect his first dollar in salary from McDonald's until 1961. He temporarily cut out such frills as membership in his country club and began holding his household payments back to the last day possible. He increased his personal bank borrowings and even borrowed on his life insurance to help cover the salaries of some of his new employees.

To be sure, Kroc was willing to grasp the McDonald's opportunity because things had deteriorated so badly at Prince Castle. But while Kroc was hoping that McDonald's would improve his financial position in the long run, he was not looking to get rich overnight. In fact, money appears not to have been an important motivator for Ray Kroc. He would tell his employees to concentrate on doing a good job, not on making money. If they worked hard and loved their work, he told them, money problems would resolve themselves. "If someone only likes making money, I'm not attracted to them," Kroc said years later. "I like anybody who likes what he's doing, because that's the thing that I treasure most."

What was motivating Ray Kroc more than anything else was the belief that he had at last found the idea that could be the foundation of the major enterprise he had been hoping to build since leaving the security of Lily-Tulip in the late 1930s. This was now 1954, and at age fifty-two Ray Kroc was still looking for the magic—something that would allow him to capitalize on his three decades of sales experience. In McDonald's, he was convinced that he had *the* sales opportunity he had trained for. He also knew it was the type of opportunity that would never come his way again. "It was practically life or death for me," Kroc said. "If I lost out on McDonald's, I'd have no place to go."

Chapter 3
THE FRANCHISING DERBY

Some enterprises succeed because those who undertake them blaze a new trail. Apple Computer grabbed a major share of the microcomputer market by introducing the first personal computer. Federal Express is the leader in overnight package delivery because it was the first to conceive of a mass market for such a service. Xerox is a leader in office equipment because it commercialized xerography. Because McDonald's enjoys such a dominant position in fast food, it is understandable why it is widely considered the creator of fast-food franchising and is sometimes perceived as the inventor of all franchising. It was neither.

When Ray Kroc formed McDonald's System, Inc., on March 2, 1955, he was among a dozen or so entrepreneurs who were seeking to extend franchising into the fledgling fast-food business. Kroc's McDonald's had no head start in franchising against the likes of Burger King, Kentucky Fried Chicken, or Chicken Delight. They were already in business. Within a couple of years of starting McDonald's, Kroc found himself in an overcrowded field that included such additional competitors as Burger Chef, Burger Queen, Carol's, and Sandy's. Furthermore, the new fast-food chains were merely applying franchising methods used in other industries since the turn of the century.

Modern business franchising was introduced in the United States just after the Civil War when the Singer Sewing Machine Company developed a chain of retail outlets by selling franchises to local operators who owned and ran the stores. But franchising did not really take hold until the early 1900s when the auto manufacturers and the soft drink companies developed their national distribution networks by franchising to local dealers and bottlers. The advantages they saw were compelling. Local investors would lay out most of the capital—and take most of the risk—in building a distribution system. Wholesale pricing was more stable than retail pricing; and in the case of the auto makers, local dealers, not Detroit, would be confronted with the problems of trade-ins and repairs. In addition, the manufacturers reasoned that they would strengthen their appeal to the retail market by placing their sales operations in the hands of local operators. In the early 1930s, the major oil companies began to see the same advantages and made a massive conversion to franchised dealerships.

Such so-called manufacturers' franchises dominated the early years of franchising. But by the 1930s, franchising began to spill over into the retailing and service industries, where it eventually experienced its greatest growth. In the early 1930s, auto parts distributors, such as Western Auto Supply Company, began building their nationally franchised chains. Drugstore chains such as Rexall, variety stores such as Ben Franklin, and grocery store chains such as IGA (Independent Grocers Association) all began to follow suit.

With the popularity of the automobile, America was becoming a mobile society, and—thanks to radio—a national market as well. Producers were establishing national brands through advertising, and retailers, too, were looking for the same brand recognition from one market to another. Their solution was in franchising their outlets.

Not surprisingly, the franchising of food service establishments paralleled the rise of the automobile. In 1924, two entrepreneurs by the name of Allen and White founded the first franchised food service chain based on their distinctive root beer syrup. Their A&W Root Beer stands catered to drive-in business, and while the stands later sold food items, the initial menu was root beer only. A&W sold its first territorial franchises for as much as $2,000 each, but the company made most of its profits on the sales of root beer concentrate and cooling equipment to its franchisees. The chain had hundreds of outlets before lack of uniformity in their menu and operations sabotaged its effort to convert to fast-food service.

Today, A&W's only remaining claim to fame in franchising comes from the business it sprouted. In 1927, J. Willard Marriott went into the food service business by getting the A&W franchise in Washington, D.C. Within a year, Marriott converted his A&W Root Beer stands to Hot Shoppe's, a popular local restaurant chain specializing in barbeque sandwiches. In time, of course, Marriott Corporation became the nation's largest hotel chain.

But it is Howard Johnson who normally gets credit for developing the first franchised food service operation when he began franchising his roadside restaurants and ice cream parlors in 1935. Johnson demonstrated to the food service business what type of leverage a chain could obtain by relying on the capital and operational skills of franchisees. Within four years, Howard Johnson's name was on more than one hundred outlets, which made his chain the dominant food service provider in the United States. Johnson's operation further established the approach to food franchising that A&W had started. Virtually all of his company's revenues came from ice cream and other food products supplied to franchisees from company-owned commissaries.

But the food service industry's franchising boom did not really develop until Harry Axene began his licensing efforts in the mid-1940s. In 1944, Axene, a farm equipment sales manager for Allis Chalmers, discovered a totally new kind of ice cream store in East Moline, Illinois, while there on a family visit. It was operated by Jim Elliott, but John McCullough, a dairy operator in Davenport, Iowa, owned the rights to the equipment and the manufacturing process. McCullough had purchased those from Harold Oltz, who had invented a freezer that chilled a liquid dairy mix in a five-foot-long cylinder and produced a continuous flow of soft ice cream, not unlike the frozen custard that vendors were hand dipping from vats. To make a cone in seconds, the operator needed only open the spigot on the machine. As Axene drove by Elliott's store he was intrigued by the long lines of customers he saw. "What are they selling, nylon stockings?" Axene asked his sister, referring to the scarcest product of the war. "No," she replied. "That's Dairy Queen."

McCullough, who had developed the Dairy Queen mix, knew that his soft ice cream product had much greater potential than one store, but he did not know how to market it. Axene did, and he persuaded McCullough to enter into a partnership to franchise Dairy Queen nationally. Axene's big break came when a Chicago ice cream cone manufacturer helped him recruit twenty-six investors—mostly from the ice cream trade—to attend a meeting at a Moline hotel. Axene prepared extensive charts describing the tremendous profit potential of a Dairy Queen franchise, but as he watched the group eagerly consume the soft ice cream samples he dished out, he knew he had a product that nearly sold itself.

All twenty-six investors were ready to pay for exclusive Dairy Queen franchises, some for territories covering entire states. Axene obliged, selling some territories for up-front fees of $25,000 to $50,000. That was just the bonus money. In addition, Axene charged franchisees

45 cents for every gallon of soft ice cream mix they bought. "Selling franchises was no problem," he recalls. "When they tasted the product, they were crazy about it."

The food franchising race began that day in Moline. With little more than a name, an uncomplicated dairy formula, and a relatively simple food service geared to a novel ice cream machine, Axene had a bonanza. He was perhaps the first to realize the instant wealth that fast-food franchising offered. He was not obliged to set standards, oversee operations, purchase materials, or market products. In fact, he needed do little more than collect his money to become an overnight millionaire.

Such easy money was certain to attract other franchisers. Drive-in food service operations were made to order for franchising because they were based on fixed menus and operating procedures that were relatively easy for beginners to master. And because they were such a departure from conventional restaurants, they attracted a wide variety of investors from outside the food service industry. Drive-ins such as Dairy Queen were particularly appealing to investors without much capital, including thousands of GIs returning from World War II and looking to make up for lost time. Many veterans got their start-up loans from the Small Business Administration. Nor was it uncommon for them to apply for Title 1 FHA loans—supposedly for expansion of their homes—and spend the money instead on food service franchises.

The astonishing growth of Dairy Queen triggered a revolution in the restaurant trade. By the time Axene resigned from Dairy Queen in 1948, there were 2,500 outlets in operation, and some franchisees had added hot dogs and other food products. By 1950, Axene had formed a new partnership with Leo Moranz, who had developed a smaller automatic freezer that was far superior to the Dairy Queen unit. The partners used the new machine to establish Tastee-Freez, which went into head-on competition with Dairy Queen. By the mid-1950s, Tastee-Freez had more than 1,500 outlets scattered around the country.

But while Axene and Moranz were developing one end of the drive-in franchising industry, Bob Wian was pioneering at the other. He had begun to franchise his full-service chain based on the Big Boy sandwich in the late 1930s, but Wian entered his heyday in franchising the carhop drive-in in the late 1940s, when a story on Big Boy appeared in *Time* magazine. "I was flooded with inquiries," Wian recalls, "to the point that I had to turn some people down."

Dairy Queen and Big Boy were on the extremes of food service franchising. A Dairy Queen outlet was based on one product, cost no more than $30,000, and was closed in the winter. By comparison, Wian franchised year-round, full-service restaurants, each requiring a capital investment of $250,000 or more. By the early 1950s, it was obvious that there was a huge void in between.

In fact, when Kroc struck his deal with the McDonald brothers in 1954, the void was already being filled. Drawn by the success of Dairy Queen and Big Boy, a number of operators had begun selling fast-food franchises that borrowed from both extremes. Two years before Kroc met the McDonalds, A. L. Tunick made the first move to extend fast-food franchising beyond the soft ice cream stands. Tunick, a scrap iron dealer, discovered a special oil cooker in a factory his company was dismantling. When the inventor of the cooker demonstrated to Tunick how his device could deep fry chicken under pressure in one-third the time of conventional deep fryers, Tunick decided to bankroll production of the cooker and build a franchised fast-food operation that would require franchisees to buy the cooker. When Tunick sold out to Consolidated Food in 1964, his Chicken Delight chain had several hundred stores.

But the largest fried chicken chain had its genesis in 1952, the year that Harlan Sanders, who ran a motel and restaurant in Corbin, Kentucky, met Pete Harmon, who ran a hamburger restaurant in Salt Lake City. The two struck up a friendship during a food service seminar in Chicago: shortly thereafter, Sanders visited Harmon on his way to a Christian church convention in Australia. When Harmon told his visitor how he was searching for a specialty item to add to his hamburger menu, Sanders replied, "I'm going to cook you dinner tonight."

The dinner that night was the best fried chicken Harmon had ever tasted. Before Sanders left town, Harmon got his secret combination of eleven herbs and spices, and within days he added the chicken to his menu. He also painted a sign on his restaurant window that read: KENTUCKY FRIED CHICKEN. When Sanders stopped in Salt Lake City on his return trip, he found that his chicken had become Harmon's hottest menu item, accounting for 50 percent of his sales. In fact, during its first year with Kentucky Fried Chicken, Harmon's restaurant sales grew threefold to $450,000; and when Harmon opened a new restaurant in 1952, he invited Sanders out to the grand opening, billing him as the Kentucky Colonel.

Harmon encouraged Sanders to franchise his chicken product nationally, and in 1954 Sanders agreed. His plan was simple: provide his recipe to restaurant operators who buy a territorial franchise to Kentucky Fried Chicken, and charge them a nickel for every bird they sold. Harmon became the first franchisee, and Jim Collins, who had earlier copied the McDonald brothers' hamburger system with his Hamburger Handout, soon followed suit. By 1986 their companies were the two largest KFC franchisees, each with more than two hundred and fifty stores.

While 1954 was a magical year in fast food for both Kroc and Sanders, they were not alone. In that same year, Dave Edgerton became the first franchisee of InstaBurger King, having obtained the franchise for Dade County (Miami), Florida, from Keith Kramer and Mattey Burns, the two Jacksonville operators who had gotten the national franchising rights to a fast-food system based on a novel automatic broiler developed by a Los Angeles equipment company. Within a year, Edgerton teamed up with Miami restaurant operator Jim McLamore.

Both had one thing in common that set them apart from virtually all other fast-food pioneers: they held degrees from the famed School of Hotel Administration at Cornell University. That alone made them standouts, because in the mid-1950s the emerging fast-food industry was attracting the mavericks of food service and entrepreneurs from a variety of other fields—and precious few operators trained in old-school ways. Still, Edgerton and McLamore became the only successful InstaBurger King franchisees by making a clean break with the conventions they had been taught. Edgerton totally redesigned the broiler to correct major design flaws of the initial equipment provided by InstaBurger King, and McLamore vastly expanded the appeal of the chain by creating a new quarter-pound hamburger he named The Whopper. By 1957, the partners had four stores in Miami, and they began franchising regionally their own revamped broiling operation and revised menu under a new name—Burger King, Home of the Whopper. A few years later, when the Jacksonville franchisers ran into financial problems, Edgerton and McLamore obtained the national rights to the Burger King System.

Edgerton and McLamore soon enticed another entrant into the fast-food race. They had approached General Equipment Company in Indianapolis to help them replace the old broilers and shake machines that had been the basis of the InstaBurger King franchise they had obtained for Miami in 1954. They especially wanted to dump the broiler, a Rube Goldberg device that featured a chain conveyor system to transport hamburgers through the broiler in metal baskets. The baskets were supposed to open at one end of the broiler for insertion of the patties, close to hold the burgers in place as they traveled over the broiler's flame, and automatically open at the other end to release the cooked hamburgers. Things did not always work that way, and the basket conveyor's penchant for total breakdown caused operating nightmares.

Edgerton designed a simpler, more efficient chain broiler without baskets, and he and McLamore turned to General Equipment to produce it. The equipment company was better known for its Sani-Serve soft ice cream machines and Sani-Shake milk shake machines, but when it began building the automated broilers for Burger King, General Equipment suddenly had a complete portfolio of fast-food machinery. The opportunity of competing with Burger King soon seemed better than supplying it. Thus, in 1957, Frank and Dave Thomas, the brothers who owned General Equipment, decided to franchise their own 15-cent hamburger chain based on a conveyor broiler, and with better financial backing, their fast-food entry—called Burger Chef—soon began expanding faster than Burger King.

Equipment manufacturers were not the only nonfood service operators who caught the fast-food franchising bug in the mid-1950s. Food producers, too, saw franchising as a natural and extremely beneficial extension of their primary business. Like the equipment vendors who entered the market, the food processors figured they could make most of their money by selling their products to franchisees. Only five months after Ray Kroc opened his first McDonald's store in Des Plaines in 1955, Bressler Ice Cream Company in Chicago opened its first 15-cent-hamburger operation, called Henry's, about ten miles away. The two were close in other respects. Henry's looked nearly like a carbon copy of a McDonald's drive-in because—indirectly at least—it was. While on the West Coast, David Bressler, one of the five brothers who owned the ice cream company, had seen Jim Collins's Hamburger Handout, one of the clones of the McDonald brothers' original store. Bressler thought he had discovered a perfect way to sell more ice cream, and he asked Collins to train his brother, Charles, so that he could get the Henry's operation started. Collins gave Chuck Bressler a three-week training session at Hamburger Handout and flew to Chicago to help open the first Henry's on the northwest side.

Nor were McDonald's and Henry's the only chains forming in the mid-1950s in hopes of transplanting to the Midwest the fast-food concept that was sweeping California. There were, in fact, at least three other Illinois-based chains. Chicago was also home base for Golden Point, another McDonald's look-alike that got off to a flashy start but was not heard from after the early 1960s. Sandy's was a Peoria-based chain started in 1957 by a few of Kroc's earliest franchisees who had copied the McDonald's System in violation of their contract. It, too, was a strong early competitor that later merged into Hardee's. And Carol's, the hamburger chain that Leo Moranz founded in Chicago in the late 1950s (and named after his only daughter), was an effort to expand beyond the Tastee-Freez franchise Moranz had started in 1950. Before the chain faded in the late 1960s—eventually to become a Burger King franchisee—Carol's opened about two hundred units.

Thus, when Ray Kroc opened his Des Plaines store on April 15, 1955, he was hardly a pioneer in fast-food franchising. Indeed, it seemed that everyone was suddenly discovering the opportunity Kroc had seen. About the only food service operators ignoring the new market were those who were perhaps the most logical candidates to enter it—the conventional, medium-priced restaurant chains. Perhaps that was because fast food was such a radical departure from food service traditions that conventional operators could not see the glamour of it. Whatever the reason, the most significant development in food service in this century did not attract the largest restaurant operators of the day, and particularly those two most oriented to a mobile market—Fred Harvey, which ran a chain of medium-priced restaurants at train and bus depots, and Howard Johnson, whose hundreds of roadside restaurants were arguably the precursor of fast-food franchising.

Even when they attempted to enter the fast-food market, the established restaurant chains were unable to comprehend the essence of the revolution that outsiders were igniting. Jim McLamore recalls a time in the mid-1950s when he was summoned to the office of Howard Johnson Sr., who wanted to inspect the conveyor broiler McLamore and Edgerton were using in their Burger King operation. The thirty-year-old McLamore, awestruck over the prospect of presenting his fast-food format to the legendary Johnson, packed up his broiler in his station wagon and drove to Johnson's office in Miami, where Johnson operated one of his commissaries. "It was like being ushered into the presence of a god," McLamore recalls. Johnson was fascinated with the Burger King concept, but his advisers quickly began adding ideas to recast it in the Howard Johnson mold. They insisted it have multiple ice cream flavors—the signature of the Johnson chain—and in addition to hamburgers there had to be other sandwiches. Eventually, Johnson's company joined the fast-food race with an entry called Ho Jo Jr's, one of the many fast-food operations sabotaged by a menu too broad and service too slow. "I took great delight—and I'm sure Ray Kroc did, too—in seeing people look at our fast-food system and try to improve on it," McLamore observes. "They didn't understand the simplicity of it, the consumer need it was fulfilling, or that the whole idea of it was fast service."

If Ray Kroc was not alone when he entered the fast-food market in 1955, he was at least armed with a unique concept. Popular images to the contrary, Kroc had not invented a 15-cent-hamburger, or a self-service drive-in, or a fast-food preparation system. What Kroc *was* inventing was a unique franchising system, one that set McDonald's apart from all the other early fast-food franchisers.

As Kroc surveyed the franchising industry he was about to enter, he saw serious flaws in the approach others were taking. As a vendor to other food franchisers, he had an objective view of the new industry that many of its other operators lacked. His background in food service encouraged him to adopt a long-term orientation to an industry that was offering many others a huge opportunity for short-term profits. Kroc's simple desire was to build a lasting fast-food business distinguished by uniformity and quality in its service and products. To get that, he demanded much more control over the system than other franchisers did, and in return he was willing to sacrifice the quick franchising profits others were making.

In the early years of building the business, Kroc exchanged dictaphone tapes with the McDonald brothers, who were also quality conscious. The single theme penetrating virtually all of his electronic epistles to the McDonalds was the self-destructibility inherent in what Kroc saw as the "franchising rackets" that made up the largest part of McDonald's competition in the 15-cent-hamburger business. Indeed, Kroc was prescient when it came to forecasting the development of fast-food franchising—how its ease of entry would lure hundreds of new outfits and how its brutally tough operating requirements would knock most of them out. "This is going to be probably one of the most competitive businesses in the U.S.," Kroc told the brothers in a 1958 tape. "And we have the only real solid approach to this business. The other ones are going to die like flies. They are rackets. They are fast-buck deals. They are a promotion. I now know of four 15-cent-ham-

burger deals, and heaven knows how many more there will be. And
they are going to be run loose as a goose. Those fellows [the franchi-
sees] are going to do any doggone thing they want to do, and the
owners of the name are just going to let them do anything they want as
long as they are getting money out of it. It will be a survival of the
fittest, and we are going to be on the top of the list of the fittest. I know
we have the only clean, honest franchise."

Essentially, Kroc's franchising formula was different from that of
other fast-food chains in several respects. The first, and perhaps most
critical, was the avoidance of territorial franchises. Kroc was determined to sell only single-store franchises and only for $950. He resisted
the basic allure of franchising that was attracting every other chain:
easy money. Selling exclusive operating licenses for large markets,
such as a state, is the fastest way for a franchiser to make money.
During Kroc's early franchising days, some franchisers were collecting
$50,000 or more simply by selling to a territorial franchisee the exclu-
sive right to use the franchiser's fast-food system in a major market.
That money was almost all gravy; the franchiser was not required to do
much to earn it. While he might have been obliged to provide some
very basic assistance in setting up the first operation and some fundamental training concerning his system of operation, most of the up-
front money collected from a territorial franchisee dropped neatly to
the franchising company's bottom line.

Occasionally, territorial franchises were pyramided, when a licensee holding a franchise for a broad territory sublicensed his rights
to others, collecting a sizable franchising fee up front from each one.
The subfranchisees, in turn, sold parts of their territories to a third level
of operators. That type of territorial licensing gave franchising a bad
name, since it opened up the field for exploitation by those seeking to
make a quick buck by selling a fast-food concept they did not operationally support.

When Kroc started McDonald's, selling exclusive territories was
the first rule of franchising. Dairy Queen and Tastee-Freez both granted
large franchising territories. Axene sold Dairy Queen territories for up
to $50,000 each, and by the time Moranz had franchised Tastee-Freez
nationally, he had only twenty-five master franchisees, all with large
and exclusive territories. Typically, Dairy Queen's master franchisees
sublicensed parts of their territories, sometimes through three or four
tiers of licensees. By the time the license was sold for an individual
store, the local operator often carried a huge burden in licensing fees.

With each franchising tier taking its cut from ice cream sales, the local store operator was stuck with a thin net margin. Rather than subsidize so many layers of franchising, many local Dairy Queen operators eventually abandoned the system—replacing the Dairy Queen sign with their own—after concluding that they had more to gain by operating independently.

Territorial franchising was by no means restricted to soft-serve ice cream. Most of the early hamburger and fried chicken chains engaged in it, too. In fact, Burger King's largest licensee, Diversifoods Incorporated, had the Burger King franchise for all of Louisiana and metropolitan Chicago. With 377 stores, its revenues exceed $500 million, making it the equivalent of a medium-sized fast-food chain. Indeed, in 1985, Burger King's parent, Pillsbury Company, acquired Diversifoods to gain complete control over its largest franchisee. The practice of territorial franchising has continued even with newer fast-food operations. Wendy's International grew rapidly in the 1970s in part because it aggressively sold large territorial franchises to major investors who were required to build new stores at a quick pace.

But even when the aims of the franchisers were honest, territorial franchising occasionally ran into serious problems. In addition to the defections Dairy Queen suffered, its territorial franchising made it extremely difficult to exert central control over the development of the chain. The large territorial franchisees, with considerable amounts of money invested in their local operations, developed their territories as they saw fit. Thus, Dairy Queens soon operated differently in different parts of the country. Some had food; some did not. They even offered different sizes of cones and types of sundaes. With little centralized supervision, the quality of local operations varied all over the map. While some operators provided a quality product and service, Axene recalls how others would "cheat" by adding water to their dairy mix and their toppings.

The real problem with territorial franchising was that a mistake in choosing a franchisee was immediately magnified. If a franchiser has a poor franchisee in one store, he has one type of problem. But if that same marginal operator has a contractual right to put up as many stores as he wants in his exclusive territory, the franchiser's quality problem becomes a nightmare.

When Axene left Dairy Queen in 1948 and later teamed up with Leo Moranz to form Tastee-Freez, the two tried to remedy some of the control problems that territorial franchising had caused. Tastee-Freez was based on a vastly improved freezer that produced soft-serve ice cream more efficiently by automatically pumping the liquid mix into the freezing barrel to replace the mix that was drawn out. By contrast, the Dairy Queen freezer required a relatively skilled operator to manually control the pump with one hand while drawing an ice cream cone with the other. While the freezer was the most expensive part of a Tastee-Freez operation, the relatively inexpensive pump was the heart of the system. Axene and Moranz devised a clever scheme for controlling their new chain by *selling* the freezer to territorial franchisees but *leasing* them the pump. If franchisees turned out to be weak operators, their damage to the system was limited by terminating their lease on the pump. In the Tastee-Freez jargon, the method of disciplining a recalcitrant operator was called "pulling the pump."

Still, the Dairy Queen and Tastee-Freez chains withered because of their inability to control their large territorial franchisees. Specifically, they missed the golden opportunity to climb aboard the fast-food bandwagon in the mid-1950s. Lacking control over their big franchisees, they could not convert their ice cream operations into food service outlets that offered uniform menus and service quality. And by failing to convert to fast food, both chains found it difficult to justify the higher cost of real estate during the 1960s. Tastee-Freez went nearly into oblivion a decade later. Though Dairy Queen made a better conversion to food service, it nevertheless lost the position it once held as the nation's dominant food franchiser.

Axene concedes that if he were to start franchising again, he would follow Kroc's more gradual approach to franchising by paying more attention to controlling quality and passing up the fast money from selling large, territorial licenses. "I'd go much slower and do everything first class," says Dairy Queen founder Axene. "We were in a hurry. We could see that money ahead of us, and we all wanted a share of it. I think he [Kroc] got his franchising ideas by watching Dairy Queen and by thinking about what would happen if he did the same thing Dairy Queen did. He avoided all that."

Kroc quickly established more control over his franchisees by selling one franchise at a time to operate only one store. While some early franchisees were granted territories for metropolitan areas such as Washington, D.C., Cincinnati, and Pittsburgh, Kroc quickly began to cut down the area covered by a franchise to a one- or two-mile radius, and by 1969 to the street address of the store. Even in his territorial agreements with early operators Kroc did not *sell* territorial rights; he *gave* them away. Nor did his territorial agreements give franchisees the right to build as many new McDonald's units in their territories as they chose to build. His territorial franchisees merely had the right to obtain additional stores *if McDonald's* chose to put additional stores in their territories. They could keep McDonald's from granting stores to anyone else in their territories, but they could not demand new stores for themselves.

Thus McDonald's could—and did—limit to just one store its early territorial licensees who had poor performance records. Strong operators, such as John Gibson and Oscar Goldstein in Washington and Lou Groen in Cincinnati, parlayed their late-1950s territorial agreements with Kroc into forty-three-store and forty-store operations, respectively, but other less dedicated territorial licensees never got beyond the first store. That is because Kroc chose to sacrifice immediate growth in their markets rather than lower the quality of the system. As a result, when McDonald's in 1971 moved to its eight-story home office building in Oak Brook, a white-collar suburb west of Chicago, it moved into the middle of a six-suburb market where it had only one restaurant. It was one of McDonald's most underdeveloped markets. The reason: Joseph Sweeney, who had gotten the territory in a deal he made with Kroc in 1957, ran a store that did not live up to McDonald's tough standards. Sweeney never got a license for a second store. The company bought back his franchise in 1968, and now Sweeney's old territory boasts fifteen McDonald's.

Of course, Kroc knew his company would start out on a more solid financial footing if he sold large territories for big up-front fees. But he also knew that investors signing those deals would want something for their money—namely, the assurance that they could pick their locations, build their own stores, and operate with little interference from Kroc. Thanks to his experience in selling Multimixers to chains such as Dairy Queen, Kroc had seen the inconsistency that results from lack of central control. Above all else, he wanted uniformity at McDonald's—a brand name that would stand for the same fast service and quality product throughout the country. And he was convinced that McDonald's could not get that unless it exercised substantial control over those to whom it granted licenses. While other chains started out permitting franchisees to deviate, conformity to operating standards was bedrock principle to Kroc from the beginning. "Now, damnit, we are not going to stand for any monkey business [from franchisees]," Kroc informed the McDonald brothers in a 1958 tape recording. "These guys want to sign a franchise, by God, it is a matter of buyer beware. Once they sign it, they are going to conform and we are going to hold to it that they do conform."

It followed naturally that Kroc disliked the idea of selling McDonald's fundamental asset—its franchise—to a wealthy investor whose operation and power might someday exceed that of Kroc's own company. "When you sell a big franchise territory," Kroc reasoned, "you give up the business to the man who owns the area. He replaces your organization, and you don't have control."

By retaining the right to determine whether a franchisee is to be granted a license to operate a second store and then another, McDonald's also retained the only carrot it could use to motivate a franchisee to follow the system's rules on quality, service, cleanliness, and value. As Kroc saw it, keeping that incentive was critical to McDonald's long-term profitability. To him, the practice of turning a short-term profit by selling exclusive territories for handsome fees epitomized the dark side of franchising. Kroc said of franchisers who engaged in the practice: "They were money hungry, and I was never afraid of them. They would not postpone making an honest, happy buck."

Kroc also resisted the temptation to make big profits by selling products and equipment to his franchisees. That policy also went against the industry's grain. Virtually all other major fast-food franchisers made a good portion of their profits on the markup on goods they supplied to their operators. Tastee-Freez sold freezers to its licensees. Dairy Queen took 45 cents out of every $1.40 gallon of mix its approved dairies sold to its operators. General Equipment provided shake machines, broilers, and most other kitchen equipment to its Burger Chef franchisees. Chicken Delight required its franchisees to purchase its chicken cookers. Howard Johnson built ice cream and candy plants to supply franchisees and operated huge commissaries that supplied store operators with much of their other food products. And Burger King's DavMor Industries (named after cofounders David Edgerton and James McLamore) manufactured broilers to be sold to its franchisees and operated commissaries that provided them with food products. In stark contrast, Kroc sold his franchisees just two $150 Multimixers and those only during McDonald's first decade.

Franchisers have to have some means of generating income, but selling products to franchisees can create the appearance—real or imagined—of a conflict of interest between the franchiser and the franchisee. In fact, the practice has led to some of fast-food franchising's most nettlesome litigation. Chicken Delight, for example, went out of business not long after it lost an antitrust suit to operators challenging a requirement that they buy only the chicken cookers made by the chain.

A greater, but more insidious, problem with supplying franchisees is that it can encourage restaurant chains to tend to their commissaries and manufacturing plants rather than to their stores. Their orientation shifts increasingly to the profits they make as suppliers, not as retailers, and as a result they begin to ignore store operations and their retail customers.

That appears to have been the case with Burger Chef, which for a period in the 1960s was the most serious challenger McDonald's had. Its parent, General Equipment, manufactured most of the $25,000 worth of equipment that went inside each Burger Chef. The chain, formed a couple of years after McDonald's, copied its 15-cent-hamburger operation, and with General Equipment's financial support it grew rapidly. By 1968, when Burger Chef was sold to General Foods, it had nearly a thousand stores, just a dozen stores fewer than market leader McDonald's. But then Burger Chef went into a tailspin. By the early 1970s, General Foods was taking massive write-offs on Burger Chef, and the chain's breakneck expansion abruptly ended. Later, Burger Chef was sold again, and while it is still in operation, it is no longer a major factor in fast food.

What accounts for such a startling demise? The most common explanation is that Burger Chef's parent looked at the chain as an outlet for its equipment and did not put the same stress on perfecting store operations. Jack Roshman, once Burger Chef's largest franchisee and later a cofounder of Ponderosa Inc., the steak house chain, cites a natural conflict of interest between Burger Chef's equipment and restaurant business. Roshman, who opened more than one hundred Burger Chefs in Ohio, argues that the Burger Chef system was based on a broiler instead of a grill because General Equipment sold a broiler, not a grill. "I always wanted a grilled hamburger [at Burger Chef], and I fought for it, because I think the American public likes a grilled hamburger better than they do a broiled one," Roshman says. "But we *sold* broilers, and so we had broilers in our restaurants."

Similarly, he argues that the best french fryer then on the market was made by a Chicago company called Keating, which supplied McDonald's. Burger Chef franchisees initially used that fryer, too, until

General Equipment began supplying one of its own, which in Rosh-man's judgment was inferior. When an equipment company is in the food service business as a means of selling equipment, Roshman says, "you tend not to buy the best products [for the fast-food chain] because you buy the ones you are making. You rationalize that your products are as good."

Ultimately, General Equipment was providing about three-fourths of all the equipment going into each Burger Chef, and Roshman believes that funds that should have been spent on improving restaurant operations were spent instead on developing new types of equipment. Roshman even suggested that General Equipment spin off Burger Chef, allowing it to make equipment purchases independently. But his opinion was not shared by Frank Thomas, who ran General Equipment along with his brother Dave. "You couldn't run both businesses well," says Roshman. "They should have allowed me the flexibility to buy equipment where I could get the best price and best product instead of forcing their equipment down my throat."

Kroc understood that selling high-priced territorial franchises and profiting on sales of supplies to franchisees shared a fundamental weakness: the franchiser made most of his or her money before the franchisee's restaurant even opened and thus was less dependent on that restaurant's success for profits. Invariably, observes McDonald's Senior Chairman Fred Turner, chains that tried to copy McDonald's, but that also made easy money selling territories and equipment to franchisees, never wound up with operations that measured up to McDonald's. Their buildings were not as sound, their products were not as good, their service was not as quick, and their stores not as clean. Turner believes that franchising practices explain why: "They didn't mind the store, because the operation of the store was not where they were making their money. When a franchiser gets most of his revenue before the store opens, whether it be through equipment sales or heavy up-front franchise fees, most of his job is done. The aftermath means less to him than it does to us."

By contrast, sales at the store meant everything to McDonald's because Kroc only sold a one-store franchise, initially for a fee of only $950. McDonald's made most of its money on the 1.9 percent of stores' sales that it collected as a service fee. There were no profits in selling territories and none on equipment either, aside from the small profit Prince Castle made on Multimixers. "Our method of collecting revenue was almost totally dependent on the sales volume of the franchised store," Turner explains. "And so our economic interests were not in conflict with the franchisee's interests, but compatible with them."

In short, while other franchisers were figuring out ways to pad their bottom line, McDonald's was concentrating on ways to pad its top line—the total revenues of all franchised restaurants in the McDonald's System. If they succeeded in doing that, Kroc repeatedly told his corporate managers, the profits of the franchising company and its franchisees would take care of themselves. Because the success of local operators was crucial to McDonald's own success, Kroc was careful to avoid doing things that put franchisees at an economic and, therefore, competitive disadvantage. McDonald's, he concluded, must play a major role from the beginning in selecting suppliers for its franchisees, but it did so to obtain the price advantages resulting from the system's broader purchasing power. Kroc then passed those price breaks directly to his franchisees, rejecting the common practice of early fast-food chains of accepting a rebate from suppliers.

While he was aware of all their other flaws, Kroc was convinced that the fundamental weakness of other franchised chains was their penchant for getting a cut of the supplier's price to franchisees. The whole purpose of a franchise system, he realized, was to obtain the benefits of cooperative purchasing so that restaurant operators in the chain could sell food at a lower price than they could if they ran their restaurants independently. "No one could accuse us of taking kickbacks, commissions, or anything of that kind unless he wanted to face about a million-dollar slander suit, because I would throw one at him in a split second," Kroc told the McDonald brothers in an early taped letter. "Our operators know which side their bread is buttered on. And the result is that they are cooperative. When you find a good selfish reason for people to cooperate with you, you are pretty sure of their cooperation."

Conversely, Kroc believed the supply practices of other chains invited rebellion from their franchisees. On that score, too, Kroc's foresight was twenty-twenty. "A great many Howard Johnson units are now bootlegging stuff [food supplies] because the prices being charged them by Howard Johnson are so completely out of line with what they can buy locally that demoralization has set in," Kroc reported to the brothers in a 1958 tape. "I mean it has set in bad. Howard Johnson is definitely on the way down."

Kroc was so adamant about rejecting the rebates that fast-food vendors customarily gave to franchisers on supplies they sold to their franchisees that he even turned down innocent gratuities from McDonald's suppliers. Harry Smargon, who had founded a tiny shortening company in Chicago in 1952, began getting orders over the phone from Kroc, who had heard about Smargon's shortening from another of his vendors. It was 1956, and Kroc had just founded McDonald's and had only three stores in the Chicago area. Still, the orders—five hundred pounds a crack—seemed big to Smargon, who decided after a few unsolicited orders that it was time to meet his new benefactor.

"Ray, this has never happened to me where a customer calls me up and gives me order after order without wanting something in return," Smargon told Kroc. "What is it that you want?" Smargon wondered if there was some business favor he could perform for McDonald's.

"Harry, I don't want you to wine me or dine me, and I don't want any Christmas presents," Kroc replied. "I want only the best quality shortening you can give me."

Smargon's company, Interstate Foods, eventually wound up as the largest supplier of shortening in the fast-food business, with revenues exceeding $100 million a year. Smargon's son Kenneth, who ran the company for a decade after it was acquired by CFS Continental, recalls how some fast-food chains wanted a penny kickback for every pound of shortening Interstate sold to their franchisees and why Smargon refused to deal with them. "They had no right to that penny," Ken Smargon says. "It was just a handicap on the operator. It was just greed." By not indulging in kickbacks, Smargon says, McDonald's showed suppliers and franchisees alike that "it was in business for the long haul, not the short haul." It is not surprising, he adds, that all the chains that once came to him seeking kickbacks no longer exist.

By refusing to profit at the expense of its franchisees, McDonald's was putting the franchisees' financial position ahead of its own. The essence of Kroc's unique but amazingly simple franchising philosophy was that a franchising company should not live off the sweat of its franchisees, but should succeed by helping its franchisees succeed. While such a philosophy has an appealing sense of human justice to it, it also made faultless business logic, because a franchising company cannot succeed without a harmonious relationship with its franchising partners.

In the end, the genius of Ray Kroc was that he treated his franchisees as equal partners. He was but one of dozens to see the mind-boggling potential of quick-service restaurants, but he had something no one else had—franchisees working on his side. Because Kroc and his company had acted in the system's interest, he was in a position to inspire franchisees to do likewise. What eventually separated McDonald's from the rest of the pack was Kroc's ability to marshal the efforts of hundreds of other entrepreneurs—his McDonald's franchisees—to work not merely for their selfish interests but for McDonald's interests. As Ray Kroc saw it, they were one and the same.

Chapter 4
THE OWNER/OPERATOR

To a large extent, the corporate culture defines how receptive managers are to change. Some companies have traditions of playing things close to the vest. They discover a winning formula and never deviate from it. Other companies make changes eagerly. Their managers continually experiment with new ideas, on the notion that what worked yesterday may not work tomorrow.

Understandably, McDonald's looks like the former. It has never strayed from the one business it knows. And it has pursued that business with a tamper-proof set of principles on franchising and an unshakable commitment to quality, service, and cleanliness that has produced a restaurant chain that is best known for its consistency from one store to the next.

But beneath this cloak of uniformity hides a corporate culture that worships flexibility. McDonald's managers take pride in their ability to "turn on a dime." Overnight they drop carefully laid plans that have been torpedoed by a shifting market. They revel in experimentation. They expect mistakes. But when things go wrong, they quickly admit problems and address them.

That trial-and-error mentality has its roots in Ray Kroc's search for his first franchisees. His franchising principles were flawless and not open for compromise, but when it came to putting them into practice in the mid-1950s, Kroc had no magic. In fact, he learned mostly by making mistakes, and his first lesson involved location.

He decided to begin building his fast-food chain in California. It was the land of the automobile. It had a superb climate, which allowed drive-ins to operate year-round. And it was the market in which McDonald's—and the entire fast-food industry—had taken root. By the time Kroc had signed the national franchising agreement with the McDonald brothers, nine McDonald's stores, including eight licensed directly by the brothers, were in operation. All but one of those (in Phoenix) were operating in California. In short, California was an ideal market to sell a franchise. "They knew more about drive-ins in California than they did in any other part of the country," Kroc later explained.

Fully half of the eighteen McDonald's franchises Kroc signed during the first year of his agreement with the brothers were for stores to be located in California. However, while franchises were easier to sell in California, franchisees were impossible to control. The stores were nearly two thousand miles from Kroc's headquarters in Chicago, and his fledgling McDonald's System, Inc., was in no position to service its West Coast operators and maintain the quality control and operational uniformity Kroc demanded. Instead, his California franchisees began taking their cues from operators who had been signed by the McDonald brothers or from independents who had plagiarized their system. Since those operators lacked any regimen, the result was a disaster. Kroc's new franchisees soon were experimenting with new products, new procedures, and new (and higher) prices. Few maintained the high standards of quality and cleanliness that the brothers had established in San Bernardino. In 1957, Kroc dispatched his young operations lieutenant, Fred Turner, to California to get his first look at the company's West Coast operations—and his first glance at a franchising system run amok.

It was obvious that Turner's trip to the West Coast was Kroc's way of teaching him what can happen to a fast-food chain when it loses control over quality. What Turner saw at McDonald's in California amounted to fast-food anarchy. It left an impression that no lecture from the boss on quality control could come close to producing. "Ray knew what I was going to see, and it must have been a delicious moment for him when I came back and he listened to what the hell I had to say," Turner recalls. "McDonald's in California was a zoo. Instead of a uniform ten-to-the-pound hamburger, I saw eight, nine, ten, and eleven to the pound, some with onions ground in the patty as an extender and some added separately [as required]. And instead of a ten-item menu, I saw a foodarama—burritos, enchiladas, hot dogs, tacos, corn dogs, chili, pizza, and roast beef. Prices were all over the lot —some stores at fifteen cents on hamburgers, some at seventeen, some eighteen, some nineteen, and some twenty-one. I saw the filthiest McDonald's I have seen in thirty years. I had been hearing Ray Kroc preach about uniformity, about a standard menu, one-size portions, same prices, same quality in every store. It had been pounded into me, and I accepted these basic tenets. But, man, when I came back from California, there was a conviction."

But Turner believes that Ray Kroc's miserable licensing experience in California in the first few years "was the greatest thing that ever happened to the McDonald's System because we could see what would happen if we let the system get away from us. We concluded from then on that you fight with maverick franchisees about price, you fight over portions, you fight about everyone using the same chocolate, and you fight about menu."

The experience in California also persuaded Kroc temporarily to suspend franchising on the West Coast and to concentrate his franchising closer to home, beginning in Illinois and fanning out to neighboring states. Fortunately, Kroc in early 1955 had begun building his own McDonald's in Des Plaines in a fifty-fifty joint venture with Art Jacobs, a home builder who was a fellow member of Rolling Green Country Club in nearby Arlington Heights. From the beginning, the store was designed to be a showcase to attract franchising prospects in the Midwest who had no idea what a self-service drive-in was all about. But, with the collapse of the franchising effort in California, the Des Plaines unit suddenly became the focal point of Kroc's licensing effort, which was now aimed at prospects in and around his hometown.

But that change in course immediately created problems of its own. Indeed, Kroc ran smack into a new fast-food rival that had the potential to deliver a crippling blow to his revised franchising plan. Unlike all other early fast-food competitors, this one had something Kroc thought only he himself had—an exclusive area franchise to the McDonald's System. It was held by Frejlich Ice Cream Company, which had obtained a local franchise from the McDonald brothers just before Kroc had signed his national licensing contract. The Frejlich brothers had paid $10,000 for a license to build four stores; and since the McDonalds had sold fourteen other limited area franchises, this one would have been a minor irritant except for one very important difference. The Frejlich license was for Cook County, Illinois—site of Chicago, perennial location for the National Restaurant Association convention, and headquarters of Prince Castle Sales and its founder, Ray Kroc. It was where Ray Kroc had trained for thirty years for the McDonald's opportunity, where he had his best food service contacts. Chicago was the obvious and perhaps the only place for Kroc to locate his headquarters for McDonald's System, Inc. It was also where Kroc now wanted to locate his prototype McDonald's store, something the Frejlich agreement prevented.

Kroc had already begun planning the Des Plaines unit when he paid a visit to the Frejlichs to sell them Multimixers. While on that sales call he happened to mention the deal he had just struck with the McDonald brothers. Right then the Frejlichs hit Kroc with the bad news.

As soon as he got back to his office, Kroc placed an angry call to the McDonald brothers. "Do you think I'm going to work on this [national licensing] and not have an exclusive?" he fumed.

Dick McDonald tried to calm him down. "Ray, there is no way we can back out of the Frejlich deal," he said. "Besides, you've got the whole rest of the country to work on."

McDonald had picked the wrong thing to say, and Kroc got hotter. "This is all my territory," he insisted.

McDonald held his ground. "No, it is all your territory except for what we sold to Frejlich," he responded.

"But I live in Cook County; how the hell can you give it to Frejlich?" Kroc screamed. "That's my headquarters!"

McDonald, calling on his ample reserve of New England stubbornness, hung up on Kroc and then fired off a short telegram with a big message: "The deal is off."

Several days later, Kroc sent his West Coast Multimixer representative, Bill Jamison, on a peace-keeping mission to San Bernardino to revive the deal with the McDonald brothers. Fortunately for Kroc, the Frejlichs were not as interested in building a McDonald's unit as they were in making a quick profit on the sale of the franchise they had just purchased. Kroc offered to buy their Cook County McDonald's license, and they agreed to sell at a slightly inflated figure—$25,000. Without hesitating, Kroc wrote out a check for that amount. "Wait a couple of days before cashing it," he told the Frejlichs, "because I don't know where I'm going to get the money."

His first McDonald's had not yet opened and already Kroc was desperate for money to salvage his franchising plan. When his initial attempts to borrow the money from banks produced nothing but a thumbs down from bankers, Kroc tried selling an equity interest in his fledgling franchising company to several investors he knew. He offered to sell any one of them half of the stock in his company for just $25,000. Only three decades later, that much equity in McDonald's would have been worth *billions,* but in early 1955, Kroc's generous offer produced no takers. Finally, Kroc lined up a bank loan to cover part of his payments to the Frejlichs, and he looked to the McDonalds for the rest. If the brothers would return the $10,000 they had collected from the Frejlichs, Kroc would borrow the other $15,000 he needed to complete the deal. The McDonalds agreed, and Kroc bought back the franchise rights the Frejlichs had obtained. While it did not really alter Kroc's plan, except for saddling him with another $15,000 of personal debt he did not need, it forever altered his opinion of the brothers whose name he was about to make famous. "The brothers were very naive and inexperienced," Kroc later declared. "They weren't businessmen at all."

With the Frejlich matter resolved, Kroc's Des Plaines McDonald's was ready to open for business on April 15, 1955. Since it was designed to lure franchising prospects as well as customers, Kroc personally made certain that the unit was a fast-food paragon. He watched over it like a mother hen. At seven o'clock every morning, he parked his car at the Des Plaines store and checked with the manager on the preparations being made for that day's business. He then walked to the train station nearby to take the Northwestern into the Loop, and at six o'clock in the evening he reversed the process. Fred Turner, now the senior chairman of McDonald's who began his career working as one of the first grillmen at Des Plaines, still recalls Kroc's walking the three blocks from the train station to the store: "Every night, you'd see him coming down the street, walking close to the gutter, picking up every McDonald's wrapper and cup along the way. He'd come into the store with both hands full of cups and wrappers. He was the store's outside pickup man."

As a result, Kroc's Des Plaines store created the same impressive sight as the San Bernardino unit run by the McDonald brothers. It looked like no drive-in that any midwesterner had ever seen. Turner vividly recalls his first impression of the Des Plaines unit: "It was so clean, so bright, so colorful. It was demonstration cooking. All the food preparation was out in the open. There was all that glistening stainless steel. And the uniforms of the crew were white and clean."

Yet, no matter how attractively Kroc maintained his Des Plaines store, the franchise he was selling did not attract the midwestern entrepreneurs he was looking for. The problem was that conventional drive-ins in the Midwest were typically low-budget, single-operator hamburger and hot dog stands that were closed five months of the year. They were not considered a serious investment, and no single McDonald's unit—not even a spotless one—could change that regional bias overnight. Kroc reacted by changing his franchising plan once more. He turned to his friends, primarily his golfing buddies at Rolling Green Country Club.

Ray Kroc was a typical suburbanite. He and his first wife, Ethel, lived in a large ranch home in one of the better residential sections of Arlington Heights, a middle-class suburb twenty miles northwest of Chicago. He spent weekend mornings performing the yardwork that gave his home a manicured appearance. Afternoons were reserved for golf at Rolling Green, where Kroc upheld a respectable golf handicap of about fifteen, despite a physical handicap of premature arthritis. He also escaped from the office every Wednesday at noon to catch lunch at the club and play another eighteen holes. Every Wednesday night, Ethel would join him at Rolling Green for dinner.

Rolling Green was the natural center of Ray and Ethel's social life. For one thing, their home was on the perimeter of the golf course. But, more important, the atmosphere of the club fitted comfortably with their lifestyle. Catering to middle-class members, Rolling Green lacked the stuffiness that distinguished the private clubs of the more elite suburbs along Chicago's North Shore. Because of its uncommonly good cuisine, the club was where Ray and Ethel most often met their friends for dinner. And it was where the personal side of Kroc's salesmanship was most visible. An extrovert and a good conversationalist, Kroc enjoyed having a good time, and he had dozens of friends at Rolling Green. While he was anything but a humorist, he laughed uproariously whenever anyone told a slightly off-color joke. Dinner get-togethers at Rolling Green often turned into impromptu parties with Kroc occupying the spotlight at the piano.

Kroc's friends at Rolling Green were mostly his peers in business—independent businessmen with small- to medium-sized companies. He did not hobnob with bankers or top executives of major corporations. Taken together, the Rolling Green crowd represented a wide variety of occupations, all outside food service. There were Art Jacobs, the home builder; Jerry Olson, a car dealer; and Tony Weissmuller, who owned a heating and ventilating business. Art, Jerry, Tony, and Ray were a steady foursome at the club. Kroc's Rolling Green pals also included club president Bill Paley, who owned a cemetery. There were the Taubensee brothers, Tom and Jack, who owned a steel service business. And there were Phil and Vern Vineyard, accountants; Chris

Oberheide, who had a coal distribution company; Bill Godfrey, a sales manager for Kelvinator; Don Coffey, who had a screw machine company; Joe Sweeney, a sales manager for Skil Tools; and Dick Picchietti, who was a plastering contractor. And there was Bob Dondanville, an advertising representative for *Ladies Home Journal*, a straitlaced occupation that belied his free-spirited character. The club's most independent thinker, Dondanville was perhaps Kroc's closest friend. When Kroc opened his Des Plaines store in 1955, these friends had really only one thing in common—their membership in Rolling Green. By 1958, they shared membership in a second club: all were new franchisees of McDonald's.

In all, Kroc recruited as franchisees eighteen members of Rolling Green during the late 1950s. In truth, they were Kroc's only hope of getting McDonald's off to a quick start in its race with a flock of early imitators, but Kroc never let his desperation show. "Ray played it low key," Weissmuller recalls. "It became known at the club that he had met the McDonald brothers in California and made a deal, but Ray didn't push people to get into it. If they wanted to talk about it, he always carried around a little portfolio with pictures and income statements [from his store]." The reaction among club members at first was anything but a rush. "Ray, you've got to be crazy," Weissmuller told Kroc when he heard that his friend was betting everything he had on a 15-cent hamburger. "There's no way you can make money on 1.9 percent."

He soon realized that while McDonald's might not produce a windfall for the franchiser, it could be a lucrative proposition for the franchisee. Kroc's numbers on his own store operation were enough to prove that. If the store did $200,000 per year—as the Kroc unit in Des Plaines did in the second year—it could generate a pretax profit of 20 percent, or $40,000, for the operator. And that profit was earned on a fraction of the investment required for a carhop drive-in. Capital investment in those operations typically started at $250,000, but an early McDonald's—including land, building, and equipment—could be opened for as little as $80,000. When the franchisee found a landowner willing to rent the space to him and a bank willing to provide a mortgage on the building, his investment amounted to no more than the $30,000 needed for the equipment, the sign, and start-up inventory, and even that could be borrowed.

Weissmuller, for example, invested only $17,000 of his own cash to get ownership of his first McDonald's store, which had the potential of earning twice that much in the first year. And other operators put up considerably less cash than that—some as little as $5,000. When word of the potential returns on McDonald's red-and-white hamburger stores began spreading around Rolling Green, Kroc no longer had to sell his friends a franchise. They were ready to buy.

During the first three years of his franchising efforts, Kroc found about half of his McDonald's franchisees from the membership at Rolling Green. The club provided an enormous initial franchising base for the new fast-food chain. Unfortunately for Kroc and McDonald's, however, the base was not solid. With few exceptions, the Rolling Green group was arguably, from McDonald's point of view, the worst collection of McDonald's operators in the chain's thirty-year history. In all but one instance, they were men who made their livings in other businesses and who looked on McDonald's as a secondary source of income. They had some of their savings at stake, not their livelihoods. From the beginning, Kroc sensed the need for the McDonald's franchisee to be the full-time operator as well, and he told that to his friends at Rolling Green. "Ray was very, very much against remote control," Weismuller recalls. "He felt the success of the business would be much greater if the individual who invested was active in the business."

The problems of the Rolling Green franchisees were many, but most of them wound up infuriating Kroc by refusing to adhere to the founder's demands for operations uniformity and store cleanliness. The greatest maverick of them all—at least when it came to the subject of uniformity of operations—was Kroc's closest Rolling Green friend, Bob Dondanville.

Two years before Kroc started McDonald's, Dondanville had moved to southern California to open a hamburger restaurant called the Choo Choo, borrowing the concept of a Chicago operator who had used a Lionel train set to transport hamburgers from the kitchen to the booths where his patrons were seated. He was the first Rolling Green member recruited by Kroc, and from the start it was painfully obvious that the free-spirited Dondanville was better suited for an offbeat format like the Choo Choo than he was for the regimen of a fast-food chain, particularly one run by a franchiser hell-bent on obtaining conformity.

While Kroc preached the need to stick to the ten-item menu he had inherited from the McDonald brothers, Dondanville found that rule far too limiting for his store in Reseda, California. He and Kroc had spirited discussions on the subject, with Dondanville insisting that for

McDonald's to broaden its consumer appeal it had to broaden its menu. Without obtaining Kroc's approval, he quickly began expanding the menu at his McDonald's. When he added roast beef, his Reseda store looked more like a roast beef outlet than a hamburger stand. Dondanville placed a huge roast in the front window between the two serving windows, donned a chef's hat, and carved the roast himself in view of his customers.

But what irritated Kroc most was when Dondanville raised his hamburger price from 15 to 18 cents. He justified it on financial grounds; like most other early McDonald's units in California, the Reseda store was barely breaking even, and Dondanville was becoming desperate. "We ate hamburgers at home for twenty-seven days in a row, and we got sick of it," Dondanville recalls. "That's when I decided to raise prices."

Kroc was furious. The 15-cent hamburger was central to McDonald's image; and while he had no power to dictate prices to his franchisees, he talked and acted as if he did. As soon as he learned of Dondanville's price increase, Kroc fired off a telegram to the Reseda store. "Take down your arches," it demanded.

Dondanville ignored it. He also ignored Kroc's frequent admonitions about shaving his beard. Kroc, a model of fastidious grooming, objected to anyone on his staff growing a beard, and the idea of a bearded Dondanville slicing roast beef in the front window of a McDonald's drive-in was abhorrent. Dondanville had grown the beard while he waited for his store to be built. His plan was to shave it on opening day, but, perhaps because he was aware of Kroc's objections to it, he kept it.

Kroc knew he could not get Dondanville to shave simply by ordering him to do so. He decided instead to use the one enticement that might produce results: publicity. Dondanville was one of the most publicity oriented of the early McDonald's operators. He advertised his store frequently in local newspapers, and his Chevrolet station wagon —customized with two steel golden arches—was a colorful traveling advertisement. Spanning the length of the car, the arches made it difficult for anyone to get inside, but, says Dondanville, "They were real eye-catchers."

Knowing that penchant for publicity, Kroc selected Dondanville's store as the site for the press announcement of the next hamburger sales milestone at McDonald's. To attract media attention, Kroc figured he would tell the local press that the Reseda operator had grown the beard just to celebrate the sales achievement by shaving it off. Kroc suggested that Dondanville sit in a barber's chair in front of the store and have his beard shaved while the new "millionth sold" sales figure was added to the McDonald's sign. Knowing that newspaper photographers could not pass up a shot like that, Dondanville agreed to the stunt. He personally served up the celebrated hamburger, added the record sales figure to his sign, chatted with reporters, and posed for pictures. He did everything Kroc wanted, save one thing—he kept the beard.

But it was not until Dondanville opened another restaurant that he did irreparable damage to his relationship with Kroc and McDonald's. Franchisees of McDonald's are prohibited from owning similar food service outlets, and Dondanville's second restaurant—called Hamburger King—was an obvious violation. Not surprisingly, Dondanville never got a second McDonald's franchise, but he holds no grudges. "I hated to take orders," Dondanville admits, "but Ray couldn't have recalcitrants like me giving him a hard time when he was trying to build a national image. McDonald's can thank God that I was such a scalawag, because it made them more careful in selecting franchisees."

While Dondanville's opposition was more colorful, he was by no means the only Rolling Green recalcitrant who wound up on Kroc's bad side. After his first two stores, Weissmuller was never granted another franchise, because he wanted to own the real estate in the third store as he had in the first two. By then, McDonald's policy called for the company to purchase or rent the property and sublease it to the franchisee. While Joe Sweeney had control over an exclusive license to develop McDonald's in six suburbs west of Chicago, he was never granted another store because, in Kroc's view, he had not properly maintained his first unit. Indeed, not long after McDonald's purchased Sweeney's store in 1968, it found out just how poorly maintained it was. On his first inspection of the unit, Michael Quinlan, now chairman of McDonald's Corporation but then a fledgling store manager assigned to run Sweeney's old store, discovered a rag wrapped around a pipe in the basement. It was soaked with an ominous-looking black liquid, and when Quinlan loosened the rag, he was shocked to uncover the source: a rotting potato plugging a hole in the pipe of the soft drink drain. It had been put there to "repair" a leak.

But the greatest friction from the Rolling Green–McDonald's connection occurred between Kroc and Richard Picchietti, whom Kroc accused of continually purchasing inferior food supplies in order to get a cheaper price. Picchietti was the first of the Rolling Green franchisees to open a store in the Chicago area. Located in Skokie—just two suburbs away from Kroc's store in Des Plaines—it was an important store for attracting other members of the country club into the McDonald's club, but it was also a source of unending frustration for Kroc.

The battles between Kroc and Picchietti began when the founder paid his first visit to the Skokie store soon after it opened. Kroc displayed for the first time his penchant for dealing firmly and vocally with shortcomings. In this case, he pulled a crew person aside to berate him for having dirty fingernails. Picchietti took it as an affront to his authority. The Skokie store was *his* store, not Kroc's, and he apparently thought Kroc had no right to interfere. "Don't you start telling my help what to do, or I'll tell you what you can do," Picchietti warned Kroc.

Kroc was stunned. As he saw it, *he* was McDonald's when it came to the matter of quality and uniformity. In Kroc's view, *every* McDonald's was *his* McDonald's because each one reflected the chain he was trying to build. "It was stupid, stupid," Kroc recalled years later. "There I was trying to help him out, and he tells me that. I put on my coat and hat and walked out of the store and never came back again." In fact, Kroc did make one more brief appearance in Picchietti's store—seventeen years later. By then, Picchietti had dramatically improved his once sloppy operation after it became apparent that his twenty-year franchise would not be renewed otherwise. Even so, it was only at the urging of his operations staff that Kroc grudgingly agreed to renew the store's license—the only one Picchietti ever got.

The operating experience with the Rolling Green group was a personal blow to Kroc, one that cost him most of his once valued friendships. When the McDonald's chain began taking off in the early 1960s, the Rolling Green operators naturally assumed that they would benefit from their ground floor involvement. They did not. While his friends were all pioneers in McDonald's, only five of the eighteen Rolling Green franchisees wound up with more than one store. Of those, only Phil and Vern Vineyard—the accountants—adequately capitalized on their early involvement in McDonald's, eventually building a twenty-one unit operation in Florida. It was Ray Kroc's clearest signal that his rule of granting franchises one store at a time and only to top-grade operators was inviolate.

McDonald's founder felt betrayed by many of his Rolling Green friends, and even in his last years he found it difficult to talk about them by name. Yet, he freely conceded the valuable licensing lesson he had learned from his experience with them. "They were all people with other types of business, and they got the opinion that they could own a McDonald's without putting time in," Kroc said. "They were absentee owners who were only interested in making money. They didn't give a damn about what the hell they sold."

But even as his investor-oriented friends were becoming a bitter disappointment, another group of franchisees was starting to expand Kroc's franchising horizon. Discovered almost by accident, these franchisees set a pattern for the type of operator on which Kroc would build McDonald's. None was wealthy or even close to it. Most were not owners of their own businesses. They were clearly not the big-time investors most fast-food franchisers sought as licensees. Nor were they even small-time investors, such as those Kroc had found at Rolling Green. They were giving up jobs in other careers, risking on McDonald's all their savings and, typically, all the money they could borrow from friends and relatives. They spent so much time working in their stores that their McDonald's became a second home. And while they yearned to be independent businessmen, most were not ready to go into business completely on their own. McDonald's was an attractive compromise: they could control their own business and still receive the support of a national system as long as they followed its basic rules. They were franchise entrepreneurs—a mix between full-fledged entrepreneurs and corporate employees—and their devotion to their stores produced the results that began creating the image of a McDonald's franchise as a license to print money.

Kroc did not get them by running advertisements. In fact, throughout its thirty-year history, McDonald's has run only a few small franchise ads in the *Chicago Tribune*. To recruit the owner/operators who built the system, Kroc relied on the cheapest form of advertising there is: word of mouth.

But the word had to start somewhere, and it started with Sanford Agate. When he first heard of McDonald's in 1955, Sandy Agate was a forty-six-year-old Chicago pressman who dreamed of running his own small business. He had even gone to night school to get a degree in optometry, but his weekend and evening practice was never lucrative enough to allow him to quit his job as a pressman. That was when his wife, Betty, decided to get a job to supplement the family's income by selling Catholic Bibles door-to-door. She chose a curious market to target—the offices in Chicago's Loop.

The idea of a Jew selling Catholic Bibles door-to-door in the heart of Chicago's financial district may not seem all that promising, but it opened a new world for the Agates. One of Betty Agate's first Bible sales calls was made at 221 North LaSalle, the building that housed the 850-square-foot office that contained the headquarters of Ray Kroc's Prince Castle Sales Division and his upstart McDonald's System, Inc. It was early in 1955, and Kroc had not been able to sell a single franchise other than the ones he had sold in California. Anyone entering his office—even a Bible peddler—had to be considered a hot prospect for a franchise.

Betty Agate's occupation fascinated June Martino, Ray Kroc's enterprising, aggressive, convivial—and slightly offbeat—secretary. "What the hell is a Jew doing selling Catholic Bibles?" she asked. "Making a living," Betty Agate replied. "Why don't you get a McDonald's instead?" Martino suggested.

Such directness was typical of Martino, but the simplicity of the sales pitch was right on target for the Agates. Sandy Agate had already been thinking of getting into the restaurant business, preferably an easy-to-learn operation. At a dinner at the Krocs' shortly afterward, the Agates got a more elaborate sales pitch from McDonald's founder, and on their way home that night Betty Agate threw her support solidly behind a fast-food gamble. "Let's reach for the moon," she told her husband.

Later that year, the Agates paid Kroc the $950 he was asking for a franchise, and Harry Sonneborn, the new man Kroc had hired to help find sites for McDonald's, told the Agates about a property for rent in Waukegan, fifty miles north of Chicago. They rejected the location, but they liked the prospect of a McDonald's in Waukegan. Like San Bernardino, Waukegan was, in Betty Agate's words, a "lunchpail town." Its predominantly blue-collar residents were the very type of clientele who initially supported McDonald's. And while Waukegan was then a town of 60,000, it had but one drive-in hamburger stand, which closed in the winter. More important, the Agates found a banker who owned a piece of property right across the street from the site of a proposed shopping center. After a sales pitch from Kroc, the banker, William O'Meara, agreed to build a McDonald's on the site and rent it to the Agates, charging them rent of 5 percent of their sales, but no more than $1,000 a month and no less than $500. The Agates did not have nearly enough money to build a McDonald's on their own, but when O'Meara agreed to take that risk, they were ready to move to Waukegan.

O'Meara never dreamed that the tiny store might exceed sales of $20,000 a month, the point where the percentage rent would hit the $1,000 cap. As it turned out, it reached that figure in the first month, prompting an angry call from O'Meara to Kroc. "Hey, that fella's doing a land office business," O'Meara said. "At this rate, he'll be a millionaire and I'll still be getting dribbles. You should be paying me more rent." Kroc was not about to change the terms. "I told you what we'd do there, and you didn't believe me," Kroc told O'Meara. "Now you believe."

Distinctly different from the Rolling Green investors, the Agates entered McDonald's playing for keeps. Agate quit his printing job to take up the spatula, and his wife worked behind the counter—the first of hundreds of husband-wife teams to operate a McDonald's. Their security deposit on the lease, the license fee, and their substantial down payment on the sign and equipment had consumed the $25,000 they had saved over the previous two decades. Knowing how tight things were, Kroc gradually informed Agate of all the costs involved in opening a new drive-in. Finally, when Agate had spent virtually all his cash, Kroc reminded him two days before opening that he needed $100 to make change.

Agate blew. "You haven't been telling me the whole truth," he shouted. "I'd never have gone into this business if I'd known all the things I'd have to do." Kroc's response made irrefutable logic: "That's why I didn't tell you." Agate tapped the family's last cash reserve— $150. He put $100 in the cash registers in the store and gave the rest to Betty for household expenses. "Stretch it," he said.

On Thursday, May 26, 1955, the Agates waited anxiously for their opening day's business. Kroc waited just as impatiently. The opening was as important to McDonald's future as it was to the Agates' financial security. While Kroc's own store was quite profitable, ringing up sales of $200,000 a year, he desperately needed a successful franchise operation in the Midwest as an example of the earning power of a McDonald's. The Rolling Green group did not provide the sales tool Kroc was looking for, partly because they were poor operators and partly because they were friends of Kroc, and as such they were less credible to franchising prospects outside Kroc's social circle. Aside from the Roll-

ing Green group, the only other McDonald's franchised by Kroc outside of California was experiencing miserably low sales. That store,
which opened in Dallas in 1956, was owned by Ross Cole and V. F.
Garrett, who had bought the fourth McDonald's franchise Kroc sold. It
averaged just $10,000 a month, and after experiencing fifteen consecu-
tive losing months, Cole and Garrett simply abandoned their bankrupt
unit. Though the arches have been removed, the red-and-white tile
structure still stands as part of a used-car business—a little known
shrine to the only complete failure of the world's most successful
franchiser. Over the years, other McDonald's franchisees have gone
under because of losses suffered outside of McDonald's and other
franchises have changed hands or locations before becoming successful. But the Cole-Garrett franchise became McDonald's only irreversible store failure, and it soured the chain on the Texas market for years.

Fortunately, the experience in Waukegan was the very opposite.
From the moment he opened his doors, Sandy Agate's McDonald's was
a gold mine. Its performance was so stunning that it took even the
optimistic Ray Kroc by surprise. On the first day, lines of customers
stretched out to the street. That morning, the driver for Mary Ann
Baking in Chicago, McDonald's first bun supplier, had warned Agate
that he had overordered by requesting 125-dozen buns. "You'll be
throwing them at each other when the day is over," he told Agate. By
five o'clock that afternoon, the store was running out of buns, and
Agate placed an emergency order. By the end of the day, Agate
counted a total take of $450. "You're over the hump," Kroc told him.

In fact, he had just begun to climb. On the next day, Friday, when
hamburger sales typically collapsed in such predominantly Catholic
towns as Waukegan, the lines stretched around the McDonald's and
down the block. Sales hit $800, and Agate's operation hit a snag: his
two cash registers were too small. By the end of the day, they were
stuffed with currency, and Agate had not thought of getting a deposit
bag from his local bank. Worried about leaving all that cash in the store
overnight, he stuffed the bills and coins into brown paper bags and
carried them home.

Totally without warning and without so much as a single newspaper advertisement, the opening of the McDonald's store—selling 15-
cent hamburgers that tasted much better than anyone expected—had
become a social event in Waukegan. Despite a steady rain, customers
on Saturday began lining up at 10:00 A.M., a full hour before opening.

The line did not break until 1:00 A.M. the next day, two hours after the scheduled closing. Agate's store had a $1,000 day, something Kroc's own store had yet to achieve.

On Sunday, demand continued, and by 5:00 P.M. Agate had run out of meat. He placed a frantic call to his meat supplier. When Agate told his customers standing in line that there would be a half-hour delay, he was aghast at their response: virtually everyone waited. "We were deliriously happy to think that we were taking in that kind of money with our only advertising being word of mouth," Betty Agate recalls.

To Kroc, the overnight success in Waukegan confirmed his instincts on the type of franchisee McDonald's needed to win the fast-food race, which was just starting. Agate was not a sideline investor but an operator with a consuming commitment to his McDonald's. He rented a house behind his store, but his store was really home. He was the first on the premises at 7:00 A.M. and the last to leave at midnight. When he took his breaks at home, he spent most of his time in the kitchen, where he had installed a window with a bird's-eye view of the store. From there he timed cars coming into and leaving the lot to gauge the speed of service at the counter. To ensure that his store mastered the McDonald's production regimen, he carefully selected the crew, preferring mostly navy chiefs from the nearby Great Lakes Naval Training Center. During peak periods, Agate barked out production orders as a skipper might order sailors to their battle stations. When he saw Agate's crew go through its paces, Kroc knew what he had to do: find more Sandy Agates.

The word of the Waukegan restaurant's blockbuster success quickly spread to would-be entrepreneurs. From surrounding towns and even neighboring states, they made the trek to the lakeside town to see for themselves what they found hard to believe. Agate's operation grossed more than $250,000 in its first twelve months, and it netted the Agates about $50,000. A few years later, the Agates bought their first home—spending more than $100,000 for a home in a posh new residential section of town. It did not go unnoticed by prospective franchisees that Kroc's first successful operator was now living in a far more luxurious residence than Ray and Ethel Kroc had in Arlington Heights.

Indeed, Agate was suddenly earning four times more than Kroc, but the McDonald's founder took that as a good sign. Unlike every other franchiser of the day, he believed that McDonald's could only succeed if its franchisees became wealthy, and now he was in a position to sell that dream. Kroc seized on every opportunity to tell the Agate story to other franchising prospects who were cut from the same cloth as Agate—independent operators willing to invest everything they had for the chance to quit working for someone else and begin working for themselves. When those prospects showed up at 221 North LaSalle, Kroc did not fail to show them the income statement of the Waukegan restaurant. So many copies of the statement were printed that McDonald's managers began using them as notepads. Agate's private financial statement became so public that Agate finally complained. Kroc's response was typically pragmatic: the statements circulated on Agate's operation thereafter identified the store only as "Gan," a none-too-subtle code name for Waukegan.

Within months of his store's opening, Agate began noticing cars with out-of-state license plates in his parking lot. Waukegan was no tourist center; the cars were owned by prospects Kroc had sent. One of them was driven by Lou Groen, a part-owner and manager of a Cincinnati restaurant. While attending the National Restaurant Show in Chicago, Groen had seen Ray Kroc's Des Plaines restaurant. He was fascinated by it, but he also knew it was a model, owned by the franchiser. "Have you sold any franchises?" asked a skeptical Groen. Kroc referred Groen to Waukegan.

Groen was immediately impressed by the line at Agate's restaurant, and he walked in to meet the operator. "I've paid off my entire investment in a few months," Agate bragged. But Groen was in the restaurant business, and he knew restaurants were not *that* profitable. "You've gotta show it to me before I will believe anything you say," Groen insisted. "If you're so successful, show me your damn tax return."

Agate took Groen to his house, sat him down at the kitchen table, and pulled a tax return from a small file drawer. "I've never made so much money in my life," he told Groen as the visitor pored over his tax return, obviously stunned by Agate's sudden wealth. Groen was sold; and while he did not know it then, the wealth he would accumulate in McDonald's would be many times greater than Agate's. In fact, Groen eventually operated forty restaurants. He now runs two, and his son Paul has two. Four of the restaurants are owned by two former employees of Groen, and McDonald's Corporation owns the rest. Groen credits Agate's candor for getting him into McDonald's. "Sandy Agate was a great salesman for McDonald's," Groen says. "He was its first rags-to-riches hero."

Groen's experience with the Waukegan store was repeated with dozens of other franchising prospects. Reuben Taylor, a truck equipment salesman from Wisconsin who had been scouting franchise opportunities, was also impressed when he saw Agate's store. When he got his franchise in Hamden, Connecticut, in 1957, he quit his job and began working full-time behind the counter. He also quickly began experiencing the same sales and profits that Agate had. Two years later, Taylor hit the jackpot with a second store in Newington—on the Berlin Turnpike between New York and Boston. It made Agate's numbers pale by comparison, and it made Kroc realize that McDonald's had far more potential than even he had dreamed. By 1964, McDonald's-Newington became the first fast-food restaurant to break $500,000 in annual sales, better than double the chain's national per-store average that year, and it launched Taylor into a career as a McDonald's operator whose family eventually wound up with 25 restaurants. They currently have 16.

In addition to out-of-state visitors, the Waukegan restaurant also attracted Agate's friends and relatives. Agate recruited his brother, Barney, for a store in Evanston, Illinois, and a brother-in-law for an outlet in Mishawaka, Indiana. Betty Agate's brother, Edward Traisman, became a five-store operator in Madison, Wisconsin.

Their tiny Waukegan outlet was becoming something of a fast-food equivalent of the Book of Genesis. But Agate's store had its greatest impact by attracting a number of Waukegan merchants who were fascinated by the lines that formed at the store every day at noon. The first was Harold Stern, who managed a women's ready-to-wear store across the street from Agate's store. When Betty Agate persuaded Stern to visit Ray Kroc in Chicago, he brought with him his close friend Mel Garb, who ran two luggage shops in nearby Kenosha. The two agreed to enter into a partnership for one restaurant in Saginaw, Michigan, which opened in 1958, but before they sold out their operations to McDonald's for $25 million more than a decade later, the Garb-Stern partnership had opened (or acquired) a total of forty-six McDonald's restaurants in Michigan, Wisconsin, Oklahoma, Nevada, and California.

After Garb and Stern got their first McDonald's franchise, other Waukegan merchants began clamoring for their own. Arthur Korf, the owner of the clothing store Stern managed, got a franchise in Asheville, North Carolina, in 1959, and with his partner, Richard Frankel, built a twenty-nine-restaurant McDonald's operation in the Carolinas and Arizona before they sold out in 1976. Fritz Casper, who, like Korf, owned a small clothing store in Waukegan, bought a franchise for Tampa, which eventually became a twenty-nine-restaurant McDonald's operation. And Bill O'Brien, a Waukegan drugstore owner, became a two-store McDonald's operator in Iowa City, Iowa.

In all, the Sandy Agate restaurant directly spawned two dozen other franchises within the first three years. If the Rolling Green investors accounted for nearly half of Kroc's franchisees in the late 1950s, the Agate contingent accounted for most of the rest. The difference was that the franchisees recruited by the Agate store were full-time owner/operators who went on to open up well over two hundred additional restaurants around the country. And many would concur with Mel Garb's assessment that the Waukegan unit provided Kroc with the nucleus of franchisees he needed to build a national fast-food chain. Says Garb: "The Sandy Agate store was the root from which the tree grew."

Curiously, despite his contribution, Agate did not make the fortune made by many others who were attracted into McDonald's by his restaurant. Three years after he opened Waukegan, Kroc granted him a second franchise. But when he asked for additional units, he was repeatedly denied them, because as the years went on he became identified in McDonald's eyes as a problem operator. Field service consultants for McDonald's gave his store low grades on their inspections, and Agate got a reputation as a "price buyer" for substituting lower-cost products than those offered by "approved" suppliers. Even Betty Agate concedes that her late husband stubbornly opposed McDonald's advice on basic operations. "I always told Sandy to play their game," she recalls. "He said, 'The hell with it, I am my own man.'"

But Sandy Agate's cola substitution put him on Kroc's bad side for keeps. After several years, Agate began insisting that Pepsi-Cola would outsell Coca-Cola in his market. In many other product areas, McDonald's gave operators leeway in selecting suppliers, but Coke was (and still is) the only approved cola. No one knows how attractive a deal Agate got from the Pepsi distributor, but when he made it in the early 1960s, McDonald's had already become an important soft drink account, and other competitors were eager to crack Coke's monopoly of it.

Agate was the first crack in the McDonald's armor on colas, but he was also the last. Although there were other reasons for Agate's being rejected for additional stores, he nevertheless became known as the one punished by Kroc for switching from Coke to Pepsi. In 1975, just after McDonald's informed him that his twenty-year operating franchise would not be renewed, Agate sold both restaurants and left the system. Since his switch to Pepsi, and the consequences it seemed to entail, no other McDonald's operator has attempted to repeat Agate's version of "the Pepsi challenge."

The incident became perhaps the most notable example of Ray Kroc's dedication to uniformity. Yet, in disciplining Sandy Agate, Kroc sent out clear signals that unauthorized deviation from the basics of the McDonald's System would never be tolerated.

By the end of the 1950s, Kroc had begun to identify the type of franchisees who worked best for McDonald's. While he continued to franchise to some investors, the smaller, more entrepreneurial operators such as Sandy Agate were obviously producing better results. They were hands-on operators, not passive investors, and because virtually all of them came from outside the food service industry, they were open for accepting and mastering the novel McDonald's System.

Kroc's franchising plan—selling low-cost franchises for one store at a time—was perfectly suited for attracting them. But it was also well suited for channeling their creativity in a direction that would produce uniform quality. In dealing with the free-spirited franchisees that McDonald's began attracting and seeking after the Sandy Agate success, Kroc walked a fine line. He would give them freedom to create and contribute ideas that he believed benefited the system, but he would not tolerate deviation from the norm when he thought it hurt the system.

That was a judgment call. But by retaining complete control over new stores—something territorial franchisers had relinquished—Kroc had the power to enforce his judgment on those aspects of the operation that he believed must be uniform. And by using that power on the first and most important of his entrepreneurial franchisees, Kroc made it clear that his judgment on the basics was not to be ignored. Says Betty Agate: "You had to realize when you were dealing with Ray that he had a head like a rock. Ray never forgot, and he never forgave."

Chapter 5
MELTING POT

"If a corporation has two executives who think alike, one of them is unnecessary."

That was Ray Kroc's reply to a student at the Amos Tuck Graduate School of Business Administration at Dartmouth College, where McDonald's executives appeared at a management seminar in 1973. At the seminar, the McDonald's founder had been denouncing the growing government threat to free enterprise, when a student asked Kroc if all his managers were required to share his conservative views. Kroc's response summarized in a nutshell his management philosophy in building McDonald's Corporation.

Fred Turner, whom Kroc had just promoted to chief executive of McDonald's, gave the Dartmouth class a more graphic example of the differences of opinion Kroc tolerated, and even encouraged, in his company. In 1972, he recalled, when McDonald's received its first negative publicity following a $250,000 contribution by Kroc to the campaign of Richard Nixon, Ray Kroc's hand-picked successor became one of a handful of corporate chief executives to vote for arch-liberal George McGovern. The news so delighted Dr. John G. Kemeny, the liberal president of an otherwise staunchly conservative Dartmouth College, that Kemeny descended on Turner at a cocktail party afterward, obviously convinced that he had found a fellow liberal lost in a sea of conservatism.

He soon learned otherwise. To illustrate his nondoctrinaire presidential voting record, Turner explained that McGovern probably had few supporters in 1972 like himself—he had voted for Barry Goldwater in 1964. Turner recalls: "Kemeny dropped me like a hot potato."

The incident illustrated the most important characteristic of McDonald's management. It is not monolithic. McDonald's corporate executives do not think alike or act alike. They do not have anything approaching similarity in their backgrounds or character traits. More important, that is by design. It appears that the only commonality Ray Kroc wanted in his corporate managers was their loyalty to McDonald's. Though adamant about obtaining complete uniformity in his fast-food operation, Kroc was not in the least interested in hiring uniform managers to get that job done.

Rather, he was interested in hiring people who were extremists of a sort—intensely interested in a certain phase of the business and extremely capable of handling it. As he built his management foundation, Kroc hired and judged people according to the way they performed in their jobs. Indeed, Kroc hired more than his share of oddballs who had little in common with anybody, and he accommodated their eccentricities because he respected their performance.

Although he is largely unheralded for it, Ray Kroc was a managerial genius. This is little known, perhaps because his seemingly arbitrary judgments and temperamental outbursts overshadowed his managerial acumen. Kroc was an intensely emotional man with extremely strong opinions on how things should work and how people should behave. He was a man with uncompromising old world values. His judgments on issues and people were black and white. But Kroc also had a keen sense of appreciation for the talents needed to make McDonald's a superior performer. As he put together his first group of corporate managers, he suppressed his strong likes and dislikes of personal traits to pick and promote people for their skills. Even when their personal habits drove him up a wall, he found ways of venting his anger to keep talented people.

In short, Kroc assembled and tolerated one of the most diverse collections of individuals ever to occupy the top management of an American corporation. And even today, the practice of recruiting extremely individual managers is a McDonald's trademark, one almost completely hidden by the chain's legendary operational uniformity. "Ray's genius was surrounding himself with individuals whose talents were absolutely necessary to make McDonald's a success, even though their personalities conflicted sharply with his own," observes Edward Schmitt, a retired vice chairman of McDonald's. "If there is one bedrock item that made McDonald's successful, it is that Ray's management philosophy has been disseminated throughout the McDonald's System."

Kroc not only hired people with diverse personalities, he gave them enormous freedom. Despite a widely held belief that he ran

McDonald's as a one-man show, Kroc delegated far more power than do most strong-minded corporate founders.

But even those close to McDonald's, including many who work for the company now, picture Kroc as something of a benign corporate dictator. To some extent, that perception is understandable because in many ways Kroc exhibited the appearance of an autocrat. There is no denying that he had extremely strong opinions on individual mannerisms. He had them in spades, and he voiced them regularly, often displaying an explosive temper. He absolutely detested dozens of personal peccadilloes—chewing bubble gum, reading the comic pages, and wearing white socks. He disliked anything that suggested a disheveled appearance—dirty or bitten fingernails, wrinkled suits, or uncombed hair. At the end of the workday he wanted to see a clean desk and a covered typewriter. He even wanted his employees to keep their automobiles clean.

His opinions on personal grooming and behavior were so strong that they became words for McDonald's managers to live by, even though some rules made no sense to anyone but Kroc. For example, he cringed when he saw an employee drinking a Manhattan, not because he did not enjoy drinking himself (he did), but because he considered it an inappropriate drink for an executive. For the same reason, casual sport coats were unacceptable substitutes for suits, and even in the summer long-sleeved shirts were required.

For the most part, his dicta reflected his personal fastidiousness. He forbade pipe smoking, likening the mouth of a pipe smoker to a volcano. "Vesuvius with halitosis," he called it. Although he allowed cigarette smoking and enjoyed it himself, he required female employees to smoke only at their desks. He believed so strongly in grooming that he easily crossed over what many others would have considered a line of personal privacy. He told some managers to cut the hairs in their nose or to clean their teeth. Facial hair of any kind was prohibited, even into the 1970s, when hair of all kinds was in vogue. When Burt Cohen, an executive in the company's franchising department, returned from a sabbatical sporting a beard, he made a point to go to Kroc's office first. "Don't worry, Ray, it's coming off tomorrow," he said. "I know," Kroc replied.

On the surface, it appeared that violations of Kroc's codes of personal conduct were grounds for dismissal. When one of McDonald's lawyers walked into the corporate office wearing a watch cap— the blue knit stocking caps many Chicagoans wear during the worst of their winter days—Kroc ordered the man fired on the grounds that managers should wear business hats, not stocking caps. The same sentence was issued to a regional real estate representative who picked up the McDonald's founder at an airport and asked him for a $2 loan to pay for the parking. Kroc was outraged that his host manager had not stocked up on cash beforehand. And when an Oklahoma field service manager in cowboy boots picked up the chairman in a dusty convertible, Kroc ordered him fired, too—after first instructing him to drive to the nearest car wash.

Such on-the-spot terminations were made on the most fleeting of emotions. While Kroc at one time or another may have ordered virtually all of his managers terminated, he never fired anyone himself. He often seemed intent on avoiding a direct confrontation with the person who was the source of the trouble. He preferred, instead, to vent his anger—and execute termination orders—through a third party. When Kroc boiled over after learning that an operations manager had put chateaubriand on his expense account, he called Gerry Newman, the company's then chief accountant. "I wasn't at the dinner," Newman recalled, "but the following day Ray called *me* and really chewed *him* out."

But the frequent termination orders were more often forgotten than they were carried out. Even Kroc recalled walking into the office of one of his managers one morning with an emergency assignment only to find the manager clearing out his desk. "What are you doing?" Kroc asked. "I'm getting ready to leave," the manager responded. "You fired me last night." Kroc had already forgotten his momentary anger with the manager the night before, and he told him to restock his desk and get to work.

Whenever someone was dismissed, it had little to do with personal code violations and everything to do with the employee's poor performance. For example, Turner recalls that he refused to execute Kroc's order to fire the Oklahoma field service consultant because he was one of his best operations men. "If Ray got hung up on one of his idiosyncrasies, I didn't let anyone go because of it," Turner says. "I fought it."

Kroc never second-guessed such decisions. In fact, most of his "firings" were never carried out because those designated to perform the deeds realized that the founder was merely venting steam. Kroc's dismissal instructions were most often given to June Martino, his long-time secretary, who wisely delayed executing them because she knew her boss likely would change his mind when he cooled off. "If he told me to fire someone, and I told him right then, 'I won't do it,' he would have fired both of us," Martino explains. "So I'd say, 'You're right, Ray, he's no good,' but a day later I'd tell him, 'I bet if you thought it over, you'd probably change your mind.' Most of the time, Ray just got mad at someone for the moment."

In short, Kroc's closest associates knew that his bark was more frequent than his bite and that at heart he was a pragmatist more than an autocrat. In fact, he was far more tolerant of differences in people than most executives who display far fewer pet peeves. If his managers were contributing to building *his* McDonald's, they were on his side— no matter how much their personalities differed from his. During the Vietnam War, when long hair was perhaps the most common antiestablishment affectation, Kroc more than once resisted an urge to confront managers with long locks. One afternoon as Kroc was leaving McDonald's headquarters with his public relations consultant, Al Golin, he glanced across the parking lot and spotted his new advertising manager, Barry Klein, whose shoulder-length hair was flying in Chicago's wind. Kroc so detested the long-hair look that Klein might have been fired on the spot had he not already played a role in the creation of the character Ronald McDonald. Instead, Kroc looked to Golin and grumbled: "The son of a bitch better be good."

Kroc not only tolerated such frustrations, he set himself up for them by hiring people who had personal traits he knew would upset him. After three decades of searching, he knew he had found a winner in McDonald's, but only if he could also find the right people to help him pull it off. Before joining McDonald's as a personnel manager in 1962, James Kuhn recalls that he had read a *Time* magazine story describing how Kroc had posted a notice at the office water cooler that anyone leaving their paper cups around the office would be dismissed. "I read that and I said, who is this nut," says Kuhn, a former McDonald's vice president. But when Kuhn started work at McDonald's he was surprised to find that "what appeared to be a totally structured and inflexible person on the surface was really very flexible underneath. The man was so interested in doing it right that if you convinced him something was right, he didn't care from whom that advice came."

Some of Kroc's managers were keenly aware of the duality because they knew that Kroc silently tolerated some of their own traits that he found objectionable. Turner recalls that on his first day on the job in 1957, Martino greeted him with rules of office decorum à la Ray

Kroc. "You have to work with your suit coat on, and there's no smoking at your desk," she advised. That was at 8:30; by 9:30, Turner's jacket was off, his sleeves were rolled up, and he was smoking his first cigarette. To get Turner's dedication to operational perfection, Kroc bent the rules: he said nothing.

He made the same unspoken adjustment in the case of Ed Schmitt, who did not fit into Kroc's strong bias for lean managers. Yet, despite his weight "handicap," Schmitt was rapidly promoted through the operations ranks and eventually to vice chairman. "Ray had the ability to recognize his own weaknesses," says Schmitt, now an owner/operator, "and surround himself with people who could fill in those voids."

The voids Kroc was looking to fill were not the typical ones found in most corporate organization charts. In fact, there were no organizations like the one he was trying to build. Since other food franchising organizations in the mid-1950s were built on the concept of selling franchises, they recruited managers oriented mostly toward sales. Kroc wanted more than that—a well-rounded organization with personnel skilled in operations, marketing, finance, real estate, equipment and building design, and food and paper purchasing. In essence, he was building the first fast-food franchising system to provide a full range of services to its franchisees. The personnel requirements of such an organization were so varied that there was no way Kroc could meet them by hiring people like himself—or like one another.

Furthermore, the fast-food concept was so new that there was no training ground for it. Even the best hotel and restaurant schools had no notion of the type of business Kroc was building. As a result, the corporate managers Kroc recruited had to be considerably different from the typical managers hired by traditional food service businesses. McDonald's was such an untested system that Kroc was forced to take a gamble on unproven talent and on extremely individualistic and slightly offbeat characters.

Those requirements happened to match Kroc's hiring preferences. Clearly, he was not interested in hiring people for their academic skills or their intellectual prowess. He rejected the deep thinkers in favor of activists, doers, and intense workers. Like him, most of the early managers he hired at McDonald's were not college graduates, because Kroc did not think a degree was any better than work experience—and common sense. Kroc even had a slight bias against college graduates entering his new company. "Most of the college men didn't expect to work that hard," Kroc said, explaining his early hiring choices. "They wanted to sit down at a desk in a bank. They thought that made them businessmen. I hired on the basis of the individual—people who would work hard and put up with difficult conditions, until we could all prosper together."

When he joined McDonald's personnel department in 1962, Jim Kuhn was greatly relieved to learn that McDonald's did not require (and still does not) a college degree for managerial slots. "The thing that I loved at McDonald's," Kuhn says, "was that they just told me to go out and get the best damn people I could get and to look at *them*, not their credentials. We hired people that would not have gotten through the door at other companies, not because they were losers but because they were not traditional."

From the beginning, Kroc also recruited people likely to enjoy working for a nontraditional company. In fact, if there was a thread that connected the personalities of Kroc's otherwise diverse managers, it was that they were ill at ease with the business establishment. They tended to have nonestablishment, nearly antiestablishment attitudes, which explains why they were attracted to a business that in the mid-1950's lacked even a modicum of prestige. When most early McDonald's managers decided to enter a business specializing in 15-cent hamburgers, "it wasn't a popular decision with the family," recalls Turner, who joined McDonald's after dropping out of premed studies during his junior year at Drake University. "I can still remember the expression on my father's face."

Turner's friends had similar reactions. Bob Rhea, a fraternity brother of Turner's at Drake, remembers that when both returned from the service, Rhea tried to put social distance between himself and his former classmate. "I figured he was cooking hamburgers in some greasy spoon, and I thought this poor bastard's down on his luck," Rhea recalls. "I told my wife I didn't want to look the Turners up, because they had two kids and it would just make me feel bad." Fortunately for Rhea, he did reestablish contact with Turner, became a McDonald's franchisee in Cleveland, and eventually parlayed that into ownership of 45 percent of McDonald's in the United Kingdom.

Kroc realized that McDonald's appeal to those seeking a nonestablishment environment virtually required diversity in management. Nowhere was that diversity more striking than in the contrast of personalities of the three charter managers and initial owners of the business: Ray Kroc, June Martino, and Harry Sonneborn. While many others later capitalized on the opportunity that Kroc was offering managers to make a significant individual contribution to the development of Mc-Donald's, Martino and Sonneborn set the trend in motion. Though their efforts were largely unheralded, they clearly were not unre-warded. In lieu of the bigger salaries Kroc believed they deserved but that he could not pay, Martino and Sonneborn were given equity in the company in the late 1950s, with Martino receiving 10 percent and Sonneborn 20 percent. Less than a decade later, when McDonald's became a public company with a hot stock, Kroc's first two partners became multimillionaires.

Both came from much more humble origins. Martino had worked as a secretary and bookkeeper for Kroc at Prince Castle Sales, and while she remained Kroc's secretary throughout her career at McDon-ald's, her role was expanded dramatically, eventually to corporate sec-retary and treasurer. Martino even became a member of McDonald's board of directors. But her principal contribution had nothing to do with her secretarial skills or her newer titles. The key to understanding how a secretary could wind up with 10 percent of McDonald's initial stock lies in understanding how critical Martino's people skills were in holding McDonald's together during the early years. With so many different personalities working in a pressurized environment, it was obvious from the start that Kroc needed an informal mediator at the center, someone who could handle personal crises, help create family unity, and most important, keep conflicting personalities from destroy-ing one another and, in the process, McDonald's. That was Martino's real job. Says Turner: "June Martino was the glue."

The word *secretary*—particularly in a 1950s setting—vastly under-states Martino's role and misrepresents her character. She was one of a handful of women who grew beyond the narrow confines of that title because she was the rare woman of her era who was not intimidated by a male-dominated workplace.

Martino had succeeded in a male environment before. Fresh from high school, she was one of two women among five hundred wartime graduates of a rigorous eighteen-month electronics course taught by the Army Signal Corps at Northwestern University, and during World War II she worked in the Signal Corps on teams that performed a variety of male-oriented tasks, from testing radar systems to trouble-shooting work on problems with airplane radios. Later, she and her husband, Lou, set up a small business that helped bring electricity to rural homes in Wisconsin.

While her experience and her blunt and outspoken demeanor were anything but secretarial, Kroc hired her because he needed a take-charge person to run his office at Prince Castle while he spent much of his time on the road. At McDonald's, her ability to make quick decisions on her own when corporate managers were on the road was critical. Kroc's young managers were always out of town—checking the performance of existing stores or developing sites for new ones—and Martino soon was coordinating communications among most of McDonald's top executives. Her position as the communications link—and her growing power in the corporate hierarchy—did not go totally unnoticed. As early as 1961, a feature in the *Chicago Tribune* reported how Kroc's secretary was a rarity in American business in that period. It read: "Mrs. Martino treats each problem with unflustered calm. She has an incisive mind which one male colleague has described as 'completely free from that pettiness which mars most women's thinking.' "

Clearly, Martino was the exceptional woman who advanced in a business career before the feminist movement took hold. But she succeeded because of the strength of her character, not by virtue of her academic credentials. Her directness in dealing with problems was disarming. Once, during McDonald's early years, she ordered a large plate of meat sandwiches to feed staffers involved in late-night meetings, and only when the delivery was made did she realize that it was a meatless Friday for the predominantly Irish Catholic managers at the meeting. Because McDonald's was then struggling just to survive, Martino refused to waste the food, and instead sought an immediate dispensation from the very top of the local Roman Catholic hierarchy. She placed a call to John Cardinal Cody.

Cody, of course, was the spiritual leader of the largest Catholic archdiocese in the United States, and McDonald's was a long way from admission into Chicago's corporate establishment. Still, Martino managed to make a minor problem sound urgent to one of Cody's aides, who quickly summoned the cardinal to the phone. Cody granted her request for an on-the-spot dispensation.

Despite the growing importance of her position, Martino remained unusually down-to-earth. Outspoken to the point of being embarrassingly blunt, Martino gave some the impression of being slightly daffy because of her affinity for offbeat subjects. For example, she is fascinated by psychic phenomena and other fringe topics such as phrenology (the study of bumps on the head). "When I talk about these things, most people think I'm cuckoo," she says. On more traditional topics, Martino's approach is—at the very least—unusual. When McDonald's went public, she suggested that the company's stores display the stock's daily quote at the serving counter. And one manager remembers how Martino described her new exercise regimen to a luncheon gathering of a dozen McDonald's managers. "Most people talk about their exercise program," the manager recalls, "but June got down on the floor and did ten push-ups to show us."

Yet, Martino was also warm and caring, and more than anything else, those were the traits that most distinguished her at McDonald's. Before she became wealthy, Martino kept adopting children (eight, over the years), despite the fact that she had two of her own. And she had no reservations about requesting aid for others. Not long after Turner became executive vice president of McDonald's, Martino made an unannounced visit to the Turner household requesting used furniture for a needy Puerto Rican family she knew. She left with a sofa crammed into her station wagon.

She showed the same personal caring on the job. Early on, when McDonald's franchisees were as poor as the company, Martino made her home available to new franchisees while they were in Chicago for training. One operator extended the offer to include his wife and five children, all of whom showed up at Martino's house with sleeping bags. Similarly, when corporate staffers had personal or family problems, it was Martino they often turned to for advice.

Because her people instincts were usually so on the mark, Martino had an enormous impact on recruitment. She succeeded in attracting such critical franchisees as Sandy and Betty Agate. She also pushed for employment of people she thought would fit well in McDonald's, and as a result she was responsible for recruiting some key employees. One of those was her own husband, Lou, who for five years ran the company's unique research laboratory. And when she was impressed with a friend her son referred to her for part-time employment during college, Martino gave him a job in the mailroom, carefully monitored his performance, and put in good words to others about his progress. The mailboy of the 1960s, Michael Quinlan, is now McDonald's chairman.

Martino's role in employment and other management decisions was intentionally subtle and at times even camouflaged. When two life insurance salesmen walked into McDonald's five-room office in 1957, all they were looking to do was sell executive life insurance and estate planning services. But they had to get by Martino first, and they began by explaining to her that their backgrounds were not typical for door-to-door life insurance salesmen. Both had law degrees and had been accountants with the IRS. Both were also polite and soft-spoken, and by the end of their introduction, Martino concluded that the two were perfect candidates to provide the additional financial skills McDonald's needed.

She walked into Harry Sonneborn's office and announced that two IRS agents were there to see him. "My heart started beating like a triphammer," recalled Sonneborn, whom Kroc had hired a year earlier to handle the company's finances. "I didn't know if they were examining me or the company." When he realized the trickery that two salesmen had apparently used to get into his office to peddle insurance, Sonneborn was not only amused by the ruse but impressed by its creativeness. He hired both men.

Not until twenty-five years later did Martino admit that the deception was hers. "If I told Harry that these two were selling life insurance, they didn't stand a chance to see him," Martino says. As it turned out, the two men were among the most important hires McDonald's made during its embryonic period: Robert Ryan, who served as McDonald's treasurer, and Richard Boylan, who retired in 1983 as senior executive vice president and chief financial officer.

Perhaps no one understood better than Martino Kroc's willingness to open up McDonald's to individuals from a variety of backgrounds. When her son's high school teacher became engaged to an Italian national, Martino sponsored him by providing the employment he needed to qualify for immigration to the United States. Luigi Salvaneschi had a doctorate in canon law and had mastered nine languages— but not English. Yet, Martino was convinced he could overcome the language barrier, and she hired Salvaneschi to work in a McDonald's she and her husband owned in a suburb of Chicago. Although Salvaneschi quickly learned the McDonald's System and became the store manager within months, his command of English trailed. One Christmas, Martino agreed to Salvaneschi's request to put a seasonal greeting on the sign in front of the store, but when she saw the message she regretted not checking Salvaneschi's plan for the Christmas sign beforehand. It read: PEACE ON YOU. Still, Martino's instincts about Salvaneschi proved accurate. He entered the corporate ranks and rose rapidly to vice president in charge of real estate, before leaving McDonald's to become an executive vice president at Kentucky Fried Chicken.

It is curious that Kroc permitted Martino so much influence. A traditionalist on most matters, Kroc was no pioneer of women's rights.

Otherwise, he would never have supported a policy that required all-male employees at McDonald's restaurants until the late 1960s. "Ray's basic personality would never have allowed a woman to get that much power," says James Kuhn, who believes that Kroc checked his fundamental instincts when he saw Martino's performance.

Martino's success at McDonald's was perhaps the first indication of Kroc's willingness to delegate authority to individuals cut from a different cloth. But the surest sign that he planned to manage McDonald's with a melting pot of personalities was the power he entrusted to Harry Sonneborn.

Harry Sonneborn and Ray Kroc were a study in contrasts. Sonneborn was Kroc's partner in starting McDonald's, and his contribution was so vital that he was nearly a cofounder. Yet, the two men shared nothing else in common. Kroc was outgoing, personable, engaging, and charming. Sonneborn was an introvert, and most McDonald's managers and franchisees considered him cold and impersonal. Kroc was an open book; Sonneborn was unusually private. Kroc was trusting of people almost to a fault; Sonneborn was the very opposite.

Furthermore, Sonneborn liked all the things in business that Kroc disliked. He enjoyed managing a company by its financial numbers, and Kroc had so little interest in finances that he could not interpret a balance sheet. Conversely, while Kroc loved the hamburger business— and routinely made personal checks on the restaurants—it would have made little difference to Sonneborn if McDonald's were selling pizza instead of hamburger. "I always thought that I could pay somebody to run the hamburger stand," Sonneborn said. "I didn't care about the quality of the food or the cleanliness of the unit. I knew it had to be done, but I didn't care about doing it. At the first fifteen stands, I was the first customer, and I gave them all a signed dollar bill. That's what I did. Then I left."

While Kroc identified with his franchisees—and they with him— Sonneborn liked the prestige of being in the company of lawyers and bankers in pinstripe suits. By contrast, Kroc viewed them as a necessary evil, an appendage to a business. Kroc saw his greatest achievement in terms of the millionaires McDonald's made out of independent businessmen. Sonneborn took greater pride in the millions that investors made in McDonald's, and his crowning moment came when he got the company admitted to what he considered the most prestigious club on earth—the New York Stock Exchange. In short, Harry Sonneborn was Ray Kroc's extremely silent partner, a financial man who stood in the shadow of the founder.

That Kroc hired Sonneborn at all is testimony to the founder's willingness to take chances on raw, unproven talent. Although an extremely bright graduate of an advanced high school program affiliated with New York's City College, Sonneborn dropped out of the University of Wisconsin and went to work instead as a salesman for his foster father's clothing plant. In the 1940s he started a couple of small garment manufacturing operations of his own, largely by employing his innate ability to persuade skeptical bankers to loan him money.

But in the early 1950s he discovered the built-in leverage of franchising. He went to work for Leo Moranz, who was then building Tastee-Freez. But when Sonneborn left after a dispute with Moranz in 1956, Don Conley, the salesman from Helmco-Lacy who was later hired as McDonald's first licensing vice president, told him to contact Ray Kroc to see if he could find a spot in his new McDonald's business. "I don't think he likes Jews," Sonneborn replied. Conley assured him that despite Kroc's repeated use of ethnic epithets, he harbored no real prejudices. (Kroc sometimes called himself a "Bohunk," in reference to his Bohemian lineage.)

Kroc hired Sonneborn because he needed help selling franchises and because Sonneborn had similar experience at Tastee-Freez and was enthusiastic enough about McDonald's prospects to work for a mere $100 a week, less than a quarter of his Tastee-Freez salary. But when Sonneborn immediately began demonstrating his expertise in making money—something Kroc surprisingly had not thought out very well—Kroc made Sonneborn the number two man in his company and gave him nearly unbridled power over its finances because he respected Sonneborn's skills in the one area of the business where he was not skilled. Kroc's trust was not misplaced. Although Sonneborn is unknown outside of McDonald's—and even now by many on the inside—he was the man who developed the formula to convert McDonald's into a financial powerhouse.

Yet, Kroc knew when he hired Sonneborn that he was hiring his opposite. It was as if he intentionally set the stage for an eventual conflict. "I didn't give a damn about money, and I didn't pay as much attention to that part of the business as I should have," Kroc conceded. "All I wanted was a winner in the hamburger business, and I sort of took profits for granted. But Harry didn't know or care a damn thing about hamburgers and french fries. When it came to what the company sold and who the franchisees were, Harry was far away from it. He was a cold, calculating money man, but I needed a guy like that."

The sharp differences in personalities among Kroc, Sonneborn, and Martino set a pattern at McDonald's. The next three critical employees—Fred Turner, Jim Schindler, and Don Conley—were no less different from one another than were the first three, and yet Kroc's eclectic approach to management continued to be extremely successful. Because each had totally different interests and traits, they wound up perfecting different aspects of McDonald's: Turner developed a restaurant operations system that would become the model for the fast-food industry; Schindler designed buildings, equipment, and signs that also became industry standards; Conley provided the diplomacy needed to recruit the extremely independent franchisees who were the foundation of the McDonald's chain. In a sense, the diversity of Kroc's managers led to the uniformity of the McDonald's System.

When Kroc began hiring the managers he needed to oversee restaurant operations, he might have been expected to turn to his peers in the food service business, all experienced and middle-aged. Fred Turner, who was only twenty-three when he first met Kroc, clearly did not fit that mold. In February 1956, Turner showed up in Kroc's office with his brother, Don; Don's father-in-law, J. W. Post; and Post's son, Joe. Don Turner had been talking with his father-in-law about investing in a food franchise. The idea was that Don Turner and the elder Post would put up the money, while Fred Turner and Joe Post would operate the store. That was when Joe spotted a small ad in the *Chicago Tribune* for McDonald's franchises. The next weekend, Fred Turner, just finishing up a two-year hitch as a clerk-typist in the army, drove to Chicago from Fort Dix, New Jersey, so that the four partners could meet with the McDonald's founder. The night before, Turner and Joe Post had scouted out the Des Plaines McDonald's for three hours, counting the surprising number of customers braving the bitter February cold to wait outside in line for hamburgers that they would have to eat in their cars. More impressive still were the types of customers they saw. "We were looking at families and family-sized orders, and that registered with us because it was something different for a carryout," Turner recalls. "There was enough business on a cold February Friday evening that even two uninitiated observers could see that it was significant."

The next day, the four partners in Post-Turner Corporation met with Kroc to hear his sales pitch on McDonald's. Kroc talked about his vision of building McDonald's volume per store to $300,000, double the first year revenue of Des Plaines, but it was the feeling that Kroc projected that influenced Turner. "I was struck by his directness and genuine enthusiasm," Turner says. "It was not an acquired enthusiasm, but a natural enthusiasm, and yet it was thoroughly credible. This guy had no secrets."

Turner, who had dropped out of Drake during his junior year, was wrestling with the idea of resuming his studies after the army, but that day in Kroc's office, Turner says, "tilted the needle" away from college. The four partners paid their $950 franchise fee and set about finding a location. In the meantime, Turner worked as a counterman at the Des Plaines store to support his wife and four-month-old daughter and learn the McDonald's System. On days off he scouted potential sites for Post-Turner, and while he found several, the four partners could never agree on one. As a result, their partnership was falling apart, and Turner's training stint in Des Plaines had run its course. For the next two months, he sold Fuller Brush supplies door to door to offices in the Loop, and the task of persuading each receptionist to let him through the front door was so humiliating that he suffered from the dry heaves each morning before work. Yet, Turner had found himself increasingly fascinated with the operation of the McDonald's food preparation system, and when an opening developed for assistant manager at a new restaurant on Cicero Avenue in Chicago, Turner eagerly took it, even though it paid only $100 a week. Turner spent his last day with Fuller Brush sitting with his sample case on a bench at the LaSalle Street railroad station, thinking about the new McDonald's restaurant.

It was the last non-McDonald's job Turner had. When the Cicero Avenue restaurant opened in September 1956, Turner threw himself into the task of learning how to manage a store. At the end of the year, Kroc asked him to come to work for McDonald's System, Inc., to help it fulfill its commitment to train new franchisees and help them at store openings. Turner soon forgot about the Post-Turner Company, which still had not settled on a site for its restaurant, and began thinking about developing McDonald's operations department.

Kroc hired Turner for his "youth, his spirit and excitement," but what he really got was a man of nearly frightening intensity. By his own admission, Turner had done few things with balance; anything worth doing was worth overdoing. He had fluctuated from one extreme to another in an apparent search for something to sustain his intensity. In his first year at Drake, he focused all his energies on his premed studies and was rewarded with a 4.0 average. But when he joined a fraternity, his commitment to study was replaced with a devotion to coed partying and cutting classes, and racking up incompletes became a steady practice. He was such a fraternity enthusiast that his fraternity brothers wanted to elect him president—just before Turner quit Drake and volunteered for the draft, disgusted with his failure to apply himself to the books.

In McDonald's, Turner's intensity and his ability to delve into the seemingly smallest of details finally found a steady outlet. And while Kroc had set the broad operating principles of quality, service, and cleanliness, Turner soon had the same control over operations that Sonneborn had over finance and real estate. Within months he was defining virtually all operating procedures, writing manuals for franchisees to follow, and developing the industry's first system for monitoring and grading the performance of franchisees in the stores. As much as Kroc himself, Turner was responsible for building into McDonald's the quality and consistency that would become the company's most visible trademark and the standard against which all other fast-food operations would be judged.

While it might be argued that Kroc was forced to give Sonneborn power in finance, an area in which Kroc had little interest, there was no such rationalization for the enormous authority Kroc gave to an inexperienced youth in the one area of the business that Kroc himself cared about. Yet, despite all his rules for how his employees should live and look and behave, Kroc motivated people to work by giving them rope. "He always gave you space," Turner says. "He never ragged you. He had a saying that you should go roamin' in the gloamin'. You knew he had a temper and was capable of blowing up at any moment, but he would listen to me, give me my day in court, and let me know what he thought. And if I was arguing my point with conviction, he usually let me have my way. [As a result], you always wanted this guy to respect your acumen. You wanted to take the initiative because you wanted to please him."

Turner's intensity was balanced by the lack of intensity in another early Kroc recruit, Don Conley, McDonald's first franchising vice president. Conley was a more traditional, easygoing salesman—a master of a smoother, softer, subtler form of salesmanship than Kroc performed. Conley rose from a shipping clerk to sales manager of Helmco-Lacy, which sold a soup warmer called the Lacy Hot Cup to restaurants and a line of fudge warmers to the same soda fountains that bought Kroc's Multimixers. Kroc knew Conley shared his belief in a better financial break for franchisees and that his soft-sell approach was made to order for selling franchises. But Kroc also knew that he was well suited to perform all the hand-holding that is necessary to keep a franchisee sold on the concept while he anxiously waits a year or more for his restaurant to be built. With a crop of prematurely white hair, Conley's look accented a soft-spoken manner that gave McDonald's franchising a credibility that other franchisers often lacked.

Conley also brought to McDonald's another desperately needed commodity—a pilot's license. A bomber pilot with considerable combat experience in World War II, McDonald's first franchising vice president doubled as the company pilot—flying managers around the country in his own single-engine Cessna 195. While that might seem trivial, it allowed Kroc and Sonneborn to travel economically and at a moment's notice into the less accessible small towns and remote suburbs where McDonald's took root. That, in turn, gave them a critical edge over upstart competitors in the race to find prime sites and negotiate real estate financing for new stores. It also provided Fred Turner invaluable assistance in building a field service team that would help train new franchisees, set up their local supply relationships, and check on their operations.

From that positive initial experience with Conley, McDonald's quickly began to appreciate the value of general aviation in building a national restaurant chain. By 1959, when the company's net worth was less than $100,000, McDonald's had added a Beechcraft Bonanza and a $70,000 Rockwell Aero Commander, a six-seat twin-engine turbo prop. The three-plane fleet gave Kroc's company a mobility none of his competitors could match. But the appearance of young McDonald's managers flying into small towns in company planes also gave the fledgling fast-food chain instant credibility among local food suppliers, property owners, and mortgage lenders, whose support McDonald's desperately needed to obtain and finance its sites and set up its restaurants. The reputation of fast-food franchisers as hustlers and hucksters was not easily overcome, and to some extent the appearance of McDonald's as an airborne company countered the here-today-gone-tomorrow image of the fast-food industry.

Of all the initial selections of building-block managers, none so clearly demonstrates Kroc's intent to choose the right talent for the job as his hiring of James Schindler to head McDonald's construction-engineering and equipment-design function. As individual as they were, Martino, Sonneborn, Turner, and Conley might have prospered in larger corporate environments. That is not true of Schindler, a genius intellect who had no tolerance for the petty requirements of corporate organizations. He was a man who could not waste time with corporate politics but who could spend hours defining such obscure concepts as his theory that man's perfection approaches only 64 percent of God's.

Even though McDonald's remained surprisingly free-form in its structure as it grew into a large corporation, the idea of working for a billion-dollar company seemed to bother Schindler. At one point during the 1970s when Schindler was particularly upset with what he believed were the shortcomings of the corporate bureaucracy, he asked for time to make a slide presentation to a meeting of the company's twenty or so senior managers, including then chairman Turner and former vice chairman Ed Schmitt. Schindler had just come back from an African safari, and he managed to blend that experience into a personal critique of McDonald's corporate structure. Schmitt recalls the scene: "He first announced what he thought of the board of directors, and he flashed up a slide of asses of zebras. Then he pictured the operations group by showing a slide of jackals picking fleas out of their hair. And then he announced the 'brain trust' of the organization—the financial group—and he showed a slide of baboons. By this time he had really intended to get us mad, but it was so funny that everyone was rolling off their chairs, and Jim was infuriated. He took his slides and left."

Schindler spoke such an arcane language—a combination of his technical jargon and philosophical ruminations—that his discourse often confused the direct and uncluttered mind of Ray Kroc. "Ray never understood what the hell Jim was saying, because he could talk in circles," Schmitt observes. "He was like a mystic to Ray, but he had complete confidence in what Jim could do because Jim had creative capacity in equipment which was unique not only to our company but to the restaurant field."

Schindler picked up most of his engineering and design skills on the job. While he continued throughout his career to take night school courses in such varied subjects as architecture and chemical engineering, he never obtained a degree. But his eclectic work experience was far more valuable than any degree. It began in grade school when Schindler tagged along to construction sites to assist his father, a plas-

tering contractor, and to study procedures used by each of the construction trades. Even while still in high school he took college-level
drafting and architecture courses, and after high school he worked in
the engineering department of Albert Pick and Company, a manufacturer of such heavy-duty food service equipment as walk-in coolers
and cafeteria counters. There, Schindler picked up skills in kitchen
layout that he later employed at McDonald's to design kitchens that set
the standard for the fast-food industry. During the war, Schindler
trained in electronics in the Signal Corps, designed tools for munitions
production, and learned how to run a lithographic printing press. He
even designed kitchens for submarines, gaining experience that was
invaluable when he arranged kitchens for the cramped quarters of the
early McDonald's buildings. After the war, Schindler became chief
engineer for Leitner Equipment Company, one of dozens of commercial kitchen "packagers" that manufacture cabinets and counters for
restaurants and install kitchen equipment made by others.

It was there that Kroc, in 1955, turned to Schindler to solve a
problem he had encountered at his new Des Plaines restaurant.
Counter sections, made of a thin-gauge steel wrapped around wood
and soldered at the job site, were buckling in the cold. Schindler
replaced them with prefabricated stainless sections that were twenty
times thicker and bolted together at the job site. Kroc recognized that
Schindler had designed them to withstand the temperature changes of
a year-round drive-in. Schindler's breadth of construction and design
knowledge and his respect for quality made a lasting impression on
Kroc, who finally put him on the payroll in 1958.

Of course, bringing together such diverse characters was only the
beginning of the challenge. The real task was getting them to work in
harmony. All had strong feelings about their work, and when their
personality differences were added to it, the mix was explosive. Kroc
had to find a way to harness that energy.

Centralizing authority might have seemed the most effective way
to prevent personality and power clashes among McDonald's maverick
managers. But Kroc flatly rejected such an organizational structure.
Having hired unique individuals who would not easily fit into a corporate mold, he decided that the only way to get them moving together
was to give each of them plenty of rope.

Creating a decentralized structure, however, was not a strategic
move for Kroc. It was a natural one. Although he possessed many

autocratic traits on the surface, Kroc was at heart a freethinker who had no desire to stifle the creativity of his young managers. He was a supreme pragmatist who understood that to get the job done, he had to let his managers do their jobs without interference from him. While he taught and counseled and even demanded in those areas where he had his deepest convictions, he did not dictate. "I don't admire dictators because I could never work for one," Kroc said. "I liked delegating authority, and I always admired people in business who could consider alternatives to their way of doing things."

But Kroc also realized that he was in no position to dictate because he was as new to the fast-food business as was everyone who worked for him. He forbade discussion of very few new ideas, such as the addition of hot dogs to the menu (because he believed "the skin covered a multiple of third and fourth classes of meat") and the addition of jukeboxes to the restaurants (which he believed would convert McDonald's from family restaurants to teenage hangouts). But those were exceptions; on most subjects, Kroc encouraged his managers to express their differences and to experiment with new ideas. "I had no previous experience in the hamburger business," Kroc explained. "In fact, none of us had dyed-in-the-wool reasons for saying anything. So, if they [his managers] had a different idea than my idea, I'd let them run with it for six months and see what it did. We differed, and I made mistakes and they made mistakes, but we grew together."

In short, Kroc harnessed the energy of his staff by unleashing it. Clashes between opposites were prevented in part because every manager had such enormous responsibility in his area that he had neither the time nor the inclination to engage in internal debates. At least in the early years, that surely was the case with the two managers who were diametrically opposite—Kroc and Sonneborn. Sonneborn had been on the McDonald's payroll for less than a year when he began proposing a major shift in corporate strategy toward investment in real estate at the restaurants. The notion of entering into leasing contracts, land purchase agreements, and building mortgages was foreign to Kroc. However, while Sonneborn was proposing a revolutionary direction for a fast-food franchiser—one loaded with enormous financial risk—Kroc surprisingly gave him freedom to do it, and that ignited Sonneborn. "Ray was a nicer fellow than I was," Sonneborn said. "He agreed with me more than I agreed with him. He involved himself in the real estate activities, but [in that area] he generally deferred to my judgment." Kroc agreed with that assessment. "I got along with Harry by staying out of his reach," he said. "Once or twice I had to remind him that while I had a lot of tolerance, I would appreciate it if he would remember that I owned the company."

Kroc seemed to understand the need for his managers to make their own mistakes—and to learn from them. Thus, despite the fact that he had a boss who was totally opposite from him, Sonneborn nevertheless was willing to put in long hours working toward the same goal as Kroc. "Harry respected Ray because Ray gave him a chance to be something and gave him the rope to prove himself," Martino observes.

As McDonald's grew, its decentralized decision making continued to attract to the company individualists who would have difficulty conforming to more traditional organizations. Thus the second generation of McDonald's managers exhibited much the same pluralism as was evident in the first generation, but they also showed the same enthusiasm for their jobs and spirit of cooperation with one another. Turner notes: "For those people who have the ability but who have not been in situations where they could demonstrate it, McDonald's became a place of opportunity with a capital O."

McDonald's diverse managers also avoided internal competition by developing a feeling of family that persists inside McDonald's today. Few executives share their personal joy and grief more than managers at McDonald's. Even when executives quit McDonald's, there is among the managers who remain a sense of loss, not unlike that created by a death in the family. When the loss is to a competitor, the parting manager has committed an unspeakable treason. That was the feeling when Donald Smith abruptly announced his departure in 1976 to become president of Burger King less than one week after being promoted to senior executive vice president at McDonald's. Yet, the bitter resentment over his leaving—and the timing of it—still lingers. Even when Smith moved back to Chicago and became president of International Diversifoods, most McDonald's executives who knew him well adhered to an unspoken rule of not associating with him.

To a large extent, the family feelings at McDonald's were an early by-product of the sense of mission that Kroc developed. Though different from one another, his managers pulled together because Kroc convinced them that they were involved in a noble undertaking— building a national chain of 15-cent-hamburger stands—that outsiders considered frivolous. They shared a common desire to prove to family, friends, and more established businessmen that they were pioneering a new industry that would someday have a far-reaching impact on American life and business.

Kroc himself believed that McDonald's had nearly a sacred mission, and he never missed a chance to rework his themes about the "fast-buck artists" in franchising and the lack of consistency and quality in "fly-by-night" fast-food chains of the late 1950s. But Kroc had more subtle ways of communicating the dedication he expected from his staff. Turner, for example, recalls how the founder bought all of his managers a copy of *What Have You Done for Me Lately?*, the Walter Schwimmer treatise on the advertising trade. While the book depicted the insatiable demands of fickle advertising clients, Kroc's protégés got another message. "I was reading Schwimmer but thinking Kroc," Turner remembers. "Ray saw McDonald's as an innovative company, and this was his way of communicating to us that we had to keep working at this thing and that yesterday's accomplishments belonged to yesterday. Everyone worked a little harder after that."

As a result, McDonald's managers treated the fast-food drive-in business as seriously as IBM treated computers, as Delta treated air travel, and as Boeing treated airplanes. The fact that the outside world was not ready to understand that only made the McDonald's sense of purpose more binding on its early managers. Kuhn observes: "When you believe in what you do, you are willing to work in many cases with people that you cannot stand. If we didn't have the strength of a mission, all the love in the world wouldn't drive us."

The sense of family was also cultivated by Kroc's refusal to separate his work from his social life. Even when McDonald's had but three employees, Sonneborn and Martino would frequently gather at Kroc's home for dinner and late-night discussions about their visions of corporate expansion. As the staff grew, the social gatherings after work among key managers continued, with Kroc typically initiating them.

The meetings that mixed social and office life remained woven into the fabric of McDonald's even when the company entered the billion-dollar class and corporate socializing became an extremely expensive proposition. Few companies invite as many managers *and their spouses* to management conventions, seminars, and conferences, all of which are designed to mix work with socializing. Indeed, each year, McDonald's spends nearly $10 million on management and franchisee meetings. And every two years, the company convenes its week-long convention of franchisees and their families from around the world. In

1994, more than ten thousand people attended the operators' convention in Las Vegas, where they conducted business but also attended lavish dinners and shows sponsored by McDonald's. And even when thousands of managers and franchisees gather at company banquets, care is taken to maintain a family atmosphere by downplaying the corporate hierarchy: there is rarely a head table.

To sustain the sense of family, McDonald's had to develop the equivalent of a corporate matriarch and patriarch. The former role was played exceedingly well by June Martino, who perhaps more than anyone else was responsible for preventing the diversity at McDonald's from turning into corporate divisiveness. Simply put, Martino was a den mother to McDonald's young managers. And while she got little formal recognition for that role, it made her perhaps the only universally liked executive in McDonald's.

She generated such affection because she played a vital peace-keeping function without regard to her own interest. That was a prerequisite for a start-up company that had no formal management and yet required closer—and potentially more volatile—relationships among employees. When a secretary was on the verge of a breakdown because she had been spurned by a married executive who had not treated their affair as seriously as she had, it was Martino who took her into her home for several days of homespun therapy sessions. When newly hired managers came into the office with rumpled suits or dirty fingernails or with some other imperfection that was certain to set Kroc off, it was Martino who caught the offending employee before Kroc did. And it was Martino who involved wives in the McDonald's family and who dealt with their frustrations over the long hours their husbands were putting in. When Kroc gave Turner a $1,500 bonus at the end of his first year, Martino grabbed the young operations manager as soon as he left the founder's office. "Come on, you're coming with me," she told Turner. "Where to?" he asked. "We're going to buy your wife a mink stole." As a result, the bonus Turner was hoping to spend on a second car went to pay for a $1,700 mink for Patty Turner. June says: "Even though they had three little kids and Fred was out of town a lot, Patty was uncomplaining. The wives did a lot when we started McDonald's, and I always thought they should share in it."

But the greatest sense of unity among McDonald's diverse managers was fostered by an uncommon loyalty to the company's patriarch, Ray Kroc. Few understood better than Kroc that a boss gets loyalty only by giving it first. Following a similar approach to that which he took toward franchisees, Kroc created that loyalty internally by setting an early precedent of generosity to McDonald's employees, many of whom took sizable pay cuts when they began working for McDonald's during its unprofitable start-up years. Sonneborn, for example, came to work for Kroc for $100 a week, after having been a $25,000-a-year vice president for Tastee-Freez. Conley's pay cut was even bigger. But when McDonald's had the resources, Kroc rewarded his early managers handsomely with stock and salary compensation.

Even before McDonald's became a moneymaker, Kroc was anything but a hard-liner on salary. To get Schindler to shift jobs in 1958, he had to pay him $12,000 a year—which was all that Kroc himself was making from Prince Castle Sales (Kroc drew no salary or expense money from McDonald's until 1961). McDonald's at the time was virtually broke, and the only way its founder could cover Schindler's salary was by borrowing against his life insurance.

Two years earlier, Kroc had willingly granted Fred Turner's request for a starting salary of $475 a month instead of the $425 that Kroc had offered. Turner had provided Kroc with a sheet listing all commuting and household expenses that he firmly believed justified the higher figure. But, in retrospect, Turner is surprised that Kroc did not object to his request for more money. "Ray wasn't taking a nickel out of the business, and without hesitation he gave me the money," Turner recalls.

But Kroc's role as patriarch transcended money matters. To a great extent, Kroc wove his managers into a tight-knit family not by telling them how to perform their specific tasks, but by teaching them fundamental principles they could identify with as a group. To virtually all of his managers—twenty to thirty years his junior—Ray Kroc was the consummate father figure.

He was always teaching his managers, and many of his lessons—like many of his tirades—did not deal directly with business decisions. They were instead rules to live by, rules Kroc believed were proper and in his managers' best interests.

McDonald's founder was deeply committed to basic, puritanical values. He believed in the work ethic. He believed that a clean and tidy appearance said something about the strength of someone's character. And while his puritanical belief in thrift also reflected his Bohemian upbringing, it was so strong that it shaped his behavior long after McDonald's success propelled him into the ranks of the nation's wealthiest men. Even in his eighties, Kroc was looking for bargains. It was not unusual for him to be driven in his Rolls-Royce to one of California's many membership discount warehouses, where, among other things, he could buy a carton of cigarettes for his wife cheaper than she could buy them at neighborhood stores. "To Ray, waste was terrible regardless of how much money you have," Turner says. "It's inefficient, unthoughtful, and selfish."

In the 1950s, when McDonald's itself was struggling to survive financially as a company, Kroc was giving his managers personal instructions in thrift. He told them the cheapest place to buy food. He advised them to clip coupons and to buy economy-sized boxes of cereal for their kids. He once circulated a memo to all staffers telling them how much cheaper it was to buy cigarettes by the carton than by the pack. Teaching thrift by example continued even after Kroc became rich. Some executives recall flying with Kroc and his third wife, Joan, in his $8 million Gulfstream jet, when they saw Kroc chastising his wife for bringing him an orange with three napkins instead of one.

But Kroc was teaching his business philosophies, too, many of which were applications of the same puritan ethic. He kept preaching to his young managers to focus only on the long-term profits that come from quality performance and not to chase short-term profits that can be obtained without dedication to details. If they did the job right, he assured them, the money would take care of itself. Indeed, his business lessons were so often repeated that well over a dozen of them have been converted to Krocisms that now adorn most of the office partitions at McDonald's corporate offices. One sample: "Success is not free; neither is failure." Another: "None of us is as good as all of us." And another: "Free enterprise will work if you will."

While Kroc was not a religious man by churchgoing standards (a Congregationalist by birth, he went to church mostly for weddings and funerals), he was nevertheless deeply devoted to his principles of living. They were black and white, and there was no room for compromise. What is curious is that Kroc was pioneering a new world of fast food on strictly old world values. "Ray Kroc," wrote columnist George Will, "was a nineteenth century man living in the twentieth century." Yet, by imparting to his managers his uncompromising principles in the manner of a father to his children, Kroc created among them a strong family bond. As different as they were on everything else, his managers nevertheless shared the founder's philosophies. "You see it in today's context, and they [Kroc's rules of living] sound like an intrusion on private rights, and I guess in today's context they would be," Turner observes. "But that was a different era. These rules were not offensive, not negative. You knew these things were important to Ray, and you accepted them."

But McDonald's managers accepted Kroc's principles of living because they did not really deprive them of any freedom in performing their jobs. Indeed, by giving his young corporate managers enormous responsibilities, Kroc encouraged them to express their diversity creatively. By acting as their patriarch, he encouraged them to pull in the same direction. Kroc had mastered the art of managing creative individuals by maintaining the delicate balance between their need for freedom and their need for guidance. "He brought out the very best in people," Turner says. "He was the best boss you could ever have."

Chapter 6
MAKING HAMBURGERS

It was the early 1960s. Jack Roshman was standing in a Burger Chef he was about to open in Springfield, Ohio. It was to be only one of more than one hundred Burger Chefs that Roshman would open in Ohio under his franchise for the entire state, but the opening in Springfield would never be forgotten. A construction crew across the street was putting the finishing touches on a brand-new McDonald's, and Roshman was intently watching the progress of the restaurant that would be his first head-to-head encounter with his arched rival.

He saw a man walking from the McDonald's to his Burger Chef, and he assumed it was the new McDonald's franchisee. It was actually Ralph Lanphar, McDonald's new area supervisor, and as he approached, Roshman was preparing to exchange pleasantries and suggest that the two new hamburger restaurants might provide each other emergency supplies of hamburgers, buns, and other fast-food staples. He knew McDonald's was gaining a reputation as "not exactly the friendliest operator around," but he nevertheless was not prepared for the greeting he got. "Hello, I'm the new McDonald's supervisor," Lanphar told Roshman. "We're going to run you out of business."

The image has stuck with Roshman for nearly three decades. To him, it reflected McDonald's unwavering commitment to building *the* superior hamburger operation and its conviction that the only thing it could learn by cooperating with competitors were bad habits. Roshman likens the operations of McDonald's to the Marine Corps—tough training, tough rules, and tough taskmasters to enforce them. "When a guy came out of Hamburger University [McDonald's training center], he was convinced he was the best damn restaurant operator in the world, and he could conquer anybody," Roshman observes. "Burger Chef had similar rules on quality, service, and cleanliness, but we just didn't get it done as effectively as McDonald's. There are no secrets in this business—a hamburger is a hamburger. I don't think we had the dedication to quality that they had."

Fred Turner rejects out of hand Roshman's analogy to the Marine Corps. To Turner, there have been far too many marketing initiatives and new product discoveries on the part of individual franchisees for McDonald's to be considered regimented. "It's one of the superficial notions about McDonald's that no one has put into perspective," Turner says. "The independent-mindedness of our operators prevents regimentation. While they stick to the basics of the system, they zig and zag by making refinements and changes, and everyone benefits from their willingness to zig and zag. The system deals with setting uniform standards, but regimentation? No way!"

His objections aside, however, there is no denying that much of McDonald's success is the result of its dedication to operating regimen. More than any other early competitor in fast food, McDonald's was deadly serious as it went about the task of defining its operations, setting basic standards of achievement, and monitoring suppliers and operators to determine whether standards were being met. While that work continues today, the fundamental shape of the operating system was built during the first decade, and Turner, more than any other individual, was responsible for building it.

It was Ray Kroc, of course, who set the policy. While perhaps underrated for his franchising and management insights, Kroc's personal commitment to quality, service, and cleanliness is legend. QSC long ago became the most popular acronym among fast-food operators, but the phrase originated with Kroc, and he used QSC to distinguish McDonald's from all other competitors in an industry that was otherwise rife with duplication. The McDonald brothers had not given him a secret recipe for hamburgers, milk shakes, and french fries. He possessed no patents, no technological breakthrough, and no new product. Kroc was not handed a Xerox or a Polaroid.

Managers of other fast-food chains knew that their food, when properly prepared, was more or less competitive with McDonald's. While there are many reasons why McDonald's wound up dominating an industry where no one had a special advantage, its competitors agree on only one: McDonald's took more seriously the task of building a uniform operating system. That created a difference where there had been none. McDonald's franchisees could be counted on to deliver the same quality of food and service time after time, restaurant after restaurant. Its competitors, by their own admission, did not duplicate that.

Achieving uniformity is the toughest single task of any franchised service business. Unlike manufacturers, which produce uniform products simply by centralizing production, fast-food franchisers sell a product produced locally by infinitely different operators. Essentially, McDonald's had but one operational secret that made it the industry standout: It found a way to obtain strict manufacturing uniformity without stifling the individual creativity of its operators through excessive regimentation. "Anybody who says they have operations as good as McDonald's is lying," declares Richard Kearns, who built the Red Barn hamburger chain into a respectable three-hundred-store operation before selling out to Servomation Corporation in 1968. "There wasn't a one of us that came close. We all had star stores that could keep up with the best of McDonald's stores, but on a companywide basis, nobody compared. Ray Kroc was never driven as much by money as he was by ego. He had such an extreme amount of personal pride that when he saw a bad McDonald's, he went berserk. He believed in QSC as a religion. All McDonald's people did." And Jim Collins, whose Collins Foods International operated two hundred and fifty Kentucky Fried Chicken restaurants, shares that opinion: "I've been to McDonald's in Tokyo, Vienna, and Australia, and I get a great sense of having the same product from each one of their locations. Most people haven't been able to bring the discipline needed in fast food to get that type of consistency, and I think that's good old hard-boiled Ray Kroc telling his operators, 'Do it my way or you won't be around.' "

In setting up its operating system, McDonald's displayed no particular genius, just tenacity. To survive today, all fast-food chains must build central organizations to develop standards of operation and train its licensees to meet them. They must be responsible for picking suppliers and setting specifications on all food products. And finally, they must monitor the system to determine that the franchisees are following standards and that suppliers are meeting product specifications.

As logical and basic as that sounds, it was a revolutionary concept in food franchising when McDonald's took that approach in the 1950s. Indeed, it is impossible to appreciate the breakthrough that McDonald's made without first understanding that before McDonald's, food service franchisers simply did not spend much time developing central organizations to supervise purchasing, to set operating standards, or to train franchisees. Most of their time and energy was spent on the one function on which McDonald's spent surprisingly little effort—selling franchises. Once their stores were opened, most franchisers focused on collecting royalties from existing units and opening new ones. From an operations standpoint, their systems were on automatic pilot.

When McDonald's began in 1955, the two largest franchised food service chains—Dairy Queen and Tastee-Freez—had already set that pattern. Because they sold large territories to franchisees who sublicensed them to local operators, it was up to the statewide franchisee to supervise store operations. Understandably, those operations varied. Some territorial franchisees checked their restaurants, some did not; some controlled the quality of their supplies, some did not.

The territorial franchisees themselves were not responsible for meeting rigid standards because the national franchiser did not enforce them. Harry Axene ran Dairy Queen almost as a one-man show. Leo Moranz, the founder of Tastee-Freez, had a staff of only five people, even after his chain had opened fifteen hundred stores. That staff included two secretaries, someone to collect royalties, someone to handle supply orders placed through the cooperative Tastee-Freez Buying Association, and someone to travel around the country to help territorial franchisees open their first stores. In fact, says Moranz, one of the reasons Harry Sonneborn left Tastee-Freez was because it did not have enough work for a man of Sonneborn's talents. "If he stayed with me, he wouldn't have been anything," Moranz says, "because I *was* the business."

Once he parceled out the entire United States to territorial franchisees, there was little for Moranz to do but collect his 10-cent royalty on every gallon of mix that operators bought from the dairies he selected. Moranz had a money machine he thought needed no oil. "I was averaging a royalty of six hundred dollars per store per year," he recalls. "That doesn't amount to anything—until you multiply that by fifteen hundred and realize that I didn't have much overhead." Moranz also made money selling to franchisees the freezers his company made, and when those profits are added to the equation, he says he earned easily over $1 million a year—a tidy sum for the 1950s. "I used to go to Palm Springs for six months during the winter," he says. "That business ran itself."

Most early fast-food franchisers operated in a similar fashion. Although they put in more hours, they nevertheless did not think about

building large operating systems to control their franchisees' operations. Harlan Sanders also franchised Kentucky Fried Chicken to large
territorial operators, and before selling out in 1964 to a syndicate
headed by future Kentucky governor John Y. Brown, Sanders's central
organization was no larger than the one Moranz had. Nor had the early
hamburger barons established any precedent for large operating organizations. Bob Wian franchised his Big Boy operation nationally with a
staff of five people because he relied on well-established territorial
franchisees to supervise their own operations.

None of the other franchisers in the 15-cent-hamburger business
had any notion of building a supervisory and support organization
similar to the one Kroc envisioned. Even competitors such as Henry's,
which possessed the financial resources Kroc lacked, were not devoting the time and money McDonald's was spending on central operations. Owned by the Bressler Ice Cream Company, Henry's provides a
classic comparison with McDonald's. It too was based in Chicago, and
it opened its first fast-food drive-in restaurant there just five months
after Kroc opened in Des Plaines. Furthermore, the unit was patterned
after Jim Collins's Hamburger Handout in Los Angeles, which itself was
a direct copy of the McDonald brothers' drive-in in San Bernardino. In
fact, Jim Schindler, the young kitchen designer Kroc later hired for
McDonald's, designed the kitchen for the first Henry's unit. With the
impressive financial backing of Bressler's, Henry's grew as fast as Mc-
Donald's at first, and strictly from a financial standpoint, it appeared
that Henry's had a much better shot at becoming the king of the 15-
cent-hamburger business. But by 1965, the year McDonald's became a
publicly held company and built its seven hundredth store, Henry's
had disappeared.

Henry's problems were all operational, and they could all be
traced to Bressler's concept of using the hamburger chain as a vehicle
to sell its ice cream. That created tremendous pressure to sell franchises and open stores so that franchisees could begin purchasing Bressler products. Conversely, there was no incentive to build an operations
team. Charles Bressler, one of the five Bressler brothers involved in the
family-owned Bressler Ice Cream Company and the man in charge of
operations for Henry's, believes the biggest problem with the hamburger chain was the lack of adequate store supervision. He recalls that
his suggestions for more manpower to upgrade store operations fell on
deaf ears. When he asked for money to start a training school similar to
the one McDonald's opened in 1961, he was told "it was too early."

When he wanted to hire Jim Schindler, he learned there was no room on the payroll. Henry's lost Schindler's kitchen design talents to McDonald's.

Even when he pleaded for a tighter screening process to select more talented franchisees who could run stores in an environment of minimal supervision, he discovered that others in his family's company were more interested in selling franchises first and asking questions later. When he went to help a franchisee open the first—and only— Henry's in Phoenix, he was horrified to discover upon arrival that the franchisee had only one arm. "Do you have a brother or a son or a wife who is going to help you in this business?" Bressler asked the new franchisee. "No," was the man's response. "I'm all by myself." To Bressler, the incident crystallized his company's approach to fast-food franchising. "You can't blame a guy for having one arm, but how in the hell can you sell a franchise to a guy who couldn't even wrap hamburgers?" Bressler asks. "I don't like to downgrade my brothers, but they just weren't into the drive-in game." Their interest in Henry's, he says, was "mostly for the ice cream game."

In sharp contrast to other newcomers to the fast-food business in the mid-1950s, McDonald's directed much of its efforts toward defining, refining, and implementing its operating system. The very opposite might have been expected, since McDonald's was starting with a surprisingly detailed system that had better than six years of market experience in San Bernardino. Yet, Kroc instinctively assumed that the Speedee Service System of the McDonald brothers could be upgraded and that he had the power to make such changes, even though his contract with the McDonald brothers clearly ran counter to that assumption. Under the contract, the brothers had to approve every change in writing, and they approved not one that way.

Kroc decided that to build a national chain—one that could be licensed to hundreds of newcomers to the restaurant business—he would have to develop a far more refined system of operation than the McDonalds had employed in San Bernardino. He needed a system that was so solid and yet so simple that it could convert novices into strong operators within weeks. Thus, from his first day of operations in Des Plaines, Kroc and his operations staff began making substantial modifications to the brothers' techniques, knowingly putting McDonald's Corporation in clear violation of its restrictive contract.

As Kroc's new managers approached it, the task of redefining the McDonald's System touched on four areas: improving the product, developing superior supply relationships, upgrading the building and equipment package, and organizing a field force to train licensees and monitor their stores. While Kroc provided encouragement and overall direction, the team that built the new McDonald's operations system consisted of Turner, equipment specialist Schindler, and Nick Karos, whose family operated a sandwich and ice cream shop called The Carousel on Chicago's North Side. Karos had been evaluating a Henry's franchise by managing one of the chain's Chicago stores, but when he became disillusioned with Henry's, he accepted Kroc's offer to work with Turner in developing field operations for McDonald's.

The work of Turner, Schindler, Karos, and Kroc's other operations specialists had its most visible results in the quality of food, the speed of service, and the cleanliness of the American drive-in restaurant. They established the operations standards for a $72 billion fast-food industry. But the impact of their efforts went even beyond that. To obtain their QSC results with a completely new food service format—one most suppliers were not geared to serve—McDonald's conducted a behind-the-scenes campaign to revolutionize dozens of businesses outside the restaurant trade, from food processing to kitchen equipment and even to major segments of American agriculture.

In fact, McDonald's greatest impact on American business is in areas that consumers do not see. In their search for improvements, McDonald's operations specialists moved back down the food and equipment supply chain. They changed the way farmers grow potatoes and the way companies process them. They introduced new methods to the nation's dairies. They altered the way ranchers raised beef and the way the meat industry makes the final product. They invented the most efficient cooking equipment the food service industry had seen. They pioneered new methods of food packaging and distribution. Indeed, no one has had more impact than McDonald's in modernizing food processing and distribution in the past four decades.

It began when McDonald's young operations team wrote the book on how to prepare the food service industry's most popular meal—a hamburger, french fried potatoes, and a milk shake. While the operation of gourmet restaurants had been elevated to an art, no one had attempted to make a science out of the preparation of the one restaurant meal that had mass appeal. More important, no one had set basic standards of food quality for such common products. When McDonald's opened in Des Plaines, hamburger meat often consisted of whatever beef parts filled the butcher's leftover bin. Similarly, no one—not even food experts in the potato industry—had discovered a way of consistently producing good french fries. Restaurants were just as likely to serve fries that were limp and greasy as ones that were crisp and golden. And though soda fountains could consistently produce a quality milk shake, the drugstore fountains were becoming economic dinosaurs, doomed by their labor intensiveness in an era of high-cost labor. Soft-serve ice cream chains were using automated machinery to replace fountain ice cream, but no chains were using the new technology to produce shakes.

McDonald's changed all that by showering the lowly hamburger, french fry, and milk shake with more attention, more study, and more research than anyone had dreamed of doing. The genesis of that work was the realization by Turner and Kroc that the McDonald's format gave them an enormous opportunity to streamline service in the same way as manufacturers had streamlined assembly plants years ago. Their desire for quality motivated them to perfect an operating system, but it was McDonald's ten-item menu that made it possible. Specialization had brought operational improvements to most major industries by the mid-1950s. One exception was food service, and the obvious stumbling block was that the industry's typical menu was so broad that it defied streamlining. McDonald's was the first to achieve efficiencies in food service in part because it was the first to benefit from specialization. "It wasn't because we were smarter," Turner says. "The fact that we were selling just ten items, had a facility that was small, and used a limited number of suppliers created an ideal environment for really digging in on everything."

McDonald's early operations staff had another advantage in their favor: ignorance of accepted restaurant practices. With the exception of Karos, most of McDonald's operations specialists did not have restaurant backgrounds. However, because the concept of fast-food service was so different, the lack of conventional restaurant training became a plus, not a handicap. Even in its current recruiting McDonald's pays no homage to the graduates of Cornell and other big-name restaurant and hotel schools. Much of McDonald's pioneering began with experiments it would not have made had its operations staff known better. "Because we lacked prior restaurant experience, nothing was taken for granted," Turner recalls. "We had to learn everything on our own."

The Turner-Schindler-Karos process of discovery set the pattern for the way the McDonald's System would continue to develop. Everything was done on a trial-and-error basis. No idea was unworthy of discussion. Most were worth trying. More important, few methods were so entrenched that they would not be changed as soon as better ones were found. In short, McDonald's business evolved as a result of thousands of operating experiments made in the real world of store operations. Says Turner: "We were continuously looking for a better way to do things, and then a revised better way to do things, and then a revised, revised better way."

Nowhere was that process followed more exhaustively than in the development of the common french fry. When McDonald's System, Inc., was formed, french fries accounted for no more than 5 percent of all potatoes sold in the U.S. market. Today, they account for more than 25 percent of it, and most industry experts would concede that the improvements McDonald's made in the growing and processing of the ordinary potato contributed greatly to that change. It also greatly enhanced the image of McDonald's, because the 10-cent bag of french fries gave McDonald's its most significant product differentiation. Even consumers who doubted that any chain specializing in 15-cent hamburgers could produce quality food were soon lured to McDonald's by its french fries. Some believe the fries were even more important in building McDonald's than the hamburger itself, an opinion that finds support in the fact that even today four out of five lunch and dinner customers at McDonald's order french fries. "A competitor could buy the same kind of hamburger we did, and we wouldn't have anything extra to show," Kroc once explained. "But the french fries gave us an identity and exclusiveness because you couldn't buy french fries anywhere to compete with ours. You could tell the results of the tender loving care."

The fabled french fries were no accident, nor were they inherited from the McDonald brothers. Instead, they were the product of continuous research. The late Gerry Newman, once McDonald's senior executive vice president and chief accounting officer, estimated that the company during its first decade spent more than $3 million on perfecting its french fries, an impressive investment for any food company but a stunning expenditure for an upstart like McDonald's.

Most of the early work involved nothing more than monitoring the cooking of fries in the restaurants and attempting to determine the precise temperature and time settings that would yield the best quality french fry every time. But what at first appeared to be a simple task soon seemed akin to unlocking the secrets of the atom. McDonald's discovered that temperature settings on the fryers had little to do with the temperature of the oil in the vat. After cold potatoes were dropped into the vat, some fryers recovered from the temperature decline much faster than others. When it became obvious that the time and temperature riddle was more complicated than he had realized, Turner intensified his investigation. "I found myself carrying a damn thermometer with me on all my store visits to calibrate the temperatures on their fry vats," he recalls.

Even when Turner developed what appeared to be optimum settings for each type of fryer, operators still found that some batches of fries were cooked throughout while other batches, fried at the same settings, came out golden on the outside but undercooked inside. The difference occurred even when suppliers did not vary and when the potato was the standard No. 1 Idaho Russet that was preferred for french fries because of its oblong shape and high solids content. No one in the industry could explain the inconsistency—not the growers, the processors, or the distributors. Like many questions McDonald's was asking in the early days, this one had not been raised before.

With experience, Turner and Karos began to realize that the answer lay in the curing the potatoes received in the store. Those stored in the basement for longer periods produced noticeably better fries than those cooked right after delivery. As they researched the idea of curing, they discovered what is now known throughout the fast-food business: potatoes used for french fries must be cured for about three weeks so that enough of their sugars can be converted into starches. Otherwise, the sugars in the potato produce excessive browning, which results in french fries that look cooked on the outside before they are fully cooked inside.

The curing discovery only encouraged Turner and Karos to look closer for other improvements in french fries. They learned from potato chip manufacturers that Idaho Russets vary greatly in their solids content, which greatly affects crispness after frying. So, Turner and Karos began measuring solids to determine the right content needed to produce a crispy french fry, and eventually they set a standard for McDonald's to accept only potatoes with a solids content of at least 21 percent. Soon Karos, Turner, and other field operations specialists were visiting McDonald's local produce suppliers with hydrometers, a floating instrument that measures the specific gravity—and thus the solids content—of potatoes immersed in a large bucket of water. The sight of young, clean-cut McDonald's field men armed with hydrometers was a startling experience for most potato distributors. Their customers had never shown up in their stores to test potatoes for specific gravity—or for anything else. "The potato guys were a rough and tough group," Karos says. "Most of them had never heard of specific gravity, but we convinced them of our need for potatoes with high solids."

Convincing local distributors was the easy part. If they had not seen hydrometers before, neither had they seen a potato order from one restaurant even approaching the three thousand pounds per week that came from the average McDonald's. But, while that was sufficient incentive for the local produce man to shape up, he could not control his own supply that closely. To get the right potato every time, McDonald's had to go to the source—growers and processors.

Eventually, Karos traveled to Idaho to trace the chain's best potato supplies to growers who followed certain planting and fertilization practices. Karos also found that most processors stored potatoes in shallow man-made caves constructed from excavated sod. The discovery was a shocking revelation to McDonald's. Its problems with rotting potatoes were not the result of excessive curing in its stores but rather of archaic practices in the potato industry, which used storage facilities that lacked any sophisticated temperature controls. Turner recalls: "If the storage area was getting too hot, they opened the door to the cave."

In 1962, the number of McDonald's stores went over the four hundred mark and its potato consumption exceeded six million pounds a year—enough purchasing power to entice the potato industry to meet its needs. It began influencing Russet growers to follow planting and fertilizing practices that would yield potatoes with high solids, and it began looking for processors willing to invest in modern storage facilities with automated temperature controls. By making those demands, McDonald's helped bring about major improvements by the mid-1960s in an industry it knew nothing about before Kroc opened his first store in 1955.

Not all the improvements in french fries came from changing the raw materials, however. Even more dramatic steps were taken to improve the frying process in the stores. Not long after the Des Plaines store opened, Dick Keating, whose company supplied McDonald's with gas fryers, suggested that Kroc visit a hot dog stand called Sam's on Chicago's North Side. It was one of scores of hot dog stands in Chicago during the mid-1950s that served a wiener with an order of fries, and like many others, this one used the so-called Chicago method of cooking french fries. Instead of cooking them for five minutes in one process, as most restaurants did, Sam's blanched the potatoes for three minutes in the morning and "finish fried" them for a couple more minutes to meet orders later in the day. The two-step process allowed the hot dog stand operator to meet peak hour demand for french fries, but Keating was convinced that blanching also produced a crispier fry. Kroc, too, became convinced, and he ordered a change from the one-step process handed down from the McDonald brothers.

Keating also wanted McDonald's to consider using the beef-fat-based shortening used at the North Side hot dog stand, and he referred Kroc to the tiny supplier of that product, Harry Smargon. Smargon had just formed his Interstate Foods Company, and because he could not afford the hydrogenation equipment needed to produce 100 percent vegetable shortening, he used the traditional process of making shortening from a blend of vegetable oil and refined beef fat. Impressed with the taste of the fries Keating had recommended, Kroc decided to test Smargon's Fry-All shortening.

For reasons even he finds hard to explain, Smargon insisted that Interstate's shortening blend produced a crisper and more flavorful french fry than one cooked in the all-vegetable shortening that had become the standard in restaurants for deep frying. When Kroc agreed with Smargon, McDonald's soon became the bulk of Interstate's business. Smargon even developed a shortening specifically for McDonald's and called it Formula 47, a reference to the 47 cents McDonald's then charged for its so-called All-American meal—a 15-cent hamburger, 12-cent fries, and a 20-cent shake.

Just how much Interstate's Formula 47 improved the french fry is a matter of individual taste. The fact is that McDonald's decision on shortening became an industry standard. Smargon's company—a three-man operation when Kroc placed his first order in 1955 but now a subsidiary of CFS Continental—sells an estimated $125 million of vegetable and beef shortening a year. It not only supplies Formula 189 to most of the 14,000 McDonald's, it sells a similar shortening to Burger King, Wendy's, Hardee's, and Jack-in-the-Box. With more than 40 percent of the market, Interstate dominates the fast-food-shortening business, which—without the influence of McDonald's—almost surely would have been controlled by Procter & Gamble, Wesson, or one of the other powers in the shortening market.

But even those changes did not satisfy McDonald's passion for refining what had by the late 1950s become its most important product. In fact, the chain, then still a break-even operation with a net worth under $100,000, began researching potato frying the way pharmaceutical companies research new drugs. In 1957, Louis Martino, June's husband, approached Kroc and Turner with the idea of converting the frying of a potato from an art to a science. Martino, who had quit his job as an electrical engineer at Motorola to operate the McDonald's unit in Glen Ellyn that he and his wife owned, had been researching the frying of potatoes in the basement of his store for several months. He was convinced that what McDonald's needed was a laboratory where he could work full time on research. Even with the improvements McDonald's had already made, Martino knew the french frying process still suffered from inconsistent results, and he believed the only answer was to make it foolproof through automation. "McDonald's believed that a kid they hired last week was able to learn by this week how to take potatoes from the raw state to the final fried state," Martino says. "It was wishful thinking."

Kroc agreed with Martino's proposal to open a small (forty by fifty feet) lab in Addison, a suburb west of Chicago. While Kraft, Heinz, and other big food processors by then all had research labs, the idea of opening a food lab in the infant fast-food business was so novel it seemed almost ludicrous. But Martino had a convenient facility to offer —the building he and an associate had constructed to manufacture the ill-fated Fold-A-Nook bench.

When Martino converted the building into McDonald's lab, he immediately began extensive experiments measuring something even labs of the big food processors had not researched: what happens to a potato during a deep-fry cycle. He put temperature sensors into a fry vat and into potato slices themselves and charted their temperature readings during the cooking process. He even cooked potatoes in dyes that allowed him to analyze thin slices of fried potatoes under a microscope. Eventually, McDonald's hired Ken Strong, a food technologist with Lamb Weston, a major potato processor, to assist Martino in his research.

After more than a year of research, Martino and Strong made a critical discovery that would automate the cooking of french fries. Even when suppliers met McDonald's product specifications and when operators carefully followed the proper cooking times and temperatures, batches of fries varied in crispness and in degree of cooking. Martino discovered how to eliminate that. His research revealed that when a batch of cold, wet potatoes are thrown into a vat of melted shortening at 325 degrees, the temperature of the oil falls dramatically, as might be expected, but settles at a different level for each batch before recovering. More important, he learned that no matter how much the temperature fell, the french fried potatoes were always perfectly cooked when the temperature of the oil in the vat recovered by just 3 degrees from whatever the low point was.

Martino's discovery was made to order for automated control. His invention was grandiosely dubbed the "potato computer," but it was nothing more than an electrical sensor that determined when the temperature of the shortening in the fry vat had regained the critical three degrees. Still, it was quickly introduced in all McDonald's stores to automate potato frying by signaling the operator when a batch of fries was perfectly cooked. The potato computer worked so well in eliminating inconsistencies that a modern version is still standard equipment on all McDonald's deep-fry vats, and Martino's principle is used to automate the cooking cycle of other deep fried products, from Filet-O-Fish to Chicken McNuggets.

The detail work McDonald's undertook on french fries was repeated on all other products, and in those areas, too, McDonald's reshaped industry standards. Kroc wasted no time converting his thirty years of experience in the dairy business into operating improvements in his new hamburger chain's milk shake operation. The McDonald brothers had always made milk shakes the way the soda fountains did —hand dipping hard ice milk base into a cup and mixing it with milk and flavoring on a Multimixer. Not only was the method labor intensive, it required large freezers for the ice milk and holding cabinets to store up to eighty milk shakes prepared in advance of peak demand. The milk shake department occupied fully one-fourth of the area of the first McDonald's buildings in California, and Kroc wanted to eliminate that.

Kroc knew that technology was emerging to make milk shakes automatically by machine, using a concentrated liquid milk shake mix. Delivered in large cans that took up much less space than frozen ice milk base, the liquid mix was poured into the machine, which froze it and automatically dispensed it as a soft ice milk base that was ready for mixing in a cup with syrup flavoring. Milk shakes no longer had to be prepared so much in advance of peak periods, which eliminated most of the storage cabinets that the brothers used in San Bernardino. Kroc used the machine in his prototype McDonald's in Des Plaines,

and it vastly changed the size and efficiency of the unit. That innovation—along with the use of a basement for storage—cut the floor
space of his store to just nine hundred square feet, compared with
sixteen hundred square feet in the McDonald's built on the West Coast
under licenses sold by the brothers.

While Kroc was not the first to experiment with the new milk
shake machines, McDonald's became the first major user of the technology. And the introduction of milk shake mix proved to be only one
of many issues on which Kroc used McDonald's purchasing power to
challenge the big dairies. "The dairies were staying with the old-fashioned ways," recalled Kroc, who criticized their managements for rejecting innovation. In Chicago, the dairies were particularly powerful
because they operated almost like a cartel of family companies, setting
prices and margins that were one-third higher than surrounding markets and generally resisting anything that might upset a very comfortable status quo.

But Kroc was determined to use his powerful weapon to force
change. Each McDonald's unit purchased better than fifteen thousand
gallons of shake mix a year—easily five times what previously was
considered a good commercial account. A regular customer of that
size was golden to the capital-intensive dairies whose plants ran most
efficiently meeting large and predictable orders. "Our volumes bog-
gled the dairy guys, and they came into Kroc's office like fish after
bait," Turner observes.

Kroc wanted the dairies to meet his demand for liquid mix, not to
push their preference for sticking with the traditional frozen base. He
demanded more efficient deliveries three days a week, when the dairy-
men insisted on retaining a five-day schedule. He wanted a mix to
make shakes thicker; they wanted to keep their thinner products. When
they gave him delivery of liquid mix in ten-gallon cans that had to be
carried by two crewmen, he wanted five-gallon cans that could be
carried by one. And, most of all, he wanted his volume purchase to
be reflected in the price, when the dairies preferred charging all customers the same high price. Kroc, who had spent a career dealing with
dairies under their rules, was delighted to put the shoe on the other
foot. "Ray got his jollies dealing with the dairy guys," Turner recalls.
"They would come into his office and he'd have a field day. He was
going to change the way they did business. He came at them forty-
seven different ways, and he won on every count."

Indeed, Kroc got everything he wanted, including a price reduction from $1 a gallon to about 72 cents. But a far more important accomplishment was the impact McDonald's had in pioneering a thicker milk shake. The first milk shake mixes were little more than diluted soft-serve ice cream mixes, but McDonald's operations chief Turner and Howard Sorenson of Elgin Dairy, one of the early McDonald's milk suppliers, developed the first mix formula specifically for milk shakes.

They spent as much time on that formula as Karos spent writing potato specifications. Most of it was spent researching the key ingredient—the stabilizer that controls the amount of ice crystals in the mix as it is drawn from the machine. Turner became so preoccupied with "crystallization" that most veteran McDonald's managers treat the term with a reverence competitors find arcane. Yet, McDonald's was introducing a type of milk shake that was foreign to most markets accustomed to thinner, more finely whipped milk shakes. By contrast, McDonald's was marketing a shake that was much thicker and colder because of its higher level of ice crystals and milk solids. Its milk shake was more thirst quenching, and Kroc believed it did not leave the consumer with the lingering aftertaste and bloated feeling associated with conventional shakes. "It wears better," he would say, meaning that the consumer would not still be tasting it three hours after drinking it. But it was the proper crystallization that was the key, and when McDonald's popularized it, the colder, thicker shake soon became the standard for the fast-food industry.

The dairy business also became one of many industries in which McDonald's pioneered modern packaging. Kroc's search for improvements from the dairies ultimately led him to what proved to be the most efficient dairy packaging material—a durable but lightweight plastic bag in a cardboard box. When Kroc first saw experimental plastic bags used to pack liquids in boxes (called bag-in-the-box by the trade), he envisioned a perfect container for McDonald's liquid milk shake mix—lighter, disposable, and more sanitary than reusable cans. Aside from being easier to move than the heavier five-gallon cans that were then standard for commercial shipments, the square bag-in-the-box containers allowed much more compact storage. That appealed to Kroc's innate sense of efficiency. "Most people would look at a delivery of milk cans and see the cans," Turner observes. "Ray would look at it and see all that air in between the cans. It drove him nuts." Bag-in-the-box was first used by Sam Lerner, whose Dairy Fresh dairy in Stoughton, Wisconsin, had never been in the mix business before and thus could use the new technology without having to dispose of an inventory of cans. Partly because of that problem, most dairies supplying McDonald's did not want to convert to the box, and Kroc responded by shifting his business to Dairy Fresh and others that adopted the new package. Eventually, pressure from McDonald's resulted in a massive shift by the dairies from cans and glass containers to the cardboard and plastic ones that are now commonplace.

However, when it came to changing entire industries, McDonald's had its greatest impact through the standards it set and rigidly enforced for its mainline product—the hamburger. Before Turner and Karos devised a formula for hamburger, there was no such thing as a typical hamburger, because standards for hamburger meat did not exist. Indeed, hamburger was the embarrassment of the meat industry, perhaps the last area untouched by the reforms triggered by Upton Sinclair's 1906 exposé *The Jungle*. While the U.S. meat industry had been sanitized and standardized after Sinclair's revelations, hamburger remained largely undefined. The government required merely that ground beef—to be designated *hamburger*—must not have a fat content greater than 30 percent.

Meat plants could drive a herd of cattle through a hole like that, and they did. What exactly hamburger contained was a mystery, but it often included cheaper soy protein additives, a meat extender that absorbed moisture and reduced shrinkage during cooking. It often contained excess blood to cover up high amounts of fat. Nitrates were used to keep the meat pink even after it had begun to turn. And beef parts that had little or no commercial value—such as tripe (stomach) and cheek—were given value by being ground into hamburger meat. "The meat formula was arrived at with a pencil," recalls Jim Williams, president of Golden State Foods Corp., which supplied hamburger to independent drive-ins in California before becoming a major supplier to McDonald's. "You would negotiate a price with the drive-in and then find a way to make it work economically. All-beef hamburger was a myth. There were very few additives that weren't used."

Turner and Karos set the toughest standard for hamburger that the meat industry had ever known, one that still produces some of the leanest hamburger to be found in either the supermarket or the fast-food industry. The U.S. Department of Agriculture still allows hamburger with up to 30 percent fat, but McDonald's standard holds fat content between 17 percent and 22.5 percent. While some hamburger even now contains nonbeef additives, McDonald's prohibition against additives is absolute. And "100 percent beef" was not used by McDonald's to encompass unwanted beef parts. The meat, Turner and Karos decided, was to consist only of 83 percent lean chuck (shoulder) from grass-fed cattle and 17 percent choice plates (lower rib cage) from grain-fed cattle. But merely setting a tough new standard was only half the task, because meat suppliers rarely met specifications on hamburger even when restaurants set them. Cheating was the rule, not the exception.

There was reason for meat suppliers to conclude that they could cheat on McDonald's. Since all meat was fresh and not frozen during the chain's first twelve years, all meat suppliers were local. Before McDonald's began converting to frozen hamburger in 1968, its number of meat suppliers hit a peak of 175. As they multiplied, some suppliers ignored the high-cost standard, hoping that the fragmented meat supply system was too difficult for McDonald's to police. They had not counted on the intensity of McDonald's commitment to its meat standard. Rather than leave the inspection of meat to visual examination—the method the McDonald brothers and most other drive-in operators used—Turner and Karos advised franchisees to have the meat routinely analyzed in labs.

Karos also prepared a fifty-item meat test that allowed operators to determine for themselves whether the meat had any additives. Franchisees were trained to grill sample patties of every meat delivery and to watch for telltale signs of doctored meat that Karos identified. Meat that was gummy or chewy and never turned brown with age was probably bull meat. If the problem was one of a lingering red color, the cause was likely "dynamite" or nitrates. Meat that gave off excessive moisture during cooking usually signaled the presence of toasted soy protein. Meat that bowed on the grill may have been improperly ground. Karos even devised a simple method of analysis that allowed McDonald's operators to perform a quick measurement of the fat content, using a small vial and hydrochloric acid.

McDonald's quickly gained a reputation as a chain that could not easily be fooled on hamburger quality, but not all suppliers picked up on that fast enough. Indeed, a few were caught in the act of cheating by Turner and Karos, who made unannounced visits during the night to meat plants suspected of cheating. When Karos noticed at one Ohio restaurant that the meat patties were giving off a gas during grilling, he immediately suspected a high bacteria count, and a lab analysis confirmed his suspicion. Karos and the store operator paid a 3:00 A.M. visit to the meat plant and discovered that leftover meat that had been picked up that day at the restaurant was being ground back into the meat bound for the store the next day. A new supplier was found within days.

Similarly, on one field service trip, Turner discovered "hamburger patties that were squirting like grapefruits when you bit into them." A lab analysis of the product showed that soy powder and water had been ground into the hamburger meat as a low-cost filler. The meat supplier received an unannounced visit from Turner at his plant early the next day. With the owner nervously eyeing his every move, Turner began looking for the soy in the most obvious places, on the theory that suppliers who are careless enough to cheat on the specifications are careless enough to expose the evidence. When Turner found the cardboard container of soy powder "hidden" under the sink where it was being mixed with water, he glared at the butcher. "You are through," he told him. The same day, Turner put out a memo to all McDonald's field consultants: "In checking meat plants, be especially mindful to look for cardboard containers under sinks with available running water."

McDonald's placed the same type of surveillance on other early suppliers. Not unlike the practices of the meat suppliers, the produce industry tolerated cheating on commercial potato orders, and McDonald's early on caught produce operators rebagging utility potatoes into bags labeled "Idaho No. 1 Russets." In time, the chain's field consultants and franchisees could spot such violations without even opening the potato sack. "If a guy was crooked enough to rebag on you, he never was smart enough to thread the string on the bag through the original holes," Turner says. "Or we would see a new bag tied with old string, and bang, we knew we had them."

During the early years, such "raids" on meat and potato suppliers were common, mainly because McDonald's standards were so uncommon. Most commercial buyers accepted whatever meat plants called hamburger and whatever produce suppliers called baking potatoes, and their lack of supervision encouraged suppliers to take shortcuts. Indeed, McDonald's caught so many violators red-handed simply because suppliers never dreamed any chain would take so seriously its specifications on such commodities as hamburger. "These were old-school guys," Turner says. "Their practice [of cheating] was widely accepted. But if they got caught by us, they were in trouble."

The trouble, of course, was losing the best account they had known. Each McDonald's restaurant ordered eighteen hundred pounds of hamburger meat per week; potato vendors could count on receiving orders for thirty 100-pound bags a week. Such orders were easily five times larger than what previously was considered a large food service account. Joan Kroc recalls that in 1959 when she and her first husband, Rollie Smith, opened a McDonald's in Rapid City, South Dakota, a disbelieving potato supplier by the name of Fred Kypers ignored their order and showed up at the store on the day before opening with one bag of potatoes. When the new McDonald's operators insisted that their thirty-bag order was accurate, Kypers emptied his warehouse of potatoes and delivered them to the basement of the new store. "They're going to rot down there," he told her. They were gone by the end of the week.

That type of volume riveted the attention of meat and potato suppliers, who began taking McDonald's standards almost as seriously as the chain did. As other fast-food chains began adopting them, McDonald's strict standards began rippling through the meat, produce, and dairy industries, changing the balance of power between commercial food suppliers and their food service customers. Before McDonald's established its commanding market presence, food suppliers were large enough to overwhelm their local food service buyers and operate in their own interest, not necessarily in the interest of the restaurants they served. McDonald's changed that with its volume. Just as supermarket chains had amassed buying power on a regional basis, the spread of McDonald's throughout the United States produced the first truly national food purchasing organization that the food service industry had known.

Indeed, it is possible that the most important service Kroc provided for his first franchisees—the one that initially built loyalty between them and McDonald's—was in coordinating the purchases of food and paper supplies and in obtaining discount prices for his volume purchases. Although he was always willing to pay a few cents more for quality, McDonald's founder was able to sell all of his suppliers on the notion that it was in their interest to price their goods to McDonald's not on the basis of the initial volumes but on the basis of the *future* volumes they would get if he succeeded in building the chain of one thousand stores he was talking about building in the late 1950s. And because he planned on giving every bit of the price discount—typically 30 percent on food and 15 percent on paper—to his franchisees as an incentive for signing and staying with him, Kroc was essentially asking his suppliers to join in a partnership with him to help build McDonald's.

Steve Barnes, at the time a salesman for Perlman Paper Company, a distributor of Dixie cups and other paper products used in food service, recalls how compelling Kroc's presentation was. "He was talking in terms of maybe someday having a thousand restaurants, and his reasoning was so very logical that he could do it, assuming he had the backing of people like Lou [Perlman] and other suppliers who would work with him," recalls Barnes, who accompanied his boss, Lou Perlman, on the sales call to Kroc's office in late 1954, several months before Kroc opened his prototype store in Des Plaines. "If he could show to potential licensees that he could buy them products through the McDonald's System at prices they couldn't get on their own, he could have a tremendous advantage in selling franchises. And so, while his first store would use only ten thousand coffee cups a year, he wanted the order priced at two hundred and fifty thousand."

Perlman agreed to those terms, says Barnes, because "Ray sold us on the potential of his becoming one of the biggest restaurant chains. He did the same thing with every guy who supplied him, and that's an insight into this man's ability to convince people that he was going to be a very big user of their products." Barnes was so impressed with Kroc's sales pitch that day that he predicted to his wife that night that "I'm going to work for this man someday." In fact, Barnes became Kroc's first purchasing coordinator in 1961 and ultimately rose to be chairman of McDonald's International. But he was only one of dozens of suppliers amply rewarded by their early faith in Kroc's plan. "Those suppliers who joined him back then and gave him price concessions he needed," Barnes says, "have since become multimillionaires because they believed in this man."

In addition to gaining price concessions, Kroc fostered an intense commitment to McDonald's from its suppliers by the way he selected and treated them. Almost all suppliers chosen by Kroc in the 1950s and 1960s were not in the ranks of the big food processors. Like Perlman Paper, Golden State, and Interstate Foods, they were tiny companies— every bit as entrepreneurial as McDonald's itself. Almost all of them are still McDonald's suppliers today, and solely on the strength of that business they have become giants in the food processing and restaurant supply trades. As Kroc's company grew it soon accounted for the bulk—if not all—of their revenues. They became nearly captive to the system. Their self-image is based more on their association with Mc-Donald's than anything else.

Essentially, Kroc redefined the entire concept of customer-supplier relations in the commercial food processing business. Along the way, his McDonald's created a whole new class of suppliers simply because the more established vendors refused to accept his concepts, whereas some aggressive upstart companies did. Indeed, after a few years, McDonald's displayed an unusually strong preference for smaller suppliers and began restricting supply arrangements with the giant food processors such as Kraft, Heinz, and Swift. In part, Turner says, that was because the brand name suppliers were more interested in tapping the larger retail market than in serving commercial and institutional accounts.

Satisfying both markets required contradictory mind-sets. The big processors were confident of their ability to create consumer demand for their packaged retail products through superior marketing. As a result, they were not accustomed to giving any one institutional food service account the type of personalized service McDonald's demanded. "Smaller companies that specialized in institutional selling have always done a better job for us than the big retail-oriented organizations," Turner observes. "To companies with a retail orientation, the institutional market is a tag-along business that gets secondary attention. That's why we ended up with our own suppliers doing their own thing."

McDonald's also encouraged closeness with vendors by giving them enormous incentives to upgrade their operations. It did so by demonstrating early on that it could be just as loyal to suppliers that met its standards as it was tough on those that did not. "Other chains would walk away from you for a half a cent," says Kenneth Smargon, son of the founder of Interstate Foods, the shortening supplier. "Mc-Donald's was more concerned with getting quality. They didn't chisel on price and were always concerned with suppliers making a fair profit. A lot of people look on a supplier as someone to walk on. But McDonald's always treated me with respect even when they became much bigger and didn't have to. That's the big difference, because if McDonald's said 'Jump,' an awful lot of people would be asking 'How far?' " Thus, even when Interstate began supplying competing fast-food chains, says Smargon, it gave McDonald's "a little bit more special care."

McDonald's loyalty was particularly surprising to commodity food suppliers accustomed to winning and losing accounts solely on price. Jim Williams, of Golden State Foods, remembers that when he was selling hamburger to other restaurants in the mid-1950s, the name of the game was being there first with the lowest price. "Everyone was beating the poor meat man over the head for a penny a pound, and we were in and out of the drive-ins every week," Williams says. "Deals and kickbacks were a way of life. How long you let a guy stretch out his payments was more the determining factor of whether you got the business than the quality of the product you were selling. Kroc brought a supplier loyalty that the restaurant business had never seen. If you adhered to McDonald's specifications, and were basically competitive on price, you could depend on their order."

Kroc's approach to suppliers was totally pragmatic. He and his operations staff were doing too many other things to waste time looking for bargains on supplies from week to week. "We were too damned busy to do that kind of stuff," Kroc said. "I told our first suppliers that someday they were going to have a helluva lot of business from us that no one would be able to take away. 'There's just one thing you have to do,' I told them, 'and that is, don't resort to any trickery. Don't think you can get by with certain things just because I'm putting my faith in you, because if I ever catch you in a lie, I'll throw you out.' "

Golden State's Williams believes that Kroc's loyalty to suppliers saved McDonald's precious time during the critical development period when dozens of fledgling competitors were trying to make a go of it in the fast-food business. "It allowed McDonald's to spend the majority of its time on operations," Williams says, "while a lot of other food retailers were spending ninety percent of their time on the supply side of the business and not taking care of the operations end."

Because it relied on a relatively few loyal suppliers who understood its system and depended on it for their growth, McDonald's could devote more of its resources to developing specifications for products that met its unique needs. That was considered absolutely essential, since Kroc and his operations managers believed that their restaurant was so unusual that existing products sold to traditional food service outlets were not geared to meeting McDonald's needs. They refused to shop for food service products that were already on the shelf. Everything was developed either from scratch or by greatly modifying existing products, and a key element in that process was McDonald's partnership with its suppliers.

Nowhere was McDonald's insistence on customizing its supplies more evident than in Jim Schindler's design of the chain's equipment and buildings. It did not take Kroc long to realize that the building and everything in it could not be based on standard food service items. From an operations standpoint, McDonald's was introducing not a new restaurant but a food-manufacturing system. Because its food volumes were as much as five times greater than those of typical restaurants and because it was relying so heavily on automated procedures that were tailored for unskilled labor, each McDonald's was a small factory. Everything about the building and equipment had to be designed for a new standard of speed, simplicity, and durability.

The McDonald brothers, of course, had started out with the same premise, but Kroc learned even in his first unit that what worked in San Bernardino was not good enough for national use. The buckling counters at Kroc's unit in Des Plaines are a case in point. When Schindler replaced the sheet metal counters with prefabricated structural steel members that were twenty times as thick, he doubled the cost of the counters to $500, but he set a pattern that McDonald's would follow in all building and equipment design. Schindler's rule: it was always better to pay more to get customization and quality than to buy the lowest priced items in stock. "To me, quality is like buying oats in the marketplace," he said. "You can always get them a lot cheaper if you run them through the horse first."

Schindler redesigned virtually every aspect of the red-and-white building McDonald's had inherited from the brothers. The changes were not cosmetic. In fact, they did not greatly change the look of the building. Rather, they ensured that a structure that worked well on opening day would not deteriorate rapidly with the heavy use McDonald's intended to give it. Few things tarnished a fast-food chain's image more than buildings that started falling apart soon after they were built. Though he could do little to remove the circus atmosphere of the original red-and-white tile unit, Schindler converted it into the most functional and durable structure the drive-in business had ever known.

Schindler insisted that specifications on all construction materials be vastly upgraded. Problems in existing units—from water leaks to sewer drainage—were corrected with continual refinements in design. Standard fixtures were redesigned to be more functional. Cabinets, for example, were raised from the floor and attached to walls to allow for easy cleaning. Even the arches were rebuilt to withstand high winds and to create the illusion that the building was suspended from the arches. Heavy structural steel replaced sheet metal to produce a more evenly curved arch, and exterior neon lighting gave way to modern fluorescent lamps placed inside the arch. After the improvements, the red-and-white McDonald's were so solidly built that Schindler would later boast that they withstood hurricanes, tornadoes, floods, and—at least in one case—a blast from four sticks of dynamite. The city of Cleveland saw the buildings' potential for protection against a bigger blast: it designated McDonald's drive-ins as official bomb shelters.

Yet, Schindler's greatest contribution was designing the first equipment package tailored for the fast-food industry. He concluded that standard cooking gear was next to useless because McDonald's was setting new records on the amount of food that could be produced in a cramped hamburger stand. "We couldn't buy standard cooking equipment because it never gave us the capacity we needed and still fit into the space we had," he explained.

In many cases, those requirements involved completely redesigning standard items. Soft drink dispensers had to be redesigned to draw 250 gallons a day—easily five times the capacity required at most restaurants—which meant vastly increasing the cooling and water handling capabilities of conventional dispensers. Heavy backsplashes were put on grills to keep crewmen from poking holes through them with spatulas, rarely a problem in a restaurant that did not cook twenty-four hamburgers every four minutes. The typical placement of grease traps in front of gas grills also created no problem in a conventional restaurant setting, but at the high-volume McDonald's, the traps soon clogged with onions and grease, and their proximity to the flame touched off dozens of fires. Schindler enlarged the traps and put them on either side of the grill, away from the flame. His changes increased the cost of the early grills from $350 to $800, but they produced the custom-made grill McDonald's needed. "I got 'fired' more often than most people around here," said Schindler, "because I was always adding to the cost of the building and equipment."

But the heating, ventilating, and air-conditioning equipment presented Schindler with his most complex design challenge: developing a compact commercial air-conditioner that could handle industrial-sized loads. McDonald's crammed such enormous food production capability into the nine hundred square feet of space in the original store that the air in the building had to be replaced every three minutes to exhaust the cooking gases. The only air-conditioning units then on the market capable of doing that were industrial units, and even if they were not prohibitively expensive, they still would have consumed half the storage space in the McDonald's basement.

Before Schindler solved the problem, early McDonald's licensees were forced to operate their stores nearly in a vacuum. Air rushed through service windows so fast that it made a popping sound. During peak demand, crew people were virtually held captive inside the store, because the negative pressure in the building made it all but impossible for anyone to open the door. Schindler worked with Mammoth Furnace Company to help design the first commercial rooftop heating and air-conditioning equipment capable of handling small industrial loads but with two-thirds of the space and expense involved with standard commercial units. Now, similar units are used in a wide variety of stores, small office buildings, and apartment units. Schindler would later observe that McDonald's "planted the seed for the development of a rooftop air-conditioning industry in the United States."

In some cases, Schindler had to design new equipment from scratch because he could not satisfy McDonald's needs even with major modifications of existing products. Thus when McDonald's decided in the mid-1960s to free up grill space by toasting the buns off the grill, Schindler's engineering team had to invent a new type of commercial toaster. The conveyor toasters that were then standard in high-volume restaurants produced a continuous stream of toasted buns, but they could not meet McDonald's requirement of toasting twenty-four crowns and heels at one time. McDonald's developed a toaster—similar to an oversized waffle iron—that could equal the volume of the largest conveyor toasters and yet fit into McDonald's batch-cooking process.

Even minor functions did not escape the attention of McDonald's equipment designers. For example, when operators complained that employee productivity in their french fry departments was suffering because the metal tongs used to fill the fry bags were awkward to handle, Lou Martino assigned one of his lab engineers, Ralph Weimer, to solve the problem. Weimer created a simple but ingenious device— a V-shaped aluminum scoop with a funnel at the end—that filled a bag of fries in one easy motion and even aligned all the fries neatly in the same vertical direction in the bag. Now, twenty-five years after its invention, Weimer's french fry scoop is still used in all 14,000 McDonald's around the world.

Indeed, the device is the most ubiquitous tool in the fast-food industry. That's because it is manufactured by Prince Castle, Kroc's old

Multimixer company, which supplies it to countless other fast-food units outside the McDonald's System. Prince Castle wound up manufacturing dozens of kitchen tools produced by McDonald's designers, including Martino's cooking computer, Schindler's toaster, and Weimer's scoop. Curiously, Kroc missed out on that particular bonanza, because he sold Prince Castle to eight McDonald's corporate managers in 1963 for only $150,000. Just three years later, the managers sold it for $900,000 to Martin-Brower, McDonald's paper goods supplier, to comply with a New York Stock Exchange ruling that the inside ownership of Prince Castle involved a conflict of interest.

Yet, the company still manufactures the equipment created by the McDonald's design team, and because it sells versions of those products to other fast-food chains, it has become a conduit for transmitting McDonald's technology throughout the food service trade. Indeed, that became a sore point with Turner, one of the eight McDonald's managers who owned Prince Castle. While on the board of that company, Turner argued that proprietary items of McDonald's should not be sold to its competitors, but he did not always win the point. Admits Turner: "We let some of our equipment expertise get away from us."

Now, however, McDonald's is more careful to protect the cooking appliances designed by its equipment engineers, who develop increasingly more specialized and sophisticated gear. For example, all new restaurants now receive the newly developed "clamshell" grill that cooks hamburgers in half the time by grilling both sides simultaneously. What started out with Schindler repairing the countertops of the first McDonald's in Kroc's Des Plaines unit grew into a construction and equipment engineering staff not unlike one that might be found in a medium-sized manufacturing company. McDonald's now employs more than 530 engineers around the world, and they owe their jobs to Schindler's insistence that McDonald's equipment and building design be an internal function.

Yet, no matter how much time McDonald's spent upgrading its supplies and automating its equipment and building, Kroc and Turner realized that such efforts were for naught if the company failed to give the same detailed attention to the way franchisees ran the restaurants. That was where Kroc's unyielding commitment to uniformity was most visible, and more than anything else, the rules that McDonald's enforced in the operation of its restaurants resulted in a consistency of service that no franchised system had ever before attained.

The first operating procedures were handed down from the Mc-

Donald brothers, but McDonald's youthful operations specialists led by Turner quickly began expanding on the fifteen dos and don'ts given to them by the brothers. Turner and Karos were so compulsive about documenting the discoveries and changes they made in operations that in a relatively short period there were few aspects of operating a McDonald's drive-in that were not contained in manuals that were easily the most voluminous in the fast-food industry. By spelling out its operations procedures so carefully, McDonald's signaled to its franchisees how serious it was about their meeting its standards. It was a signal many other early fast-food franchisers were not sending.

Within months of joining McDonald's, Turner had drafted a 15-page mimeographed manual, followed quickly by a 38-page effort. But after a year of daily consultations with operators, Turner in 1958 produced a 75-page operations manual, printed and bound. Other manuals would follow (Karos turned out a 200-page work in 1961; and the current operations manual is a four-pound, 750-page affair), but it was Turner's third volume that set McDonald's on its course of documenting in detail all the knowledge it was gaining from the collective operating experience of its franchisees. While other chains virtually ignored franchisees once their stores were opened, McDonald's studied everything they did, trying to learn what worked and what did not.

Turner essentially tried to convert running a restaurant from an art to a management science. His third manual contained fully ten pages of sample forms that operators could use to track inventory, prepare cash reports and other financial operating statements, compose work schedules, and make sales projections. Soon, McDonald's was flooding franchisees with forms requiring them to dissect their business into its financial components. In addition to calculating their profits, licensees were asked to determine what percentages of their sales were going to labor, to various food items, and to nonfood supplies and certain other operating expenses. Such figures were compiled for the entire system so that individual franchisees could compare their cost percentages against the average. Using Turner's system, operators could quickly break down their sales of such key items as hamburgers, shakes, and fries to determine the amount of food and nonfood supplies they should have consumed. It was an invaluable tool for detecting pilferage, quality control problems, and errors in yields.

But most of the manual was aimed at defining the operating techniques that Turner believed held the secrets of high volume. He made it clear that there was a right way and a wrong way to run a McDonald's and that McDonald's would view disdainfully licensees who did not adhere to the chain's standards. Indeed, that view was communicated in a rather presumptuous opening sentence. It read: "Herein outlined is *the* successful method." Turner also revealed his personal commitment to details. "High-volume McDonald's will always have an old mother hen cluck-clucking around from one corner to another, never being satisfied," he wrote. "YOU MUST BE A PERFECTIONIST! There are hundreds and hundreds of details to be watched. There isn't any compromising. Either, (A) the details are watched and your volume grows, or (B) you are not particular, not fussy, and do not have a pride or liking for the business, in which case you will be an also-ran. If you fall into the 'B' category, this is not the business for you!"

Turner applied that philosophy to the manual itself: it was crammed with minutiae. It told operators exactly how to draw milk shakes, grill hamburgers, and fry potatoes. It specified precise cooking times for all products and temperature settings for all equipment. It fixed standard portions on every food item, down to the quarter ounce of onions placed on each hamburger patty and the thirty-two slices per pound of cheese. It specified that french fries be cut at nine-thirty-seconds of an inch thick. And it defined quality controls that were unique to food service, including the disposal of meat and potato products that were held more than ten minutes in a serving bin.

The manual also defined those specialized production techniques that made the operation of McDonald's like an assembly line. It described the flow of production and provided a specialized job description—and detailed operating methods—for two shift managers and for each of the production "stations" occupied by the nine-man crew: three window men taking orders, a grill man, a milk shake man, a french fry man, two bun wrapping men, and a cleanup man. Grill men, for example, were instructed to put hamburgers down on the grill moving from left to right, creating six rows of six patties each. And because the first two rows were farthest from the heating element, they were instructed (and still are) to flip the third row first, then the fourth, fifth, and sixth before flipping the first two.

Indeed, the manual was at times too detailed. It specified prices for all products, a violation of current restraint of trade rules, and its all-male job titles were intentionally discriminatory. Though not spelled out in the manual, an unwritten rule during McDonald's first decade prohibited the hiring of women in the restaurants. It was rationalized on the grounds that many tasks—such as carrying hundred-pound sacks of potatoes up from the basement—were too strenuous for women. But that was a thinly veiled disguise for the real reason: Like the carhops in conventional drive-ins, female crews, Kroc feared, would attract too many teenage males who would convert McDonald's into another high school hangout. That ran directly counter to Kroc's plan of establishing McDonald's as the first family-oriented drive-in, and thus the unwritten rule against women was as sacred as the written (and still enforced) prohibitions against jukeboxes, cigarette machines, and public telephones. "I had made up my mind," Kroc once told a reporter, "that all hamburger joints had jukeboxes, telephones, and cigarette machines, and that your wife and my wife wouldn't go to a place with leather-jacketed guys and smoke-filled rooms."

Preserving the "antijoint" restrictions was one of Kroc's highest priorities. During its first few years, when McDonald's had difficulty generating cash to meet payrolls, Kroc resisted the temptation of obtaining easy income from vending machines. It is likely, too, that he objected to the vending industry's reputed connection with organized crime. Kroc recalled how he told one vending machine salesman of his policy against jukeboxes and cigarette machines, and the salesman replied, "That's your decision, but I wouldn't change my mind if I were you." Kroc caught the underlying message: "He meant that if I changed my mind and went to a competitor for a better price, I wouldn't be around anymore."

Yet, the characteristic that was possibly most responsible for creating the family image Kroc was looking for was the cleanliness that McDonald's built into its operating system. Most independent drive-in operators gave cleaning standards short shrift, but nothing in Turner's 1958 manual comes across so clearly as the stringency of the requirements on cleanliness. Half of it was devoted to describing recommended procedures on cleaning. Even competitors concede that McDonald's uncommon dedication to running a clean restaurant set a standard in the industry that others aimed for but seldom hit. Says Jim Collins of Collins Foods: "McDonald's is still the cleanest operation in the business."

Turner's manual specified that *every day* the windows had to be cleaned, the lot hosed down, and the garbage and waste cans scrubbed. Every other day, all stainless steel in the store, including such typically ignored areas as exhaust stacks, had to be polished. Every week, the ceiling of the store had to be washed. Mopping floors and wiping counters became nearly a continuous process, and the cleaning cloth became an essential tool for every crew member. "If you've got time to lean, you've got time to clean" was perhaps the first Krocism that infiltrated the entire system and shaped its operations philosophy.

It was clearly Ray Kroc who gave McDonald's its passion for cleanliness. Personally fastidious, Kroc set the priority on cleanliness by the way he operated his own restaurant in Des Plaines. He worked on weekends as the store's cleanup man—hosing down the lot, cleaning the trash cans, and scraping gum off the green concrete in front of the store with a putty knife. It made an indelible impression on both Turner and Karos, and what impressed them most was Kroc's insistence on cleaning areas no one else thought about. "I saw Ray spend one Saturday morning with a toothbrush cleaning out the holes in the mop wringer," Turner recalls. "No one else really paid any attention to the damned mop ringer, because everyone knew it was *just* a mop bucket. But Kroc saw all the crud building up in the holes, and he wanted to clean them so the wringer would work better." Karos adds: "Ray practiced what he preached in his own store, and that's how he instilled in Fred and me the meaning of QSC."

At times, Kroc's desire for cleanliness even colored his judgment on hamburgers. At a staff Christmas party in 1958, Dolores Conley, the wife of licensing vice president Don Conley, pleaded with Kroc to eliminate pickles on all hamburgers unless otherwise requested by the customer. "A lot of people don't like pickles," she told Kroc, "because you step on them all over the parking lot." That hit Kroc's hot button. He had picked up his share of pickles at his Des Plaines store. Thus, on the following Monday, Kroc ordered Turner to send another of his ubiquitous memos to all operators, this one on the subject of pickles. "After experimentation and considerable thought and conversation with operators," the memo read, "it has been deemed advisable to eliminate the pickle from the McDonald's hamburger." Only six months later did Kroc realize that was an overreaction. The pickle was reinstated on all McDonald's hamburgers and has remained a standard feature since.

Even when he no longer worked at Des Plaines, Kroc was a self-appointed cleanup man for McDonald's. On his frequent visits to restaurants, Kroc commonly picked up wastepaper on the lot before going inside to see the franchisee. "It was sometimes embarrassing to visit a store and see Ray get out of the car and start picking up the guy's lot," Don Conley observes. "But it demonstrated to the operators that if cleaning the store wasn't beneath the boss, it shouldn't be beneath anyone else."

A dirty restaurant never failed to send Kroc into orbit, but his fiery temper became a remarkably effective tool. "When Ray read out an operator with a dirty store, you could hear him six blocks away," Karos says. " 'You're in the wrong business, and you ought to sell out,' he would tell them. After he got through reaming a guy out, he would talk to him like a son, and tell him he knew he could do better. He always had the capacity to see that a guy could turn it around. He was very compassionate."

But Kroc showed little compassion for those who threatened the system by repeatedly violating procedures that Turner and Karos developed. As a result, McDonald's was as intense about enforcing its operating standards as it was about developing them. Kroc was convinced that the honor system was not appropriate for the McDonald's System. Indeed, his electronic epistles to the McDonald brothers in the late 1950s make it clear that Kroc had a fundamental distrust of franchisees left to their own devices. His taped messages to the brothers leave no doubt that from the beginning Kroc realized that a national food service chain had to require operator conformity to a very strict set of standards. "We have found out as you have that we cannot trust some people who are nonconformists," Kroc told the brothers in March 1958. "We will make conformists out of them in a hurry. Even personal friends who we know have the best of intentions may not conform. They have a difference of opinion as to various processing and certain qualities of product. So, from the standpoint of growth on the firmest kind of foundation, the only way that we can positively know that these units are doing what they are supposed to do . . . is to make it so that they can have no alternative whatsoever. You can't give them an inch. The organization cannot trust the individual; the individual must trust the organization [or] he shouldn't go into this kind of business."

With that conviction, Kroc introduced a level of supervision that was unknown in the fast-food industry. It started in January 1957 with the hiring of Turner, who was instructed simply to "visit the stores." Given his intensity, Turner converted that into his personal mission. After just two months on the job, he drafted a seven-page, single-spaced "field service report" form to use in evaluating a franchisee's performance on his restaurant visits. It reported on the cleanliness of the building, the quality of its food, the times and temperatures followed in cooking, and the time it took to serve customers.

Turner's first store evaluation was of a McDonald's in the Champaign-Urbana area in downstate Illinois, and it was easily the most thorough report ever made on the performance of a single drive-in. There was only one problem: Kroc could not bring himself to read it. "He turned the pages, but that was just for my benefit," Turner recalls. "I could see he wasn't reading it. Ray just wouldn't read a long report. I swear, he never read our annual report."

On the next report, Turner solved the problem by summarizing the entire report in grades (A, B, C, D, or F), which were written in the upper right corner and covered four subjects, the top one for service, the next for quality, a third for cleanliness, and finally a grade for overall performance. Soon, subject categories were abbreviated to SQC, but two years later Kroc asked Turner to put quality first in the grading system, and QSC—the universal symbol of performance in the fast-food trade—was born. In the mid-1960s, Kroc tagged on a "V" for value, but for antitrust reasons operators have never been given a formal grade on that, because as independent businessmen they are free to price their products as they choose. Still, the initial rating system has remained intact for three decades, and store grades still constitute the bottom line of McDonald's annual operator review.

By the late 1950s, as Karos and others joined Turner's staff, the job of visiting and evaluating restaurants was made a full-time position: field consultant. Initially, the field consultant was not primarily an inspector of system quality but a consultant to operators—helping to train personnel, open new stores, line up local suppliers, improve operations, and even develop local marketing programs. But as other McDonald's departments began providing such specialized assistance, the field consultant became a specialist in inspecting stores to determine their level of compliance with operating standards. By the mid-1960s, the grades Turner developed were being used to appraise whether operators should be granted licenses for additional stores. The field consultant's report suddenly had real teeth to it, and experience in the position of field consultant became a prerequisite for advancement through McDonald's line management.

Today, McDonald's employs more than 330 field service consultants, each of whom does nothing but visit and evaluate some twenty-one restaurants several times a year. On each visit, they and the store managers complete pages of reports that focus on QSC&V, sales, and profits. In 1992 alone, McDonald's spent more than $27 million on its field service operation. More than any other factor, the store grades determine the company's judgment on a licensee's "expandability," and now a B grade on existing stores is considered necessary for a licensee to get additional stores.

No other aspect of McDonald's has been more extensively duplicated than its field service operation. But, while they copied the chain's field service methods, many competitors—by their own admission—did not demonstrate the same zeal in enforcing their standards. That zeal was evident in the 1950s in the way Turner and Karos, then in their mid-twenties, related to McDonald's first crop of operators, most of whom were twenty years their senior. Turner recalls how in the first couple of years on the job he invariably was asked the same two questions upon meeting a new franchisee on a visit to his store: "How old are you?" and "How long have you been with McDonald's?" He even started wearing a hat because he thought it made him appear older. Yet, Turner quickly overcame the age issue by convincing franchisees just how seriously he took his job. "I was not undiplomatic, but I was serious as hell," Turner recalls. "And because I knew what I was doing—and was putting in the hours—I gained the respect of operators."

Turner's command of the details of a completely different food service operation allowed him to fend off challenges by many early franchisees, who could not match his expertise. He stood his ground even when the battle involved operators who were Kroc's friends from Rolling Green. "I had some classic debates with those guys," he remembers. "They had a better way of doing things, and they were going to convince me that the entire system should do it their way."

Turner recalls how he had a running feud with Tony Weissmuller, a Rolling Green alumnus with a McDonald's unit in Aurora, Illinois, over how to handle french fries to reduce breakage. To support his method, Turner cited results of tests he had performed with other operators, but Weismuller would not change. Others might have found the matter laughable, but, Turner says, "it became my cause. I spent hours arguing with him, sometimes until midnight." Yet, such encounters clearly left an impression on other operators about the commitment that Turner, Karos, and other operations managers had about enforcing standards. It apparently left a positive impression on Weissmuller, too. He offered Turner one-quarter of his new Ann Arbor franchise if he would manage it, one of dozens of job offers Turner received from franchisees. "If I didn't get a job offer a month from the operators, I used to feel I wasn't doing my job," Turner says.

Turner, of course, could not have enforced the standards as aggressively as he did without the continuous backing of Kroc. The founder's support may have been even more critical for Karos, whose style had some of the flamboyance that Kroc himself displayed. Karos even initiated a practice of taking photographs of extremely dirty units to document the franchisee's transgressions. (The practice is still followed in McDonald's.) Occasionally, Karos's penchant for dramatization drew some furious responses from franchisees. When he noticed McDonald's litter strewn about the yards in the neighborhood of a store in New Jersey, it was obvious that the operator had ignored the system's requirement for policing the area within a two-block radius of the store. Karos picked up all the litter he could carry, marched into the franchisee's office, and dumped the trash onto his desk. "How can you let this stuff go on your neighbor's lawn?" he screamed. Only years later did Turner tell Karos how close he had come to a pounding at the hands of the franchisee, a six-foot-four-inch, 250-pound ex–football player. "He was ready to stomp on you," Turner confided.

Despite such clashes, the bulk of the work of the first field service consultants involved instructing franchisees on the fine points of the operating system. By 1957, McDonald's was making rudimentary training films, the first of which was photographed by licensing chief Conley and featured Turner as the "actor" demonstrating the hamburger system. Homemade training films soon were replaced with professional ones, and by 1961 McDonald's was ready to launch a training program that would capture the imagination of the fast-food industry and the public as well—the formation of Hamburger University.

Previously, McDonald's had been attempting to instruct licensees solely through in-store training. "We had to have a classroom atmosphere to teach some of these guys the operating philosophy and the theory of the McDonald's operation," Karos says. "You couldn't do that in the field."

No other chain had even thought of opening a full-time training center. Yet, to Turner and Karos, it was the obvious missing element that would round out McDonald's commitment to uniform operations. Obvious or not, it was not universally supported within McDonald's. Sonneborn was opposed to spending the $25,000 that was budgeted (and the $100,000 that was actually spent) to build a training center in the basement of a McDonald's restaurant. The basement would contain a classroom—complete with equipment models—where a full-time instructional program on the McDonald's System would be offered. Despite Sonneborn's opposition, Kroc supported the plan, and in February 1961, McDonald's matriculated the first fifteen-man class at Hamburger University at a new store in Elk Grove Village, a suburb northwest of Chicago. Karos served as the school's first dean.

Hamburger U. gave McDonald's more than a leg up on competitors in training. From the day he opened his own store in Des Plaines, Kroc had been eager to add a touch of class to the negative image generated by a hamburger that sold for 15 cents. By 1961, there was still an overwhelming public perception that nothing priced so cheaply— least of all anything as pedestrian as a hamburger—could have quality. Nothing so frustrated Kroc as the low-quality image that was associated with the 15-cent price. In 1962 he ordered the price removed from the McDonald's sign, and when Dick McDonald sent Kroc an illustration of the McDonald family crest, Kroc had it added to the sign as a symbol of quality, replacing Speedee, the boyish chef character that the McDonald brothers had developed to designate the Speedee Service System. When others insisted that the crest was gaudy, the search was on for a more stylish corporate symbol. Turner fiddled with a new logo, based on the V in the Cadillac insignia, and Schindler used that to sketch a logo that pictured the slanted roof line of the store piercing a line drawing of the golden arches in the form of an M. (In 1968, the roof line image was dropped and the McDonald's name was added to derive the current logo.)

But in the early years, nothing better promoted a McDonald's quality image than the media coverage generated by Hamburger University, complete with photos of licensees in white uniforms marching to class. The press, of course, might easily have made Hamburger U. appear a publicity stunt, too hokey to be serious. Al Golin, the public relations consultant Kroc hired in 1957 to help him publicize McDonald's, recalls how *Life* magazine sent reporter Nancy Fraser and a photographer to the Elk Grove Village store to prepare one of *Life's* celebrated photo stories on Hamburger U. The piece gave McDonald's instant prestige that no other fast-food chain had. Newspapers around the country followed *Life's* story with their own articles on the school, and a *CBS Evening News* feature on the training center gave McDonald's its first network television coverage. But after the *Life* article appeared, Fraser admitted to Golin that *Life's* original intention was to write a tongue in cheek satire of a company that was taking the plebian hamburger a bit too seriously. But after observing the instruction at Elk Grove Village for a week, Fraser changed her slant. "I realized how dedicated you all are to Hamburger University," she told Golin. "It didn't deserve to be put down."

Hamburger University was not puffery. While some snickered about its Degree of Hamburgerology, McDonald's was serious about it. Karos developed a detailed, two-week curriculum for the first class. In the basement classroom of the Elk Grove Village store, Karos instructed operators on such fine points as the type of potatoes McDonald's required and the formula it used for hamburger meat. He also used cutaways of all McDonald's equipment to demonstrate to operator trainees how each machine was constructed and how it operated. The school even had a Hollymatic patty manufacturing machine to show trainees how the company's hamburgers were made by suppliers.

Competitors soon realized the benefit of classroom instruction, too. Now all major fast-food chains have training schools. Yet, none has come close to matching the resources McDonald's continues to devote to formal instruction.

In 1968, McDonald's opened a $500,000 Hamburger University with two large classrooms, both equipped with state of the art audio-visual equipment. But in 1983, McDonald's moved Hamburger University to a $40 million facility that rivals the training centers of the nation's airlines. With seven separate auditorium classrooms, each capable of seating from 60 to 300 students, the new Hamburger University has an overall capacity for 750 people. Each classroom contains computer equipment for automated recording and scoring of exam answers, and each is also equipped with translation booths that allow foreign operators to attend the same courses as their American counterparts. The school's equipment labs contain functioning grills, fryers, shake machines, and all other types of cooking and refrigeration equipment. And its thirty member faculty consists of specialists who teach the Advanced Operations Course, which includes team-building and interpersonal and management skills. Furthermore, the school is the only one in the fast-food industry that offers thirty-six hours worth of courses that are university accredited by the American Council of Education. The university even includes a 227-room lodge where students live during training.

Given its commitment to uniform standards, the McDonald's System hardly seems to provide room for individual initiative. In fact, one of the least understood characteristics of the system is that its fascination with uniformity exists side by side with its lesser known—but equally strong—respect for the creativity and judgment of its franchi-

sees. "True, we have procedures that do not allow for a lot of tolerance," Turner concedes. "But anyone who concludes that we march
around regimenting operators and managers in fourteen thousand restaurants contributes to the most superficial notion of McDonald's. Anyone who meets our operators knows there is no way those guys could
be regimented."

The real secret to McDonald's successful operating system is not
found in its regimen but in the way it enforces uniform procedures
without stifling the entrepreneurship of franchisees. As such, McDonald's is something of an American response to Japan's management by
consensus. Without the freedom of franchisees and suppliers to exercise their entrepreneurial instincts, to test their own ideas on new
products and procedures, and even to challenge the corporation head-
on, McDonald's might still have attained its celebrated uniformity, but
at a terrible price. It would lose the grass-roots creativity that diverse
franchisees and suppliers provide. It would, in short, lose touch with
the marketplace.

Turner realizes that perhaps more than anyone else in McDonald's, and thus the father of the operations system is the first to concede that his offspring had a serious limitation. The rules could
provide only a framework, and that alone could not unleash the real
potential of any franchising system—the human ingenuity of hundreds
of independent businessmen. In essence, the secret to McDonald's
success was that its nearly fanatical operations specialists, led by Kroc
himself, recognized that the chain's operating system—easily the strongest in the fast-food business—was not enough.

It was his five-spindle Multimixer that led Ray Kroc to McDonald's in 1954. Before that, Kroc demonstrates the device at his booth at the National Restaurant Show (1). He sold ten Multimixers to Dick and Mac McDonald for use in their novel fast-food drive-in, including the one shown above inside the brothers' San Bernardino restaurant (2).

The first McDonald's was an octagonal structure built by the McDonald brothers in 1940 and shown here (3) in 1949, one year after the brothers converted the unit from a conventional carhop drive-in to the world's first self-serve, fast-food restaurant. The operational genius of the duo was Mac McDonald (4); his younger brother Dick specialized in marketing. Dick (right) and Mac (center) discuss a new neon sign for their drive-in with an executive with Southern California Edison (5).

4

The key to the early McDonald's operation was the all-male crew, each man trained to perform one task. Here, the crew of Art Bender (center, seated), the first counterman of the McDonald brothers and first franchisee signed by Ray Kroc, is shown in front of Ray Kroc's Des Plaines Restaurant (6).

The McDonald's building has undergone dramatic change since Kroc opened his first unit in Des Plaines, Illinois, in 1955, now preserved as a museum (7). More than one thousand buildings of the original Golden Arches design were built in the 1960s (8), but beginning in 1968, McDonald's revamped all of its outlets, and the Golden Arches unit gave way to a mansard-roofed building that accommodated the chain's first indoor seating (9). Today's McDonald's exhibit a more individual design, such as this ultramodern restaurant opened in New Orleans in 1983 (10).

11

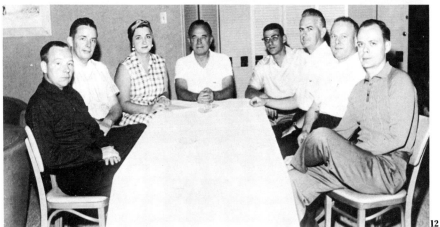

12

From his modest 1950s office in Chicago's Loop (11), Ray Kroc assembled the fast-food industry's first complete management team, shown here in an informal group meeting (12). Left to right, they are company attorney Tom Casey, accountant Dick Boylan, corporate secretary June Martino, Ray Kroc, real estate and financing specialist Harry Sonneborn, licensing director and pilot Don Conley, construction and equipment expert Jim Schindler, and operations chief Fred Turner.

Kroc's first three hires proved to be his key partners in building McDonald's foundation. Secretary June Martino is shown inside her McDonald's store in suburban Chicago (13); operations expert Fred Turner was one of the first grill men at Kroc's store in Des Plaines (14); and Harry Sonneborn developed the financial strategy that made him president of the chain and put McDonald's on the New York Stock Exchange in 1966. On the day McDonald's went on the big board, Sonneborn (left) sampled the company's product with NYSE President G. Keith Funston (right) (15).

To promote his chain, Kroc (16) relied on the press-agentry methods of publicists Al Golin (left) and Max Cooper (right), shown here celebrating McDonald's 15th Anniversary in 1970 with President Fred Turner and Chairman Ray Kroc.

17

18

19

20

More than any other fast-food chain, McDonald's relies on its franchisees for marketing innovations. Herb Peterson (17), a franchisee in Santa Barbara, developed the Egg McMuffin; Lou Groen (18) discovered the Filet-O-Fish sandwich to boost the flagging sales of his Cincinnati franchise; and Pittsburgh franchisee Jim Delligatti (19) invented McDonald's most recognized product, the Big Mac.

But the chain's most legendary franchisees were John Gibson (left) and Oscar Goldstein (second from right), who are shown with McDonald's executives at the opening of one of their restaurants in Washington, D.C. Gibson and Goldstein created Ronald McDonald to cultivate the children's market, and that, along with their operational excellence, allowed them to build a forty-three-restaurant franchise (20).

21

22

From the beginning, McDonald's executives took to the air to expand the chain from town to town. The first corporate plane was a Cessna 195, owned and piloted by Don Conley, the chain's licensing director. Shown with the plane are Dick (left) and Mac (right) McDonald, along with Dolores Conley, Don's wife (21). By the early 1970s, McDonald's had advanced to a Gulfstream II jet, which Herb Lotman (left) and Lynal Root (right) used extensively in 1973 to run a custom slaughtering operation that kept McDonald's supplied with hamburger in a beef shortage (22).

Chapter 7
MAKING MONEY

By 1957, Ray Kroc had assembled all the elements he needed to make McDonald's a winner. His franchising plan gave entrepreneurs an opportunity to get a business of their own without having to pay excessive franchising charges or to make unfair purchasing commitments. Word of his franchisees' success was attracting attention from scores of prospective franchisees who were willing to invest their life savings to cook hamburgers. His arrangement with outside suppliers was giving dozens of tiny but innovative companies a chance to make a fair profit on high-volume orders without having to pay a kickback to Kroc. McDonald's highly disciplined operations system was ensuring a higher standard of quality, service, and cleanliness than the drive-in industry had ever seen.

There was only one flaw in Kroc's plan—McDonald's had no way of making a profit. Kroc was romancing the fast-food business. The salesman in him was attracted to the volume potential and consumer appeal of a good 15-cent hamburger. The old world thrift in him was fascinated with the efficiency of assembly-line food service. He was determined to convert what he found in San Bernardino into a respected national chain and change the way the food service and food processing industries did things. But making money was not part of the romance. Although he became one of the country's wealthiest men, with an estimated worth of $600 million when he died in 1984, he never talked of accumulating wealth. He was not driven by acquiring money. He never analyzed a business by its profit and loss statement, and he never took the time to understand his own company's balance sheet.

As a result, he had not charted a plan to make McDonald's profitable. Kroc had been too generous to the McDonald brothers, too concerned about the success of his franchisees, and too honest in arranging for supplies. Most of his company's income was coming from the 1.9 percent service fee it assessed franchisees on their food sales. But one-quarter of that (0.5 percent) had to be turned over to the McDonald brothers. He made no big up-front fees for territorial licenses. His initial franchise fee was only $950, and when it was raised in 1956, it went only to $1,500. (It is currently $45,000.) He made no large sum on supplying McDonald's operators with food and equipment. His Prince Castle Sales Division provided them with $150 Multimixers, and Kroc's company claimed a small marketing margin on that. On principle, Kroc had rejected all the conventional means of making money on franchising, but he had not replaced them with a moneymaking scheme he found palatable.

Indeed, everyone was making money on McDonald's except Ray Kroc's company. Its stores were averaging $200,000 in annual sales in the late 1950s, but of that McDonald's got only $2,800 in retainable service fees. Another $1,000 went as a royalty to the McDonald brothers, and the average franchisee was making an operating profit of up to $40,000. McDonald's take was not nearly enough to cover the cost of providing minimal services to operators, let alone to support the extensive operations team Kroc was organizing. If McDonald's had relied solely on Kroc's financial formula and still provided the same level of service, the company in 1993 would not have become one of the country's most profitable retailers with a net income of $1 billion on systemwide sales of $23.6 billion. In short, Kroc's concept for building McDonald's was financially bankrupt.

What converted McDonald's into a money machine had nothing to do with Ray Kroc or the McDonald brothers or even the popularity of McDonald's hamburgers, french fries, and milk shakes. Rather, McDonald's made its money on real estate and on a little-known formula developed by Harry J. Sonneborn. Sonneborn was the former Tastee-Freez executive Kroc hired in 1956, and he worked for McDonald's for just ten years. During that period, he was Ray Kroc's partner—his extremely silent and obscure partner. While Ray Kroc would become legend in American business, Harry Sonneborn would barely be known outside a small circle of McDonald's veterans. In fact, most current McDonald's employees have no idea who Harry Sonneborn was or what he did. But without his financial formula, McDonald's would never have become a viable competitor in fast food, to say nothing of achieving its powerhouse position. "Harry alone put in the policy that salvaged this company and made it a big-leaguer," Kroc

conceded months before he died. "His idea is what really made Mc-
Donald's rich."

To Al Golin, McDonald's longtime public relations consultant, the
Kroc-Sonneborn duo was the classic case of "Mr. Outside and Mr.
Inside." Kroc, the colorful and amiable founder who gave McDonald's
its public image, was such a strong figure that his personage totally
overwhelmed that of Sonneborn, whose impersonal style and preoccupation with only the financial side of the business relegated him to
being a behind-the-scenes operator.

Yet, Sonneborn's real estate investment strategy remains the most
important reason why McDonald's now boasts a financial position that
is not close to being equaled in the food service business. As the man
who served as McDonald's top financial officer during its first decade,
Sonneborn must be credited for converting the flawless Kroc-Turner
operating system into a highly profitable corporation. He did that by
finding a novel way to make money that did not conflict with Kroc's
concept of fairness to suppliers and franchisees. Instead of charging
higher fees for the franchise or raking off a percentage on goods sold
by suppliers to franchisees, Sonneborn conceived of the idea of
making money on real estate that McDonald's would lease to its franchisees.

Far from conflicting with the interests of McDonald's franchisees,
Sonneborn's moneymaking formula fit perfectly into Kroc's concept of
forming a partnership with his franchisees. It did so by solving the
biggest single problem encountered by the entrepreneurial operators
Kroc began recruiting after his Rolling Green friends: finding the funds
to pay for the land and McDonald's red-and-white building. Had Kroc
sold multistore franchises covering large territories, as Wendy's, Burger
King, and other franchisers have done, he would have attracted powerful investors with resources to build their own stores. By franchising
one store at a time, Kroc controlled the quality of operations, but the
independents he attracted as licensees had neither the $30,000 then
needed to acquire the one-half-acre store site nor the $40,000 needed
to build the structure. Nor were most capable of borrowing those
funds.

Sonneborn proposed a strikingly simple solution. McDonald's
would form a separate real estate company—called Franchise Realty
Corporation—which would locate and lease restaurant sites from landowners willing to build McDonald's units, which would also be leased
to the company. Franchise Realty would enter into twenty-year im-

proved leases with these property owners and then sublease the store to the franchisee, charging a markup for the real estate services it was providing.

Sonneborn had proposed a similar real estate plan when he was at Tastee-Freez, but Moranz had rejected it. He could afford to, because Tastee-Freez had a source of income that McDonald's did not—a percentage of its dairy suppliers' revenues from all ice cream mix sold to franchisees. McDonald's problem, Sonneborn says, was that "fundamentally, the company couldn't make a profit on its franchise income because the bulk of it was expensed as overhead."

The beauty of McDonald's taking a "sandwich" position on real estate—leasing from the property owner and subleasing to the franchisee—was that it produced a predictable profit. In fact, Sonneborn had developed a formula that provided for a substantial profit—better than McDonald's would make if it sold equipment and food supplies to licensees. In his negotiations with property owners, Sonneborn refused to cave in to their demands for rents based on a fixed percentage of store sales and insisted on McDonald's paying flat monthly rents, typically in the area of $500 to $600. In subleasing the store to the franchisee, he marked up McDonald's lease costs, initially by 20 percent and then by 40 percent. Thus, on a store costing McDonald's $600 a month in rent, McDonald's charged the franchisee a minimum of $840 per month. Furthermore, in calculating the franchisee's base rent, Sonneborn even added an interest charge on McDonald's real estate investment. "We had developed a formula for subletting that was unbelievable," Sonneborn boasted. "We would have a major real estate investment."

As long as the subleased store stayed in business, it would provide McDonald's at least the 40 percent real estate margin. McDonald's real estate costs were fixed for twenty years, since there were no escalators in any of the leases Sonneborn signed. Furthermore, all subleases with franchisees were on a "net net" basis, meaning that franchisees—not McDonald's—were responsible for paying property insurance and taxes, both of which were certain to increase over time. Thus all McDonald's rental income in excess of its fixed leasing costs expanded the bottom line. "It was retainable money," Sonneborn said. "There were no subsequent expenses."

But the best part of the formula was that the 40 percent markup on the lease was only the *minimum* rent paid by the franchisee. It would give McDonald's enough money to cover its overhead costs on servicing franchisees. Most of the profits to the company were to be made on a second feature of the rental plan, which calculated the operator's rent as a percentage of his store's sales—initially 5 percent. The operator was required to pay McDonald's either the fixed base rent or a percentage rent, whichever was higher. Sonneborn had found a way for McDonald's to claim some of the profits that resulted from growing sales at its stores. Indeed, he had achieved the best of both sides of the rental agreement—refusing to pay a percentage rent to property owners but insisting on getting a percentage rent from operators. "I didn't justify it to anybody," Sonneborn said. "That was the deal—take it or leave it. I never went through the exercise of telling the franchisees what their rental factors were. This was the rent."

Franchise Realty also produced an immediate cash flow. As soon as McDonald's began subletting real estate to franchisees, it began requiring them to pay a $7,500 security deposit, half of which was refunded in the fifteenth year and half in the last year of a twenty-year franchise. (The security deposit was raised to $10,000 in 1963 and is currently $15,000.) In the meantime, McDonald's had use of the money, and within a year Sonneborn began using it to extend his real estate gambit to the second phase: ownership of the property. At first, that involved leasing the land and owning the building, using some of the deposit as a security on the ground lease and some for a down payment on the mortgage on the building. By the early 1960s, however, Sonneborn was going after total ownership, purchasing the land under a ten-year installment contract with the property owner and financing the building through a bank mortgage.

The plan was a daring one. McDonald's was getting ownership of land and building without using any of its own money. It used the franchisees' money for down payments, and it borrowed the rest from landowners and banks. It was leverage in the extreme, but Sonneborn's scheme was certain to be lucrative if it worked. It was also obvious that Kroc had found a partner who more than compensated for his own shortcomings in finance.

Sonneborn's approach to business was totally financial. His principal interest in being in business was to make money. He shared none of Kroc's enthusiasm for the operation of McDonald's drive-ins. His talents at financial negotiations and his keen appreciation for the interests of all parties to a deal could have been applied in any business, and Sonneborn would have been as content to apply them in the clothing business—his initial field—as in the hamburger business. In fact, he viewed the food service business merely as a vehicle for making money in real estate. As such, he was the perfect counterbalance to Ray Kroc. He clearly had the motivation to make money that Kroc lacked. While Kroc had no reservations about demanding that franchisees meet McDonald's standards on QSC, Sonneborn had no reservations about demanding that they pay a rental fee commensurate with the quality of the services they were receiving from the company. "I never overlooked the aspects of finances with regard to the business," Sonneborn explained. "The name of the game was to make a profit."

Profit was not the only contribution of Sonneborn's real estate play. Kroc and Sonneborn believed that control of the real estate also gave McDonald's the type of control over the franchisee that it wanted but could not get from a franchise agreement. Dozens of court cases have since defined the rights of the franchisee and the powers of the franchiser, but franchising was not well recognized in law in the 1950s. What was to prevent a franchisee from taking down the McDonald's sign, changing the restaurant name, and withholding his royalty fee? What power did McDonald's have to discipline the recalcitrants in its operator community who did not want to abide by the rules on menu or operating standards? In a battle with such malcontents, Sonneborn said, "I never thought the franchise contract was worth the paper it was written on. It appeared that it could never stand up in a legal action. It would be the big corporation against the little individual, and the corporation would never win that."

Such was not the case with a lease. It was a time-honored legal document, and McDonald's quickly made compliance with its operating standards one of the requirements of its lease. "We connected the lease to the franchise so that any violation of the franchise could create termination of the lease," Sonneborn explained.

Subsequently, the courts refused to consider suits on leases separate from a franchise agreement, and McDonald's later considered both documents as part of a package. Still, Sonneborn's thinking was extremely appealing to Ray Kroc in the mid-1950s when he was having such difficulty with the Rolling Green and California franchisees, most of whom owned their units and leased the property from landowners. In fact, when Sonneborn presented his real estate plan in 1956, Kroc approved it more for the control he thought it gave him over franchisees than for the profit it generated for his company. "I have finally found the way that will put every single McDonald's we open under our complete control," an excited Kroc reported to the McDonald brothers in early 1957, as he explained Sonneborn's plan. "It [the franchisee's sublease] says that if at any time McDonald's System, Inc., notifies Franchise Realty Corporation that the operation does not conform in every way to the McDonald's standards of quality and service, this lease will be canceled on thirty-day notice. Now we will have a club over them, and by God, there will be no more pampering or fiddling with them. We will do the ordering instead of going around and begging them to cooperate."

Clearly, however, the most important benefit of the real estate connection was that it was the least offensive way for McDonald's to make money. Like any other business, franchise companies must generate profits, but unlike other businesses, they are often perceived as beneficiaries of ill-gotten gains. Selling a franchising territory for a huge fee is perceived as profit not earned. Franchisers who make money by supplying their franchisees with products they manufacture are seen as benefiting from a conflict of interest. And franchisers who take a percentage of the sales of supplies they arrange with third-party vendors are perceived as raking off some of the savings of volume purchasing that should accrue to the franchisees.

Sonneborn had found not only the most profitable way for a fast-food chain to operate but also the purest method of generating profits from franchising. McDonald's was not making a profit at the franchisee's expense, which made Sonneborn's plan legally sound. In a series of "tie-in" cases during the 1960s and 1970s, courts consistently ruled against franchisers for requiring their franchised operators to purchase equipment and supplies from them on the grounds that it constituted an illegal conflict of interest. Yet, at the same time, McDonald's requirement that franchisees rent real estate from the company withstood legal challenges. Courts ruled that selecting and controlling locations was an integral part of running a restaurant chain and that control of that function by the franchiser was natural and did not place the franchiser's financial interest in conflict with that of its franchisees.

Indeed, in McDonald's case, the real estate connection actually put the franchiser's financial interest in harmony with that of its franchisees. That is because under Sonneborn's real estate formula, McDonald's made little profit from its real estate operations until its franchised stores reached the higher sales volumes that caused franchisees to convert from paying the minimum base rent to rents based on a percentage of their sales. Initially, the percentage rent figure was set at 5 percent, but in 1970, it was increased to 8.5 percent. McDonald's must wait until its stores reach percentage rent before it begins earning a substantial return on its investment, but given the volume growth pattern of the average McDonald's unit, the wait is not long.

Thus the big benefit of real estate control is the economic incentive it provides McDonald's to foster superior operations. While other franchisers made big profits up front by selling franchises and opening new stores, Kroc's franchising plan made McDonald's profitability dependent on its ability to encourage franchisees to improve their operations and increase their sales. That motivation was greatly intensified under Sonneborn's real estate program, because the moment franchisees began paying percentage rent, the rental portion of any increase in sales dropped directly to McDonald's bottom line. In short, Kroc's fascination with QSC finally made economic sense. Senior Chairman Turner explains: "Our income became more dependent on building volume at existing stores than it was on building new stores."

In the eyes of numbers men like Harry Sonneborn, the real estate connection was golden. After McDonald's became a public company, Sonneborn enjoyed telling securities analysts that McDonald's was a real estate company, not a fast-food company. And long before that, he would use that line to steady the nerves of prospective lenders, who were comfortable making loans on real estate but anxious about lending to companies in the risky food service business. Of course, Sonneborn's observation was an overstatement that understandably infuriated Kroc. But, viewed coldly and narrowly from a numbers perspective, there is more truth to Sonneborn's remark about real estate than anyone at McDonald's cares to acknowledge.

Indeed, few companies have benefited more from the 1960s and 1970s real estate boom than McDonald's. Because the company obtained most of its suburban real estate holdings just as the nation's suburbs were being developed, it acquired properties at bargain prices. While McDonald's, like everyone else, had to pay the rising prices for new real estate acquisitions, it held the real estate cost of its existing stores constant, either because it had a long-term flat price lease with an option to buy or because it owned the property outright. By comparison, its competitors, which had overlooked the real estate play in the 1960s, were stung by escalating real estate costs in the 1970s.

While McDonald's real estate costs remained relatively level, its real estate income soared because of the impact inflation had on food prices, store sales volumes, and of course, percentage rents. For McDonald's, the double-digit inflation of the 1970s was a blessing, not a curse. Even though it had the negative effect of increasing the cost of the McDonald's hamburger from 15 cents in 1967 to more than three times that by 1980, the percentage rent that McDonald's receives from all its stores meant that the chain was collecting 8.5 percent of an inflating sales base.

The exquisite timing of McDonald's real estate investment also achieved Sonneborn's objective of building a valuable real estate portfolio. Because of the stunning growth in land values, Sonneborn's policy eventually led to a real estate empire that is the envy of all retailers. Today, McDonald's owns the property at 69 percent of its U.S. units and 35 percent of its international restaurants (the rest are leased by the company). In 1982, the net book value of McDonald's property and equipment exceeded for the first time that of the merchandising group of Sears, Roebuck and Company, making McDonald's the owner of the most valuable retail real estate in the world. By the end of 1991, the net book value of McDonald's property equaled $8.8 billion, and the market value was greater still.

But the real economic value of McDonald's real estate is in the rental income it produces. McDonald's earns about 39 percent of its net income from the 29 percent of the nonfranchised units that it owns and operates, but the rest of its income comes from franchised restaurants. And about 90 percent of that profit comes from its real estate operations.

The key to Sonneborn's accomplishment, however, was not merely discovering the real estate connection but rather figuring a way to make it work. In 1956, when he formed Franchise Realty, the odds against McDonald's having any success in real estate investment were enormous. Kroc had started McDonald's in 1954 with an equity investment of $1,000, and when the company decided to go into developing its own real estate three years later, its net worth still amounted to a mere $24,000. That type of a balance sheet—tied to a corporate plan of franchising drive-ins specializing in 15-cent hamburgers—was not likely to send property owners scurrying to their bankers for mortgage money to build red-and-white drive-ins that they could lease to McDonald's. And a couple of years later, when McDonald's began purchasing land under ten-year installment contracts and constructing buildings, its chances of obtaining mortgage money on its own were even smaller. As a rule, bankers did not want to finance start-up companies like McDonald's, and they were even less enthused about bankrolling restaurants because of their high failure rate.

Despite such monumental odds, McDonald's found a way to charm property owners into signing leases and bankers and insurers into making mortgages. It did so by converting the McDonald's character into a split personality. On the one hand were the clean-cut, detail-oriented operations managers who thought of little else but hamburgers, french fries, and milk shakes. On the other was a group of financially oriented managers and real estate brokers with virtually no interest in hamburgers but a consuming interest in making real estate deals and a talent for persuading developers and bankers to take a gamble. While the public saw the operational character of McDonald's simply by observing the spit-and-polish regimen of the McDonald's unit, the deal-making, risk-taking financial side operated behind the scenes.

The real estate team was an extremely diverse group of people. Surprisingly, it included Kroc, who had a unique capability to deal with both sides of his company. He negotiated as many real estate deals as Sonneborn did, selling property owners on McDonald's with the same enthusiasm for 15-cent hamburgers that he displayed in selling franchises. Kroc's instincts in selecting good locations were uncanny, and scouting for new restaurant sites was a constant preoccupation. Even after McDonald's had built one of the retailing industry's most sophisticated real estate departments, Kroc regularly contributed suggestions on new sites. The *Editor & Publisher Market Guide,* an inch-thick directory listing all newspapers in the United States and describing the population and commerce of the towns in which they are located, was Kroc's constant reading companion. All marketers use the guide in locating new outlets, but few knew it more intimately than Kroc. Copies of it were kept on his Gulfstream jet, and Kroc quickly turned to it if he spotted from the air a small town that looked like a good site for a McDonald's. Even in the founder's late seventies, long after he had turned over the reins of the company to Turner, the *E&P Guide* was Kroc's evening reader. "Ray practically slept with that thing," notes Wilburn H. "Wib" Sutherland, former McDonald's real estate vice president. And when Kroc spotted a town that might support a new McDonald's, he was on the phone the next day to Sutherland asking him to investigate the site.

Yet, McDonald's real estate and financial group was dominated by

Sonneborn, who spoke the language of lawyers, bankers, and real estate brokers. Sonneborn was deft at playing their game. He had a banker's appreciation for numbers and a lawyer's appreciation for contracts. And his skills in negotiating financial deals go a long way to explain how McDonald's overcame its formidable obstacles in real estate. A man who showed little emotion, Sonneborn never revealed how eager he was to find property owners willing to build McDonald's units, and that reverse psychology worked magic. Sonneborn's attitude was one of superiority: the property owner should be grateful that McDonald's was even considering his site. "Harry was a real negative salesman," Don Conley recalls. "He would always tell a property owner that he had other pieces of property to look at in the area, and that while his property looked good, it wasn't the greatest."

Even when McDonald's was in no financial position to make demands on property owners, Sonneborn made them. He flatly rejected landowners who wanted escalator clauses or leases based on a percentage of sales. Those who watched his negotiating tactics marveled at his ability to put the property owner in a weaker position by exercising the most critical of all negotiating skills: the ability to say "no deal" whenever the other side's demands conflicted with his. By projecting such confidence, Sonneborn convinced property owners and bankers that McDonald's had more financial substance than its balance sheet indicated. "Harry negotiated as if he had a position of strength even when his position was really one of weakness," observes Richard J. Boylan, retired senior executive vice president and chief financial officer.

Yet, Sonneborn also knew when he had to compromise to make a deal. Indeed, on many occasions he compromised far more than anyone else would have. Sonneborn believed that the cheapest way for a growth company to finance itself was on borrowed money, and he was able to borrow money that other fast-food companies could not get because he was willing to pay more to get it. As McDonald's grew, Sonneborn made tougher demands on loan prices, but in the beginning he believed that the interest rate was one area where he had to make concessions. Even when the rates were painful, Sonneborn rarely missed an opportunity to borrow money. In 1957, Kroc sent him down to Peoria, Illinois, where a broker had introduced the McDonald's founder to Harry Blanchard and Carl Young. The two were longtime associates in the retailing and brewing businesses, and they had just started a company to make high-risk real estate loans that the banks refused to make. Sonneborn met with Young and the two briefly talked about the one store location in Peoria that the Blanchard-Young partnership had agreed to finance. But Sonneborn quickly sensed that he had struck a bigger money well. "If you're willing to finance this store, why not finance six of them," he told Young. "I can show you a lot of other sites."

Young agreed, and when the site inspection was completed, he and Blanchard decided to lease the land at all six locations and loan McDonald's the money to finance the construction of the stores. Sonneborn had hit a jackpot. McDonald's had only thirty-nine stores in operation at the end of 1957, and it owned property at none of them. Here was a single deal that would expand the chain 15 percent and give McDonald's its first equity in drive-in buildings. Furthermore, Blanchard and Young were willing to make their loan at 7 percent, just 2 points above what then was the average rate for commercial real estate loans. There was one hang-up: McDonald's would have to repay $40,000 in principal on each store, but Blanchard and Young would actually loan McDonald's only $25,000 on each. That was their security blanket, and it converted the effective interest rate to a whopping 18 percent. These boys may have been from Peoria, but only Chicago's mob bosses were charging higher rates than that on their juice loans. Still, Sonneborn made the deal because it was McDonald's first crack at big time money, and if the company met its obligations on that mortgage, it would lead to other big loans. On those, he was certain McDonald's would be in a position to get better rates, but it had to be willing to take the first costly step.

The loan from Blanchard and Young set the pattern for financing McDonald's. While Sonneborn would never again be forced to pay rates that bordered on usury, he nevertheless signaled his intention to finance growth through excessive borrowing that made McDonald's easily the most leveraged company in the fast-food business. But because of Sonneborn's creative financing, McDonald's grew much faster than chains that thought it prudent to avoid "excessive" debt. White Castle had started in the hamburger business thirty years before Kroc, and, like McDonald's, it built a reputation for strong restaurant operations. But its growth was stymied by conservative financing. Indeed, the only thing that explains White Castle's failure to capitalize on its head start in the hamburger business was founder E. W. "Billy" Ingram's strict policy against borrowing. As recently as the early 1980s, White Castle boasted a balance sheet that had not even a dime of long-term debt. Yet, the other side of the ledger showed the price of In-gram's fiscal conservatism: White Castle operated only 230 stores.

Equally important as his acceptance of debt was the sophisticated financial team Sonneborn built at McDonald's to implement his daring real estate scheme. By the early 1960s, the company's real estate repre-sentatives were flying around the country in three corporate planes looking at hundreds of potential sites. Unlike the operations group, which purposely recruited managers without traditional restaurant ex-perience, Sonneborn's full-time real estate staff was composed of ex-tremely experienced professionals. Six of his eight top real estate specialists had been recruited from Standard Oil of Indiana, Gulf, and other major oil companies, which were then leading all other chains in the acquisition of real estate in the burgeoning suburbs. Meanwhile, Kroc had built another network of about eight outside real estate bro-kers who spent most of their time hunting for McDonald's sites, some-times under arrangements that gave them an exclusive to develop real estate in a territory. While these internal and external teams sometimes collided, they nevertheless had complete support from either Kroc or Sonneborn, and with that they demonstrated a boldness in securing sites that was uncommon among upstart fast-food companies. They doggedly pursued property owners who might be interested in build-ing a McDonald's unit on their land, often contacting twenty prospects for every deal they made.

Sonneborn had also hired a separate team of financial specialists who were just as aggressive in searching for mortgage money. In calling on banks, they demanded to see bank presidents, talking grandly about deals that would pay the bankers unusually high interest rates on mortgages, hefty loan commitment fees, and extraordinary compensat-ing balances. They followed any tip or contact that might lead to institutional money. In their desperate search for funding, they also ran risks by dealing with developers whose reputations were something less than pristine. In short, when it came to real estate and finance, McDonald's achieved Kroc's expansion goal by traveling in the fast lane.

The speed of McDonald's financial development is evidenced by the way it advanced from one real estate stage to the next. Initially, it approached property owners with a simple "build to suit" real estate offer, known only in McDonald's as a "top lease." Under that arrange-ment, the landowner obtained a mortgage and built a $40,000 McDon-ald's unit on the property and leased it to McDonald's for twenty years for about $700 a month. For the property owner, the risk was substantial. McDonald's was unknown, the 15-cent-hamburger business was novel, and the landowner was building a structure that had no other conceivable use.

But Sonneborn and his real estate team took advantage of a number of things in their favor. Chief among those was that Kroc had targeted the suburbs for development because of McDonald's orientation to the family market. "Look for schools, church steeples, and new houses," Kroc would advise his real estate team. Fortunately, when McDonald's entered the suburbs, it was virgin territory for commercial developers. Vacant land on main thoroughfares was everywhere. Home builders were rapidly developing the suburban residential areas, but development of retail properties lagged. The only national retailers aggressively bidding for suburban land were the oil companies, who were putting gasoline stations on every major corner. There were no Kmarts, no 7-Elevens, no Pacific Stereos, and no Midas muffler shops or Toys "R" Us units. The shopping malls were a decade away. "Once land is built on, it's virtually gone, because it takes a long time before you can afford to tear something down," observes Richard Schubot, a former McDonald's franchisee in Palm Beach, who in the 1960s was a real estate broker who put more property deals together for McDonald's than anyone else. "In the late 1950s, it was much easier to find vacant land because there just weren't the uses for it that there are today."

With only one major competitor for commercial property, McDonald's real estate strategy came down to offering property owners better deals than they could get from the oil companies. They had been accustomed to little competition for land and were bidding bottom dollar for leased real estate, typically paying monthly rents that on an annual basis amounted to 7 percent of the market value of the land and building. Of course, the oil companies were triple-A rated, and McDonald's was little more than a future promise, which made it difficult even for established landowners to get mortgages on the drive-ins. Yet, McDonald's overcame that handicap by making an offer that was hard for some landowners to refuse: annual lease payments equaling 10 percent of the market value of the property. "We were offering landowners a return they could not duplicate," Schubot says. "Their greed set in. They were willing to turn heaven and earth to get the store financed."

McDonald's also made a point of going after parcels of land that

the gasoline marketers passed over. Oil companies invariably demanded corner sites to get the higher traffic they generated. But the
design of the typical McDonald's—with parking in front of and on both
sides of the store and with a driveway that curved around the building
in the shape of a U—was well suited for properties in the middle of the
block, which were half the cost of corner sites. Indeed, McDonald's
often preferred the mid-block locations because they avoided the
congestion at corner traffic lights that often blocked access to the
McDonald's drive-in. "There were far more properties available in
the mid-block," Sonneborn recalled. "This was all vacant property,
and all the owners had to show for their control of the land were real
estate taxes they had to pay on it. We came along and offered a return
they couldn't get anywhere else."

Still another key to the company's success in persuading property
owners to take a gamble on a McDonald's unit was the decision not to
keep the real estate function strictly internal but to rely also on entrepreneurial real estate brokers. They knew their local real estate markets and investors better than McDonald's did, and with a hefty
commission available on each new site, the brokers had a strong financial motive to make deals.

No broker took better advantage of the opportunity than Dick
Schubot, a young and inexperienced Cleveland broker who began
making deals for McDonald's in 1958. Before he became a McDonald's
franchisee, Schubot completed about 250 real estate leases for Mc-
Donald's during the 1960s, roughly one-quarter of all the stores the
company built during that decade. He became a master at locating
McDonald's sites, largely by making the task a seven-days-a-week operation. He studied local markets more closely than even McDonald's
own real estate staff, and he took a brassy approach in negotiating with
property owners and their lawyers. As he developed each new market
in Ohio and surrounding states, he began by taking extensive aerial
photographs that would allow him to spot quickly the main automobile routes and the schools and church steeples that indicated the
presence of suburban families. Schubot then would drive around the
market in a rented auto, mapping the streets and observing the traffic
flows. Ultimately, he built a small library of aerial and street maps, and
he no doubt surprised many brokers when they called him offering
their clients' property to McDonald's and he began reciting over the
telephone more information about the sites than they had.

Schubot's method of negotiating relied on the same use of arrogance as Sonneborn had mastered. When he got the first inkling of interest from a property owner, Schubot laid out his inflexible demands. "I represent McDonald's, but you pay me the commission," he would tell the property owner. "I will give you all the service you need to make this a final deal—find you a contractor, meet with your banker, and negotiate with your lawyer—but if you want to cut my commission, go find yourself another tenant." It was tough talk for a broker representing a company few people had heard of, but the reverse psychology was disarming—and effective. "I almost defied them to make a deal with me," Schubot says.

Schubot gained a reputation for delivering on his full-service promise. When the property owner went to the banker for a mortgage on a McDonald's unit, Schubot was there making his own pitch to the banker, and if the banker refused to make a loan, Schubot advised the property owner—in the banker's presence—to find another bank. When a city planning board threatened to withhold a building permit from another landowner seeking to construct a McDonald's, Schubot showed up at the zoning board meeting with a stenographer. "What in the world are you doing?" the zoning board chairman asked Schubot. "She's taking notes," Schubot replied, "so that when you give me trouble on this, I have a record I can use to sue you." The property owner got the permit.

Schubot was equally unorthodox in some of his site selections. In 1964, he brought to McDonald's a signed lease on a piece of property on the southern edge of Ithaca, New York, that clearly did not meet Sonneborn's requirements for locations on high-traffic streets with nearby "anchors" on either side that would attract customers. While Schubot's Ithaca site was on a high-traffic street, it had little else to recommend it. It was five miles from Cornell University, the market McDonald's was obviously courting. Nor did its "anchor" compensate for its remoteness: it was surrounded by a junk yard.

Sonneborn rejected the deal, but Kroc overruled him. Yet, when McDonald's could not find a franchisee to take the store, and when the company's own operations department rejected the location, Sonneborn had the last say. "I have a deal for you," he told Schubot. "I'm going to give *you* the Ithaca franchise." By then, even Schubot had begun questioning the site, but as he walked out of Sonneborn's office, Kroc motioned to him to enter his. "Show him who you are," Kroc advised. "Take the deal."

Schubot did just that, hoping that the dearth of restaurants near the Cornell campus would encourage students to travel the five miles to McDonald's. His reasoning was sound; the students came in droves. Schubot even had to hire private guards with walkie-talkies to direct traffic into the lot. In its second year, the store's volume exceeded $500,000, double McDonald's average store volume for the mid-1960s.

Finding good sites and property owners willing to lease them was not the only—or even the most formidable—challenge McDonald's faced in implementing Sonneborn's real estate policy. A far more demanding task was finding money to finance its real estate purchases. While Sonneborn started Franchise Realty in 1956 on the notion of leasing both the property and the building from the landowner, he quickly raised the ante by including ownership of land and buildings in his plan.

Given McDonald's weak financial condition, the idea of ownership seemed even more preposterous than controlling real estate through long-term leases. Taking an ownership position required McDonald's to obtain mortgages from bankers, who were considerably less risk oriented than property owners. "The fundamental concept of banking is that you only lend money to people who don't need it," Sonneborn said. "The people who need money aren't good risks, and bankers are not in business to lend money to people who are not good risks."

To compensate for the bankers' reluctance, Sonneborn relied on the greater desire of property owners to make deals. He proposed that McDonald's sign a long-term lease on their land, providing they offer their land as collateral on the mortgages McDonald's arranged with the banks to finance its buildings. Sonneborn knew that no bank would have anything to do with a mortgage secured only by the building, since the structure had utility only as a McDonald's restaurant, and bankers, more than anyone else, had serious misgivings about the viability of a chain selling 15-cent hamburgers. But if Sonneborn could persuade property owners to relinquish their first right to the land if McDonald's defaulted on the mortgage, bankers might listen.

To say the least, it was a presumptuous proposal, but McDonald's surprisingly found property owners willing to accept it in order to obtain the attractive rents the chain was willing to pay on the land. Furthermore, McDonald's stores were establishing an enviable track record. Although few franchisees were making the annual pretax profits of $50,000 or more per store being earned by such high-volume operators as Agate in Waukegan; Taylor in Newington, Connecticut;

and Gibson and Goldstein in Washington, D.C.; few were taking a beating. Indeed, only one store—the Cole-Garrett franchise in Dallas—had gone under.

By the late 1950s, McDonald's solid track record was encouraging a growing number of landowners to lease their property to McDonald's and subordinate their land titles to a bank that would loan McDonald's money to build the unit. Almost immediately after instituting that plan, Sonneborn took the next logical step: purchasing the land itself. Once Sonneborn's Franchise Realty started leasing property to franchisees, it also began requiring them to put up a security deposit, which has been raised to $15,000. That, of course, not only provided a much needed cash infusion, it allowed Sonneborn to begin to think of buying land under ten-year installment contracts, using the franchisee's security deposit as a down payment. The idea was so bold that only a no-nonsense money man like Sonneborn would have had the nerve to propose it. After all, Sonneborn was using the franchisee's own cash to make a down payment on land that McDonald's would buy and lease back to the franchisee. The balance due on the land contract was borrowed in effect from the property owner, who was still being asked to give up his or her first right to the land so that McDonald's could obtain a mortgage on the building. As long as McDonald's continued selling hamburgers, Sonneborn had a self-generating real estate empire. "This was all operating on pure leverage—other people's money," Sonneborn would later boast. "We didn't have a nickel in it."

But the move toward purchasing property shifted the burden on McDonald's from finding landowners willing to make deals to finding bankers willing to make loans. Here, too, McDonald's early real estate specialists showed surprising creativity and brashness. In 1959, Sonneborn hired an inventive, thirty-one-year-old real estate lawyer by the name of John Jursich and assigned him the full-time task of scouting out mortgage money. Jursich's age belied his experience. Having received his law degree from De Paul University at age twenty-two, he had already been practicing real estate law for nine years and had also developed an extremely persuasive style. In fact, even before he joined McDonald's, Jursich was raking in handsome commissions by lining up mortgages for the chain while employed at a mortgage brokerage firm. Sonneborn had an obvious choice—make Jursich rich or hire him.

Jursich's style was not unlike Schubot's. He did not plead for mortgage money; he dared bankers not to give it to him. When he started scouting for mortgage money, McDonald's had not been getting to first base with big city banks. Kroc had already shifted his business and personal accounts to American National Bank after Chicago's Harris Bank refused to provide him with the $25,000 loan he needed when he started McDonald's. Later, he was rejected on a loan request by David Kennedy, then an executive with Continental Bank and later secretary of the treasury in the Nixon administration.

Instead of fighting what he considered a losing battle for multistore mortgages from big Chicago lenders, Jursich narrowed his initial search for funds to the small town banks and thrifts, where he went after mortgages only for individual stores built in their local markets. Because virtually all McDonald's units during the first decade were being opened in suburbs and small towns, Jursich's quest for mortgage money simply followed the same path. He reasoned that local bankers had an economic interest in supporting a McDonald's store in their towns, because it created roughly thirty-five new jobs.

Jursich also made a very appealing proposition to the small bankers. He knew they had more deposits than they could lend locally and that their excess funds were being invested in the low-rate certificates of deposit of the money center banks. So Jursich played to their desire for better rates the way Schubot lured landowners with above-average lease prices. "Everybody's basically got some thievery in them," Jursich observes. "I gave them a chance to be a thief." Many of Jursich's early mortgages came from savings and loans, which specialized in 5 percent home mortgages and which longed for—but rarely made— higher-rate commercial real estate loans. Jursich began dangling in front of S&L presidents a 7 percent rate on ten-year mortgages, plus a commission fee of 5 percent just to make the loan. Some were so eager to make such a relatively rich loan that they put aside their traditional concerns about the high-risk restaurant trade. In more than one case, the S&L executives were so naive about drafting a commercial loan commitment that they accepted Jursich's selfish offer to write it for them.

Jursich lured small town bankers with the same terms, plus a bonus—the promise that the McDonald's operator would maintain his business deposits at whatever local bank would loan McDonald's the $40,000 mortgage for the building. Jursich even showed bankers the deposit records of existing McDonald's operators, which revealed average deposits in the $15,000 range. Then, he posed one key question: "Name another customer willing to keep one-third compensating balances in the bank as a condition of the loan."

Jursich's style was as persuasive as were his terms. Like others on the real estate staff, he flew into a small town on the company airplane, and that alone helped to debunk the "joint" image that many bankers initially had of all fast-food operators. Jursich showed up at the bank in a three-piece suit carrying a large briefcase stuffed with color photographs of new McDonald's units, sales histories of individual restaurants, and other information to document the mortgage. He refused to see anyone but the bank president. "I was looking for a loan that was not in the bank's rulebook, and vice presidents always follow the book," Jursich explains. "The only guy willing to deviate is the CEO."

By refusing to budge from that demand, Jursich sometimes caused commotion in the bank. When the executive vice president of Tucson Federal Savings and Loan greeted the McDonald's visitor instead of the S&L's chairman, Jursich was told that the ninety-year-old chairman worked only an hour a day and never directly on loans. Jursich was threatening to leave when the chairman entered the bank, obviously delighted to learn that an executive with some new Chicago company insisted on seeing *only* him. At lunch, the old-guard chairman regaled Jursich with stories of how he was Pancho Villa's banker during Mexico's revolutionary war and ran money for him across the border. As the two came back from lunch, Jursich understood the glare he was getting from the young executive vice president he had spurned. By then, it did not matter. Jursich's loan had been approved by the chairman.

Jursich had no reservations about challenging bank presidents head-on. When the president of a bank in Mobile, Alabama, turned thumbs down on a McDonald's loan, Jursich began paging through the bank's annual report. "Is this the current list of your directors?" Jursich asked. "It is," the banker replied. "Good," said Jursich. "I'm going to call them." "What the hell for?" the bank president wondered. "You may not like this loan, but I bet your directors will," Jursich answered as he began making his exit. With that, the bank president motioned him back, and minutes later the mortgage was approved.

If such tactics were unconventional, they were employed only because McDonald's was in no position to make a standard case for a loan. Jursich and other McDonald's real estate representatives produced the hamburger chain's balance sheet only when it was abso-

lutely demanded by lenders and property owners. The company's real
estate reps and mortgage brokers could talk and act big time, but the
company's financial statement simply did not carry the same message.
It was obviously an embarrassment for anyone looking for a loan.
While its restaurant sales were encouraging, its corporate income was
virtually nonexistent, thanks to its heavy spending to develop the system. And even by the late 1950s the new real estate strategy had not
been in place long enough to begin to fatten up the company's anemic
bottom line. At the beginning of 1958, when Sonneborn started searching for funds to buy real estate, McDonald's had a net worth of only
$24,000. It had earned $26,000 the year before, but most of that came
from one-time licensing fees charged to new franchisees. The year
before it had lost $7,000. McDonald's had only 38 restaurants, most of
them at sites where it had no control over the real estate. The company
was looking to add 50 units in 1958 and, either through lease or outright ownership, to control the property at all or most of those new
locations. That would amount to $3.5 million worth of real estate. Even
on a thousand-to-one shot, no betting man would wager that McDonald's could build such an impressive position on such a flimsy financial foundation. Amazingly, McDonald's pulled it off, and in the next
two years it managed to quicken its new construction pace. By the end
of 1960, the chain had 228 restaurants in operation, and it controlled
the real estate at all but 56 sites. By then, the value of real estate leased
or owned by McDonald's totaled $16 million.

That feat was not achieved solely by the brashness of Sonneborn's
real estate team or even by the enthusiasm of Ray Kroc. When McDonald's made its play for ownership of real estate, it began dealing with
hard-nosed, skeptical investors and financiers, and they could be hus-
tled only to a point. As he got deeper into real estate, Sonneborn
realized that he needed to obtain financing from institutions and other
large investors willing to finance ten or more restaurants at one time.
Financing single locations with property owners and banks was simply
too time-consuming, and it was restricting McDonald's growth.

But in shifting his search for financing to institutions, Sonneborn
knew he had to make McDonald's balance sheet much more present-
able to the institutional lawyers and accountants who were now going
to scrutinize it. Sonneborn's plan amounted to the first attempt by a
fast-food operator to enter the financial big leagues, but in 1958, Mc-
Donald's balance sheet was strictly minor league material. Without a
decent financial statement to show investors, Sonneborn's real estate

strategy was a pipe dream. His answer was simple: develop new accounting methods that would yield better-looking statements.

Sonneborn was desperate to paint McDonald's in a better light. Indeed, in making his very first real estate deals, he had already fudged on some of the figures for Kroc's Des Plaines store—the only financial track record McDonald's then had to show to investors. Years later, Sonneborn would concede that the financial statement on Des Plaines had been altered. "I understand expenses and overstated profits," Sonneborn said. "When you are trying to sell something like that [a real estate deal], you need a really good financial statement, and the Des Plaines statement wasn't that good."

Of course, Sonneborn knew that McDonald's corporate statements could not be so crudely rearranged. But just as two cooks convert the same meat and potatoes into different tasting hamburgers and fries, two accountants—both using legal numbers—can come up with balance sheets and income statements that portray a company differently, for better or worse. Sonneborn needed the former, and to get it, he turned 180 degrees away from his aggressive real estate specialists to a behind-the-scenes manager who had total grasp of the business through its numbers and who could use those numbers to McDonald's benefit. Sonneborn turned to an accountant and lawyer, Richard J. Boylan. When Sonneborn hired him in 1958, Boylan had completed an eight-year stint with the Internal Revenue Service. Having worked in both the income and the estate and gift tax divisions, Boylan had become an expert in real estate accounting, appraisal, and taxation. Here was a man, Sonneborn thought, who knew how to improve McDonald's financial numbers as much as the law would allow.

Within weeks of joining McDonald's, Boylan was using IRS valuation techniques to dramatically increase the company's reported net worth. Just as the IRS had concluded that the future lease payments to a deceased's estate had a present value, Boylan assumed that McDonald's future net rental income from its franchisees also had a present value that should be reported as an asset. Since that value was roughly ten times McDonald's rents from franchisees in any given year, Boylan had discovered a miraculous way of adding instant wealth to the balance sheet. The only problem was that the concept of capitalizing leases was not then embodied in so-called GAAP accounting—the Generally Accepted Accounting Principles that govern virtually all corporate accounting.

But Boylan reasoned the GAAP accounting failed to disclose legitimate real estate values that McDonald's was building. Since its leased property was being marked up when it was sublet to franchisees, it created a future income stream that grew every time McDonald's opened a new unit. Boylan succeeded in convincing Doty and Doty, McDonald's Chicago-based accountants, to blaze a new trail by capitalizing the leases and reporting their future income stream as a corporate asset. It inflated the company's assets like a balloon. In 1960, McDonald's balance sheet showed total assets of $12.4 million, nearly four times the amount of the previous year. Most of the increase was the result of a one-line entry mysteriously called "Unrealized Increment from Appraisal in Valuation of Assets," which represented $5.8 million worth of capitalized leases.

Nearly half of the company's assets were contained in a figure that most accountants would have disallowed. By 1964, as McDonald's prepared to take its stock public, the company retained a Big Eight accountant—Arthur Young and Company—to satisfy Wall Street. But the respectability that came with the Big Eight name carried a major tradeoff. Arthur Young would have nothing to do with the capitalization of leases, and McDonald's was forced to remove from its balance sheet in 1964 some $17.4 million in assets reported the year before. That slashed McDonald's reported assets almost in half. But by then the capitalization of leases had performed its task of dressing up McDonald's balance sheet for executives from major lending institutions that Sonneborn had been courting for multistore financing packages since the late 1950s. "We were going to investors who would look at our balance sheet and find nothing there," Boylan recalls. "We had to develop some way of showing the earning power we were building in real estate."

Boylan applied equally innovative accounting to improve McDonald's reported earnings. While McDonald's was growing rapidly and many of its franchisees were doing well, the company's earnings were miserably low, because the costs related to expanding the system invariably showed up before new restaurant revenues. And in 1958, as McDonald's plunged into the real estate business, its profits all but disappeared. Although total sales of the system had more than doubled to $10 million that year, McDonald's net income was a mere $12,000, less than half of what it had been the previous year. "I can't raise money with these earnings," Sonneborn complained to Boylan. "We have to do something about them."

Boylan took aim at the rapidly escalating costs of developing real estate. He could do nothing to cut those costs, but he could make them look less menacing on the income statement. Following GAAP accounting, McDonald's had been expensing real estate development costs as they were incurred, but Boylan argued that they should be reported nine months later, the time it took to develop a site. Expenses should be matched to revenues they generate, he reasoned, and real estate expenses generated no revenues until new stores were open. For the same reason, Boylan also capitalized interest expenses on real estate loans during the construction of a store and amortized those costs over the twenty-year life of a franchise. Since both changes delayed reporting of expenses that were growing rapidly with McDonald's aggressive expansion, Boylan's so-called developmental accounting worked magic on McDonald's income statement: they produced reported earnings where there were none before.

Neither of those adjustments were then acceptable under standard accounting, but again Boylan persuaded Doty and Doty to permit them, and by 1960 the first results of Boylan's program appeared on McDonald's income statement. That year, the company reported $109,000 in net income—nearly ten times the 1958 figure—and much of the growth resulted from innovative accounting. The fact that Boylan's accounting did not square with GAAP did not bother Sonneborn. It was the financiers—not the accountants—whom he was trying to impress. "It was the greatest accounting gimmick ever devised," Sonneborn observed, referring to Boylan's capitalization of future lease income. "The bankers were bemused and befuddled by it because they had never seen it before, but it surely helped us get some loans."

McDonald's, of course, disclosed its accounting changes, but the numbers they produced on the bottom line of the income statement were far more prominent than the footnotes that detailed the novel accounting Boylan used. "We fully disclosed everything in the footnotes, but people don't read the footnotes," explained Gerry Newman, McDonald's former senior executive vice president and chief accounting officer. "Our numbers were funny numbers, but without them we never would have gotten the loans to expand, because we didn't have real profits." Boylan disagrees strongly with that assessment. "Every number in our financial statements was fully explained and supported by accounting principle," he argues. "There was nothing funny about them. Funny numbers are imaginary numbers, and our numbers were not imaginary."

Boylan's work was not a violation of basic accounting concepts, just a deviation from standard practices. In fact, all of his changes were rationalized using long-standing accounting philosophy, and years later some of his innovations began to make sense to other accountants as well. Indeed, a couple were finally adopted as generally accepted principles of accounting, including his capitalization of interest on construction debts.

While the new accounting gave McDonald's more respectable financial statements, it did not eliminate the fundamental money problem—lack of cash. It is axiomatic that young companies with big plans experience periodic cash crunches, but many early fast-food franchisers defied those odds. To them, fast-food franchising required little investment to produce immediate profits on the sale of franchises, and most never made the investment in operations necessary to generate profits over the long term. They got into the business, made their quick profits, and vanished.

While Kroc resisted the temptation to chase those short-term profits, his plan to build an elaborate operating system meant weathering six years during which McDonald's made almost no money. Through 1960, the chain's restaurants had sold an impressive $75 million worth of hamburgers, fries, and milk shakes, but McDonald's had managed to earn a mere $159,000 in accumulated profits during its first six years. By the end of 1960, the company had 228 units in operation, well above any other hamburger chain in the new fast-food business, but its net worth stood at a mere $95,000. And if it had not been for Boylan's accounting, the company would have reported a *negative* net worth. Ray Kroc still was not drawing a McDonald's salary, and only $1,000 a month from Prince Castle and $500 a month from his restaurant in Des Plaines kept the bill collectors away from his door. Sonneborn, the highest-paid officer, was making only $27,500, modest compensation for a president of a company employing forty people. Other executives' salaries showed similar restraint, ranging downward to the $10,500 that Fred Turner was paid as vice president of operations.

As modest as its salaries were, they nevertheless occasionally exceeded the company's meager cash flow. In fact, meeting the weekly payroll was never taken for granted. Sonneborn's new real estate policies were boosting revenues, but they were barely keeping pace with the skyrocketing manpower costs involved in supporting the chain's twin commitment to operational perfection and real estate investment. Paydays were often preceded by frantic calls from June Martino to franchisees to collect royalties due. When more payroll funds were needed, licensing vice president Conley made emergency calls to prospective licensees who were on McDonald's growing waiting list for new stores. If they could send in all or part of their $10,000 security deposit immediately, Conley would tell them, he could "lock in a location" that had just become available.

Such payroll crises developed despite Sonneborn's orders that no invoices in excess of $1,000 could be paid at one time and that no bills could be paid until enough receipts were set aside to pay wages. Yet, Sonneborn himself made it difficult for accountant Gerry Newman to balance the corporate checkbook. Sonneborn, who spent most of his first five years with McDonald's on the road looking for real estate, typically carried several blank checks to use for down payments on property. At times he forgot to tell Newman about the checks he wrote on his trips, and by the time Newman found out about them, the bank account was empty.

On one such occasion, money was so short that even the typical emergency cash generators could not overcome it. McDonald's senior managers were all out of town, and at 3:00 P.M. on Friday, Newman realized that the company's close calls on cash had finally gotten too close: there was no way to meet the payroll for the week. Newman was faced with the prospect of writing checks that would bounce or admitting to employees that the company coffers were bare. Neither prospect was particularly pleasant, so Newman wrote a staff memo that was as creative as Boylan's accounting. Although he had no authority to make payroll policy, Newman announced an immediate change from weekly to semimonthly payrolls. The cash crisis was over because that Friday's payday was simply eliminated. From that day on, McDonald's has paid employees semimonthly instead of weekly.

As nettlesome as the company's periodic cash crunches were, they paled by comparison to the financial crisis that turned up at Sonneborn's office in early 1959 in the form of a mechanics' lien. A construction contractor in Milwaukee was looking to be paid for services performed for a developer by the name of General Associates, Inc., which was building some stores for McDonald's. At first, Sonneborn paid little attention to what easily might have been a late payment, but days later a similar mechanics' lien appeared, and soon Sonneborn was swimming in mechanics' liens—all of them filed against General Associates. Suddenly, McDonald's was confronting the downside risk of Sonneborn's real estate policies. If a store failed where McDonald's merely had a franchising relationship, McDonald's lost only the service fees it was receiving. The big losers were the franchisee, who was out of business, and the real estate owner, who was stuck with a vacant, single-purpose building. But as soon as McDonald's took an interest in the property, it also took a bigger risk of a real estate loss.

Just how potentially threatening that risk was became evident with the shocker delivered by Milwaukee-based General Associates. Its president, Clem Bohr, had agreed to purchase land and begin constructing nine McDonald's drive-ins, using the security deposits of franchisees as down payments on the properties, all of which were to be bought under ten-year contracts. Bohr planned to persuade the property owners to subordinate their interest in the land to the banks from which General Associates was to obtain the mortgages on the red-and-white drive-ins it proposed to build. McDonald's, in turn, agreed to buy the properties—land and buildings—from General Associates on a ten-year installment plan. It was just the type of deal Sonneborn was looking for. With little front end investment, McDonald's for the first time would get ownership of both land and building at a restaurant site.

But what looked good on paper soon turned into a nightmare for Sonneborn. Bohr acquired the property using franchisee security deposits as down payments and hired contractors who began building the units. But, for reasons McDonald's never learned, he never got mortgages to pay for the buildings. By spring of 1959 he had not paid the building contractors a dime. They had completed more than half of their work on the buildings but were refusing to finish. Worse, Bohr was nowhere to be found.

McDonald's was suddenly in danger. Bohr's program—seven new units in Wisconsin and two in Ohio—was the largest real estate deal Sonneborn had made to date. It amounted to a 10 percent expansion of the McDonald's chain in early 1959. At about $40,000 a restaurant, the debt to contractors alone—to say nothing of the balance owed the landowners—came to nearly $400,000. In addition, franchisees had already put up $15,000 in security deposits for down payments at each of the nine sites, which meant an additional commitment of $135,000. In all, the Clem Bohr deal, which looked so tantalizing in the waning months of 1958, had by early the next year become at least a $500,000 liability for tiny McDonald's. Kroc's company did not have that kind of money or any reasonable chance of raising it. Here was an unexpected demand for twenty times the company's net worth.

While Sonneborn might have argued that the liability was Bohr's and not McDonald's, the contractors were coming to McDonald's to demand payment. Likewise, the franchisees had given their money to McDonald's, not Bohr, and they too would make their claim against the franchising chain. Sonneborn could sense an imminent flood of lawsuits, and he could picture McDonald's drowning in it. If he did not come up with about $500,000 in cold cash within a month or two to head off the trouble, McDonald's would become one of dozens of forgotten upstart companies that each year are victims of what securities analyst Robert Emerson calls the fast-food industry's "Endless Shakeout." And the worst fate of all would be Ray Kroc's, because just when it appeared that he had captured the entrepreneurial magic he had sought for more than three decades, his McDonald's—and his dreams of riding the wave of a revolution in American lifestyles—would be in bankruptcy court.

It is little wonder that Fred Turner recalls the period as "trauma time" for McDonald's. The Clem Bohr debacle created such tension that it even rattled Sonneborn, who typically was so calm under pressure that his coolness was widely interpreted as arrogance. There was no arrogance now. "I'm telling you, I almost committed suicide," Sonneborn recalled. "There seemed no way to get the company out of this mess. I had many sleepless nights over it."

To stay out of court, McDonald's needed an immediate cash infusion to pay off the contractors. Sonneborn turned to perhaps the surest source—the company's suppliers. They were already benefiting from the stunning food sales the new chain was racking up at its drive-ins, and they had almost as much at stake in the survival of McDonald's as the company itself had. Sonneborn approached five of them—Continental Coffee, Perlman Paper Company, Honey Hill Dairy, Mary Ann Baking, and Interstate Foods—hoping to persuade each to purchase $25,000 in debentures from McDonald's. He did not even have to sell them. "Louie Kuchuris [the owner of Mary Ann Baking, the bun supplier] didn't even want the debentures," Sonneborn recalled. "I had lunch with him, and he wrote out a check on the spot. If it had not been for the loans from those purveyors, McDonald's would not have lasted another five minutes."

But the $125,000 infusion only bought Sonneborn the time he needed to find institutional financing. He had been searching for the big money for real estate expansion for months and had had no luck. If he could not tap the money markets to finance McDonald's growth, what chance was there for him to find institutional money to keep the chain out of bankruptcy? Yet, in retrospect, the Bohr incident was the best thing that could have happened to McDonald's. Now, Sonneborn was *compelled* to find institutional money. He devoted every working moment meeting with insurers, real estate brokers, and investment bankers on LaSalle Street, Chicago's financial center. He even went to the pension funds of such unions as the Teamsters and Amalgamated Butchers, where he was turned away. "I had feelers out all over town, and I went to anybody who would listen to me," Sonneborn recalled. "I wasn't proud; I was a beggar."

He pursued every tip he got, and one of them led Sonneborn to the office of E. E. Ballard, president of All-American Life and Casualty. By 1986, a subsidiary of U.S. Life, one of the nation's largest insurers, All-American in 1959 was a small but aggressive insurer that Ballard had formed just seven years before. He listened to Sonneborn, who made no mention of the Bohr calamity, and was intrigued by the idea of a 15-cent-hamburger chain. Days later, his son became interested in a McDonald's and visited Ray Kroc to talk about a franchise. Kroc seized the opportunity from that contact to interest the older Ballard in a somewhat larger commitment. Although the two had never met, Ballard, who lived less than a mile from Kroc and occasionally golfed at Rolling Green, had heard of Kroc's new restaurant chain some time before. And now, when Kroc asked to pay a visit to the Ballard home, the insurance president gladly agreed.

It was Kroc's chance to save his young company, and he turned on the charm. "It was Ray's fire that really got me interested," Ballard recalls. "I'll never forget his knowledge of the details of the business. He knew exactly what he was going to do and how he was going to do it. I liked his neatness, the way he stood and talked."

The next day, Ballard asked a couple of officers of his small insurance company to investigate McDonald's finances. They did not uncover the Bohr problem, but their report to Ballard was anything but encouraging. "McDonald's didn't have anything in the way of assets," Ballard recalls. Still, he recommended to his board that All-American provide McDonald's enough mortgage money to finance all nine buildings at the sites Bohr had begun to develop. In all, the ten-year mortgages totaled $260,000—all at 6 percent. Ballard reasoned that the loans were really low-risk commitments, since the property owners at the sites were subordinating their ownership of the land to the mortgages being made by All-American. Since the land was at least as valuable as the buildings All-American was financing, it was more than sufficient collateral on the loan. If McDonald's defaulted, it would be the landowners who would lose.

With Ballard's support, the loan was approved. McDonald's had found a savior in All-American. Ballard never knew how close the chain had come to bankruptcy. In fact, he never sent anyone to inspect the stores that All-American was financing. "It sounds like I was easy on them, but I was a little like Ray Kroc," Ballard says. "I believed in doing business with people who had enthusiasm for what they were doing. Ray was determined to make a go of it, and I just knew he would."

It was the first institutional financing in the fast-food business, and Sonneborn fully understood the efficiency of it. With one stroke of the pen, McDonald's had obtained financing for nine stores. For about as much time as the chain invested in negotiating with property owners and small town bankers to obtain financing on one store, it could nail down a multiple-store loan with an insurance company or other big-time money manager. If McDonald's was really going to build a national chain, it could no longer finance its stores one at a time. "As fast as we were wanting to expand, we just didn't have the time to look for property, run the business, and still find single-store mortgages from local banks," Sonneborn said.

More than anyone else, Sonneborn realized the urgency of gaining access to the major money markets, and All-American provided the all-important break. There is a sheepish character to institutional lending. Major lenders—particularly in real estate—like to put their money where other institutions have similar loans. Now, Sonneborn could approach other insurers for loans and proudly point to the presence of All-American's mortgages on McDonald's balance sheet. Soon he had received a similar loan commitment from another Chicago-based insurer, Central Standard Life.

While a couple of medium-sized loans from midwestern insurers were an impressive catch, they did not give McDonald's the financial credibility Sonneborn wanted. It was still a drive-in chain, a fledgling competitor in a fast-food industry that lacked respectability in establishment money circles. Until McDonald's overcame that stigma, it would be living on the razor's edge, always chasing mortgage money and never assured of getting it. So, Sonneborn now set his sights on bigger game—eastern money. Specifically, he wanted to nail down a $1 million loan from a highly established lender. At that moment,

McDonald's really did not need that much money, but Sonneborn wanted the prestige of such a loan on the balance sheet.

What appeared to be the big score came quickly and almost effortlessly. Months after he completed the mortgage deals with All-American and Central Standard, Sonneborn made contact with a wealthy Manhattan investor. The investor was impressed with McDonald's real estate strategy, and he was contemplating a commitment bigger than anything Sonneborn had dreamed of. Sonneborn rushed to New York to close the deal. When he walked into the office of the investor's attorney, he saw the check on the attorney's desk that confirmed how serious the investor was. It was carefully placed so that Sonneborn could read it from the other side: "Pay to the order of McDonald's, $22,000,000."

Bingo. Earlier that year, McDonald's was close to bankruptcy, and now it was getting a loan that was 350 times greater than that year's net income. For $22 million, it could build more than two hundred restaurants—doubling the size of the chain. "I've got it made," Sonneborn thought, as he greeted the lawyer. Just then, the telephone rang. It was the investor. "I want to make a few minor changes in the agreement," he told Sonneborn over a speaker phone. He then proceeded to change everything, and the new terms were so unfavorable that Sonneborn could not possibly sublet the new properties to franchisees at anything approaching a reasonable percentage of sales and still make money. "When I first met you fellows," Sonneborn said as he stood up from his chair, "I thought I was dealing with businesspeople. Now I have come to the conclusion that I am dealing with nothing but crooks." With that, Sonneborn left the lawyer's office. His bravado concealed his disappointment. Sonneborn was devastated. He had hoped to be leaving the lawyer's office to celebrate. He went instead to his hotel room and threw up.

Sonneborn's disappointment did not last long. His search for a big loan had netted dozens of contacts, and it was only a matter of time before one of them would open the door to the financial arena in the East. Not long after the New York deal collapsed, Sonneborn met his man. His name was Milton Goldstandt, and he was an unlikely contact to big eastern money. For one thing, he was a Chicago native. For another, his business was selling life insurance, not making loans. But Kroc had heard that Goldstandt might be helpful in locating money, and he suggested that Sonneborn follow up on the tip.

When he did, Sonneborn learned that Goldstandt was not a typical life insurance agent. He was the largest producer for John Hancock, and although he was an independent agent, he was so influential at the Hancock that he had direct contact with its senior management, including those who ran the investment side of the house. In the words of a longtime Boston banker, Goldstandt was a "bird dog" for the Hancock. In selling life insurance to wealthy clients, he heard of scores of new companies that needed financing, and he brought the better-looking prospects to his good friend Lee Stack, John Hancock's senior vice president in charge of all investments. During the 1950s, Stack was one of the insurance industry's most innovative portfolio managers, developing a number of new, higher-interest investment vehicles. Among other things, Stack had pioneered deals that allowed wealthy investors to obtain tax breaks by purchasing rolling stock and leasing it to railroads. Clearly, Stack was not cut from the same cloth as most of his counterparts at other life insurers who viewed as a crapshoot investments in any company that had less than triple-A rating.

When Sonneborn briefed Goldstandt on McDonald's need for institutional money, the insurance salesman immediately brought the matter to the attention of Stack, who at age sixty-five was just retiring from the Hancock. That did not matter, however, because he was becoming a partner in the brokerage firm of Paine Webber, where he intended to remain very active in finance and in constant touch with friends in Boston's closely knit financial fraternity. They included Dick Wilson, Stack's counterpart at State Mutual Life Insurance; John Gosnell, chief of investments at Paul Revere Life Insurance; and Bill Brown, a commercial loan officer at First National Bank of Boston. Although all were involved with institutions known for their conservatism, Stack's friends shared his willingness to accept more risk to get bigger returns. They avoided pure venture capital plays in brand-new companies, but they were on the lookout for young companies that had survived the shakedown cruise and were ready to head for the high seas.

After months of prospecting, Sonneborn finally had struck a financial vein that contained the payoff he was looking for. Quickly, he arranged mortgages on about fifteen restaurants with John Hancock, and he got some good-sized loans from Bill Brown at the First of Boston. But he knew this was the chance for the big score, and in early 1960 he went for it: he proposed a $1.5 million loan with some equity added as a bonus. Stack took the proposition to John Hancock, but he could not persuade his former employer to take the deal. On its face, a loan of that size—fifteen times greater than McDonald's net worth in 1959—was an insane risk, particularly for an institution investing the money of policyholders who look to life insurance for long-term security. McDonald's was anything but a safe bet.

When Hancock turned thumbs down, Stack turned to Wilson at State Mutual. Wilson was intrigued, and he called into his office a rising star of his investment group, twenty-nine-year-old Fred Fedelli. Fedelli was a novice at making risk-oriented deals, but he had no trouble analyzing the twenty-five-page prospectus on McDonald's that Stack handed to him. Even if the chain's growth projections were overstated by 100 percent, Fedelli thought, McDonald's could repay the loan. But the big inducement was the bonus Sonneborn was willing to pay if the insurers made the high-risk loan—20 percent of McDonald's stock. Wilson and Fedelli concluded that McDonald's deserved a first-hand inspection, particularly since Stack was recommending the deal. Since neither had even heard of McDonald's before, it was decided that Fedelli would fly to Chicago to investigate.

Days later, Fedelli was in Sonneborn's office, getting a pitch on how McDonald's was building an impressive position in real estate. It was Sonneborn's favorite argument. "Harry kept telling me not to worry," Fedelli recalls, "because if the restaurants failed there was still all this value in the real estate McDonald's controlled. He didn't know much about the restaurant operations. He looked at them as a way to establish a real estate empire." The argument was appealing, and Fedelli was taken by Sonneborn's sophistication in finance. Yet, Fedelli also knew there was no way he was going to recommend a loan to any food service company simply because it controlled valuable real estate. The loan McDonald's wanted would be unsecured, and subordinated to all other debt. If McDonald's went bankrupt, State Mutual would be last in line for a share of any assets. Thus the restaurant operation was the key, Fedelli concluded. If it were weak, there could be no loan.

During the next two days, Fedelli flew around the Midwest on McDonald's Aerocommander, visiting twenty McDonald's. When the trip was over, his mind was made up on the loan. "I couldn't believe it," he recalls. "You could get a drink, fries, and a hamburger for less than fifty cents, and the food was good. This was real value. The places were all clean, and the parking lots were picked up. I figured it couldn't have been a setup, because we went to so many different units, and at every one I saw the same thing."

When Fedelli returned to Boston, he persuaded his father and brother to drive three hours with him to see the nearest McDonald's, in Newington, Connecticut. Before he recommended the loan, Fedelli wanted to look at one more store, this one on his home turf, not that of McDonald's. He had unwittingly picked a store that was becoming legend among McDonald's operators. Located on the Berlin Turnpike midway between Boston and New York, the store was run by Reub Taylor, and it was breaking all McDonald's sales records. When other stores averaged $250,000 a year, Taylor's unit was the first to top the $500,000 mark. "We got there at eleven-thirty, and the parking lot was already jammed," Fedelli recalls. "There were two serving windows and fifty people in each line."

That sealed it. Fedelli was determined to persuade Wilson to make the loan. It was not Sonneborn's real estate arguments that won him over, but Kroc's commitment to operating basics. "If the parking lots had been dirty, if the help had grease stains on their aprons, and if the food wasn't good," Fedelli insists, "McDonald's never would have gotten the loan, regardless of what Harry Sonneborn said about real estate."

With Fedelli's glowing report to go on, Wilson recommended the loan to his investment committee. But, because of the risk, State Mutual wanted to include a partner in the deal, and Fedelli called John Gosnell at Paul Revere, who agreed to take half of the $1.5 million loan at 7 percent, and both insurers would split the 20 percent equity kicker. As part of the deal, Stack and Goldstandt would split a finder's fee of 2.5 percent of McDonald's stock.

Taking that type of loan would not be an easy decision for the entrepreneurs of McDonald's. Their equity was the result of six years of hard work, and it is difficult to give up any ownership, not to mention 22.5 percent. Some managers on the real estate staff, such as John Jursich, argued that Sonneborn was giving the company away for no reason, because McDonald's was getting all the mortgage money it wanted in smaller loans from local bankers. He was so upset over the move that he left the company soon afterward. Even Kroc was upset about the equity giveaway. "Ray was madder than hell," Sonneborn recalled. But Sonneborn's response persuaded Kroc to go ahead with the deal. "You've got to remember, Ray," Sonneborn said, "that seventy-eight percent of something is a lot better than one hundred percent of nothing, and nothing is what we've got now."

At the time of the loan in 1960, no one knew the value of 22.5 percent of something that Sonneborn had bartered to enter the financial big leagues. But when McDonald's went public five years later, it was clear that the insurers had made their best loan ever. On the day McDonald's went public, State Mutual and Paul Revere each owned $3.3 million of the chain's stock. During the next decade, both sold off all of their McDonald's holdings, not wishing to press their luck any further. Together, the insurers took capital gains on the stock of just under $20 million, and of course, their $1.5 million loan to McDonald's was paid off at the end of its fifteen-year term.

Buoyed by his McDonald's coup, Fedelli became one of the insurance industry's most progressive portfolio managers, and by 1979 he had risen to the presidency of State Mutual. Now, he recalls the McDonald's loan as the best investment he ever recommended. "It was a high just to persuade a group of older, conservative insurance directors that they should take this loan," he says. "It was as risky as anything they had ever seen up to that point." To keep his ego in check, however, Fedelli need only to remember that he also sold off all of State Mutual's McDonald's stock by the mid-1970s. While that produced a stunning capital gain of $12 million, Fedelli's loan to McDonald's would have been a veritable gold mine had State Mutual kept its 150,000 shares of McDonald's stock, then equal to 10 percent of the company's equity. Adjusted for splits, that much McDonald's stock today is worth more than $975 million.

Using twenty-twenty hindsight, Sonneborn had paid dearly for the prestige of a $1.5 million loan from major eastern insurers. He was so proud of the financing that he did not spend any of the borrowed capital for six months. Instead, he kept it as a very valuable dab of dressing on McDonald's balance sheet—something the company could use to obtain mortgage money from bankers who previously were hesitant to loan money to the chain. Now, when those bankers looked at McDonald's financial statements and saw a huge loan from established insurers, they were much more willing to finance McDonald's stores. If a company already has debt, Sonneborn realized, it's easier to get more.

The insurance loan gave McDonald's the access to institutional money that no other fast-food chain had. While Kroc's clean-cut operations specialists were distinguishing McDonald's as the industry's most advanced operator, Sonneborn's equally aggressive financial group was putting the company a decade ahead of its competitors in solving the most troubling problem facing the fledgling fast-food chains once the easy franchising money ran out: raising capital for expansion. While other companies struggled to obtain financing to build stores faster, McDonald's was the first to finance multiunit packages, the first to obtain major institutional loans, and the first to raise money by selling stock. Eventually, Burger King had sold out to Pillsbury, Burger Chef to General Foods, Pizza Hut and Taco Bell to Pepsico, Red Barn to Servomation, Big Boy to Marriott, and Hardee's to Imasco. By then, McDonald's had become a public company well on its way to financial independence. More than any other reason, it was the unpublicized financial savvy of Harry Sonneborn that explains why McDonald's remains today one of only two major fast-food chains whose stock—and destiny—is not controlled by a larger corporation. (Wendy's International is the other.)

Additional financing would not come easily. Indeed, the search for institutional money had really just begun when State Mutual and Paul Revere made their $1.5 million loan in 1961, and for the next ten years the financing of McDonald's growth was anything but guaranteed. But Sonneborn knew the hardest part was over because he could point to his first big loan as justification for even bigger loans from other institutions. He had opened the door to the big money, and during the 1960s and early 1970s, McDonald's walked through that door to finance the most massive store expansion in the history of retailing. "They gave away a lot of stock on the $1.5 million loan," concedes Dey Watts, a lawyer for the Chicago firm of Chapman and Cutler, which represented the two insurers on the loan and later was retained by Sonneborn as McDonald's outside attorney. But in return, Watts adds, "They got strong financial sponsorship that made everything else easier for them. If responsible institutions like this were going to give them seven percent money unsecured, why wouldn't others lend them money secured by hard real estate? This loan gave them credibility in the financial arena. They essentially built the company on it."

Chapter 8
THE BUYOUT

Dick McDonald was waiting for a response on the other end of the line. There was none. Ten seconds of telephone silence seemed like an eternity, and McDonald worried that he had lost the connection with his Chicago franchiser. McDonald had just informed Ray Kroc that he and his brother, Mac, wanted $2.7 million to sell the rights to their trade name and fast-food system to Kroc's company. They would accept no notes or multiyear payout; they wanted one payment—in cash. The brothers figured that would give them each $1 million after capital gains taxes were paid, and that was the figure they were determined to net from their role as founders of the fast-food industry.

McDonald could not wait any longer for Kroc to respond. "Are you still there, Ray?" he inquired. "Didn't you hear that racket?" Kroc answered. "That was the sound of me falling from the LaSalle-Wacker building to the pavement."

Kroc was burning up, but he refused to show his anger. "Dick, that's a hell of a price," Kroc continued pleasantly. "Tell me, what will you settle for?" That brought out the Yankee trader in Dick McDonald. "If we don't get $2.7 million," he countered, "we can't do it. That gives $1 million for Mac, $1 million for me, and $700,000 for Uncle Sam. We won't take a penny less."

At that moment, the ill feelings toward the McDonald brothers that Kroc had been harboring for a couple of years turned into outright contempt. Surely, he thought, the McDonalds knew that his company did not have the type of money they were demanding. Kroc was convinced that the brothers were simply taking a flier. "They put their figure high enough so that if I raised the purchase money, they would be very satisfied," Kroc explained years later. "But they thought I didn't have a chance of getting it."

That presumption was sound. The $2.7 million figure appeared outrageously high. The buyout discussions had begun in early 1961, and all 228 McDonald's had had sales the year before of $37.8 million. Of that the brothers had received 0.5 percent—or $189,000—which was their royalty for allowing Kroc's company the exclusive right to franchise their trade name and hamburger system. To forsake their right to uncertain future income from McDonald's, the brothers were demanding nearly fifteen times their current royalties.

Clearly, McDonald's had no way to generate such funds on its own. The company's meager $77,000 profit in 1960 did not even match the $100,000 the McDonald brothers earned that year at their San Bernardino drive-in. Furthermore, having just completed the $1.5 million loan with the Boston insurers, Kroc's company was already so deeply in debt that the chance of borrowing the purchase amount was almost nil. The company's $5.7 million in long-term debt was nearly twenty-two times greater than its skimpy $262,000 in equity. It was hard to fathom how McDonald's balance sheet could carry any more debt.

Still, by 1961 the buyout of the brothers had become an imperative for Kroc. In his haste to obtain the national rights to franchise the fast-food system that the McDonald brothers had developed, Kroc had donned a legal straitjacket. Company lawyers who later analyzed his contract with the brothers were astonished by its restrictions. Although Kroc was entering a totally new field—one that was changing daily and that, therefore, required enormous flexibility—his company legally had no room to maneuver.

The contract treated Kroc solely as a national licensing agent of the brothers, empowered only to sell licenses. There was not the slightest indication that Kroc's role was to develop a supply system, to supervise the operation of the licensed restaurants, to develop new products, procedures, and equipment, or even to select new sites for drive-ins. Indeed, it suggested that these functions were *not* part of Kroc's role. It was assumed that the fundamental elements of the brothers' system, which had worked in San Bernardino, needed no refinement when the system was exported to other markets around the country. Kroc had no authority to modify the system to meet the requirements of those new markets. The brothers' licensing agent, the contract read, "shall neither alter, modify or otherwise change, add to or delete from any portion of the said component parts of McDonald's Speedee System without the prior written approval" via registered letter from the McDonald brothers.

During the seven years that his McDonald's System, Inc., sold licenses for the brothers, Kroc repeatedly asked for approval of changes he deemed necessary. He rarely obtained verbal permission and never once got approval in writing as the contract required. Kroc knew that if he followed his contract to the letter, he had no chance of success in building a national hamburger chain. He concluded that the lawyer for the McDonald brothers was so intent on "protecting" them that he had drafted an unworkable contract.

Kroc did the only thing that any extreme pragmatist would do: he ignored the document. Indeed, his first official act as the national franchiser of McDonald's—selling his first franchise to himself—violated a provision in the contract that prohibited him from being a McDonald's licensee. But he concluded that the only way he could get a showcase store to display to prospective franchisees was to build one himself. Nor did his prototype store in Des Plaines conform to the McDonald brothers' design. In fact, it deviated from it on dozens of points—from its innovative use of milk shake machines to replace the brothers' hand-dipping procedures, to its heavier stainless steel counters designed by Schindler, to the use of a glass and stainless steel "winterfront" that enclosed a small area in front of the stand to shelter customers during Chicago's bitter winters. Kroc had even violated the contract by installing a furnace in the basement, since the San Bernardino store had no need for either a basement or a heater. While the brothers presumably understood the need for such basic changes, they never approved them in writing. Kroc was dumbfounded. "They just wouldn't answer me on the changes I proposed to make," Kroc explained years later. "There I was running the business, and the owners of the system wouldn't cooperate with me. So I said, 'The hell with 'em.' "

As McDonald's expanded, the contract violations multiplied. Although McDonald's remained surprisingly true to the brothers' formula during the first five years as far as outsiders could see, it had made hundreds of detailed changes designed to improve operations—all of them without written approval from the McDonald brothers. The brothers stubbornly refused to condone even minor changes. "If you have something that's successful and you start tinkering with it, it's a big mistake," Dick McDonald explains.

While the McDonalds never once threatened to use the violations of the contract to pull the licensing rights away from McDonald's System, Inc., neither did they lift the contractual cloud that hung over Kroc. If the McDonald brothers, for whatever reason, wanted to press a suit challenging the legitimacy of Kroc and his company as their franchising vehicle, there were plenty of grounds. Sonneborn desperately needed to remove that contractual risk in order to find additional major league financing.

In fact, the $1.5 million loan from State Mutual and Paul Revere was probably a fluke that would not be repeated until the company got contractual freedom. Even before the loan was approved, Dey Watts, then the attorney for the insurers, analyzed the company's agreement with the brothers and threw up a red flag. The McDonald brothers, he says, "had Ray and his company wrapped up so tight they couldn't breathe. It was obviously a business risk to lend to an entity that could not manage its own affairs. If McDonald's was living with that franchise agreement today, I doubt there is anything they sell that would be in compliance with it." The insurers accepted that risk only because they got 20 percent of McDonald's stock, a grant Kroc and Sonneborn vowed never again to make.

But McDonald's exposure under its master franchising contract went beyond financing. If the McDonald brothers won a suit charging Kroc with breach of contract, they could force his company to remove their name from its restaurants. Since the brothers held all of McDonald's franchises, Kroc would have to renegotiate a new agreement with all his franchisees, and they might just as easily decide to operate as direct franchisees of the brothers—not of Kroc's company. Fortunately, Sonneborn's real estate program was giving McDonald's control of the property at an increasing number of its outlets, which made any shift in franchiser allegiance difficult for the operators at those locations. But, while control of real estate blunted the risk of a suit by the brothers, it did not remove it. "It was a godawful contract," remembers Frank Bernard, an attorney with the firm of Sonnenschein, Carlin, Nath and Rosenthal, who had just been retained as McDonald's first legal counsel when he began advising Kroc to revise his contract with the brothers. "If Ray jeopardized his master license by violating the terms of the contract, it could put him out of business."

By 1960, Kroc's contract with the McDonald brothers was becoming threatening for another reason: it was approaching expiration. There were only four years remaining on its ten-year term, and although Kroc had an option to renew it for another ten years, renewal could be denied on the grounds of one of many technical violations of the original. Even without filing a lawsuit, Dick and Mac McDonald might attempt to deny renewal of the agreement in order to regain complete control over McDonald's franchisees. Kroc's company would be thrown into such disarray that its very survival would be at stake.

With the need for legal stability becoming critical, McDonald's in 1960 began renegotiating its contract with the brothers. Kroc wanted the term of the contract extended to ninety-nine years and the conditions modified to give him complete power to make changes in the franchised operations and a new authority to open nonfranchised stores operated by McDonald's. It was during the renegotiation process that Kroc ran head-on into Frank Cotter, the attorney for the McDonald brothers. Years later, Kroc would still recall Cotter for two things—first, as the brother of Jayne and Audrey Meadows; second, as his mortal enemy. As Kroc sought a freer hand in running McDonald's, Cotter gave him fits. "Cotter hated Kroc as much as Kroc hated him, and we were caught in the middle," recalls Dick McDonald.

Cotter would have none of the wording changes Kroc's lawyers proposed. "He was tough as nails," Frank Bernard says, recalling Cotter's insistence that the language of the original contract not be changed in the contract extension. Cotter took the same inflexible stance with his own clients, who were far more willing to yield. As Cotter saw it, Dick McDonald says, "Kroc wasn't going to get one iota of control. He was still just selling franchises and that was it."

Cotter's resistance to change was easy to understand from a legal standpoint. The only thing the brothers had that justified their 0.5 percent royalty was the control of the name and system that they gave Kroc to license. If Kroc made changes in that system over time, he could claim at some point that the system was his, not theirs. Kroc could merely rename his chain, relicense its operators, and cut the brothers off at their knees. So, Cotter insisted on a contract that gave his clients the upper hand if the Kroc-McDonald relationship ever wound up in court.

The overriding flaw was that the document was based on distrust, and businesses cannot survive on such a foundation. The contract worked only in the worst environment for business—the courthouse. It did not give McDonald's the flexibility to succeed in the marketplace. Kroc, of course, knew that, and the more he thought about the confining contract he had signed in 1954, the hotter he got. "What Ray wanted was control, so that he didn't have to come to us for anything," McDonald explains. "He felt that we were sitting in California getting a lot of money from McDonald's and really not doing anything for it. I could understand his feelings. In his position, I would feel absolutely the same way." Yet, the brothers followed their lawyer's advice anyway. "You should listen to your lawyer the way you listen to your doctor," McDonald reasons. "If you have an attorney and you don't listen to him, you might as well do your own legal work."

After tough negotiations, Kroc won only minor concessions. The new contract permitted "such changes in the blueprint plans which do not materially alter the basic design, size, layout or appearance" of the McDonald's drive-in. A second concession—allowing McDonald's to operate some units on its own without a franchisee—was far more important. Still, neither altered the fact that Kroc was in violation of the agreement for any changes he made in the McDonald's System without the approval of the brothers.

But it was the debate on the length of the revised contract that produced the greatest bitterness between Kroc and attorney Cotter. Kroc insisted on a contract that made McDonald's the national franchiser for the next ninety-nine years. Cotter would agree to only a twenty-year term, and to Kroc that constituted the last straw. "He just doesn't understand the trust we have in each other," Kroc told the McDonald brothers in a dictaphone tape. "He thinks twenty years is enough, but that boy's got a few things to learn." On that demand, the brothers for once refused to follow Cotter's advice. On February 5, 1960, they signed an agreement granting Kroc the national franchising rights for ninety-nine years.

But by then the damage was done. When he met the brothers in 1954, Kroc had a sincere admiration of their entrepreneurship, and in the early years their relationship was close. Kroc wanted to replicate with his franchisees the type of first-class operation the brothers ran in San Bernardino, and the brothers respected Kroc's efforts in that regard. But a once warm relationship gradually turned cool. Kroc was continually upset by what he thought was the brothers' naïveté toward business. He saw himself doing everything for them while they gave him precious little support in return. But the renegotiation of the contract had finally turned the Kroc-McDonald relationship icy cold. Kroc failed to get the freedom of operation he deemed essential, and now both he and Sonneborn were receptive to advice from their attorney. Says attorney Bernard: "Everybody by then was in agreement that if they ever wanted to make a real success of this business, they had to get the McDonald brothers out of their hair."

It was the pressing need for freedom that made Kroc accept acquisition terms he considered grossly unreasonable. Yet, the only demand that really upset him was the brothers' insistence on a cash purchase. That aside, Kroc believed the $2.7 million purchase price—though steep when compared to McDonald's size in 1961—was a bargain over the long term. Kroc had long talked confidently about building a chain of 1,000 stores, and with 250 already in operation by mid-1961, that goal no longer was as ludicrous as it had once seemed. McDonald's was growing at the rate of 100 new stores per year, and at that clip the 1,000-store mark would be reached before the end of the decade. Even if annual per-store sales did not grow beyond the current $210,000, it was likely that Kroc's company would be paying the brothers better than $1 million a year by the late 1960s.

If that progression made Kroc eager to buy the brothers out, it made the brothers even more eager to sell. Their royalty stream was subject to regular income tax rates, and at $1 million a year the brothers would have a huge annual tax liability. But a more menacing threat was the tax burden their estates would have to carry at the time of their death. "Dick, you and your brother had better stay healthy," one tax attorney told Dick McDonald, "because if you die in five years and you are earning royalties of one million dollars a year at the time of your death, Uncle Sam is going to value your estate at five times that. Where's your wife going to come up with that money? She'd have to sell everything she owns."

The McDonalds quickly decided that they were better off to convert their future royalty income—taxed at rates in excess of 50 percent —into a $2.7 million capital gain taxed at just 25 percent. That would give the brothers a tax-paid nest egg of $1 million each. The brothers knew that much greater wealth would be theirs simply by holding on to the rights to their fast-food system, but they saw nothing in great wealth but great worry—primarily about taxes. Dick McDonald would later reflect that he never regretted passing up the fabulous wealth that he and his brother would have earned by maintaining the McDonald's tie. "I would have wound up in some skyscraper somewhere with about four ulcers and eight tax attorneys trying to figure out how to pay all my income taxes," McDonald observes.

Clearly, the brothers' passion was simply to live comfortably, and they had that goal in hand. "From the time we had our broken-down theater in the Depression, I wanted complete financial security," McDonald says. " 'Boy,' I thought, 'how marvelous it would be never to have to worry about paying the rent.' Well, that day came. My brother and I had a garage full of Cadillacs, a home in Palm Springs, one in San

Bernardino, and another in Santa Barbara. I remember Mac asking me, 'What the hell can we do with five million that we can't do now?' "

Once Kroc accepted the acquisition terms, Bernard was instructed to begin work on a purchase agreement. But work on the buyout had just begun when Kroc ran into a major obstacle. He had called the brothers to nail down some final details on the acquisition when he made a casual reference to his plans for the brothers' drive-in in San Bernardino. What had made the $2.7 million price particularly appealing to Kroc was his belief that McDonald's would be getting ownership of the brothers' San Bernardino store. It was generating a profit of $100,000 per year, and that alone was worth about a third of the total acquisition cost.

"What do you mean, San Bernardino?" Dick McDonald asked. "San Bernardino is in this deal," Kroc insisted. "The hell it is," McDonald snapped. "But you said it was," Kroc demanded. "No, I did not, at no time," McDonald replied, explaining that he and Mac had always planned on giving their store (but not the property) to two longtime employees.

Kroc was furious with McDonald. He had counted on getting the store's cash flow, and he was convinced that that was part of the initial acquisition package. "Hell, I guess the deal is off," Kroc said as he hung up the phone. He could contain his rage no longer. "I closed the door to my office and paced up and down the floor calling them [the McDonalds] every kind of son of a bitch there was," Kroc reflected years later. "I was so mad I wanted to throw a vase through the window. I hated their guts." His mind raced through all the times when he had wanted their approval on changes and they had withheld it. He thought of the territorial franchise they had sold to the ice cream company in his hometown. He thought of their difficult lawyer. He thought of the seventy-hour weeks he was working and of the money the brothers were making—many times his modest 1960 income of $20,000. He thought of how rarely the brothers came to Chicago because they refused to fly. He had tolerated them for years, but now the brothers had gotten on Kroc's wrong side, and with Ray Kroc, that was always a permanent shift.

Despite his parting words to McDonald, Kroc never once thought of calling off the deal. "It was a lot of money to pay for a name," Kroc observed. "I suppose I could have called it 'McDougall's' and started over. But I was getting old—too old to fart around. I decided to take their deal anyway."

Agreeing to the McDonalds' cash price was one thing. Finding the money to pay for it was another. Had Sonneborn not lined up a $1.5 million loan a year before, there would have been no buyout because McDonald's would have been in no position to raise the cash the brothers were demanding. The buyout could be financed only by arranging another major borrowing. Furthermore, the loan would have to be completed within a matter of a few months. The value of the McDonald's franchising rights was growing daily, and the $2.7 million asking price would not stay on the table long.

The money from the first loan had already been committed to store expansion, but it provided McDonald's with its first contact with a pool of establishment money. Sonneborn wasted no time in trying to tap it again. He called John Gosnell, the senior investment officer at Paul Revere Life Insurance, which had provided half of the $1.5 million loan. Under that agreement, both Paul Revere and State Mutual had first right of refusal on any additional institutional financing McDonald's wanted to make. Gosnell quickly informed Sonneborn, however, that another large loan to McDonald's would concentrate too much of the insurer's investments in one company. But Paul Revere also now owned 10 percent of McDonald's, and it was in Gosnell's interest to find an investor who would welcome Sonneborn.

Gosnell knew just such an investor. His name was John Bristol, a Manhattan-based money manager who supervised investments for large trusts, particularly those of private universities and charitable foundations. Like his counterparts at State Mutual and Paul Revere, Bristol was always on the lookout for somewhat riskier investments that would produce higher yields than triple-A bonds. "We always thought we had the quality investments without the dressing of a fancy rating," Bristol explains.

Gosnell could not have picked a better candidate to provide the $2.7 million McDonald's needed. Aside from being more risk oriented than other institutional money managers, Bristol was enamored of McDonald's real estate play. He had invested his clients' money in hundreds of gasoline stations, which he purchased from major oil companies and leased back to them. Thus when Harry Sonneborn showed up in Bristol's New York office and began talking about McDonald's real estate, he was talking Bristol's language. "People in the East didn't understand the fast-food business, and the hamburger itself didn't have a good reputation," says Bristol, who had not heard of McDonald's when Sonneborn approached him for the $2.7 million loan. But Bristol was fascinated by Sonneborn's concept of mixing real estate and hamburgers. "Harry was very impressive to an investment man," Bristol observes. "He got across the idea that McDonald's was building substantial value in real estate and that the franchisee was on the hook to lease property from them for a much longer period than it would take McDonald's to pay off its real estate purchases. Harry knew that business."

At last, Sonneborn had found someone who fully appreciated the merit of his real estate plan. Fortunately, Bristol also controlled the big money Sonneborn needed to raise—and fast. Among other things, Bristol managed the investment portfolio of Princeton University, which even then was valued in excess of $100 million. He also managed the trust funds of such other private schools as Colby College, Howard University, Syracuse University, the Institute of Advanced Study at Princeton, and Swarthmore College. Bristol also managed investments for a variety of charitable foundations, such as the Good Will Home Association; the Samuel S. Fels Fund, a charity set up by the founder of the Fels-Naphtha soap business; the New World Foundation, founded by the granddaughter of Cyrus McCormick; and the Bulletin Contributionship, the charitable foundation for the old *Philadelphia Bulletin*. He even handled investments for the pension fund of Sharpless Corporation (later part of Penwalt) and the profit-sharing fund of J. Walter Thompson.

It was an extremely diversified clientele, and one that was much more likely to be investing in AT&T bonds. Yet, after hearing Sonneborn's pitch, Bristol decided to recommend to all twelve of his major clients that they make the $2.7 million loan to a hamburger chain none of them knew.

Sonneborn had been searching for old-line eastern money for more than three years, and in John Bristol he found it in spades. Here was the type of money that had been earning interest for at least a half-century, and Bristol was about to introduce it to the brand-new world of fast food. Bristol devised a loan package under which Princeton would put up $1 million while the eleven other college, charitable, and pension funds that Bristol managed would split up the rest. To sell the loan to his clients, he drafted a well-researched financial analysis of McDonald's, predicting that the chain might eventually have fifteen hundred units nationwide. Under a complex bonus plan that was built into the loan proposal and calculated on McDonald's sales growth, Bristol estimated that over the fifteen-year life of the $2.7 million loan, the investors could get back on their investment anywhere from $7.1 million to $9 million—a return ranging from 150 percent to 225 percent.

Given that, Bristol strongly recommended the loan, and soon he had separate approvals from all his major clients. As McDonald's lawyers hurried to wrap up the negotiations that would allow the company to break free of the McDonald brothers, Kroc and his managers developed an internal nickname for Bristol's clients: the Twelve Apostles.

They had good reason to be overjoyed. Sonneborn had defied the enormous odds against a thinly capitalized company like McDonald's attempting to take on such a heavy debt. But the loan from the Twelve Apostles was even more unusual because of the way it was structured. Easily one of the most intricate private placements ever made, the $2.7 million financing accomplished several conflicting goals. Sonneborn had succeeded in resisting the demand for an equity kicker similar to the one that had been provided to State Mutual and Paul Revere. An equity bonus to the lenders seemed to be an essential inducement for a loan of this size and risk, but Kroc, Sonneborn, and Martino were dead set against further diluting their ownership. To solve that, Sonneborn opted for a bonus payment plan, which provided the investors with all the added incentive they needed to make the loan and gave McDonald's plenty of incentive to pay it off early. Remarkably, the loan package achieved all this while still improving McDonald's cash position.

Under the proposed agreement, McDonald's would borrow $2.7 million at 6 percent interest and pay off the loan with monthly payments equal to 0.5 percent of the chain's total food sales. That was the same amount McDonald's was already paying each month in royalties to the McDonald brothers. The length of time it took McDonald's to pay off the entire principal and interest on the $2.7 million at that rate of repayment would determine the length of a bonus period in which McDonald's would make additional monthly payments to the lenders as an incentive for making the loan. The monthly bonus payments also would be equal to 0.5 percent of McDonald's sales. Thus if it took McDonald's eight years to pay off the principal and interest on the loan, as Bristol projected, it would pay the lenders the bonus for *another* eight years. Since McDonald's growth might be explosive in the bonus period, it was likely that the size of the bonus would be several times greater than the loan.

Richard Boylan, the accountant Sonneborn had hired to help

manage finances, added a subtle final twist to the loan that would greatly ease McDonald's severe cash squeeze. He proposed that McDonald's would defer 20 percent of the payments due during the loan repayment and bonus phases to a third period that would begin when the first two were completed. Thus, while McDonald's would *owe* the lenders 0.5 percent of the sales during the first and second phase, it would actually *pay* them only 0.4 percent at the time and withhold the remaining 0.1 percent until the third period, when, presumably, McDonald's cash crunch would have abated. In short, McDonald's would be buying out the McDonald brothers through a loan that required McDonald's to pay 20 percent less per month to the lenders than it presently was paying in royalties to the brothers. By any measurement, the deal was a grand coup for Sonneborn. As soon as it appeared to be consummated, he and his wife, Aloyis, along with others involved in arranging the loan, celebrated with an impromptu vacation in Las Vegas.

The celebration was premature. Sonneborn had just settled in at the crap table when he got an emergency call from June Martino: the loan had been killed. A committee of executives representing the twelve institutional lenders had gathered in New York to give what was expected to be a perfunctory approval of the $2.7 million McDonald's financing. Instead, they had decided that a loan to a food service company was simply too risky.

Sonneborn immediately called Bristol and requested a meeting with the investor group the next morning on Wall Street. He boarded a red-eye flight to LaGuardia, and on the plane he put together a presentation he hoped would rescue the loan that he knew was crucial to McDonald's future. Without freeing itself from the McDonald brothers, his company would never be able to finance its national expansion in time to maintain its edge on Burger Chef, Burger King, and Kentucky Fried Chicken—all of which were pursuing their own plans for building national fast-food chains.

Sonneborn arrived in New York at 9:00 A.M., unshaven and without any sleep the night before. He grabbed a helicopter shuttle in order to make it to his 10:00 A.M. meeting in the Wall Street office of Dean Mathey, an investment banker who specialized in oil investments and who had helped form Louisiana Land and Exploration, one of the country's largest independent oil explorers. Mathey also was chairman of Princeton University's investment committee. As soon as Sonneborn arrived, he knew he was in trouble. "Would you like a drink?" Mathey asked. It's ten o'clock in the morning, Sonneborn thought. Why is this guy trying to give me whiskey, if not to confuse me?

Quickly, Sonneborn knew who had organized the last-minute opposition to the loan. "Mr. Sonneborn," Mathey began, "we are turning down this loan because we are not about to lend money to anybody in the food service business. The percentage of failures in the restaurant business is higher than any other."

Sonneborn had heard that objection on dozens of his other attempts to finance McDonald's, and he was ready for it. "Mr. Mathey, I think you misunderstand the real nature of McDonald's," Sonneborn answered firmly. "We are not basically in the food business. We are in the real estate business. The only reason we sell fifteen-cent hamburgers is because they are the greatest producer of revenue from which our tenants [McDonald's franchisees] can pay us our rent. There is nothing else that will produce the volume that food sales will, and all of our leases are based on a percentage of food sales. You can see the sales results of our units. That's the proof of what I'm telling you."

For about an hour, Sonneborn continued to explain the real estate side of the business and to deny the significance of the food side except as a producer of rent dollars. It revealed just how sharply Sonneborn's approach to McDonald's differed from that of Kroc. Kroc was caught up in the romance of the hamburger business. Sonneborn was not. Viewing McDonald's as a real estate company was close to heresy for the chain's founder.

Heretical or not, Sonneborn's view of the business was the only one that appealed to a financially oriented executive like Mathey. After making his appeal, an exhausted Sonneborn told the group that he had been up all night and needed to use the bathroom. "I was scared to death that the loan was lost, and it was written all over my face," Sonneborn recalled. When the group made its decision on the loan, one member decided that Sonneborn should not be kept in suspense any longer. Standing at a urinal in the men's room, Sonneborn learned McDonald's fate. "Harry, you made one hell of a case," the committee member told Sonneborn. "We've just approved your loan."

Within weeks, the brothers were showing close friends and business associates the $1 million checks that each received from the buyout. The moment the deal was completed, Kroc unleashed the frustrations that had built up during his seven years of dealing with the brothers. He hopped on a plane to Los Angeles, bought a piece of property at Fifteenth and E—one block away from the brothers' seminal fast-food drive-in—and ordered the construction of a brand-new McDonald's store. It had only one purpose: to put the McDonald brothers' unit out of business. The brothers were forced to take down the McDonald's sign—since Kroc's company now owned their trade name —and the original McDonald's was renamed the Big M.

While on the West Coast to select the new site, Kroc paid a visit to Art Bender, McDonald's franchisee in Fresno, who more than anyone else understood the roots of Kroc's frustrations with the brothers. Bender had been with McDonald's from the beginning, serving as the first counterman for the brothers when they converted their San Bernardino drive-in to a fast-food business in 1948. The brothers had loaned his services to Kroc to help him get Des Plaines opened in 1955, and one year later Bender became Kroc's first franchisee. As Bender and Kroc reminisced, it was clear that Kroc could not let go of his anger at the brothers. "Art, I'm normally not a vindictive man," Kroc told Bender. "But this time I'm going to get those sons of bitches."

Kroc had his way. The brothers had rebuilt their octagonal store in 1955 to give it the new red-and-white look and the golden arches that Dick McDonald had developed. Kroc's store just one block away looked exactly the same and featured the exact same menu and food preparation techniques. The only difference was that the new store now carried the McDonald's name.

That made all the difference. Many of the patrons of the first unit assumed that it had been moved to the new site and they moved their business there. The new San Bernardino McDonald's experienced relatively modest sales, but it nevertheless had a devastating effect on the original McDonald's. Sales at the Big M—now controlled by two long-time employees—plummeted as soon as the new McDonald's opened in mid-1962. In 1967, the store that had set the food service business on its ear by ringing up annual sales of better than $400,000 during the 1950s reported a meager $81,000 in sales. In early 1968, it was sold to Neal Baker, who runs a local fast-food chain specializing in hamburgers and tacos. But Baker could not turn the unit around and he closed it in 1970. Today, the only remnant is the sign that the brothers had erected in front of their drive-in. Instead of broadcasting the number of hamburgers sold, it now reads THE MUSIC BOX, the name of the music store that occupies the site of the birthplace of the fast-food industry.

Where are the McDonald brothers today? Mac (Maurice), the operations specialist on the team, died in 1971. Richard, who much preferred dreaming up new marketing concepts, lives in Bedford, New

Hampshire, where he retired after selling out to McDonald's. Although he has lived quite comfortably by any standard, McDonald became the first of dozens of managers, operators, suppliers, and investors who missed out on millions simply by pulling out of McDonald's too early. Obviously, he benefited by investing his $1 million in cash, but no new investment was likely to come close to the one he gave up.

If McDonald had not sold his right to the 0.5 percent of McDonald's sales that was due him and Mac under their ninety-nine-year contract with Kroc, he would have become one of the country's wealthiest men, almost as wealthy as Ray Kroc. Since the brothers sold their rights for $2.7 million in late 1961, McDonald's restaurants have rung up a total of $198 billion in sales. The royalty payments that would have been due the McDonald brothers had they not sold out come to a total of $990 million. Today, the McDonalds would be earning more than $109 million a year in royalties on their fast-food system. Although Kroc could not have known it then, on the day he bought out the brothers, he had gotten all the revenge he needed.

Much more important was the fact that Kroc's company now had its freedom. It did not come cheaply. Although McDonald's paid off the $2.7 million loan in five and a half years—almost three years sooner than Bristol had projected—its bonus payments to Bristol's clients still brought the total cost of the financing to $14 million. Yet, without the freedom to expand with big league financing, to add new products to the menu, and to change the look of the drive-in to respond to the demands of the market, McDonald's almost surely would have been one of dozens of also-rans in the fast-food business. In short, when the buyout was completed on December 28, 1961, McDonald's had the flexibility it needed to attempt to dominate the industry the brothers had created.

At that moment, McDonald's was easily the industry's largest chain, but at least a dozen other chains still had a shot at becoming the dominant competitor over the long term. With only 323 restaurants in operation in forty-four states—fully two-thirds of which were in states bordering the Great Lakes—McDonald's was still a long way from establishing its hegemony in the fast-food market. In fact, most of the country's consumers still had not been told about McDonald's, much less been sold on it. But as it ended its ties to the brothers who had started it all, McDonald's now had the opportunity to market the chain as it saw fit. It wasted no time exploiting it.

Chapter 9
PARTNERS

The buyout of the McDonald brothers had given Ray Kroc complete control over his McDonald's franchised restaurants. His team of field service lieutenants enforced operating discipline the way no other fast-food chain could. His franchise plan was airtight—franchisees were given no exclusive territories, just one restaurant at a time, and if they failed to toe the line they got no additional restaurants. Kroc's corporate staff controlled all standards for restaurant operations. Harry Sonneborn had even given McDonald's control of real estate, something no other franchise chain had yet considered. And, thanks to Sonneborn's financial maneuvers, McDonald's had the money to expand without being at the mercy of financiers.

In fact, by 1960 McDonald's was ready for its first major move outside franchising and toward complete control over some restaurants—as both owner and operator. In 1959, McDonald's had backed into ownership of a franchise when it took over a failing unit in Brentwood, Missouri, from Milo Kroc, a distant cousin of the founder. But one year later, the chain opened the first four of its so-called McOpCo (McDonald's Operating Company) units—four new company-owned and company-managed stores in Columbus, Ohio. A shopping center developer had offered to develop the four sites for McDonald's provided the stores were operated by the company instead of a franchisee. McDonald's agreed because Sonneborn liked the real estate deal and because Turner wanted some company-controlled outlets as training ground for his field consultants.

But Ray Kroc hoped the very presence of the four "controlled units," as he referred to them, would encourage wayward McDonald's franchisees to clean up their act. At times, it appeared that only practical considerations kept him from building an entire chain of company-owned stores devoid of franchisees. "If I felt that if we could finance the things and grow rapidly enough, I would darn near be in favor of never selling another franchise," Kroc told Dick and Mac McDonald at the time. "Even a good licensee operation," he added, "will never be as good as a company-controlled unit because when a guy has some of his money in the place, he wants to have something to say about that place."

If financing made a chain of company-owned stores a fantasy, Kroc nevertheless was now in a position to dictate all McDonald's policy from his corporate office on the twentieth floor of 221 North LaSalle. In fact, viewed from the outside, centralized control seemed to be a passion with Ray Kroc.

That was not the view from the inside. To be sure, Kroc had demanded and obtained a level of control over unit operations that was unparalleled in franchising. But when it came to keeping McDonald's in touch with the market, Kroc had an innate sense—a salesman's sense—that the promotion, advertising, and new product development could not be dictated by a corporate staff. To succeed in marketing, Kroc believed, McDonald's had to reach out and respond to each market. Marketing ideas had to come from the grass roots, not the blue sky. In short, Kroc realized that for McDonald's to capitalize on the market opportunity it now had, his company had to rely on the creativity of its partners—its franchisees and suppliers.

There were two good reasons for that. For one thing, the mass-marketing of a national fast-food chain was clearly not the science that operations was. It was an art—one that no one knew anything about. When McDonald's ran its first television advertisements in a handful of markets in the late 1950s, it was entering virgin territory. Restaurants did not advertise at all on television and not much anywhere else. Food service businesses relied mostly on word of mouth promotion. Their formal marketing programs had not advanced beyond ads in the Yellow Pages and on sandwich boards. Thus, when it came to marketing, Kroc correctly thought that the more new ideas he could get flowing into his company—no matter what the source—the better off he was.

But there was a more pragmatic explanation for Kroc's reliance on his partners for advertising and new product development: McDonald's corporate staff had focused so hard on operations and finance that it had developed very little expertise in marketing.

Clearly, Kroc himself was not particularly gifted in advertising and new product development. Although obviously sales oriented, he was at his best when he was making a sale face to face. He had no command of how to use advertising media, and even when McDonald's began to develop that skill, Kroc was not a central part of the process.

While Kroc's personal search for new products was a constant preoccupation, it was also a source of continuous frustration. He instinctively knew that new products could be used to broaden the appeal of McDonald's, but he himself was not blessed with a new product touch. The only consistency to his new product ideas for his fast-food chain was in their dismal record of failure.

Kroc was absolutely convinced that a dessert was needed to round out the McDonald's menu, and during the late 1950s he proposed brownies, strawberry shortcake, and pound cake. When he introduced pound cake, he predicted that individual stores would sell as many as a thousand of the 15-cent "loaves" a day. As it turned out, cake sales throughout the entire chain never reached that level, and the product was unceremoniously dumped from the menu. When he added kolacky to the menu at some stores, his judgment was based on personal tastes acquired through his Bohemian upbringing. Unfortunately, the mass market did not share Kroc's enthusiasm for the Eastern European pastry.

Sensing a need for a nonmeat product for Fridays, Kroc concocted a sandwich consisting of grilled pineapple and two slices of cheese on a toasted bun. Attempting to preserve McDonald's all-hamburger image, he made the new product sound like a natural extension of the hamburger line. He called it the Hulaburger. Like his other food inventions, the Hulaburger bombed. Despite his status as a master salesman, Ray Kroc was no new product genius.

Nor was Kroc as devoted to building a marketing staff as he was to hiring operations and real estate specialists. The company's first marketing chief was Don Conley, who functioned primarily as licensing vice president and secondarily as corporate pilot. In marketing, he had little time to do much more than provide a few newspaper and billboard ads and direct-mail promotions, some of which featured paintings by Austin White, well known for his Rockwellesque artwork for Coca-Cola. While McDonald's paid $100,000 for five paintings, it was hardly a big budget advertising commitment, since the company did not advertise itself but rather provided the materials to franchisees to use in their local media.

Although the name McDonald's is now synonymous with high-powered television advertising, the company's ad program was anything but high-powered during its first decade. It did not appoint its first advertising director, John Horn, until 1961, and it was not until 1963 that it ran its only national ad before becoming a public company—a one-page advertisement in *Reader's Digest*. It was not until then that it produced its first television commercials, which consisted of two thirty-second animated spots showing "Archie McDonald" dancing around a McDonald's counter. A similar character called Speedee had been developed by the McDonald brothers and added to the drive-in's sign, but Horn had the character redesigned and renamed because it closely resembled Speedy Alka-Seltzer, a name no food service chain wanted to be identified with. Even those spots, however, were run only by a few franchisees who bought the commercials from the company and purchased television time for them in local markets. McDonald's —now the nation's third largest television advertiser—did not retain its first major advertising agency, D'Arcy Advertising, until 1964 and did not develop a national advertising program until 1967, the year it formed a marketing department.

Despite the absence of aggressive corporate marketing, McDonald's Corporation nevertheless played a key role in marketing by setting the tone for its partners to follow. Operationally, McDonald's was in a position to build the country's first nationwide restaurant chain, and Kroc was determined not to blow that opportunity for lack of creative marketing. Although Kroc demanded strict uniformity in operating standards, experimentation by franchisees with new products and promotions was encouraged and rewarded, not stifled. And while McDonald's did no national advertising, Kroc prodded franchisees to do more and more local advertising. By 1959, the franchise contract required operators to spend 2.5 percent of their sales to promote their stores. The new rule made McDonald's one of the first of the new fast-food chains to mandate advertising expenditures by its franchisees. (The advertising contribution was raised to 4 percent in 1969.)

More important, Kroc taught his franchisees a lesson in aggressive promotion by the way he personally sought press publicity for McDonald's. In 1957, Kroc retained the Chicago public relations firm of Cooper, Burns and Golin to obtain press publicity for his new hamburger chain. The fee—$500 a month—was not large even by late-1950s standards, but for a company of McDonald's size (1957 revenues of $243,000), it was an enormous amount to spend just to get its name in the newspaper. Indeed, Harry Sonneborn was furious that Kroc would spend so much on what he believed was a frivolous expense.

But Kroc argued that McDonald's was not a typical consumer business, not even a typical restaurant. The unique speed of its service combined with the fishbowl effect of the drive-in's design made a visit to a McDonald's an entertainment event—the customers' first glimpse of a commercial kitchen in action. "McDonald's," Kroc repeatedly told his franchisees and managers, "is not in the restaurant business; it's in show business."

To publicize that, Kroc could not have picked a more appropriate team than Max Cooper, Ben Burns, and Al Golin, and the $500 a month he paid them resulted in some of the best free advertising a company ever got. Today, it is fashionable for public relations firms to consider themselves financial relations specialists. They talk about their clients' price-earnings ratios and return on equity, and the best of them know how to use the business press to get to their primary audience: investors. By contrast, Kroc had retained a more traditional public relations firm, one whose unabashed purpose was to get publicity for publicity's sake. "It was post-press agentry and pre-public relations," explains Cooper, now a McDonald's franchisee in Birmingham, Alabama. "There was an interim period called 'publicity,' and that's what we did."

Cooper and Golin were particularly suited to publicize a venture with an entertainment angle and with an owner who possessed a show business flair. Cooper had formed the firm in the mid-1950s by specializing in writing gag lines as a means of getting his local show business clients quoted in Chicago's gossip columns, primarily Irv Kupcinet's column in the *Sun-Times* and Herb Lyon's "Tower Ticker" column in the *Chicago Tribune*.

Golin, too, had been schooled in press agentry, spending most of his pre-McDonald's career as a publicity agent for MGM in the post–World War II days when the studio referred to such specialists rather shamelessly as "exploitation" people. Golin's job at MGM—touring with film stars to promote their movies—converted him into the classic publicist Kroc wanted: the kind who spends his time looking for ways to get his client's name in the newspaper rather than figuring ways to keep it out. Golin remembers picking up Clark Gable at a Chicago train station along with a since-forgotten actress who complained of the tedium of dealing with fans demanding autographs. "Honey," said Gable, "things only get tedious when they stop asking you."

Kroc's new public relations firm followed Gable's philosophy in publicizing McDonald's. Within a few years of getting the account,

Cooper, Burns and Golin succeeded in getting stories run on McDonald's and Kroc in scores of local newspapers, in nationally syndicated newspaper columns, and finally, in 1961, in the press agent's big-time arena: *Time* magazine.

Some of their methods seem outlandish by today's standards, but they regularly got McDonald's media attention for a fraction of the cost of advertising. As trivial as some of their techniques appeared, the Cooper-Burns-Golin publicity campaign was cleverly designed to make the name of McDonald's synonymous with hamburgers.

Not long after they got the account, Kroc's name began appearing regularly in Chicago's gossip columns along with whimsical witticisms designed to catch the reader's eye—and to plug McDonald's. "Ray Kroc, boss of the McDonald's drive-in chain, says a chiropractor is a slipped-disk jockey," read one gag line published in Lyon's column in the *Chicago Tribune*. And Kup's column in the *Sun-Times* featured the following: "Ray (McDonald's drive-in) Kroc observes that there's nothing more exasperating than a wife who can cook and won't—unless it's a wife who can't cook and will!"

McDonald's publicity team also prepared press kits showing operators how to get the same free newspaper coverage for McDonald's in their markets. Among other things, they contained press releases highlighting McDonald's impressive hamburger production figures and presenting them in a colorful context. The amount of flour used to bake the buns that McDonald's has sold would fill the Grand Canyon, one release said, while another noted that the ketchup used by the chain would fill Lake Michigan. Invariably, the releases calculated how many times the billions of hamburgers sold would stretch to the moon.

Eventually Turner would halt what he disparagingly called "burgers-to-the-moon publicity," but it fascinated reporters for years. Even *Time* magazine fell victim to such a trivial pursuit when it began its 1973 cover story on McDonald's by noting that the 12 billion hamburgers McDonald's had sold could "form a pyramid 783 times the size of the one erected by Snefru." And, *Time* continued, "If all the cattle that have ever laid down their lives for McDonald's were to be resurrected for a reunion, they would stand flank-by-jowl over an area larger than Greater London."

Cooper, Burns and Golin also attempted to establish McDonald's as the world's unquestioned authority on hamburgers—a position they then exploited mercilessly to generate publicity. Each year, for example, McDonald's published a "national" hamburger survey that reported—down to the tenth of a decimal—how many hamburgers the "average American" consumed in a week. No one else had such figures, and even the American Meat Institute accepted them as gospel. McDonald's never revealed that its hamburger statistics were based solely on interviews with a couple of hundred Chicagoans surveyed by its publicity agents.

Surprisingly, such trivia was eagerly consumed by the public and the press. Everyone had taken hamburgers for granted; here was an outfit that took them seriously. Publicist Golin explains, "No one expected hamburgers to be big business, and so there was shock value to McDonald's numbers."

In dozens of other cases, McDonald's got free publicity simply by tracing the origin of the hamburger to a period before its popularly accepted genesis—the St. Louis World's Exposition in 1904. According to Cooper-Burns-Golin news releases, the product originated with Russian sailors who popularized in the port city of Hamburg, Germany, one of their staple meals—sandwiches made of raw scraps of beef. That the story made for good publicity was more important than the fact that it was not universally accepted. When McDonald's served up a hamburger to the mayor of Hamburg in a mid-1960s publicity stunt to celebrate the "return" of the product to the city of its birth, the German mayor had an easier time swallowing the hamburger than he did McDonald's story of its beginnings. "What is *this* hamburger?" asked the burghermeister. "*I* am a Hamburger." The quote—and McDonald's name—appeared in newspapers throughout Germany the next day.

But the key to McDonald's extensive press coverage was not so much its clever press agents as it was its colorful founder. Kroc could charm reporters with his dream of building an empire based on 15-cent hamburgers. Recognizing that Kroc's personality attracted press coverage, Golin dogged journalists, hoping just to get their agreement to meet Kroc. He was convinced that if he could get that far, Kroc's salesmanship would win the day. Golin says: "Ray was a public relations man's dream."

The big break came in 1959 when Golin lined up an interview for Kroc with Hal Boyle, the late Pulitzer Prize–winning feature writer for the Associated Press whose column was then the most widely syndicated feature in the United States. Golin realized how Boyle had earned his reputation as New York's most disorganized journalist. For months, he called Boyle each week to determine if he had gotten the

McDonald's press kit he had sent. Each week Boyle misplaced it, and Golin dispatched another—a half dozen in all.

But he finally succeeded in persuading Boyle to meet with Kroc, and the McDonald's founder readily agreed to make a special trip to New York. To be safe, Golin showed up a day early to remind Boyle of the interview. "Are we still all set for the interview tomorrow?" Golin asked Boyle. "With whom?" Boyle asked. Golin, mustering his patience, calmly reminded Boyle of the lunch date he had with Kroc the following day. "I can't make it," Boyle demurred. "That's the annual AP lunch, and I have to be there." Golin suggested an alternative interview in the morning in the editorial office of the AP, and Boyle consented.

When Kroc showed up at Boyle's desk the next morning, he walked into the typical bedlam of an open city room. With dozens of reporters rushing to meet late-morning deadlines, phones were ringing and typewriters were clacking. But Kroc, whose high-pitched voice typically was raised several decibels above normal in an unconscious reaction to a slight hearing problem, had no trouble communicating over the din of city room traffic. And when he got into his sales pitch on McDonald's, it was obvious that Kroc had captured more than just Boyle's attention. One by one, the typewriters around Boyle's desk were silenced as reporters gathered around to hear about 15-cent hamburgers.

Suddenly, Boyle's desk was surrounded by a dozen AP staffers, some asking how they could get a McDonald's. Boyle had showed little interest in McDonald's at first. But, Golin says, "when he saw the reaction of other reporters, he knew he had something." The interview went on for an hour and a half, and the next day Boyle's column carried a glowing feature on McDonald's that appeared in more than six hundred newspapers. "I put the hamburger on the assembly line," Boyle quoted Kroc.

It was the first national press that the chain had received, and within days the company was flooded with franchise applications. Recruiting McDonald's licensees had never been a serious problem, but national publicity was creating a "problem" of too many applicants. The waiting list of approved applicants swelled to well over one hundred, and some of them waited two years for a restaurant.

Boyle's article had a domino effect. McDonald's was suddenly showered with free publicity it could not buy at any price. Reporters from other national news organizations who had been courted by Golin without success soon were hounding him for interviews. *Time, Life, Newsweek, The Wall Street Journal,* and *Forbes* all wanted interviews with Kroc, and he never failed to spellbind them.

Interviews with Kroc, however, were not the only means of generating free publicity. Charity was another. Franchisees were advised to become involved with the favorite charities of their local newspapers —a surefire way of getting mentioned in the press coverage of any fund-raising activity. Press kits from Cooper, Burns and Golin were sent to operators suggesting different community relations programs to appeal to different markets. For example, donating hamburger profits to pay for band uniforms was suggested as a way to appeal to a family-oriented market while at the same time obtaining the support of an army of youthful volunteers to promote adult patronage for the drive-ins. The kits also contained suggestions on how to get press coverage for the programs and particularly on how to stage press photos.

Indeed, the more picture possibilities a charity provided, the better. During the late 1950s, Turner and other managers toured Chicago's Loop in a vehicle called the "Santa Wagon," an ice cream vending truck converted into the rolling likeness of a McDonald's drive-in, complete with golden arches. The managers grilled hamburgers and made coffee, and at stops along the route they fed the streetcorner Santas of the Salvation Army. A photo of the Santa Wagon always made the Chicago papers.

Golin concluded that such community involvement was a far more efficient form of promotion than advertising was. "At first, the stores were too scattered for the operators to pool their resources for cooperative advertising," Golin recalls. "They had to promote individually, and they couldn't afford to reach the same market with advertising that they were reaching for a lot less money with community relations."

Supporting a visible charity was not just a cheap form of advertising, it was better. For a drive-in chain looking to appeal to a family market and seeking respectability in an industry burdened with a questionable reputation, the community involvement by local operators produced the type of image-boosting publicity that McDonald's needed. Yet, their early community service work had a single motivation: selling hamburgers. "We got into it for very selfish reasons," Fred Turner remembers. "It was an inexpensive, imaginative way of getting your name before the public and building a reputation to offset the image of selling fifteen-cent hamburgers. It was probably ninety-nine percent commercial."

But what started out as a corporate marketing strategy soon grew into a grass-roots movement. Local franchisees began developing their own ways to promote their stores through charitable deeds. In a few years, the corporation acted merely as a clearinghouse for community relations ideas developed—and proven successful—by local operators. When one licensee struck public relations paydirt with a practice of contributing free orange drink for local organizations to sell at fundraisers, McDonald's operators throughout the country began sponsoring "Orange Bowls," so called for the automated glass mixers used to dispense the orange drink. Since uniformed crewmen dispensed the drinks, it was an effective way of showcasing McDonald's fast service.

Once operators got turned on to the idea of community involvement, there was no turning them off. Their participation in local benefits—from bands to schools to scouts to hospitals—became something of an epidemic inside the McDonald's System. When advertising became a practical and affordable marketing tool for McDonald's, community involvement took on a meaning outside of promotion.

Most of McDonald's community work is initiated by local operators and without pressure from the company, which itself gave more than $700,000 to charities in 1991. Still, most operators treat community relations as a sine qua non of a McDonald's franchise, and public relations expert Golin believes that is explained by a fundamental psychological need. "It gives individual operators a sense of personal identity in a business where that identity can easily be lost," he reasons. "By getting involved in a community charity, an operator can get individual recognition and become 'Mr. McDonald's' in his hometown."

Whatever the motivation, the community relations work has become one of the most powerful weapons in McDonald's impressive marketing arsenal, and it was individual franchisees who made it so. For example, it was the operators—not the company—who developed and expanded McDonald's most visible charity—Ronald McDonald Houses. Located adjacent to children's hospitals, the houses provide free or low-cost room and board for families with children requiring extended hospital care. The idea was conceived by Elkman Advertising, the ad agency for McDonald's operators in Philadelphia, in response to a plea from former Philadelphia Eagle linebacker Fred Hill. Hill, whose daughter Kim had been hospitalized for leukemia, realized the hardship on families with hospitalized children and was seeking support to build a home away from home for them in Philadelphia. The McDonald's operators raised $50,000 for the first Ronald McDonald House, which opened in Philadelphia in 1974. Today, there are 162 Ronald McDonald Houses in 12 countries—all sponsored by local franchisees—that have served more than 1.5 million family members.

When Ray Kroc died in 1984, the company created Ronald McDonald Children's Charities (RMCC), a charitable foundation to continue Kroc's legacy of giving back to communities by helping children and families. Since its inception, RMCC has awarded more than $100 million to thousands of children's organizations.

When the operators took control of McDonald's community relations work early on, it was but the first sign that they intended to dominate McDonald's marketing—at least during the first critical decade when the chain formed its image with consumers. After his early disappointments with investor-oriented franchisees, Kroc by the late 1950s had begun to shift the focus of licensee recruitment toward struggling entrepreneurs. Because they had everything at risk in McDonald's, Kroc thought, they were more motivated to work behind the counter themselves and adhere to McDonald's operating regimen. But, while it was adopted for operating reasons, the new licensing policy was also paying unexpected dividends in marketing. The entrepreneurial franchisees were suddenly coming up with all the good marketing concepts. Kroc was not about to resist them, because the local operators were promoting McDonald's far more effectively than was his Chicago staff.

Why its franchisees became such an innovative and influential force in McDonald's marketing is a matter of speculation. One explanation is that most McDonald's operators did not come from traditional restaurant backgrounds and thus were not bound by the industry's tradition of word of mouth promotion. Indeed, many had left backgrounds in sales and advertising to become McDonald's licensees, and to them, promoting McDonald's was not unlike marketing any other product. If McDonald's marketing was more creative, it was only because the franchisees did not know any better.

It also appears that McDonald's operators realized that marketing was their one opportunity to vent their individual creativity in a system that otherwise offered little chance for self-expression. Everything else —right down to the temperature required for french fries—was prescribed in the manual, and Kroc objected to any deviation from the chain's operating regimen. And once he saw the marketing skills of some of his entrepreneurial franchisees, Kroc essentially made an unwritten pact with them based on a simple trade-off: their strict adherence to McDonald's operating rules in exchange for nearly complete freedom in marketing.

Once he displayed his belief in aggressive promotion, Kroc's franchisees put McDonald's on the road to becoming the food service industry's most creative marketer. No single franchisee discovered the mass-marketing potential of McDonald's, but one of the most important of the system's advertising innovators was Jim Zien. Although Zien owned the Criterion in St. Paul, one of the most popular restaurants in the Twin Cities, he was not a conventional restaurateur. His primary business was operating movie theaters, and by the time he opened his first McDonald's in Minneapolis in 1958, he owned seven theaters. Like other theater operators, he used newspaper advertising extensively, but he also had his own ideas for promoting films playing at his small-town theaters. "We would put banners on automobiles advertising pictures and drive through the town all day," Zien recalls. "Advertising was just in my blood."

When he opened his first McDonald's, the idea of advertising it came naturally. "I had something really unique in McDonald's," Zien explains, "but relying on word of mouth would take too damn long to build the business." Thus, Zien did something other restaurant operators—including most McDonald's franchisees—had not considered. He decided to spend 3 percent of sales on advertising his new store, and he asked Patty Crimmins, the McDonald's operator in St. Paul, to contribute a like amount to a cooperative advertising fund. When Crimmins agreed, the two began chipping in $600 a month each to support an advertising campaign. Since Zien wanted a much bigger promotional splash than he could make by relying on the few stock newspaper ads provided by McDonald's, he turned to Jaffe, Naughton and Rich, a local ad agency, to produce a more sophisticated ad campaign.

Even Al Jaffe, one of the partners in the firm, could not understand why Zien wanted to spend any money advertising a 15-cent hamburger stand—much less $1,200 a month. "I had seen this funny-looking store going up, and I wondered why someone would want to desecrate the neighborhood like that," Jaffe says, recalling his first impression of Zien's new drive-in. "When he wanted to advertise it, I figured he knew something I didn't."

But Zien's break with restaurant convention went beyond aggressive advertising. With Zien's encouragement, the Jaffe agency decided against advertising in print, the primary medium for the limited restaurant advertising that was done in that era. Jaffe reasoned that Zien and McDonald's were really selling an entirely new concept in eating out, one that could not be conveyed well through newspaper ads.

So Jaffe bet all the Zien-Crimmins kitty on a single campaign in a medium then rarely used for restaurant advertising—radio. To make the ad memorable, the agency decided to write a simple jingle—the first of dozens of upbeat McDonald's advertising tunes that would eventually weave their way into the American pop culture. Sid Rich, another partner in the agency, wrote the first one for Zien in 1958, highlighting the single most distinctive feature about the new McDonald's unit—its bargain price for a hamburger, french fries, and a milk shake. "Forty-five cents for a three-course meal," the main lyric read, "sounds to me like that's a steal." Rich's simple jingle became a surprise hit in Minneapolis. "It was just corny enough for people to pick up on," Jaffe remembers. "Before long, everyone in town was singing it."

The radio jingle immediately lifted annual sales at Zien's Minneapolis unit to $315,000 by 1959, fully 61 percent above the national average. In the following year the unit topped all other McDonald's restaurants in sales. When Zien told other marketing-oriented franchisees about the success of the ad, they asked for a tape of it, and Zien provided it—for only the cost of the tape. Soon the ad was running in Washington, Connecticut, and other markets, and when Zien began promoting the McDonald's hamburger, french fry, and milk shake combination as "the All-American Meal," franchisees from around the country picked up on the slogan, making it McDonald's first systemwide advertising theme. The free exchange of Zien's promotional ideas set a precedent that remains a key principle in McDonald's marketing today: that all franchisees are partners, and what one develops to improve his or her local operation is provided freely to all operators to improve the system's performance, with no royalty going to the franchisee who discovered the concept.

In 1959, a year after his radio spot went on the air, Zien broke new ground again by putting his advertising message on the medium that now consumes most of the McDonald's System's $600 million advertising and promotion budget—television. Television was never used for restaurant promotion, even by larger chains, but Zien saw it as the means of reaching the segment of the market that he believed was the key to unlocking all others. "I knew if we could get the kids, we would get their folks, too," Zien says. "If the kids asked to go to McDonald's, the old man was going to say 'okay' because the food was so cheap."

Other franchisees around the country had already begun to appreciate the importance of children as a marketing target. While many adult consumers initially resisted McDonald's because of the lower-quality image conveyed by its 15-cent-hamburger price, McDonald's attracted children because it sold their favorite foods in an environment that gave them a chance to place their own orders and to be entertained by watching the cooking process. But what Zien further realized was that television was really the only medium through which to reach children.

In fact, television was a perfect vehicle for a local children's advertiser in the late 1950s. The networks and television syndicates had not yet seized control of kids' television. Locally produced children's shows were among the highest rated programs on daytime television, all of them hosted by local television personalities idolized by young viewers, who responded favorably to their product endorsements. Better, kids' television was a remarkable buy: one-minute spots cost no more than one-fourth the prices charged by prime-time programs.

It was so good that Zien soon directed his entire advertising budget to purchase time on three kids' TV shows in Minneapolis. Each featured the cartoons and the Our Gang comedies that were standard children's TV fare, and each host played to a studio gallery of adoring young fans. Three days a week, Zien and Crimmins purchased advertising time on all three shows, and because the hosts made on-air promotions for McDonald's, the two franchisees paid next to nothing to produce the spots.

Word of Zien's success with kids' programming spread quickly throughout the system, and by the early 1960s McDonald's operators in more than a dozen markets had taken a major position in supporting local children's television. But, in addition to TV, other operators perfected other forms of advertising and promotion, and their innovations also began filtering through the McDonald's chain.

Like Zien, Jim Pihos, a sales promotion manager for Ryerson Steel before becoming a McDonald's licensee in Milwaukee, quickly dedicated 3 to 4 percent of sales to advertising, and he, too, teamed up with the other operator in town—Peter Weitzman—to fund a cooperative ad campaign. But Pihos also devoted much of his ad budget to direct mail, saturating the market around his store on the South Side with twenty thousand direct-mail pieces distributed every quarter—each one offering a free hamburger with no requirement of purchase. His direct-mail pieces, many of which were developed for him by licensing director Conley using the Austin White artwork, never failed to draw a response rate less than 50 percent—a phenomenal pull for any direct-mail program—and they quickly helped establish his first restaurant as an above-average performer. In the process, Pihos helped establish direct mail as an effective local marketing tool for other McDonald's franchisees.

Meanwhile, another former industrial salesman by the name of Reub Taylor was using his marketing skills to establish a McDonald's stronghold in the Northeast, where new product and service concepts do not easily take root. In addition to New England traditionalism, Taylor had to contend with the fact that he was operating in the power base of what was then the nation's largest food service chain—Howard Johnson.

Taylor's specialty was perfecting point-of-sale marketing—service at the window. He believed McDonald's quick-service format would be lost if service at the order window was not courteous and efficient, and he developed a detailed tape recording to train his window crewmen. "I wanted them to be outgoing, to greet customers properly, and assemble their orders speedily," Taylor recalls.

The tapes covered every aspect of dealing with the customer during his or her fifteen seconds at the McDonald's window. Crewmen were instructed to initiate each order with a polite question: "May I have your order, please?" No customer was to leave the window without a crewman saying, "Thank you very much, and please come again." Window men were also taught the most efficient sequence for filling the order. Taylor remembers that the tape even informed trainees to "give the clean-looking hamburgers to the women and the messier hamburgers—the ones with the mustard and ketchup showing through the wrappers—to the truck drivers."

The success of Taylor's service methods could not be questioned. His stores consistently performed well above average, and his third unit, in Newington, Connecticut, was the legendary store that persuaded State Mutual's Fred Fedelli to recommend the $1.5 million loan that put McDonald's into the big-time financial arena. With sales regularly double that of McDonald's national average, the restaurant in 1964 became the first unit in the system to crack the $500,000 mark in annual sales, and franchisees—even from other chains—were coming from all over the country to see how Taylor's window crew could courteously process more orders than anyone in the fast-food trade had thought was possible.

Taylor's tape recording was such an effective training tool that Fred Turner asked if he could have it as a basis for making a more professional training film on window service. When that began circulating throughout the system, McDonald's crewmen around the country were following most of Taylor's guidelines on window service. And today there are few fast-food chains that do not follow the procedures Taylor pioneered in Connecticut.

But few franchisees had greater impact on shaping McDonald's marketing than the two entrepreneurs who had made the deal with Kroc in 1956 for the exclusive franchise of metropolitan Washington, D.C.: John Gibson and Oscar "Goldy" Goldstein. Gibson, a Miller Beer distributor for northern Virginia, and Goldstein, an owner of a tavern and delicatessen that was served by Gibson's company, became the most successful franchisees in McDonald's history by running their Washington operation—known as Gee Gee Corporation—in much the same way that Kroc and Sonneborn ran the corporate office.

Goldstein supervised all operations with the same type of fascination with details as Kroc had. Gibson, meanwhile, brought to the partnership the same type of financial and real estate acumen as Sonneborn brought to McDonald's Corporation. Because Gibson and Goldstein had purchased their franchise before McDonald's entered the real estate business and because they had the resources to finance their first restaurants, Sonneborn gave them permanent control over real estate in their territory. Thus, while other operators were renting property from McDonald's Franchise Realty after 1958, Gee Gee leased or owned all its store sites directly and paid McDonald's only a service fee of 1.9 percent of sales. If they could generate sales, they would have a gold mine.

Goldstein was the generator—and McDonald's most promotionally minded franchisee. From the day Gee Gee opened its first unit in Alexandria, Virginia, in July 1957, Goldstein hounded executives at Kal, Ehrlich and Merrick, the advertising agency that Gibson had used for his Miller distributorship. Kal, Ehrlich and Merrick was then one of Washington's premier advertising agencies, and had it not already developed a fine relationship with Gibson's beer business it would never have stooped to accept a hamburger drive-in account. "Look what's happened to me," moaned the late Bill Mullett, the half-brother to partner Harry Merrick Sr., who inherited the McDonald's account by virtue of his involvement with Miller. "After all of these years, I end up advertising for a hamburger stand."

Getting the account was only the beginning of Mullett's frustration. Many entrepreneurs want to promote beyond their means when they just get started, but Goldstein took that inclination to extremes. When the first store opened, he told Mullett he wanted McDonald's to advertise on Washington television stations, on most major radio stations, and in the *Washington Post*. Mullett could not believe that Goldstein did not understand the fundamentals of advertising, which dictated against buying media coverage that could not possibly help the business. "Goldy was driving Bill crazy with his requests," recalls Harry Merrick Jr., who acted as an assistant to his uncle on the account. "They would meet underneath the stairs of the first unit, sit on ketchup cases, and argue about what to do about advertising. Goldy always wanted all the things that only a major advertiser can handle."

For a couple of years, Mullett was successful in persuading Goldstein to spend his advertising money on smaller radio stations and newspapers. But, by early 1960, Gee Gee had expanded to five restaurants in the Washington area, and Goldstein finally persuaded the agency that McDonald's was ready to tackle the big-time Washington media. WRC-TV, the NBC affiliate in town, had just aired what appeared to be the perfect vehicle—a new show called *Bozo's Circus*. It was a particularly fitting vehicle for advertising a franchised chain, since the Bozo program itself was a franchised operation. It had been created by Larry Harmon, who had purchased the rights to Bozo from Capitol Records and developed a television program format to fit the clown's character. At its zenith, the show had been franchised in most major television markets, and in each one the local station hired a person to play Bozo according to Harmon's format.

Goldstein loved the idea of sponsoring the show, because it appealed to the market segment—children—that was fast becoming McDonald's most important. And though Goldstein did not know it at the time, the character of Bozo in Washington would be played by an extremely likable young television announcer who would become a local children's idol. His name was Willard Scott, now the weatherman on NBC's *Today Show*.

At the time, Goldstein was taking a gamble with a rookie. Scott had never played a clown. Indeed, at age twenty-five, he was not a veteran of anything. When he got the part as the local Bozo, Scott had just broken into television and was learning the ropes as a junior announcer at WRC-TV. He had not even polished that act. "The staff announcers at the station passed around a china egg to the guy who had just made a boo-boo on the air, and it seemed like Willard always had the egg," Merrick recalls. He and others at the agency made a practice of watching a particular spot in which Scott performed a voice-over for one of Kal, Ehrlich and Merrick's clients—Stibham Tire Stores. As the addresses of the tire stores flashed up on the screen, Scott had six seconds to say, "There are seven Stibham Tire Stores to serve you in Washington, D.C." Invariably, what came out was closer to "Steven Stibham Stire Stores," and Scott wound up with the egg again.

But when he put on his Bozo clown suit, Scott became a pro. His ability to be childlike on television made him an immediate smash with kids in the Washington market. Scott developed his own tricks to give the clown a unique personality. And when it came to endorsing products, Scott as Bozo had the power to deliver the children's market. There was nothing subtle about his sales pitch; Scott's appeal to children was a direct plea to "get Mom and Dad to take you to McDonald's." Yet, his tone was always happy, innocent, and sincere. "Willard was an incredible salesman as Bozo," remembers Barry Klein, then a young copywriter for Kal, Ehrlich and Merrick who wrote most of the Gee Gee spots.

Goldstein was so pleased with the popularity of the commercials that he quickly asked Scott to play Bozo at the opening of Gee Gee's next restaurant—a second unit in Alexandria. The response stunned everyone, even Goldstein. Several thousand people came out to see Bozo. The traffic backed up for two miles in either direction, and kids with their parents were lined up for blocks.

Bozo had become a star in Washington, but more important, he had become *McDonald's* star. Like other aggressive marketers, Gee Gee was spending more than 3 percent of sales on advertising, most of it on Bozo. On the strength of the clown's popularity, Gee Gee's annual per-store sales grew 30 percent in the next four years to $325,000—50 percent above McDonald's average. And by then Gibson and Goldstein had opened twenty-five restaurants in the Washington area, making them easily the biggest franchisees in the system. When operators in other markets saw that performance, they began sponsoring their own local Bozo clowns.

But in early 1963, the Bozo bandwagon in Washington came to a screeching halt: WRC executives decided to give their kids' show the ax. Bozo's popularity had slipped somewhat, and the show, which aired between five and five-thirty, was no longer considered a suitable lead-in to Chet Huntley and David Brinkley. Bozo was canceled, and overnight the McDonald's franchise in Washington had lost its spokesman. "Goldy almost went nuts," Klein remembers. "He called up Channel 4 [WRC-TV] and vowed that he would never buy another minute of time on the station."

Kal, Ehrlich and Merrick tried everything to preserve the marketing momentum Bozo had created. Lacking another kids' TV star, they tried other local television personalities as McDonald's spokesmen to appeal to the adult market, and they used popular disc jockeys to appeal to teens. In fact, they tried almost anyone who had name recognition. Nothing worked. "Finally, we decided that if we couldn't find another spokesman, we would make another one ourselves," Merrick says.

Goldstein's promotional team—Willard Scott, Harry Merrick Jr., Barry Klein, and others at the Kal, Ehrlich and Merrick agency—decided that the only way they could recapture the magic they had with Bozo was to come up with another clown. But, Merrick says, the decision involved a major departure in McDonald's advertising. "We didn't have a vehicle—a live television show—to create the character," Merrick explains. "We would have to establish the new clown by producing our own television commercials."

To date, all McDonald's television commercials had been relatively simple, involving little more than writing a script for a kids' show host to read on the air. Gee Gee was now entering a new and more complex field of television production that no other fast-food franchisee had dreamed of. It was 1963, and even McDonald's Corporation was only that year producing its first thirty-second animated television spot for franchisees to use locally.

Nevertheless, Goldstein insisted on moving forward on the clown project. Janet Vaughn at Kal, Ehrlich and Merrick designed a costume that, Klein remembers, "was as commercial as anything I have ever seen." The hat consisted of a tray with a Styrofoam burger, a bag of fries, and a milk shake. The shoes were shaped like buns, and the nose was fashioned out of a McDonald's cup. The belt buckle was made of a Styrofoam hamburger, and on film, the clown magically pulled hamburgers out of his belt.

The agency proposed calling the clown Archie McDonald, a reference to the Golden Arches, which had become a symbol of the chain.

But there already was an Arch McDonald in the Washington market—a veteran broadcaster for the old Washington Senators—who would surely object to the commercial use of his name. Finally, Willard Scott, who would again play the clown character, used a simple rhyme to name him: Ronald McDonald.

The difficulty, however, was not in creating the clown but in making him as popular as Bozo without the benefit of a children's television show. "We weren't at all sure that by working only through commercials we could establish Ronald as a warm-blooded character," recalls Harry Merrick Jr.

The agency tackled the problem with commercials that told a short story, a practice McDonald's follows today. They contained a lesson on safety or courtesy in addition to a plug for McDonald's. To enhance their appeal to kids, the spots pictured Ronald McDonald on a child's level, not as a father figure. "The concept was that Ronald did everything kids like to do," Scott recalls, "and the commercials showed him roller skating, biking, swimming, or playing baseball. Ronald was their pal."

Ronald McDonald made his television debut in Washington in October 1963, and Scott, now acting as the first Ronald McDonald, quickly showed the same magic touch with children that he displayed as Bozo. By the mid-1960s, the McDonald's franchise in Washington was spending $500,000 a year on advertising—most of it on Ronald McDonald. It was more than any other local or national fast-food chain was spending on advertising, more than even McDonald's Corporation itself. Goldstein also used Ronald McDonald to open each new store it built, and his personal appearances never failed to create traffic jams.

By 1965, Goldstein was convinced that he had discovered in Ronald McDonald the perfect national spokesman for the chain, and he offered the clown free of charge to Max Cooper, the publicist who by then had been hired as McDonald's first director of marketing. Surprisingly, Cooper turned him down. "I told him the outfit was too corny and not up to our standards," Cooper recalls. "Goldstein reminded me that his was the most successful market in the system." After reflecting on that, Cooper decided not to argue, and he proposed a national Ronald McDonald to Harry Sonneborn.

"Are you crazy?" Sonneborn told Cooper. "What are we going to do with a clown?" Cooper was accustomed to Sonneborn's rejecting his ideas the first time around, so he marshaled the figures on the Washington market and made a dollars-and-cents argument for Ronald that was more up Sonneborn's alley. This time, Sonneborn approved, and in 1965 Ronald McDonald made his first national appearance, just as McDonald's embarked on its first nationwide television advertising campaign. In time, network television commercials featuring Ronald would create the only commercial character in the United States with a recognition factor among children equal to that of Santa Claus.

That, in turn, succeeded in giving McDonald's hegemony in the children's market. Seeking dominance there seemed trivial to many fast-food chains in the early 1960s, but by the 1970s they were admitting that they had miscalculated the importance of the children's segment. Indeed, no other marketing factor has been more important in distinguishing McDonald's as the leader in fast food than its early decision to appeal to children through advertising. And when McDonald's principal rivals belatedly tried appealing to the market they had forsaken years before, none was able to weaken the loyalty of children to McDonald's. Even today, McDonald's commands 40 percent of the fast-food visits of children under seven years old, well above its 33 percent overall share of the fast-food market.

After the Minneapolis and Washington experiences, most operators around the country appreciated the value of television as a fast-food marketing tool, but most still could not afford their own TV marketing campaign. Zien and Gee Gee were unique cases—operators with enough restaurants in one market to justify television coverage and with enough money to pay for it. But by the early 1960s, Kroc had ceased giving out the exclusive rights to metropolitan markets that both Gee Gee and Zien had. Instead, he divided up major markets among as many as a dozen or so smaller operators. While that resulted in better control over QSC, it limited McDonald's marketing muscle by restricting the power of its marketing innovators—local franchisees. In most markets, no single-store operator could muster enough money for television.

The obvious answer was to pool the advertising dollars of all stores in a market, but the operators in the most obvious market for such cooperation—Chicago—stubbornly rejected the idea. No other market was better suited for cooperative advertising because none had more franchisees fragmenting the market. But it was the market where Kroc had sold franchises to so many of his independent-minded and investor-oriented friends from Rolling Green Country Club. They were no more interested in supporting cooperative advertising than they were in adhering to Kroc's QSC standards. Not surprisingly, the stores in Chicago were not as successful as stores in Washington, Minneapolis, Connecticut, and other markets with operators who advertised aggressively.

Nick Karos, the field consultant hired after Fred Turner, was determined not to repeat the Chicago experience in Cleveland, where his brother Gus had opened a restaurant in 1958. As soon as new licensees started operating in the Cleveland-Akron-Canton television market, Karos began selling them on the idea of a cooperative. Further, he and Fred Turner began influencing the selection of operators for the Cleveland market to find those who would be likely to support the concept of an advertising co-op. "You couldn't force anyone to join a cooperative, but [in Cleveland] we tried to brainwash them a little," Karos recalls.

By summer of 1961, there were six operators in the market—enough to implement the co-op strategy. When the six licensees got together for their first meeting, Karos was there giving one final pitch for the idea of pooling resources to buy marketwide television coverage that no one operator could afford. The operators were receptive to the idea, not only because they had been presold on it, but because average restaurant sales were declining, from $256,000 in 1960 to $220,000 in 1961. The Cleveland-area operators decided to chip in $7,000 each (or 3 percent of sales) to pay for advertising on a local kids' television show. McDonald's first multioperator advertising cooperative—complete with bylaws and elected officers—was formed. Although the Cleveland operators did not know it at the time, they had formed an organization that would be a model for all other regional and national operator advertising cooperatives in the system—now the source of virtually all McDonald's advertising dollars.

The Northeast Ohio Cooperative retained a local advertising agency, Nelson Stern, which suggested that the best television vehicle for McDonald's was Barnaby, a hobo clown character played by Lynn Sheldon, who hosted a cartoon show carried on WKYC, the local NBC affiliate. Barnaby began pitching McDonald's hamburgers on TV on a Thursday, and by the following Sunday some operators were running out of meat and buns. The Cleveland market stopped its slide, and by 1964, per-unit averages climbed back to the $256,000 level.

If the experience in Cleveland was not dramatic enough to convince all McDonald's operators of the need for regional cooperatives, the turnaround in Los Angeles did. No other McDonald's market in the country showed the miserably low sales volumes of the stores in Los

Angeles. While the McDonald's System as a whole was boasting a per-store sales average of $200,000 per year by 1963, the restaurants in the southern California market—the birthplace of McDonald's and the fast-food format—were averaging a mere $165,000. In part, that was because McDonald's was confronting so many independent competitors who had copied the McDonald brothers.

In May of 1962, Ray Kroc moved to Los Angeles, partly to take personal charge of a renewed effort to crack a southern California market that should have been a natural habitat for a fast-food chain. He asked Karos to be his operations chief for the region, and Karos quickly began telling operators in California the story of the success of the Cleveland co-op. They had every reason to be skeptical because others had come from Chicago suggesting miracle cures for the problems in L.A., none of which had worked. Marketing director Max Cooper had even suggested that the solution lay in reaching commuters when they were most vulnerable—trapped on the L.A. freeways. He hired an airplane to fly over the freeways during heavy drive times and flash McDonald's messages from neon signs installed on the wings. The market did not budge.

When Karos finally succeeded in organizing franchisees into an advertising cooperative, it lacked the resources to fund television advertising, partly because L.A. TV was too expensive and partly because the operators were too poor to contribute more than 1 percent of their sales to the co-op program. "It became clear," Karos remembers, "that we were either going to go on TV in Los Angeles or go broke there." With that conviction, Karos wrote an urgent memo to Turner suggesting that the only way for McDonald's to register in the minds of the market's six million consumers was through "continuous mass stimulation" through television advertising. He suggested that the company itself contribute to help its franchisees in L.A. raise enough money for a television campaign. In 1964, McDonald's did just that, contributing $187,000 to supplement the local operators' advertising fund.

It was the first time the corporation had spent any money on television advertising, and it paid immediate dividends. That year, average store sales in L.A. soared 22 percent, and in 1965 sales grew another 21 percent. When the impact of television advertising in Los Angeles became known, there was no longer any doubt within the McDonald's System that television was the key to opening up the mass market and that licensee cooperatives were essential to funding a television blitz. Operators in other markets quickly began organizing their own cooperatives, and by 1967 franchisees in all major markets in the United States had formed locally controlled advertising co-ops, each with its own ad agency.

In that same year, McDonald's had also created a formal national television advertising program. But by forming local advertising co-operatives first, the operators had taken the organizational action needed to ensure that advertising at McDonald's—which from the beginning had been a grass-roots effort—would remain under local operator control as it moved to the national networks. Even as McDonald's total advertising and promotional budget grew to more than $1 billion by 1992—the largest and most powerful marketing program behind a single brand name—the local operators, working through 165 regional cooperatives and their 48 independent ad agencies, continued to control all advertising funding, approve all media purchases, and exercise a significant influence over the long-term direction of all advertising and promotional programs.

While McDonald's television advertising has the uniform look of any corporate program, it is in fact the product of corporate marketing working in concert with regional operator cooperatives, each with its own promotional priorities and concepts. Indeed, the regional advertising cooperatives continue to provide the operators with their most powerful check against the influence of the corporation.

But the operators' enormous influence in marketing would not be restricted to advertising. By showing much more creativity than the corporation, they seized control of yet another important marketing tool that McDonald's has since used better than most chains to broaden its market—new products. Kroc's miserable experience in attempting to add desserts to the menu presaged a broader failure by the corporation in new products. Not until the Quarter Pounder was added in 1972—an idea of Fred Turner and new product director Al Bernardin—did McDonald's corporate management succeed in creating a new product winner. Since then, the only major new product added by the company was Chicken McNuggets, also inspired by a Turner suggestion. All other major new products can be traced to the experimentation of local franchisees. "I kept plugging away," recalls Bernardin, who helped develop a variety of unsuccessful products for the company—from strawberry shortcake to fried clams. "But my success in all of our different concepts was not too stellar. Why they kept me on I sometimes wondered."

The franchisees' superior track record in new products is partly explained by the fact that they were closer to the market than were corporate staffers and could see new product opportunities better. But they were also looking harder. Outside of Ray Kroc's desperate search for a dessert, McDonald's corporate headquarters was anything but a hotbed of new product activity in the early days, in part because Turner and other operations people were fearful that new products might disrupt the efficiency they had worked so hard to achieve. Thus, for most of its history, dedication to new products resided with certain product-oriented franchisees who stubbornly pushed their inventions on company managers who were not easily sold on them.

That grass-roots process began in the early 1960s, when an operator in Cincinnati decided that developing a new product was a matter of survival. Lou Groen's one restaurant in Cincinnati was surviving on a shoestring and Groen believed the problem was that the neighborhood around his store was predominantly Roman Catholic. On meatless Fridays, those potential customers were bypassing his McDonald's in favor of a nearby Frisch's restaurant, one of the full-service drive-ins owned by Dave Frisch, the area's Big Boy franchisee. Frisch served a popular halibut sandwich, and Groen was convinced that the business McDonald's was losing to Frisch's on Fridays was affecting his unit on other days as well. "A lot of customers felt that if I didn't want their business on Friday, then I could forget about getting it on other days of the week," Groen says. "I had to have a damn fish sandwich."

But when he suggested adding the new product, McDonald's operations specialists denied the need for fish. "They kept reminding me that people in other markets were knocking down the doors for McDonald's hamburgers," Groen says. That did not change Groen's mind. He marshaled statistics on fish sales of competitors, estimated the sales he had lost for lack of a fish product, and calculated the costs involved in adding one. He prepared an audiovisual slide presentation to demonstrate how a fish product could be cooked at a McDonald's unit. He then flew to Chicago to make his pitch to McDonald's managers and to cook for them the fish sandwich he proposed—halibut, dipped in a pancake batter, deep fried, and served on a bun.

Impressed with Groen's thoroughness, McDonald's executives in Chicago approved his request to test the fish sandwich. The market reaction was immediate. Groen's average gross on Friday soared from $100 to as much as $500, and the Friday fish trade helped boost hamburger sales the rest of the week. Within two years, the volume at his once-struggling restaurant climbed 30 percent. Groen says: "Fish was the only thing that saved me from going broke."

McDonald's executives from Chicago and licensees from all over the country came to Cincinnati to see how Groen prepared the new product. What they saw was a complicated process. Groen began hand cutting the halibut into two-and-a-half-inch sticks as early as Thursday morning for Friday business. The battering and blanching of the fish would continue until 3:00 A.M. Friday. It was anything but a process tailored for McDonald's assembly-line operations. "There was no way we could live with that kind of operation in all our stores because it was such a mess," recalls Al Bernardin, now a franchisee in California. "It just didn't fit into our orderliness."

The success of Groen's test, however, ended the antifish bias at McDonald's, and the company quickly decided to test its own fish product. Since McDonald's had no capability to develop such a product, Bernardin called several prospective fish suppliers, but the only one to return his call was the late Bud Sweeney, an account executive with Gorton Corporation, a big name in retail frozen fish but then a tiny factor in the institutional market. Eager to land Gorton's first major commercial account, Sweeney interrupted a business trip and returned to Chicago when his office informed him of McDonald's call. The next morning he showed up in Bernardin's office with a batch of fish samples. "Al was more impressed by our responsiveness than he was with our products," Sweeney recalled.

Still, Sweeney got the business; how he did it is a case study in what McDonald's looks for in a supplier, and it set a critical precedent for supplier involvement in the chain's development of new products. If Sweeney created a good first impression with Bernardin, it was his follow-up that put McDonald's into the fish business and Gorton into McDonald's. From the beginning, he became something of an unpaid product development consultant to McDonald's in finding the right fish sandwich. Instead of Groen's homemade product, McDonald's required a fish product that was cut and battered in the plant and delivered frozen to its stores, ready for the deep fryer. In addition, Sweeney advised that the halibut that Groen was using was impractical for a national restaurant system because the fish was in limited supply and subject to wild price fluctuations.

However, Sweeney quickly offered a number of alternatives, and he spent the next three months testing each of them in McDonald's stores. He was no idle observer of those tests. In fact, Sweeney started spending most of his workdays running the fish department at the test store in suburban Wheeling, and during the busy periods he picked up a spatula and flipped hamburgers. He serviced his other accounts in his spare time. "I started incurring the wrath of my peers at Gorton who began asking why I was spending all of my time at McDonald's," he remembered.

But Sweeney's persistence—and Gorton's perseverance—were only beginning to be tested. Three months of testing produced nothing McDonald's wanted. Sweeney arranged for Kroc and Turner to visit his company's headquarters in Gloucester, Massachusetts, where Gorton's top brass listened to McDonald's objections to the existing products. Virtually all frozen fried fish used a coarse corn breading that overwhelmed the taste and texture of the fish, and McDonald's wanted Gorton to develop a finer breaded coating, not unlike Lou Groen's batter. It would mean developing new breading technology from scratch. That was a tall order from a chain that had only two hundred restaurants, but Sweeney convinced Gorton that McDonald's was certain to grow into a major commercial account.

Sweeney spent another three months in McDonald's stores testing other new products developed by Gorton, until a breaded clam strip was singled out as the best. Yet, when Sweeney prepared it for a group of McDonald's managers, President Harry Sonneborn offered some none too encouraging words: "You'll never see a seafood product in a McDonald's." While McDonald's agreed to expand the test of the deep fried clams, marketed as the "Deep Sea Dory," the five-store test gave Sweeney no more encouragement than Sonneborn had. The product bombed.

Sweeney refused to concede defeat. He went back to putting in thirty hours a week in the Wheeling store to come up with a fish product better suited to McDonald's fast-food system. After another three months of testing—fully one year after he got the initial call from McDonald's—Sweeney, working closely with Bernardin, had a fish sandwich he thought was a winner. It was made from cod, which was more plentiful and stable in price than halibut. It had a tartar sauce made from a recipe Bernardin had borrowed from Paul Burnet, the head chef at Chicago's famed Palmer House Hotel. Sweeney served the fish on a steamed bun and even added a personal touch—a small slice of melted cheese. "While I worked for a fish company, I really didn't like the taste of fish in those days," he said. "The only way I could tolerate it was with a slice of cheddar."

The product in 1962 was approved as the first chainwide addition to McDonald's menu, but Sweeney's job in introducing it had just begun. He found local distributors for the frozen fish, helped select the necessary freezer equipment, and aided McDonald's equipment designers in developing a fish fryer. Then he traveled around the country convincing McDonald's operators of the need to add fish to their menus.

McDonald's expected that type of involvement from Sweeney, but it also rewarded him for it. Gorton got all the fish business when McDonald's successfully introduced Sweeney's fish sandwich throughout the country, but it was obvious that the business was going to Sweeney more than to Gorton. Four years later, when Sweeney left Gorton, some of McDonald's fish business started shifting to Booth Fisheries, Sweeney's new employer. Gorton's percentage of McDonald's business fell to about 50 percent until the mid-1970s, when Gorton brought Sweeney back as its independent consultant on the McDonald's account. By the time of his death in 1989, he had succeeded in building back Gorton's share of McDonald's $60 million annual fish business to 80 percent.

The introduction of fish brought McDonald's unique marketing partnership full circle. The idea had originated with a single franchisee reacting to his local market. It had been converted into a national product by McDonald's Corporation, which changed it to fit the requirements of the operating system it had designed. And it was manufactured by an independent supplier showing the same commitment to McDonald's needs that its employees and franchisees had. It amounted to a near-perfect utilization of the power of a franchising system.

Some fast-food franchising systems were becoming overly centralized with all power in the hands of the franchiser, who supplied all products and equipment. Others were totally decentralized with all power in the hands of large territorial franchisees who made their own operating and marketing decisions. McDonald's was striking a balance. The Chicago franchiser insisted on nearly complete control over certain tasks—enforcing operating rules, training, designing equipment, and financing—which benefit most from centralization and standardization. Yet, it was giving its franchisees enormous freedom to work on those tasks—advertising, promotion, and new product development—where the operators' proximity to the consumer was a definite advantage. And instead of exposing itself to all the conflicts of interest involved in supplying its franchisees, McDonald's was developing nearly captive suppliers willing to develop new products by reacting to the company's operating requirements and the franchisees' marketing instincts.

Just one decade after Kroc opened his prototype store in Des Plaines, McDonald's had achieved dominance over its competitors. But Ray Kroc's greatest achievement was not at all obvious. He had built not a company but a system of independent companies all pursuing the same goal, each dependent on the other. Indeed, the synergy that was developing between all the parts of McDonald's was so different and unexpected that Kroc himself was only beginning to grasp the significance of it. In the late 1950s, it seemed that Kroc wanted all control to reside in his company. But as his chain began expanding its horizons with new products and new promotions, he was discovering the creativity of his company's independent franchisees and suppliers. They were becoming full-fledged partners in the business, and McDonald's was realizing that it could not dominate the quick-service restaurant business without relying on them. Slowly, almost imperceptibly, McDonald's partners—its franchisees and suppliers—were coming into their own.

Chapter 10
GOING PUBLIC

Building McDonald's was a consuming passion for Ray Kroc. It was not a career. It was his life. There was no separating his persona from his business, and in the early 1960s an event in Kroc's personal life triggered changes in his business that fundamentally altered the course of both. Just as he was on the verge of attaining the business triumph he had sought so long, Kroc was overwhelmed by an unexpected joy. He was in love.

He had been married to Ethel since 1922, but when he went to Minneapolis in 1957 to negotiate the franchise for that town with Jim Zien, he laid eyes for the first time on the woman he knew someday he would marry. Her name was Joan Smith, and she was the organist at the Criterion, Zien's popular St. Paul restaurant and lounge.

From the time he had been a professional piano player in his early twenties, Kroc had admired anyone with talent at the keyboard. The nightclubs in Chicago that featured pianists were among his favorite social retreats. So, it was not at all surprising that Kroc had trouble keeping his mind on his franchising discussions with Zien and off the Criterion's organist. Joan Smith was not only talented at the keyboard, she was a stunningly attractive blond in her late twenties. Kroc was infatuated.

It might have gone no further had Zien not agreed to hire Rollie Smith—Joan's husband—as manager of his first McDonald's restaurant and to split the profits evenly with him. When that restaurant's sales exploded, Rollie got a bonus of $12,000 in the first year, more than double what he had been making as a railroad engineer for the Milwaukee Road. A year later, when he and Zien went together fifty-fifty into a McDonald's franchise in Rapid City, South Dakota, Rollie and Joan became members of the McDonald's family and followers of its patriarch, Ray Kroc.

Although he saw Joan infrequently during the next few years, Kroc knew that his marriage of thirty years had to be ended. In his autobiography, *Grinding It Out*, published in 1977, the McDonald's founder recalled having long telephone discussions with Joan about the progress of the franchise in Rapid City, but it was obvious that his interest went much further. "I would be tingling with pleasure from head to toe when I hung up the receiver," Kroc wrote. And Joan recalls today that "when Ray and I met, we both knew that someday we wanted to get married. It was unspoken, but it was there."

By late 1961, it was spoken as well: Kroc decided to divorce Ethel and propose to Joan, and she accepted. Since he had received his first salary from McDonald's ($75,000) only that year, and had agreed to give Ethel their house and $30,000 a year in alimony, Kroc could finance his divorce only by selling off his best asset next to his stock in McDonald's—his 100 percent ownership of Prince Castle Sales. Harry Sonneborn arranged a $150,000 loan from American National Bank in Chicago, which allowed eight McDonald's managers (excluding Sonneborn) to buy Prince Castle and give Kroc the money he needed to start a new life. Looking for a fresh start, Kroc decided to move to California. He and Joan picked out a house in the Woodland Hills section of Los Angeles and began planning their marriage.

Then the pangs of conscience began tormenting Joan. The idea of her divorce from Rollie did not wear well with Joan's family, particularly her mother and daughter. "They liked Ray, but they kept on saying, 'What will poor Rollie do without you?' " Joan remembers. The final blow came from Joan's fourteen-year-old daughter, Linda. "If you marry him," she told her mother bluntly, "forget that you have a daughter."

Joan hastily called off the wedding. Kroc was crushed. But his move to California was still on. He now owned a home there and was still looking to start a new social life following his divorce. Furthermore, Kroc liked the newness of southern California and the willingness of its people to accept innovation. Observed Gerry Newman, McDonald's former chief accountant: "Ray was attracted by the glamour of California because there was always a little show business in everything he did."

Kroc moved to California in May 1962. A year later, Joan changed her mind and mustered enough courage to fly to St. Paul and convince her mother that "she could still love me if I married Ray." But her mother was prepared to give her a far more disturbing message. "I talked with Ray this morning," Joan's mother said. "He's getting married."

The second Mrs. Kroc was Jane Dobbins Green, a script assistant to John Wayne. Kroc had met her on a blind date and married her within two weeks. It was a rebound and an admission that Kroc was uncomfortable living alone. "I married Jane, and that was a convenience," Kroc would admit years later, "but I still thought about Joan all the time."

While the events that put Kroc on the West Coast were personal, the move had an enormous impact on his Chicago-based company. To outsiders, it must have appeared that the sixty-year-old entrepreneur was pulling back from McDonald's just when his goal of building a national chain was within reach.

Nothing was further from his mind. Kroc was not entering into a self-imposed exile. He was assuming personal leadership of an assault on the West Coast—potentially the most lucrative market for McDonald's, but until then easily the most disappointing. When Kroc moved to California, his company was just beginning to rediscover a market it had all but abandoned in 1957 as a reaction to its maverick West Coast franchisees that it could not control from its remote Chicago base. After a four-year moratorium, McDonald's began building units again in California the year before Kroc arrived. But by mid-1962, the chain still had only sixteen units in operation there, and it was not close to achieving the market penetration it needed to stand out from the myriad independent operators who had freely copied the McDonald brothers' concept. With average annual sales nearly 20 percent below the chain's national average, California was still a disaster area for McDonald's.

Capturing the West Coast market now became the linchpin of Kroc's strategy for building a national chain. No matter how much success McDonald's enjoyed in the Midwest and the East, Kroc understood that without the West Coast, his company could not be a viable competitor in fast food. Thus he converted a personal setback into a positive plan to build a powerful West Coast base for McDonald's that could provide franchisees in California the same close field supervision that had made the chain a standout everywhere else.

Skimming some of the cream from the Chicago staff, Kroc transferred to California operations specialist Nick Karos, construction boss Bob Papp, and personnel manager Jim Kuhn. And in 1964 Kroc transferred purchasing expert Steve Barnes to Los Angeles to become Mc-

Donald's first regional manager. The McDonald's founder was assembling a shadow corporation—a Mini Mac—in Los Angeles, and he intended personally to supervise work on the final link in his national chain. He could afford to do that, Kroc figured, because he had his trusted operations chief, Fred Turner, back in Chicago. "You run McDonald's east of the Rockies," he told Turner, "and I'm going to run it west of the Rockies."

Because of that division, Turner's scope and sophistication in managing McDonald's operations grew impressively during the first half of the 1960s. Thanks to Sonneborn's breakthrough in finance, McDonald's was adding one hundred new restaurants a year—easily twice as many as its largest hamburger rivals—and Turner's power over operations was expanding just as quickly. In purchasing, he increasingly centralized sources of supply. He also upgraded the chain's unique training program, expanding it well beyond Hamburger University to a growing base of McOpCo units. By 1963, Turner was overseeing McOpCo units in Chicago, Boston, Los Angeles, Atlanta, and Columbus, Ohio. Two years later, McDonald's established regional offices in all five cities under a sweeping reorganization plan. With nearly seven hundred restaurants in forty-four states, the chain by 1965 could maintain its unparalleled supervision of its franchised operations only by adopting a decentralized structure that put managers closer to the market.

Even with this spreading infrastructure, Turner was struggling to recruit enough talent to maintain the strict enforcement of standards. In his travels he was forever on the lookout for recruits. He tried hiring airline ticket clerks, even fellow passengers—anyone who seemed service oriented and willing to learn a new service format. He hired a social worker, a railroad clerk, an insurance salesman, a bank teller. Indeed, he sought recruits from almost any field—except the traditional food service business. "They accepted all the norms of operation that we weren't accepting," Turner explains.

Because Kroc and Turner thought alike and communicated so well, the founder's move to California during this period of explosive growth did nothing to weaken their unity of purpose. But gradually the development of a West Coast McDonald's headed by Kroc accentuated the already natural division of the company into two camps: those who rallied around the operations oriented Kroc and those who most identified with financial chief Harry Sonneborn.

That alone would not have been damaging were it not also for the fact that by moving to the West Coast Kroc became even more involved in operational issues and less and less interested in finance and administration. Yet, those were precisely the issues that became critical as McDonald's became a medium-sized corporation, and they propelled Sonneborn into a position of power in the chain that rivaled the founder's. While Kroc became enamored of operations on the West Coast, Sonneborn took charge of running the corporation. As he did so, it created a potentially disruptive confrontation between Kroc, who saw McDonald's primarily as a hamburger operation, and Sonneborn, who viewed it as a real estate venture.

The confrontation did not erupt into open battle until the mid-1960s, but it took root in a relatively inconspicuous change that accompanied the $1.5 million loan McDonald's obtained in 1960 from the Boston insurers. To satisfy the insurers, McDonald's combined into a new corporation—McDonald's Corporation—the two related companies it had operated separately: McDonald's System, Inc., the operations group that Kroc supervised, and Franchise Realty Corporation, the real estate subsidiary managed by Sonneborn. While Sonneborn was made president and chief executive officer of the new company, the designation meant little to Kroc. As founder, 52 percent owner, and inspirational leader of McDonald's, there was no doubt in his mind who was boss. "Making Harry CEO had no significance to Ray," Turner observes. "Harry took it very literally."

With Kroc on the West Coast, Sonneborn used his new title to steadily tighten his grip on the reorganized corporation and ever so gradually change its character from an operations oriented company to a financially oriented one. Indeed, between 1962 and 1966, the period of Kroc's California gambit, Sonneborn was chief executive not only in name but also in fact. That happened in part because financial controls were inevitably becoming more important as the company grew, but also because Kroc wanted nothing to do with finances. "Whenever we had discussions of financial situations, it would just turn Ray off," recalls Dick Boylan, Sonneborn's chief aide who later became McDonald's chief financial officer.

In the early 1960s, Sonneborn had used his financial expertise to shape McDonald's overall direction and, more important, its rate of growth. Sonneborn's approval on major new expenditures was tougher and tougher to get. "It wasn't that people were not inclined to give input on the budget, but input with Harry meant that people were asking for something that he didn't want to give," Boylan remembers. "Harry was tight with the buck."

Each year, Sonneborn strictly controlled the number of new stores to be added to the system, largely by limiting the number of staffers in the real estate department. Initially, Sonneborn's penurious ways did not restrict the expansion of the chain. But in addition to approving the number of new restaurants, he also approved each location, often rejecting good sites because he believed their prices were exorbitant. He refused to approve acquisition of land costing more than $50,000, and he continually pressured his real estate managers to negotiate tougher leases. Boylan recalls: "The guy might come in having worked out a real estate deal calling for a payment of a thousand dollars a month, and Harry would say, 'It's fifty dollars too much; go back and renegotiate.' "

As competition for suburban commercial property increased, some McDonald's corporate managers began realizing that Sonneborn's inflexible $50,000 limit on site acquisitions was forcing the company to make deals on secondary sites two or three blocks away from the best retail spots. It seemed clear to them that Sonneborn was appraising locations for their potential real estate appreciation, not for their potential hamburger sales.

Dick Schubot, the independent broker who easily led all others in making McDonald's real estate deals in the 1960s, attributes part of his success to his practice of going around Sonneborn to get approvals on sites directly from Kroc. With Sonneborn routinely rejecting his deals, Schubot would build up an inventory of potential sites for Kroc to approve during his trips back to the Midwest. On those occasions, he took Kroc up in a plane to view a half dozen sites from the air during the day, and he worked in a hotel room all night preparing papers on the properties. The next morning he would hand the founder completed leases to sign, and invariably Kroc approved them. Schubot says: "Harry looked only at the pure dollar cost of the real estate instead of lost income [from hamburger sales] by not making deals for more expensive property."

But Schubot's end run around Sonneborn was the exception, not the rule. As time went on, the McDonald's president steadily increased his hold on the purse strings. And what elevated Sonneborn's position to its peak—and set the stage for his ultimate confrontation with Kroc

—was the one event in the life of a corporation that invariably in-creases the significance of all things financial: going public.

Given Sonneborn's controlled growth plan, McDonald's did not need new equity capital to fund the company's development. The initial motivation in going public was the desire of the principal owners of the company to sell some of their stock. By 1965, Ray Kroc (with 52.7 percent of the stock), Harry Sonneborn (with 15.2 percent), and June Martino (7.7 percent) were already millionaires, but their millions were tied up in a stock with no public market. While their yearly salaries had recently become respectable, they were far from extrava-gant: $115,000 for Kroc, $90,000 for Sonneborn, and $65,000 for Mar-tino. All three agreed that the time had come to convert some of their wealth in stock into wealth they could spend. Sonneborn said: "Going public was the only way that Ray, June, and I could cash in on our work."

From the initial planning in early 1964 until the sale of stock on April 15, 1965, Sonneborn supervised every aspect of the public offer-ing. In the process, he became deeply involved with lawyers, auditors, and investment bankers. Even worse, as far as his relationship with Kroc was concerned, Sonneborn became enamored of them. He sur-rounded himself with trusted legal, banking, and economic advisers who shared his financial perspective on business. He also selected a new law firm—Chapman and Cutler—because he was impressed with its financial expertise. He appointed as a director Lee Stack, the invest-ment adviser who introduced Sonneborn to eastern money, and re-tained Stack's brokerage firm—Paine, Webber, Jackson and Curtis—to manage the public offering. Sonneborn also retained a Big Eight ac-counting firm, Arthur Young and Company, replacing Doty and Doty as the company's auditors. Fred Turner observes: "Harry began to feel his CEO oats."

Indeed, Sonneborn began thinking of himself as something of a corporate power broker. Before the chain's stock offering, he explored taking the company public by merging it with one already publicly held. That route to the stock market was less expensive and less taxing to McDonald's owners, who would be swapping their equity for a public company's stock in a tax-free exchange. With that in mind, he approached Chicago-based Consolidated Food Company (now called Sara Lee Corp.) and United Fruit in New York. Many times McDonald's size, such huge food processors would have loved to use their financial muscle to snare the leader in the high-flying fast-food business. But there was a catch-22 to Sonneborn's proposal: he wanted McDonald's to be the surviving entity of a merger—the tail that wagged the dog. "They thought I was crazy," Sonneborn recalled.

With the merger route ruled out, Sonneborn opted for a public offering of 300,000 shares of McDonald's common. All the stock would be offered for sale by the company's major shareholders, namely, Kroc, Sonneborn, and Martino as well as Paul Revere and State Mutual, which were looking to cash in some of the stock they had received as a bonus for their $1.5 million loan.

Despite McDonald's growth and the go-go stock market of the mid-1960s, Paine Webber did not have an easy time putting a syndicate together to underwrite the chain's offering. Most blue-chip, blue-blooded investment banking firms, such as Morgan Stanley and Goldman Sachs, turned thumbs down on the deal. "It's hard now to conceive that investment bankers didn't fall all over themselves to get into the syndicate," says Harry Fisher, the Paine Webber partner who managed the McDonald's account. "But all of the big boys on Wall Street wouldn't touch it with a ten-foot pole. Their attitude was that this was a fly-by-night outfit."

Part of the problem was that the major brokerage firms were all in New York, the one major market that neither McDonald's nor the other emerging fast-food chains had captured. Astonishingly, though McDonald's was now a national operation with more than seven hundred stores, many of the big-name investment bankers were hearing the company's name for the first time.

Furthermore, there was no existing stock on Wall Street whose performance could be used as a guide in appraising McDonald's. Today, Kentucky Fried Chicken, Burger King, Pizza Hut, and most other major fast-food chains are all part of publicly held companies, and their performance is continually scrutinized by a legion of securities analysts who specialize in fast-food stocks. But before McDonald's, no fast-food company had ever gone public. Up against such obstacles, it was all but impossible for Paine Webber to sell McDonald's to other major investment bankers in New York. "This wasn't a railroad or a steel company or an automobile company, but a business no one on Wall Street had ever heard of," Fisher explains. "And in 1965, the investment banking business was one of the most hidebound, traditionalist businesses in this country."

While some of Wall Street's largest firms eventually participated in the offering, they took a relatively small portion of it, which reflected the lack of interest in the new issue among their big institutional investors. But Paine Webber, along with about a dozen regional brokerage houses that participated more enthusiastically in the underwriting, began to sense an interest in McDonald's stock among thousands of their smaller, individual investors looking to buy a hundred shares or less. In short, McDonald's stock was attracting the same type of grass-roots patronage that its hamburger enjoyed. Indeed, during the early years, as much as 80 percent of the company's stock would be held by individual investors. By contrast, institutions now control about 55 percent.

The McDonald's offering also benefited by flawless timing. In 1965, the stock market was in the grip of the go-go fever. Without examining the companies behind them, many investors assumed all new stock issues had merit and would automatically be propelled upward by one of the greatest bull markets in American history. "It didn't make sense, but every new issue was going through the roof," Fisher recalls. "People who didn't know what McDonald's even did were likely to buy the stock because they felt they could sell it the next day and make a profit."

As the April 15 offering date approached, it was clear that the fever had spread to McDonald's stock. Brokers had already begun allocating shares among customers flooding them with orders. Sonneborn knew that the interest in McDonald's stock was soaring, and he negotiated with his underwriters a price that was at the high end of the new issue market. At $22.50 a share, the stock would hit the market at just under seventeen times McDonald's 1964 earnings, an impressive premium for a nine-year-old company in a new industry. But the industry was so new that there were bound to be some last-minute jitters inside the syndicate. Days before the sale, Sonneborn was called by executives at Paine Webber, who were pressing him to reduce the price to under $20. "I absolutely refused," Sonneborn recalled. "What I told them was not fit to be printed."

Sonneborn's convictions were justified the minute the issue began trading over the counter. The stock was oversubscribed—by an enormous margin. Brokers were telling even their best clients that they were unable to cut them in. By the end of the first full day of trading, the price of the stock had soared to $30. Within a week, it climbed to $36, and it hit $49 within weeks. Suddenly, McDonald's had the hottest stock on the street.

The stock market had vaulted Kroc, Sonneborn, and Martino into the ranks of the superrich. Kroc realized a $3 million gain on the sale of his stock to the public, Sonneborn $1.2 million, and Martino slightly more than $300,000. But the stock's torrid performance gave the three McDonald's executives much greater wealth in the equity they still held. Within weeks, Ray Kroc—a middle-class suburbanite when he founded the chain just a decade before—owned $32 million in McDonald's stock. Sonneborn, who made $125 a week when he went to work for Kroc, controlled $8.5 million. And June Martino, who started as a secretary, held $5 million.

Yet, some McDonald's managers believed it was now up to the underwriters to explain why they had "blown the market," short-changing the selling shareholders by taking the stock public at a price well below what the market was apparently willing to pay. At a higher offering price, of course, there may have been little market for the stock, but that point was hard to communicate to McDonald's. During the early years, Fisher says, "everyone in McDonald's was a neophyte on how the stock market worked. It used to rankle me." At the closing a week after the initial offering, when the underwriters presented McDonald's with the funds from the equity sale, the brokers' reception was cool. "Normally at the luncheon after the closing, you celebrate and everyone is happy," Fisher says. "But at this one, we didn't have the normal drunken luncheon." And even today, executives at McDonald's—no longer neophytes on the market—feel that the cold-shoulder treatment they gave the brokers was justified. "Let's face it," Turner says, "Paine Webber underpriced the stock."

The process of going public did more than expand Sonneborn's power. It gave him his first real public exposure as the man who ran the nation's biggest fast-food chain. With Kroc on the West Coast, it was Sonneborn's turn to be in the corporate limelight, and, to the surprise of those who had watched "Mr. Inside," he relished his new role.

As a publicly held company, McDonald's finances had a much higher profile. Sonneborn, for example, began making speeches before the Society of New York Securities Analysts. And one year after he took McDonald's public over the counter, his exposure on Wall Street increased further when he took the company onto the New York Stock Exchange. It was the crowning achievement of his business career.

There was good reason for such pride. Going public is a relatively simple feat; meeting the financial standards for inclusion on the New

York Stock Exchange was an entirely different proposition. Here was the market where the shares of General Motors, U.S. Steel, and AT&T were traded, and by entering this arena McDonald's overnight claimed the credibility and respectability it had long sought—and that no one else in the fast-food business had. In 1985, McDonald's would achieve the ultimate in respectability by becoming the first service company to be added to the prestigious list of the Dow Jones 30 Industrials, but the process of getting to that pinnacle began on the day the company was listed on the New York Stock Exchange.

Sonneborn made the most of it. It was as if a populist had entered the exclusive realm of the industrial establishment. To publicize the event, Sonneborn sent hundreds of McDonald's hamburgers to the traders on the floor. Earlier, he had given the directors of the NYSE an even clearer sign of his company's nonestablishment bent by insisting that his wife, Aloyis, and McDonald's secretary-treasurer, June Martino, be invited to the luncheon the exchange was hosting for McDonald's in the all-male directors' dining room. When the McDonald's chief was informed that the dining room's all-male code had been broken only once—for Queen Elizabeth—and that the directors were not ready to make an exception for McDonald's, Sonneborn objected. "If its good enough for the queen, then its good enough for my wife," he insisted. The NYSE officials held their ground. "In that case," the McDonald's president threatened, "we don't list our stock."

That was overkill, and the exchange executives quickly relented. But in the excitement of that day, a far more significant aspect of the ceremonies was overlooked: Ray A. Kroc, the founder, was not present. Kroc had passed up the event in favor of a cruise around the world with his second wife, Jane. His absence underscored his lack of understanding and, more important, his lack of enthusiasm for finance. "Ray was over his head on the business of going public," Turner says.

But Kroc's absence also reflected his growing disenchantment with Sonneborn. Kroc was avoiding the NYSE's reception for McDonald's for the same reason he was avoiding a return to corporate headquarters from his office on the West Coast. Were he to resume working side by side with his partner of ten years, Kroc feared, his growing resentment of Sonneborn would almost certainly explode.

From the outside, the rift between McDonald's chairman and its president was not easily perceived. Indeed, it now appeared that Sonneborn was the supreme power at McDonald's. During McDonald's first two years as a public company, it was Sonneborn—not Kroc—who functioned as the front man. Once an obscure figure, Sonneborn now wanted to move out from the founder's shadow.

When Prince Philip came to Chicago as part of a U.S. fund-raising tour for Variety Clubs International, it was Sonneborn who appeared in the newspaper photos with the prince after Sonneborn donated two "Sunshine Buses" to the charity to be used to transport crippled children. Similarly, when officials in St. Louis invited McDonald's executives to the dedication of their massive Gateway Arch, it was Sonneborn who showed up.

The invitation to St. Louis was a simple gesture of recognition of the growing importance of the Golden Arches on the U.S. landscape, but Sonneborn seized the opportunity to gain the type of publicity for McDonald's that Kroc was a master at generating. On the day before the dedication of the Gateway Arch, he proposed that the McDonald's restaurants in St. Louis donate $100,000 to help pay the cost of relocating to the base of the Arch the Spanish Pavilion at the 1964 New York World's Fair. Sonneborn knew that was a pet project of Mayor Alphonso Cervantes, and his offer immediately earned him a position next to the mayor at the dedication ceremonies as well as generous local television coverage for both Sonneborn and McDonald's.

The city's civic leaders afterward decided to take over the funding of the project rather than allow an outsider to take credit for it, but McDonald's had already gotten the publicity Sonneborn was looking for. "Harry Sonneborn appeared to be so conservative," observes former marketing director Max Cooper, "but he had a hidden tendency to be a showman."

Indeed, after taking McDonald's stock public, Sonneborn had become so enamored of his newfound spotlight that he played a surprisingly critical role—more important even than that played by Ray Kroc himself—in establishing what would become McDonald's most visible activity: network television advertising. The subject was raised at a meeting of multiple-store operators in 1964, and it was promoted even more strongly at the first national convention of all McDonald's operators in Hollywood Beach, Florida, in 1965. There, marketing director Cooper argued for the formation of a national advertising cooperative —similar to the regional cooperatives that had been so successful.

Purely from the standpoint of cost efficiency in purchasing media, there was not yet a strong case for national television. With fewer than eight hundred restaurants at the end of 1965, McDonald's had not penetrated enough markets to justify the cost of network advertising. It meant buying much more media coverage than the chain needed. Yet, Sonneborn simply overlooked that in the fall of 1965 when Max Cooper came across an offer from the National Broadcasting Company for three and a half minutes of national television for only $75,000—a one-quarter sponsorship of Macy's Thanksgiving Day Parade.

Curiously, Cooper had rejected the deal only three weeks before, when advertising manager John Horn rushed into his office announcing that he had "a hell of a good deal from NBC." Horn was speechless when Cooper, normally promotion oriented, began laughing. "Are you nuts," he said to Horn. Later, Horn tried again. "Max, I just can't understand why you're rejecting the Macy's deal," he told Cooper defiantly. "What do you mean?" Cooper answered. "The Macy's parade," Horn said. "I told you about it the other day." "Macy's?" Cooper cried. "I thought you said Mason's."

Cooper hurriedly presented the NBC offer to Sonneborn, who this time defied his penchant for cost cutting. Sonneborn enjoyed parades, and as a native New Yorker he had particularly fond memories of the annual Macy's Thanksgiving Day Parade. He did more than approve the company's first purchase of network advertising; he asked publicist Al Golin to figure a way for McDonald's to be in the parade—perhaps with its own marching band.

With the parade just several weeks away, that seemed out of the question. But when Golin contacted Macy's, he learned of a situation made to order for an eleventh-hour parade entry. A high school band from Pennsylvania had failed to raise the money it needed to travel to New York and was forced to cancel its appearance. Sonneborn quickly agreed to sponsor the band in the parade, provided they sport McDonald's Golden Arches logo on their uniforms.

He told Golin to find the biggest drum he could and have McDonald's name printed on its skins. Golin's luck continued. He had heard of a drum maker in Dodge City, Kansas, who had made the largest drum in the world for the University of Texas; when Golin contacted him, he was told that the university happened to be looking for a buyer for the drum. The drum maker fashioned the drum with new skins bearing the McDonald's name and logo and shipped it to New York just in time for the Macy's parade.

Sonneborn clearly had violated Macy's prohibition against using participation in its parade for commercial purposes. But by the time the band showed up on parade day—displaying McDonald's brand everywhere—it was too late for Macy's officials to do anything about it, and Sonneborn knew it. "That parade is planned a year in advance, and they can't throw someone out at the last minute," Sonneborn said. "But when they invited us to sit in the viewing stand, I wouldn't go. Max went, and I let him take the heat; I always believed in giving ulcers, not getting them."

Fortunately, just one year earlier Cooper had hired D'Arcy Advertising in Chicago to produce television spots to be distributed to local operators. Those spots were now used for McDonald's network debut.

At Cooper's urging, D'Arcy had begun working on commercials featuring the clown that had taken the Washington market by storm. But while Cooper and D'Arcy agreed that Ronald McDonald should be the hamburger chain's national advertising spokesman, there were long discussions on whether he should continue as a clown. A clown was perhaps too old-fashioned. Since the western was then the most common television fare, some at D'Arcy proposed converting Ronald into a cowboy. Others argued for a spaceman to capitalize on the popularity of the nascent space program. "Those were the most ridiculous meetings I ever attended," recalls Paul Schrage, then a media buyer for D'Arcy and now senior executive vice president and chief marketing officer for McDonald's. "Here we had a guy in Washington who was knockin' 'em dead, and the agency was looking at all these different characters. In the end, sanity prevailed."

But while Ronald was kept as a clown when he was promoted to McDonald's national spokesman, the actor who played him—NBC's Willard Scott—was unceremoniously dumped. Schrage went to Washington to audition Scott for the part he had developed, but Scott remembers how he sensed that it was "one of those token auditions. You can tell when you're being stroked." The agency planned to produce commercials featuring an extremely active Ronald, and it concluded that Scott was simply too heavy to handle the part.

Scott was devastated. He knew that being the national spokesman for McDonald's was his chance to move from local to network TV commercials, and he could not believe he was being denied a role he had earned. He had helped to create the clown character, and all of his commercials for Gee Gee in Washington featured a very active, childlike Ronald. "The good Lord has rewarded me a thousandfold since then," Scott says. "But getting that part meant a lot to me then, and it was total disappointment. It was the first time I was really screwed by the mass media."

Scott was rejected in favor of Coco, an internationally known clown with the Ringling Brothers, Barnum and Bailey Circus. Because Coco spoke Hungarian, D'Arcy cast him as a nonspeaking Ronald in commercials based on the theme "McDonald's is your kind of place." Put to the melody of "Down by the Riverside," McDonald's first national advertising slogan was the only one it used that was not based on original music. The first D'Arcy commercials all featured Ronald McDonald, and the most popular one showed the clown landing at a McDonald's drive-in on a flying saucer shaped like a hamburger. It was this batch of spots, produced primarily for local markets, that was rushed into network service for NBC's telecast of the Macy's Thanksgiving Day Parade in 1965.

It was a strange time of year to introduce on network television a hamburger chain that did most of its business in the summer. But Cooper sold Sonneborn on Macy's parade by arguing that it might stimulate sales just when the chain's drive-ins entered their winter doldrums. When Kroc founded McDonald's, he was determined to counter the drive-in industry's tradition of closing down for the winter. It would take all the determination Kroc could muster. The chain's franchisees were struggling to break even in the wintertime. While they rang up impressive annual volumes in excess of $200,000 in the late 1950s and early 1960s, the bulk of their sales were crammed into the summer months. In San Bernardino, the McDonald brothers boasted annual volumes twice as large, but they never faced winter weather. Kroc had immediately modified their building design by developing a so-called winterfront, a removable aluminum and glass enclosure that was added to the serving window area during the winter season to protect customers from subfreezing temperatures. Still, with monthly volumes seldom breaking $12,000 from December through February, some of Kroc's franchisees began questioning the wisdom of winter operations.

Advertising on the Macy's parade was a watershed, not only because it was the first time a fast-food chain had broken into the networks, but because it broke McDonald's out of its winter doldrums. The Macy's parade commercials produced immediate results. Instead of entering their typical seasonal decline, store sales in the following month of December spurted 8 percent.

The parade produced some longer-term marketing results as well. When McDonald's publicist Golin met afterward with Bernie Sklar, then the Macy's parade director, and Arch Robb, who then headed

program specials for NBC, they began discussing the company's participation in the following year's parade and the possibility of a permanent McDonald's band. Robb suggested that a possible director might
be Paul Lavalle, the musical director of Radio City Music Hall, who had
long talked about forming an All-American marching band consisting
of high school band members from around the country. Golin put the
idea into action, and the next Macy's parade featured McDonald's own
All-American Band, composed of two high school marchers from each
of the fifty states and directed by Lavalle.

The quick sales payoff McDonald's received from its Macy's
parade commercials made it receptive for another sales pitch from the
networks. McDonald's participated in the Macy's parade the next year,
and a week after that D'Arcy informed Cooper of an even bigger—but
riskier—television network buy. CBS was offering two minutes on a
Sunday afternoon telecast of a brand-new postseason football game,
and the network had assured Cooper that it would promote the event
heavily to produce the type of viewership needed to justify its lofty
advertising price—$200,000 for two minutes, more than double what
NBC had charged for three and a half minutes on the Macy's telecast.
And the parade was an established program, while the football game
was a new and untested sporting event.

Worse, both NBC and CBS were televising it, diluting its rating
potential. Both networks argued that the game's popularity would surprise everyone, but other major network sponsors were not convinced.
By late December, just a couple of weeks before the game, CBS still
had spots available. When McDonald's pressed for a price concession,
the network gladly offered the two-minute spots for just $170,000, and it
even threw in a couple of free spots on its Saturday morning kids'
programs. To cover himself, Sonneborn insisted on buying a one-minute spot on NBC's telecast of the game for $75,000. More experienced
television advertisers might have seen that as a white elephant sale, but
the discounts were enough to tempt a novice like McDonald's to make
what turned out to be the most important—and rewarding—network
television buy it has ever made.

The game's popularity stunned even the networks. No one cared
that the contest was a woeful mismatch of football talent that pitted
Vince Lombardi's Green Bay Packers' powerhouse against the Kansas
City Chiefs of the upstart American Football League. All that really
mattered was that the game had become the object of so much media

hype that it was transformed into professional football's version of the World Series: the Super Bowl.

The results of the Macy's parade had made McDonald's a network enthusiast; the response to its eleventh-hour decision to advertise on the first Super Bowl converted the chain into a television fanatic. The telecast of the 35–10 Green Bay victory was watched by 41 percent of the households in the United States, easily the highest-rated program of the year and one of the most popular in the history of television. And because McDonald's was the only sponsor of both network telecasts of the game, it was the only one benefiting from its total drawing power. Seldom has an advertiser purchased more efficient television time and received such an immediate sales boost. McDonald's national average per-restaurant volume in January—normally one of its worst sales months—jumped 22 percent over the levels of the preceding year. While some of that gain was the result of the chain's first price hike on its hamburger—from 15 to 18 cents—easily half of the increase could be attributed to its network exposure on the Super Bowl.

McDonald's was hooked on network television. For at least two years, operators and corporate managers had discussed forming a national advertising cooperative similar to the ones formed in most regional markets. By the time of the Super Bowl promotion, the creation of an advertising cooperative to buy national television time was academic. When the company petitioned all operators in 1966 to contribute 1 percent of their sales to a national advertising fund, better than 95 percent of the chain's franchisees agreed. Suddenly, a company that had spent $75,000 on national advertising in 1965 would enter 1967 with a network advertising budget of $2.3 million, or nearly 1 percent of the $266 million in sales generated by the chain's nearly one thousand restaurants.

But the company would not control the fund. It was local franchisees—not the company—who had introduced television to McDonald's. They had controlled local advertising spending through regional advertising cooperatives, whose directors they elected. And in 1967 the operators maintained the same control over all national advertising when they set up OPNAD, the Operators National Advertising Cooperative.

While the operators would eventually set up other organizations to preserve their influence over McDonald's, none matches the importance of OPNAD or better illustrates the power McDonald's operators have retained through collective decision making. Elected by their fellow franchisees from their region of the country, the forty-two operator members of the OPNAD committee approve all national advertising budgets, purchase of media, and review all advertising programs.

That makes OPNAD a force not only in McDonald's but in network television. Given its positive early experiences with national television, McDonald's became something of a television addict. As a result, McDonald's franchisees control one of the most powerful network advertising funds in the United States. In 1991, McDonald's spent $572 million on national advertising, more than 66 percent of all of its worldwide advertising and promotional expenditures. It is the largest network advertising budget for a single brand name, and because every penny of it is approved by McDonald's operators, it is also the most democratically controlled media program in the advertising industry.

Chapter 11

McDonald's East, McDonald's West

Each Christmas season during the 1960s, Lou Perlman, the amiable supplier of all paper products used by the system, hosted a Christmas party for McDonald's executives and their spouses. The Perlman party was the highlight of the company's social calendar, and as the chain grew and its corporate managers became more specialized, it offered a rare occasion for the McDonald's family to get together. In 1965, it also offered Ray Kroc a chance to bring his second wife, Jane, to Chicago to meet all his managers.

Jane had already met the executives at Kroc's West Coast office, but she knew few of the executives in Chicago. Yet, she knew enough about office politics to be curious about one thing, and she knew she could find the answer from June Martino. Just before the managers came forward at the Perlman party to introduce themselves, Mrs. Kroc whispered her question to Martino: "Tell me which ones are Ray's men and which ones are Harry's."

By the mid-1960s, the division between Kroc and Sonneborn had spread throughout management. It was not that the members of the two sides were becoming rivals; they were not. But they were taking separate cues from two bosses—Kroc and Sonneborn—who were becoming bitter rivals. Indeed, the split between the heads of McDonald's East and McDonald's West was so severe that it could not help but lead to a perilous division within the ranks between Kroc's men, who controlled operations, and Sonneborn's men, who controlled the purse strings.

The Kroc-Sonneborn rivalry had its genesis in the distinct character differences of the two men, but for years they had maintained a peaceful—and constructive—coexistence. That changed almost the moment McDonald's went public. Although Sonneborn's corporate talents resulted in McDonald's making industry-leading moves into real estate, into institutional financing, onto the New York Stock Exchange, and into network television, the act of going public unleashed other characteristics in McDonald's president that pitted him directly against the entrepreneurial Kroc.

By 1965, Sonneborn had become a professional executive, the type of manager who could boss a *Fortune* 500 company. He was running in an elite financial circle, rubbing elbows with other chief executives, surrounding himself with big-name legal and financial talent. He had even redecorated the corporate offices at 221 North LaSalle Street—the headquarters of McDonald's East—to conform to traditional corporate standards. With plush dark green carpeting and dark mahogany paneling, the remodeled offices looked more like those of an establishment law firm than the headquarters of an antiestablishment fast-food chain. There were red leather chairs in the board room and sconces on the board room walls. There was nineteenth-century artwork, including a Renoir, in the executive suite. A sign next to the receptionist's desk carried the latest quote on the company's stock.

More important, Sonneborn was running McDonald's more like a traditional corporation. Personal and informal relationships that previously had bound everyone in McDonald's headquarters into a close-knit family gave way to bureaucratic structures and organization charts. Freewheeling decision making at all levels was replaced by formal management reviews.

At the top, Sonneborn established a so-called troika of executive vice presidents reporting to him—Boylan in finance; Turner in operations, marketing, and training; and Pete Crow [a real estate specialist whom Sonneborn had recruited from Standard Oil of Indiana] in real estate and construction. The new organization sharply divided responsibility into three equally powerful sectors, and when they did not see eye to eye, things did not get done. There was also a proliferation of staff departments. People who had nothing to do with hamburgers—accountants, attorneys, auditors, and investment bankers—were playing a much bigger role.

Much of this bureaucratization was the necessary fallout of going public. Merely producing reports to the Securities and Exchange Commission and to shareholders required dozens of staff people whom McDonald's had never needed before. By themselves, such trappings of corporate power need not preoccupy top management and interfere with its operations. But that is exactly what happened under Sonneborn's rule once McDonald's went public. Sonneborn was running the company as a professional manager. Kroc wanted it run as an entrepreneurial endeavor. Sonneborn was playing it safe on expansion, protecting the base that was built; Kroc wanted to continue taking major expansion risks to build a much bigger base. Sonneborn was responding to his constituency of bankers on North LaSalle Street and Wall Street; Kroc responded only to consumers. Sonneborn saw accountants and lawyers as vital to the operation of a public company; Kroc barely tolerated them as a necessary evil. Kroc got even closer to store operations while he was in California; Sonneborn—never close to stores or operators—became more distant from both. Even their styles of dress now clashed: Kroc bought more expensive sport coats while Sonneborn took to wearing pinstripes.

"When you go public, the role of attorneys, accountants, and tax people necessarily becomes larger," Turner observes. "Ray was well suited to get those professional influences back in line so that they didn't take over the life of the company. But Harry was smitten with it. Legalese, accountingese, and SECese became his dominant language. It got us out of whack, and it got Harry in trouble with Ray."

Kroc was becoming openly contemptuous of the cautious management style that Sonneborn had adopted. Sonneborn, in turn, was contemptuous of Kroc's failure to appreciate that McDonald's was now a public company—answerable to shareholders—and no longer the private empire of a hamburger baron. Things had to be done through corporate structures, not on the whim of the founder. And, he reasoned, it is the chief executive officer who has the final say on how corporations should be run. That was Sonneborn's title, and he now wanted the managerial prerogatives that normally go with it.

Kroc was unalterably opposed to that thinking. He was the founder and still 43 percent owner of McDonald's. It was *his* company. In fact, he looked at every restaurant as *his* McDonald's. When it practiced *his* Quality, Service, Cleanliness, and Value credo, he took personal pride in it. When it failed, he took it as a personal insult. Kroc believed McDonald's was answerable to the public—but his public were the customers who bought the hamburgers, not the investors who bought the stock. Nor did the founder have much interest in corporate titles. It was fine with him for Sonneborn to be called chief executive officer, as long as everyone knew that Kroc was still the boss.

After McDonald's went public, Kroc and Sonneborn had a simple, albeit unorthodox, manner of handling their differences: they didn't speak to each other. Here was a phenomenally successful fast-food chain, but the chairman in California and the president in Chicago talked to each other through an intermediary. That thankless task went to June Martino, the only person in McDonald's who admired the warring partners equally.

In their last two years together, Martino was the only communication link between Kroc and Sonneborn, and she invariably toned down their rhetoric to make palatable what one had to say about the other. When the misunderstandings between the two were on the verge of open warfare, Martino defused the powder keg, sometimes taking blame for not properly communicating a message when, in fact, her communication was flawless.

When one partner got down on the attitude of the other, Martino pictured things in a brighter light. When Sonneborn brooded about quitting because he could no longer tolerate Kroc's flamboyance or his quixotic temper, Martino was there to lift his sagging spirits. "You know Ray," she would tell Sonneborn. "He's been that way for years, and you can't change him. Let Ray holler and tear his hair out. You know what you are doing, and you know it's right." Conversely, when Kroc confided in her that he wanted to fire Sonneborn, Martino reminded him of Sonneborn's accomplishments. "McDonald's is a successful company with Harry in his position," she told Kroc. "Why change it now?"

Had it not been for Martino's acting as a human buffer, the Kroc-Sonneborn partnership never would have lasted as long as it did, and McDonald's would have suffered as a result. Indeed, even if Martino had done nothing else for McDonald's, her role as peacemaker alone would have earned for her the 8 percent of McDonald's stock that she owned when the company went public. Yet, even now, Martino has bittersweet memories of her role in keeping Kroc and Sonneborn together. "I liked and respected both of them for what they were, and it was a torment for me," Martino says. "I was constantly walking on a teeter-totter."

But the differences between Kroc and Sonneborn transcended their clashing management styles. In time, even Martino's diplomacy could not cover up the raging policy disputes, every one of which could be traced to the partners' conflicting ideas of what business McDonald's was in—hamburgers or real estate.

Kroc believed that if hamburger sales went down, McDonald's went down with them. His perspective was that of a classic retailer: if the company was diligent in building the top line, the bottom line would take care of itself. Sonneborn took the very opposite approach. If hamburger sales went bust, he reasoned, McDonald's always had property to fall back on. His method of building the bottom line was to strictly control expenses. And as McDonald's began making good profits in the mid-1960s, Sonneborn became preoccupied with protecting those profits—avoiding the risk of overexpansion and reducing debt by financing a more modest but safer expansion plan entirely out of the company's cash flow.

In fact, after McDonald's went public, Sonneborn lost even the one umbilical cord that tied him to the stores—real estate. "Harry was turning real estate over to Pete Crow, and he became even more removed from operations," recalls then operations chief Turner. "Previously, he had been in the field, making real estate deals and communicating with operators. But when he no longer did that, he began spending all his time with professionals [in the investment and legal communities]." Even Sonneborn conceded that whatever interest he ever had in hamburger operations eventually disappeared. "I told Ray that he should take care of the food end of the business," recalled Sonneborn. "I didn't want a damn thing to do with it. I didn't even eat hamburgers."

By the mid-1960s, Kroc's and Sonneborn's conflicting philosophies were producing scores of disputes on how to run the business. Even seemingly minor disagreements grew into battles. When Kroc, for example, sold franchises to a half dozen of Jane Kroc's relatives, he waived the requirement for them to put up a $15,000 cash security deposit on the real estate and took a personal note instead. Sonneborn knew it was wrong and rightfully protested. But it didn't stop there. In fact, Chapman and Cutler, the law firm Sonneborn picked in the early 1960s to represent McDonald's, wrote a legal opinion supporting Sonneborn's position on the subject. At that point, Kroc loaned Jane's relatives $100,000 for their security deposits. But he never forgot the humiliation of the wrist-slapping he got from his own president and his own company's legal counsel.

Kroc was also annoyed by Sonneborn's increasing absence from the Chicago office. He spent much of 1966 at his home in Mobile, Alabama, writhing in pain from a severe bout of sciatica. Sonneborn spent months on his back on a sofa at his home on the Fowl River, conducting all his business by telephone. Directors even flew to Mobile that year to attend a board meeting at Sonneborn's estate. Kroc, who tolerated the pain of his own arthritis, had difficulty accepting anyone else's illnesses. "When Harry came into Chicago, he'd go to his office, take care of what he needed to get done, and then leave again. No one knew when he was in, and no one knew when he was gone," Kroc recalled. "There was no leadership in Chicago."

However, none of the disputes between Kroc and Sonneborn came closer to the heart of their fundamental disagreement than their opposing views on how fast McDonald's should expand. Until the mid-1960s, expansion was not an issue because the United States was a virgin market for fast-food operators. McDonald's had many more growth opportunities than it had resources, and the risk of failure was small, if only because McDonald's had so little to lose.

But after the company went public, that changed. Suddenly McDonald's was in a position financially and operationally to expand at a much greater rate. However, because it had attained a measure of financial success, it also had more at stake if the expansion backfired. For the first time, it was possible for Kroc's faith to run headlong into Sonneborn's numbers. Kroc saw the sky as the limit; Sonneborn saw it as the excess.

Although he had made very bold and risky financial maneuvers to get his real estate program going, Sonneborn began exercising much stricter financial discipline. It could well be argued that Sonneborn's tight-fisted controls were essential for a company being guided by a founder whose strong suit clearly was not finance. But by the mid-1960s his financial strictures seemed out of place and unnatural in a burgeoning fast-food chain that had experienced only a single unit failure.

Instead of increasing new store openings each year as McDonald's financial base expanded, Sonneborn did the very opposite. After authorizing a record 116 new restaurants during 1962—the year McDonald's was flush with funds from its $1.5 million loan from insurers—he reduced the number of new stores built in each of the next three years. The biggest cut came in 1965, the year McDonald's expanded its financial horizons by going public. At precisely the time when most companies shift into high gear, Sonneborn put McDonald's into neutral.

While the chain by the end of 1965 was still several times the size of most of its rivals, with 731 units, it had added only 81 new outlets that year, down from 107 the year before.

The slowdown would have been much more pronounced had it not been for Ray Kroc's group of young tigers on the West Coast. With the founder's blessing, they openly flouted Sonneborn's restrictions on expansion and real estate spending. Kroc and his California managers began buying much higher-priced restaurant sites than were being purchased by any other region—sometimes paying more than double the $50,000 that Sonneborn had set as the ceiling price. In part, that was because California property was more expensive, but it was also because Kroc refused to settle for secondary locations, something managers in other regions were sometimes forced to do.

Furthermore, Kroc was expanding his California real estate group much faster than Sonneborn was expanding his in Chicago. As a result, the California region remained largely unaffected by the slowdown in construction that affected the rest of the company. Between 1964 and 1967, when Sonneborn was putting a lid on new store expansion, Kroc's California group accounted for fully one-third of all new stores added to the McDonald's System. In short, while Kroc was turning McDonald's West into a hustler, Sonneborn was putting McDonald's East on hold.

The East-West differences went well beyond expansion. Indeed, they seemed to be evolving into two separate companies. McDonald's East was more formalized; McDonald's West was freewheeling. McDonald's West was risk oriented; McDonald's East was becoming the company's safety net. And while Sonneborn's stewardship tended to stifle experimentation, Kroc's fostered it. Even the camaraderie among their managers reflected the differences between Kroc and Sonneborn. "The guys in California had good esprit de corps and were socializing with each other almost every weekend," Turner observes. "Social life in Chicago was disappearing once Ray left."

McDonald's on the West Coast also became a testing ground for new concepts, particularly in design and construction. To satisfy his passion for adding a touch of class to the hamburger drive-in, Kroc poured money into landscaping that was lavish by comparison to anything else in the fast-food business, including elsewhere in McDonald's. More attractive exterior lighting was added along walkways and on the perimeters of the lots to offset the stark neon look of the stores. Decorative walls were built to enclose unsightly storage and waste collection areas. New types of building materials, such as adobe blocks, stone, and brick, began replacing the standard red-and-white tiles on the exteriors of new buildings.

But perhaps the most significant departure was the addition of large patios with seating and canopied tables. A few McDonald's previously had squeezed limited seating into the enlarged winterfronts—called Metros—that were being added in the early 1960s. But until Kroc's West Coast group began building patios with extensive seating, McDonald's had remained almost exclusively a drive-in. Food was either carried out or eaten in parked cars. In California, the introduction of patios, attractively lit and landscaped, changed the image of McDonald's from a drive-in to a restaurant. And in southern California's climate, patio seating was a year-round feature, not a seasonal frill.

Technically, of course, Ray Kroc had the power to dictate that the changes taking place in California be adopted around the country, Sonneborn's opposition notwithstanding. But Kroc was too much of a pragmatist to risk the management confrontation that would have ensued. Instead, he led by example, not by decree, and he used California as the example of the original thinking he wanted to see throughout McDonald's. "There was always a tremendous strain on all of us who were loyal to many people back in Chicago," recalls Jim Kuhn, then Kroc's personnel director on the West Coast. "It was not that Ray was hostile, but he began to view a lot of the people in Chicago as a bunch of bureaucrats. And he would repeatedly say, 'If those guys tell you, "Don't go ahead with something," do it anyway.' He didn't want to divide the company. He went his own way and said to himself, 'In time, they will follow.' "

Nevertheless, it did create a division between the managers loyal to Kroc and those who reported to Sonneborn, and it was particularly uncomfortable for managers in California who had to get approvals for changes from corporate headquarters in Chicago. Robert Papp, the construction manager Kroc transferred from Chicago to California, recalls how he had to "walk on a tight wire" between two opposing forces. "Ray wanted to see action and progress, while Chicago was being caught up in red tape," Papp says. "I had Ray pushing me from one end to go ahead and make changes in the building, and I had Chicago telling me that I couldn't make changes. Ray would say, 'Screw Chicago; I'm telling you to do it.' "

Papp rationalized his changes in construction as best he could, sometimes fibbing to Chicago that the California code required certain design modifications. But it became clear that Sonneborn did not approve of the experimentation taking place on the West Coast. His position was simple: Why monkey with a building design that works, particularly when the modifications are adding to the cost?

Eventually, Kroc had his fill of Chicago's resistance to the design improvements he wanted, and he dispatched Papp to the Windy City to be interviewed by Sonneborn for the position of McDonald's vice president of construction. Kroc, of course, was endorsing Papp for the job, but as a gesture of goodwill he let Sonneborn make the appointment. But when Papp showed up at Sonneborn's office to keep an early-morning appointment, Sonneborn made him wait outside his office— all day. The following morning, Papp got the same treatment.

At noon, he was so annoyed that he took a cab to O'Hare and flew back to California. "What the hell are you doing here?" Kroc demanded the moment he laid eyes on Papp. "I had some problems in Chicago, Ray," Papp replied and related the story of his cold shoulder reception from his new boss. Kroc immediately called Sonneborn and unleashed his rage. "Ray's office was at the far end of the building from mine, but I could hear him all the way down the hall," Papp says.

Within a week Papp was back in Chicago to start his new job. It was just three years since he had left corporate headquarters for the West Coast office, but when he returned he sensed he had entered a different company. "When you needed certain things or certain people to do something new, they weren't available," Papp recalls. "The attitude to new ideas was that 'you can't do it that way.' "

The philosophy against change was enforced at corporate headquarters by increasingly sophisticated reporting procedures that eliminated entrepreneurial decision making. Observed Gerry Newman, who as the company's chief accountant was well placed to witness the growing mounds of red tape: "In the Sonneborn era, everything was controlled. We were a financial organization, and everything was controlled. We were a financial organization, and everything had to justify a return on assets. Everything had to have a purchase order, initialed and counterinitialed. Bob Ryan [treasurer] and Dick Boylan [chief financial officer] reviewed every real estate contract. And paperwork sat on the desks sometimes for weeks, because people could only handle so much."

Not everyone in Chicago, however, was resisting change. Kroc still had stalwarts there, and chief among them was Fred Turner. But Sonneborn's status quo management was wearing on Turner, who was slowly slipping into depression. The creation of five new regional offices by 1965 had moved many of Turner's day-to-day operational management duties outside of Chicago, leaving Turner's desk uncharacteristically clear. The action was in California, and Turner was isolated from it and especially from his mentor, Ray Kroc.

He began quietly entertaining a half dozen offers from other fast-food chains and a few lucrative propositions from major McDonald's franchisees. Turner had devoted all of his working life to McDonald's. He was known among Chicago staffers as the golden boy who could do no wrong in the founder's eyes. That he was even considering a move was a sure sign that the morale in Chicago among those in the Kroc camp had sunk to the bottom.

There were even times when Turner must have felt branded as a noninnovator by Kroc because of his association with McDonald's East. On several occasions Kroc scolded him for resisting his new product ideas, particularly desserts, on the grounds that it would upset store operations. The worst rebuke was a public one—at the Perlman Christmas party in 1966. Turner had been stubbornly objecting to the founder's addition of strawberry shortcake to the menu, and Kroc finally had enough. With his wife, Patty, and a couple of dozen McDonald's managers within earshot, Turner got a dressing down he will never forget. "You're getting too damn negative," Kroc insisted. "You've been against every damn dessert I've tried, and now you're against shortcake. Well, let me tell you something, Fred Turner, this is going to succeed in spite of you."

By the time his tirade ended ten minutes later, Kroc was pounding on Turner's chest with his finger. Embarrassed managers had left the room. Turner, dressed in a tuxedo, was speechless. When the party was over, Turner and Patty quietly left with Litton Cochran, the franchisee in Knoxville. Cochran, a good friend, had accompanied the Turners to the party, and they had planned to leave whenever Turner signaled to Cochran that they had stayed long enough. The drive home was solemn—until Cochran spoke. "Fred," he said, "I think you waited a little too long to give me the high sign."

Aside, perhaps, from his brief stint as a Fuller Brush salesman, it was the darkest time in Turner's life. He was being labeled by Kroc as a conservative on new products, when he knew—and Kroc knew—that the real opportunity McDonald's was missing was not in expansion of the menu but expansion of the chain. "I felt estranged from Ray, let down by Ray," McDonald's senior chairman recalls. "His influence wasn't being felt the way it should be. I wondered, 'Why is he letting us drift?' The retrenchment bothered me. I was disillusioned."

Indeed, Turner and other Kroc loyalists stuck in Chicago were becoming convinced that McDonald's—after building a splendid base —was blowing its golden opportunity to build a major nationwide food service chain. Burger Chef and Burger King were now expanding at a faster rate, gaining ground on the hamburger leader. And Sonneborn increasingly was showing signs that he no longer cared about the business. Instead of working the twelve-hour days that were typical before McDonald's went public, he was now on a nine-to-five schedule.

Mel Garb, a long-time McDonald's franchisee, recalls that in late 1966 he stormed into Sonneborn's office to complain about the one new store he had been granted in Detroit after Kroc had promised him three. He knew Sonneborn was a tough negotiator, and he expected a donnybrook. But when Garb charged in, followed by then franchising vice president Ed Bood, he was stunned to see Sonneborn—obviously suffering from another bout with sciatica—reclining as far back as his chair would go. "The answer is no," Sonneborn joked. "What's the matter, Melvin?"

"You guys are liars," Garb shouted, gearing up for the confrontation he was sure would follow. But Sonneborn was out of character. "I have never lied to you," Sonneborn said calmly, disarming Garb, who knew the statement was true. Still, he pressed his case. "Ray promised me some stores in Detroit," said Garb, who then ran six stores in Saginaw, Michigan, about seventy-five miles north of Detroit. "Here I get a letter for one store. What am I going to do—send somebody down there to supervise just one?"

Sonneborn did not argue. Instead, he instructed Bood to grant Garb the right of first refusal on the franchise to any new store McDonald's built in Detroit. McDonald's had not granted metropolitan territories for years. Anyone with any faith in the future of McDonald's knew that Sonneborn had given Garb a fortune. Indeed, Garb had gotten more than he had ever dreamed of getting from the normally tight-fisted Sonneborn. The entire Detroit area had only fourteen McDonald's, and Garb now had the right to accept any new stores built to fill in the market.

Garb went immediately to Turner and offered him a 25 percent interest in his Detroit operation if he would manage it. "I'd like to take it," he told Garb, "but the way this company is going, I think if they called me back to save it, I'd have to come back." Garb was stunned.

"The guy's unhappy there, and we make him an offer like this and he turns it down," Garb told his franchising partner, Harold Stern. "How nuts can a guy be?" (In 1968, Garb and Stern sold all of their Michigan and Nevada stores and the Detroit territorial franchise back to the company for $2.5 million, and today what was once the Garb-Stern territory in metropolitan Detroit has 139 McDonald's.)

Turner refused Garb's offer because he could see that the relationship between Kroc and Sonneborn was falling apart. Something was bound to give—and soon. It was increasingly apparent that Sonneborn believed McDonald's was nearing its peak in market penetration. And that put him on a collision course with Kroc, who believed McDonald's had just scratched the surface of the fast-food market.

After the 1965 lull, new store construction picked up momentum in 1966 with the addition of 126 new units, an increase of better than 50 percent over the preceding year. Kroc's managers were eager for another large increase in 1967, but Sonneborn was in no mood to satisfy them. Fearing a severe recession in the U.S. economy, he once again applied the brakes, cutting the size of the real estate staff in late 1966. The real estate cuts virtually ensured that McDonald's would add far fewer restaurants in 1967 than in 1966. That alone was enough to enrage Kroc, but Sonneborn, by late summer of 1966, was adding fuel to the fire by openly predicting a recession for the economy and a slowdown for McDonald's. In a two-week period, McDonald's stock dropped more than seven points. Turner recalls: "Ray was livid."

Sonneborn seemingly was countering the entire McDonald's System, which was primed for accelerated expansion. Real estate specialists in each of the company's five new regions had identified dozens of sites that could support a new McDonald's. The regional television advertising being financed by the new operator cooperatives was stimulating enough consumer demand to justify many more restaurants. Throughout the first half of the 1960s, average store volumes had not budged from $200,000. But in 1966 they soared to $275,000—nearly 40 percent above the average of three years earlier. With advertising, McDonald's was breaking through to new segments of the market, and its success was spurring competitors to expand at faster rates and encouraging others to enter the suddenly glamorous fast-food business.

In such a setting, Sonneborn's retrenchment seemed unreal. "We were contracting, and it was so unnatural," Turner recalls. "Those who were tuned into the marketplace knew it was wrong. We were listening to Harry's financial arguments, but they didn't make any sense to us. He was almost talking depression, and I began picturing him with an apple cart."

While those in the Kroc camp were convinced that Sonneborn was losing what little faith he had in the hamburger business, the McDonald's president was ordering the slowdown solely on economic grounds. His fears of impending recession were real, and, more than anyone else in the company, he knew how exposed to it McDonald's was. "My concern was the potential exposure of the company in a recession," Sonneborn explained many years later. "We were completely leveraged. All of our expansion had been done on borrowed money. If we suddenly had just a few restaurants fail on us, and we had to pick up their lease payments, we would have been in trouble. If you don't have to take that risk, why take it?"

Sonneborn was not the only one who thought the wheels were coming off the economy and that a more conservative expansion plan was now prudent. The country had experienced an economic growth rate that was unprecedented in the post–World War II era. But there was growing concern that the economy was overheating. Already, interest and inflation rates—though mild by 1970s standards—were soaring to levels contemporary businessmen had never known.

Among those concerned was Allen Stults, a former McDonald's director and then chairman of American National Bank of Chicago, one of the first banks to loan McDonald's money. As much as anyone, Stults understood the long-term potential of McDonald's. Still, he agreed with Sonneborn that the economy might be headed for a severe recession, one that could put a heavily leveraged company like McDonald's in danger—no matter how well it ran its restaurants. Stults was one of Sonneborn's most trusted financial advisers, and the two agreed that if McDonald's continued expanding at the 1966 rate, it could become badly overextended if a recession developed in 1967. "McDonald's financial reserve was practically zero, and a pause in the rate of expansion at that period was sound," Stults explains. "Harry and I wanted to get the company into a stronger financial condition so that it would have a base for a more rapid expansion rate later on. We were passing up additional growth, but we were getting the assurance that we could withstand an economic shock."

Even though that economic shock did not come until three years later—when McDonald's was strong enough to withstand it—Stults still believes that Sonneborn's planned slowdown for 1967 was proper. "Isn't it beneficial to have life insurance even if you don't die during the term of the policy?" Stults asks.

Even within McDonald's there were signs that justified Sonneborn's cutback. One was store performance. While average sales were growing, expansion in previous years had left McDonald's with a disturbing number of losing and marginal restaurants in isolated and undeveloped markets. Part of the problem could be traced to the deterioration in the quality of franchising after Ray Kroc moved to California. McDonald's had opened 335 new units from 1961 through 1963, more than doubling the size of the chain, but its franchising department was clearly not up to the task of finding qualified franchisees for all those stores. It "solved" the problem by compromising the licensing standards Kroc had carefully developed. Despite the founder's early setbacks with his Rolling Green friends, investors were coming back into McDonald's franchising picture. Furthermore, some applicants were granted licenses solely on the grounds that they were related to existing franchisees. And candidates without sufficient capital were given breaks in reduced licensing fees, while anyone with enough money was granted a license with few questions asked. "Ray knew from experience the qualities an individual needed to be a successful McDonald's operator, and after talking with a fellow for a half hour, he could tell whether he had them or not," observes J. Kenneth Props, the company's ninety-one-year-old former director of licensing, who started his second business career by joining the real estate department at McDonald's in 1962 after thirty-five years as a marketing manager at Standard Oil of Indiana. "But," Props adds, "the people put in charge of franchising after Ray moved west had no concept of what was needed to screen licensees."

The problem was bad enough by 1964 for Sonneborn to create what he called his "whitewing" department (a reference to street sweepers) and to name Props as its head. Sonneborn was asking Props to unload twenty-four McDonald's units that were losing an average of $1,000 a month. All were owned by the company, some because of takeovers from operators who threw in the towel and some by virtue of the licensing department's inability to franchise them. After a full year of searching for buyers, Props had sold only two of the distressed units. Fortunately, however, Sonneborn had developed a so-called business facilities lease agreement six years earlier to rescue the restaurant McDonald's had taken over from Milo Kroc, and now Props latched on to that instrument to solve his problem. Instead of selling the stores to new franchisees, he found operators willing to take over the remaining twenty-two stores under favorable leasing terms and with a security deposit of only $5,000, one-third the normal deposit. Still, given the whitewing department's experience, "Sonneborn had reason for his slowdown on new construction," Props says. "He just failed to see that the real weakness was not in the market for new stores but in the inability of the licensing department to turn out the right franchisees."

Yet, Sonneborn would have battled with Kroc over expansion even if there had been no concerns about recession or marginal stores. Kroc was willing to gamble everything the company had won to date because he was convinced that a much faster rate of expansion was the closest thing to a sure bet. Sonneborn's mind-set was exactly the opposite. "When you start a company, you borrow with a single purpose—to reach a position to get out of debt," Sonneborn explained. "When we had no money and we were dealing only with other people's money, we had nothing to lose by gambling on expansion. But when it was our money we were gambling with, I had a problem with that. Then when you play a numbers game [on expansion], you're playing Russian roulette."

Thus Sonneborn in early 1967 developed a long-term plan that allowed for an "orderly expansion" of new restaurants even after the predicted recession was over. It scheduled just two hundred units per year for the next decade, a rate Sonneborn determined could be financed completely from McDonald's cash flow. At the end of that period, he figured, McDonald's would have a potful of money in the bank and zero debt. The only drawback was that the plan woefully underestimated McDonald's potential: By the end of 1977, Sonneborn's McDonald's would have had just under three thousand stores—two thousand fewer than it actually had by then.

Kroc saw Sonneborn's construction slowdown as proof of his president's lack of appreciation for McDonald's past operational achievements and a lack of faith in its future. From the beginning, Kroc admitted years later, he had suspected that their different perspectives on the business would someday tear his partnership with Sonneborn apart. "I didn't give a damn about money, and I took the profits for granted," Kroc explained. "All I wanted was to make McDonald's a winner in the hamburger business. That was the thing I romanced. But Harry was strictly a financial man. He didn't know a damned thing about hamburgers. I couldn't talk to him because he couldn't talk operations. That's what made us drift apart. I was afraid Harry was turning McDonald's into a cold, calculating business."

In the end, it was the very success that the two partners had worked so hard to achieve that was now pulling them apart. As long as McDonald's struggled, Sonneborn and Kroc had an equal desire to expand. But once the chain achieved a level of financial success, Sonneborn's desire to make even more money no longer equaled Kroc's desire to sell even more hamburgers. "Harry got into the business for what he needed in money, and when he made that money, he quit," Kroc said. By comparison, Kroc, who worked at McDonald's until the day he died at age eighty-one, was driven by something other than the hundreds of millions he made. His entire ego was wrapped up in how McDonald's was perceived by consumers. Said Kroc one year before his death: "If I were going to live to a hundred, I'd be down here [in the office] every day of the week."

Aside from their differences over expansion, Sonneborn and Kroc had other major battles in 1966. One involved pricing of the McDonald's hamburger, which remarkably had remained at 15 cents for nearly two decades. Kroc wanted to increase it to 18 cents to respond to inflation, and he believed that McDonald's quality would keep consumers loyal. Sonneborn argued that the 15-cent price was part and parcel of McDonald's appeal and that modifying a winning marketing formula was folly. Their positions were so entrenched that the only way to resolve the dispute was to take the one step executives typically avoid at all costs. Sonneborn took their pricing dispute to the McDonald's board of directors.

In recent years, corporate boards have become somewhat more involved in setting policy, but in the mid-1960s they were invariably rubber stamp operations, and it was unthinkable to air management disputes before the board. That Kroc and Sonneborn even considered taking the pricing conflict to the board was itself a sign of how serious their differences were. "Instead of taking on Ray one on one," Turner observes, "Harry made the mistake of making the boardroom a battleground."

As the pricing issue went to the board, the dynamic reaction between Sonneborn and Kroc approached meltdown. They put Gerry Newman on the spot by asking him to draft an economic analysis of the pricing issue that they could present to the board to support their respective positions. Newman took the only practical way out of the mess: he wrote two economic analyses, one favoring a price increase, one opposing it.

But the battle in the boardroom became almost surreal when Sonneborn—concerned that his positions on pricing and other contentious issues were properly documented—insisted on recording board meetings on tape. When word of that spread throughout McDonald's, everyone in the system knew the end was near. Turner says: "We had an open little society at McDonald's; recording what people said was something totally foreign."

What was even more unusual was Ray Kroc's position in the boardroom battle. He was desperately looking for supporters. Though the founder still owned 43 percent of McDonald's stock after the company went public, his own board of directors appeared decidedly pro Sonneborn. Because Kroc had concerned himself solely with operational matters, the board of directors until now had had little meaning to him. It was Sonneborn who was preoccupied with corporate administration, not Kroc, and the board was composed of executives who were much closer in their thinking to McDonald's president than to its chairman.

In addition to Kroc and Sonneborn, the board consisted of two other insiders—Dick Boylan, Sonneborn's right hand in finance, and June Martino, who walked the tightrope between her two bosses. The two outsiders were both Sonneborn designates and close financial advisers—Allen Stults of American National and Lee Stack of Paine Webber. "There really wasn't anyone on the board Ray could count on for support," observes Donald Lubin, a current director of McDonald's and a partner in Sonnenschein, Carlin, Nath and Rosenthal, the Chicago law firm McDonald's now retains as its legal counsel.

Lubin's firm previously had held the McDonald's account but lost it in the early 1960s when Sonneborn selected another Chicago law firm—Chapman and Cutler. But Chapman and Cutler were considered Sonneborn's lawyers, and when McDonald's management structure was on the verge of rupturing in 1966, Kroc went to Lubin for legal help. Lubin's experience in becoming a director and recapturing the prestigious McDonald's account underscores the potential value of even the slightest professional contact. Although it did not seem like a big opportunity at the time, Lubin had opened a small crack in McDonald's door shortly after the company went public. June Martino had called him out of the blue to ask a simple question on behalf of a personal friend who wanted to know the residency requirement to obtain a marriage certificate in Nevada. Lubin called a county clerk there, and within five minutes telephoned Martino with the answer. Impressed with such speedy service, Martino then asked Lubin to draft her will. Soon, that was followed by an even bigger plum—drafting a will for her boss, Ray Kroc.

Before long, Lubin was doing all of Kroc's personal legal work, and in January 1967, that led to an assignment corporate attorneys dream about. Lubin had become aware of the problems developing between Kroc and Sonneborn, but he was still not prepared for a telephone call he got while in New York on business. It was Ray Kroc. He had at last decided to act. "I have a problem with Harry," Kroc told Lubin. "He wants out and I want him out. I want you to negotiate a settlement with him. You're the company's new legal counsel."

Lubin was stunned. He was only thirty-three years old, and he was still several years away from being a full partner in the firm. But Kroc was impressed with the young lawyer's skills, and he did not hesitate to appoint Lubin as a McDonald's director—his first move to reinforce his position with the board.

There was no real threat that a palace coup could be engineered by Sonneborn. Kroc still held better than 40 percent of McDonald's stock, and if it came down to a fight, there was no doubt that Kroc and shareholders friendly to him would win it hands down. However, while Kroc now clearly wanted Sonneborn out of office so McDonald's could regain momentum, a public battle over policy was the last thing he wanted. To oust Sonneborn, the McDonald's chairman would have to work with his board of directors.

Now Kroc's oversight in maintaining his influence with his own board was putting him in an uncomfortable position. If it came down to having to fire Harry Sonneborn, the decision would have to be made by a McDonald's board that appeared more partial to Sonneborn than to Kroc. Firing Sonneborn was one decision the present board would not easily make. "Ray didn't feel that he had any allies on the board," Lubin recalls. "The board would have had to fire Harry, and at that point it would not have been sympathetic to Ray's desire."

Not all the directors agreed with Lubin's analysis. Indeed, American National's Allen Stults, who was seen as a Sonneborn ally, insists that Kroc's support on the board was never in doubt. And if it had come down to a vote between Kroc and Sonneborn on any policy, Stults insists, he and other board members would have stood solidly behind the chairman. "The board was not pro Sonneborn," Stults says.

"It was pro Sonneborn's policy of financial stability. Had Ray's expansion rate continued, McDonald's would never have built a financial base to expand subsequently as fast as it did. But it was Ray Kroc who built the company. His ideas and his philosophy were sound, and they had the total support of the board. To suggest otherwise is totally ridiculous."

Whether accurate or not, Kroc *perceived* that he faced a Sonneborn-controlled board, and he was determined to reconstruct a board more sympathetic to his wishes. When he asked Lubin for other director candidates, McDonald's new lawyer suggested David Wallerstein, the former president of Balaban and Katz, the movie theater chain that was the forerunner of Plitt Theaters. Wallerstein seemed a perfect candidate. He was more retail oriented than financially oriented. Like Kroc, he was an entrepreneur. Furthermore, he was in the entertainment business and had the type of showmanship Kroc admired. He also had experience on a major board, having served as a director of ABC after it acquired Balaban and Katz. After a brief meeting, Kroc was prepared to name Wallerstein to the McDonald's board to further dilute the influence of Sonneborn.

Kroc was itching to get back in complete control of his company. It was now clear to all directors that Kroc was fed up with his stalemate with Sonneborn and was ready to make a change in top management. Director Allen Stults made an eleventh-hour attempt to salvage the Kroc-Sonneborn partnership. In private meetings with Kroc, Stults argued that losing a man of Sonneborn's financial expertise was a mistake and that Kroc would be hard pressed to replace him from within. "You have to have somebody to run the company, Ray," Stults said. "You appointed Harry as CEO because you didn't want to run it day to day, and the fact that he is an able CEO has been demonstrated."

Kroc and Stults discussed the matter several times over lunch, and when those sessions were over, it was obvious to Stults that Kroc was in no mood to reconcile. "It's gone too far," a somber Kroc told Stults. "Harry's got to go."

"Who in the world is going to take over?" Stults inquired. Kroc did not hesitate. "We'll put Fred Turner in there," he shot back. "He's a smart guy, and he can learn. He can do it."

After all of his maneuvering with the board to prepare for a final confrontation with Sonneborn, Kroc discovered that his partner was in no mood to fight. Instead, he was ready to resign. He had tendered his resignation the year before, citing his sciatica. Kroc had refused his resignation then, but in early 1967, when Sonneborn offered it again, the founder readily accepted it. Later on, Kroc would remember firing Sonneborn. In fact, his partner beat him to the punch. Before he died, Harry Sonneborn conceded that he had lost his desire to run McDonald's. "I had outlived my usefulness at McDonald's," he explained. "I had accomplished everything I ever wanted to do there, and I wanted to live my remaining years in peace."

Today, Harry Sonneborn is all but forgotten inside McDonald's. In part, that is because McDonald's is now dominated by operations executives who do not share Sonneborn's notion that McDonald's is a real estate company that happens to sell hamburgers. Sonneborn also did little to enhance his place in McDonald's history by casting his ultimate vote of no confidence: He had so lost his faith in McDonald's that when he resigned in 1967, he sold all his stock—the largest block next to Kroc's—for an estimated $12 million. Although he did well in reinvesting that, he missed the enormous investment opportunity he would have had merely by holding the 170,000 shares (or 11 percent) of McDonald's that he owned when the company went public. At today's prices, that stock would be worth more than $720 million.

His resignation at age fifty-one was so bitter that when he retired to Mobile, his relationships with most McDonald's executives were severed, and his achievements were virtually stricken from the corporate record. Although no one but Kroc was more instrumental in shaping McDonald's foundation, his portrait was nowhere to be found among the paintings of McDonald's corporate managers that adorn the walls of the company's executive suite. Not until 1983 did Fred Turner commission a painting of Sonneborn for the management gallery, a first step to restoring the former president to his place in the company's history. But Turner, more than anyone, knew how tightly Kroc clung to final judgments on people: he waited until after Kroc's death in January 1984 to hang Sonneborn's portrait.

By 1967, Turner and Kroc had developed the closest thing there is to a father-son relationship, and when Sonneborn resigned it was obvious that Turner would be his successor. Still, Kroc had nearly waited too long. Turner himself was close to leaving the company, which seemed to be losing faith in itself. Although he was only thirty-five, no one else was more experienced in the McDonald's fast-food system and no one else—other than Kroc—had greater faith in its potential. But neither was anyone more frustrated by Sonneborn's rule. For months Turner had bottled up that frustration, and at a dinner meeting

at the Whitehall Hotel, where Kroc notified his young protégé of Sonneborn's resignation and his selection as successor, the emotions
came pouring from Turner's face in tears he could not hold back.

Some were tears of joy. Nearly from the day he was hired by Kroc,
Turner had dreamed of being McDonald's president. But Turner was
also unleashing pent-up anger over Kroc's failure to confront Sonneborn sooner. "Where the hell have you been?" Turner demanded.
"Why didn't you do something sooner?"

It was hardly the response Kroc had anticipated. Yet, Kroc knew
that Turner was releasing the same frustrations as Kroc himself had
been keeping under a lid. "It couldn't have been done sooner," Kroc
replied. "Things like this need time to be resolved."

Chapter 12
HIGH GEAR

It was nine o'clock in the morning and Ray Kroc had had just two hours of sleep the night before. Still, as he walked to the podium to address a convention of McDonald's operators in the fall of 1968, he felt invigorated—and very anxious. He had looked all over for Joan Smith, but he could not see her in the audience.

Ray had not seen Joan since she broke off their engagement seven years before. He had not seen her, that is, until the night before. Like other operators, Joan and her husband, Rollie, who earlier that year had become a franchisee in Winnipeg, Manitoba, had come to San Diego the day before the convention. But unlike the others, Joan had wound up in Ray Kroc's hotel suite after a dinner party.

It was an innocent rendezvous, if only because it was chaperoned by Carl Erickson, Kroc's chauffeur. For hours Ray and Joan sat at the piano playing old favorites, and they fell in love all over again. "Throw another log on the fire, Carl," Kroc would say every half hour—until 4:00 A.M., when Rollie called asking for Joan to come home. Joan's mother, who had made the trip hoping to prevent just such a rekindling of Joan's romance with Ray, insisted that Rollie and Joan leave San Diego first thing that morning. "This is like throwing gasoline on a fire," she told Joan.

Kroc was determined not to let Joan slip away a second time. He had told her the night before that he was prepared to get a divorce and marry her, and Joan had said she was ready to do the same. But when he could not spot her in attendance at his opening speech, he was worried that she had gotten cold feet again. There was one way to find out for sure, and Kroc tried it. "I'd like to recognize all of our brand-new operators in Canada," he began. "Why don't they all stand up so everyone can see them."

As he suspected, Joan was nowhere in sight. But Kroc soon realized that did not matter. When Joan left San Diego, she was following her mother's wishes regarding Ray Kroc for the last time. "When they took me out of town that morning," Joan says, "they didn't know that the die was cast, but it was. I was going to marry Ray."

As abruptly as he had announced his intention to divorce Ethel for Joan seven years before, Kroc now announced his intention to do the same with Jane. Right after the convention, key managers, directors, franchisees, and suppliers gathered in Fort Lauderdale to send off Ray and Jane on a round-the-world cruise on the *Kungsholm,* a Scandinavian ship. A bon voyage party on a chartered yacht had been planned for months, and Kroc could not back out now. At first he thought of beginning the cruise and jumping ship when the boat reached its first port, but by the time he got to Fort Lauderdale he had decided not to make the cruise at all and to announce his divorce instead. The McDonald's clan still gathered that night on the seventy-two-foot yacht, but as they cruised along the innercoastal waterway, the party was like nothing they had expected. People gathered in groups whispering the news that had stunned them. Jane was in tears, being consoled by her friends. Lou Perlman was walking around bemoaning how he just had a $200 champagne, fruit, and flower basket delivered to Kroc's cabin on the *Kungsholm.* The party on the yacht that night, recalls director Don Lubin, was McDonald's version of *Ship of Fools.*

Once more, Kroc's personal life was affecting his company's destiny. After Sonneborn had resigned, Kroc had resumed the chief executive's role. He had even delayed for a year the announcement of Fred Turner as the company's next president, hoping to give him added time to grow into the role. Yet, Kroc was convinced that he needed a strong president to replace Sonneborn, someone who shared his faith in McDonald's and his commitment to quality, service, cleanliness, and value. Although he would remain intimately involved in McDonald's, he was not going to be the type of founder who refused to relinquish power until it was too late.

Now, one year after Sonneborn's departure, Ray Kroc had the best reason of all to turn the reins of his company over to Fred Turner: he was going to start a new life with Joan. "Ray was the classic entrepreneur, except he didn't make the classic mistake of hanging on too long," observes Harry Fisher, the former partner of Paine Webber who served as McDonald's investment banker for more than a decade. "Ray came back to Chicago at the right time [to take over from Sonneborn], but when he knew he had the right people in the saddle—particularly Fred Turner—he had the good sense to bug off."

Given the experience he had had with Harry Sonneborn, it is perhaps surprising that Kroc was ready so soon to turn over chief executive power to someone else. But Kroc was certain he had picked the man who could get McDonald's moving again, because he knew that no one shared his grand vision of McDonald's more completely than Fred Turner.

Once again, however, the founder had not attempted to install his clone in the presidency. To casual observers, Ray Kroc and Fred Turner were as different from each other as were Kroc and Sonneborn. Outward appearances were critical to Kroc, who was always nattily dressed. Turner had considerably less interest in appearances, and it showed. At the dedication of the new $500,000 Hamburger University in 1968, June Martino pulled the new McDonald's president aside to tell him that Director Allen Stults observed that Turner's pants were too baggy. Turner knew that the source of that complaint was really Kroc.

Kroc was comfortable as a public figure, and he made no attempt to conceal his growing fortune. Turner kept his profile almost as low as Sonneborn's, and the typical symbols of wealth were ostentatious by his standards. He and his wife, Patty, continued to live in their middle-class suburb even when they easily could have moved into one of the exclusive enclaves of Chicago's business elite. And while he briefly tolerated Kroc's wish that he be chauffeured to work, Turner quietly dismissed the Cadillac limo because it did not square with his concept of a hamburger chain as an egalitarian enterprise.

Kroc was well suited to running a hamburger chain because he was a showman, and he understood there was a strong element of show business in McDonald's. Turner has none of Kroc's panache. Although every bit as strong willed and decisive, he is more at ease operating behind the scenes. He does not court press attention; indeed, he seems to try his best to avoid it. And when he grants interviews, he lacks Kroc's flair for colorfully summing things up. His demeanor is serious, and he eschews the black and white oversimplifications that make for easy reading—all traits that have made him vulnerable to reporters who choose to exploit his candidness.

In 1979, syndicated business writer Dan Dorfman wrote an article for *Esquire* magazine that recited Wall Street's perennial concern that the fast-food market was saturated and McDonald's growth would be stifled. Their concerns always proved to be unfounded, and Dorfman's analysis was so trite that other executives might have breezily glossed over it and steered the writer into a more productive direction. Turner took each concern seriously, almost combatively, and unsuspectingly fell into Dorfman's trap. "I found him defensive, often tense, and angry at times," Dorfman wrote. "On occasion, when confronted with an especially tough question, he would hesitate, rise nervously, and then pace back and forth as he replied. Through a three-hour interview . . . he repeatedly responded to questions by closing his eyes, turning his head away, putting his right hand over his face and massaging it. Clearly, he struck me as a man with a lot on his mind." Turner declined press interviews for the next two years.

Although he has run McDonald's longer than Ray Kroc did, Fred Turner has never outshone the founder. In part, that is because Turner insisted on deflecting most of the spotlight onto Kroc. "Fred's a modest man, and he may have learned a lesson by watching what happened to Harry Sonneborn when he tried to overshadow Ray," observed McDonald's Director David Wallerstein. "But Fred also had such love and respect for Ray that he wanted Ray to continue to be McDonald's personality. That was important, because most big companies don't have personalities anymore."

Throughout the 1970s, the founder remained the chief spokesman for McDonald's, and as the chain sprouted thousands of outlets, Kroc played the key role in maintaining its image as a colorful and human organization. It was Kroc who stole the show at new restaurant openings. It was Kroc who gave the major public speeches and appeared before the television cameras. And in most newspaper and magazine stories, it was Kroc—not Turner—who was quoted. Kroc was also McDonald's best contact with its second most important public—its franchisees. His office in San Diego (he moved it there from Los Angeles in 1974) was visited each week by a dozen or so franchisees looking for Kroc's advice.

Turner was by no means subservient to Kroc, but he did nothing to dispel the notion that McDonald's founder was still "the boss" of the chain. He referred to him as such; and even on matters of seemingly little consequence, Turner made certain that the boss had his way when he really wanted it. While Turner wound up having the final say on multimillion-dollar projects, he insisted that Kroc make the final determination on all executive salaries and bonuses, because he knew Kroc wanted the privilege of knocking $1,000 or so off one manager's bonus and adding it to another's. At times, accommodating Kroc's small wishes required considerable creativity. When National Guard troops killed four peace demonstrators at Kent State University in 1970, Kroc insisted that all flags at McDonald's fly at full staff. But a panicky operator in one university town notified Turner that students—the heart of his customer base—were demanding that he and other merchants fly their flags at half staff in honor of the slain demonstrators. Turner took the operator off the hook without riling the founder: he told the franchisee to back his bun supplier's truck into the flagpole and knock it down.

Yet, Turner's deference to Kroc went beyond outward appearances. Kroc was his mentor, and when Turner called him on an almost daily basis, he did so because he wanted input from a man whose retailing and operations genius he genuinely respected. Thus, although Kroc remained on the West Coast after Turner became president, he continued to play an extremely active role in the company. He remained the chief advocate of new products to expand the chain's appeal, and he suggested hundreds of locations for new restaurants. More than anyone else, he monitored sales reports on new outlets, and he continued personally to pester operators whose restaurants were below par on QSC&V.

In cases where he was convinced that a new policy was right, Kroc rammed it through. In late 1969, for example, he ordered that the territorial boundary of a new franchise be reduced from a three-mile radius around the store to a single street address. The old territory had been considered part and parcel of a franchise, but, years ahead of everyone else, Kroc envisioned instances in which McDonald's units might be located within a couple of blocks of each other. "He pushed it and pushed it, and none of us could understand why," Turner says of Kroc's insistence on the change. "We only adopted it because he was pushing so hard."

In short, Turner's approach to Kroc restored the harmony that was missing in the mid-1960s, when McDonald's was dangerously split into two camps. No small part of the new harmony was the close personal relationship that had developed between Turner and Kroc. "Fred became the son Ray never had," observed Director David Wallerstein. "Basically, Fred worshiped Ray, but he could handle him. He had the knack of selling something to him by letting him think it was his idea. He handled him the way a son handles a father." Director Allen Stults added: "Fred was amazing in his treatment of Ray, because he wasn't play acting when he called out to California to see what 'the boss' was thinking, and yet at the same time he has been every bit as strong in running McDonald's as Harry was."

Still, Turner was so overshadowed by Kroc's public presence that outside McDonald's he was virtually unknown—even by a business community that should have known the chief executive of an $11-billion-a-year enterprise. Such a fate might be deserved had Turner been merely a caretaker for a powerful founder. While that may well be the image, the reality is vastly different.

Even as Ray Kroc continued to receive the public adoration as the chief architect of McDonald's stunning success, he was quietly letting Turner call virtually all the shots. Turner wasted no time exercising that power, and his decisions were anything but those of a caretaker manager. Indeed, during his first five full years as president—from 1969 through 1973—Turner directed more changes than McDonald's had experienced in its previous fifteen years. Kroc clearly had given McDonald's its roots, but Turner so vastly changed things that the McDonald's that emerged at the end of that period bore only a passing resemblance to the McDonald's that had entered it. David Wallerstein declared: "The modern McDonald's is strictly the creation of Fred Turner."

When Turner became president in 1968, McDonald's was at the watershed that young companies inevitably reach when they succeed in the first phase of their development. It was attempting to make the difficult transition into a major corporation. When Turner took over, McDonald's seemed unwilling to make that transition. The fast-food industry was now exploding, but McDonald's onetime dominance in the market was being severely challenged. Other competitors appeared just as ready and able to become the ultimate industry leader.

In fact, some of McDonald's biggest competitors seemed more intent on becoming the new leader than McDonald's was on preserving its lead. In 1967, Burger King's expansion program finally broke the one hundred new restaurants per year mark, equaling for the first time the expansion pace of McDonald's. While that gave Burger King only slightly more than one-third the number of locations that McDonald's had, the Miami-based chain that year potentially became the industry's best financed competitor by virtue of its acquisition by Pillsbury Corporation, the third-largest packaged foods company. By outward appearances, Burger Chef was mounting an even greater challenge. At the beginning of 1968, its expansion program had closed the gap between it and McDonald's to less than one hundred stores. And during the same year, General Foods, the number two food processor, followed Pillsbury into the business by laying out $20 million to buy Burger Chef.

The corporate race into the high-flying fast-food industry was on. In a few years, virtually all the food processing giants would have a stake in the business. Ralston Purina acquired a West Coast drive-in called Jack-in-the-Box. Borden's was developing a new hamburger chain called Burger Boy. Consolidated Foods had bought Chicken Delight. Great Western, the sugar-based conglomerate, bought Shakey's Pizza. Servomation, a company specializing in institutional feeding, bought Red Barn, an impressive fast-food entry originating in Ohio. And Marriott Corporation, having failed at its fast-food effort—the conversion of its famous Washington, D.C., Hot Shoppe's to Hot Shoppe Juniors—was having much better luck with a new fast-food operation called Roy Rogers.

Furthermore, scores of new companies were hoping to cash in on what was quickly developing into a fast-food craze. It was now fashionable for celebrities to lend their names to fast-food chains. Minnie Pearl's popularity with the Grand Ole Opry was used to promote Minnie Pearl Chicken franchises in the South, and character actor Arthur Treacher gave his name to a fish and chips chain. Another new entry called Carson's was trying to capitalize on the popularity of talk-show host Johnny Carson. As it turned out, Harry Sonneborn's slowdown, timed for a recession that never materialized, left McDonald's in an extremely precarious position—a leader caught off guard by explosive growth in its business. "Competition was popping up all around us," Turner recalls. "You almost had a new chain a week."

With such competitive pressure, it was anything but certain that McDonald's could maintain its market leadership and its corporate independence at the same time. Others in Ray Kroc's position might have been tempted to take their capital gains and seek shelter in the arms of a well-heeled corporate parent. In fact, within months after selecting Turner as president, Kroc had a golden opportunity to do just that. He, Turner, and Dick Boylan had been invited to dine at the New York apartment of conglomerateur Nate Cummings, the domineering chief executive of Consolidated Foods and the architect of its acquisition strategy. The walls of Cummings's apartment at the Waldorf-Astoria were covered with impressionist art that never failed to affect executives of companies Cummings was scouting. "I felt like a fly in the spider's web," Turner remembers.

Ever so tactfully, Cummings broached the subject of acquisition. "Is there some way we could bring our companies together?" Cummings asked Kroc, politely suggesting a "marriage" and carefully avoiding terms, such as *takeover,* that came closer to describing the arrangement he had in mind. "You've got a marvelous company, and that is a great compliment," responded a guileless Kroc. "The problem is that we just wouldn't consider something like that unless we were the surviving company, and I'm afraid that managing a company like yours is just more than we could handle." Recalls Turner of Cummings's reaction: "His jaw just dropped. I'm sure he had been turned down before, but that had to be the most memorable turndown Nate Cummings ever had."

Kroc's response was more meaningful in the message it conveyed to McDonald's young president. The founder was not in the least interested in selling out, and he was obviously giving Turner the green light to shift McDonald's into high gear. Turner's strategy simply called for expanding McDonald's at a pace that no fast-food executive, even Kroc himself, thought was possible.

Securities analysts were already talking about the saturation of the fast-food market, but Turner did not believe it. "There was pent-up consumer demand throughout the system, and all of our markets needed more outlets," Turner says. "And to be more competitive, we also needed the additional advertising dollars that new stores would generate. Everyone on the operations side of the company knew it. The operators knew it. I knew it. The growth in our volume averages per store suggested it. It was screamingly apparent."

But if expansion was an obvious solution to the competitive challenge, Turner's notion of expansion caught everyone—most of all McDonald's competitors—by surprise. In his first two years as president, Turner doubled McDonald's real estate and construction staff to implement his bold plan to increase the chain's store openings over a five-year period from 100 new units a year to 500 a year. While Burger Chef and Burger King had begun matching McDonald's old expansion rate, they did not come close to keeping up with the new pace: 211 new restaurants in 1969, 294 in 1970, 312 in 1971, 368 in 1972, 445 in 1973, and finally 515 in 1974.

By 1974, McDonald's had a nationwide chain of three thousand restaurants—three times larger than what Turner inherited when he became president five years before. But, even more important, McDonald's had reestablished its hegemony in the fast-food business at a critical period when competitive market positions were being delineated for the long term. Indeed the timing of McDonald's expansion was prescient. Its new restaurant program was exploding just as its biggest competitors were making the mistake of easing off.

Reacting to a shakeout in the fast-food business, Pillsbury slowed the aggressive expansion of Burger King, and by 1974 it had been left behind in McDonald's dust—two thousand stores behind the industry leader. Jim McLamore, the cofounder of the chain, who had sold out to Pillsbury hoping to find the funds to catch McDonald's, stepped down from the presidency of Burger King, disappointed that Pillsbury had pulled back. McLamore believes that the events in fast food from 1969 through 1972 largely explain why McDonald's by 1991 held a 2.2 to 1 lead in hamburger sales in the United States (2.8 to 1 worldwide) over second-ranked Burger King. "We had been tracking McDonald's by about forty months in the late 1960s, and our rate of growth was actually much higher than theirs," McLamore recalls. "But one of the mistakes Pillsbury made was that it suddenly held the growth of Burger King back between 1969 and 1972, and McDonald's picked up a great advantage. Ray Kroc recognized, to his everlasting credit, that that was precisely the time to go faster in this business."

But in light of the disaster that was developing at General Foods' Burger Chef, Pillsbury's managers had good reason to wonder whether a food service operation was a good mix with their traditional food packaging businesses. Most of the huge food processors that took the plunge into fast food in the late 1960s were surprised by the complexity of managing the business and disappointed by their results. Servomation virtually destroyed the once promising Red Barn operation it had acquired, because it failed to provide the chain sufficient capital to get through the developmental period when profits are low or nonexistent. Similarly, Ralston Purina embarked on an ill-fated national expansion of Jack-in-the-Box and later was forced to retreat to the chain's strong base in the Southwest.

But none of the industry's newcomers was more bitterly disappointed than General Foods. When Burger Chef sold out to General Foods in early 1968, it had 850 stores, compared with 970 for McDonald's. But it was rapidly closing the gap, opening new units at the astonishing rate of 300 a year—three times the pace that Harry

Sonneborn had set. "We had just increased our potential for even faster growth by enlarging our field staff and by opening new territories, but we had more growth potential than we could finance," recalls Robert Wildman, the former executive vice president of Burger Chef. "We sold out to General Foods because we thought they could finance our faster growth. It didn't work out that way."

Initially, General Foods did pump massive resources into Burger Chef, but it also made the critical mistake of eliminating its fifty-four-man field staff, which scouted new properties and supervised new store development. Some of the chain's field men were making more money than the General Foods managers who were dispatched to Indianapolis to run the chain. The General Foods executives assumed they could eliminate the hefty salaries of the field men by replacing the entire field real estate staff with independent real estate brokers. When word of that spread, brokers flooded Burger Chef with property proposals. But many of those sites were ill suited for fast food, and by eliminating its field men, General Foods began losing its grip on the new store development program. By 1971 it was obvious to everyone that Burger Chef's expansion program was out of control: General Foods brought new store development to a screeching halt and took a $75 million write-off on its fast-food operation.

In a single year, General Foods had managed to lose more money in the hamburger business than McDonald's had earned in the preceding decade. Burger Chef was never again a serious threat to McDonald's. The chain never expanded beyond the peak of twelve hundred units that it reached in the early 1970s. After a series of additional fast-food setbacks, General Foods sold its hamburger chain, and today Burger Chef—a division of Hardees—has less than one hundred restaurants in operation.

The red ink pouring out of Burger Chef was a clear signal to the food processing giants and conglomerates that the fast-food business was not the source of easy money that they had thought it was. In fact, it revealed a major flaw in the concept of a large and diversified company attempting to manage a fast-food operation in the same way as it ran its manufacturing divisions—from a corporate headquarters.

The packaged foods companies belatedly discovered that there was an enormous difference between the management of manufactured foods sold to grocers and foods prepared and sold directly to customers at a fast-food outlet. In the former, manufacturing is centralized and more easily controlled, and the sale to the consumer is indirect and depends highly on branded advertising. In the latter, production is decentralized and difficult to control, since each store is a self-sustaining production unit. Furthermore, the sale to the consumer is direct and depends highly on local service. "Burger Chef just did not fit well into General Foods' management structure," Wildman observes. "They were used to running a Jell-O factory, filling up boxes and building demand through advertising. Our business was foreign to General Foods managers, who were inexperienced in dealing directly with consumers and with service people. When General Foods managers were assigned to Burger Chef, they felt as if they were being sent to Siberia."

Kroc had avoided a similar fate by steadfastly insisting on McDonald's independence. But simply avoiding acquisition did not eliminate the risks Turner was taking with his massive expansion program. Even if it remained independent, there was no guarantee that McDonald's might not lose control of its growth in the same ways as General Foods lost control over Burger Chef.

Yet, Turner knew that McDonald's had the industry's best field service operation. Burger Chef, by comparison, had one of the worst. McDonald's had also organized itself on a regional basis in 1965; and as soon as Turner embarked on his massive expansion program, he began boosting McDonald's regions, increasing the number of regional offices from five in 1967 to eight in 1973. More important, Turner vastly increased the regional manager's authority. Where previously final decisions on new restaurant sites and new franchisees were made by McDonald's headquarters management, Turner ordered that those decisions would now rest solely in the regions. Regional managers were given powers nearly equal to those of presidents of independent regional chains. Their decisions on franchising and real estate matters were the final word.

In a few years, Turner had replaced Sonneborn's relatively centralized management style with one of the most decentralized structures in corporate America. Yet, in a service business where the final product was produced in the field, decentralizing power actually increased McDonald's control over expansion. Managers were closer to where the action was and thus could make better informed judgments. Their decisions were tailored to the unique operational problems and growth opportunities of their local markets. In short, McDonald's took the very opposite management approach that the packaged food companies followed in fast food. In food service, Turner notes, "the closer decision making is to the stores and to the marketplace, the better are the decisions that managers make."

The fact that McDonald's decentralization plan helped maintain the chain's high level of control over service quality and site selection was quickly evident from the sales performance at its stores. While average store volumes at Burger Chef and other rapidly expanding chains plummeted in the late 1960s, McDonald's sales per store soared from $333,000 to $621,000 during Turner's first five years, even as the number of locations tripled.

Maintaining control was only one of the challenges of McDonald's massive expansion program. It also created an obvious financial burden. Sonneborn had thought he had solved McDonald's capital crunch, but he had been building a total of only one hundred new units per year. Turner each year was *raising* by one hundred the number of new restaurants added to the preceding year. But it was not just the size of the expansion program that strained McDonald's finances. Instead of leasing land for new stores, which had been Sonneborn's practice, Turner ordered the chain's managers to begin buying all new unit sites that were available for purchase, and almost overnight McDonald's began taking title to the property on two-thirds of its new stores.

Although acquiring land might be more expensive initially than leasing it, payments on land purchases eventually end when the property is owned free and clear. Lease obligations endure, Turner reasoned, and as the business succeeds and the value of the land grows, leasing costs are bound to increase—perhaps three to fourfold—as leases expire and are renegotiated. "It was a no-brainer, an obvious thing to do," Turner explains. "You make more money on a new store for the first five years by leasing. But after that, you make more money by owning."

The land acquisition strategy reflected the type of long-term profit perspective that was typically absent from other corporations, which in the late 1960s and 1970s were maximizing each quarter's profits. Yet, it involved considerable near-term risks, because it nearly doubled the amount of capital McDonald's had to lay out for each new store. That meant carrying a much heavier debt load. Indeed, Turner's gamble on real estate made Sonneborn's pale by comparison. On the other hand, the payoff was much bigger, too. Today, McDonald's owns the land at 69 percent of its domestic restaurants, whereas other chains continue to lease the great bulk of their store sites. As the fast-food industry matures, they face major escalations in their rents as their twenty-year land leases approach expiration. Thus, while Sonneborn taught all fast-food chains the benefits of real estate leasing, Turner put McDonald's in the enviable position of being the world's largest owner of retail property.

Still another feature of the expansion program that greatly increased its financial burden was the overhaul McDonald's decided to make in its building, which had not undergone fundamental change since Dick and Mac invented the design in the early 1950s. As a result, virtually all McDonald's depended exclusively on carryout orders placed at their front service windows. But, following the lead of Ray Kroc, who had launched an extensive patio seating program in California, Turner now decided that the system was finally ripe for a mass conversion to indoor seating. "We were confronted with a more discriminating fast-food market, and customers were looking for more accoutrements," he says. And by the late 1960s, environmentalism was giving McDonald's another reason to add seating. "The red-and-white tile building with golden hoops going through the roof was becoming a period piece." Turner explains. "The arches in the roof were not seen as benefiting the American landscape anymore."

The new design, introduced in 1968, was a dramatic departure from the old one. The Golden Arches, the very signature of McDonald's, came off the building (but remained on the sign). Red-and-white tiles were replaced with brick. The slanted roof gave way to a more contemporary mansard roof. But easily the most dramatic—and potentially traumatic—change was the expansion of the building to accommodate fifty seats. "We had grown up as a carryout drive-in," Turner observes, "and we were turning ourselves into a restaurant."

The change was traumatic in financial terms as well, both to franchisees and to McDonald's. It cost $50,000 to remodel existing stores to the new format, and by asking its franchisees to pay for that, McDonald's was attempting what no other fast-food franchise had dared—to encourage franchisees to make a whopping reinvestment in their units. McDonald's sold the concept by convincing franchisees that seating would increase their sales by at least 20 percent and that the profits from that would pay for the investment in three years.

Those projections proved to be conservative, but there was no guarantee that franchisees would believe them. However, by the late 1960s, the company had built up considerable credibility with its owner/operators on reinvestment issues. Its traffic building projections supporting much smaller investments in such things as fish fryers and winterfronts had been right on the money. Thus, when the company made similar claims for the remodeling program, most franchisees had faith in the accuracy of its sales projections. In essence, the conversion program was massively capitalizing on something McDonald's had developed that many other franchisers ignored: the trust of its franchisees.

McDonald's, of course, was leading the way in supporting the conversion, since all new stores after 1968 were built with the new design. That, however, only further aggravated the pressure that was building to finance Turner's expansion effort. The new McDonald's building cost $100,000 a copy—double the cost of the red-and-white striper—and when that was added to the new costs involved in buying land and the costs related to the sheer size of the new store program, it soon became clear that the task of financing McDonald's expansion was going to be monumental.

Despite that, Turner paid little attention to the financial challenge. Rather, he simply turned the problem over to Dick Boylan, the company's chief financial officer. Typically, it is the financial executive who informs the chief executive how much capital he has each year to devote to expansion, but in 1968 Turner was in no mood to hear about the capital constraints from his top financial executive. Turner recalls: "I just told Dick, 'I'm buying; you get the money.' "

From then on, an interesting relationship developed between Turner and Boylan, who previously was Sonneborn's right-hand man and had been considered by some insiders a prime candidate to replace him. Indeed, Sonneborn himself preferred Boylan as his successor, and he placed him on McDonald's board in 1961. Given Boylan's close association with Sonneborn, Turner might have been expected to replace him. Instead, Turner relied on Boylan even more than Sonneborn had and gave him considerably more latitude over McDonald's finances. Turner never overruled Boylan on financial matters; indeed, he tolerated Boylan's preference for reporting primarily to the board of directors and for keeping Turner minimally informed on what he was doing in finance. Boylan had such autonomy in his area that Turner, when introducing his top management at shareholder meetings or to security analysts, would occasionally note that "Dick Boylan is our senior executive vice president in charge of finance, and he reports to his wife, Rose."

Turner had good reason for granting Boylan such sweeping powers. A novice himself in finance, Turner needed Boylan to supervise the funding of his expansion program while he busied himself oversee-ing all its operational aspects. For Boylan's part, his newfound powers in financing may well explain why he remained at McDonald's after losing the presidency to Turner. "I let Dick do his thing by staying out of his hair," Turner says. "Consequently, he let me do my thing. He could have fought me and made things difficult. He was disappointed —thought he should have been made president and, I'm sure, felt that he was far more qualified. But we developed a close personal regard for one another and an arm's length business relationship. We had a truce."

The unexpected cooperation between Boylan and Turner—with one controlling finances and the other overseeing everything else— was nearly as critical a turning point in McDonald's as the replacement of Sonneborn. Had Turner taken over finance, he would have raised much of the expansion money by selling McDonald's stock, which seemed to be the cheapest way of raising capital. "My view was that stock financing was free money," Turner recalls. Boylan's view was diametrically opposed to that. "It's a hard point to get across, but selling stock is the most expensive form of financing for a growth company," Boylan argues. "By borrowing, you lock in a rate and even-tually pay off the loan. But you are never through paying for an equity financing, because the dilution of the stock is permanent, and you pay dividends on the new shares forever."

By favoring 100 percent debt financing, however, Boylan's policy in financing the expansion matched Turner's strategy in making it: both chose a plan that produced the best long-term result, not the easiest short-term gain. Still, it was not easy for many in McDonald's to understand the concept. The company had a high-flying stock with an attractive price-earnings ratio. A stock financing seemed easy and in-volved no payment of interest. "I had to fight constant pressure to sell stock," Boylan recalls.

The soft-spoken and mild-mannered Boylan seemed at first to be a pushover for the strong-willed Turner. Yet, on financing, Boylan was unrelenting and unyielding. Despite growing pressure from Turner and the company's investment bankers for additional stock offerings, Boy-lan financed McDonald's ambitious expansion program by taking one debt issue to market after another. Indeed, he expanded the com-pany's long-term debt from $43.5 million at the end of 1968 to $353 million by the end of 1974. And during that period, McDonald's raised only $65 million of equity. That represented Boylan's only compromise to Turner, and it remains the only stock ever sold by McDonald's. All other public offerings of McDonald's stock, including the initial one, consisted of blocks sold by Kroc and other major shareholders.

In some respects, Boylan's heavy borrowing was the riskiest part of the expansion gamble. If the expansion worked, Boylan's leveraged financing ensured that the fruits of McDonald's success would be reserved for existing shareholders. But McDonald's was also building a massive debt servicing liability, and if there were any reversals in the fast-food market, the company could wind up in a dangerous cash squeeze.

McDonald's was headed in a financial direction totally opposite from the course charted by Boylan's mentor, Harry Sonneborn, who had planned a steady reduction of the company's debt. Under Boylan's direction, McDonald's easily led the food service industry in the standard measurement of leverage—the ratio of long-term debt to shareholder equity. Conservatives believe a one to one ratio is pushing your luck in a high-risk industry such as fast food. Boylan had taken McDonald's well beyond those limits. By 1973, McDonald's had 40 percent more debt than equity.

But Boylan carefully projected the McDonald's earnings five years into the future to ensure that the company did not borrow itself into bankruptcy. When analysts and directors argued that McDonald's had to sell $100 million in stock to keep its debt and equity in better balance, Boylan pulled out charts showing how the company would increase its equity by that amount within months even without a stock financing—by *earning* it.

In retrospect, Boylan's financial planning seems prescient. He had scheduled McDonald's heaviest borrowings for the first half of the 1970s, when McDonald's was financing its biggest growth spurt. Thereafter, he reasoned, growth rates would slow, and McDonald's would gradually reduce its debt as it generated more income. As it turned out, Boylan did his heaviest borrowing when interest rates were relatively low, and McDonald's debt began to level by 1979 when most of its expansion could be financed from profits. That is precisely the time, of course, that the prime rate soared to 20 percent. And by avoiding the sale of stock, Boylan ensured that all of McDonald's fabulous growth benefited existing stockholders. Anyone who held McDonald's stock has gained over the years by eleven stock splits (and one stock dividend) which *alone* have increased by 372 times the value of a share of

McDonald's stock bought in the first public offering in 1965. A single share of McDonald's stock bought at $22.50 almost three decades ago is worth more than $10,000 today. "There was risk involved," observes Harry Fisher, McDonald's former investment banker. "But McDonald's decision to go the leverage route as opposed to the equity route in its financing was an exquisite decision."

But, while he let Boylan draft that financial strategy, Turner did anything but shy away from the financial community. In fact, he began displaying the same intense curiosity there that he had always shown in operations. Turner quickly picked up the jargon of Wall Street and soon was putting together sophisticated presentations to securities analysts, who found him surprisingly candid in discussing McDonald's shortcomings instead of glossing over them. Yet, he insisted on approaching Wall Street on his terms, and because his roots were far removed from established financial circles, those terms were unorthodox.

Fisher recalls how McDonald's president battled with investment bankers on interest rates they set on the company's debt offerings. He rejected their established formulas for pricing based solely on what interest rates were being paid by companies carrying a similar Standard and Poor's rating. On one occasion, when investment bankers tried arguing Turner off his demand for a lower rate by pulling out their spreadsheets showing what "similar" companies were paying, Turner grabbed their papers and tore them into pieces. "I don't give a damn about other companies," he roared. "We are McDonald's!" To Turner, the exercise was no different from negotiating the best price on meat and potatoes, but it caught the buttoned-down investment bankers off guard.

Turner was demanding the same type of respect for the fast-food business that investment bankers gave to more established industries. That was a tall order. During the late 1960s, fast-food stocks were considered a crapshoot. Some had produced windfalls, but many more had yielded sobering losses. As such, investment bankers looked at fast-food companies as novelties.

Turner insisted it was a serious business, and he was annoyed when McDonald's was misunderstood by Wall Street, particularly by his company's own brokerage firm—Paine Webber. Fisher remembers vividly how he persuaded Turner to travel to New York to meet his boss, Tom Wenzell, head of Paine Webber's investment banking division. As Fisher describes it, the blood flowing in Wenzell's veins was bluer than the water in Strauss's Danube. He was a "double H," Fisher says, referring to Wenzell's undergraduate and law degrees from Harvard. He was president of the Audubon Society, lived in Connecticut, and spoke with an eastern accent that bespeaks old money. He was Turner's image of investment banking—schooled in Standard Oil, AT&T, and U.S. Steel, but a snob when it came to fast food.

Fittingly, Wenzell took Turner to dinner at a private room at the 21 Club. As long as the discussion remained on Wall Street, Wenzell was on solid ground, but when he tried to inquire politely about Turner's business, the stage was set for a collision between a midwestern populist and an eastern elitist. "I understand that you sell a lot of Coca-Cola in McDonald's stores," Wenzell politely inquired. "Is that true?" "Yes, it is," Turner confirmed. "Well," Wenzell continued, "just what do you do to dispose of all those bottles?"

Turner's back stiffened at a remark he regarded as an insult. Here was a man whose firm was pocketing handsome commissions on one of Wall Street's hottest stocks, and he did not understand that McDonald's dispenses Coke from a machine and serves it in paper cups. "How in hell can you be my investment banker?" Turner bitterly demanded. "You've never been inside a McDonald's." The dinner ended abruptly, and although Paine Webber kept the McDonald's account, Turner never forgave Wenzell for his faux pas.

Even as Turner was attempting to change Wall Street's concepts about McDonald's, he was undergoing a metamorphosis of his own. For a man who rose up the McDonald's ladder by searching for the right temperature to cook french fries and for the perfect level of ice crystals in milk shakes, Turner proved to be a surprisingly quick study on financial matters and a fascinated player of the corporate money game. In some respects, he was becoming more financially adept than his predecessor. By purchasing most real estate at new restaurant sites, Turner plunged McDonald's deeper into real estate than Sonneborn had ever dreamed of doing. But he also saw an entirely new profit stream that Sonneborn had not seen. Unlike Sonneborn, who preserved McDonald's almost exclusively as a franchising operation, Turner concluded the moment he took over as president that McDonald's was missing a golden profit opportunity by not running more units on its own, claiming the operating profit that normally goes to the franchisee.

Turner also concluded that for the company to run restaurants in a market successfully, it had to obtain the management economies of operating a large cluster of units in certain markets. Since most major markets were already franchised, the only way to build a profit center around company-operated stores was to buy out some of McDonald's largest and most successful franchisees. Thus, beginning in late 1967, even as he was revving up McDonald's new unit construction efforts, Turner supervised the most ambitious corporate buyout program ever undertaken in franchising. The timing was right for it. A growing number of veteran McDonald's operators had become millionaires—on paper. Now they were looking to convert their wealth in McDonald's franchises into wealth they could spend.

The fact that McDonald's had a hot stock gave Turner the perfect buyout tool—one that provided a tax-free exchange for the operator and an acquisition bargain for McDonald's. "Some of our operators had tremendous wealth but no money," Turner explains. "And we were using McDonald's stock that was trading at twenty-five times earnings to buy restaurants for seven times their earnings. There was tremendous leverage and earnings growth." McDonald's was in a position to pick the very best markets, and no one was more suited for the role of cherry picker than Turner, who understood McDonald's operating strongholds better than anyone.

Yet, the major purchase that led the way to a massive expansion of McOpCo, the subsidiary that runs the company-owned restaurants, was negotiated by Kroc, not Turner. It involved the buyout of the premier franchise in the system—the forty-three-unit Gee Gee franchise in Washington, D.C., owned by John Gibson and Oscar Goldstein. The news of the Gee Gee sale was certain to stimulate the already hot pursuit for a McDonald's franchise. The partners sold their Washington operation for a cool $16.8 million. Gee Gee's franchise covered only metropolitan Washington, and yet the purchase price was six times what Kroc had paid only five years earlier to buy the national master franchise from the McDonald brothers. It was within a few million of what Pillsbury and General Foods had paid for Burger King and Burger Chef.

Given the size of the deal, Kroc wanted to buy the partners out with stock, and he was outraged when Gibson and Goldstein demanded cash. "When you want cash, you want my flesh," Kroc roared. Nevertheless, because Gee Gee had had such a strong operations team and because it also had the unique right to develop all of its own real estate, Kroc was eager to reclaim the only franchise that paid no rent to

McDonald's. So, as he had done with the McDonald brothers five years before, Kroc caved in to the sellers' demand for cash. But he never forgave Gibson and Goldstein for being so adamant about refusing to accept stock. Not long after the deal was completed, Goldstein called Kroc from his retirement home in Florida, complaining about boredom and asking for another franchise. Kroc flatly refused him. "Goldy," Kroc told him, "when you demanded cash, you entered hell."

The acquisition of Gee Gee was the beginning of a wave of buyouts by Turner that converted dozens of McDonald's pioneering franchisees into instant millionaires. In the process, McDonald's picked up experienced managers to run its mushrooming McOpCo operation. Turner bought the seven units in Minneapolis owned by Jim Zien, one of the system's most proficient marketers. In two separate acquisitions, be bought out the franchises of Mel Garb and Harold Stern, who sold their forty-two restaurants in such scattered markets as Michigan, Nevada, California, and Oklahoma. He acquired the sixteen-restaurant franchise of Jack Penrod in south Florida, and the twenty-one unit operation in the Tampa–St. Petersburg area that was owned by Phil and Vern Vineyard.

From 1967 through 1976—the era of the buyouts—Turner and Kroc negotiated the acquisition of 536 stores from McDonald's franchisees for a total of $189 million in cash and stock. When they were finished with their buying spree, McOpCo's base of stores was half as large as McDonald's franchised operations. The acquisition binge had also given McDonald's an important third profit leg—the earnings from company stores—to supplement the income the company made from real estate and from the franchise and service fees it collected from franchisees. In 1993, the 4,161 company- and affiliate-run restaurants accounted for 70 percent of McDonald's revenues. But the acquisition of so many franchised units carried the potential for changing the fundamental character of McDonald's. In his first five years, Turner's buyout program had lifted the percentage of McOpCo units from 9 to almost 33 percent of total McDonald's outlets. To be sure, McDonald's needed additional company-owned stores simply to groom new managers for a chain that was growing exponentially. But Turner's expansion of McOpCo clearly went well beyond that.

The McOpCo stores had already become an important source of profits, and Turner was convinced McDonald's had a golden opportunity in expanding their contribution to the company's bottom line. "Fred's acquisition program did not square with the old philosophy that the company stores existed primarily as a training ground for McDonald's managers," observed former Senior Executive Vice President Gerry Newman. "The philosophy now was to make much more money on company stores. It was a fork in the road."

It was a potentially dangerous fork. Turner was having too much success in buying franchised operations and expanding them. Acquiring earnings so easily and relatively cheaply could have become addictive. Indeed, given the easy profits that Turner was buying, it must have seemed tempting to continue running the McOpCo percentage higher and higher until McDonald's changed from a franchiser into an operator of company-owned stores.

Turner saw the danger. In the early 1970s, he suddenly realized that his expansion of McOpCo had gotten out of hand and was now threatening the good of the entire system. It was stretching McDonald's management beyond practical limits, and company-store operations in some major markets began to suffer. Lacking the incentive and drive of entrepreneurial owner/operators, company-run stores rarely equaled the profit margins of franchised units. While company operations could succeed in strong markets that yielded above-average volumes, they often ran into profit problems in markets that produced average sales or in tougher, central-city markets that presented a host of special operating challenges. In marginal markets, it was becoming clear that the above-average dedication of an owner/operator was critical to profitability. "When we hit twenty-five percent company-owned, I thought we could handle thirty-three percent," Turner recalls. "I went too far."

Turner might have resolved the problems by expanding McDonald's home office and regional management staff even faster, but he rejected the option. "If you have too many company stores, you are no longer sufficiently oriented to the backbone of the system, which is the franchised community," Turner reasons. That is exactly what happened in Washington, D.C., where company stores vastly outnumbered franchising units. Turner admits: "We started doing a poor job servicing licensees there, and we didn't really relate to them."

Turner did not like the trend. By becoming a chain of company-operated units, of course, McDonald's could claim all of the profits, instead of splitting them with millionaire franchisees. But Turner concluded that while a predominantly company-owned retail operation might produce high profitability in the short term, it would compromise McDonald's competitive superiority—and jeopardize profits—over the long term.

He decided that McDonald's had to remain primarily a franchising business. Quickly, Turner capped the company-operated portion of McDonald's stores at 33 percent, and he began scaling it back to 25 percent by slowing the acquisition program and shifting more new stores toward franchisees. The company-store percentage has remained in the 25 percent range since the mid-1970s. "Running a McDonald's is a three-hundred-sixty-three-days-a-year business [the restaurants are closed only on Thanksgiving and Christmas], and an owner/operator, with his personal interests and incentives, can inherently do a better job than a chain manager," Turner says.

Despite its scope, McDonald's buyout program did nothing to reduce the influence of its franchisees. Indeed, Turner attempted to strengthen the chain's commitment to the concept of owner/operators. Whereas previously local McDonald's franchises could be 50 percent owned by investors who did not play a direct role in the operation of the stores, Turner required that 100 percent of any new franchise be owned by a full-time operator.

Furthermore, even as McDonald's was buying out some of its strongest franchisees, it was allowing others to have a profound impact on the direction of the system. More than ever it seemed that independent-minded franchisees were challenging the company to make changes to improve operations. At times, those improvements were made only because some feisty franchisees were ready to go to war over their beliefs. A case in point was Tom Christian, a franchisee in Elkhart, Indiana. In the mid-1960s, Christian became the first operator to violate one of Ray Kroc's most sacred rules: he hired a woman in his store.

At the time, unemployment was practically nonexistent in Elkhart, and Christian was having nearly an impossible time meeting McDonald's requirement of an all male crew. "I had been scraping the bottom of the barrel in hiring all males," Christian recalls, "and I figured that hiring the best female help available would be better than hiring the worst of the males."

Careful to avoid a repeat of the problems created by the carhops in the older drive-ins, his first female hire was the wife of his preacher and the next several were housewives with school-aged kids. He even enforced informal rules designed to avoid the types of problems McDonald's feared it would encounter with mixed crews. "The aisles were narrow in the old stores, and I had all kinds of rules against bump and run," Christian says. "Hiring females was a breakthrough, and I didn't want to blow it—for their sake or mine."

Christian had overnight solved his staffing problems and discovered that his female employees made better than average McDonald's crew persons. That did not impress McDonald's. As soon as the company's field consultant spotted women in the Elkhart store, he told Christian to fire them. Christian refused. Six months later, the field man repeated his demand. This time Christian became a little more militant. "If the company really is this opposed to hiring women," he told the supervisor, "I want to see it in writing. If you won't do that, don't mention hiring women to me again."

The letter never came, and by the late 1960s, franchisees throughout the system began following Christian's lead in defying the all male hiring code. With its operators dictating a new de facto policy, McDonald's in 1968 finally conceded to operator demands on employing women in the stores. But if McDonald's now endorsed hiring female crew members, the chain's tradition of the marinelike, all male crew did not die easily. The new female policy distinctly favored the more matronly. Hairstyles had to be short and simple and makeup kept to a minimum. False lashes, eye shadow, colored fingernail polish, iridescent lipstick, rouge, and "excessive use of strong perfumes" were prohibited. The operations manual even noted that "women with serious complexion problems should not be scheduled for window work." All jewelry, aside from wedding rings and watches, was disallowed, and operators were advised that female employees should be scheduled to finish work by 5:00 P.M. Even their duties were narrowly defined by the new policy to lighter tasks, such as taking orders and wrapping hamburgers. Noted one advisory to operators: "Bear in mind that certain jobs, such as the grill, require far more stamina than most women possess."

Some of the criteria on hiring the first female crew persons were so discriminatory that they could not be published in the operations manual. "We figured that the first women we hired should be kind of flat-chested," Kroc recalled. "We didn't want them to be attractive to the boys. And the first woman manager we had wore glasses and flat shoes. She swore like a trooper. But she got the respect of all the men in the store." But Kroc's worst fears that attractive female crew members would convert McDonald's into a teenage hangout proved unfounded. Today, McDonald's crews are 56 percent female, and fully 46 percent of all units are managed by women.

As Turner expanded the system, franchisees might also have lost their influence in the one area where they had traditionally made their greatest contribution—marketing. In a large national retailing system, new marketing programs tend to be developed centrally. The ideas of individual franchisees—though they reflect real market experiences—are typically too far removed from decision makers to be noticed. Yet, the very opposite occurred at McDonald's during Turner's building spree, and the clearest evidence of that was visible in the area of new products.

Far from losing their grip over new products, franchisees became even more innovative and influential in expanding the once-limited McDonald's menu. Indeed, during Turner's first five years as president, McDonald's franchisees introduced so many successful new products that they began changing the definition of a fast-food drive-in. With the exception of its addition of the fish sandwich in the early 1960s, the chain had not deviated from the limited menu handed down by the McDonald brothers. But by the early 1970s it was marketing two new hamburger products, and it had finally found successful dessert items as well. And franchisees were experimenting with a wide range of products that opened up an entirely new market everyone in the fast-food business had ignored—breakfast. Yet, with the exception of the Quarter Pounder, the stream of successful new products introduced during this period originated not with McDonald's but with individual franchisees.

That was surely the case with the item that touched off the new-product rampage—a double-decker hamburger that sold for more than twice the price of McDonald's regular hamburger. Introduced systemwide in 1968, it was the brainchild of Jim Delligatti, one of Kroc's earliest franchisees, who by the late 1960s operated a dozen stores in Pittsburgh. Despite the fact that Delligatti had an exclusive territorial franchise for metropolitan Pittsburgh, he had struggled with sub-par store volumes. Delligatti was convinced that the only way to broaden his customer base was to broaden McDonald's menu.

He used every opportunity to lobby with other multistore operators and with the chain's top managers about the need to improve lackluster sales by introducing products aimed at a more adult-oriented market. In 1967, Delligatti's persistence won him permission from McDonald's to test a large sandwich he developed that featured two hamburger patties and sold for 45 cents. He called it the Big Mac.

Delligatti did not invent the sandwich. Bob Wian, the founder of the Big Boy drive-in chain, virtually built his entire franchise around a double-decker sandwich with two patties of ground beef separated by a center section of bun and smothered with lettuce, pickles, onions, cheese, and a mayonnaise-based sauce. Delligatti had managed a drive-in in the early 1950s in southern California, where Wian first popularized the Big Boy, and he was one of dozens of operators there who copied it. Thus, when he started looking for new menu ideas for McDonald's, a near copy of Wian's Big Boy sandwich quickly came to mind. "This wasn't like discovering the light bulb," Delligatti admits. "The bulb was already there. All I did was screw it in the socket."

Still, persuading the chain's management to attempt to sell a new hamburger—particularly one selling for better than twice the price— was no mean feat. Although Fred Turner was aggressive in expanding the chain, he was nearly reactionary when it came to expanding the menu. A stream of new products, he feared, would throw a monkey wrench into the finely tuned store-operations system he had helped to perfect. It was only because Delligatti had the complete support of Ralph Lanphar, the regional manager in Columbus who ran interference for him with higher-ups, that he got corporate permission even to test the Big Mac. And the permission McDonald's finally granted was something less than sweeping. Delligatti could test the product only at his Uniontown restaurant and only if he used McDonald's standard bun. But, after three days, even casual observers could see that the bun was too small and the sandwich too sloppy. So, Delligatti ignored McDonald's caveat and ordered an oversized sesame seed bun cut in three pieces. Within a few months, the new Big Mac was increasing the Uniontown store's sales by better than 12 percent.

Soon it was in all of Delligatti's units, and at each one the sandwich produced the same healthy sales gains. McDonald's managers and dozens of operators began descending on the Pittsburgh franchisee looking for information on his new sandwich. The chain hurriedly added the Big Mac to other test markets, and when it scored 10 percent or better sales gains in every one, the new product was put into nationwide distribution by the end of 1968.

By the very next year, sales of the Big Mac accounted for 19 percent of all McDonald's sales. Even more important, the new hamburger had greatly expanded the chain's potential market by attracting adults who previously had overlooked McDonald's. Almost overnight it became the most recognized of all McDonald's menu items, a new and powerful focal point for the chain's marketing. Its advertising popularized the notion of an irresistible "Big Mac attack," and schoolchildren around the country were reciting a jingle listing its seven ingredients.

Not surprisingly, Delligatti's success with the Big Mac brought a tidal wave of new product experimentation by local McDonald's franchisees, each hoping to have the type of impact on the system that Delligatti had. Litton Cochran, a multiunit franchisee in Knoxville, argued that a dessert was nearly a requirement for success in his market, and he persuaded Turner to let him attempt to crack the dessert barrier that Ray Kroc had erected with his string of product failures.

Cochran concluded that Kroc had overlooked the obvious dessert. If the hamburger and french fries had become the All-American Meal, he reasoned, no dessert was more all-American than apple pie. From his youth, Cochran had loved a deep-fried apple pie his mother always made for him after school "to tide him over" until dinner. Shaped in a half-moon, the pie consisted of apple filling between two pieces of pie dough that were pinched together at the edges. Fried pies were a favorite in the South, and because they were so easy to make into single-serving portions, they were perfect for a fast-food operation. Initially, Cochran's mother and sister made the pies for his units in Knoxville, but he quickly turned to a commercial supplier when the idea spread to other stores throughout the South. "People down South," Cochran explains, "just have to have dessert after every meal." By 1970, however, Cochran's fried apple pie had become a standard at all McDonald's in the United States—and Cochran entered the ranks of legendary franchisees.

Not all new products conceived by franchisees had such success. In 1967, Nick Karos, the pioneering operations specialist who had become a franchisee in Cleveland, proposed testing a roast beef sandwich similar to one being successfully marketed by Arby's. When Turner flatly refused to grant approval to test the product, Karos went around him to Kroc, who he knew was likely to approve a new product even after his president had turned thumbs down. Karos was right, and when his McDonald's in suburban Northfield introduced a roast beef sandwich, Karos hit the jackpot. The store's sales grew 33 percent in one year, and the new sandwich was accounting for 15 percent of total volume.

That got Turner's attention, and in 1968, McDonald's decided to introduce the sandwich throughout the system. But instead of adding ovens to all McDonald's units to bake the roast as Karos had done, the chain decided to "McDonaldize" the preparation process by deep frying the product in a bath of oil. Jim Schindler even designed a unique automated roast beef fryer, which he called a Tepidarium, and with Turner's blessing the world's first—and only—deep-fried roast beef made its debut.

Unfortunately, the sandwich introduced nationwide was drier and less flavorful than the product Karos was baking in Cleveland. Even so, the new product was an immediate hit, ringing up 7 percent to 9 percent of all store sales within weeks. Quickly, McDonald's decided to expand the new roast beef sandwich to all its restaurants. But just before the product's being rolled out nationwide, accountant Gerry Newman discovered a fatal flaw. The chain had not properly calculated the shrinkage factor on roast beef and could not make money on the 59-cent sandwich no matter how many it sold. Unwilling to move to a higher price point, Turner ordered the roast beef product killed. Unfortunately, he had already ordered one thousand roast beef slicers —one for every store—and McDonald's now had a warehouse full of the slicers that could only find a market in a white elephant sale. The company took a $300,000 write-off. For Turner, it was a costly lesson. With more than one thousand restaurants in operation and hundreds more being added each year, McDonald's could no longer afford to add new products systemwide without careful analysis.

Still, such failures did not discourage the new product search. In fact, McDonald's now seemed eager to entertain suggestions from every corner—even from the board of directors. When director David Wallerstein suggested that the chain introduce a large-sized order of its popular french fries, he was initially greeted with skepticism. "If people want more fries," Kroc told him, "they can buy two bags." But Wallerstein insisted that the consumer's psyche doesn't work that way. Buying two bags seemed gluttonous, he argued; buying a large box— initially costing 75 percent more for 60 percent more fries—did not. Yet, Wallerstein's approach had the same beneficial impact of selling more of the chain's highest-margin item.

Refusing to accept rejection, Wallerstein conducted a personal two-day survey of a McDonald's store in Chicago, and reported to Kroc a discovery that amazed him: all customers consumed *all* of their fries. Coming from anyone else, such unscientific research might have fallen on deaf ears, but Wallerstein had impressive credentials on large-sized snacks. As president of Balaban and Katz theaters, he had introduced to the movie theater industry the larger-sized orders of popcorn in boxes, which eventually replaced the small bags that were standard. He had also pioneered buttered popcorn, which itself led to larger and larger containers. Thus, when he heard of Wallerstein's research, Kroc approved the new large fry product in 1972, and today fully half of all french fries sold at McDonald's come in the large order.

Yet, clearly the biggest product breakthrough involved not just a new product but a new meal, and it was McDonald's franchisees who led the way to it. Fresh from his success with the Big Mac, Delligatti in 1970 asked McDonald's for permission to begin testing the idea of selling simple breakfast items at his one downtown store. He opened the unit at 7:00 A.M. and started selling coffee, doughnuts, and sweet rolls. A year later, he expanded the breakfast menu with pancakes and sausage. "We were paying rent, utilities, and insurance twenty-four hours a day, but we were only open for business for half that time," Delligatti reasons. "We had all those morning hours before 11:00 A.M. to do some business."

Even with his limited product selection, Delligatti began doing 5 percent of his business at the downtown store at breakfast. Unlike all other new products to date, these additions generated totally new business that took nothing away from existing menu items. Still, keeping a McDonald's open from 11:00 A.M. to midnight was backbreaking work for most operators, and none was eager to extend their hours unless they found a new breakfast item that produced double-digit sales gains.

That product came in late 1971, the discovery of Herb Peterson, an operator in Santa Barbara. Peterson had managed the McDonald's account for D'Arcy Advertising before he decided to become a franchisee. He spotted the same opportunity in breakfast that Delligatti had seen. The difference was that while Delligatti's breakfast products involved adding standard items to the McDonald's menu, Peterson believed that to launch an entirely new food line, such as breakfast, McDonald's needed something unique and yet something that could be eaten like all other McDonald's items—with the fingers. His solution came when he started modifying an Eggs Benedict sandwich that was being marketed by Jack-in-the-Box, a West Coast chain.

By Christmas of 1971, Peterson had been working on the product for months. He had experimented with prepackaged Hollandaise, which he rejected as too runny. He replaced it instead with a slice of cheese, which when melted on a hot egg produced the consistency he was looking for. He also had to develop a foolproof way of preparing an egg on a grill to give it the appearance of a poached egg. Poaching eggs did not fit with McDonald's assembly line production process, but Peterson solved the problem by developing a new cooking utensil—a cluster of six Teflon-coated rings—that was placed on the grill to give eggs the rounded shape of an English muffin. When he added grilled Canadian bacon, Peterson had a breakfast product perfect for a sandwich-oriented fast-food chain.

Kroc was celebrating Christmas that year at his new ranch just north of Santa Barbara, and Peterson asked him to stop by the store. When Kroc showed up, Peterson was ready with a demonstration of his surprise new product, complete with a flip-chart presentation to explain its economics. It was not economics that sold Kroc. He had just finished lunch before stopping by Peterson's store, but he devoured two of the new egg-bacon-muffin sandwiches anyway. At Kroc's request, Peterson two weeks later packed the Teflon rings in a briefcase and flew to Chicago to prepare his new breakfast sandwich for the rest of McDonald's senior managers, all of whom responded as positively as Kroc had.

McDonald's was ready to test the product nationwide, as soon as it settled on a name. Peterson favored calling it McDonald's Fast Break Breakfast, but the name had been copyrighted—though never used— by Nabisco. McDonald's had not yet reached the level of marketing sophistication that involved building an inventory of brand names. Peterson's concoction was homespun, and its name would come the same way. As the Turners and Krocs dined out one evening, Patty Turner suggested calling it the Egg McMuffin. The name stuck.

It took nearly four years to roll the Egg McMuffin out nationwide. Part of the problem was that the Egg McMuffin, although suitable as the center of a breakfast menu, was not suited to be an entire breakfast menu. But when Delligatti's hotcakes and sausage were perfected and when scrambled eggs were added as a third option, McDonald's by 1976 had finally expanded throughout the system a breakfast menu that distinguished it from its major fast-food competitors, which did not introduce commercial breakfast items until the mid-1980s. By then, McDonald's—thanks largely to the inventiveness of its franchisees— had a monopoly on breakfast. Accounting for 15 percent of its sales, the breakfast menu provides the biggest single reason for the enormous sales lead McDonald's restaurants maintain over their competition. (In 1991, the average McDonald's restaurant generated sales of $1.66 million, compared with $1 million and $852,000, respectively, for Burger King and Wendy's.)

Even before it introduced breakfast nationwide, however, McDonald's had established the dominance in the fast-food industry that it enjoys today. In Turner's first five years as president, McDonald's had been converted into a new type of chain. A limited-menu, counter service, drive-in operation had been replaced by a full-menu, sit-down restaurant. A chain with regional strongholds was transformed into one with a powerful national presence, and in the process McDonald's had left its competitors in its wake. In 1974, as McDonald's was dedicating its three thousandth store, Burger King had just exceeded the one thousandth mark. Burger Chef had slipped—permanently—to under one thousand units. And while Dave Thomas had begun setting his sights on becoming a new market leader, his Wendy's chain was only five years old. Because its catch-up strategy forced it to sell large territorial franchises to wealthy investors, it was in no position to duplicate McDonald's base of entrepreneurial operators.

Only five years before, McDonald's was losing momentum. It seemed only a matter of time before it would be overtaken by more aggressive competitors, now under the wing of corporate giants. In the next half decade, fast food would change from a fledgling business to a major industry. McDonald's entered that period as the leader facing fast-closing competitors. It emerged from it as a leader without peer.

More important, it accomplished its transformation without compromising its fundamental strength—Ray Kroc's philosophy of franchising. The chain had not lost touch with its entrepreneurial franchisees. More than ever, the system was benefiting from their grass-roots marketing skills. It had also stayed out of the clutches of some conglomerate that would have imposed foreign values. In short, McDonald's had taken a huge gamble to regain dominance in the fast-food market without losing control of its destiny—and it had won.

When Fred Turner was selected as McDonald's president, more than a few observers questioned the wisdom of entrusting the fate of the corporation to a man whose primary achievement had been perfecting hamburgers, milk shakes, and french fries. But by the early 1970s, any doubts about Turner's abilities as chief executive were long since gone. "Fred grew in stature as a manager as his company grew," observes investment banker Harry Fisher. "He didn't fit the cookie-cutter B-school mold. And he certainly wasn't getting the type of recognition that other corporate builders of the day were getting. But he had a better track record than most of those guys. He is the chief architect of the modern McDonald's."

To be sure, Turner was working from a powerful base built by Kroc and Sonneborn. In fact, a casual observer might conclude that he was swept to success by the irreversible forces of a burgeoning fast-food market. "Yes, Fred Turner caught the tide just at the right time," noted Director David Wallerstein. "But he also knew how to ride the tide. Not everyone knows how to do that. That's where management comes in."

Chapter 13
MEDIA MAGIC

By the late 1960s, McDonald's had virtually everything it needed to pull off Fred Turner's ambitious expansion program. It had become the food service industry's most proficient buyer of real estate. It had developed all the financial muscle it needed to do the job. A decentralized regional management structure was allowing it to control the operations of a burgeoning national chain. And the new Hamburger University put McDonald's in a class by itself when it came to food service training.

Curiously, the only missing link was marketing. Although McDonald's is now one of the world's mightiest consumer marketers, until Turner became president it had relied almost completely on its franchisees when it came to marketing. The Chicago company had not even organized a marketing department.

As innovative as their advertising and promotional programs were, the local operators had done little more than scratch the surface of the market by appealing to budget-minded families—McDonald's most obvious market segment and the easiest one to attract. Yet, with his massive expansion project, Turner was stretching the chain well beyond that traditional niche. Suddenly, McDonald's faced a much more formidable marketing challenge—cultivating a national mass market. That task far exceeded the marketing capabilities of local franchisees. Without a sophisticated and centrally coordinated advertising effort aimed at broadening McDonald's appeal, Turner's expansion could yield disastrous results.

By the end of 1967, the average McDonald's restaurant had an annual volume of only $291,000, and that average had built up slowly over the previous decade from just under $200,000. Since Turner was planning on tripling the number of outlets in five years, per-unit sales could plummet—perhaps to unprofitable levels—unless McDonald's began attracting new customers.

The expansion of the menu was attracting more adults, just as the addition of seating was beginning to appeal to consumers who would not consider eating at a window service drive-in. But McDonald's not only had to *be* a broader-based, fast-service restaurant, it had to be *perceived* as one as well.

Turner was convinced that the only way to do that was with massive network television marketing, the one area where McDonald's— and every other fast-food chain—had limited experience. The new president was fond of telling managers and franchisees that if marketing alone were the sole determinant for success, the most successful fast-food chain would be the one that put all of its advertising money into three outlets: ABC, CBS, and NBC. While McDonald's fell short of that, it nevertheless made a major shift in 1968 toward network television.

Just the year before, the chain's franchisees had created the Operators National Advertising (OPNAD) fund by pledging to contribute 1 percent of their restaurant sales to a national cooperative advertising program, in addition to the 2 to 3 percent that they were contributing to their local advertising co-ops. The creation of OPNAD suddenly opened up the networks to McDonald's. Almost overnight, the company had raised $3 million to spend on national advertising in 1968, and given the growth curve the chain was on, that would prove to be only a modest beginning. By 1974, when Turner's expansion drive hit peak stride, OPNAD's annual network television budget approached $20 million, and during the next decade it grew steadily to a stunning $180 million in 1985. When local station spots are added, McDonald's total TV advertising expenditures that year hit $302 million, the third largest television budget of any marketer (after Procter & Gamble with $779 million and Phillip Morris with $485 million) and at that time the largest TV budget spent to promote a single brand. Clearly, McDonald's new national and regional advertising cooperatives were putting the chain in position to use the most powerful advertising medium in a manner the food service industry had never known.

But money alone was not the answer. Some central coordination of the marketing effort was now a top priority, because the creation of a national brand image was the one thing McDonald's franchisees—as marketing oriented as some were—could not do on their own. Until 1968, the Chicago franchiser had concentrated on enforcing uniform operating standards and on financing the chain's growth. But now, Turner was intent on making his company a skilled national marketer as well, and to do it quickly, he turned to the outside for help.

That meant relying heavily on McDonald's first major advertising agency, D'Arcy Advertising in Chicago. Turner hired Paul Schrage, the media buyer D'Arcy assigned to the McDonald's account, and asked him to organize the company's first marketing department. Schrage quickly pulled other creative talent in from the outside, including Barry Klein, the new national advertising manager. Since the early 1960s, Klein had been with the Kal, Ehrlich and Merrick agency in Washington, D.C., which had created Ronald McDonald for John Gibson and Oscar Goldstein. In fact, Klein had written and produced virtually all the Ronald McDonald spots that the agency developed for the two Washington franchisees.

The new corporate marketing team took a unique approach to food service advertising. It differed even from the innovative advertising McDonald's operators were running locally. Previously, most restaurant advertising was focused solely on product and price, but Schrage and creative executives at D'Arcy took aim at a far more elusive but potentially more rewarding target: image. They wanted to sell hamburgers the way Miller sells beer. McDonald's now was attempting to extend to network advertising an old Kroc homily: "We're not in the hamburger business; we're in show business."

From the time he met Kroc, that attitude had affected Paul Schrage. "Ray always told us that anyone could make a hamburger and that we had to do more," recalls Schrage, now a senior executive vice president of McDonald's. "So when it came to national advertising, we felt we had to add something to our message that was different. We wanted to position ourselves with an extra dimension—a charm or warmth that no one else had."

Even the early network commercials from D'Arcy demonstrated a softer sell by being as entertaining as they were informative. The first commercials introducing the Big Mac communicated a big hamburger message while avoiding a serious, and potentially boring, description of a product most people consider fun to eat. Thus D'Arcy depicted the new double-decker burger as a three-story monument, so larger than life that a guide wearing a pith helmet was needed to point out all its components to a group of tourists. The agency gave the same light touch to McDonald's reputation for cleanliness in a commercial featuring a monocled army colonel giving a McDonald's a white-glove inspection. Even when D'Arcy took on McDonald's most important product—its french fry—it did so in human terms. One of the agency's most effective spots showed a young boy walking through a park eating a bag of McDonald's fries, feeding a couple to a squirrel, and stuffing the empty bag in his pocket. The message was not the product, but the enjoyment it creates.

Nevertheless, Schrage had barely settled into his new job when he decided that most of D'Arcy's creative energies were being absorbed by its biggest account—Standard Oil of Indiana—and that the agency was unwilling to commit enough creative resources to give McDonald's the attention it was now demanding. "They didn't see the future we saw," he says.

Thus McDonald's in 1969 began a search for a new advertising agency. Rather than requiring the candidates to prepare exhaustive bids, Schrage merely asked them to answer ten questions, including one about whether McDonald's possessed a "unique selling proposition," an attraction so strong it outweighs all the others. Unique selling proposition was a popular television advertising concept perfected by Rossier Reeves at the Ted Bates Agency, who argued that in a fast-moving and crowded medium such as television, advertisers were wise to communicate only their product's strongest feature—over and over again. The Bates agency literally hammered that message home with a classic ad showing how Anacin relieved the pounding of a headache.

But Keith Reinhard, who prepared the McDonald's proposal for Needham, Harper and Steers, concluded that no single selling proposition appealed equally to McDonald's different target markets—kids, parents, and young adults. Thus Reinhard proposed a network campaign that projected what he called McDonald's "unique selling personality," within which, he told Schrage, "we will develop selling propositions that vary depending on whether we're talking to moms, dads, or kids."

Reinhard's thesis was based on extensive consumer research that Needham conducted just to prepare its bid. "We invaded the McDonald's stores with our research people," Reinhard recalls. Needham's consumer research showed that while different segments of the market favored McDonald's for different reasons, the one perception common to everyone was that McDonald's was not a typical eating out experience, but rather a fun place for families to go. In fact, it was perhaps the only restaurant chain that treated eating out as a family event by offering something for everyone—action and finger food for kids, quality food and low prices for parents, and an uncommon attention to satisfying basic consumer needs of cleanliness and convenience. Thus, Reinhard argued, McDonald's advertising had to project a personality of sensitivity, warmth, and fun.

Such concepts were meaningful elsewhere in retailing, but they were foreign to restaurant advertising, which had not ventured beyond the hard sell of product and price. Television advertising was practically nonexistent in food service in 1970, but a simple extension of the industry's standard advertising philosophy would have resulted in TV commercials driving home a message about McDonald's low prices and showing plenty of close-ups of steaming hamburgers. Reinhard was talking about positioning McDonald's as something of a benevolent institution—a place that had an "uncanny" understanding of new consumer needs and offered a "happy experience" to boot.

It was the unique approach that Schrage was looking for, and it landed the account for Needham. Within a demanding three-month deadline, the agency developed what McDonald's concluded was a superior program. "All of our consumer research was showing us that a trip to a McDonald's was an event for each member of the family that could be likened to an escape to an island of enjoyment," Reinhard recalls. "Kids could see the mountains of french fries, moms could escape from meal planning, and dads could escape the hassles of business."

The agency rushed into production on a dozen new television commercials, all riveted to the island escape theme. Choruses sang an enchanting melody inviting viewers to "Come to the McDonald's Island." Aerial shots of McDonald's restaurants made them appear as safe harbors in a sea of traffic. Fred Turner was so enthused after he saw the first batch of Needham spots that he called back a *Wall Street Journal* reporter who had interviewed him on a story the day before. Turner told the reporter he wanted to revise his sales projections— several points upward.

The agency was ready to roll with the new spots two weeks ahead of its three-month deadline when the roof fell in. A McDonald's field consultant checking on stores in Oklahoma saw a highway billboard that put the new campaign into a cocked hat. It read: "A&W Root Beer —Your Island of Pleasure." A&W had used the slogan only for a regional campaign, but McDonald's lawyers insisted that the legal risk of running with the island campaign was simply not worth taking. Needham had two weeks to replace it. "We panicked," Reinhard recalls.

"We were sitting there with nothing as a backup, not even something we could warm up."

Reinhard scrambled into action. He was in Los Angeles working on more McDonald's Island commercials when he heard the bad news, and he asked Gordon Fenton, a senior copywriter at Needham, to meet him in New York the next morning and to schedule a meeting with Sid Woloshin, one of the country's best composers of advertising tunes. Woloshin agreed to work on a new McDonald's tune, while Reinhard and Fenton went to their hotel room to work through the night writing lyrics. They decided they only had one line from the island song that was usable: "We're so near yet far away, so get up and get away—to McDonald's." They wrote new lyrics around that and took it to Woloshin, who had already come up with some fresh melodies, which he played on the piano for them.

One stood out. Upbeat and uplifting, it was a nearly perfect fit with the lyrics Reinhard and Fenton had drafted. They quickly got the new theme song recorded in a New York studio and rushed back to play it for Barry Klein and Matt Lambert, another McDonald's marketing manager. It floored them, particularly when the singers moved into the refrain: "We're so near yet far away, so get up and get away—to McDonald's." "That's tremendous," Lambert shouted. "I felt a chill. But what was that they were saying?"

It was a huge problem—the key phrase in the whole song and no one could make out the lyric, "We're so near yet far away." But when Reinhard tried drafting a new line, he ran into a creative dead end. Nothing worked. In desperation, he went back to the consumer interviews Needham had made in researching McDonald's. There, the word *break* kept popping up. Some customers talked about a "break from the routine." Others about a "break from preparing meals." Others about a "break on prices." The word *break* somehow had to be in the new theme. By now, virtually everyone in the agency was trying to help Reinhard out of his bind, and a one-line note from Al Klatt, head of Needham's advertising review board, provided the solution. Scribbled on the note was Klatt's two-cents worth: "You deserve a break today."

That did it. "You deserve a break today, so get up and get away—to McDonald's." Not only did the new lyric fit comfortably—and understandably—with Woloshin's music, it created a general musical theme that could be used in dozens of commercials with different messages aimed at different market segments. Within a year, the new theme became the best known commercial song on television and, in fact, one of the most identifiable advertising themes of all time. It was so popular that pop singer Barry Manilow inserted it into his concert act, which led music critics to mistakenly refer to Manilow as the author of "Break."

The "break" commercials put McDonald's well ahead of the rest of the fast-food pack in advertising. No competitor had a commercial theme song nearly as popular or memorable. But Needham's creativity in distinguishing McDonald's network advertising did not stop with the theme song. Unlike virtually all other fast-food advertising—before or since—the product was almost never sold directly or separately, but rather as part of a package of positive human experiences to be gained from a McDonald's visit. Needham's advertising formula became known in McDonald's as "food, folks, and fun," and it remains the backbone of all of the chain's advertising campaigns.

But food-folks-fun advertising meant more than showing people having a good time at McDonald's. Indeed, most commercials told short stories designed to portray the character of the company paying for them. The story lines eventually became so strong and the product references so subtle that Schrage insisted on introducing each spot with a title and the McDonald's logo so there would be no mistaking whom the ads were for. "We were getting so deep into communicating our personality that we were losing communication of our identity," Schrage explains.

In each "break" spot, Needham avoided a hard sell in favor of a softer, lighter, and sometimes humorous message that countered the negative images of fast food. They were effective because no one expected advertising of this kind from a fast-food chain, and none of McDonald's competitors was attempting anything close to it. In "Butler," one of the early Needham efforts, a butler uses a Rolls-Royce to fetch a McDonald's hamburger, fries, and a soft drink and delivers the lunch on a silver platter to a millionaire boss who is obviously delighted to get change back from his dollar. In "Train," a family in a car hurrying to get somewhere is stopped by a freight train at a railroad crossing and their frustration builds until they spot a McDonald's. Dad bolts from the car and returns with the family's lunch just as the train clears the crossing.

Even when Needham tackled a serious topic like cleanliness, it turned it into one of the most entertaining and best known of the "break" commercials. It was a breakthrough for fast-food advertising, putting it in the same class as the big soft drink ads that featured

Broadway quality musical productions. Its $130,000 production budget also broke new ground for food service advertising, but McDonald's approved it because it agreed with Reinhard that to *project* quality food and service, McDonald's advertising had to *be* quality.

"Clean" also departed from all other food service commercials because it showed no food. Instead, seven crewmen danced around a mock-up of a McDonald's store singing a new lyric of "break" that Reinhard had initially roughed out during his all-nighter at the hotel in New York: "Grab a bucket and mop / Scrub from bottom to top / Before we open the door / Put a shine on the floor."

The theatrical nature of Needham's McDonald's commercials even made them vehicles for budding actors who later became movie or television stars. The trend began with the "Clean" commercial. One of the singing crewmen was John Amos, who later starred in ABC's *Roots* and the CBS sitcom *Good Times.* And long before her Oscar-nominated performance in *Tootsie,* actress Teri Garr played the lead in a McDonald's commercial as a mother who spends a morning shopping for a party dress for her young daughter, then rewards her patience with a visit to McDonald's. Michael J. Fox also starred in a McDonald's spot before becoming a teen idol.

Needham added the same theatrical flair to the Ronald McDonald spots by creating a fantasy setting of McDonaldland and filling it with a host of new storybook characters—the Hamburglar ("Every hero needs a villain," Reinhard explains), Mayor McCheese (the cheeseburger character), Officer Big Mac, and the Grimace (who devours milk shakes). While the characters never achieved as much recognition as Ronald McDonald, they became popular enough that Schrage got the idea of introducing them as playground equipment at a McDonald's store. The idea of such a playground was not completely new. George Gabriel, a franchisee in Bensalem, Pennsylvania, built the first children's playground at a McDonald's in the late 1960s. But when the McDonaldland characters were added to the concept, its popularity mushroomed, and such so-called Playlands soon became the new centerpiece of McDonald's strategy for dominating the children's market. Today, Playlands are set up in 40 percent of McDonald's units worldwide, and Don Ament, an erstwhile set designer for Walt Disney who designed the set for Needham's McDonaldland spots, built a profitable business on supplying most McDonald's stores with playground equipment.

By the mid-1970s, McDonald's marketing had changed dramatically from the 1960s, when local operators had dominated the chain's advertising and promotion and when creativity in marketing moved from the stores up. With the success of its network commercials based on the "break" theme, McDonald's Corporation for the first time became a world-class marketer. The prolific use of soft-sell television ads was seen as the key to doubling per-unit volumes in five years, to $621,000 in 1973, and they put McDonald's on the road to becoming one of the most powerful of all television advertisers. Each year, the chain's corporate marketing department supervises the production of some 160 new television commercials at an annual cost of more than $35 million.

Clearly, power in marketing was shifting toward the corporation, which was now defining the McDonald's image, producing most of the chain's television spots, and developing its overall marketing themes. A strong central marketing effort was badly needed by the late 1960s, but now there was a danger that all marketing power would reside in the hands of corporate managers. What had always made McDonald's marketing so relevant was that it reflected the strong influence of franchisees, who were closest to the consumer. But the phenomenal success of its network marketing suddenly created the risk that McDonald's might forget that its innovative approach to advertising was rooted in the franchisee community.

Fortunately for McDonald's, that did not happen. Indeed, the very advertising cooperatives that allowed McDonald's marketing to enter the network era now became the key to protecting the franchisees' clout in marketing. As might be expected, creative input on national network spots now came almost exclusively from McDonald's corporate marketing department and its national advertising agency. But in determining local advertising and promotional campaigns, which account for 57 percent of all McDonald's marketing, local franchisees working through their 165 local advertising cooperatives have remained dominant. And through OPNAD, franchisees have kept a firm grip over all network media buys, while at the same time helping to shape McDonald's network advertising strategy.

Even on the creative side of network advertising, franchisees are not without influence. By the mid-1970s, pressure from McDonald's was already building on Needham to develop more product-oriented commercials. In its food-folks-fun advertising formula, the agency was putting most of the stress on the latter two elements, and franchisees began clamoring for a restoration of the balance and particularly for a spot featuring the chain's best-known product—the Big Mac. "I remember how we were bemoaning the fact that McDonald's insisted on a Big Mac commercial that actually talked about all the ingredients in the product," Reinhard says. "How boring can you get?"

In their frustration, Reinhard and Dan Nichols, another creative manager on the account, began jotting down all seven ingredients in a single word. "Then we thought of trying to make a game out of this," Reinhard says. What resulted was a tongue in cheek commercial with an actor rapidly—and flawlessly—reciting all ingredients in the Big Mac: "Two all-beef patties special sauce lettuce cheese pickles onions on a sesame seed bun."

The commercial did not catch fire and had a very brief run. But it grabbed the fancy of Max Cooper, McDonald's former publicist who had become a multistore franchisee in Birmingham, Alabama. He concluded that what was missing from Needham's Big Mac commercial were real consumers playing the game. So, Cooper instructed his local advertising agency to produce a radio commercial consisting of actual recordings of customers at his stores attempting to recite the Big Mac ingredients. Anyone doing it correctly in four seconds got a free Big Mac. Those who botched the recital wound up on Cooper's radio spots.

The ads were an instant hit in Birmingham. Within weeks, radio stations were cosponsoring contests to recite the Big Mac tongue twister, and Cooper eventually made a man-on-the-street TV commercial showing customers attempting the "two all-beef patties" slogan. Schoolchildren all over town had it memorized. More important, sales of Big Macs in Birmingham soared 25 percent.

Soon, operators in other southern markets had picked up on the idea, and as word of their success reached McDonald's corporate marketing department, Needham decided to remake its original network commercial, this time featuring real customers reciting the Big Mac ingredients. The ads had the same effect nationally as they did in the South, so strong, in fact, that McDonald's still employs the "two all-beef patties" line in commercials it runs on the Big Mac today.

But when it came to national McDonald's marketing, local franchisees found their greatest creative outlet, not in product advertising, but in advertised promotions. During the 1960s and 1970s, virtually all of McDonald's promotions—including those that eventually made their way onto the national networks—originated with local advertising cooperatives, which are controlled totally by local franchisees. Even if none of the promotions developed locally are exported to other markets, their impact on McDonald's marketing is significant, because as a group the local advertising co-ops outspend the national cooperative (OPNAD) by a wide margin—$324 to $248 million in 1991.

Thus many of McDonald's local co-ops are among their market's largest and most sophisticated advertisers. Most employ their own advertising agencies, which report to the franchisee-controlled cooperatives, not to the company. McDonald's relies primarily on a single agency for network advertising (the chain also retains Burrell Advertising for spots aimed at a black audience and Conill Advertising for campaigns geared to the Hispanic market), but local franchisees employ a total of sixty-five ad agencies, each of which develops promotions and related advertising geared for local markets.

But the real power of the local cooperatives is found in their penchant for running in *their* markets successful promotions developed by *other* local co-ops. The local cooperatives act as a creative conduit by spreading good home-grown promotional ideas from co-op to co-op throughout the McDonald's System. And when locally developed promotions prove successful in individual markets, they are sometimes picked up by McDonald's Corporation and carried in all markets via network television. As a result, when it comes to promotions, McDonald's national advertising continues to have a strong grassroots character.

Because it is so widely used as a St. Patrick's Day promotion, the mint-green Shamrock Shake sold in more than two thousand McDonald's units each year has the appearance of a promotion that came down from corporate marketing. In fact, the idea originated in the early 1970s with Hal Rosen, a franchisee in Connecticut. In 1977, McDonald's Regional Advertising Manager Dick Brams, working with the Kansas City co-op's local advertising agency—Bernstein, Rein and Boasberg—had an even greater impact on the system when it conceived of packaging a hamburger, french fries, and a soft drink in boxes designed as circus trains, which were collected to form a set. Marketed under the name "Happy Meal," the circus train promotion was an instant hit with children. Since 1979, the Happy Meal has become McDonald's most important promotion, one offered several times a year worldwide. In 1992 alone, the chain promoted ten national and seven regional separate Happy Meals, all with different themes.

When a local promotional campaign suddenly spreads throughout the McDonald's System, it can create an unexpected windfall for the supplier of the promotion and at the same time give an enormous boost to the prestige of the ad agency that developed the promotional advertising—and perhaps conceived of the promotion—for the local franchisee cooperative. The very possibility of a local promotion going national gives suppliers and advertising agencies more than the usual incentive for making the promotion work in the local market.

For example, when the Boston co-op wanted to promote McDonald's new breakfast menu, it arranged a tie-in with another Boston company, Gillette, which was looking to promote its new Good News razor. But what started out purely as a local promotion quickly became a national one when other McDonald's co-ops got word of its drawing power. Gillette had bargained for a Good News promotion only in Boston, but it wound up with a national promotion when it inadvertently tapped into the McDonald's System: To the delight of its razor marketers, Gillette distributed 20 million samples in the Good News promotion—before they ran out of razors.

An even bigger domino effect was triggered when the Los Angeles advertising cooperative began experimenting with a new promotional game device in the late 1970s. The local co-op and its ad agency— Davis, Johnson, Mogul and Colombatto—decided to experiment with games as a means of increasing customer counts, and it approached Simon Marketing, a California promotion firm that specializes in such traffic builders. Simon developed a game that involved distributing game cards to all customers. By scratching a coating off the card, customers determined on the spot whether and what they had won. Largely on the strength of the games, McDonald's units in Los Angeles quickly became the system's leaders in average store volume.

But the real instant winner was Simon Marketing. When McDonald's co-ops elsewhere around the country heard of the success of game promotions in Los Angeles, they wanted their own game. And in 1981, McDonald's Corporation turned to Simon to develop a national instant winner contest called "Build a Big Mac." With $8 million in potential prizes, the contest increased McDonald's volume nationwide an incremental 6 percent. That triggered a game card mania in the fast-food business, and within a year of "Build a Big Mac," airlines, supermarkets, and other retail chains also had their own instant winner game cards—many of them from Simon Marketing.

The advertising agencies of the local McDonald's co-ops benefit from a windfall of a different sort when they develop a promotion that gets picked up by McDonald's Corporation for national distribution. The prestige that goes with producing a national advertising and promotional campaign for a media leader such as McDonald's can do wonders for expanding the client base of a local advertising agency. As a result, the McDonald's System in effect has sixty-five local agencies competing with one another for a shot at a national promotion. "When they're all developing their own promotional ideas, the system gets a reservoir of hot promotions that no one else has, because no other organization is structured like ours," says Schrage. "In other organizations, promotions come down from the mount. But marketing is really a local challenge. That's why many of the best marketing ideas are always going to come from the field."

Of course, this decentralized structure of McDonald's marketing could easily result in a lack of planning, wasted resources, and a cacophony of advertising messages in the marketplace. McDonald's tries to avoid that by bringing the operators' local advertising agencies into the corporate planning process. Twice each year, McDonald's meets with principals at all forty-eight agencies and with members of the OPNAD committee to thrash out new marketing plans and review the performance of current ones. And each year, the same group, along with presidents of all 165 local co-ops, meet to discuss an annual marketing plan and budget, which divides the coming year into eight to ten periods during which different products will be stressed in advertising.

The plan also identifies the timing of some eight to ten different national promotions, and before launching each one, corporate marketing sends a "blue-book" to all local co-ops detailing the promotion and requesting a commitment on participation by a certain date. While many promotional ideas may be initiated locally, they must be packaged and sold to operators centrally, simply because the chain's promotional might makes advance planning essential. Because local participation is optional, any promotion may be a dud if enough operators choose to ignore it. But each promotion also has the potential for being the type of blockbuster manufacturers must prepare for months in advance. When the system ran a Happy Meal promotion in 1983 featuring Mattel's popular Hot Wheels toy cars, it was so widely supported by local co-ops that McDonald's purchased just over one-third of Mattel's worldwide production of the tiny die-cast cars—forty-four million vehicles. Schrage says of the need for careful market planning: "If we didn't do it our marketing would be in a shambles."

Central planning and coordination, however, does not translate into complete central control. McDonald's may have become a marketing machine, but it still has many drivers. Indeed, it is in the area of marketing that McDonald's franchisees retain their most powerful check over the corporation. Since McDonald's operators contribute virtually all of the chain's advertising budget, it is natural to expect them to want some control over it. But while other franchised systems obtain most of their marketing funds the same way, their franchisees seldom have as strong a voice in shaping advertising programs.

The principal vehicle for the franchisees' influence over McDonald's national advertising remains OPNAD, the eighty-two member committee composed of forty-two elected franchisees and forty McDonald's regional ad managers. With each franchisee getting one vote and each ad manager getting a half vote, control of OPNAD is solidly in the hands of McDonald's owner-operators.

Although OPNAD is unknown outside the McDonald's System, it is one of the most powerful advertising bodies in the United States by virtue of the fact that it controls a national advertising budget that now exceeds $572 million. Yet, OPNAD works like no other organization in advertising's big leagues. Indeed, its decision-making process is so open and so democratic that it defies the laws of business management. OPNAD approves advertising spending the way a legislature passes laws—through open and sometimes heated debate and, finally, by member vote.

The OPNAD committee meets quarterly and approves by vote every expenditure McDonald's makes on national advertising. OPNAD meetings typically run for three days as members of the committee review each network purchase tentatively negotiated beforehand by McDonald's and its national advertising agency. Then the debate begins. On special purchases, some committee members question the quality of the program or its compatibility with the McDonald's System. Others worry that it is not directed at the market McDonald's may be trying to reach with that type of program, and they pressure the agency to defend its projections of the show's likely cost per rating point. And though the committee does not approve routine program selections, it takes the agency to task in "post-buy analyses" whenever the show's Neilsen ratings fall short of the agency's projections, driving the rating point cost well above the forecast. Still others argue that the mix of advertising media is wrong and that the system ought to be devoting more money to some and less to others.

Over the years, OPNAD's influence on the noncreative side of McDonald's advertising has been profound. It has argued for more thirty-second spots and against sixty-second spots favored by the company and the agency. It also put McDonald's on nationally syndicated radio when the company and its agency recommended only a steady diet of network television. At the same time, OPNAD often rejected attempts by the company to increase—from next to nothing—McDonald's expenditure on national print advertising. The committee has also pushed for more sporting events in the McDonald's program mix and has vetoed some special programs the company and agency wanted to buy. And although it offers no creative input on network commercials, OPNAD nevertheless is shown most commercials, and its collective opinions of current spots influence the production of new ones.

OPNAD, in short, is no rubber stamp. Its members are typically multiunit operators and veteran advertisers in their local markets. They "run" for OPNAD office, and because franchisees typically serve on the committee an average of five years, they become expert enough on network advertising to challenge the corporation and its agency.

As a result, OPNAD sessions are intense. The committee may wind up approving 90 percent of what the company recommends, but it modifies the remaining 10 percent, and the battle over those expenditures often becomes heated. "Most McDonald's operators underestimate the power that they have on the corporation through OPNAD," says Irv Klein, a veteran franchisee from New York, who has served two terms as OPNAD chairman. "We don't have control over the creative process on individual ads, but over the years we influence what the corporation puts on the tube."

But OPNAD's influence goes well beyond its role of buying network time. It also influences McDonald's overall advertising strategy, and McDonald's and its agency are ill-advised to ignore suggestions from OPNAD members regarding the long-term direction of McDonald's advertising. During the late 1970s, for example, criticism began building within OPNAD and throughout the franchisee community regarding the types of ads that were coming out of Needham, Harper and Steers. For many operators, there was too much McDonald's personality coming through and not enough McDonald's product. Needham seemed permanently wed to its food-folks-fun approach even though Burger King and Wendy's were stepping up their campaigns with harder-hitting, more innovative advertising that was focused squarely on products.

Needham's response was weak. It changed the theme songs of its campaigns, but the content still honed in on the happy experience theme. "We have the best quality food available in our industry, but we were doing a lousy job of communicating that fact to our consumers because we were advertising too much of everything else," argues Ernie Trefz, a forty-two-store McDonald's operator in the New York City area. "We were selling a lot of happy, jumping people."

Part of the problem was that Needham's initial success with McDonald's had elevated the creative genius most responsible for it—Keith Reinhard—to the presidency of the agency. That pulled Reinhard off the account, and as Schrage, Turner, and others saw it, Needham's work for McDonald's never reached the level of creativity it had before. When Schrage complained and demanded a change in account managers, Needham offered only two candidates in a year's time—one who rejected the job and one who was a marketing executive at Burger King. "Good God," Schrage told Needham in response to the Burger King prospect. "No way."

Meanwhile, the demand from OPNAD for harder-hitting, product-oriented advertising was becoming intense. And in late 1981, McDonald's top management voted unanimously to dump Needham and switch to Leo Burnett, the chain's current national agency. (In 1990, Needham was rehired to handle part of McDonald's advertising, and Burnett continues to do the rest.)

How much of a role OPNAD played in forcing that change is debatable, since both McDonald's management and its franchisees wanted Needham out by the time the move was made. Clearly, top management at McDonald's initiated the move, and when they approached OPNAD with their decision, it was an easy sell. But it was franchisee discontent with Needham's "personality" advertising in the late 1970s that triggered the forces that led to the shift in agencies. "The corporation is sensitive to the wishes of the operator community, but not out of fear for what the operators can do," says Klein. "Over the years we've found out that when the operators galvanize themselves about something, they're usually right."

But local franchisees need not work through OPNAD or press McDonald's to change national agencies to have an impact on the direction of the system's advertising. They have other options that have a more direct impact on their markets. Although it almost always has the look of a national corporate effort, the fact is that most McDonald's advertising and promotion is carried on local, not national, media.

And through their 165 local cooperatives, McDonald's operators have the same control over how local ad money is spent as OPNAD has over national advertising budgets. In fact, by working through their local cooperatives, operators potentially have more influence over advertising at the local level than OPNAD has at the national level. At the local level, the franchisee-controlled cooperative—not the company—hires the local advertising agency, which responds to the needs and wants of its client—the local operators. Thus, at the local level, operators have direct control—not merely over spending but over the content of commercials and promotions. And if the operators are dissatisfied with any of the ads and promotions supplied to them by the corporation, they have the power at the local level to do something about it.

That is true even of the smaller cooperatives that clearly lack the resources for making their own commercials and are forced to obtain all their locally run spots from corporate marketing. Only about half of the 160 TV commercials produced each year by McDonald's, Leo Burnett, and DDB Needham wind up on network television, and the rest are not carried equally at the local level. Instead, local McDonald's co-ops can select from the corporate advertising "menu" those spots they wish to sponsor for local viewing and pass over commercials that turn them off. In some markets, certain corporate-produced commercials may be huge hits with local co-ops that run them seemingly to the exclusion of anything else. Yet, in other local markets, the same commercials—rejected by local operators—will not run at all. As a result, McDonald's television advertising can vary considerably from one region to the next, and the ability of local operators to choose the types of commercials they want shown in their markets constitutes to be one of the most powerful checks local franchisees have over McDonald's corporate marketing. Says Turner: "When most of the operators fail to use a commercial we produce, they are delivering an important message."

The same popularity poll takes place on nationally produced promotions. When California operators introduced operators elsewhere to the instant-winner game promotions, McDonald's and Simon Marketing began turning out a steady stream of them for national use. Increasingly, local franchisees began to grumble that the game promotions were cheapening McDonald's image, and they registered their opposition by refusing to sponsor the games locally. When McDonald's attempted to run against such stiff resistance in early 1983 with a "Million Dollar Taste Game," operators around the country turned thumbs down. The game ran in less than half of U.S. markets, and McDonald's has promoted only one other national game since.

The fact is that McDonald's and its national agency have little incentive to produce national commercials that its own operators will not also run locally. Thus, while franchisees have no direct input into the creative process in McDonald's national commercials, their freedom of choice in selecting which ads to run locally gives them something close to a pocketbook veto power over what McDonald's and Burnett or Needham create in advertising.

In such major markets as New York, Chicago, and Los Angeles, local advertising cooperatives are large enough that operators can take the veto process one step further. When McDonald's national agency produces ads that turn off the big regional co-ops, they do not hesitate to replace them with their own locally produced spots.

When McDonald's introduced Chicken McNuggets nationwide in 1980, for example, operators in the New York cooperative wanted what they believed were stronger ads for the product than those coming out of corporate headquarters. With a $16 million annual advertising budget, the 320-member cooperative had a media budget of a medium-sized company, and it ordered its local agency, Rosenfeld, Sirowitz and Lawson, to produce its own McNugget ads.

The ads, showing a hostess walking through a McDonald's and passing out free samples of McNuggets, were coordinated with an actual thirty-day free trial program in which McDonald's operators in the area gave out free McNugget samples to customers at dinnertime. RS&L won McDonald's Outstanding Agency Award for the campaign, and the ad was picked up by many other co-ops around the United States. Because they each paid the New York cooperative for part of the creative cost of the ad, the New York operators not only wound up with an alternative to the corporate McNugget spots, they covered their production costs in the process. A year later, the co-op produced even more lavish product-oriented commercials pitting the Big Mac and McNuggets in a popularity contest, and the names of consumers "voting" for their favorite were entered into a drawing for prizes.

That type of marketing freedom is not cheap. It cost the New York co-op $500,000 to produce its two Big Mac/McNuggets spots when it could have obtained corporate-produced commercials at no charge.

Still, many agencies hired by McDonald's larger regional co-ops like to encourage their clients to produce their own commercials, particularly when they are convinced that they can improve on what is coming down from the corporation and its national agency. As a result, the McDonald's System winds up with one national agency and half a dozen major local agencies who see themselves warming up in the bullpen to take over on the national account whenever the starter begins to stumble.

Not all McDonald's cooperatives are large enough to demonstrate independence in advertising production, but as the chain expands, more and more local cooperatives enter the ranks of the big-time marketers. Indeed, thanks to McDonald's decentralized structure for funding advertising, marketing is perhaps the one area of operation where the power of the franchisee actually *increases* with the size of the system. In other areas, the reverse is true. As McDonald's grows, the economics of centralized purchasing and distribution become greater. And the corporation's power in real estate, construction, design, and restaurant operations becomes nearly absolute as the system applies its celebrated standards of uniformity to a broader base.

But in making the critical determination of how the system will attract its customers, McDonald's operators continue to exercise their strongest check over corporate management. Fortunately for McDonald's, that is also the one area where ideas from franchisees are needed most. When McDonald's entered the national network advertising market in the late 1960s, its corporate marketing staff quickly took charge of one of the country's most powerful and most creative advertising programs. But it was continuing input from local franchisees—who had inspired McDonald's marketing from day one—that kept the chain's massive marketing machine tuned in to a changing fast-food market. Says Schrage: "Our operators are entrepreneurs, but we tell them where their store goes, what their sign looks like, and what type of service and products they are going to have. We give them operations manuals until they can't see straight. Marketing is their one last bastion of freedom, the only place where they can freely express themselves. McDonald's would not work if they didn't have that."

In recent years, the impact of local franchisees on McDonald's advertising and promotion has noticeably diminished. Most promotions are being generated from corporate marketing, not by local franchisees. And in response to more aggressive advertising from Burger King and Wendy's, McDonald's local cooperatives tend to march to the corporate marketing drummer in their use of local television advertising—hoping to gain the maximum impact of a system of operators speaking with one voice.

But while that type of marketing efficiency may be expedient in today's competitive environment, McDonald's runs the risk of losing the grass-roots flavor that has distinguished its marketing for four decades. Franchisees who become accustomed to following the corporate initiative on advertising and promotion may forget their heritage of local initiative and lose their creative edge just when the system may need it most. Marketing chief Schrage sees the risk, but he adds, "We'll never forget our history of grass-roots marketing. Never."

Chapter 14
"McDonaldizing" the Suppliers

By the time Fred Turner's expansion program had hit its full stride in the mid-1970s, McDonald's had brought sweeping changes to the food service industry in the United States. It had led the revolution that was making the practice of eating out as common as eating at home. And with its ubiquitous network television commercials, McDonald's had introduced brand name marketing concepts to an industry previously devoid of them.

Yet, one of its most significant accomplishments remained largely unknown—even to this day. McDonald's had changed the nature not only of the food *service* industry; it had changed the nature of the food *processing* industry as well.

In fact, it had almost single-handedly built an entirely new wing of the food processing trade. When traditional food processors were unwilling or unable to supply the food goods McDonald's demanded, Kroc's company responded by developing completely new sources of supply. It developed entirely new food processing methods. It pioneered new and much more sophisticated food distribution and packaging systems. And it did it all by relying on small suppliers that were outside the mainstream of America's food processing industries, because only nonestablished vendors seemed willing to help McDonald's break food service traditions that had stood for decades.

Thanks to business they now get from McDonald's, the system's suppliers have grown into some of the world's largest food processors and distributors, and yet they remain unknown to most consumers. Outside McDonald's, very few people know the $1 billion-a-year company that is now the world's largest manufacturer of hamburgers or the

$650 million-a-year potato processor that dominates the french fry business. And the largest processor of cheese for cheeseburgers and the biggest producer of fried fruit pies are even more obscure. Names like Keystone Foods (the hamburger leader), Martin-Brower (the biggest fast-food distributor), Schreiber Cheese (which supplies 65 percent of the 130 million pounds of cheese consumed by McDonald's each year), Jack Simplot (the french fry king), and Bama Pie (the leader in fried fruit pies) obviously lack the brand name recognition enjoyed by the likes of Kraft, Heinz, and Del Monte. Nor do they reside in the stable of products owned by such highly visible food processing giants as General Foods, Beatrice, and General Mills. The fact is that in the critical area of supply, McDonald's built the world's largest restaurant operation by relying on lesser knowns and unknowns of the food processing business. It had the same affinity for entrepreneurial suppliers as it did for entrepreneurial franchisees.

The reliance on unknowns was not by design. The traditional food processing giants had their shot at getting McDonald's business, and most blew it. Swift and Armour might have been the suppliers for all of McDonald's hamburgers had it not been for their refusal to extend credit to Ray Kroc when he opened his first store. When Hires failed to live up to a price commitment made by a former salesman, McDonald's shifted its root beer flavoring business to a lesser-known syrup maker, R. W. Snyder. Early on, Kraft had all of McDonald's cheese business, but it lost all but 25 percent when it failed to heed the company's demands for a sharper cheddar flavor. The beneficiary of that shift was tiny L. D. Schreiber, a Green Bay, Wisconsin, cheese manufacturer that has grown into a major supplier on the strength of McDonald's business. Similarly, Heinz had 90 percent of McDonald's ketchup and pickle business until 1973, when it refused to supply the chain with ketchup during a tomato shortage. Today, Heinz claims less than 6 percent of McDonald's $65 million ketchup account. And Bays, a branded leader in English muffins, lost McDonald's business not long after it was chosen to supply its product to the first stores that tested the Egg McMuffin. When McDonald's demanded a more evenly cut and uniformly shaped muffin, Bays managers replied that it only made English muffins with irregular shapes and cuts, and to make them any other way would compromise the company's muffin-making tradition. Now, less-recognized names, such as East Balt and West Baking—some of McDonald's bun makers—produce the nearly 30 million dozen English muffins McDonald's uses each year.

Thus, while McDonald's did not start out with a bias against the big name food suppliers, it wound up with one primarily because its demands were more than other restaurant chains were accustomed to making and more than large food suppliers were accustomed to answering. When McDonald's wanted exclusive products, it found too many large processors unwilling to provide anything but the standard products they sold to everyone else. Maximizing their current productive capacity was a far safer bet than building new capacity and gambling on future business from McDonald's.

But the problem went beyond economics. It also involved service. When McDonald's demanded special attention it was the smaller suppliers who were willing to take the extra steps. "The big companies tended to be complacent and to have poor follow-up and high personnel turnover," explains Lynal A. Root, the senior vice president who oversees McDonald's $8 billion of annual purchases of food and paper products. "But the smaller suppliers had more to lose and more to gain from our account. They appreciated the business more and responded faster. I never met an officer from Kraft until they had lost more than fifty percent of our cheese business."

Yet, McDonald's preference for entrepreneurial suppliers was not without significant risk. After Turner began setting new expansion goals, it was questionable whether McDonald's stable of small vendors was up to the task of supplying a chain that was attempting to walk away with the fast-food market. McDonald's was no longer a cozy regional drive-in operation but a complex nationwide system with thousands of restaurants. It needed suppliers with national distribution, with economies of high-volume production, with technical sophistication, and with the financial wherewithal to expand as rapidly as McDonald's was expanding. All those traits were more likely to be found in the established market leaders, not in the upstart independents that McDonald's was depending on.

Furthermore, McDonald's was gambling with small suppliers even when it was clear that a fast-food chain's supplier connections were going to be critical to its competitiveness. Even by the late 1960s it was becoming apparent that the fast-food business—especially the hamburger segment—would develop in another decade into a market dominated by a few powerful leaders, all of whom could produce an acceptable hamburger, market it aggressively, and deliver it through a nationwide network of modern stores.

By then, the battle between the titans of fast food would increasingly be one of efficiency of supply, and the winner would be the competitor whose suppliers had the lowest cost production, the highest level of technical expertise, and the greatest desire to innovate. There was no guarantee that McDonald's could achieve that type of dominance by casting its lot with smaller, entrepreneurial suppliers and then attempting to make them into giants on its own. When compared with the potential supply networks of other fast-food chains, which were either supplied by the major names in the food processing business or owned by them, McDonald's supply system did not seem to hold much promise for becoming the industry's powerhouse.

In fact, that is exactly what it became. Far from winding up with a disorganized cluster of independent suppliers, McDonald's created what even most of its competitors concede is the most integrated, efficient, and innovative supply system in the food service industry. Today, that system is increasingly responsible for preserving McDonald's as the industry's standard setter on uniformity of product. In the 1950s, McDonald's achieved its extraordinary consistency by devoting more attention than anyone else to field service and training at the store level. But, beginning in the late 1960s, the chain began shifting some of the labor involved in food preparation at the stores back to the food plants that supplied them. Products were produced in a more standardized fashion and in a manner that made food preparation in the store nearly foolproof. Production was concentrated in huge plants devoted exclusively to McDonald's. By the mid-1980s, McDonald's had converted its distribution system into the marvel of the food processing business.

It had reduced its beef suppliers from 175 to just 5, all of which run hamburger plants that are among the largest and most efficient in the meat-processing business. Its 175 local produce suppliers—which provided fresh potatoes, but often not the kind or exact number McDonald's had ordered—were replaced mostly by Simplot Company, whose four huge frozen potato processing plants dominate the french fry business. And today, virtually all items used by a McDonald's store are delivered in single-batch shipments made twice each week by trucks dispatched from mammoth distribution centers that warehouse most food and paper goods McDonald's uses.

But McDonald's wound up with much more than supply efficiency. It had also developed in its suppliers a commitment to serving the system that is rare among any outside suppliers. As Senior Chairman Turner puts it, the chain's suppliers became "McDonaldized."

Because McDonald's started with tiny suppliers and grew with them, the chain typically accounts for the vast majority of their business, and in many cases its suppliers handle no other accounts. Thus the suppliers became as dedicated to maintaining and improving the quality of that system as they would be if they were owned by McDonald's. They not only monitor their own quality control, they check on the quality of other suppliers in the system. They maintain their own quality assurance staffs, which regularly visit the restaurants to determine that products are being properly prepared and stored. They even check the company and take issue with corporate managers when they believe the integrity of the system's network is threatened.

And they are expected by McDonald's to meet a standard of responsibility and accountability that companies usually reserve only for their own employees. Ted Perlman, chairman of Perlman-Rocque, which owns four of the U.S. and four of the international distribution centers that purchase, warehouse, and deliver all products to more than one thousand McDonald's units, recalls how he implemented a *company* decision to convert the McDonald's french fry bag to a cheaper, thinner paper. But the new paper bag proved to be too pliable in the store, which resulted in french fry crews putting too many or too few fries in the bag. When Turner found out about it, his rage was directed not only at the McDonald's manager who had ordered the change. He also took Perlman to task, insisting that *he* should have known better than to fool with McDonald's most important product. Perlman, whose company purchases all the paper products used in the McDonald's System, never forgot the lesson about the extraordinary dedication McDonald's demands from its suppliers. He says: "My whole role in life is not letting McDonald's consciously make a mistake."

McDonald's suppliers started showing a special commitment not only to maintaining quality but to improving it. Since the 1960s they have been an integral part of McDonald's new product program. Most of McDonald's new products were made possible only because suppliers were willing to risk making a substantial investment in new production technology, an investment that would go down the drain if the new product failed. Jim Williams, chairman of Golden State Foods, one of McDonald's largest suppliers, observes that his employees' preoccupation with improving existing McDonald's products and dreaming up new ones is so strong that they virtually see themselves as McDonald's employees. "When a young guy comes to work for this company, he sees nothing but the McDonald's logo on all the products we touch, and he hears nothing else but serving the McDonald's customer," Williams says. "It's no wonder we have to remind our people that the company they actually work for is Golden State."

How did McDonald's do it? In a word, the answer is loyalty. While it started with small suppliers, it allowed its suppliers to grow with the system by being intensely loyal to those who were willing to reinvest in new capacity and in new technology designed to improve their quality and efficiency. McDonald's carefully avoided a common food service practice of shopping around from week to week to find the supplier with the lowest price. It made unusually tough demands on suppliers, but those who persevered and met them were rewarded with above-average profits on McDonald's burgeoning business.

In short, it commanded intense loyalty from suppliers by giving it to them first. No supplier has lost McDonald's business simply because someone new came in with a better price. And yet, McDonald's is under no legal requirement to stay with any of its suppliers. Its "contracts" with suppliers are made only on handshakes, never in writing, even with those companies whose businesses are totally dependent on McDonald's. While that often bothers the suppliers' bankers, it is not something that concerns the suppliers themselves. "You've got to be deaf, dumb, and ignorant once you have McDonald's business to lose it," Perlman says. Golden State's Williams adds: "If you lose McDonald's business, it's a self-inflicted wound."

If the absence of written supply contracts penalized anyone, it was McDonald's. In 1984, the company lost a major breach of contract suit to Central Ice Cream Company, which supplied an ice cream product McDonald's marketed in the early 1970s as Triple Ripple. When Kroc, on a handshake deal with Thomas Cummings, the owner of Central, agreed to introduce the product in all the chain's stores, virtually everyone at McDonald's believed the founder had finally discovered the winning dessert item he had been searching for since the late 1950s. The product had the look of a winner—a swirl of vanilla, strawberry, and chocolate ice cream in a sugar cone that was wrapped and protected by a clear plastic top. It sold for only 25 cents. "It was a neat product," Turner says. "We thought we'd sell a zillion of them."

However, while millions of consumers tried it once, the cone generated little repeat business. To most people it was a novelty item, and to Kroc it was yet another dessert bomb. But this bomb produced a megaton blast. When the chain discontinued Triple Ripple after sales

TRY 'EM

I'M "SPEEDEE"

Speedee Says:

"A Delicious Meal anytime, Morning, noon or nite!"

McDonald's ALL AMERICAN MEAL

| 100% PURE BEEF | CRISPY, GOLDEN | THICK CREAMY | |
| Hamburger | Fries | Shake | **45**c |

In little more than a decade, marketing at McDonald's progressed from a late 1950s newspaper ad for the All-American Meal (23), to local television spots with NBC's Willard Scott as the first Ronald McDonald (24), to network advertising that revolutionized marketing in the food service industry. This 1969 "Clean" commercial (25) was one of the first network spots to employ the "You Deserve a Break Today" theme.

23

24

25

26

27

28

McDonald's developed entirely new production techniques for the food processing business to meet its volume requirements and quality standards. Ray Kroc inspects a McDonald's french fry line with potato supplier Jack Simplot (26), whose company built modern warehouses to clean and store the Idaho Russetts used in McDonald's fries (28) and helped develop a new process for making frozen french fries (27). McDonald's also developed new technology to produce the world's first cryogenically frozen hamburger patties (29), and its bun suppliers operate some of the world's largest and most efficient bakeries (30).

29

30

31

32

33

34

35

36

37

When Ray Kroc married Joan Smith (31) in 1968, he pulled back from the day-to-day management of his chain. He entrusted strategic direction of McDonald's to his protégé, now Senior Chairman Fred Turner (32). Turner began building an operations-oriented management team that included Ed Schmitt (33), who explains new McDonald's kitchen equipment to franchisees and managers attending a biannual McDonald's operators convention; McDonald's USA President Ed Rensi (34), who serves up the fifty-billionth McDonald's hamburger to Dick McDonald in 1984; forty-one-year-old President Michael Quinlan (35), who is shown with an eighty-year-old Ray Kroc; and Senior Executive Vice President Gerry Newman (36).

On Ray Kroc's 70th birthday in 1972, Senior Executive Vice President Paul Schrage presented the founder with the Ronald McDonald Award normally given to licensees for their marketing achievements. In Kroc's case, the inscription reads: To the all-time Mr. McDonald (37).

Nothing distinguishes McDonald's from all other retailers in the United States more than its unique success in exporting its American service concept to foreign markets. In dedicating the chain's first restaurant in Europe (Holland) in 1970, Kroc personally demonstrates his fetish for cleanliness that seems to puzzle all onlookers except for McDonald's International Chairman Steven Barnes (right), who casts a knowing smile (38). McDonald's of Canada Chair-

man George Cohon, shown behind the counter of one of 638 Canadian units, built McDonald's most profitable foreign operation by stressing an all-Canadian approach to staff and suppliers and even switched his citizenship from the United States to Canada (39).

In Japan, McDonald's fifty-fifty partner, Den Fujita, rejected the corporation's advice to build the first Japanese McDonald's in the suburbs and instead located the first store in the busy Ginza shopping district of Tokyo. Here, he cuts the ribbon at the dedication of that unit with Ray Kroc (40), and soon afterward, the restaurant (41) became one of the top performers in the McDonald's System. Bob Rhea, then chairman of McDonald's U.K. (42), is shown (right) with partner Geoffrey Wade, Ray Kroc, and Fred Turner at the 1974 opening of the first of two hundred McDonald's in the U.K.

In expanding abroad, McDonald's exported its American menu and fast-food system, but tailored its marketing to local tastes. An ad in a German newspaper (43) stresses the European desire for clever and humorous advertising and counters criticism that McDonald's is changing German restaurant traditions for the worse. The ad declares: "Every food culture has its malices," and explains that even traditional restaurants have their shortcomings.

McDonald's involvement in community charities around the world has its greatest expression in its 160 Ronald McDonald Houses in 12 countries, such as this one located in Charleston, South Carolina (44).

Jede Eßkultur hat ihre Tücken.

43

44

McDonald's was the first of the fast-food chains to open a training school. In 1961, students marched to a single Hamburger University classroom located in the basement of this suburban Chicago McDonald's (45). Today, franchisees and managers attend this $40 million training center that has no equal in the food service industry (46). Ray A. Kroc (47) died in 1984, but the fundamental principles on which he built the world's largest food service chain remain bedrock doctrine at McDonald's today.

of the product fell to a fraction of a percent of store volume in three years, Central charged that McDonald's had violated Ray Kroc's verbal promise to market Triple Ripple in all McDonald's stores. The ice cream vendor retained ace trial lawyer Jerry Spence, who had won the Karen Silkwood case against Kerr-McGee Corporation, one of a number of his victories in big civil suits against corporations. With the colorful Spence conducting a show, Central won a stunning $52 million judgment against McDonald's, which later settled the case for nearly $15.5 million.

Had McDonald's signed a written contract with Central, its lawyers no doubt would have put in all the standard escape clauses to protect the chain from such a suit. But Kroc was not the type of businessman who believed that trust with his partners could be ensured by a contract with them, and that philosophy remains strong at McDonald's today. Thus, despite the negative judgment in the Central Ice Cream case, the chain stuck to its no-contract policy with vendors, preferring to base its faith in suppliers on something more than a written instrument.

Nowhere is McDonald's unusual supplier dedication more evident than in the development of new or improved products. Over the years, suppliers have become almost extensions of McDonald's product development department, willingly investing millions of dollars to develop new products or more efficient processes. The carrot has always been the knowledge that if the new product or process worked, McDonald's would give its developer all the new business it could handle.

The tradition of supplier involvement in new products got its start with Bud Sweeney, the account executive with Gorton Corporation, which captured 80 percent of McDonald's fish business after Sweeney helped develop the chain's Filet-O-Fish sandwich in the early 1960s. The same personal commitment by suppliers was shown later on with many other new products, and in each case McDonald's demonstrated the same intense loyalty in return. By giving his company more than one-half of its 1.8-billion-pound annual (unprocessed) domestic potato business, McDonald's made Jack Simplot the world's largest supplier of frozen french fries (over 1 billion pounds of fries and hash browns per year). Like Sweeney, Simplot got that business by demonstrating an unusual dedication to meeting McDonald's needs.

When he approached McDonald's in the early 1960s with an idea to improve the consistency of its french fries, Simplot was already a major potato grower. Yet, he still ran Simplot Company like an entrepreneur looking to make his first million. So it was not unusual for Simplot to consider taking a $400,000 gamble in an attempt to solve McDonald's biggest problem with using fresh potatoes—the fact that the best potato for french fries, the Idaho Russet, was available on the fresh market only nine months out of the year. Commonly used for baked potatoes, the Russets were harvested in the fall and maintained in cold underground storage throughout the winter. But they could not survive the heat of the summer, and for those three months McDonald's and all other food service chains turned to the California white potatoes that were harvested in the spring.

Unfortunately, the whites did not yield as crisp a french fry, and when Simplot proposed developing a cold storage network to supply McDonald's with Russets in the summer, the chain jumped at the chance. For Simplot, it obviously meant more McDonald's business. Through local produce distributors, he already supplied about 20 percent of the system's potatoes, but if his novel storage plan worked, he could wind up with much more than that. So, he spent $400,000 to put three hundred carloads of potatoes in cold storage around the country, enough to last McDonald's through the summer. Storing Russets through the summer had never been done before, and there were no guarantees from McDonald's. If the potatoes did not keep, it was Simplot's loss, not McDonald's.

Taking such a risk was totally in character for Simplot. After starting out with a tiny scrap iron business he started at the age of fourteen, Simplot had built his business by taking one gamble after another on unconventional ideas. He sold his scrap iron business to buy a pig farm, and a windfall profit in the hog market gave him enough money to buy a potato farm. But when he heard of a new electric machine that replaced manual sorting of potatoes, he sold the farm and became one of the country's first automated potato sorters.

That led Simplot into trading potatoes, then onions, and then into producing dried onions using a novel vegetable-drying machine. Nobody had tried producing dried potatoes before, but when World War II began Simplot found quick success turning out potato flakes that the army used for making mashed potatoes. By the end of the war, he ran fourteen plants making dried potatoes. His demand for potatoes to keep the plants running was so great that he went into potato farming on a grand scale and was among the first to try fertilizing a potato crop to improve its yield. When fertilizer proved too hard to get as the war progressed, Simplot went prospecting for it and discovered the largest phosphate mine in the western United States. And when the army stopped buying dried potatoes after the war, Simplot tried salvaging his potato processing business by pioneering a new concept: frozen potatoes.

In each case Simplot had gambled and won, but his novel idea to supply McDonald's with fresh Russets in the summer backfired. Virtually all of the stored potatoes went bad through a series of foul-ups, and Simplot was stuck with a $400,000 loss. It was his first big setback, but Simplot's response told McDonald's just how serious he was in getting more of their business. He immediately returned to McDonald's with an even bolder solution for the summer Russet famine: convert the chain from fresh to frozen french fries.

By the mid-1960s, Simplot had become the country's largest producer of frozen french fries, but that was not saying much because the potato market was still better than 95 percent fresh. Simplot needed a big customer like McDonald's to crack the market's resistance to the new technology. At a convention of potato growers he had met Steve Barnes, who was then McDonald's purchasing director. Simplot succeeded in getting Barnes interested in the idea of substituting frozen potatoes for fresh ones, at least during the summer months. Barnes persuaded Simplot to take his proposal directly to Harry Sonneborn, then the president of the chain. "He laughed at us," Simplot recalls. "The only thing he was interested in talking about was fresh potatoes."

The opposition to any tampering with McDonald's french fries was understandable. More than anything, the chain was known for its fresh french fries, and no frozen fry then on the market—not even Simplot's —came close to matching them in color, crispness, and taste. But when Simplot got the cold shoulder from Sonneborn, Barnes suggested that he take his case for frozen fries to a higher authority—Ray Kroc. Kroc, an expert at improving the chain's supply lines, was already keenly aware of the distribution problems involved in supplying his burgeoning national chain with fresh potatoes. Kroc knew it would be impossible to improve on the best batch of McDonald's fries, but he also knew that it was getting harder to maintain quality control on fresh potatoes. By the mid-1960s, the chain was buying potatoes from 175 local produce suppliers, and many of them were not adverse to fattening their margins by shipping McDonald's cheaper and lower-grade Russets than the chain had ordered. Wisely, Simplot argued for frozen fries not on price but on quality, which was all Kroc cared about. "I told him that frozen fries would allow him to better control the quality and consistency of McDonald's potato supply," Simplot says. "They were having a hell of a time maintaining potato quality in their stores. The sugar content of the potatoes was constantly going up and down, and they would get fries with every color of the rainbow."

In fact, even before Simplot approached Kroc with his frozen fry proposition, the McDonald's chairman had transferred Ken Strong from the chain's equipment lab in Addison, Illinois, to start up a food lab at Kroc's new ranch just north of Santa Barbara. Strong's first assignment was to begin research work on frozen fries, because Kroc knew that for McDonald's to convert to frozen french fries, it needed a frozen product that could not be distinguished from a fresh one, and there was nothing close to that on the frozen potato market. A food technologist with better than a decade of experience in research at Lamb Weston, a major potato supplier, Strong's background was perfectly suited for the task. At Kroc's request, Ed Traisman, a McDonald's franchisee in Madison, Wisconsin, was also researching the frozen french fries. The brother of Betty Agate, Traisman was one of a couple of dozen entrepreneurs who became franchisees after watching the success of Sandy Agate in Waukegan. But Traisman had previously been head of dairy and cheese research at Kraft, and Kroc wanted to tap that food expertise to solve McDonald's potato problem.

Both Strong and Traisman appreciated the fundamental aversion potatoes have to being frozen, and both understood how it alters their molecular composition and destroys their taste. They understood, too, that the potato industry's standard method of producing frozen fries had really not come to grips with the problem. That method involved blanching the peeled and cut potatoes in hot water and then quick-frying them in shortening before freezing. The frozen fries were then "finish fried" in the restaurant, but even processors recognized that their frozen fries were not as flavorful or as crisp as fresh fried spuds.

After months of detailed research, Strong and Traisman separately concluded that the problem was faulty processing. Traisman determined that the water retained in the potato before freezing formed ice crystals in the frozen potato that ruptured the cooked starch granules in the potato, robbing it of both structure and flavor when deep fried. If that moisture was removed from the blanched potato before freezing, he learned, most of the problems of freezing were eliminated. While he succeeded in getting a patent on the discovery, he nevertheless provided all of his research freely to Strong and McDonald's. Meanwhile, Strong had concluded that the long blanching cycle used in the traditional processing method cooked the potato too much. A good deal of its flavor was left behind in the processing water. Also left behind were the potato's natural sugars, which give french fries a golden brown color and crisp texture. Conventional frozen fries had neither.

Strong attacked both problems by designing a new frozen fry manufacturing process that replaced the long hot-water blanch with a shorter steam blanch that did not wash out the sugars and other flavor components. And instead of immediately frying the blanched potatoes in oil, he developed a system to dry them with hot air to remove more of the moisture, thereby eliminating the destructive effect of freezing. With the conventional process some of the moisture was removed by frying the prefrozen potato. But Strong concluded this involved too much cooking in the plant and not enough in the store, and the result was a finished fry that was not crisp. By drying the prefrozen fry with air and then running it through a very quick frying cycle before freezing, Strong reduced the moisture substantially—without reducing the crispness of the finished product.

Strong's method produced a french fry that even skeptics of the frozen product conceded was as good as the fries McDonald's had been making from fresh Russets. The process was also different enough that McDonald's got a patent on it; and Simplot, whose proposal to Kroc on frozen fries could not have been better timed, enthusiastically volunteered to build a production line to put Strong's frozen potato process to work. Simplot's company had already begun making its own improvements in the frozen fry in an attempt to sell the product to Kroc, and some of its improvements were not unlike those Strong had designed into his system. Simplot was so convinced that his team could convert Strong's process into a commercial operation that only a year after his cold storage loss he was ready to stake nearly ten times as much on a new McDonald's gamble.

On a handshake agreement with Kroc, Simplot invested $3.5 million to put the experimental frozen fry process into a production line with the capacity to turn out twenty-five thousand pounds of frozen fries an hour. There were no guarantees. If Simplot had not successfully implemented Strong's process to produce high-quality french fries, he could have suffered a loss on an order of magnitude greater than the cold storage fiasco. Indeed, another major Idaho processor of potatoes—Lamb Weston—had been approached by McDonald's on frozen potatoes even before Simplot contacted Kroc, and it was not interested in taking the risk on Strong's new process. But Simplot was undaunted. "I figured, hell, if the old man [Kroc] didn't take these fries, I would expand the plant for myself," he explains. "It gave me a good excuse to build the kind of frozen french fries plant I wanted."

The gamble paid off—in spades. Soon, Simplot's only concern was keeping up with McDonald's demand. The chain originally had thought of using the frozen fries only during the summer months, but by the time Simplot cranked up his new line, McDonald's had decided that Strong's "Mac Fries" were good enough to substitute for fresh year round. The chain converted to frozen as fast as Simplot could expand production.

Within a year of starting up the first frozen fry plant, Simplot brought a second one on stream. By 1972, McDonald's conversion to frozen fries was complete, but Simplot's potato bonanza had only just begun. When McDonald's successfully converted to frozen fries, every major chain in the food service industry followed its lead and began searching for a way to duplicate Strong's process. Simplot modified the McDonald's process slightly and began supplying Wendy's and other fast-food chains with high-quality frozen fries. McDonald's was revolutionizing the potato industry, and Simplot was capitalizing on his McDonald's connection to become the largest potato processor in the United States.

His company's four frozen fry plants in the United States supply McDonald's each year with about 450 million pounds of french fries, more than 50 percent of McDonald's business (Lamb Weston and Carnation supply the remainder). Combined with the business it gets from other major fast-food chains, Simplot Company now controls 30 percent of the commercial market for processed potatoes. What was a fledgling frozen fry operation when Simplot first talked with Ray Kroc in 1965 has grown better than twentyfold into a $650-million-a-year frozen potato processing business.

McDonald's shift from fresh to frozen french fries was further evidence of the potential creativity inherent in a franchising system in which all participants—company managers, franchisees, and suppliers —contribute to the solution and provide the benefit of their different experiences. It also provided proof that the effects of that cooperative creativity were now reaching well beyond McDonald's itself. The chain's conversion to frozen fries had a stunning impact on the nation's potato industry. Today, nearly 25 percent of the nation's potato crop goes into the production of frozen french fries, compared with only 2 percent in the late 1950s, and McDonald's alone accounts for about one-quarter of total frozen french fry production.

Only a few years after Simplot and McDonald's began converting the potato business from fresh to frozen, another group of entrepreneurs had an even bigger impact on the nation's food processing industry by taking a huge gamble to get McDonald's meat business. Their names were Al Justin, Jack Catt, and Herb Lotman, and until they got the brainstorm of trying to convert McDonald's from fresh to frozen meat, they were minor players in the meat-processing business. Catt was an independent meat broker who sold products for a variety of suppliers, including Polarized Meat Company, a processing company Justin had formed in Scranton, Pennsylvania, to produce frozen portion-controlled meat entrées for cafeterias, hospitals, and other institutional customers. Lotman and his father ran a small Philadelphia deboning company that had supplied Polarized with boneless beef.

In the late 1960s, all three were looking for new business. Justin had recently sold Polarized and was looking for a new challenge. Catt was looking for a new account to replace Polarized. And Lotman was looking for something to save his family business. When Iowa Beef introduced the concept of deboning meat at the meat packing plant and supplying supermarkets with prime cuts in boxes, it eliminated the middle-man function Lotman's company performed—buying meat left over after supermarket butchers removed their prime cuts and deboning that for use by various meat processors.

But it was Catt, the national meat broker, who understood that McDonald's by the late 1960s had developed a serious problem with fresh meat. Thanks to its geographic expansion, McDonald's depended on 175 local meat suppliers to deliver fresh hamburger to its stores three times a week. Even with the system's constant monitoring of beef suppliers and its frequent inspections of its suppliers' plants, maintaining quality control over such a fragmented supply network had become a horrendous task. Even when plants *supplied* hamburger that met the chain's specifications, there was no guarantee that the stores would *serve* hamburger that met the standards.

One continuing fear was that large hamburger shipments delivered to a store on Friday to last the weekend would not be consumed by Monday if, for example, a major storm wiped out the weekend trade. In such an event, franchisees were instructed to discard the leftover meat; but there was always the possibility that some operators would risk serving bad meat to avoid an economic loss. Kroc had nightmares about it. "I'd wake up in the middle of the night from dreaming that we had bad beef and thousands of customers with upset stomachs," Kroc remembered. "I wondered how the hell we'd get over something like that."

But the resistance elsewhere in McDonald's to changing to frozen meat was even stronger than the initial opposition to converting to frozen fries. No one considered frozen meat as good as fresh. Freezing robbed meat of its flavor and evaporated its natural juices. It also gave it a tougher texture. Indeed, the frozen meat alternative was so bad that McDonald's stubbornly took the risks associated with fresh meat even when its beef supply network had become nearly unmanageable. As early as 1965, Catt began calling regularly on McDonald's to sell frozen meat, and just as regularly he was turned away empty-handed.

But in 1967 he suddenly made headway. He persuaded Don Devitt, then McDonald's purchasing director, to approve a limited test of frozen meat using a process Justin had developed that involved cryogenically freezing the meat at temperatures below minus 200 degrees. That would freeze the meat so quickly, he thought, that the juices would be sealed in rather than evaporate as they did in a conventional freezer.

Catt and Justin entered into a partnership to produce frozen meat for the McDonald's test, and they brought Lotman into the venture because he had the one thing they were missing—a meat plant with spare capacity. Each partner invested $250,000 into their new company—which they called Equity Meat Company—and that seed capital was used to purchase and refine the freezing, grinding, and patty manufacturing equipment needed to produce frozen hamburgers for the three-unit test Devitt had approved. If the test failed, Equity was out of business, and its partners were out $250,000 each. For Justin, that was no major loss, since he had sold Polarized for $8 million. But it was all the savings that Lotman and Catt could muster. Even when Lotman cleared out his bank account he came up short in meeting his contribution to Equity's capital. He made up the difference by selling his sailboat.

Yet, it was not until Equity was set to begin work on developing a frozen hamburger patty that the three owners realized how risky their venture really was. The trio had flown to Chicago to work out final details of the test with Lynal Root, who had replaced Devitt in purchasing. When Root introduced them to McDonald's newly appointed president, Fred Turner, it was obvious that Equity had made an extremely narrow crack in McDonald's door.

Lotman will forever remember the encounter: "Fred told us he hated frozen hamburgers. He recounted the times when he was a grill man [in Kroc's Des Plaines unit] that he would put a few boxes of frozen hamburgers in the freezer as a reserve supply. He remembered how they got dehydrated and how he would cut his fingers in trying to pry them apart with a spatula. He told us that frozen hamburgers were never the way for McDonald's to go."

Turner was getting worked up, talking louder and emphasizing his points by pounding on the table. Then he gave the Equity partners his requirements. "He said the only way he *might* consider frozen hamburgers would be if we could develop a frozen patty that was quicker and easier to cook, was as juicy and more tender, and which shrank less in frying than a fresh hamburger," Lotman recalls. "I almost had a heart attack right there. I had just hocked everything I had to get involved in this, and the president of the company is telling us the project is dead before it starts. It was a very quiet flight back to Philadelphia."

No major meat company would take such a risk. Even if Equity's founders figured a way around the dehydration problem with cryogenic freezing, the other criteria for the test seemed unreasonable— and unreachable. Perhaps Turner was asking for miracles, but Equity's partners were in no position to say they could not work them. Their only other choice was to lose their investment. "Fred Turner's words actually made us more determined than ever to accomplish what he wanted," Lotman observes.

The group spent the next nine months at Lotman's plant working seven days a week, twelve or more hours a day. They refined the cryogenic freezing technique and tested a variety of coolants before settling on liquid nitrogen. They analyzed the effects of different freezing speeds. They experimented with a number of different meat-grinding techniques and eventually even developed the meat processing industry's first computerized blending system to produce consistently the right mix of lean round and chuck meat and higher-fat plates. And they tested different cooking temperatures to find the right one for their frozen patties.

The quality of the hamburger they finally produced surprised even them. They discovered that cryogenic freezing sealed in the meat's juices so well that with certain cooking techniques the resulting fried hamburger was larger and juicier than one made with nonfrozen meat. They also learned that the supercold ice crystals of liquid nitrogen broke down certain fibers in the meat and produced a more tender hamburger. And the meat was frozen so solid that the patties could be stored loosely in boxes and handled like poker chips in the store. There was no need to separate them with wax paper to keep them from sticking together. Even skeptics such as Turner conceded that Equity's partners had produced a frozen hamburger that was actually an improvement on a fresh one.

Nevertheless, the initial three-restaurant test nearly stopped the frozen hamburger project dead in its tracks. The first test unit was in Minneapolis, and Catt and Lotman were on hand when the hamburgers arrived by truck from Equity's Philadelphia plant. When Lotman opened the box, his heart sank. The hamburgers were frozen—together. The cooling system on the truck had failed just long enough for the ice on the surface of each hamburger to thaw and then refreeze. Since no paper was used to separate them, the patties were bonded together in one solid brick. It didn't matter that the problem had nothing to do with Equity. Given McDonald's sensitivity on frozen beef, any snafu with the first shipment of frozen patties could stifle the chain's desire to experiment further.

The store manager must not find out, Lotman thought. He and Catt managed to work up a sweat in the store's walk-in freezer, frantically prying the hamburger patties apart with screwdrivers. Turner's description of the problems of frozen meat at the Des Plaines store was now hauntingly prophetic. As the lunch hour approached, Catt carried shipments of the separated hamburgers to the grill, avoiding any hint of his panic, and Lotman kept chipping away at the frozen patties in the back room. Somehow, they made it through the lunch hour without the store manager suspecting any hitch. "If we didn't keep up with the lunch hour rush, we might have killed the test right there," Lotman recalls.

More important, the frozen hamburgers in the test won approval from the only judges who counted—consumers. Most of those surveyed tasted no difference in the meat, and a notable minority sensed an improvement. And, aside from the shipping foul-up on the first day, the frozen products vastly simplified the distribution and preparation of McDonald's hamburgers. Cooking time was reduced from four minutes to three and a half, and the hamburgers shrank less.

McDonald's operators, who had the final say on purchasing, raced to adopt frozen meat. By 1973, just two years after the test began, virtually all stores in the system had converted from their local fresh meat suppliers to one of several new frozen hamburger plants. Equity was in no position to satisfy that demand. It had, however, agreed to a standard condition that all McDonald's suppliers accept: if a supplier develops a new product or production process exclusively for McDonald's, it must make that technology freely available to any other supplier McDonald's designates. Ray Kroc had long maintained that suppliers were part of the McDonald's System, too, and like everyone else, they must put the system's welfare first.

But the sharing of trade secrets by suppliers is perhaps the ultimate sign of faith that suppliers have in McDonald's sense of loyalty. There was nothing to keep McDonald's from giving the lion's share of the business stemming from one supplier's breakthrough to another supplier, and no one took a greater risk on that score than Equity. It had a gold mine in its new frozen meat processing method, but only if McDonald's gave it most of the business.

Equity gladly took that risk. By the time it entered into its product development agreement with McDonald's in 1970, the chain's track record of enriching its suppliers was already well known. Once small vendors had grown huge, and their entrepreneurial owners had become millionaires. Lou Perlman's Martin-Brower Company had gotten all of the chain's paper distribution business. Harry Smargon's tiny shortening company had become a multimillion-dollar operation. Taylor Freezer rose from one of the pack to a power in the milk shake machine business by agreeing to design a vastly improved automated machine that allowed McDonald's operators to produce milk shakes as fast as tavern owners can draw a beer. By 1970, Taylor had already established its commanding lead in the burgeoning milk shake machine market by getting all of McDonald's business and the lion's share of the orders from other fast-food chains. Small local bakeries, such as those owned by Dick West and Harold Freund, grew into major commercial baking companies solely on McDonald's business. And the potato empire Simplot was building on the strength of McDonald's loyalty had become legend in food processing.

Thus Equity willingly turned over the secrets of its cryogenic hamburger production to four meat suppliers that McDonald's considered the best of the local companies supplying stores with fresh meat. They included Golden State in Los Angeles, Otto and Sons in Chicago, Anderson Meat in Oklahoma City, and Pabst Meat Company in Minneapolis. Together, they could accomplish McDonald's national conversion to frozen meat much faster than Equity could working alone.

Yet, Equity hardly suffered by sharing its secret. Within just two years, McDonald's fragmented meat supply network was reduced to just five frozen meat producers. Of those, Equity has consistently gotten the largest share of McDonald's meat business. Today, its two meat plants supply nearly 40 percent of the more than 490 million pounds of hamburger meat consumed annually by the McDonald's System. From a standing start in 1970, Equity has become the world's largest hamburger producer. Now known as Keystone Foods, most of its stock is owned by Northern Foods, a London-based diversified food processor. But Lotman, who before landing the McDonald's meat account was running a struggling $4 million-a-year meat deboning company, remains the chairman and 100 percent owner of Keystone, which in 1990 reported sales of more than $750 million—all of it from McDonald's.

Keystone might have grabbed an even bigger share of the commercial hamburger business had it chosen to process for other fast-food chains. But if his company was dedicated to meeting only McDonald's needs, Lotman reasoned, Keystone might have a shot at developing yet another meat product for the chain if the system ever added another meat entrée. In 1980, Keystone got that opportunity. It came in a telephone call from Lynal Root, who informed Lotman that his company had been chosen as the supplier for a new fried chicken product McDonald's was developing. The chain had been testing chicken for a decade, and it had not found the answer. Now, the company believed it had found it in the form of irregularly shaped pieces of chicken—battered and deep-fried—and it wanted Keystone to mass produce them.

McDonald's earlier failures with chicken were becoming a problem. Americans were eating proportionately less beef, and the fastest-growing meat alternative in the American diet was chicken. Thus finding a suitable chicken entrée for McDonald's occupied much of the time and effort of Rene Arend, the European chef (from Luxembourg) who performed his craft at the exclusive club in the Whitehall Hotel in Chicago. On his extended trips to Chicago from the West Coast, Kroc lived at the Whitehall and struck up a friendship with Arend. They talked for hours about food—Kroc fascinated by Arend's skills as a continental chef, and Arend fascinated by the empire Kroc had built on feeding the masses. For years Kroc tried to hire Arend. The chef's answer was always the same: "Ray, what can I possibly do for you? I am a chef, not a hamburger man."

Arend was not the only one puzzled by Kroc's desire to hire him. Turner was completely opposed to it. But Kroc was always pressing for the development of new products, insisting that individual store volumes could only continue growing if McDonald's improved existing products and developed a broader menu with less reliance on hamburgers. And he thought Arend brought the outside perspective McDonald's needed to develop unique products that were not likely to emerge from managers and operators who had grown up in the fast-food trade. Perhaps he could develop special sauces. Perhaps he could do something with chicken. Perhaps he could develop a new dessert. To that, Turner responded wryly, "What are we going to serve—bananas *flambeaux à la mode?*"

In 1976 Arend finally decided to take Kroc up on his standing offer to become McDonald's chef. He quickly began work on a chicken entrée, and at Kroc's suggestion he developed a "chicken pot pie" similar to McDonald's deep-fried fruit pies. It flopped in a test. He developed a steak sauce, but the steak sandwich it accompanied was tested and scrubbed. He worked on fried chicken, using special chicken cuts that resulted in larger pieces. But the test product entered a crowded fried chicken market where McDonald's needed more than a modest product improvement.

Despite his string of failures, Arend's work attracted the attention of one of his initial skeptics—then Chairman Turner. Ray Kroc had asked Arend to help develop a new onion product called Onion Nuggets, bite-sized chunks of battered and deep-fried onions. But the variety of onion supplies made it impossible to control quality, and when Turner saw Arend on the way to his office one morning, he told him to quit working on onions. "But, Rene," said Turner, "why not try chicken nuggets instead?"

That morning, Arend cut up a chicken into bite-sized pieces—similar to the Onion Nuggets—and then battered and deep-fried them. By late afternoon he had some chicken nuggets ready for Turner to sample. Turner loved what he tasted, but he also realized the technical hurdles such a product faced. The principal one was that no one had developed a mechanical method for deboning and cutting a chicken into bite-sized filets.

To solve the problem, McDonald's quickly turned to Banquet

Foods, one of the largest suppliers of frozen chicken dinners. But Banquet relied on old meat-grinding technology used in making sausage, and its version of nuggets had the look, texture, and processed flavor of a chicken sausage cut into pieces. Even their diamond shapes looked artificial.

To solve the nugget problem, McDonald's clearly would have to develop a new technology and take an entirely new approach to the chicken business. In developing Chicken McNuggets, Turner might have relied totally on his company's product development department since the idea for the product had come primarily from within. When suppliers helped develop frozen fish, frozen fries, and frozen meat, McDonald's had a small product development staff. But by the 1980s, McDonald's product development department had grown to fourteen staffers with a wide variety of expertise in food preparation. Nevertheless, Turner recognized that most of McDonald's food processing expertise resided in its captive supply network, and to solve the production problems of chicken nuggets rapidly, he now decided to tap the full strength of that network.

He called Gorton's Bud Sweeney, who had developed McDonald's Filet-O-Fish sandwich. Turner wanted to "borrow" Sweeney from Gorton for about six months of crash work on the chicken nugget problem. "No way, Fred. This is going to involve a cast of thousands, and I couldn't handle the bureaucratic bullshit," Sweeney replied, envisioning how such a major new product development would get caught up in layers of McDonald's establishment that had not existed when he developed the fish product nearly two decades before. But the chicken nugget project was Turner's baby, and Sweeney's attitude was unacceptable. Turner got nose to nose with the fish supplier as he delivered a terse response: "Bud, you've become a very poor listener."

Sweeney got the message. He agreed to work on the project, but only if he could hand pick the McDonald's people he wanted helping him as leader of a Chicken McNugget SWAT team and only if he reported directly to Turner himself. The McDonald's chairman agreed to the unorthodox arrangement, and the Chicken McNugget SWAT team quickly established its independence from McDonald's bureaucracy. Indeed, superiors of some members of the team who had dropped in on its meetings to learn about the nugget development were told to leave.

Still, the SWAT team became one of the best examples of how McDonald's uses its partnership with suppliers to develop new products. Sweeney committed the breading and battering skills of Gorton, which had solved the breading problem on fish. He relied heavily on McDonald's product development and quality assurance departments to provide insight into the type of product the company wanted and to monitor consumer reaction to the product in market tests. He counted on chef Arend to develop the four sauces that would accompany the chicken nuggets. Finally, he relied on Keystone to help solve the biggest problem—finding an efficient way to cut chicken into small, boneless pieces.

No one had ever attempted to mass produce chicken in that manner before. Since chicken was always sold in much larger parts, the technology to produce commercial amounts of nuggets did not exist. After weeks of investigation, Sweeney had about given up on finding a solution to mechanically cutting chicken meat into the five different shapes that are produced when chicken is hand cut into bite-sized chunks. But Victor Wortman, a McDonald's quality assurance manager, insisted that the process had to be mechanized for McNuggets to work economically in McDonald's, and working with Bud Kivert from Keystone, he made the key technical breakthrough. The two greatly modified a hamburger patty machine to cut the deboned chicken meat into nuggets that gave them a texture similar to that of a chicken part cut by hand. Keystone still had to rely completely on manual deboning of the chicken on production lines utilizing more than one hundred chicken cutters, but it developed methods of greatly automating the line, increasing its productivity nearly threefold in a few years. While other members of Sweeney's group worked on solving the meat problem, Daryl Otten, a manager in McDonald's product development department and a member of the SWAT team, worked with Gorton to develop a unique tempura coating that gave the nuggets the appearance of being freshly battered at the store.

Thanks to the division of labor involved in the teamwork approach, McDonald's was able to rush Chicken McNuggets to market in record time, capitalizing on the competitive advantage it suddenly had with a unique product that could not easily be duplicated. McNuggets entered their market test in Litton Cochran's stores in Knoxville in March 1980, just five months after Sweeney accepted the assignment as SWAT team leader. Almost immediately, McDonald's sensed it might have the hottest new product since Herb Peterson's Egg McMuffin. The new menu item was accounting for up to 20 percent of sales at the fifteen test outlets. Thus, even before McDonald's had committed to expanding McNuggets to other markets, Keystone rushed to build a new plant to manufacture the new chicken product.

The plant was completed in just one hundred days at a cost of $13 million—an investment that was made with no more assurances than Lotman had fifteen years before when he invested every penny he had in frozen hamburger production. His only guarantee was a belief in McDonald's commitment to its dedicated suppliers. "McDonald's would never hurt a supplier," Lotman says. "If they ask you to do something like this and it didn't work out, they would find something for us to do with that plant."

As it turned out, neither Lotman nor McDonald's had to figure out what to do with the plant. By the time it opened, franchisees were clamoring to get McNuggets, and the plant was on a seven-day-a-week production schedule not long after it opened. By the time McNuggets went into national distribution a year and a half after the initial test in 1980, McDonald's had to find a second producer—Tyson Foods—to handle the demand. Just as it had shared its technology in frozen hamburgers, Keystone gave its secrets on making McNuggets to Tyson, which quickly contributed improvements of its own. It developed an entirely new breed of chicken it called "Mr. McDonald," which was specifically designed to increase the efficiency of the nugget-making process. Nearly twice as large as the standard supermarket broiler, Tyson's new chicken further reduced the deboning problem by increasing the meat yield from each cut. Keystone, of course, quickly began encouraging its suppliers to follow Tyson's lead. Within a few years, as other competitors began copying McNuggets, the market for deboned pieces of chicken—once a fraction of chicken demand—became a fast-growing segment of the poultry industry. "We absolutely revolutionized the chicken business," Sweeney boasted.

Not surprisingly, Lotman's company wound up getting 65 percent of McDonald's chicken business, which converted it into a major chicken producer. Within just three years of their national introduction, the bite-sized nuggets were accounting for fully 7.5 percent of McDonald's domestic sales, making McNuggets one of the most successful menu additions in the history of the fast-food industry. With more than $700 million in McNugget sales in 1985, McDonald's—king of the hamburger business—became the second-largest chicken retailer in the food service trade behind Kentucky Fried Chicken—king of the chicken business. (In 1990, chicken sales from McNuggets and chicken sandwiches came to $685 million.)

Interestingly, it took KFC another three years before it finally introduced its own version of chicken nuggets, and that perhaps is the most important lesson in the McNugget story. Its suppliers' technological expertise had given McDonald's the ultimate competitive advantage—a proprietary product that could not easily be duplicated, even by the leading competitor in the fried chicken market. It was apparent early on that McDonald's had a winner in McNuggets, but it was also apparent that its competitors were powerless to respond because the product was not a marketing innovation but a technical one. That reflects a subtle but significant change in the nature of competition in the fast-food industry in the 1980s. As McDonald's attempts to squeeze labor out of its stores by moving more product preparation back to the processing plant, it creates the opportunity to develop unique new products based on its suppliers' processing skills. As a result, suppliers of fast-food chains are now a critical part of their new product effort—and a key to improving their competitive position. And in the case of McNuggets, McDonald's suppliers for the first time became the focal point of new product development.

But McDonald's reliance on nearly captive suppliers for technological breakthroughs goes beyond new products. Indeed, it was suppliers—driven by the prospect of increased McDonald's business—who played the key role in organizing McDonald's supply lines and making its distribution system one of the most advanced in all of retailing.

During the 1960s, a McDonald's unit was something of a depot for delivery trucks. The bakery truck unloaded buns three days a week. The dairy truck came every other day. Meat suppliers made deliveries five times a week. There was a truck for ketchup, one for Big Mac sauce, one for fish, one for potatoes, one for frozen pies, and another for syrups. In all, a McDonald's store received twenty-five separate deliveries every week, most of them from different local suppliers. Inevitably, the chain's operators carried a heavy inventory burden, and as the system grew, its fragmented distribution system threatened to grow out of control.

In the area of paper goods, Lou Perlman saw the problem before anyone else, but he also saw a huge business opportunity in trying to solve it. Perlman's company—Martin-Brower—was a small local distributor of paper products to cafeterias and other institutional food service outlets until it got the business to distribute Dixie paper cups to Ray Kroc's first restaurant in Des Plaines. But Perlman, who knew Kroc

going back to his old days with Lily-Tulip, sought a bigger role in
McDonald's right from the start, and to get it he changed distribution
methods that were common throughout the food service business.
Typically, national restaurant suppliers, such as Dixie, used distributors, such as Martin-Brower, only to generate and invoice orders, not to
deliver the goods. Restaurants were notoriously risky accounts, and
food and paper manufacturers relied on distributors to take the risk of
nonpayment. But their goods normally were "drop shipped" directly to
the food service customer from the plant, rather than being shipped to
a distributor's warehouse for local storage. Since most distributors
were regional, national manufacturers used dozens of different distributors throughout the country. The system allowed manufacturers to
lock in their customers and protect their profit margins, because the
regional distributors were beholden to the national manufacturers, not
the restaurants that were the ultimate source of their business.

Perlman rearranged the relationship by distributing paper goods
on behalf of his new *customer*—McDonald's—and not his *suppliers*.
Ted Perlman, who was only eighteen years old when his father showed
him Kroc's Des Plaines restaurant, recalls: "Ray's concept of a national
chain excited my dad. He figured that Ray was going to need paper
products wherever he went, and the more products he could pull
together in a single delivery, the easier it was going to be for the stores,
and the more sales he was going to have."

Lou Perlman's innovation was twofold. First, he proposed to serve
as McDonald's distributor not just in Chicago but nationwide. That
would allow him to buy large quantities of paper products himself,
store them in a warehouse, and ship them to McDonald's outlets
through common carriers. By purchasing paper for all McDonald's
stores, Perlman could negotiate much better prices than a typical distributor supplying stores in only one region. Instead of negotiating a 3
percent discount on a supply for a single market, he could negotiate
perhaps a 5 to 7 percent discount on a national supply contract. The
savings more than offset any additional costs in shipping from a central
warehouse, and the plan allowed Perlman to spread freight costs
evenly through the McDonald's System so that every operator paid the
same price for paper goods. "Dad's idea was to change the entire
industry around," says Ted Perlman. "It didn't make sense for all of
these shipments to move from the factory direct to the local McDonald's stores."

But warehousing and shipping paper products from a central location led Perlman to a second distribution innovation: warehousing a variety of paper products and other dry goods that were required by McDonald's. That meant that products from different manufacturers could be shipped in single truckloads, and in quantities that met McDonald's needs, not the manufacturers' distribution needs. For example, a manufacturer might drop ship to a McDonald's store five seventy-five-pound drums of dehydrated onions—enough to last two months. The syrup supplier might ship forty-eight cases of concentrate, also a two-month supply. Sugar was shipped in two-month quantities as well. The problem was that the McDonald's store itself became a warehouse, solely because manufacturers could not justify smaller shipments. But by combining *all* dry goods into his shipment of Dixie cups, wrappers, and napkins, Perlman could afford to deliver smaller quantities of each item. Thus he continually looked for more items he could buy, warehouse, and deliver in his single shipment to McDonald's stores.

Kroc saw to it that Perlman's company benefited as much from Perlman's innovation as McDonald's did. As McDonald's grew, the once tiny Martin-Brower flourished, eventually becoming the nation's largest distributor of food service supplies. Today, McDonald's accounts for 58.7 percent of Martin-Brower's $2 billion in distribution revenues. With about 50 percent of McDonald's distribution business in the United States, Martin-Brower long ago became McDonald's largest supplier.

Indeed, as Perlman was finding new products to add to his distribution list—from cleaning compounds to Coca-Cola—he became McDonald's most critical supplier, even by the early 1960s. Perlman was almost as much a part of McDonald's as was Kroc himself. He was so close, in fact, that McDonald's eventually demanded and got an open book relationship, so that Kroc could guarantee to his franchisees that McDonald's was giving them the lowest price it could.

Ted Perlman recalls that the books came open not long after an incident in Fred Turner's office in 1961. Ted Perlman and his father were visiting with Turner, who was reviewing a letter he had gotten from Dick McDonald, who had just discovered that the schools in California were buying Dixie cups cheaper than McDonald's was. "Lou," Turner asked, "do we get any discounts on cups like that?" Stone-faced, Perlman replied that McDonald's got a standard discount of 5 percent on paper cups.

Annoyed by that, Turner called Jerry Beatty, Dixie's Chicago manager, and put him on the speaker phone as he asked him why Mc-Donald's couldn't get a discount similar to the one Dixie gave to California's school boards. "What is the discount that Lou gets?" Turner asked coyly. "He gets the standard five percent and then he gets seven percent more," Beatty answered. Perlman recalls: "Our hearts sank all the way down to the main floor of the building. But Fred just looked at Dad and said, 'Well, Lou, I caught you, didn't I?'" From then on, McDonald's went on a cost-plus arrangement with all of its major suppliers, and their books came wide open.

But Perlman was not the only supplier looking for ways to profit by innovating McDonald's distribution system. In fact, what Perlman was doing to consolidate McDonald's distribution of dry goods, Golden State was doing with food products. Golden State was a small meat supplier to restaurants and hotels in southern California when it began supplying the handful of McDonald's stores on the West Coast in the late 1950s. It was founded by Bill Moore, an entrepreneurial and expansion-oriented supplier who became fast friends with Kroc when the McDonald's founder moved to California in 1962.

Yet, Moore's growth ambitions nearly put his company under when he tripled the size of his meat plant and warehouse in 1962 and failed to find enough business outside of McDonald's to keep it running profitably. Curiously, Moore's solution was to concentrate exclusively on McDonald's, which was planning a massive expansion in California under Kroc's direction. "We shot craps with McDonald's, risking our future on the hope that they would build the stores they said they would," explains Williams of Golden State.

But even McDonald's new store construction in California could not solve Golden State's overcapacity problems. So, Moore tried getting a bigger piece of the McDonald's pie by adding other food products to his deliveries of meat to the chain's stores, duplicating in food distribution some of the economies Perlman was getting in paper. Thus, along with producing meat, he began buying, warehousing, and delivering frozen fish, cheese, pickles, ketchup, soft drink syrups, sauces, and potatoes—nearly every item on the McDonald's menu board. And when frozen meat was introduced and Golden State was chosen as one of McDonald's five remaining meat suppliers, Moore's company expanded its distribution territory well beyond the relatively restrictive boundaries of its fresh meat deliveries.

Eventually, Moore introduced the ultimate in distribution efficiency to McDonald's—and the food service industry. By delivering so many food items with its own fleet of trucks, Golden State could begin to deliver dry goods even more competitively than Martin-Brower, and in 1973, Moore's company took the paper distribution business for the McDonald's southern California cooperative away from Martin-Brower. Not surprisingly, Martin-Brower quickly responded by moving as much into food distribution as Golden State had moved into nonfood products.

Other McDonald's distributors—building from a base of meat or produce—followed the two leaders toward total distribution. Herb Lotman's company, for example, branched out from hamburger manufacturing into food and paper distribution. By the mid-1980s, McDonald's and its suppliers had converted the fast-food industry's most fragmented distribution system into its most concentrated. From about 200 distributors supplying the system's 1,500 restaurants in the United States in 1970, McDonald's concentrated its domestic distribution into 10 companies, 4 of which (Martin-Brower, Golden State, Keystone, and Perlman-Rocque) handle all supply deliveries to more than 85 percent of the chain's 9,000 U.S. units. Together, the distributors supply all McDonald's units from 37 huge regional distribution centers, which receive shipments from all 275 manufacturers supplying the system and which warehouse everything a McDonald's unit uses—better than four hundred separate products. It has cut the shipments to McDonald's stores down from twenty-five per week to only eight per month, reduced its distribution costs by 5 percent, and greatly reduced the inventory burden of each McDonald's operator.

In addition to achieving these efficiencies, the consolidation of the supply lines has also resulted in tighter control over purchases. Operators order from just one source of supply, typically once a week, and in some cases an operator need only project his or her total sales for the coming week and the distributor's computer system calculates the optimum order for each item—from pickles to fries to ketchup—based on the individual restaurant's typical mix of products sold and its current inventory of each item. Each month the operator receives a single report of all purchases, and that, along with his or her own detailed inventory and sales reports, is used to determine whether the store is getting the proper yields—whether crews are putting the right amount of ketchup on the hamburger and french fries in the bag. Billing is also handled centrally, and the bill is paid by a single electronic transfer of funds from the franchisee's bank account to the distributor's.

Yet, even as McDonald's supply system was concentrating into more powerful entities, its franchisees were consolidating their purchasing power to increase their clout over suppliers. Beginning with the same Cleveland cooperative that revolutionized McDonald's advertising by pooling the promotional funds of franchisees, regional operator co-ops began in the early 1960s to perform the same type of consolidation in their purchasing that suppliers were achieving in their distribution. While individual operators previously dealt with suppliers one on one, their power over suppliers did not compare with the clout franchisees had when they used regional cooperatives to select suppliers and negotiate prices collectively.

In fact, the development of the cooperatives and the concentration of the supply side of McDonald's are intertwined. On the one hand, the regional cooperatives gave franchisees the power they needed to deal on a more even basis with larger and more powerful suppliers. On the other, the cooperatives themselves became a force in centralizing purchasing decisions and made it easier for McDonald's to convert to larger suppliers and distributors. That conversion would have been all but impossible if McDonald's had to convince every franchisee in the system on the merits of Lotman's frozen meat or Simplot's frozen fries or on the efficiencies of Golden State's total distribution system. The regional cooperatives allowed McDonald's to make its pitch for such changes to a select group of operators sitting on the purchasing committees of the regional cooperatives.

The cooperatives became so powerful in their own right that McDonald's purchasing department could no more force its supply preferences on franchisees than the marketing department could dictate regional advertising programs. It took a decade for McDonald's to convert the system to the total distribution concept, because cooperatives would not approve the new distributors as fast as McDonald's wanted. In some cases, the co-ops overruled the supplier choices McDonald's had made. In others, they initiated their own supplier changes when they decided as a group that the service from an existing supplier had fallen below par.

Often it is other suppliers in the system who detect the winds of such operator discontent and go after the business of a supplier who has fallen out of favor with McDonald's or its purchasing cooperatives. Thus the suppliers, too, fit neatly into the system of checks and balances that govern the relationship between corporate managers and franchisees. Their performance is checked not only by the company and the cooperatives but by other suppliers in the system.

Indeed, a major incentive for McDonald's suppliers to continually upgrade their products is the threat that other suppliers in the system will move after weak links in the supply chain. In short, McDonald's suppliers play hardball with each other—not by undercutting one another on price, but by competing on improvements in product quality.

When Bill Moore's Golden State decided to concentrate exclusively on supplying McDonald's, it began looking in 1970 for other things to manufacture for the system in addition to frozen hamburger patties. It decided that it could make a strong play for supplying milk shake and soft drink syrups to McDonald's operators on the West Coast. The syrups were coming from several other suppliers back East, and Moore was convinced he could improve on their quality—the only factor that would encourage McDonald's to change. Thus Golden State built a syrup research operation in Los Angeles and even hired a top chemist from Nesbitt, a leader in the flavorings business. After developing new flavors, it built a modern syrup production line at the plant without any commitment from McDonald's that it would get any flavoring business. But when Golden State convinced McDonald's managers and the West Coast operator cooperatives that it had developed superior flavors, it wound up with McDonald's syrup business in the West.

Golden State did the same thing when it heard rumblings within the system that McDonald's and some operator co-ops were dissatisfied with the quality control at Conway, the New York company that made McDonald's tartar and Big Mac sauces. As the distributor of all food and paper supplies to operators in the West, Golden State knew firsthand the mounting complaints from operators about the quality of the sauces from Conway. "We were having a lot of recalls on the product, and McDonald's was beating them over the head to improve," recalls Golden State's Jim Williams. "They made a fatal mistake of thinking that the system needed them."

Sensing a major new manufacturing opportunity, Golden State made a move on Conway's McDonald's business. It built a sauce manufacturing operation in Atlanta and took the business away from Conway in the Southeast, and in time other McDonald's cooperatives approved similar changes for their regions. Today, Conway is no longer a McDonald's supplier, and the McDonald's sauce business is split between Golden State, McCormick, and Kraft. Through its expansion into distribution and from there into the manufacturing of other products for McDonald's besides hamburger, Golden State emerged as the system's second largest supplier, behind Keystone. Moore's aggressive strategy in pursuing McDonald's business not only salvaged his company but converted it into a major food supplier with sales approaching $1 billion in 1993—all from McDonald's.

But Golden State eventually realized that the supply system's checks and balances work both ways. In 1976, Williams's company lost the McDonald's distribution business in northern California to Martin-Brower, largely because Golden State's management staff had not grown fast enough and its distribution service in that location began to suffer. "It was the best lesson we were ever taught, and we decided we owed it to the system to keep ourselves well staffed," Williams says. "We never lost another McDonald's account."

Earlier, Martin-Brower was taught a similar management lesson. When it was acquired by Clorox in 1972, a Clorox-installed management team decided that McDonald's needed some "price discipline" and that Martin-Brower's profit margins needed some fattening to bring them more in line with the margins the company makes on consumer products. That message did not sit well with McDonald's, particularly since it was being delivered by new managers at Martin-Brower whom it did not know. Clorox had installed a new manager with no distribution experience above Martin-Brower chairman Mel Schnieder, who had built the company with Lou Perlman. In disgust, Schnieder quit, and while Clorox kept Perlman's son as vice president in charge of the McDonald's account, it was clear that top management intended to call the shots on McDonald's. But when the new team met with Fred Turner, the McDonald's chairman delivered a very blunt message: "I want you to know one thing. McDonald's only deals with Ted Perlman."

The message did not sink in. Clorox managers continued interfering on the McDonald's account until Perlman quit a year later, formed his own distribution company with partner Bob Rocque, and went after McDonald's distribution business held by Martin-Brower. When Perlman-Rocque solicited the franchisees of several McDonald's co-ops in the Midwest, their only sales pitch was that they were committed to serving McDonald's and no one else. Before Clorox found a management team with a similar attitude at Martin-Brower, it lost a considerable amount of McDonald's business to Perlman-Rocque, which now controls 25 percent of McDonald's distribution and also performs all of the chain's purchasing of paper products—the very service on which Perlman's father built Martin-Brower into a big-time distributor. In 1980, Martin-Brower was sold by Clorox to Dalgety, which has since protected its McDonald's business from further erosion.

While McDonald's has developed through its vendors what amounts to another set of eyes and ears to monitor the system's performance, its suppliers' commitment to the system does not translate into subservience to McDonald's Corporation. For a group that depends on McDonald's for most of their sales, the chain's suppliers are surprisingly independent, perhaps because McDonald's initially selected entrepreneurial suppliers instead of large and established companies. As a result, it wound up with suppliers who are not hesitant to challenge McDonald's corporate managers when they believe their decisions run counter to the welfare of the system. In addition to the restraints provided by its franchisee community, the power of McDonald's Corporation is checked by its own supplier network.

Indeed, suppliers have not been afraid to confront even the founder of the chain. When Jack Simplot was invited by Ray Kroc to sit on the McDonald's board of directors, his behavior was not what might be expected of a man whose potato empire was based on supplying McDonald's. In fact, at his first board meeting Simplot objected to Kroc's proposal to buy a corporate jet. "If I owned stock in a company that bought an airplane," Simplot told the board, "I'd sell my damn stock." Kroc responded by purchasing the jet with his personal funds and leasing it to the company for $1 a year.

But even much smaller suppliers have had the gumption to take on McDonald's when they were convinced that its corporate managers or franchisees were in error. Bama Pie is just a fraction the size of Simplot Company, but founder Paul Marshall is no less independent-minded than Jack Simplot. And even though Bama gets fully half of its sales by supplying all the apple and cherry pies sold by McDonald's in North America, Marshall has not let that restrict his entrepreneurial freedom.

Marshall is perhaps the classic McDonald's supplier. Before getting the chain's business in the late 1960s, he ran a small pie factory that supplied only the Oklahoma market. But when he paid an unannounced sales call on McDonald's just as the chain was searching for a pie supplier, Marshall suddenly found himself in the unaccustomed position of having more potential business than he could finance. When he could not scrape up the $250,000 he needed to build a new plant to handle the system's needs, McDonald's interceded with his local bank to get Bama a loan for the plant.

Yet, Marshall refuses to be McDonald's handmaiden. When franchisees from Florida paid a visit to his big Tulsa plant, which turned out 150,000 frozen pies an hour, Marshall locked them out because at a dinner the night before they had committed an unpardonable sin— insulting his hometown and his fried pies in the same breath. The next morning, Senior Vice President Lynal Root was on the phone trying to get Marshall to change his mind. He refused. "I was eating three meals a day before I met you guys, and I think I can keep eating three meals without you," he huffed.

The incident was smoothed over, but a similar one occurred a few years later. That was when a McDonald's product development specialist had spent about a year off and on at the Bama plant attempting to develop a biscuit freely using Marshall's equipment. But she was also insisting on employing a manufacturing process Marshall was convinced would not work. When he had seen enough, Bama's owner had no qualms about expressing his displeasure. He sent the young product manager packing. "It was the one time," Marshall says, "that I felt McDonald's was trying to throw its weight around."

Few major commercial customers would tolerate suppliers making such challenges, but in dealing with entrepreneurial suppliers, McDonald's is willing to trade off subservience to obtain an objective appraisal of the chain's performance. "Most suppliers just roll over and do what you want them to do," Root says. "Only your real friends will tell you when you are wrong. I don't want our suppliers sitting there always saying, 'Go ahead, go ahead.' They have a responsibility to tell us when we're wrong."

Because of that attitude, McDonald's suppliers have steered the company away from a number of disasters. There is no better example of that than the fast action Herb Lotman took in the summer of 1973, when federal wage and price controls threatened to curtail the chain's supply of hamburger. Because the controls froze the price of beef at packing plants and food stores but did nothing to restrict the live cattle price, prices for beef on the hoof rose to levels that eliminated the meat packer's margin.

Fortunately, Lotman immediately saw the danger, and he quickly warned Root that the packers around the country were losing money on every kill and were certain to begin closing down soon. But Lotman also had an ingenious solution: a custom slaughtering operation. If

McDonald's itself bought the live cattle and sold the animals to meat packing houses at a lower price that allowed them to make a profit on their slaughtering operation, Lotman figured the chain could get around the problem without turning to importing beef or to a black market that was beginning to develop. It meant that McDonald's—not the packers—would subsidize the loss on every animal.

To fund the operation, all franchisees in the system were asked to contribute 5 percent of their August sales, which provided $5 million in capital for the Lynal Root Agency, the corporate name of the emergency beef-buying project. Lotman and Root then nearly took up residence in McDonald's Gulfstream jet, traveling 8,500 miles each week between twenty different packing houses participating in the custom slaughtering operation. In the eight-week period from the time Lynal Root Agency went into operation until the price controls on beef were lifted, Root and Lotman had traveled 66,000 miles and purchased 76,000 head of cattle for a net subsidy of $3.8 million.

More important, they had kept McDonald's supplied with hamburger at a time when grocers' meat counters were nearly empty because meat packers around the country had closed their doors. In fact, because McDonald's became one of the few outlets in the United States where consumers could find hamburger during the waning months of the price freeze, the chain's sales surged nearly 15 percent, and operators recovered their beef subsidy and then some.

In many ways, Lotman's critical role in solving the beef crisis symbolizes how totally involved McDonald's suppliers are in the McDonald's System. Because of the way the chain has defined its relationship with its suppliers, McDonald's interests are indistinguishable from their interests. When the beef crisis ended, Ray Kroc offered to pay Lotman a consulting fee of $150,000 to compensate him for the two months of full-time work that he had devoted to the beef purchasing project. Lotman, however, reminded Kroc that while he helped McDonald's he had also ensured that his own company's meat plants—totally dependent on McDonald's business—remained open. Lotman charged a considerably lower consulting fee than Kroc had in mind: $1.

"People ask me how I sleep knowing that I have but one customer and no supply contract," Lotman says. "My answer is that a supply contract is only as good as the people who sign it, and if those people have an honorable intent, you don't need a contract. With McDonald's, I have never needed a contract."

Chapter 15
THE PUBLIC CHALLENGE

The sales at McDonald's units in Atlanta had begun to fall in 1976, and every franchisee knew why. Although it had yet to reach the public media, a wild rumor was spreading around town that McDonald's was adding worms to its hamburger meat.

The rumor was grotesquely menacing. Such a grossly inaccurate story had an existence of its own. It was a fantasy that needed no support from reality, and the plain truth was insufficient defense. McDonald's was supplied by the cleanest meat plants in the United States. It had greatly elevated the meat industry's standards for quality and purity of hamburger by eliminating all fillers and additives. Its standard for bacteria in meat was tougher than the one enforced by the U.S. government. But using that information to counter a ludicrous rumor served only to give the story a hint of credibility.

It was better not to breathe a word about it to the press, and that was the order Fred Turner gave to his corporate public affairs managers just before he went on a hunting trip to Missouri. But the pressure from the Atlanta franchisees to do something about the rumor became intense, and the public affairs managers at McDonald's concluded that they could not sit idly by. Against Turner's orders and without consulting McDonald's outside public relations expert, Al Golin, they decided to hold a press conference in Atlanta to deny a rumor that had not yet appeared in print. That was damaging enough. But the real bombshell came when a local franchisee, responding to a reporter's question, admitted that his sales had been badly hurt by the talk of worms.

What was a local problem became a global one overnight. The newspaper wires and television and radio networks carried a story the next day about how the sales of the largest hamburger chain were being depressed by a rumor about worms in its meat. When Turner saw the story in the St. Joseph, Missouri, *News-Press*, he immediately knew the massive scope of the damage. "My heart stopped," he recalls. "It gave the rumor some credence, and it gave it momentum."

Indeed, publication of the story was now delivering a blow to McDonald's sales throughout the Southeast, and a stream of denials by McDonald's did little to deflect it. Ray Kroc's response was clearly the most effective rebuttal. Unfortunately, McDonald's did not get it out to the press soon enough. "We couldn't afford to grind worms into our meat," cracked the chain's founder. "Hamburger costs a dollar and a half a pound, and night crawlers cost six dollars." Kroc was not the only one who saw humor in the story. On that week's broadcast of NBC's *Saturday Night Live,* Jane Curtin referred to the episode on the show's satirical news report. McDonald's top executives, Curtin intoned, flatly denied the rumor that the chain adds worms to its meat. But, she added, they were at a loss to explain why the cut halves of a Big Mac crawl in opposite directions.

Unfortunately, humor could not undo the damage. The rumor depressed McDonald's sales for months. In time, Turner fired the public affairs manager who had ignored his order, and he assigned other managers to research the rumor. After months of investigation, they concluded that the apocryphal story originated from a national magazine article about someone promoting franchises in worm farms, declaring his intention to become "the McDonald's of worm farming." That knowledge provided no solace to Turner, who even today cannot bring himself to speak of worms, preferring instead to refer to "the four-letter-word rumor."

Perhaps more clearly than any other incident, the Atlanta episode revealed that by the mid-1970s, McDonald's had begun to pay the price of its enormous success. When it was a young company introducing a brand-new concept in food service, it could do no wrong in the public eye. Consumers and even McDonald's competitors were awed by the quality and consistency that Kroc's managers and franchisees were bringing to a food service business that had never known nationwide uniformity and standardization. Every town in the country wanted a McDonald's. And when they finally got one, the city fathers were invariably impressed by how the McDonald's franchisee became so intimately involved in the community's well-being. A monotonous string of quarterly sales and profit gains of 20 percent or more had made McDonald's stock one of Wall Street's darlings. And Ray Kroc was universally admired as a man who had given his fellow entrepreneurs a good shot at becoming millionaires.

But when Fred Turner's expansion program had achieved everything that could have been expected of it, the public attitude toward McDonald's changed. With thousands of restaurants throughout the United States, with a commanding lead in the burgeoning fast-food market, and with a fabulously wealthy owner and hundreds of rich franchisees, McDonald's had become an institution. Its television commercials were so pervasive and so sophisticated that it was easy to forget that McDonald's was still nothing more than a large cluster of small entrepreneurs. It was a marketing power. And a visit to McDonald's no longer was a new experience. It was, in fact, commonplace and expected. As publicist Al Golin puts it, "McDonald's wasn't that cute little company anymore."

Nor was it any longer benefiting from the American penchant to pull for the brash young competitor challenging old ways. By virtue of its astonishing success, McDonald's was instead becoming victimized by the counterbalancing penchant to be skeptical of power. "The only publicity we ever had during the early years consisted of wonderfully warm stories, but now we were being viewed as an institution, and people take pot shots at institutions," Golin says. "Our bigness was now bad. In fact, all the things that made McDonald's successful—its predictability, uniformity, and controls—were perceived by some people as lacking individuality, stamped out and mass produced. We were tagged as part of a plastic society some social observers were condemning. For the first time, we were on the defensive."

Such criticism could have been expected. McDonald's impact on consumers was now so extensive that the chain had become the most visible retailing organization in the world. Everything it did of any consequence wound up in print, as did thousands of things that had no consequence at all. It had become an easy target. "McDonald's became so widely known," Golin says, "that any mention of it in the local press—even in the most isolated places—could have worldwide implications."

Nevertheless, McDonald's was not at all prepared to handle that notoriety or respond to the public and private challenges it inevitably created. Its expertise was totally wrapped up in operating its stores, not in defending the system from public attack. "It was such a shock to have our legitimacy questioned," Turner says. "It was an era in which we were the nouveau riche company that was extremely naive about the social and political establishment."

Nowhere was that naïveté more evident than in the first national attack on McDonald's credibility—the criticism of Ray Kroc's $250,000 personal contribution to the 1972 campaign to reelect Richard Nixon. Had Kroc had any idea of the controversy that would develop from the Nixon campaign's fund-raising effort, there is no doubt that he would never have taken the risk of making such a visible contribution. Although Kroc was concerned about what he perceived as the country's drift toward a social welfare state, he was not even remotely involved in the American political process. He had never before made any notable political contribution, and he rarely offered his views on politicians, even to his confidants. "Ray's political-interest index was unusually low," Turner says.

Yet, the clear conservative-liberal split in the 1972 Nixon-McGovern campaign briefly aroused a sense of obligation in Kroc to defend a free enterprise system that had given him so much. Furthermore, Kroc was now among the conspicuously wealthy, who are prime targets for all political fund-raising efforts. Thus, when Kroc was asked to attend a Republican fund-raising dinner hosted by Bob Stuart, the chairman of Quaker Oats, and featuring Secretary of Commerce Maurice Stans, the McDonald's founder had already decided to contribute $25,000 to the president's campaign. But as one of the country's most accomplished salesmen, Kroc's biggest weakness was that he was easily swayed by other polished salesmen. And at the fund-raiser that night, Secretary Stans's salesmanship obviously wooed Kroc. "After Ray heard Stans speak," Turner says, "he just decided to add another zero to his contribution."

What was done on impulse soon was pictured as a carefully crafted strategy to influence the Nixon administration's policies to favor McDonald's. The allegation was that McDonald's was attempting to prevent an increase in the minimum wage, which covers a small army of young workers employed at McDonald's restaurants. McDonald's franchisees were among hundreds of businesspeople lobbying against an increase, as well as for passage of a law exempting part-time students from the minimum wage. The controversial student exemption legislation was quickly dubbed "the McDonald's bill" by its opponents—a connection largely attributed to the flap over Kroc's donation to the Nixon campaign. (An extremely limited exemption was eventually passed by Congress.)

But the controversy over Kroc's Nixon contribution was triggered by what otherwise would have been an obscure decision by the Wage and Price Control Board to allow McDonald's request for a price increase on its new Quarter Pounder hamburger. Nixon's price controls posed a particularly serious problem for the new, hot-selling Quarter Pounder. In the middle of the product rollout, Kroc declared that the sandwich should have two pieces of cheese instead of one. That change could only be justified economically by adding four cents to the Quarter Pounder's introductory price, and Turner reasoned that since the product had been upgraded in quality and cost, its price could be increased under the price control guidelines. But when McDonald's law firm refused to sign the registration statement on a pending securities offering unless McDonald's received formal approval for the Quarter Pounder's price increase, Turner reluctantly agreed to present the matter to the Wage and Price Control Board.

That put the issue in the public forum. While the Price Board approved McDonald's request, the ruling did not escape the watchful eye of Jack Anderson. One of Anderson's syndicated columns linked the Kroc contribution to the Price Board decision and also accused McDonald's of influence peddling on the minimum wage issue. Before McDonald's knew it, the Kroc contribution was being wrapped up in the panoply of campaign excesses that were tied to Watergate. Kroc, who had never intended his contribution to support any specific policy—least of all one as controversial as restricting minimum wage— was astonished by the avalanche of negative publicity his big donation to the Nixon campaign had caused.

While Turner knew that Kroc's contribution and his decision on pricing the Quarter Pounder had innocent motivations, the effect of the publicity nevertheless was devastating. A company that never had anything but the most pristine image was suddenly receiving crank telephone calls and being flooded with negative—and sometimes threatening—mail. Turner even received a letter bomb. Fortunately, his secretary called McDonald's security personnel when she saw some wires protruding from the unopened package.

Once again, McDonald's was completely unprepared to handle such a radical change in its public perception. "It was demoralizing and embarrassing," Turner recalls. "It tainted us a bit. 'My God,' we thought, 'how will this affect the self-image of our operators and managers and their families?' There was an implication that we had done something wrong."

Even before the Nixon contribution had embroiled McDonald's in a national controversy, the chain had begun to get a taste of negative publicity generated by a series of fierce battles that sprang up at the local level. The first, and one of the most threatening, took place in Cleveland in 1968 when McDonald's came under bitter attack from a loose coalition of black activist groups led by a militant named David Hill. McDonald's had already begun a nationwide search for its first black franchisees, but that effort was initially unsuccessful, and McDonald's had franchised only four units to blacks when Hill called for a boycott of McDonald's in Cleveland. Before the chain had time to react, hundreds of black demonstrators were picketing the six white-owned McDonald's on the town's predominantly black East Side.

It was the worst time and the worst place for McDonald's to become involved in a racial controversy. Martin Luther King Jr. had just been assassinated, and Cleveland was one of the most racially divided cities in the country. It had elected the first big city black mayor, Carl Stokes, but rather than ease racial tensions, Stokes's mayoralty aroused them. Stokes had courted the support of the Black Panthers and other militant groups and in so doing had fanned the fires of prejudice that burned in the hearts of thousands of politically active residents on the town's mostly white West Side.

The city was racially split—East Side against West Side—and McDonald's became one of the first victims of that division. Hill and the other black groups refused to remove their pickets until McDonald's removed the white franchisees from the six black neighborhood stores. The pickets became violent, intimidating patrons by carrying night sticks and wearing ammunition belts and eventually by hurling rocks through store windows, an escalation that forced McDonald's temporarily to take over the operation of the stores. The company brought in experienced managers from its newly acquired forty-three-restaurant Gee Gee operation in Washington to run the six Cleveland units and relieve the besieged franchisees.

Bob Beavers, the veteran black corporate manager from Washington whom McDonald's selected to supervise the reopening, might well have qualified for battle pay. To prevent a riot, the police had pulled back from the pickets, and before he entered the area of his first unit, Beavers got some frightening advice from a white Cleveland police sergeant. "I suggest that you change your hotel and change your name," the sergeant told him. Then, to Beavers's astonishment, the officer handed him a revolver. "If you have to use this," he told Beavers, "shoot to kill."

McDonald's quickly began negotiating with the black coalition, but even those talks took place in an environment of intimidation. Carl

Stokes had provided an office at City Hall for a negotiating session between McDonald's corporate managers and representatives of the black groups, but that turned out to be something less than neutral turf. When Ed Bood, McDonald's vice president of franchising, showed up at the meeting two doors down the hall from the mayor's office, he was greeted at the door by "guards" from the coalition forces wearing bandoliers. Hill and the other black militants at the meeting demanded that they be appointed agents of McDonald's to supervise the selection of black franchisees for the stores. In return they wanted a "commission." While Bood—supported by all the white licensees involved— agreed to refranchise the stores to blacks, he rejected Hill's terms. Only later did he realize how menacing the meeting was: one of the coalition representatives sitting across from him was holding a gun under the table. "Carl Stokes," Turner recalls, "did not help matters."

Only when Dr. Kenneth Clement, a black physician, publicly called the boycott a "shakedown" did the tide turn in McDonald's favor. Clement was the genius behind the campaign to elect Stokes, but following the election he broke with the mayor. Not long after Clement spoke out, the boycott of the McDonald's units ended, and black franchisees were soon found for all six restaurants. Clement's description of the boycott seems to have been justified. Hill was later convicted of blackmail stemming from his efforts to force the sale of McDonald's restaurants in Cleveland to blacks, and was later a fugitive living in Guyana.

As bad as the Cleveland blowup was, however, it did not do nearly as much damage as McDonald's suffered when it got involved in another local controversy in 1974 with New York City's elite. McDonald's had erred in the Cleveland imbroglio by not anticipating the problem and recruiting black franchisees earlier. But when well-to-do residents on New York's Upper East Side began picketing a new McDonald's site at Sixty-sixth Street and Lexington Avenue, the chain committed a less forgivable public relations mistake: not realizing soon enough when it was beaten.

The construction of a McDonald's at Sixty-sixth and Lexington was part of a new strategy to begin penetrating an urban market McDonald's had ignored during its first fifteen years, and the development of Manhattan was a top priority in implementing that plan. The chain had already built ten new units in Manhattan, and when McDonald's leased the site at Sixty-sixth and Lex, it must have thought that a new unit in such a fashionable neighborhood was certain to be a gold mine. It was more like a land mine instead. In fact, the company might have had better luck trying to get a permit to build in Central Park than to get the approval of the chic residents around Sixty-sixth and Lexington. On one corner was a historic armory building, on another an exclusive apartment high-rise, and on a third the home of the Cosmopolitan Club, an old-line women's social club whose registry was cluttered with the names of New York's blue bloods. Around the corner was the Manhattan residence of David Rockefeller, the chairman of the Chase Manhattan Bank. Indeed, the neighborhood claimed some of New York's most influential residents—writers, brokers, lawyers, and corporate executives.

When he heard that McDonald's had purchased the funeral home on the corner of Sixty-sixth and Lexington and planned to erect a small office building with a McDonald's on the main floor, architect David Beer immediately organized the Friends of Sixty-sixth Street to fight the project. McDonald's, displaying a midwestern naïveté about the influence of New York's social elite, merrily proceeded to build as if no opposition existed. "There was a little sense of arrogance on the part of McDonald's local managers," recalls Howard Rubenstein, a top New York public relations consultant later hired by McDonald's to represent the chain. "McDonald's position was that it owned the property, that it was properly zoned, and that the company had a legal right to build a restaurant there and could not be stopped."

They had badly underestimated the power of the group being organized by architect Beer. Within weeks, Beer had collected the signatures of some fifteen thousand area residents on a petition against the McDonald's unit. The opposition included such influential residents as Mrs. David Rockefeller, Arthur Schlesinger Jr. and Theodore White, the author of the *Making of the President* books.

When McDonald's refused to meet with the Beer group, the protestors began to display their real power—connections. Footage of the pickets marching at the McDonald's construction site became a regular feature of local television news broadcasts. Editorials began appearing in the *New York Times* and elsewhere bitterly denouncing the McDonald's store as a potential eyesore in the midst of one of Manhattan's most attractive neighborhoods. And the New York brokerage house of Baker, Weeks and Company abruptly removed McDonald's from its list of recommended stocks on the grounds that it had saturated the easy suburban sites and would now have to tackle much more difficult urban locations.

Still, McDonald's—and particularly Turner—refused to cave in. The heat from the anti-McDonald's group reached a fever pitch when Mimi Sheraton, then the food editor of the *New York Times*, wrote a scathing critique of McDonald's in a *New York Times Magazine* cover story under the rather inflammatory title, "The Burger That's Eating New York." It came in the midst of the battle over Sixty-sixth and Lexington, and Sheraton summarized all of the neighborhood group's claims—that the McDonald's unit would become a magnet for unsavory characters as well as an unsightly haven for litterbugs—but she did not stop there. Indeed, that story merely provided Sheraton a launching pad for a diatribe that hammered McDonald's for Kroc's contribution to Nixon, for questionable accounting, for wrecking landmark buildings, and for underpaying its youthful crew members.

But her most vitriolic critique was of the chain's food: "McDonald's food is irredeemably horrible, with no saving graces whatever. It [hamburger] is ground, kneaded, and extruded by heavy machinery that compacts it so that the texture is somewhat like that of a baloney sausage, and it becomes rubbery when cooked. Once cooked, the burger is insulated in a soggy bun, topped with pickle slices that seem recycled, or dehydrated onion flakes, or shredded lettuce that is more like wet confetti, and one or another of the disgusting sauces. Potatoes may be crisp but they have no taste. The shakes (significantly not called milk shakes) are like aerated Kaopectate."

McDonald's considered the critique a malicious fabrication, but it decided against pursuing legal action in order not to draw even more attention to the article. Yet, Turner remained convinced that Sheraton had done a "hatchet job" on McDonald's food, which aided the cause of the Friends of Sixty-sixth Street. "The food editor of the *New York Times* knows something about food," Turner argues. "She had to know that her statements were fiction."

Sheraton's story also referred to another recently published article in *Barron's* that lambasted McDonald's accounting practices. Written by Abraham Briloff, professor of accounting at City University of New York, it, too, appeared to be part of the fallout from the bomb the New York establishment had dropped on McDonald's. In his article, which referred to the battle over Sixty-sixth and Lex in its lead paragraph, Briloff argued that McDonald's was overstating its reported net income through questionable accounting, primarily the "pooling" method of accounting, which allowed companies to account for acquisitions by blending the financial statements of the acquired operations with those of the acquiring company. Briloff happened to be one of the growing number of critics opposed to pooling, and McDonald's happened to be one of the hundreds of acquisitive companies using the procedure, in this case to account for its string of acquisitions of franchised restaurants. Briloff argued that pooling grossly understated the true costs of those acquisitions and thus overstated net income. While pooling was later rejected by the accounting profession as a means of accounting for the acquisition of small companies by large ones, it was nevertheless one of the generally accepted principles of the profession when Briloff used McDonald's to gain a forum for his assault on pooling.

In the same article, Briloff insisted that McDonald's overstated income by failing to report as a corporate expense some $8 million in stock that Kroc had given to some of his company's employees and their families in commemorating his seventieth birthday in 1972. It was one of the most magnanimous gestures a corporate founder had ever made to his employees, and McDonald's top managers benefited mightily. Turner alone got $1 million worth of stock from Kroc, and his wife, Patty, got an equal amount. The senior executives and their wives each got $125,000. But Briloff argued that such a gift by a principal corporate shareholder should have been deducted as a company expense—that in essence Kroc was giving the money to McDonald's, which in turn was giving it to employees as compensation for their work.

While McDonald's defenses of the Briloff allegations were sound enough to protect its accounting from further attack—particularly from the ultimate enforcer of accounting propriety, the Securities and Exchange Commission—the article nevertheless did the type of damage chief executives of public companies have nightmares about. It delivered a vicious blow to the stock. On the day it was published, McDonald's stock plunged nine points—or 19 percent. That alone reduced McDonald's market value by more than $357 million. "That's when I got religion," Turner recalls. "I realized that the opponents of Sixty-sixth and Lex were better at making war than we were, and I surrendered. But I swore that someday I'd get even."

Rubenstein, McDonald's public relations consultant on the New York dispute, conveyed Turner's truce terms: Remove the pickets and drop the multimedia campaign, and McDonald's will quietly drop its plans to build a store at the contested location. The controversy ended, and today McDonald's owns a two-story office building at Sixty-sixth and Lexington that is a tribute to the power of neighborhoods with powerful residents. Instead of housing a McDonald's, its ground floor retail space is occupied by The Forgotten Woman, an elegant boutique for women of larger sizes. Rubenstein says of the entire affair: "It was one of the most brutal confrontations any community has ever organized against a business."

Eventually, Turner got his pound of flesh from the New York establishment. Although there was never any direct evidence, he and others at McDonald's believed that such a well-orchestrated campaign against the Sixty-sixth and Lexington store had to be the masterstroke of someone with better connections to New York's power brokers than architect David Beer. Turner concluded that the real architect of New York's anti-McDonald's resistance was Margaret Rockefeller, the wife of the Chase Manhattan chairman.

While executives at Chase Manhattan later assured Turner that the bank was not involved in the opposition movement, Turner nevertheless counterattacked using the only weapon at his disposal—McDonald's banking business. Before the six-month battle over the Sixty-sixth Street location in 1974, Chase Manhattan was not a major lender to McDonald's. But as McDonald's began expanding abroad and as it outgrew its oldest banking ties to American National Bank and First National Bank of Boston, the chain began giving Chase some of its international business—until Turner intervened in 1982. And since then, McDonald's began giving increased attention to other banks in addition to Chase, including First Chicago, First of Boston, and Citicorp.

Retribution, of course, was no long-term solution for the image problems McDonald's had begun to encounter in the early 1970s. It was the impressive scope of its operations that was making McDonald's such a visible public target, and the chain's only answer to its new outside challenges had to lie in learning how to adapt to the consequences of its own size.

During the first half of the decade, McDonald's had exhibited all the signs of corporate adolescence—aggressive growth mixed with an awkward public presence, boundless but untamed energy, and boldness that lacked some of the wisdom of experience. But McDonald's was really in no position to continue making the mistakes of youth. It had become too powerful to be so undisciplined. Because it had grown faster than most companies, it now had to mature in record time, too.

The maturation of McDonald's took nearly a full decade, and in many respects it was a far more complicated—though considerably less celebrated—process than Ray Kroc's founding of the chain and Fred Turner's massive expansion of it. In a relatively short period, McDonald's had to make a complete transformation. It had to learn how to be comfortable with a new level of media scrutiny. It also had to realize that to avoid the type of media bombardment it was getting, it needed a decision-making process that was sensitive to community needs, to political risks, and to social issues. Until now, McDonald's priorities involved little more than building as many quality hamburger operations as it could. More than anything else, that explains why it found itself unprepared for a dangerous rumor about its food, an explosive racial protest, high-society pickets, and charges of influence peddling.

Remarkably, McDonald's managed to turn all of those negatives into positives. By the late 1970s, in fact, the chain was responding to challenges on each of those fronts and was already seeing the favorable results of a more enlightened approach to the outside world.

Shocked by the connections that some journalists had made to his $250,000 contribution to Nixon's reelection effort, Kroc never again made a political contribution anywhere near as large or as potentially controversial. In fact, he refused to give another nickel to a presidential campaign and made almost no other political contributions of any significance. The one exception was a $45,000 donation to the campaign in 1976 to elect James Thompson as the Republican governor in Illinois. But when Thompson went back to Kroc for financial support for his successful reelection bid two years later, he walked away empty-handed. Since the Nixon affair, Kroc told Thompson, he had come to view contributions to politicians somewhat like the support parents give their kids. "My job is to get them to college," he told the governor. "Now, I've helped you get through college in politics. From now on you're on your own."

While Kroc curtailed his political largess, however, McDonald's began using the political process more skillfully to get its message across to government bureaucrats and lawmakers. It coordinated those efforts better and increased the professionalism of its governmental contacts by creating a government relations department in 1975.

The new department carefully avoided involvement in issues where the political risks outweighed the rewards. Minimum wage was clearly one such issue. Previously, McDonald's had helped organize a lobbying effort by dozens of local McDonald's franchisees in an attempt to influence federal minimum wage legislation. But in 1977, when individual franchisees waged a grass-roots campaign against an increase in the minimum wage by contacting their local congressmen, McDonald's Corporation and its government relations department stayed clear of the issue. "There's a lightning rod aspect to McDonald's and minimum wage," Turner explains. "Let's face it, we have a conflict of interest there, and we should keep our nose out of it."

Instead, the new government relations unit focused on issues with more positive overtones. For example, McDonald's began countering the "junk food" label that some critics had extended to fast-food products. It had an outside consulting firm conduct a study of the nutritional value of its food; and it concluded that a meal of a hamburger, french fries, and a milk shake provided a large percentage of the recommended daily allowance of key nutrients—clearly enough to constitute an important part of a well-balanced diet.

Unfortunately, the regulations of the federal Food and Drug Administration contained such extensive labeling requirements that it effectively kept fast-food chains from communicating nutritional information to consumers. The FDA rules allowed McDonald's to print a detailed nutritional analysis of each item on its menu boards or individual product packages and wrappers. However, they prevented a more logical and efficient dissemination of that information through the distribution of brochures at the store. "We were getting a bad rap on nutrition, but we couldn't communicate the positive information we had," says Clifford Raber, McDonald's vice president of Government Relations.

In 1978, Raber succeeded in driving that point home to staffers of the Senate Subcommittee on Nutrition. Ironically, the chairman was none other than George McGovern—the candidate Nixon had defeated in 1972 with the aid of some big donations from Ray Kroc and scores of other wealthy businessmen. But by 1978, McDonald's was in the center of an issue McGovern might use to deliver a message that would go over well with his many farmer constituents in his native South Dakota—that American-grown beef, potatoes, and dairy products were, in fact, wholesome.

Thus when Raber offered to work closely with the subcommittee to determine whether government bureaucracy was preventing nutritional information from reaching the public, he found a sympathetic ear. Largely because McDonald's pledged its full cooperation, the subcommittee decided to hold hearings into the matter in February 1979, and Raber's efforts were immediately rewarded with the type of coup that government relations specialists dream about. In opening the hearing, Senator McGovern flatly declared that fast food was good food. Coming from a longtime advocate of more nutritional diets and from a liberal not known for making statements supporting big business, that was news. That evening, all three TV networks carried the story, and the support the hearings generated for better communication of nutritional information eventually brought action from the FDA, which in 1982 relaxed its policies to allow McDonald's and other fast-food chains to distribute brochures containing nutritional analyses of their typical meals without requiring the labeling of each wrapper, something everyone agreed was impractical.

But more important than McDonald's growing sophistication in national politics was its new sensitivity to the type of local political muscle that it encountered—and badly underestimated—in its 1974 battle in Manhattan. After that experience, McDonald's developed a policy to assess a community's political environment carefully before building a new unit and respond to any resistance early—before positions on either side became public and intractable.

That was a major change in the attitude of top management. "At Sixty-sixth and Lexington, McDonald's instinct was to fight back," says Rubenstein. "Ray Kroc and Fred Turner were adamant about not backing out. They believed McDonald's was a good business, a good neighbor, and that the community was wrong. But they learned that there are more than just business and legal considerations in picking new locations—that you must also consider the community's political reaction to them."

An erstwhile aide to former New York Mayor Abe Beame, Rubenstein is one of the better connected public relations specialists in New York, and after the Sixty-sixth and Lexington battle ended, he continued to represent McDonald's to help prevent such blowups at other new stores in the city. Similar specialists were assigned the same role in other markets, and while McDonald's has since had its share of disputes with zoning boards and other local officials on new units, it never again allowed a local protest to get so out of hand.

In New York, Rubenstein used his political contacts to give McDonald's an early warning system for detecting community opposition to new stores. He was equally resourceful in dealing with resistance whenever it developed. When he detected neighborhood opposition to a plan to put a new McDonald's in Brooklyn, Rubenstein photographed the site chosen for the new restaurant—a dilapidated building housing a porno movie theater. When a high borough official took a look at Rubenstein's photographs, he promised to silence any local resistance to the new store. "Go ahead and build," the official told him. "If you think I'm going to support some porno theater in order to keep out McDonald's, you're crazy."

Nowhere did McDonald's respond to any of its public challenges more aggressively and creatively than it did to the minority franchising issues raised by the racial confrontation in Cleveland. When black groups began picketing the white-owned McDonald's on the city's East Side in 1968, Bob Beavers had already been on the job six months as McDonald's new director of community action and development, responsible for recruiting black and other minority franchisees for the system. But the task was complicated by new licensing rules, introduced when Fred Turner became McDonald's president, that required that all new franchises be totally owned by the operator of the store without the support of outside investors.

The new policy reflected solid operations experience, but it severely limited the chain's flexibility in solving its minority licensing problem. Under McDonald's licensing rules, a franchisee could borrow only half of the $150,000 (now $500,000) he or she needed to buy the license, kitchen equipment, store furnishings, and McDonald's sign—everything a franchisee must pay for to open a new restaurant. But very few potential black operators had savings of $75,000. Even when qualified blacks inquired about McDonald's franchises, white regional licensing staffs, says Beavers, "automatically tuned a lot of them out" because they did not fit their notions about how a licensee should look, talk, and dress, and about the amount of formal education he should have. Black entrepreneurs who had raised themselves up by the bootstraps—and from the ghetto—had considerably less polish than the white entrepreneurs who were making it big in McDonald's, and unfortunately that, too, was keeping some of them out of McDonald's.

Cleveland changed everything. In fact, it became a catalyst for one of the most dramatic breakthroughs ever made by minority groups into American business. From only four in 1969, the number of black franchisees in McDonald's soared to nearly fifty by the end of 1972—approaching 10 percent of the system's operators. "Cleveland made people in the regions aware of the danger and sensitized them to the need to move a lot faster on minority licensing," Beavers says.

Easily as important as any attitude changes, however, were the sweeping licensing changes McDonald's made at the corporate level to create opportunities for black entrepreneurs who lacked the capital to become McDonald's franchisees. Working through the Small Business Administration and the Office of Minority Business Enterprise, McDonald's helped black businessmen secure SBA-guaranteed loans to raise most of the capital needed to open a McDonald's. The company also granted minorities exceptions on its 50-percent limit on borrowed capital, allowing black candidates to purchase their franchise and equipment with as little as $30,000 in up-front cash, or about 20 percent of the total investment.

But the most radical exceptions McDonald's made to recruit black franchisees were its so-called zebra packages. In the late 1960s, the company allowed eight black operators each to obtain a McDonald's store with the help of two white Chicago investors who put up the money to buy the franchise and the equipment. It violated what was now McDonald's most fundamental licensing rule, the requirement of 100 percent ownership of the franchise by the operator of the store. It also ignored the long-standing rule that McDonald's owners live in the market where their restaurants are located. The two investor-owners of the eight zebra franchises were in Chicago, but their stores were scattered all over the country.

McDonald's was assured by the white investors that the equity in the eight stores would eventually be transferred to the black operators. But the investors broke their promise, and the zebra packages quickly changed from being a minority licensing solution to a minority licensing disaster. After double-crossing the black operators, the two white investors began cheating everyone else—including each other. Bills to suppliers went unpaid. The eight units fell months behind in their franchising fees and rents to McDonald's. Eventually, the two investors each hired his own bag man, who every day raced to the eight stores hoping to beat the other owner's revenue collector to the till. "We had stretched or broken every licensing rule we had—everything that was proven to be successful—in order to franchise to blacks," notes Burt Cohen, senior vice president in charge of McDonald's franchising. "It all came back to haunt us."

Things got so convoluted that Cohen spent a full year untangling the zebra agreements—cajoling bank lenders and unpaid suppliers and working out new financing for the black operators. In the end, McDonald's wound up losing $500,000, but the eight blacks wound up controlling their own restaurants, and the two whites were forced out.

If stretching the franchising rules for blacks produced some excesses, it also allowed McDonald's to create what may be the most important economic opportunity for minorities that exists in America outside of entertainment and professional sports. The number of minority owner-operators in the system has grown from the 50 recruited in the first three years of Beavers's special licensing effort to 762 today, not including another 28 blacks who are on the list of 116 applicants currently in training. Together, McDonald's black franchisees own and operate better than seven hundred McDonald's stores, or fully half of all black-owned franchised restaurants in the United States. Even the cloud over the zebra franchising deals had something of a silver lining. While six of eight black operators in those deals did not make it and their stores were refranchised to other blacks, two of them became millionaires: Herman Petty, a five-unit McDonald's franchisee in Chicago, and Lonear Heard, an owner/operator of six McDonald's in Los Angeles.

But the black franchising program was no handout. Once inside the system, black operators had to meet the same standards as everyone else to stay in. Fully a third of the first fifty black operators recruited by Beavers failed or were terminated within a couple of years. In fact, the community relations risk McDonald's took by drumming some blacks out of the system was potentially as explosive as the charges in Cleveland that it had refused to let them in. Says Beavers: "For McDonald's, minority franchising could have been a catch-22 situation."

Fortunately, the opportunity to succeed was all that most of McDonald's black franchisees wanted. Many of the original fifty are still in the system, and many of those have amassed the same type of McDonald's fortune that white franchisees have built. Narlie Roberts was a construction contractor without a high school diploma when he took over one of the six Cleveland stores that changed from white to black hands in 1969. He became one of the most highly regarded operators in the system, with eight stores in Cleveland that averaged 40 percent above the national average. After his death, his widow sold all but one of his stores. Similarly, Lee Dunham also outperformed the national average at his eight units located in Harlem, where he once patrolled the streets as a New York cop. Dunham has since sold his Harlem units. He now operates two restaurants in New Jersey and one on Broadway in New York City. Those volumes are not anomalies. The average volume of the mostly urban stores of McDonald's minority operators is higher than the per-store volume of white franchisees.

The minority operators, however, were not the only beneficiaries of the new recruitment program. By successfully enlisting black and Hispanic entrepreneurs, McDonald's penetrated urban markets more effectively, simply because good minority franchisees understood how to market to inner-city communities better than good white franchisees did. When Herman Petty became McDonald's first black franchisee in 1968, he took over the store from a white operator in Chicago's predominantly black South Side. Petty had worked at two full-time jobs for six years to bankroll his McDonald's—running a barber shop by day and driving a Chicago Transit Authority bus on the graveyard shift. He knew everyone in the community at his first McDonald's. His barber shop was only five blocks away, and he made certain all his customers spread the word of his shift from barber to restaurateur. He carried the McDonald's message to all the churches in the area—and even provided free hamburgers at church socials—because he knew the churches were the community's centers of social activity. He met with community groups and local businesspeople, and he spruced up a once poorly maintained store until it glistened.

His community-oriented marketing brought overnight results. In one year, Petty doubled the store's volume to $500,000 a year. Now he had enough money to buy a second unit from a white franchisee just down the street from the Chicago Transit Authority car barns, where Petty had dozens of friends from his bus driving days. The marketing approach was the same, and so were the results.

As Petty expanded his McDonald's base on the South Side, his restaurants began having a noticeable impact on the black communities themselves. Convinced that deteriorating neighborhoods could be restored by new businesses, he built some new stores in the middle of areas badly victimized by white flight. When he decided to open his third McDonald's, the storefront businesses in the area he selected for his new unit had all been shuttered. The one remaining center of activity—the Shell station on the corner—was in the process of closing. But Petty struck a deal with the local alderman, promising to build his McDonald's if the city improved lighting and refuse collection in the neighborhood, added new sidewalks, and repaired the alleys behind the store. When the Shell station owner saw a McDonald's going up, he decided to remodel and expand his station instead of closing it.

Franchisees of Popeye's Famous Fried Chicken and Church's Fried Chicken began regularly visiting the new McDonald's, amazed by the friendliness of Petty's crews and the activity at the registers. While the area had one of the highest crime rates in the city, Petty told the chicken operators that he had yet to call the police. The seats were not carved up and the walls had no graffiti. Courteous service, Petty had learned, produced orderly customers. Indeed, nearly 40 percent of his customers were white—salesmen, construction workers, and others passing through the neighborhood looking for a place to eat where they felt no intimidation.

Soon, Petty's McDonald's had two new competitors down the street—a Church's Fried Chicken and a Popeye's. The vacant building across the street was refurbished and converted to a medical center, and one by one the storefront businesses that had been closed by whites were reopened by blacks. "There is no such thing as a bad community," Petty observes. "You just have to concentrate on bringing the good out."

Petty's McDonald's units on Chicago's South Side also have proven to be a stabilizing influence on the youth of the area. By the early 1980s, his operation employed nearly five hundred workers—virtually all of them black and getting their first work experience. Petty made certain it was a positive experience—for his young workers and for his stores—by investing heavily in training. He hired a woman with a master's in education as his full-time training instructor and opened a classroom in the basement of his third store. Because most job applicants are underprivileged, Petty's training goes beyond cooking hamburgers. Racial animosities are "washed out of their heads," Petty says. "We train our people to realize that everyone is a human being and we all have to treat each other that way. We tell them what working is all about and where money comes from." Although Petty's demands are tough and the starting pay is minimum wage, he has never advertised for help. "People who have worked here come back asking me to take on a younger brother or sister, because they know they'll be trained well and will get respect," Petty says. "They tell us that McDonald's helped them face the world."

Thanks to the success of black operators like Petty, McDonald's never again came under the type of racial attack it encountered in

Cleveland. Its record on minority licensing has even protected the chain from legal challenges. When Charles Griffis, a four-store black operator, sued the company in 1982, claiming he was being denied additional outlets because of racial discrimination, he gained national press coverage as well as the support of one of two competing regional chapters of the National Association for the Advancement of Colored People, which called for a black boycott of McDonald's. But the national leadership of the NAACP refused to condone the boycott, presumably because it was impressed by the mountains of statistics McDonald's presented to the court on the Griffis case. Among other things, McDonald's noted that 60 percent of new franchises sold in the Los Angeles area since Griffis got his last store in 1980 went to blacks and Hispanics and that black operators in the region were granted new stores with two-thirds greater frequency than whites. The court granted McDonald's motion for a summary judgment in its favor, and the company purchased Griffis's stores and refranchised them to other minority operators.

But of all McDonald's responses to the public challenges it began to encounter in the 1970s, none was more difficult for the company to make—or more crucial to its long-term success—than its response to the press. In many respects, McDonald's was becoming America's most visible business.

Yet, after the damaging Atlanta rumor, the battle of Lexington Avenue, the controversy over Kroc's political contributions, and the negative articles in *Barron's* and the *New York Times Magazine*, McDonald's did what most public companies do when they get burned by the media—it retreated to a corporate bunker. Senior executives were rarely available for interviews, and the company often ducked inquiries from the press. Even less frequently did it take the initiative to create media coverage. "There was a feeling that permeated the entire organization that the press was out to get us," recalls Communications Senior Vice President Dick Starmann of the late 1970s media mentality at McDonald's. "It was never a written policy, but it was understood that you avoid getting your name in the paper."

But that buttoned-up approach to the media also kept McDonald's from generating the positive coverage that it had received in the early days when Ray Kroc charmed his interviewers. Indeed, McDonald's became so distant from the press that it nearly lost credibility with the media. Thus, on the few occasions when it did surface, such as in 1978 when Fred Turner consented to his *Esquire* interview with business writer Dan Dorfman, the result was coverage that was distinctly anti-McDonald's. Not long after the Dorfman piece ran, however, McDonald's finally decided to tackle its publicity problems head-on. "We decided we had nothing to be ashamed of," Starmann recalls. "For God's sake, we had a great story to tell."

The first move was to upgrade the company's public relations function. A communications department was finally created in 1974, but the first officer in charge of it was the company's former legal counsel, who had no experience in dealing with the press. After the Atlanta experience, he was replaced with a marketing executive, who converted the department into a full-line communications section, bringing together for the first time all public, press, and community relations functions into one group.

But it was not until Starmann became the public relations chief in 1981 that McDonald's media relations began to change. Starmann had risen through the marketing ranks at McDonald's, and while he had no formal public relations training, he nevertheless held the trust of top management. By contrast, the media manager who was caught up in the Atlanta rumor controversy was a professional press relations specialist who was not held in high esteem by top management. "The media relations manager was operating in the blind—someone called in after a decision was made and told him to make a statement," Starmann says.

But in 1981 that changed. Starmann was included in every top-level meeting involving decisions affecting the company's public image. More important, he was asked for his opinions on the media impact of different courses of action. The communications department staff had already been expanded to thirty-five people, three times the size of the staff in the mid-1970s. And now the department is given the autonomy required for an objective—and credible—media relations effort. Once under the wing of McDonald's Marketing Department, Starmann, as head of Communications, now reports directly to Jack Greenberg, McDonald's vice chairman and chief financial officer. As a result, the company's press relations team is better prepared to respond to media challenges that once caught it off guard.

McDonald's campaign to turn around its press relations went far beyond crisis management. By 1980, the company had decided to tell its story once again, and for the first time in years its top managers became accessible to the press. The chain even revived the publicity agent tactics that Al Golin had successfully employed years ago to capitalize on the magic media touch of founder Ray Kroc. Once again it was staging media events and creating feature photo opportunities. When the company signed a contract to open McDonald's units at up to three hundred navy bases around the world, Ronald McDonald posed for pictures in front of an aircraft carrier. Similarly, on the tenth anniversary of Ronald McDonald Houses, the children and parents staying at the seminal Ronald McDonald House in Philadelphia stood in front of ABC television cameras and, on cue, opened the network's morning show by shouting "Good Morning, America."

But the most widely covered media event McDonald's ever staged took place at the Grand Hyatt in New York on November 21, 1984, when the chain served its 50 billionth hamburger. There, the company invited reporters to witness Ed Rensi, then president of McDonald's USA, cook the celebrated hamburger and serve it up to Dick McDonald, who had cooked the first McDonald's hamburger thirty-six years before. The opportunity for pictures and nostalgic interviews proved irresistible. More than two hundred journalists from around the world showed up, and the electronic media crammed their television gear onto three separate camera platforms. The story ran on all network news shows, in virtually all U.S. daily newspapers, and in *Time* and *Newsweek*. Golin says: "It was a return to the showmanship of Ray Kroc."

But it was its responses to potential public relations disasters that most distinguished the new McDonald's press relations from the old. In 1982, McDonald's confronted just such a challenge when microbiologists at the federal Centers for Disease Control published a paper suggesting a link between two outbreaks of intestinal illness and a rare bacteria thought to be isolated in the meat of a "major fast-food chain." When a Miami reporter correctly identified the chain as McDonald's and reported that in his story in the *Miami Herald,* McDonald's suddenly was faced with an issue possibly more damaging than the worm rumor.

But the result was different, largely because of the way McDonald's reacted. CDC had quietly begun its research after a rash of intestinal disorders was reported in Traverse City, Michigan, and in Medford, Oregon. Of the nearly two dozen residents in each community complaining of intestinal flu symptoms, most had recently eaten meat at the local McDonald's. But long before the CDC made the cases public, McDonald's itself had launched a massive investigation of the incidents, working each step of the way in close cooperation with the CDC.

A task force of twenty-five McDonald's managers, including operations specialists, microbiologists, food technologists, and quality assurance inspectors, descended on the two affected stores to inspect grills, vents, filters, freezers, and other equipment and to examine their products and preparation methods. Nothing was found to indicate any bacteria problem. The same intensive examination was made of the chain's meat plants, and nothing irregular was found there either. In fact, CDC inspectors admitted that the quality control measures taken at the plants were among the most stringent they had ever seen.

Thus, by the time the cases became public, McDonald's was armed with research indicating that the only link between its stores and the intestinal disorders was a statistical correlation, and even that might be explained simply by McDonald's overwhelming penetration of the American food service market. At the time, 16 million Americans ate at McDonald's every day—over 6 percent of the U.S. population—so it was not unlikely for a high percentage of the residents near any store to have eaten at a McDonald's within the four-day period of the two outbreaks. And if there had been extensive exposure to bacteria problems at either store, many more people would undoubtedly have been affected. Furthermore, neither McDonald's nor the CDC's investigation could prove any causal connection, and when McDonald's took that story public, it had obviously learned a lesson from the Atlanta debacle. Whatever caused the problem, the company flatly declared, it could not be attributed to McDonald's food. Soon that was followed up by an even stronger response delivered by Vice Chairman Edward Schmitt, who was interviewed on network television while he sat down to eat a Quarter Pounder at a McDonald's restaurant. His message was clear and firm: "You bet it's safe to eat at McDonald's."

The CDC eventually did report that the likely cause of the intestinal problems was bacteria present in McDonald's hamburger meat that had been cooked at below-standard temperatures. That conclusion—based largely on the discovery of *one* hamburger patty containing the rare bacteria—is still disputed by McDonald's today, and the CDC never developed what it considered conclusive proof. It had, however, discovered a new and extremely puzzling disease apparently related to meat. It has been seen sporadically since, although never again related to McDonald's.

While the incidents briefly affected McDonald's sales in the two areas, the effect was modest and short-lived. Still, McDonald's had avoided a public relations nightmare only because its treatment of this meat controversy was 180 degrees different from the one it faced in Atlanta. It has responded publicly only *after* gathering all the facts through an exhaustive research effort. Furthermore, its media response was carefully prepared and delivered in a controlled setting by a senior executive of the company. And the company's media relations officer was intimately involved in every aspect of the company's investigation. More important, it had conducted itself responsibly, taking the position that it had nothing to hide and wanted to find the cause of the problems as much as the CDC did. In fact, Dr. Alan A. Harris, a Chicago epidemiologist and a consultant to McDonald's, suggests that the CDC might never have been able to make its conclusion had McDonald's not provided so much information. While that conclusion ran counter to the company's, McDonald's nonetheless benefited from its cooperation. "There is no question that the company's cooperation improved the tenor of some of the health authorities," says Dr. Harris. "And that affected how they communicated the matter to the public."

But the CDC episode was but a mild prelude to the crisis McDonald's confronted on July 18, 1984. At 7:30 that evening, Starmann and his wife, Kathy, had just been seated at their table at the International Club, the exclusive restaurant in Chicago's Drake Hotel, where they planned to celebrate Kathy's birthday. The Starmanns had no sooner placed their dinner order than a telephone was brought to their table. It was a call from their thirteen-year-old son, R.G., who had just seen a television news bulletin about a shooting at a McDonald's restaurant in California.

A shooting in a McDonald's sounded like a local story—something worth following but not a crisis demanding immediate corporate attention. Yet, minutes later there was a second call—four people were confirmed dead in the California shooting. Soon, another call took the count to six, then another to eight.

This was no local story. Before dinner was served, the Starmanns were rushing to their car for the thirty-minute drive to McDonald's home office in Oak Brook. On the way, the death toll in California kept mounting. By the time he arrived, Starmann's mind was racing to analyze the consequences of the bloodiest massacre in the history of an American corporation. John Huberty had walked into a McDonald's in San Ysidro late that afternoon and begun spraying it with bullets from his carbine. Before he was felled by the bullet of a police sharpshooter, Huberty had killed twenty-one innocent people at the McDonald's store—customers, crew people, and passersby.

McDonald's had never faced anything as tragic as the slaughter that had just taken place at its restaurant in the poor Mexican-American border community of San Ysidro. Still, it raced into action as if it had already had a few drills on mass murders. Within minutes of reaching his office, Starmann was on the phone to marketing chief Paul Schrage and then President Michael Quinlan. Schrage decided that the chain should suspend all advertising for at least four days, and Starmann immediately communicated that message to reporters pressing the company for a reaction. Then, for fifteen straight hours the next day, Starmann gave press interviews—seventy-one in all—and appeared on every network television newscast that night. A day later, he met with top McDonald's executives to discuss various courses of action. With Fred Turner out of the country, the major decision was Quinlan's: approving a $1 million contribution to the survivors' fund organized the day before by Joan Kroc, who donated the first $100,000.

That night a team of senior McDonald's executives flew to San Ysidro to attend the funeral that was held the next day for eight of the victims. On the way out, Starmann argued that the store had to be closed, but others had reservations that such a move might communicate defeatism. Worse still, it might appear to be grandstanding, and the McDonald's executives were so cautious about being branded with that charge that their plan to attend the funeral was not publicized.

But any hesitation on closing the store quickly disappeared when the McDonald's representatives attended the funeral, toured the neighborhood, and met with Monsignor Francisco Aldesarro, the spiritual leader of the Catholic community. "The community was treating the store as a shrine," Starmann says. "People were bringing flowers and statues there and lighting candles and votive lights as they prayed. To reopen that McDonald's—with so much human emotion attached to the site—would have been absolutely wrong."

Ed Rensi decided that the store should be permanently closed, but McDonald's had to avoid any appearance of capitalizing on a human tragedy by staging a media event. Thus Starmann advised regional manager Steve Zdunek to have crews remove the McDonald's sign at 3:00 A.M. on Monday, before television cameramen and newspaper photographers could capture the closing on tape. "Should I tell the police?" Zdunek asked. "Hell, no," Starmann warned. "That's the biggest source of leaks there is."

Five weeks later, after extensive discussion with community leaders, McDonald's donated the property to the people of San Ysidro to allow the city fathers to decide what to do with it. Throughout the crisis, observed then Executive Vice President Donald P. Horwitz, one rule applied to all McDonald's decisions: "We decided to do what we thought was morally right, not what was necessarily legally correct nor financially sound nor even proper from a communications standpoint. We had a moral obligation to do the right thing, no matter what the right thing was."

Clearly, McDonald's, once confused by the publicity risks of its global operations and notoriety, had at last become prepared to confront them. While it had not sought favorable publicity on San Ysidro, McDonald's handling of the crisis generated hundreds of positive letters to the chain. It also produced scores of complimentary newspaper editorials.

Even in the minds of San Ysidro residents, McDonald's had succeeded in separating its image from the memory of the worst tragedy in the community's history. Indeed, McDonald's enjoys more support in San Ysidro than ever. Today, the chain operates a new store just three blocks from the old one, and its sales are running higher than those of the outlet it replaced.

Chapter 16
CHECKS AND BALANCES

As threatening as its public controversies were, McDonald's during the mid-1970s faced a private challenge that was potentially more menacing. It came from within, from the very people who were benefiting most from the fast-food bonanza McDonald's had created—its franchisees.

Apart from being a more dangerous threat, it was also easily the most surprising. When McDonald's entered the ranks of major corporations, it should have expected the public attacks. But McDonald's franchisee community seemed its least likely source of trouble. More than any other franchiser, Ray Kroc had made his franchisees an integral part of McDonald's fast-food system. They were legitimate partners in the enterprise and were given ample opportunity to express their creative energies.

They were also rewarded as partners. Indeed, McDonald's was orchestrating the greatest dispersion of wealth that the free enterprise system had ever seen. By the mid-1970s, most franchisees were fast approaching annual net profits of $100,000 per store. Those with several units were millionaires. In fact, since its beginning, McDonald's has put well over one thousand of its franchisees, suppliers, and managers into the millionaire ranks. To outside observers, any attack by the franchisees on McDonald's appeared to be the closest thing to financial suicide.

But the franchisee-franchiser issues that developed in McDonald's in the mid-1970s were far more complex than that. The group of franchisees—some fifty in all—who became actively involved in an organized attack on McDonald's had a variety of individual motives. But a common denominator for almost all of them was the cumulative impact on the McDonald's System of Fred Turner's massive and phenomenally successful expansion program.

The success of that program had given some veteran operators wealth they had never dreamed was possible. But to a man, that wealth was wrapped up in their McDonald's stores, many of which were approaching the end of the twenty-year terms of their initial franchises. Multistore operators who had gotten only average grades on store operations were beginning to worry whether their franchise agreements would be rewritten for another twenty years. Some of these weaker operators apparently believed that the only way to protect their interest was to cause McDonald's enough grief that it might buy them out rather than kick them out.

While this small band of self-serving operators was stirring up trouble on the surface, discontent was quietly spreading underneath, affecting hundreds of franchisees who had a valid complaint: They were losing touch with the company.

For many veteran operators, Turner's expansion was something of a blow to their pride; they began feeling that they were no longer in the Kroc-Turner inner circle of fast-food pioneers who had built McDonald's. In 1971, McDonald's had moved its corporate offices from the familiar confines of 221 North LaSalle Street in Chicago to a new eight-story building in suburban Oak Brook. The expansion of corporate staff that accompanied that growth created new bureaucratic layers between the franchisees and McDonald's top echelon. Previously, they had been directly accessible to almost all franchisees, but with eleven hundred franchised operators in 1975, it was impossible for Kroc and Turner to maintain such close personal ties. In the minds of many old-line operators, McDonald's was only making that situation worse by bringing one hundred or more new franchisees into the chain each year—a practice that remains in force today as a means of replenishing the system with new vigor and fresh ideas.

Moreover, when McDonald's in 1965 adopted a regional organization with the establishment of five major new offices outside Chicago, it laid the groundwork for an important change in its relations with franchisees. And when Turner in 1968 shifted the final responsibility for real estate acquisition and new store development to the new regional offices, the fate of franchisees was in the hands of youthful regional managers. For longtime operators, that seemed to signal the end of their old-boy connections with Kroc, Turner, and other senior officers at McDonald's. Now, regional managers less familiar with the older operators were empowered to determine where all new stores would be built and whether they would go to existing franchisees, to new franchisees, or to McOpCo, the company-owned restaurant operation. The growth of McOpCo—from 9 percent of all units in 1968 to 31 percent of all units in 1975—was itself a perceived threat to some franchisees. While the expansion of McOpCo had been achieved primarily through acquisitions that had enriched a select group of franchisees who were selling out, the franchisees who wanted to remain in the system began to worry that McDonald's would continue its drift away from franchising.

But of all the franchisee-related problems caused by rapid expansion, none was more serious or more real than "impact," what operators called the loss of sales at existing McDonald's units that was caused by the opening of a new McDonald's nearby. During the 1960s, the United States offered so many virgin markets for fast-food operators that impact was never a concern. Indeed, McDonald's back then did not even build a new store unless it had an exclusive market area of at least fifty thousand residents. If an operator could not make a go of it, he had no one but himself to blame.

But by 1975, impact was a legitimate issue. Senior Executive Vice President Gerry Newman, McDonald's chief accounting officer, who knew the financial statements of operators more intimately than did anyone else, believed that 30 percent of all new stores by then had some measurable impact on sales at nearby stores. Not everyone at McDonald's accepts that estimate, citing the fact that per-store sales during this period were growing at extremely healthy rates, thanks in part to the expansion of the menu. Still, Newman speculated that in about 5 percent of all new stores, the impact on other nearby McDonald's was severe enough to reduce their profits.

Put all of these expansion forces together, and the result was that franchisees increasingly began feeling distant from the company that Ray Kroc had built. "It was more in their perception than in reality, but in their mind operators lost the ability to converse with the top management," Newman observed. "They thought that Fred Turner and Ray Kroc were inaccessible and that if they tried to bypass the regional managers, all expansion opportunities for them would be cut off. And with the expansion of McOpCo, some operators looked at the corporation and said, 'You are no longer just my landlord and licensor, you are now also my competitor.' The seeds of dissent began with the regionalization of the company and were aggravated by the expansion of the system."

Like the unexpected public criticism, the internal dissent caught top managers by surprise. It began in 1975 when about twenty-five multistore operators invited Kroc, Turner, and other senior officers to a meeting they proposed in Atlanta. On the surface, there was nothing suspicious about it. Kroc and Turner had attended such impromptu bull sessions before, listening to complaints about impact and the reduced operator contact with top management. The franchisees involved in the Atlanta meeting badly erred in not signaling in advance that this meeting was different—and much more serious.

Without such warning, Kroc, Turner, Newman, Vice Chairman Ed Schmitt, and Marketing Chief Paul Schrage all declined the invitation. "In the early years, I had been to these meetings before, and they degenerated into bitch sessions," Turner says. "We felt we had heard all of this before." McDonald's dispatched Senior Vice President John Coons to the Atlanta meeting to represent the company, but Schmitt believes that the rest of top management's absence "indicated an attitude of indifference toward what the operators felt were legitimate problems."

McDonald's blew a golden opportunity to nip a potential franchisee revolt in the bud. When the operators compared notes in Atlanta, the rough outlines of an organization began to form and the group agreed to meet again in Florida. There, a committee of seven was "elected" to represent the group in a private session with Ray Kroc. Kroc initially agreed to the meeting on one condition—that Bob Kinsley, an operator from Colorado whom Kroc found particularly objectionable, not be part of the committee. Unfortunately, he was, and the operator group refused to remove him. The meeting with Kroc never came off. "Had Ray met with the committee," says Don Conley, the former McDonald's licensing manager who was now himself one of the dissident franchisees, "there never would have been a McDonald's Operators Association."

That was the name the group chose at their next meeting in Colorado in mid-1975, when they incorporated and officially designated themselves as members of an independent operators' organization that would act as permanent adversary counsel to McDonald's Corporation. The operator community in McDonald's was abuzz. All signs were pointing to the one confrontation that McDonald's could least afford—an open battle with its own franchisees.

The McDonald's Operators Association, or MOA, was not a collection of rookie operators. In its ranks were some of the oldest and largest McDonald's franchisees. Don Conley, who had left his position as McDonald's licensing vice president to become a four-store franchisee in suburban Chicago, was elected as its president, but by most accounts he was little more than a figurehead. The real powers behind the organization were Richard Frankel, a twenty-three-unit owner from North Carolina, and Max Cooper, the twenty-two-unit operator in Birmingham and the former partner of publicist Al Golin. MOA's membership was concentrated in the Southeast, but it solicited members throughout the country and succeeded in landing some. One early vice president of the group was Ron Lopaty, whose family now operates twelve McDonald's in California and thirty-two in Tennessee. Furthermore, MOA had all the trappings of a permanent organization—a full-time executive director and a monthly eight-page newsletter.

In the first issue of that letter, MOA left no doubt that it intended to live up to its billing as an "adversarial" group. Its fundamental tenets contradicted the basic franchising principles Kroc had instilled in McDonald's. Among other things, MOA declared that operators had an automatic right to have their twenty-year franchises renewed. It insisted that all new units in a market be awarded only to existing franchisees in the area. Any major store improvements, the group argued, should be paid for by the corporation, reversing the long-standing McDonald's practice of requiring reinvestment by the franchisee. MOA further demanded that any proposed new unit that might have a measurable impact on an existing McDonald's must not be built.

In essence, the members of MOA were declaring that the further development of McOpCo and expansion of the franchising base must be stopped. Instead of having franchisees compete with one another, MOA's members wanted guaranteed expansion, lifetime security for their operations, and a shelter from competition. In short, they wanted to destroy the very foundation of McDonald's—the delicate system of checks and balances between corporate managers, franchisees, and suppliers. If McDonald's power balance had shifted toward the company during Turner's expansion, MOA now wanted to shift it excessively in the opposite direction.

The demands of MOA were so contrary to McDonald's principles that even today there is dispute within McDonald's regarding just how serious the challenge was. Turner is probably in a minority of McDonald's executives who tend to diminish its significance. He argues that MOA represented a minority of wealthy, self-centered operators, most of whom were looking to sell their stores to the company and were creating pressure to drive up the buyout price. Indeed, Turner was so outraged that in a speech at the 1976 Operators Convention he sardonically dubbed MOA the "Millionaire Operators Association."

But most McDonald's executives accept the analysis of Ed Schmitt. At its peak, MOA had only fifty signed members; but Schmitt estimates that fully one-third of all franchisees were secretly "MOA sympathizers." Furthermore, he believes MOA's members and supporters wanted to be more than adversaries of McDonald's and in fact, were after a significant role in the corporation's management, ending forever McDonald's powerful check on its own franchisees. "If MOA succeeded," Schmitt concludes, "it could have ripped the very fabric of McDonald's apart." Even if the group achieved a considerably smaller measure of success, Schmitt says, the impact on McDonald's would have been catastrophic. Make no mistake about it, Schmitt says, "the period from 1968 to 1975 was one of dynamic growth for McDonald's, but it was also the breeding ground for the greatest schism we ever faced."

If the goals of MOA were so outrageous, why did Schmitt and other McDonald's managers take the challenge so seriously? The answer lies in the fact that many of MOA's charges had more than a small element of truth. To be sure, many operators were using MOA selfishly. Many knew that their store operations were so substandard that there was no hope that their franchises would be renewed for another twenty years. For them, MOA was a means of bidding up the price McDonald's would have to pay to buy the troublemakers out of the system. And, in fact, McDonald's easily squelched criticism from that segment by purchasing their stores.

But that response did not deal with the real challenge. Even if most members of MOA had only selfish motives, the fact was that some of their charges rang true with dozens of operators who remained loyal to the system. And the primary reason for that was regionalization. When McDonald's created five regional offices in 1965, it was responding to a retail chain's need to keep decision making close to the market. But by 1975, the number of regions had grown to twelve and the powers of regional managers had been steadily expanded. Furthermore, McDonald's had not set up sufficient corporate structures to oversee the regions and to keep decisions of regional managers from becoming arbitrary and unfair.

Some regional managers seemed more interested in building new restaurants than in determining the impact those units would have on existing stores. Others were showing a decided preference for assigning new stores to McOpCo rather than to franchisees. "Some regional managers began operating under the theory that if you open a new store, you might as well open it first as a company unit, and if it doesn't work out, you can sell it to one of the franchisees," said Gerry Newman. "They misread the signals."

Nor was there any guarantee that the ideals of fairness to which Kroc and Turner were deeply committed were evenly transmitted to regional franchising and real estate staffs. Indeed, some managers appeared callous toward the legitimate interests of franchisees, and there was little a franchisee could do about such treatment. McDonald's had set up no formal avenue of appeal for franchisees who felt wronged by a regional manager's decisions on building a new store or awarding a new franchise. The big profits in McDonald's are made by franchisees who can leverage their management expertise with a multistore operation, and some operators began to blame regional managers for keeping them from the wealth McDonald's promises.

McDonald's also had failed to measure empirically the probable sales damage a new unit would have on an existing one to determine whether franchisee concerns about impact were valid. Its focus was on building the chain, not on protecting existing franchises. "In a period of explosive growth, the company necessarily became introspective," Schmitt says. "It focused on how to develop its structure, secure its people, train its managers. But in the process, we forgot the very essence of our system—we forgot our licensees."

In most cases, the shift in priorities was a natural consequence of expansion, not a deliberate attempt to profit at the expense of franchisees. Unfortunately, however, not all excesses of regional managers were so guileless. Indeed, just when some MOA members began making seemingly wild charges about payoffs on real estate at the regional level, McDonald's turned up a major fraud that gave those charges immediate credibility.

The fraud involved a regional real estate manager in the Southeast who enriched himself by acquiring property under an assumed corporate name, marking up its price, and quickly reselling it to the company to pocket a handsome personal profit. While McDonald's bought the property, its inflated price was ultimately the burden of the franchisee, since his minimum rent was based on what the chain paid for real estate. Because the manager possessed a talent for acquiring properties at bargain prices, he could afford to mark them up 10 to 25 percent without creating suspicion. It was only when the thief became greedy

—marking up real estate by as much as 100 percent—that franchisees in the region began complaining. For months, franchisees in the Southeast screamed about excessive prices being paid by McDonald's on real estate, but while their complaints were investigated, nothing improper was immediately found.

By the time the fraud was finally uncovered, the damage to McDonald's relations with operators in the Southeast had already been done. McDonald's own investigation revealed that the real estate manager had practiced his middle-man routine for nearly a decade, and had collected more than $1 million in illegal profits.

But the real estate swindle only accentuated a management problem that McDonald's had allowed to continue too long in its Southeast region. While regional managers in other markets were occasionally excessive in using their newfound powers, the boss of the Southeast region in the early 1970s had caved into the demands for new stores and other favors from established franchisees who were running subpar operations. When that regional manager was replaced, operators in the Southeast suddenly confronted a new manager who refused to overlook their shortcomings. When that management shock was compounded by the real estate swindle, it is little wonder that MOA initially took root in the Southeast and found virtually all of its early members from within the ranks of franchisees in that region.

While other regions did not have such critical problems, they were not entirely free of abuses either. Indeed, perhaps the most serious effect of the expansion was that some regional managers gradually began treating franchisees less as independent businessmen than McDonald's employees and, in the worst cases, as subordinates. Nowhere was that more evident than with McDonald's field service consultants, who monitor store performance to ensure that the chain's high operating standards are being met. The field service operation of McDonald's was rightfully the pride and joy of its creator, Fred Turner, because it was the one thing that distinguished McDonald's as a superior operator.

But Turner had conceived of field service as something more than a regular inspection of stores that resulted in an overall store grade of A through F. In addition, it involved regular consultation with franchisees, and that was really the key to McDonald's operational prowess. Through consultation, field service managers could pick up tips from experienced franchisees and pass on those secrets to less experienced operators. Well executed, McDonald's field service operation was a massive information exchange that continually improved store performance.

But during the new store construction boom, McDonald's field service in some areas deteriorated to little more than a white-glove inspection. Some field consultants had become condescending and superior. In part, that may have been because expansion had resulted in the hiring of many new field consultants who lacked experience in consultation. It was easy for them to see their role purely in terms of inspection—measuring temperatures on grills, calculating holding times on products, and determining whether windows were cleaned daily.

When Ed Rensi, now president and CEO of McDonald's USA, appraises his own performance as a twenty-two-year-old field service consultant in Ohio during that period, he is candidly self-critical. He recalls how he once gave a D grade to a store operated by Lou Groen, the legendary Cincinnati franchisee who pioneered the fish filet sandwich. Groen had flunked Rensi's inspection because he had used a new cash register system that was not approved by the company and had made an unauthorized change in the store's front counter. Pointing his finger a couple of inches away from his field consultant's nose, Groen gave Rensi a much deserved dressing down. "Don't you ever let the bureaucracy of that damned grading form of yours stifle my ingenuity," he shouted. Rensi now concedes Groen's point. "I was being an autocrat, and Lou deserved better from me," he says. "From that day on, I busted my ass to prove myself to that man."

But Rensi admits that his performance with Groen was typical of the attitude being taken by many younger field consultants during the expansion era. "The field service organization had become too heavy-handed," he says. "We were telling franchisees what was wrong with their operations instead of telling them, 'Here's the problem, here's a solution, and now let's try to fix it together.'"

Yet, by the time McDonald's recognized the problems, dissent within the system had already begun to spread. MOA's members were actively lobbying Congress to pass national legislation severely limiting the franchiser's right to terminate or refuse to renew franchises. While that was serious enough, it was only the beginning of the group's legal challenge. In fact, MOA members and sympathizers began taking their grievances to the one place where McDonald's had never been challenged by its franchisees—the courthouse. During the mid-1970s, a half-dozen major lawsuits were filed by McDonald's licensees who were seeking to rewrite the ground rules of their compact with the system. Some challenged McDonald's ability to require its licensees to rent real estate from the company. Others attacked the company's authority to terminate franchisees for gross QSC violations or to refuse to renew poor performers at the end of the twenty-year licenses. To McDonald's, those were fundamental prerogatives. If such suits were lost, McDonald's would never again be the same.

Thus, in 1975, McDonald's was reaching yet another watershed. It had to learn how to live with its success—to manage the impressive new size of its franchising system without sacrificing the fundamental principles that made it franchising's most successful company. The year was its twentieth anniversary, and it had reason to celebrate its market dominance. Systemwide sales in 1975 alone had soared 28 percent to $2.5 billion, and the company reported a 32 percent increase in income during what for almost everyone else was a recessionary year. But it was in no position to savor the triumph over its competitors because the threat from within was creating a pervasive sense of unease. "I was a poor boy from Ohio who made good because of McDonald's," Rensi says. "This was my family, and my family was being ripped apart. It was happening before my very eyes, and I was helpless to stop it."

Had McDonald's not been organized on Kroc's principles of fairness toward franchisees, its managers might not have been nearly as sensitive about MOA's charges, and McDonald's might not have responded until it was too late. But from the 1950s, Kroc had drilled into his managers a philosophy that set McDonald's apart from all other franchisers. Thus, when MOA stunned Kroc's managers, they responded more aggressively than they had to any of McDonald's outside challenges.

Indeed, they met MOA head on. As soon as the maverick organization was formed in 1975, Schmitt and Turner personally interviewed each of the twenty officers and directors of MOA. Most of their complaints could be traced to a breakdown in communication between franchisees and the company. During the early years, McDonald's had been an extremely effective clearinghouse of information, but contact between company managers and franchisees was always informal. As the system mushroomed, those circuits became overloaded. Running through all of MOA's complaints, Schmitt observes, "was a thread of complete uncertainty on the part of the operators, a lack of confidence in their ability to have an impact on the system's future patterns of development."

Schmitt and Ray Kroc proposed sweeping changes to restore the balance of power by giving franchisees new and more formal avenues of communication with McDonald's management and important new tools to check the corporation's growing power. It was a brilliant maneuver. Schmitt was turning MOA's attack into a constructive instrument. The franchisees needed new powers to continue to be an effective force, and it was in McDonald's interest to provide them. The concept was the very essence of Ray Kroc's franchising formula: stronger franchisees produced a stronger franchising company. In effect, Schmitt's answer to MOA merely required adapting Kroc's original franchising philosophy to a much larger system.

But Schmitt could not restore the old balance without finding some way of checking the power of McDonald's increasingly influential regional managers, and that was an extremely risky proposition. When Fred Turner pushed decision making down to the regional level, he gave McDonald's an enormous competitive advantage over other national fast-food chains by allowing it to be as responsive to local market conditions as local retailers are. Its regional managers were not encumbered by corporate rules that they knew were not appropriate for their markets.

As a result, McDonald's regional managers became as resourceful and entrepreneurial as the chain's franchisees. They, too, began developing unique marketing concepts that were proven in their markets and expanded throughout the chain. Working in concert with Paul Schrage, Jim Zien, a onetime franchisee who had become a regional manager in San Diego, developed and successfully tested the first Playland. In 1982, Jim Klinefelter, the regional manager in Minneapolis, developed a mini McDonald's known as McSnack after he realized how many shopping mall locations there were in Minneapolis that could not support a full-sized McDonald's but could support a unit that took up one-tenth the space of a conventional store. Similarly, Larry Ingram, the regional manager in Dallas, was answering a local market need when he built the first drive-thru window in 1975 at a McDonald's store in Oklahoma City, minutes from Tinker Air Force Base. Ingram's drive-thru was responding to a new regulation prohibiting airmen traveling off-base to get out of their cars unless they were in uniform. But when the drive-thru increased the store's sales by 28 percent in the first year, McDonald's quickly realized that its attraction went well beyond the military. Today, about 90 percent of McDonald's free-standing units in the United States have drive-thru windows that account for over 50 percent of their sales.

McDonald's was not about to jeopardize such local market creativity by eliminating the autonomy of regional managers. But it did have to begin dealing with the excesses of regional management that appeared during the early 1970s. Everyone was appraising the performance of franchisees, but the checks against excesses of the regional managers were clearly insufficient. And because the regions were growing so rapidly, positions were being filled with younger and less experienced managers. The setting was ready made to produce conflicts between veteran franchisees and young regional managers on a superfast track. "There was improper supervision of our field generals," recalls Michael Quinlan, McDonald's fifty-year-old chairman. "Top management didn't really know what was going on in the regions, partly because corporate management was spread too thin and partly because the regional managers just weren't talking enough to them about what the hell they were doing. Nor were they asking for advice from operators on whether their decisions were right or wrong. It was a very autocratic environment."

Quinlan knew that environment well, because he was perhaps the prototype McDonald's fast-tracker. He was hired in 1963 by June Martino, whose son John was a fraternity brother of his at Loyola. The connection landed Quinlan a part-time job as McDonald's mailboy and stockroom manager, which paid his way through college. At age twenty-three, Quinlan began full-time work in 1968 in McDonald's largest region—Chicago—which happened to be run at the time by Ed Schmitt. Impressed with Quinlan, Schmitt put him through the paces. In five years in the region, Quinlan moved from being an administrative assistant to assistant store manager, to store manager, to field consultant, to area supervisor in charge of five McOpCo stores, and finally to district manager in charge of St. Louis. In 1973, Quinlan took over the helm of the Washington, D.C., region, then McDonald's largest with 360 stores. Quinlan was only twenty-eight and less than a decade removed from his days as a mailboy, yet he was now the operations boss of one-eighth of the stores in the McDonald's System.

Despite his youth, he was treated like a senior manager. In his three years as Washington's regional manager, Quinlan approved the construction and licensing of 210 new stores with no one looking over his shoulder. He was not even visited by a senior corporate executive until he had been on the job in Washington for fifteen months. And like every other regional manager of that era, Quinlan was the absolute power in Washington. "There wasn't any structure to audit the regional manager's decision-making abilities," he says. "Oak Brook wouldn't see a mistake in regional licensing until a year and a half after the fact. It was a loosey-goosey process, and we didn't give a damn whether the licensees liked it or not."

Thus part of McDonald's response to the MOA challenge involved giving regional managers a modest amount of added supervision—checking some of their excesses without curtailing any of their creative freedom. A new senior management position of zone manager was created, and each executive appointed to it was responsible for overseeing the performance of five regions. The training of field consultants was vastly upgraded, and the job returned to being one primarily of consultation, not inspection. And while field consultants still perform an annual "full field" inspection and grading of each store's performance, the criteria for assigning different grades were defined more sharply so that evaluations would be more objective.

But Schmitt, who organized the overall response to MOA, realized that the key to restoring the balance of power in McDonald's was not to be found in making regional managers weaker and less effective but in making franchisees stronger in their relationship with the company. The operators, Schmitt determined, needed both collective and individual mechanisms for checking the power of McDonald's. As a collective force, he proposed a critical change in an operator advisory board that Turner had recently created to define and promote the operators' position on policy issues. Schmitt's version of the National Operators Advisory Board was not unlike Turner's except that now NOAB was to be composed of two franchisees from each region, *elected* by the operators and no longer appointed by the company. Its scope would include all policies affecting the relationship between the franchisees and McDonald's. Its role would be advisory only, but as the official representative of franchisees on matters of policy, NOAB's opinions could not be easily ignored. Advisory or not, NOAB would have power if it wanted to use it. When chairman Turner approved the plan, McDonald's became the first company voluntarily to reverse what appeared to be the natural order of franchising: It gave power back to its franchisees.

McDonald's new approach to dealing with individual franchisee grievances came from a suggestion by Ray Kroc, who borrowed a concept that could be traced back to third-century Scandinavian royalty. The kings of Sweden, Norway, and Denmark had then begun using advisers to plead the case of common people who had complaints about the treatment they received at the hands of the kings' ministers. They were called ombudsmen, which meant "all the people's man." In McDonald's, Kroc thought, the ombudsman could function as a neutral third party to investigate complaints of any franchisee who felt harmed by the decision of a regional manager, primarily on questions of awarding new stores or on matters of impact.

More than anything else, NOAB and the ombudsman were the keys to diffusing MOA's strength, and both have become permanent features of McDonald's franchising structure. From the beginning, it was clear that the NOAB's directors would be accountable only to the franchisees and would in no way be influenced by the company. In fact, the first chairman of the group was Art Korf, a franchisee who had been a prime organizer of MOA.

The new advisory group quickly spurred McDonald's into action on a number of key issues. While the company had already begun changing policies in response to MOA's complaints, NOAB encouraged it to take bolder corrective measures. NOAB, for example, played a key role in reforming the field service function. And it pressured McDonald's to develop a clearer policy on expansion, one that gave operators better notice of expansion plans, a detailed evaluation of their own expandability, and more equitable treatment on the matter of impact. "They kicked us around the schoolyard on impact," Quinlan says, "but they made us a better company."

Perhaps more important, NOAB has checked the company whenever franchisees *perceived* threatening action from Oak Brook. In 1979, for instance, the company proposed a completely new master franchise agreement called "compact." It was designed to remove the potential for subjective interpretation of the license, and when each provision of the new contract was approved piece by piece over a one-year period, none of McDonald's top executives realized how harshly the document might be viewed in toto.

But when NOAB grabbed hold of compact, the sparks started to fly. The group found the new license so objectionable that it decided to fight the company all the way to the courthouse. It hired a law firm and sent out an emergency request for contributions of $50 per store from franchisees. Within weeks it had a legal warchest of more than $100,000, and it was obvious that that was just the initial ante. McDonald's took the prudent course: it buried compact.

While NOAB was protecting the collective rights of franchisees, the newly appointed ombudsman was even more effective in protecting the rights of individual operators. Over time, his or her advisory judgments on franchisee complaints were taken almost as gospel—not only by franchisees but by the company, which is under no obligation to follow them. In part, that reflects McDonald's desire to make the ombudsman position meaningful. But it is also a tribute to the absolute neutrality of the man who held the post from its beginning through 1991—John Cooke.

Cooke had served McDonald's in delicate positions before. As the company's labor relations chief in the late 1960s and early 1970s, Cooke stood toe to toe with local labor unions that had tried organizing McDonald's stores on some four hundred separate occasions. Technically, Cooke's job was to communicate with the crews of the stores being organized—to educate them on unions and to listen and respond to their complaints.

In practice, Cooke's job was to keep the unions out. McDonald's saw itself as an entrepreneurial operation, and no one believed more fervently than Cooke that unions threatened the creativity of McDonald's entrepreneurs. "Unions are inimical to what we stand for and how we operate," Cooke insists. "They don't believe in ever letting the work force get excited about what they are doing. And they peddle the line to their members that the boss will forevermore be against their interests."

Cooke translated that passion into a powerful union resistance movement. He organized a "flying squad" of experienced McDonald's store managers who were dispatched to a restaurant the same day that word came in of an attempt to organize it. He trained managers on how to deal with employees and union representatives. He worked with McDonald's field operations teams to make sure employee grievances were dealt with promptly. When union pickets blocked deliveries of food to the organized store, as they did in San Francisco, Cooke's group lined up alternative shipments.

In short, Cooke gave no ground to unions, and they eventually concluded that a McDonald's store was not a likely target for a successful organization effort. Of the four hundred serious organization attempts in the early 1970s, none was successful. As a result, McDonald's stores today are strictly nonunion shops.

The ombudsman's task required the same toughness from Cooke. In more of the fifty or so cases he reviewed each year, Cooke dealt with operator complaints about the adverse impact of new stores or about the award of a new store to another operator. They are issues on which franchisees have a lot at stake, and they often pit one franchisee against another. A ruling in favor of an operator who has been turned down on a new store means ruling against an operator who has been awarded that store. For Cooke, it was almost a no-win situation, but his decisions, though technically only advisory in nature, were rarely overruled by the court of last resort—the chairman of McDonald's.

That was so because Cooke fulfilled his role with a neutrality that belied the fact that he was a McDonald's employee. His decisions were made only after a methodical two-week investigation that always included a personal visit to the local market. In each case, he called in a franchisee from another market to investigate the case with him. And his opinions, sometimes running up to forty pages, read like legal decisions.

He was as detached from McDonald's management as he was from the complaining franchisee. He refused to discuss his investigations with McDonald's managers, and he revealed to no one his batting average, that is, the percentage of his rulings in favor of franchisees or in favor of the company's regional managers, whose decisions typically trigger a franchisee's protest. "Neither Fred Turner nor Ed Schmitt has asked me about a case," Cooke observed. "I am thankful for that because I have been prepared for the last sixteen years to say, 'It's none of your business.' "

Not all of the responses to MOA stemmed from the interviews Turner and Schmitt conducted with its leadership. While Schmitt was orchestrating the organizational changes to increase the power of franchisees, other managers dealt with the economic issues that were causing the more general operator unrest that MOA exploited. Some of the most effective work was done by Gerry Newman, who in 1975 took to the road, meeting operators in each of McDonald's regional offices. The sessions began at 7:00 A.M., went through lunch, and rarely ended before 11:00 P.M. One by one, every franchisee in the region who had a complaint got a private audience with Newman.

Their most common complaint concerned the negative impact on older stores that was being caused by new McDonald's units built nearby. In more than two-thirds of the cases, Newman offered a solution. Sometimes that involved nothing more than granting rent relief to operators who were losing money. The company had started the practice of temporarily reducing rents to troubled operators in the 1960s, but by the mid-1970s, many more McDonald's franchisees were running marginal or losing operations, most of them at new stores that had not yet reached their ultimate sales potential. Responding to that, McDonald's granted more than $5 million in rent relief to about three hundred operators in 1975, the year MOA was created.

But rent relief did nothing to improve a troubled operator's sales. So Newman devised a plan for financing capital improvements designed to increase a weak store's marketing potential, including such additions as drive-thru windows and Ronald McDonald Playlands.

Newman's financing scheme was a no-lose proposition for franchisees. Licensees normally are responsible for financing store improvements, but Newman told the troubled operators that McDonald's would loan them $50,000 to pay for the store additions, and if they failed to boost their store's annual volume by $150,000 within two years, the operator did not have to repay the loan.

During the first year, some 225 operators accepted the so-called Newman-Texas 150. That was the name given to Newman's financing arrangement, because so many of the capital improvements loans were granted in Texas, a market that McDonald's was slow to enter. When a McDonald's unit in Dallas went under in the late 1950s, then president Harry Sonneborn decided that the market was naturally hostile to a McDonald's drive-in, and the chain stayed out of Texas for years. When it reentered in the late 1960s, it encountered other problems, including a court order that kept it from using the name McDonald's in Houston until it bought the rights to the name from a local drive-in chain that took the last name of its owner—George McDonald. By the time McDonald's began expanding in Texas in the 1970s, the market was a Burger King stronghold, and dozens of McDonald's franchises there might not have survived the tough early going had it not been for Newman's program.

Newman's loan program applied to all troubled operators—not just MOA members—and it was undertaken strictly because of Newman's initiative, not because of some corporate strategy. That was in the best tradition of the Kroc-Turner brand of management, which rejects organizational charts and encourages executives assigned to one area to take action in someone else's bailiwick when they feel strongly enough about something. Curiously, such crisscrossing rarely yields management conflict, largely because most McDonald's managers understand the basic rule of power at McDonald's: authority goes to those who seize it. Thus, by filling what he believed was a void, Newman, the company's chief accountant, became a specialist in licensee relations, a marketing advocate for Playlands, and a financier of capital improvements at marginal McDonald's units.

Nor was the Newman-Texas 150 a quick-fix program that was shelved as soon as the MOA heat was off. It worked so well, in fact, that it has become a permanent part of McDonald's franchising program. In the 1980s, Newman met with nearly two thousand franchisees looking for help in financing store improvements, and he made his guaranteed loan to half of them, most to finance Ronald McDonald Playlands. In all but a handful of cases, the Playlands increased sales by $150,000 within two years, giving the operator sufficient profit to pay back the loan.

Newman's investments paid off handsomely. The program turned some 400 stores from losers to winners, and that dramatically cut the number of units needing rent relief. Here was Kroc's interdependence formula at work. By increasing sales of weak stores, McDonald's made more money on the 11.5 percent of sales it charges operators in franchise fees and rents. And when Newman saw how the Playlands he financed had lifted the sales of weak stores anywhere from 15 to 35 percent within a matter of months, he decided to expand his Playland financing program to healthy units as well. Indeed, Newman more than anyone else deserves credit for expanding the novel Playlands to as many as 4,900 of McDonald's more than 14,000 restaurants worldwide.

Being more involved in helping some of its troubled operators, however, was only part of the changes McDonald's made to respond to the economic complaints that were coming from franchisees. And just as it had with Newman's reinvestment loans, McDonald's itself came out ahead by striking a new balance with its franchisees. For example, when it dealt squarely with the problem of impact—the most critical of the franchisees' concerns—it developed a more enlightened expansion policy that resulted in better new store locations for McDonald's and better treatment for operators by eliminating the subjectivity and apparent favoritism that had become part of decision making on new units.

For the first time, McDonald's clearly defined and articulated standards that franchisees had to meet to qualify for additional stores. An "expandable" franchisee was one whose existing units had regularly earned at least a B grade on QSC. He or she also had to have sufficient financial and management resources to support expansion, in addition to a good record of community involvement and an attitude of cooperation with the company and other franchisees. Under a more clearly defined policy, operators began meeting with regional managers once a year for a complete appraisal of their existing units and their chances for additional stores. When shortcomings were found, franchisees were told exactly what remedies were needed for them to be considered "expandable."

To counter charges that regional managers were reneging on new store promises, Schmitt required McDonald's field bosses to put such promises in writing or to stop making them. And from here on, franchisees would receive an annual review of the region's three-year plan for new stores. Operators were now asked for their opinions on proposed new sites, but more important, they were assured that in the awarding of new units serious consideration would be given to expandable operators whose existing units were most severely impacted by them.

Understandably, the policy required McDonald's to upgrade its analysis of a new store's marketing prospects, including its potential for stripping away sales from existing units. Until the mid-1970s, McDonald's picked new store sites on the basis of census tract information on the number of residents near a site and with the help of state highway department studies measuring the automobile traffic passing by it.

Yet, those studies often produced inaccurate forecasts of a site's sales potential. Sites along highway routes to airports, for example, were an early favorite because of their unusually high traffic counts. But the restaurants were usually low-volume units because people racing to meet airplanes typically were a poor market to tap for hamburgers. Conversely, basing site selection solely on the number of residents living in an area ignored thinly populated areas that nevertheless attracted shoppers and workers.

Even worse, the traditional market analysis gave no indication of the new store potential in McDonald's most saturated areas. By the early 1970s, McDonald's had proven that stores could be successful in areas with fifty thousand residents. Thus locating new stores was mostly a matter of building in areas that had more than fifty thousand people, which was assumed as the saturation level. The problem with that was obvious: What if the saturation level turned out to be a lot less than fifty thousand?

The work on improving site selection began quietly a couple of years before MOA raised the issue of impact. Curiously, the initiative did not come from the obvious source, McDonald's real estate department, but rather from Marketing Chief Paul Schrage. Just as accountant Newman had filled a vacuum by promoting Playlands, Schrage moved into a real estate void to answer a nagging question: Is McDonald's hitting market saturation?

A good many Wall Street security analysts had already concluded that it was, but the analysts had no special marketing insights to back them up. So, Schrage created a new group within the marketing department to analyze the market area of new stores more scientifically. Statistical analysis of restaurant sites was unknown in the fast-food business, but the new group quickly began applying trading area surveys commonly used by the big supermarket chains. They conducted interviews of hundreds of customers at each store to determine where they lived, and the census tracts that accounted for the bulk of a store's customer base were used to define its market area. That information could be used to identify markets where new stores could be built without impacting the business of existing units. But regional managers accustomed to relying on their instincts in selecting new sites resisted using the new technique. However, when MOA spotlighted the impact problem in 1975, that resistance collapsed, and trading area surveys became commonplace. Surprisingly, they showed that McDonald's most penetrated markets could easily support many more stores. Yet, when the regional real estate staffs began raising too many unanswered questions about measuring the impact of specific new stores, Jim Rand, vice president and McDonald's director of marketing research, realized that he needed a more powerful device to forecast the sales potential of each new store. The only problem was that the trading area survey was then the state-of-the-art tool.

If McDonald's still wanted to grow by penetrating the market further with many more new stores, it had to pioneer improved ways for analyzing sites. Thus Rand devised a new survey that asked customers at existing stores for much more detailed information. In addition to determining where they lived, he asked them to identify precisely where they were before their McDonald's visit and where they were going afterward. Rand also grouped the data in smaller and better defined segments than census tracts, and he even isolated the number of trips to a specific McDonald's that were contributed by such nearby traffic generators as schools, offices, and shopping malls.

Rand called his invention the "trip pattern survey," and it was clearly a more sophisticated tool than anyone had ever devised for identifying the sources of retail trade. When the new information was put on a map, with different colors denoting different sources of business, it created a graphic picture of a store's annual sales. From a location standpoint, at least, it held the secrets of each McDonald's store: how many of its sales dollars came from the residents within three minutes of the store, how many from the shopping mall a mile away, and how many from the three office buildings down the street.

More important, the trip pattern survey could forecast the revenues a new store would draw from the sales generators of existing McDonald's in the area. In short, Rand and his team could now estimate that a new store built at location A would take $150,000 a year away from an existing store at site B and perhaps $75,000 to $100,000 each from stores located in sites C and D. By the late 1970s, such detailed forecasting was being used by McDonald's regional managers in awarding new restaurants to expandable operators whose existing units were most affected by new ones.

The new research not only helped defuse the impact bomb, it helped uncover hundreds of new locations. In fact, McDonald's was becoming one of the nation's most expert retail site analysts, and in the process it was proving that the saturation issue that fascinated Wall Street was a bogeyman. Thanks in part to its new market survey techniques, the minimum population per store in McDonald's most penetrated markets fell from fifty thousand in the early 1970s, to twenty-five thousand by the end of the decade, to somewhere in the high teens today. In Chicago, for example, McDonald's learned it could locate a store on the fifth floor of Water Tower Place (a high-rise shopping center on Michigan Avenue), another in a high-rise apartment building six blocks to the south, and three more in between.

When does McDonald's reach saturation? In the mid-1980s, Ed Schmitt enjoyed the shock value in telling people that there were more General Motors dealerships in the United States than there were McDonald's restaurants. His point was that McDonald's could not be near saturation when the number one automotive brand has more outlets than the number one hamburger chain. And McDonald's success in its most saturated markets seems to underscore that.

Taken together, the ombudsman program, NOAB, and all the other franchising and operating reforms of the mid-1970s made McDonald's an even more effective franchising system by creating tools that allowed for better management of the chain's impressive size and scope. McDonald's managers were better able to deal fairly with individual franchisees, and they, in turn, now had the means for reversing unjust decisions, particularly on new stores. Indeed, Ray Kroc's concepts of equity with his franchising partners were now more evident inside McDonald's than ever before.

Thus it is not surprising that the McDonald's Operators Association by 1977—just two years after its formation—had lost all of its punch. Having lost its constituency inside McDonald's, MOA had to look elsewhere for support. In fact, it survived only by joining a broader organization—called the National Franchisee Association—which began soliciting members and representing operators of all national franchised chains.

While MOA had been eliminated, the operator lawsuits that it spun off were still around, and until they were eliminated, too, the MOA threat was still present. The suits struck at the very underpinnings of the McDonald's System. They challenged the company's right not to renew a license at the end of its initial twenty-year term. They took issue with its right to require franchisees to lease their real estate from McDonald's. And they contested the company's right to terminate franchisees who had failed miserably in following McDonald's uncompromising QSC standards.

Until the mid-1970s, McDonald's had succeeded in staying out of the courtroom, preferring marketing battles over legal ones. In its first two decades, the company's only major court case was the suit it brought against Sandy's, a fast-food chain started by four Peoria businessmen who were partners in one of McDonald's earliest franchised units. Encouraged by their success at their one McDonald's unit in Champaign-Urbana, the four partners founded a fast-food chain that appeared to be a carbon copy of a McDonald's. It was also an apparent violation of a provision of the McDonald's contract prohibiting franchisees from operating similar restaurants and from using elsewhere trade secrets learned at McDonald's. McDonald's won the case on appeal, establishing new case law that extended trade secret protection to the rather nebulous area of fast-food franchising. (Sandy's was later acquired by the Hardee's chain.)

While legal action between the company and its franchisees was

the exception in the 1960s, it nearly became the rule during the turbu-
lent MOA years when McDonald's suddenly found itself embroiled in a
dozen major lawsuits with its franchisees. In part, they were individual
extensions of MOA's collective attack, and MOA's lawyer, W. Yale Mathieson, wound up representing some of the franchisees bringing suit.
But McDonald's phenomenal success had also made it a highly visible
and potentially lucrative target for all lawyers with a good practice
representing franchisees. In fact, during the 1970s, McDonald's tangled
regularly with an outspoken advocate of the rights of franchisees—
Harold Brown, an attorney from Boston. Brown's record of winning
suits for franchisees was legend, and even the title of his book conveys
his bias: *Franchising: Trap for the Trusting.*

As it entered the courtroom, McDonald's found precious little
comfort in the existing case law on franchising. One after another,
franchised gasoline dealers won court actions against oil companies
that required their dealers to buy tires, batteries, and accessories only
from them. Such so-called tie-in arrangements, the courts declared,
violated federal prohibitions against restraint of trade by putting franchisees in economic bondage. By the mid-1960s, the principle was
extended to fast-food franchising. The landmark opinion came in a
class action against Chicken Delight (*Siegel v. Chicken Delight.*) The
1970 ruling declared illegal Chicken Delight's requirement that franchisees purchase pressure cookers, fryers, and a wide range of supplies
from the company. Since that was how the chain made most of its
money, the decision delivered a crippling blow. Soon afterward,
Chicken Delight was out of business.

The tie-in rulings pertained only to supplies that McDonald's—
thanks to Ray Kroc's foresight—did not sell to its franchisees. Still, they
fostered an aura of uncertainty about the propriety of franchising. The
Federal Trade Commission was becoming critical of the franchiser's
power. Legislatures in a number of states began passing laws restricting
a franchiser's right to terminate existing franchisees or to deny the
renewal of expiring licenses. Such a bill was introduced (though never
passed) in Congress by Abner Mikva, a representative from Illinois.
"The public perception of franchising was that of a coercive system in
which giants force franchisees to act to their economic disadvantage
and solely for the franchiser's profit," notes Allen Silberman, a partner
with Sonnenschein, Carlin, Nath and Rosenthal, McDonald's counsel.

Given that environment, McDonald's might easily have ducked its
legal battles. Virtually all of them were being waged by sub-par opera-

tors who had gone to court to keep McDonald's from terminating their franchises for failure to meet QSC standards. McDonald's could have sidestepped the suits simply by allowing the marginal operators to remain in the system. By choosing to fight instead, McDonald's was knowingly exposing itself to a wide range of antitrust charges that were certain to be raised by any licensee being drummed out of the system.

The fact that the company did not back down suggests that its responses to MOA were being guided by ideas about the system's welfare, not by notions of corporate convenience. McDonald's made a clear distinction between franchisees who were disenchanted with their diminishing influence on policy and franchisees who were using MOA as a shield to cover up grossly inadequate operations. Its conciliatory responses to the former and combative responses to the latter were surprisingly consistent. Giving all operators new powers to check a franchising company that had grown too powerful had the same positive effect as eliminating a handful of operators who were giving McDonald's a bad name.

Furthermore, when it came to protecting the operating basics, McDonald's had always refused to compromise with anyone. More so than any other franchiser in America, it insisted on tossing out the rotten apples—no matter what the legal and public relations cost. "Success in franchising is a very fragile thing," observed Donald Horwitz, the company's former executive vice president in charge of legal affairs. "And because we were so successful, we had more to lose and thus had more incentive to take action against operators ignoring the very things that made us successful."

McDonald's took action against weak operators in two ways. In cases of gross violations of the company's QSC standards, it sued franchisees for default of their license agreement, and some of those franchisees sued McDonald's—claiming everything from price fixing to illegal tie-ins. The other half of the major franchisee lawsuits were triggered by McDonald's decision not to renew a marginal operator at the expiration of his or her twenty-year license.

In 1975, when McDonald's earliest licenses expired, the company announced a unique policy on renewal. To be renewed, operators had to maintain stores with at least a C average on QSC, and their management organizations had to be strong enough to perpetuate that operating level for another twenty years. The licensee also had to exhibit a willingness to reinvest in capital improvements and to cooperate with his or her fellow franchisees by contributing to their local advertising cooperative. As a result, marginal franchisees who were not technically in default of their existing licenses nevertheless would not have those licenses renewed. Since many franchisees had anticipated automatic renewal, McDonald's renewal policy was certain to cause as much consternation among marginal operators as its default notices caused among operators being terminated for gross QSC violations.

The policy was unheard of in franchising. Fast-food franchisers typically went out of their way to retain even mediocre franchisees because they are the source of all franchising income. By contrast, McDonald's was using renewal to upgrade the quality of its franchisees. "That was very scary for operators to think about," Horwitz says. "How would we do that and get the support of the system at the same time? It was the toughest operator-company problem McDonald's had ever seen—bar none."

Yet, McDonald's exercised extreme care in implementing the policy. Operators were given three years' notice when they were not being renewed, and the company even lined up prospective buyers for their franchise. McOpCo was prohibited from buying the store of a nonrenewed operator. A committee of senior executives was set up to decide each renewal by majority vote, preventing individual biases from influencing the outcome. In fact, there were even cases of franchisees who were renewed against the personal wishes of Ray Kroc. Furthermore, the numbers alone indicated that the renewal process was being used only to screen out the weakest of the system's franchisees: Overall, 91 percent of operators who have been up for renewal have received new twenty-year licenses.

No matter how fairly McDonald's executed its policies on eliminating weak operators, it was certain to set off legal fireworks. And given the ominous trends in franchising law, it is surprising that McDonald's won any of its legal entanglements with franchisees. The actual tally is perhaps the closest thing there is to a legal miracle: it won all of them.

Indeed, the McDonald's franchising cases established important legal precedents. Previously, court rulings on franchising described practices that were so unfair to franchisees that collectively they gave franchising a bad reputation. The McDonald's cases had the very opposite effect. The courts essentially used them to define franchising practices that were equitable, and taken together they created a body of case law that gave franchising a degree of legitimacy it had never before had.

In the process, McDonald's also placed a protective legal shield around the franchising tenets that made up the foundation of its fast-food system. For example, it convinced the courts that its requirement that franchisees rent their property at their stores from the company did not constitute an illegal tie-in with its franchise agreement. The company successfully argued that, in contrast to supply tie-in arrangements, the property "supplied" to franchisees was an integral part of the restaurant operation. Its success as a fast-food chain, McDonald's contended, depended on its ability to control the selection of store sites and to retain control of the building even if the franchisee left the business. Furthermore, the courts concluded that McDonald's rented property to operators at rates that were competitive.

McDonald's also succeeded in convincing courts of the fairness of its renewal policy. Repeatedly, courts declared that its contract with franchisees clearly specified only a twenty-year commitment and that franchisees could not read into that a lifelong guarantee. Even more important, McDonald's defended its right to terminate franchisees for failing to meet its QSC standards. The company never terminated a franchisee without first offering either to find a buyer for the restaurant or to buy the store itself at market value and resell it to a new franchisee. Still, a number of terminated operators—on the advice of their lawyers—had rejected buyout offers that went as high as $550,000 for a single store. They opted to seek legal damages instead, and in every case they wound up losing. A franchise that they could have sold for hundreds of thousands of dollars just before the termination of the license was worthless afterward—and not one of the suing franchisees walked away from the courthouse with so much as a nickel in damages.

McDonald's showed no compassion to operators who had violated its standards and spurned its leniency. When Bob Ahern, a franchisee from suburban Chicago, rejected McDonald's offer of acquisition in favor of a lawsuit challenging the company's decision not to renew his franchise, he became one of the more notable targets of McDonald's righteousness. Although McDonald's won the case, it could not evict Ahern from the premises, since he was one of a handful of early licensees who owned his store property. But it wasted no time relieving him of its most valued possession—the McDonald's trade name.

At 5:00 A.M. on the day after the court's decision, Shelby Yastrow, McDonald's general counsel, showed up at Ahern's store with a crew to remove the Golden Arches and the McDonald's sign. Yastrow even strapped a small set of arches to the hood of his car and hauled them back to his office to show his colleagues that he had claimed his prize. Ahern renamed his hamburger restaurant Berney's, but he soon found new respect for the power of the McDonald's name and the wrath of its managers against those who were thought to have abused it. McDonald's opened a lavish new franchised unit—complete with an indoor Playland—a block and a half from Ahern's place. Berney's was out of business within the year.

But clearly McDonald's most significant QSC verdict came in 1982 in the case of Raymond Dayan, who sued McDonald's in Illinois court to prevent the company from terminating his exclusive license for Paris, France. Since Dayan was claiming that he had not violated the company's QSC standards and McDonald's was terminating him simply because it thought he had, the Dayan case was the only "pure" QSC case ever to go to trial.

With twelve McDonald's restaurants already in operation in Paris and a license to develop the entire market, Dayan had a lot to lose. But so did McDonald's, which considered Dayan's units an eyesore and an international embarrassment. Indeed, McDonald's in Paris was considered "a QSC wasteland" by everyone else in the system. The company's strict specifications on food products had been blatantly ignored. Hamburgers were prepared without all of the standard ingredients. Food was held so long and served so cold that McDonald's managers inspecting the stores found it difficult to eat. Standard cooking equipment was either missing or poorly maintained, and the grills were improperly calibrated. Food was stored next to cleaning compounds.

Veteran managers insist that they have never seen McDonald's units maintained in a filthier state: cooking oils were rancid and black, layers of grease covered the floors and walls, litter was strewn about the store, and grease dripped from the vents into cups hung from the ceiling. In fact, the stores were so unclean that McDonald's franchisees elsewhere around the world began hearing complaints about them from their own local customers who had seen Dayan's restaurants while visiting Paris.

Understandably, pressure built within the system to remove Dayan. George Cohon, then president of McDonald's of Canada, wrote a letter to Turner about Paris, insisting that "it is time to remove the cancer." Turner advised Cohon to take action himself, and McDonald's Canadian president attempted to negotiate a buyout of Dayan's restaurants and his Paris license for $12 million, an offer Dayan would later regret turning down. Months later, McDonald's terminated his license, and Dayan countered with his suit for injunction.

That Dayan chose the courthouse over a settlement was predictable; his one-quarter partner in Paris was attorney Mathieson, the lawyer for MOA. But the opinion the court wrote deciding the case was something no one expected. The Illinois Circuit Court ruled in McDonald's favor, a decision that was influenced by different sets of photographs of the Paris stores: those presented by McDonald's, showing filthy and dilapidated outlets; and those from Dayan, showing gleaming units. But there was yet another critical difference in the photographs that McDonald's lawyers quickly drew to the attention of the court. McDonald's pictures, taken in the summer when the chain terminated Dayan's license, showed foliage on the trees outside. Dayan's pictures showed trees with no leaves. His pictures, the court determined, had been taken in the fall, after termination notice had been given and Dayan had finally taken time to clean the units.

Not surprisingly, the court was not pleased with the attempted ruse, but it seemed even more annoyed at what it concluded was Dayan's abuse of the McDonald's System. Few court opinions—least of all in the area of franchising—have been so supportive of a corporation taking action against an individual. In justifying its termination of Dayan, McDonald's had obviously convinced Circuit Court Judge Richard L. Curry that it regards its QSC standards as sacrosanct. Said one McDonald's veteran when he read Curry's opinion: "He must have gotten ketchup in his blood."

In his opinion, Judge Curry flatly rejected Dayan's claim that McDonald's wanted to reclaim its Paris franchise to pocket the substantial profits that Dayan was making in the French market. "Far more realistic . . . is the conclusion that McDonald's herculean effort in this case is motivated by a zeal to rid itself of a cancer within its system before it grows and further infects the 6,900 store organization," Curry wrote, adding that "if Dayan, the grade 'F' operator in Paris, can thumb his nose at the system and its standards, then so too can operators everywhere."

But Curry reserved his harshest criticism in summing up his judgment in favor of McDonald's: "As though he were intent on writing his own chapter to the infamous *Ugly American* saga, Dayan takes this immensely attractive and uniquely American franchise to Paris, he masquerades it as the real thing while delivering a product vastly inferior to what has made it a success in this country, he belittles the standards and expectations of his adopted city, he fools the customers who are attracted by McDonald's name, he cons the man he calls his friend [Steve Barnes, former chairman of McDonald's International], he ignores and disregards the critical operational standards he had agreed to uphold, he fleeces his operation in order to enhance his return, he entreats the court to ignore facts and to embrace fantasy, and at the close of his case he argues that it is his financial benefactor who is engaged in a 'scam.' Within the context of this case, no pun is intended when I note that plaintiff does not stand before the Court with clean hands."

When Judge Curry's decision in the Dayan case was handed down in 1982, it effectively brought to an end the franchising turmoil that had begun in the middle of the previous decade. McDonald's had confronted the new crisis head-on. It emerged a stronger, more intelligent, and more sophisticated franchiser. When it needed to adapt Ray Kroc's principles of fairness to a larger and more complex system, it was willing and able to bend. When it had to protect those principles from attack by those who ignored them, it was ready to wage war.

In a period of turbulence and confusion, bitterness and opportunism, McDonald's had displayed both compassion and fury, and, incredibly, it had picked the right moment for each. It had applied Ray Kroc's knack for blending a deep sense of fairness and honesty with devotion to discipline and hard work. Like a schoolmaster, Kroc had drilled those principles into his young managers and franchisees. More than anything else, it was the soundness of Kroc's franchising philosophy that had allowed McDonald's to weather its external and internal storms of the 1970s.

Kroc's principles had withstood the test of time—and the test of law. Donald Lubin, the partner in the Sonnenschein law firm who has been a McDonald's director since 1966, believes that the key to McDonald's unique and unblemished record of success in franchising cases is basically attributable to the "genius of Ray Kroc," and particularly to his instinctive decision not to make his money by selling high-cost franchises or by supplying his franchisees at a profit to himself. "Sometimes, you argue law based on factual quicksand," Lubin says. "It is much more difficult to establish what might be good law when your facts are lousy. We always had some really good things going for us factually, because Ray did not choose the easy way to make money.

In everything he did, his interests were consistent with the interests of his franchisees."

Ray Kroc worked at his office in San Diego until just a few months before his death in January 1984, at the age of eighty-one. Although he held the title of senior chairman and founder for the last decade of his life, he never stopped working full-time for McDonald's. He enjoyed calling Chef Rene to conspire behind Fred Turner's back about some new product. He watched over the company restaurant just outside his office window like a hawk. When the sky began turning dark, he phoned the manager to remind him to turn on the lights. He studied how fast the cars moved past the drive-thru window, and he pondered how its single cash register handled 40 percent of the store's business while the six registers inside handled the rest. (The insight led to the installation of another window at many drive-thrus, one to handle payment and one for dispensing food.)

But when the complications of two strokes finally put him in the hospital a few months before his death, Kroc sensed he would never again return to work. It upset him that he was still on McDonald's payroll, even though he was no longer physically able to earn his $175,000 yearly salary. When Fred Turner paid him a visit, Kroc from his hospital bed asked Turner—his friend, his protégé, and his son through corporate partnership—to take him off the company payroll.

On his flight to San Diego, Turner had listened to newly discovered dictaphone tapes that Kroc and the McDonald brothers had exchanged in the 1950s, when Kroc was setting up the McDonald's System. In them, the McDonald's founder laid out his basic organizational and operational concepts, and perhaps more than ever before, Turner appreciated just how much of the system's fundamental strength could be traced to Ray Kroc's uncomplicated but honest philosophy of entrepreneurship. Turner did not hesitate in replying to Kroc's payroll request. "No way, Ray, no way," he said. "You've earned your pay for the next hundred years."

Chapter 17
EXPORTING AMERICANA

It's a fever that sooner or later hits all successful corporate executives. Call it empire building. Call it corporate power brokering. Call it executive suite egotism. At some point, a company with a magic touch in one business assumes it can transfer its expertise to another.

Diversification fever ran particularly high in the United States in the late 1960s and early 1970s, and Ray Kroc had a good case of it. As early as 1962, Harry Sonneborn had talked him into buying a restaurant on the South Side of Chicago called Hottinger's. It featured a German beer garden complete with an outdoor bandstand and lawns that looked like putting greens. Sonneborn thought it was unusual enough to franchise an upscale hamburger restaurant and tavern, one whose principal product was an extra large hamburger served on rye bread.

It was McDonald's first diversification. Staffers at the fast-food chain soon became involved in a turnaround effort to make Hottinger's a showcase to impress potential franchisees. Al Bernardin, McDonald's new product manager, took over the operation of the new restaurant. Gerry Newman, McDonald's chief accountant, did Hottinger's books. June Martino even cleaned the washrooms at the restaurant to prepare the place for a wedding reception. And Harry Sonneborn pitched in by working as the restaurant's maître d' on busy weekends.

But the concept was flawed. Too much of the restaurant's overhead was tied up in outdoor dining, a dangerous proposition in Chicago. Even in the summertime a wind shift could send cold breezes off Lake Michigan and empty the packed beer garden, leaving some three dozen outdoor waitresses, bartenders, and band members with little to do but wait around for the end of their shifts to collect their pay. Thus, eighteen months after Sonneborn bought it, Hottinger's folded, and the hope of spinning off a second franchised food chain was dashed. It was a sobering lesson on the risks of diversification. Altogether, Kroc, Sonneborn, and Martino, the three McDonald's owners who had invested in the restaurant, lost $1.3 million on the venture. Indeed, some McDonald's veterans believe the beginnings of the Kroc-Sonneborn fallout can be traced to the Hottinger's fiasco.

But Hottinger's did anything but dampen Kroc's enthusiasm for duplicating McDonald's success elsewhere. He continued to romance other fast-food businesses. He came close to buying Taco Bell and Baskin Robbins, both of which were later acquired by others. Kroc also tried to buy Marie Callendar's, a California chain of pie shops, but when the company rejected his price, he decided to start his own pie shop chain, which he named Jane Dobbins Pie Shops, after his second wife. Kroc built two of the pie shops in the Los Angeles area in 1968, hoping to develop a new fast-food concept he could franchise. He spared no expense. Both were beautiful stores with dining rooms that wrapped around huge, Ferris-wheel-like pie ovens that filled the restaurant with the aroma of freshly baked pies. Kroc even hired a pie consultant at $50,000 a year. But after two years, the two pie shops were still big losers, and Kroc, who in the meantime had divorced Jane and married Joan, lost interest and closed them.

Kroc had the same unhappy experience with Ramond's, the opulent hamburger emporium he developed in the late 1960s in his search for another business to franchise. Featuring a broader menu of sandwiches than the standard hamburger fare at McDonald's, Ramond's was aimed at an upscale urban market. The restaurants were lavishly decorated, and the first two units were located in markets where McDonald's at that time did not go—just off Rodeo Drive in Beverly Hills and near North Michigan Avenue in Chicago. But without a gourmet hamburger to match its lush decor, Ramond's was a concept that was doomed from the start. Both stores were closed within two years, and Ray Kroc's record in developing new restaurants—not unlike his record in new food products—remained unblemished by success.

But Kroc's dabbling with other fast-food formats did not compare to the plunge he almost took into the amusement park business to compete head to head with his World War I comrade, Walt Disney. Kroc had met a promoter on the West Coast by the name of Henry Steele, who sold him on the idea of McDonald's opening a Disneyland-like theme park just northeast of Los Angeles. Based on a western theme, the project was known inside McDonald's as Western World.

When Kroc told the company's officers and directors about his grand scheme for a theme park on a couple of thousand acres of untouched California countryside, they were flabbergasted and, to a man, opposed to the idea. After seeing the land, a rugged but inaccessible terrain that was used in filming *The Lone Ranger* television episodes, McDonald's then director David Wallerstein tried to talk Kroc out of his bold plan.

Better than anyone else associated with Kroc, Wallerstein knew the magnitude of the project he was contemplating, and he knew Kroc was grossly underestimating it. Fifteen years earlier, Wallerstein had been asked by his friend Walt Disney to take a look at vacant land in Anaheim, California, as he related his scheme for a theme park. Disney told Wallerstein, then an executive with ABC, that both NBC and CBS had turned him down on investing in the park and now Disney was turning to the smallest and weakest of the networks for help. Impressed with the plan, Wallerstein and a few associates persuaded the network's board to take a one-third interest in the park and assist in its financing to obtain an afternoon children's show and prime-time feature program Disney proposed making for television. For ABC, which was starving for programming, the deal produced two hit shows (*Mickey Mouse Club* and *Wonderful World of Disney*), and of course, Disneyland's smashing success created a theme park industry. ABC also received concession rights for snack foods in the park in return for its participation.

But no one entering that industry was willing to compete directly with Disney before Kroc proposed doing it. And now Wallerstein was convinced that the move was foolhardy and would deprive McDonald's of funds it badly needed to support Turner's massive store expansion. "Ray thought you could pull a theme park out of the woodwork," Wallerstein says. "But I knew what Walt had gone through. He had the finest technicians in the country working on that park for years. We didn't have those creative resources, and we didn't have an ABC backing us."

Still, opposition from Wallerstein and other directors did not deter a stubborn Kroc. He was enthralled with the project. However, he agreed that initially he would get options on the land—fifteen hundred acres—using his own money. McDonald's hired consultants to conduct feasibility studies on Western World, which indicated that the first phase of the park alone would cost more than $30 million.

As McDonald's drifted closer to a "go" decision on Western World, the outside directors became more opposed to it. And when Kroc announced his divorce from Jane and his marriage to Joan, they believed the time was right for dissuading Kroc from his costly and risky scheme. "After Fred became president, Ray was unsettled in his life and was looking for other things," says director Don Lubin. "But when he married Joan, there was no further need for diversions." Thus, when Lubin, who was both McDonald's outside counsel and Kroc's personal attorney, suggested that Western World should be scrubbed in light of all the changes going on in Kroc's personal life, the founder agreed. Virtually everyone in the company believed that McDonald's had just dodged a bullet.

Yet, as disconcerting as Western World was to him, Turner caught his own case of diversification fever when he took the helm of the company. In the late 1960s, he launched his own search for another growth business, particularly one where McDonald's might apply its impressive franchising and real estate development skills. Investment bankers marched a parade of acquisition candidates by him, and Turner entertained every one. He looked at buying hotels, steak houses, barbecue chains, and florist shops. He even considered buying a major stake in the Chicago Bears professional football franchise that was being offered for sale by owner George Halas.

He also caught Kroc's amusement park bug. He looked into acquiring the troubled Astro World theme park in Houston, built by Judge Roy Hofheinz, who had developed the Astrodome. But Turner was more intrigued with an amusement park proposed by Tom Klutznick, son of the former secretary of commerce and the developer of Chicago's Water Tower Place, the luxury high-rise hotel, condominium, and shopping center. Even as Water Tower was being developed, Klutznick had dreams of a more ambitious project—an amusement park the size of Disneyland, but under one roof. It was never built, but for a moment Turner was intrigued by the idea.

It took two years for Turner to get his acquisition fantasies out of his head, and when he did, he had more appreciation for what he already had in McDonald's. "I spent a lot of time looking into each opportunity," he recalls, "but each time I kept thinking, 'Oh, hell, that's not as good a business as the one we're in.' "

In retrospect, it is fortunate that McDonald's flirtation with diversification never became a heavy affair, because it is unlikely that it would have found another business with profits matching the 20 percent or better return on equity that McDonald's had reported for each year since Turner became president and eventually chose internal growth over diversification as a long-term strategy. The false starts in diversifying had at least forced McDonald's to study both routes, and "the better choice was obvious," Turner says. "The hamburger business was a business we knew, and it was a marvelous business. Our orientation from then on was to stick to our own knitting."

But by the beginning of the 1970s, it was also becoming obvious that McDonald's by the end of the decade would become a cash machine generating many more dollars than it could prudently spend on its domestic hamburger business. If diversification was ruled out, the only other alternative was to do what no American retailer had ever done—successfully expand its service worldwide. "The rationale for going international was as simple as determining that the market was there," Turner says.

That understates the significance of the move. The market was there for a lot of American services that never capitalized on it. It was there for Neiman-Marcus, Saks Fifth Avenue, and other high-fashion department stores that remained essentially domestic operations. It was there for J. C. Penney and Sears, Roebuck and Company and other American mass merchandising chains that stuck mostly to their home base. And it was there for dozens of specialty chains that revolutionized American retailing in the 1970s, but which somehow did not export the concept.

In 1970, when McDonald's made its first big push abroad, it was indeed treading on foreign soil. Aside from the international oil companies, which were marketing a commodity product whose raw material they controlled, retailing was primarily a native business. Occasionally U.S. retailers would test the waters in Canada, but rarely did they go outside North America. Even massive Sears, easily the most international of all American-based retailers before McDonald's, in 1986 derived only 11 percent of its merchandising sales from foreign operations, all of it from Canada and Mexico. In the mid-1960s, a few fast-food chains began to experiment with foreign operations, but those were notable neither for their scope nor their success.

Thus, when McDonald's began expanding internationally, it encountered none of the dozen or so hamburger competitors it battled in the States. But the market was even more virgin than that. Most countries had no locally based fast-food outlets either. Indeed, eating out—an increasingly routine experience for Americans—was an uncommon experience in most foreign markets. In Europe particularly, restaurants were still locked into traditions of full linen service, waiters in black tie, wine stewards, and multicourse meals. There were virtually no family restaurants, and thus for the middle class eating out was always a special occasion.

To succeed abroad, McDonald's had to introduce a major cultural change. To a lesser degree, of course, the chain had faced the same challenge in the United States two decades before. "For the old-timers, one of the really stimulating things about going international was that it meant pioneering again," Turner says.

But McDonald's abroad was doing more than pioneering everyday food service to the middle classes. It was attempting to export something that was now endemic to American life but totally foreign everywhere else. Quick service food was uniquely American. So were drive-ins and self-service restaurants. And the food it was exporting was as different as was its method of retailing. Hamburgers, french fries, and milk shakes were an integral part of American culture, but they were not mass marketed in most foreign countries. Indeed, in Japan and other Far Eastern countries, McDonald's was faced not only with the task of introducing the hamburger but with an even more fundamental challenge of establishing beef as a common food. All things considered, the job of going international seemed even more complicated than diversifying.

Despite that, McDonald's success abroad is one of the best-kept secrets of American business. In the business press, the story has been buried under daily reminders of the growth of the U.S. trade deficit and repeated stories about the bombardment of the American market by cheaper and better-manufactured imports. Yet, in the last fifteen years, while old-line U.S. manufacturers were losing their grip on world markets, McDonald's was establishing its presence around the globe. While Japanese and German auto producers were devouring the American market, McDonald's was quietly becoming the number one food service chain in Japan and Germany, not to mention the U.K., Canada, and Australia.

Indeed, McDonald's Americanization of the global food service industry is one of the most promising developments in U.S. trade relations. McDonald's, after all, is exporting what has become the centerpiece of American industry—the service sector. It is leading the way in exporting America's well-developed systems for conveniently serving consumer needs, and if its success thus far is any indication of the potential, the service sector could join the high-tech and agricultural industries as a prime source of American exports.

Once its orphan child, McDonald's International is now the fastest-growing segment in the system and the best hope of future growth. In 1992, McDonald's generated $8.6 billion in food sales outside the United States or fully 39 percent of its $21.9 billion in worldwide system sales. Ten years before, only 19 percent of its sales came from overseas. Now, the shift to international is accelerating. Of the 675 restaurants added to the system in 1992, fully 480 were built outside the United States, and in the last four years alone McDonald's has entered fifteen new foreign markets. As a result, by the end of 1992, a total of 4,134 of McDonald's 14,000 restaurants—1 in every 3—were located in one of sixty-five foreign countries where McDonald's operates.

In many of those countries, McDonald's is now the leading food service chain. That is the case in Japan, where by mid-1992 there were 865 McDonald's restaurants; in Canada, where there were another 642 units; in Germany, where there were 391; in the U.K., which had 445 McDonald's; and in Australia, with 304. In fact, by the end of 1992, sales of McDonald's International approached the *domestic* revenues of McDonald's largest American competitors, and fully 44 percent of the company's 1992 operating income came from outside the United States.

What is more surprising than the scope of its success abroad is that McDonald's cracked the international market with more or less the same formula it had perfected in the United States. Given the enormous lifestyle differences between domestic and foreign markets, a unique approach to international expansion might have been expected. McDonald's might have greatly modified its system to adapt to foreign cultures. Instead, it stuck to the basics of its system and changed the cultures to fit it. "People told us that we'd never be able to franchise abroad or buy real estate or sell hamburgers," observed former Executive Vice President Brent Cameron. "We just plowed dumbly ahead using the same old system that we had in the U.S. It was like reliving history."

Indeed, whenever McDonald's International departed from its tried-and-true franchising methods, it stumbled. In issuing its first foreign license in 1965, for example, McDonald's sold John Gibson and Oscar Goldstein, its legendary Washington franchisees, the rights to develop the Caribbean under a so-called developmental franchise.

That meant that McDonald's provided no field supervision of the Caribbean stores, developed no real estate, and set up no suppliers. All of that was to be done by Gibson and Goldstein, and instead of charging the typical 3-percent service fee and 8.5-percent rent, McDonald's collected a mere 0.5 percent of the sales of the Caribbean stores in addition to a one-time franchise fee of $10,000 per unit. The Caribbean franchise put up some twenty-five restaurants in Puerto Rico, Panama, Nicaragua, Honduras, and El Salvador, but when Goldstein pulled back from daily involvement in the venture, it lost his operational expertise. The financially oriented Gibson was running the show, and when he ran it into the ground, McDonald's—with a stake in only 0.5 percent of the Caribbean revenues—had little incentive to pull it out of its dive.

Developmental franchising was plainly not the secret to McDonald's franchising success in the United States, where the chain carefully scrutinized the operations of all its franchised units, built a sophisticated supply system, developed all of the store real estate, and made its money by earning a sizable percentage of a store's sales. The Caribbean franchise had been sold by Sonneborn, and it clearly reflected his loss of faith in McDonald's. In early 1967, months before his departure, Sonneborn all but gave away the potentially lucrative Canadian market under developmental franchises sold to George Tidball, who got the franchising rights for western Canada, and George Cohon, who got the license for eastern Canada. They paid only $7,500 to $10,000 per unit and 1 percent on sales to McDonald's, and by the time Turner bought back both territories in 1970, both franchises were losing money. Tidball had gotten caught up in a confusing array of sublicensing arrangements with investors not involved in store operations, while Cohon, though a dedicated operator, proved to be insufficiently capitalized to develop a commanding presence in the eastern Canadian market.

Turner concluded that McDonald's Corporation had to be as heavily involved overseeing its foreign restaurants as it was in its American operations, but that type of involvement was worthwhile only if McDonald's had a lot more at risk than 1 percent of international hamburger sales. So, Turner deemphasized the developmental licensing approach when he launched McDonald's international drive in earnest in 1970. But he, too, erred by departing from the McDonald's franchising formula. Selecting The Netherlands as the initial market for development, he entered into a fifty-fifty joint venture with the country's leading supermarket chain, Albert Heijn. McDonald's now had a major stake, but it also had a corporation as a partner, rather than an individual owner-operator—the only type of franchising partner it would accept in the United States. The idea was to use Heijn's expertise in setting up food supplies in Europe, but whatever McDonald's gained on that score it lost by not having a local entrepreneur running the stores.

Turner also ignored the chief management lesson that McDonald's had learned in the United States—that operations-oriented hamburger chains are best built by operations-oriented managers who are promoted through the ranks. While McDonald's new president was placing operations specialists into every other line position, he hired an outsider to implement the corporate plan to develop the foreign market. He was a seasoned management consultant with thorough knowledge of international markets, but unfortunately, many of the early mistakes McDonald's made abroad can be attributed to the fact that the consultant it hired had no background in McDonald's operations and thus little appreciation for the subtleties of its fast-food system.

Whatever the cause, The Netherlands experiment turned into a series of small mistakes that added up to a long-term disaster. Following the American experience, the stores were built in the suburbs. However, all the retail action was urban because the central cities in Europe had not deteriorated as they had in America, and the suburbs were devoid of commercial development. And instead of introducing the standard McDonald's menu, the joint venture eliminated the popular Quarter Pounder and added a couple of Dutch favorites—applesauce and deep-fried chicken croquettes. "We got spooked into thinking that we had to have indigenous foods," Turner says.

It took years for the Dutch stores to overcome those early mistakes, even after McDonald's bought out the Heijn interest in 1975. But if the perennial losses of the Dutch operation became a tribute to McDonald's persistence abroad, Holland would also prove to be a valuable learning experience.

In fact, far from deterring McDonald's from its plan to develop the international market, the early disappointments abroad encouraged it to redouble its efforts. It quickly became obvious that McDonald's—though now wildly successful in the United States—could take no shortcuts in developing foreign markets. But as McDonald's began applying the lessons of its initial miscues in the Caribbean, Canada, and The Netherlands, it became apparent that the vision of an international chain was no mirage.

Nowhere were the fruits of the learning experience more rewarding than in Canada. As soon as Sonneborn sold the two Canadian franchises for a song, Ray Kroc started regretting it. Indeed, when he made his first trip to eastern Canada in 1968 to dedicate McDonald's first store there in London, Ontario, he immediately offered to buy back the exclusive development rights for the territory from George Cohon and his partner, Ted Tannebaum.

Cohon and Tannebaum had paid just $70,000 for the rights to build their first seven units in eastern Canada, but at a dinner on the eve of the first unit's grand opening, Kroc stunned those gathered by announcing his offer to pay all of the partners' debts plus $1 million to buy back their exclusive territory. The partnership had yet to sell its first hamburger and already it was looking at a possible bonanza.

As Kroc spoke, Cohon's father jabbed his son. "God, is he serious?" he asked. "He wouldn't say it if he didn't mean it, Dad," the younger Cohon replied. But Cohon did not give the offer a second thought. "I didn't get into McDonald's to open one store and sell," he says. "Besides, if Ray was offering a million, the franchise had to be worth a lot more."

It was. Only two years later, Turner—eager to get out from the developmental licenses and invest more heavily in Canada—offered to buy back the eastern territory. The partners by then had fourteen restaurants, but their operation was losing $1 million a year, and since McDonald's was getting only 1 percent of sales, it had little incentive to turn things around. This time, Cohon agreed to sell in a series of deals totaling $6 million. He was convinced that Canada was as good a fastfood market as the United States, but he needed to raise McDonald's visibility in Canada by building many more stores, and an infusion of capital from Oak Brook would accomplish that.

But, as some McDonald's directors saw it, Turner was paying dearly to buy a losing business. Criticism of "Turner's folly" increased a year later when Turner bought out Tidball's franchise in western Canada, which also was losing money at nineteen stores. Overall, McDonald's paid $15 million to acquire forty-three losing Canadian stores, and the fact that Turner in the process had acquired the rights to develop new units throughout Canada did not impress his critics. "People who did not understand my desire to make the Canadian deals thought Canada was the land of snow and moose," Turner explains. "But those who had seen how dynamic Canada's cities were, they understood."

But Turner also knew that Cohon had built a strong operations team and would stay on as president of McDonald's Canada to direct an all-out assault on the market. It was not unusual, of course, for U.S. companies to operate Canadian subsidiaries and consider Canada little more than an extension of the American market, but Turner wanted to take a different approach. The secret of McDonald's success in the United States was due in large measure to the chain's reliance on independent local operators with freedom to develop their markets as they saw fit. Thus Turner gave Cohon the same leeway as an exclusive franchisee, plus the one thing he lacked—enough capital.

Cohon used that freedom to make his McDonald's operation seem as Canadian as a Canadian-owned company. While McDonald's major American suppliers were all nearby, Cohon insisted on developing all new Canadian suppliers and on conducting his company's banking only with Canadian institutions. Furthermore, more than half of McDonald's stores in Canada are franchised—every one to a Canadian operator. "We sell to Canadians, make our profits from Canadians, and we support the Canadian economy by buying from Canadians," Cohon reasons.

But McDonald's Canadian president went well beyond that. He got considerable local press coverage by becoming personally involved in Canadian charities and civic activities. When Eaton's Department Store announced that it could no longer afford to support its seventy-seven-year tradition of its annual Christmas parade in Toronto —Canada's equivalent to the Macy's parade—Cohon made front page news by organizing a fund-raising effort to save the parade. He also became deeply involved in politics, even to the point of helping to organize political fund-raising dinners and of developing close political friendships that went all the way to the top of government. One of those friends, then Prime Minister Pierre Trudeau, appointed Cohon to the board of directors of the Canadian postal service. Cohon also began talking like a Canadian, making typically nationalistic comments on how "Washington can't think of Canada as its fifty-first state" and observing that "our lakes are all getting polluted because of all the stuff coming from the United States." But without question, Cohon made his most dramatic effort to project a Canadian image in 1975: he became a Canadian citizen. "McDonald's is an integral part of the

Canadian economy," Cohon says, "and it's important that McDonald's expands internationally with citizens of the local countries."

Cohon argues that his shift in citizenship was made simply because he intends to stay in Canada and wants the right to vote in its elections. Nevertheless, it has obviously enhanced his ability to position McDonald's in Canada as a Canadian-run operation, and that has had its own marketing benefits. In his frequent speeches at universities, Cohon makes a point to publicize his company's patronage of Canadian suppliers, but occasionally he takes some heat from students who complain that the company is still 100 percent American-owned. "But I'm a Canadian citizen," he commonly replies. "And while you were born into it, I adopted it by choice." Says Cohon: "It usually stops them dead in their tracks."

Cohon's all-Canadian operation and his penchant for gaining favorable coverage in the Canadian press did wonders in countering the resistance McDonald's might have expected—particularly in the eastern provinces—to anything that further Americanized the Canadian culture. Still, a good local image alone was not enough to crack the Canadian market.

Frustrated by a string of losing years and by his failure to raise his stores' average sales volumes to anything approaching those in the United States, Cohon and Turner agreed that a much bolder measure was needed. Thus, in 1971, Cohon took a step McDonald's had never taken in the United States and likely would not have taken in Canada if the operation had been run out of Oak Brook: he cut prices 20 percent across the board. "We had to do something dramatic to get Canadians to come in and try the product," Cohon says.

It worked. Per-unit sales jumped 25 percent in one year, and even when normal pricing was restored two years later, sales in the Canadian stores continued to improve. And with heavy funding from its corporate parent, McDonald's Canada was the only fast-food chain aggressively building stores in Canada in the early 1970s. By the end of the decade, it had nearly a monopoly in Canada's fast-food market—one that turned Turner's acquisition a decade before into solid gold. In 1993, McDonald's 674 units in Canada recorded average sales of $2.3 million (Canadian dollars) per unit, almost 15 percent above the chain's worldwide average and highest of any major operation in the system. In that year alone, McDonald's Canada generated a pretax income of $83.6 million—more than five times what Turner paid for it.

Success in Canada clearly proved the wisdom of extending to

international operations the same franchising concepts and local operator control that was the secret of McDonald's success in the United
States. But it did not prove that an American fast-food retailer could
make it big in a completely different culture—with an American
franchising scheme, an American menu, and an American concept of
an entrepreneur on the premises. McDonald's Japan did that.

And of the three ingredients, it was the entrepreneur McDonald's
chose as its partner in Japan that was the most critical element to its
success there. His name is Den Fujita, the founder and owner of a
Japanese import company specializing in handbags, shoes, and ap-
parel. Most outsiders think of the Japanese as exporters, not importers,
and they picture Japanese businessmen as team players, consensus
decision makers, traditionalists, and lifetime loyalists of one of Japan's
corporate giants. Fujita did not fit the mold.

He was, in fact, as much of an opportunistic entrepreneur as Ray
Kroc. He had started his own company at age twenty-five, importing
golf clubs and Florsheim shoes. But he decided that women were a
better target for Western imports, since they reorder every time the
winds of fashion shift. And when the big name European designers
became international brand names for mass-produced garments and
accessories, Fujita correctly foresaw a huge market for anyone capitalizing on the Japanese woman's fascination with designer name tags.
His company became Japan's largest importer of boutique fashions
from such designers as Christian Dior, and even today Fujita is the
world's largest commercial buyer of Dior handbags.

Through his trading representative in Chicago, Fujita had learned
of McDonald's interest in international expansion, and from his many
business trips to the States he was familiar with the popularity of American fast food. He also was convinced that the time was right for the
Japanese culture to absorb yet another Western concept.

But Fujita wanted to run McDonald's in Japan as a Japanese entity
autonomous from McDonald's headquarters in Oak Brook, because he
was certain that Japanese consumers would not satisfy their desire for
Western products if it meant buying them from an American company.
"All Japanese have an inferiority complex about anything that is foreign, because everything in our culture has come from the outside,"
he observes. "Our writing comes from China, our Buddhism from Ko-
rea, and after the war everything new, from Coca-Cola to IBM, came
from America." But he argues that Japan's admiration for anything

Western is tempered by another side of the Japanese psyche. "Japanese people are basically anti-foreigner," Fujita explains. "We don't like the Chinese, we don't like the Koreans, and we especially don't like the Americans because we lost the war to them."

Fujita's conclusion: American fast food could be a big hit in a Japanese culture seeking to identify with the success of the West, but the company that attempts to sell it must look 100 percent Japanese— from the boss down to the crews in the stores. In short, the Japanese might buy the American hamburger, providing it wasn't positioned as an American import. "If I insisted that this was something that came from America, the Japanese would say, 'This is American, and we don't like it because we don't like Americans,'" Fujita explains.

Fujita had the entrepreneurial credentials McDonald's was now looking for abroad. So, in 1971, it agreed to form a Japanese joint venture with McDonald's controlling 50 percent and Fujita and Daiichiya Baking Company splitting the other 50 percent. Fujita was made president and chief executive of McDonald's Japan, and he soon bought out Daiichiya's interest. From the beginning Fujita called the shots in introducing McDonald's to Japan. Confident that he could import a concept as foreign as the hamburger to a culture whose diet was oriented to fish and rice, he insisted that there was no need to tailor McDonald's menu to Japanese tastes in the way McDonald's had attempted—unsuccessfully—to localize its menu in Holland. Rather, he decided to sell the hamburger to the Japanese as a "revolutionary" product. He gave lectures on it at universities and attracted considerable press coverage by making outrageous statements about the hamburger's properties and by revealing his plans to put hamburger outlets throughout Japan. "The reason Japanese people are so short and have yellow skins is because they have eaten nothing but fish and rice for two thousand years," he told reporters. "If we eat McDonald's hamburgers and potatoes for a thousand years, we will become taller, our skin will become white, and our hair blond."

Fujita also ignored McDonald's advice to begin building his stores in the suburbs. The lesson about suburban sites in Holland was not yet clear, and managers in Oak Brook were still insisting that the chain should build its foundation in each new foreign market on the same suburban foundation that supported McDonald's success in America. Fujita strongly disagreed. McDonald's first unit in Japan, he argued, had to go in the Ginza, the international shopping bazaar in downtown

Tokyo. It is where all new imported products get their initial exposure to the Japanese market. It is also the place where one million people pass each day, including thousands of Americans. "I figured that American tourists eating hamburgers in the Ginza would be an eye-catcher," Fujita says. "Japanese seeing that would think, 'Americans are eating it; it must be good.'"

But the crowded Ginza posed one major problem. New retail space there was precious and rents were prohibitive. Yet, through his contacts at Mitsukoshi, Japan's largest and oldest department store, Fujita succeeded in getting five hundred square feet of ground-floor space in what had been the purse department Fujita supplied. Though it would open to the street, the space was still only one-fifth the normal size of a McDonald's store, but Fujita made it work by designing a compact kitchen and by using stand-up customer counters instead of seats.

But the terms of the lease were even more restrictive. Mitsukoshi did not want McDonald's to disrupt its normal retail business, and it allowed just one day—a holiday—for construction of the store. Fujita had from 6:00 P.M. on Sunday to 9:00 A.M. on Tuesday to construct his tiny McDonald's—thirty-nine hours to complete a construction job that normally takes three months.

The location was too good to pass up, and Fujita accepted the terms. To prepare, he rented a warehouse on the outskirts of Tokyo where his construction engineers and crews began practicing how to assemble a McDonald's unit in record time. Detailed procedures and schedules were set for each of the seventy workmen. They went through three trial runs—assembling the store, tearing it down, and doing it all again. On the third try, the crew got their time down to thirty-six hours.

Fujita telexed Chicago that the grand opening of McDonald's first Japanese store was set for Tuesday, July 20, 1971, and Ray Kroc and the other McDonald's officials showed up in Tokyo on Saturday, the 17th. The next morning, one of the visiting McDonald's managers, Ken Strong, asked to see the store. Fujita happily took Strong to the window at Mitsukoshi's where workmen would begin construction that evening. "Here's where it goes," Fujita said, beaming as he pointed to the best window in all of Tokyo. "But where's the store?" Strong asked.

Strong could not believe Fujita's explanation. "Mr. Fujita, grand opening is the day after tomorrow," Strong warned. "How can you make it?" "Ah, Mr. Strong," Fujita reassured, "we will do it." When he went back to the hotel, Strong related the story to an incredulous Kroc. "We're in big trouble," he told Kroc. "We're opening in two days and nothing is there."

The construction crew performed their well-rehearsed maneuvers flawlessly, and when the McDonald's founder showed up for opening ceremonies, the store was ready. But it was when the store opened for business that the real magic began. The unit rang up $3,000 on the first day, and within a few months it set a new McDonald's record with a one-day volume of $6,000. The internationalization of the McDonald's hamburger had begun.

The expansion program that followed in Japan was as frantic as the construction of the first store. Fujita liked reminding Kroc that both of them had been born in the Year of the Tiger, and he wasted no time proving that he could expand McDonald's in Japan as boldly as Kroc had in the United States. Even before the first store opened, Fujita started a Hamburger University in Japan to train store managers, and he quickly assembled a staff of twenty headquarters people to supervise an expansion program that has never been equaled by a new McDonald's franchise. Three days after the first store opened, Fujita opened another in Shinjuku-ku, near one of Tokyo's commuter train terminals. A day later, he opened a third unit. After just eighteen months, Fujita's team was operating nineteen McDonald's throughout Japan, virtually all of them in urban centers. And all of them succeeded by marketing only standard McDonald's fare. "Japan was really the acid test," Turner says. "After that we realized that the American menu could fly abroad and that modifications were not needed or at best would be minor."

But Fujita was careful to make marketing modifications that were needed for an American retailing concept to succeed in Japan. He made it clear that McDonald's Japan was run by the Japanese. He was quick to advertise on television, and he made certain that the spots had a Japanese flavor. Convinced that McDonald's would have better luck selling the new hamburger product to Japan's youth, he aimed virtually all his advertising at children and young families. "The eating habits of older Japanese are very conservative," he explains. "But we could teach the children that the hamburger was something good." Fujita even changed the pronounciation of the name of the restaurants because he knew how difficult it was for Japanese to pronounce Mc-

Donald's. The change made pronunciation simple: Makudonaldo. For the same reason, Ronald McDonald became Donald McDonald in Japan.

Fujita's adaptions were not always so easy for his American partner to accept. On one visit to Japan, Turner was visibly upset when he caught a glimpse of the interior of a unit in a university area. Decorating the walls were poster-sized pictures of leather-jacketed members of a motorcycle gang "one shade removed" from Hell's Angels. Fujita tried to calm McDonald's senior chairman. "Turner San, you don't understand, this is very Western and young Japanese people like Western," he told Turner. "But, Den San, we are not a hangout place and this looks like a motorcycle gang hangout," Turner replied. "No problem, Turner San," Fujita said. "Japanese people don't understand the fine points."

While Fujita had enormous freedom in marketing, McDonald's would not allow deviation from its proven operating principles. Yet, in some respects the Japanese management culture was too regimented for the McDonald's System. Although McDonald's stores rely heavily on the type of teamwork and uniform operations the Japanese are known for, Turner also knew the chain was equally dependent on the differences it encourages among its individual store operators and the unique approaches they take to their markets. That was the key to McDonald's grass-roots creativity.

Duplicating that creativity was not easy in the Japanese management system, where seniority determines advancement, where decisions are made collectively, and where the "good" employee is someone who does exactly what he or she is told to do. When he first visited Japan, Turner noticed immediately how McDonald's Japanese store personnel followed the operating manual to the letter. The grill men were a good example. Turner says: "We've been trying to get twenty-eight thousand grill persons to lay the first row of patties four inches from the left of the grill, closer to the heating element. But in the U.S., with our Yankee mentality, you watch these grill men and they don't give a damn what the system says, because they've got a better way. But in Japan, you tell a grill man only once how to lay the patties, and he puts them there every time. I'd been looking for that one-hundred-percent compliance for thirty years, and now that I finally found it in Japan, it made me very nervous."

When Turner realized that the system was more threatened by Japanese regimentation than it was aided by it, he decided that Mc-

Donald's had to introduce more than an American hamburger to Japan. It needed to influence Japan's management culture.

While all of Fujita's fifteen hundred managers are Japanese, his company is not run in typical Japanese fashion. In part, that is because Turner placed one of his own managers in Fujita's operation. John Asahara, a Japanese-American who worked with Fujita's company from its beginning, was responsible for introducing the American management techniques that McDonald's has found critical to success in fast food.

With Fujita's blessing, Asahara built a young and creative operations team, which he sheltered from the potentially stifling influence of Japanese management culture, where most power rests with more traditional senior executives. In fact, when operating decisions at McDonald's Japan ran counter to top management desires, Asahara was the one who took the heat. Continually on the lookout for young and aggressive operations managers, he encouraged their promotion ahead of more senior staffers—a direct challenge to Japanese traditions of promotion by seniority. He even convinced the Japanese company of the wisdom of using part-time assistant managers. The practice is critical to efficiently managing the demand peaks and valleys of a fast-food operation but it is totally foreign to the Japanese, who equate management to full-time, lifelong employment.

Yet, Asahara accomplished everything not by communicating the dictates of the American partner but by patiently teaching that American operating concepts—at least in fast food—produce the efficiency that the Japanese respect. Although he is an influential figure in McDonald's in Japan as an operations consultant and senior vice president, Asahara maintains an extremely low profile. In short, he walked a fine line—bending traditions without challenging them. Said Asahara: "I keep my mouth shut and I look like any other Japanese. Nobody outside McDonald's knows I exist over here [in Japan]."

The marriage of an American menu and operating system with Japanese marketing concepts has produced the most successful example of an American retailer taking root overseas. The chain's success in Japan demonstrated that an American fast-food hamburger system was exportable to a totally foreign culture. In 1983, revenues of McDonald's in Japan exceeded those of the country's largest native restaurant chain, the two-thousand-unit Sushi Company. And Fujita's company is showing no signs of letting up. By 1993, McDonald's in Japan had 1,040 restaurants and total annual sales of more than $1.6 billion, and Fujita surpassed Canada in 1988, taking the lead in McDonald's International.

More important, however, Fujita's success made it clear to McDonald's that to succeed in retailing abroad it needed a partnership that could give McDonald's a homegrown flavor in each foreign market without deviating from the fundamentals that made McDonald's work in the United States. Indeed, its partnership in Japan gave McDonald's a model it could use in licensing throughout the world—dependence on a local entrepreneur with a substantial ownership position in a joint venture and even more autonomy than that of franchisees in the United States. In short, Japan proved that the key to success in the international market was the same as it was at home: local control by local owner/operators.

The policy resulted in such a diverse array of local joint-venture partners that McDonald's—now the most international of all retailing organizations—is anything but a typical multinational corporation. Rather, it is a loose federation of independent local retailers who happen to market the same thing—a well-defined fast-food menu and operating system—but who tailor their marketing approach to their country's different cultures. Although McDonald's foreign partnerships vary from country to country, the chain entered most foreign countries by forming a joint venture which involves 50 percent ownership by McDonald's and 50 percent by a local entrepreneur who runs the foreign operation as a mini-McDonald's. In some cases, the stores in those countries are owned and operated by a joint-venture company, but in other cases they are licensed to local franchisees, who have the same relationship with the local McDonald's company as franchisees in the United States have with McDonald's in Oak Brook.

Aside from their entrepreneurial bent, no two foreign partners have similar backgrounds or even similar arrangements with McDonald's. Paul Lederhausen, the first licensee in Sweden, where McDonald's has sixty-eight units, was a Swedish wholesaler of American-made restaurant equipment who discovered McDonald's on his many trips to the States. Daniel Ng, the joint venture partner of the McDonald's seventy-one-restaurant operation in Hong Kong, was a chemical engineer who did research for seven years at Chicago's noted Institute of Gas Technology before he returned to his native Hong Kong and became a venture capitalist. Robert Kwan, the joint-venture partner with fifty-two stores in Singapore, had a small wholesale toy operation before taking an equity interest in McDonald's Singapore. Peter

Rodenbeck, the partner in Rio de Janeiro, was an investment banker in Rio. Saul Kahan, one of McDonald's partners in Mexico, was a new-car sales manager in Mexico City. Obviously, in selecting its foreign owner-operators, McDonald's applied one of the most important lessons learned in the United States—that entrepreneurs from other fields typically do well in McDonald's and traditional restaurateurs often do not.

In English-speaking countries, McDonald's capitalized on the chance to enter into joint ventures with entrepreneurs who knew the McDonald's System cold—its American franchisees. Bob Rhea, Turner's longtime friend and five-store licensee in Cleveland, became an equity partner in the U.K., and Donn Wilson, a six-store operator in Dayton, became McDonald's managing director in Australia. But in both cases, McDonald's was careful to include a native influence. Geoffrey Wade, an English investor with real estate experience, became a minority owner in the U.K. company, and Wilson selected Peter Ritchie, an Australian real estate specialist, as his second in command; and when Wilson resigned as managing director of McDonald's Australia in 1974, Ritchie succeeded him.

Even when McDonald's entered a new foreign market through a wholly owned subsidiary, it opted for local control and autonomy. It selected the experienced Dutch food service executive Tony Klaus to run its German affiliate. When a plane crash in the Swiss Alps claimed the lives of Klaus and top international managers, McDonald's promoted a young and inexperienced German operations manager to become the new managing director rather than send a more experienced American replacement. Thus Walter Rettenwender, at the age of twenty-seven, took over the helm of a German subsidiary that was already McDonald's third-largest foreign operation with forty-two stores and annual sales exceeding $40 million.

Despite their diverse backgrounds, there are some common threads that run through most of McDonald's managing directors overseas that provide insight into the chain's unique success on foreign soil. For example, while most of the international partners are foreign by birth, virtually all of them are not traditionalists in their homeland. Indeed, most have an affinity for American business practices and American entrepreneurs, and most have spent considerable time in the United States.

"Coming to the States was like getting a vitamin injection," recalls Swedish partner Lederhausen, who saw his first McDonald's while on one of many trips to Greenville, South Carolina, where the barbequing equipment he sold in Sweden was manufactured. "Americans seemed more alert, more aggressive, and were more willing to try new things." And Australian Chairman Ritchie took his job with McDonald's because he wanted to be involved in an American business. "I always admired the U.S. approach to things," he says. "American companies seemed more efficient and aggressive than Australian companies."

Furthermore, McDonald's succeeded in attracting abroad the same type of independent-minded entrepreneurs Kroc had recruited in the early days of the chain—people willing to take a huge gamble introducing food products and systems that were unknown in their countries. When he told friends of his shift from venture capital to fast food, Hong Kong's Ng recalls that "the pessimism was pervasive. The consensus was that the Chinese eat rice, not hamburgers. But since I was Chinese, I knew Chinese people at least didn't hate the hamburger, and I concluded that if I could sell the best quality product in a clean environment and at a reasonable price, I'd have a chance." When Lederhausen gave up his profitable restaurant equipment wholesaling trade and invested all his savings in developing McDonald's in Sweden, he encountered—and ignored—similar skepticism. Former customers warned him that Swedes would not eat hamburgers, and journalists asked why he wanted to introduce "plastic food" to Sweden. "Hamburgers are wholesome food," he insisted, "just like Swedish meatballs, only flat."

By recruiting local entrepreneurs as its partners abroad, McDonald's was in a splendid position to operate as a local retailer, avoiding the distasteful image of a huge American multinational corporation with designs on a global market. That was vital because retailing is by its nature a local enterprise. And McDonald's was particularly vulnerable to local resentment, since it was attempting to change part of the native culture—what people eat. Den Fujita had shown that the way to convert foreigners to American eating habits was by first allowing its management abroad to be influenced by the very foreign culture it wanted to change. "We don't bill our international operation as an American company, because people abroad are sensitive about Americans owning their local businesses," observed former Executive Vice President Brent Cameron, who became the second president of McDonald's International. "Americans didn't understand that sensitivity until the Arabs came over and started buying *our* businesses."

Yet, expanding through local partners was only half of the secret to franchising abroad. Giving those partners nearly complete freedom to develop local approaches to the market was the other. "Other guys who run American subsidiaries in Australia can't believe the autonomy I'm given," says Ritchie. "In fact, I never cease to be amazed by it myself."

There are even times when Ritchie has hesitated to use the power he knows he has. Even though he is free to make his own real estate deals without interference from Oak Brook, he felt compelled recently to get Turner's personal approval of a downtown site in Sydney that he wanted to buy because the deal was big even by McDonald's standards: $4.5 million. That was two or three times higher than some of the most expensive restaurant sites in Europe. Thus, when Turner was visiting Australia, Ritchie insisted on taking him around the site several times. When the inspection was through, Turner broke a long silence. "Why are you showing me this?" he asked. "You haven't asked me for a real estate approval for ten years. Why start now?"

In giving such free reign to its foreign partners, McDonald's was choosing action over bureaucratic review and allowing its youthful foreign presidents to learn by making their own mistakes. It seems a reasonable approach for international operations, and yet other fast-food chains rarely operate that way. Rettenwender, former director of McDonald's Germany, noted that German managers of other American-owned fast-food chains invariably have to clear their decisions through layers of decision makers at corporate headquarters in the United States. By contrast, Rettenwender was shocked when he was given the complete power at age twenty-seven to decide for himself how to spend the advertising budget, what products to promote, how many new stores to open, and what property to buy. "I was given the responsibility before I was really ready for it," he said. "But that makes you grow into the job fast. It was like learning to swim by being thrown in the water. At first you're almost drowning, but then suddenly, *Freischwimmen*—you swim free."

Even when the decisions of its foreign partners run counter to the preferences of its managers in Oak Brook, McDonald's nearly always yields, particularly in areas of marketing. Giving marketing freedom to franchisees was nothing new to McDonald's, but because of the cultural differences that existed in foreign markets, local partners had to have even greater leeway in marketing.

Den Fujita used that freedom to create the impression in Japan that McDonald's was almost a Japanese invention. McDonald's in Oak Brook might strongly suggest a new marketing tack, but the Japanese president insists on making the final decision. When Oak Brook wanted the Japanese affiliate to participate in an international soccer game promotion, Fujita flatly refused because soccer is not a popular game in Japan. Still, he telexed Oak Brook the following: "Regarding soccer, will seriously consider." McDonald's corporate managers long ago had broken that particular Japanese code, and Fujita's message came in loud and clear. "It is against our custom to say no," Fujita explains. "So when I say 'seriously consider' to Oak Brook, it means 'screw you.'"

But while Fujita kept the McDonald's System intact, some of the chain's international managing directors initially did not follow his lead and used their autonomy to make major changes in menu and store format that no franchisee could make in the United States. In Australia, the menu was designed to cater to Australian tastes; as a result, Ritchie's initial units featured English-style fish and chips instead of the regular McDonald's Filet-O-Fish sandwich. The biggest seller was not a hamburger but a fried chicken product that was unknown in McDonald's in the United States but at one time contributed 30 percent of McDonald's sales in Australia. And the most popular hamburger was one containing lettuce, tomato, and mayonnaise—the way most Australians prefer hamburgers. By contrast, the regular McDonald's hamburger—garnished with pickles, onions, ketchup, and mustard—accounted for less than 1 percent of sales. Australians obviously had difficulty accepting McDonald's notion of putting pickles on all its regular hamburger products. "We had pickles all over the store—sticking on the ceiling and the walls," Ritchie says. "If we put up a wall mural of Ronald McDonald, he would have pickles in his eyes by the end of the day."

But gradually the Australian managers realized what Fujita had discovered early on: McDonald's had better luck changing local eating habits than adapting its menu to fit them. The sales of McDonald's units in Australia are now dominated by the same hamburger products as the chain delivers in the United States. Meanwhile, the fried chicken offering has recently been replaced by Chicken McNuggets, while the lettuce and tomato hamburger and fish and chips product were dropped from the menu. And Ritchie now estimates that less than 5 percent of his customers remove the pickles from their hamburgers.

The Australian president attributes that change to the influence McDonald's has on children, whose tastes are not yet biased against the American menu. As they grew up, McDonald's succeeded in winning more customers over to the standard American menu, and when McDonald's Australia finally revoked the menu modifications it had made, its operation moved into the black after eight consecutive losing years.

McDonald's Germany went through the same learning process, only on a grander scale. Because the market was so bound by traditions, McDonald's initially felt compelled to change its food and store design to appeal to the German consumer. A hamburger was not known as a food item but a resident of Hamburg. Hard rolls were everywhere, but soft, spongy hamburger buns had never been seen. Milk shakes consisted of flavoring mixed with milk, and when McDonald's served up what it considered the real thing, German consumers voiced a common complaint—the drink was frozen.

To adapt to those cultural differences, McDonald's entered the German market in 1971 with a modified menu that included a fried chicken breast product designed to reduce the culture shock. Beer—the national beverage—was added at all the units, and local managers even toyed with the idea of adding bratwurst. The stores, too, were given a German look for fear that a typical American fast-food design would be criticized as artificial. Thus store interiors featured dark colors, an extensive use of wood, and low-intensity lighting. Since German rents were four to five times higher than comparable real estate costs in the United States, the units were typically built small—with forty seats instead of the usual hundred or more. Even in the larger units, seating areas were divided by wooden partitions to preserve the darker, genial ambience the Bavarians call *Gemutlich*. One unit in Munich even looked like a copy of a German beer hall.

But if the changes made the stores look native to Germany, they made them foreign to McDonald's. Since chicken was then not part of the standard menu in American stores, McDonald's had not automated its preparations, and the chicken product sold in McDonald's Germany was inconsistent in quality. McDonald's beer, priced well below the brew in taverns, attracted a younger, hangout crowd—including some motorcycle gangs—but the dark interiors and cozy stores did nothing to invite the passerby. Worse still, they did not appeal to the market McDonald's most wanted to tap—families. Although restaurants were plentiful in Bavaria, where McDonald's took root in Germany, they ignored the family market. "The German public is not a kid-loving public," observes Rettenwender. "There are restaurants where a dog is more welcome than a kid. Unfortunately, our first restaurants were not children oriented either."

Only when the McDonald's units in Germany began to look more like those in the United States did they begin to build volume. After Ray Kroc made a visit to Germany and was shocked by the darkness of the interiors, the restaurants were remodeled to make them much lighter. The all wood look was scrapped, partitions were removed, walls were painted with bright colors, and lighting levels were raised. Eventually, larger stores were constructed as well. To further attract families, high chairs were prominently displayed in the stores, and all standard McDonald's tools for marketing to children—from Ronald McDonald Playlands to birthday clubs—were adopted as well.

The menu also became standard McDonald's fare with the elimination of chicken and the addition of the Quarter Pounder. Beer is still sold in all of the 496 German McDonald's, but only because the real estate in so many of the early units is owned by Germany's brewers, which insist on their products being sold as a condition of the lease. Still, beer prices were raised above those at taverns to combat the hangout image, and today beer represents less than 1 percent of sales. As a result, the once low-volume German units began reaching the sales averages of American stores. And McDonald's Germany, which failed to turn a profit in its first six years, contributed $8.4 million dollars in 1991 to McDonald's operating income, seven times more than it did in 1980. "It seems that any detour we made from the standard McDonald's didn't work," Rettenwender explained. "We realized it was better to stick with the system and, if necessary, wait for the German consumer to accept it."

Nor was the Australian and German experience unique on that score. In effect, McDonald's realized that it could *only* be successful abroad if it stuck to the very same menu and store design that worked at home. "McDonald's is an American food system," reasoned Steve Barnes, former chairman of McDonald's International. "If we go into a new country and incorporate their food products into our menu, we lose our identity. We're neither fish nor fowl."

Rather than change their menus or their stores, McDonald's foreign partners made major changes in marketing to sell the American system. Among other things, advertising went back to the basics—back to the 1950s, when even in the United States McDonald's was explaining what its fast-food system was and how it worked.

But it got even more basic than that. In Germany, for example, McDonald's introduced its hamburger with billboard and newspaper ads that touted "the most revolutionary idea since the beefsteak" and pictured oversized diagrams of the product with arrows depicting the different ingredients. The need to explain the foreign menu even led to the development of marketing innovations that McDonald's eventually applied in the United States. While it now commonly uses photographs of products on menu boards outside the restaurants and on serving tray mats used inside, both were pioneered by McDonald's Germany. "In the U.S., advertising had to differentiate McDonald's from its competition, but McDonald's had no competition in Germany," said Jurgen Knauss, managing director of Heye, Needham and Partner, McDonald's German advertising agency. "Our total promotional concept had to be based on explaining an unknown range of food products."

But the German agency also attempted to tell the McDonald's story with a European style of marketing that the German consumer would be more likely to accept. Once McDonald's Germany realized that the system itself had to remain unchanged, Knauss says, "we decided to let it wear a European suit."

That meant developing totally new advertising for the German market, not merely remaking American ads. For one thing, McDonald's Germany gears 60 percent of its advertising toward print, poster, and billboard media, which are used sparingly by the chain in the States. But since German television permits advertising only in four five-minute segments each day, it obviously could not be the dominant advertising medium. In fact, McDonald's Germany uses advertising at cinemas almost as much as it uses television.

More important, the style of advertising became distinctly European. Appeals that border on fantasy were preferred to a pure dose of realism. Humor was chosen over serious or boastful appeals. "Everything in the U.S. is oversold as 'the best,' " Knauss says. "We tried giving McDonald's a European personality by letting consumers feel we aren't taking ourselves too seriously." Hence, the television introduction of Chicken McNuggets featured a man in a white suit jumping up and down and singing the German McDonald's theme song—not as a man would sing but as a chicken might. And a popular German billboard showing a McDonald's hamburger claims: "Always caviar is Kase." *Kase*, the German word for "cheese," doubles as a denunciation of an idea that "stinks." Knauss says of the approach: "We never want to position McDonald's as an American company changing the German culture, but rather as a company that feels it's German."

But McDonald's Germany reserved some of its most creative—and most European—advertising for an effort to deflect criticism of the chain by persuading German opinion leaders that McDonald's was not denigrating the German culture by introducing a crass American food concept. In one of a series of full-page advertisements reminiscent of the Volkswagen Beetle ads of the early 1960s, McDonald's directly challenged German misconceptions about the chain by noting that, among other things, it is not a typical American multinational operation but rather the product of German franchisees, German workers, and homegrown food. One ad, picturing one of McDonald's German franchisees together with his wife, daughter, and the family dog, was titled, "A typical American big business," and another, picturing an executive with his tie in his soup at a fine German restaurant, was captioned: "Every eating culture has its problems." Explained Knauss of Heye, Needham and Partners: "We tried to take a sophisticated knock at the solar plexus of our opponents."

In the U.K., McDonald's Chairman Bob Rhea, now retired, faced an entirely different marketing challenge. The hamburger was known only too well by the English as a low-quality product. "The hamburger served here was so bad that almost anything had to be better," Rhea says. "Yet, a hamburger of American parentage could be perceived as a superior product, because America was an expert at making it." Thus Rhea introduced the McDonald's hamburger with ads proclaiming "The United Tastes of America," a slogan that also capitalized on the English fondness for anagrams.

But slogans did not begin to address McDonald's real problem in the U.K. While low-cost food service was available in countless fish and chips outlets and at hundreds of Wimpy hamburger stores and in pubs throughout the U.K., their quality was so consistently bad that some local food service experts told Rhea that the English consumer obviously did not demand—or deserve—anything better. Rhea disagreed. "I thought the British people had been terribly disappointed by the quality of food because they weren't getting value at a low-cost eatery," he says. "And absolutely no one was merchandising food service to the family market. There was a huge gap we could fill."

Prior to starting the English joint venture with McDonald's in 1974, Rhea and his wife, Ida, visited McDonald's Germany, and Rhea quickly concluded that duplicating in England the small stores being built there would not convey the quality image he wanted. Ida concurred. "Let's build something we can be proud of," she said. "If we're going to go broke at this, let's do it quick."

Rhea was going to be burdened with the same high real estate costs McDonald's was paying in Germany, but instead of compensating with smaller stores, he built them as big as—and sometimes bigger than—American McDonald's. He also made them more lavish than anyone in Oak Brook imagined was possible. Most of his outlets were given travertine marble façades. And following a suggestion from Ray Kroc, Rhea lined the entire fronts of most McDonald's in England with planters containing fresh flowers. But the crowning touches were reserved for the interiors. Brass railings and mirrored walls were placed throughout the stores. Limed oak and mahogany often replaced plastic furniture, and cushions on chairs were made of plasticized fabrics instead of plain vinyl. Murals, woven fabric panels, and other wall coverings became almost standard, and some of the larger units even featured chandeliers and tapestries. By the time he opened his tenth English McDonald's, Rhea was so hooked on improving interiors that he hired a full-time designer.

However, unlike the early stores in Germany, the new units in England still looked like McDonald's—like the best McDonald's ever built. They were also the most expensive: $2 million or more to build and equip—three to four times the cost McDonald's was accustomed to in the States in the mid-1970s. Indeed, they were so expensive that throughout the system the stores in England were dubbed "Rhea's monuments." But, from the start, Rhea had determined that the only alternative to establishing McDonald's in England was to build better stores and pay for them by generating bigger volumes. "I wanted to enter the market with a splash in order to overcome the bad reputation of the local hamburger," Rhea explains.

At first, Rhea was nearly drowned by his own splash. The super stores did not immediately win over the conservative British. As bad as "pub grub" seemed to Rhea, the portions served at the taverns were huge by comparison to what McDonald's was serving. "People were always asking us, 'How much do I get with my order?' " recalls Paul Preston, an American who worked for Rhea in Cleveland and managed the first English store in Woolwich, ten miles from central London. The Englishman, says Preston, now managing director of McDonald's U.K., was concerned about getting value for his money, "but quantity was a huge part of the traditional value statement, and consumers didn't get as much at McDonald's as they did in the pubs."

The Woolwich store seemed like a disaster. It grossed just $300,000 in the first year—half of what American outlets were averaging at that time on much smaller investments—and its losses topped $150,000. Nor was the bottom line of the second store any better. So, Rhea turned in desperation to giveaway promotions, which drew crowds but no repeat business. Occasionally, they even backfired. When McDonald's promoted free milk shakes to children attending a Saturday matinee at a local cinema, the store was swamped by more than three hundred kids. "Our adult customers were actually trapped inside the unit," Rhea recalls. "We couldn't make shakes fast enough, and we gave the kids anything to get them out."

Overall, the English joint venture lost $10 million in its first five years, but Rhea refused to cut his construction frills. In fact, in 1976 he started building new stores in even higher-priced real estate in London's West End—the shopping, theater, and tourist center. There, Rhea learned what Fujita had decided five years before: no matter what the cost, McDonald's was better off entering a new country in the most visible and commercial areas downtown.

The West End stores were immediately profitable, and that, in turn, justified Rhea's first use of television. By then he knew exactly the void in the market McDonald's had to fill, and the thirty-second spots were crammed with messages which were right on target. All of them contained plugs for McDonald's "triple thick" shakes, which were a big hit from the start in England, partly because they satisfied the British taste for sweets and partly because they were viewed as superior to the flavored milk drinks the English once called milk shakes. Each spot also promoted "crisp fries," which were clearly different from the soggy products served in fish and chips outlets. And they always contained a plug for carryout trade, because the only way to generate above-average volumes was to take advantage of the break consumers got on carryout orders, which were not subject to the 15 percent sales tax levied on food consumed in the store. But, most of all, the TV ads positioned McDonald's squarely in the middle of the biggest void in the market: the family segment.

The television ads—featuring original music to a quality-oriented theme ("There's a difference at McDonald's")—had an immediate impact. Even sales at the initial low-volume stores jumped 10 percent almost overnight. From then on, Rhea put virtually all his marketing money into television, and the business it generated repeated. Encouraged by the trend, McDonald's U.K. built fifteen McDonald's in 1977—more than double the number of existing stores—and it has never added fewer units since. By mid-1986, it had two hundred units, and Rhea's gamble had paid an enormous personal reward when McDonald's Corporation bought out his 45 percent interest for $38 million. Obviously, claims by local food service operators that British consumers showed no trade loyalty proved to be as invalid as predictions that the proper British would only eat with knife and fork. "It turned out that the British food service customer was no different than anyone else," Rhea says. "And the commonality of appeal of a McDonald's hamburger was astounding."

Overcoming the local problems in marketing overseas, however, was not nearly as complicated or as frustrating a task as grappling with the problems created by a foreign food supply system. When McDonald's took its fast-food concept abroad, it encountered a food processing industry that was light-years removed from the supply network it had carefully constructed in the States.

Worse, foreign food processors lacked even basic skills that were taken for granted in the United States, where manufacturers, even before McDonald's, were capable of high-volume, automated production. In Europe, bakers were not accustomed to producing buns in quantities McDonald's wanted, and their notion of quality bore no resemblance to McDonald's. For hundreds of years they had produced buns with hard crusts, an irregular shape, and large air pockets—the result of a lower-cost mix with high water content. McDonald's demanded something they had never seen: uniform, soft, resilient buns with more flavor.

The situation was the same across all food groups. Meat plants knew nothing of high-volume hamburger production, let alone cryogenic freezing. Dairy plants did not have the same level of sanitation. Nor was there anything resembling a frozen french fry production line. Steve Barnes notes: "The U.S. was twenty-five years ahead of many of our foreign markets in every aspect of food production—growing, processing, distribution."

There were major raw material differences as well. Most European cattle were grass-fed, while in the United States McDonald's relied on a mixture of grain-fed and grass-fed stock. Russet—the premium potato for making french fries—was not found outside North America. But the biggest difference was the attitude McDonald's encountered among foreign food producers. Most considered McDonald's quality standards "too good for consumers," Barnes recalls. "They wanted to know why we wanted to 'spoil' people. I heard those words from the German, English, and French—people I thought were oriented to quality."

It was a fascinating turnabout. In other industries, European producers projected an image of "old world quality," but when McDonald's entered the European market it was faced with the prospect of either importing most of its food supplies or rebuilding the European food chain.

Some of McDonald's foreign partners abroad took the first option. Fighting a battle to upgrade the hamburger's image in the U.K., Rhea refused any compromise on the quality standards he had maintained at his stores in Ohio. Nor was he willing to hold up development of the U.K. market to give local suppliers time to upgrade. So, he initially imported some of his food supplies and kitchen equipment from the United States. Even when a dock strike suspended shipments of some suppliers, Rhea airlifted frozen french fries from McDonald's supplier in Canada to avoid relying on domestic products he thought were inferior. "We became master importers," Rhea says. "We decided we were going to duplicate the McDonald's System as it existed in the U.S. or die trying."

But an import strategy could not be sustained, since it was driving up some food costs in the U.K. operation by 35 percent. Eventually, Rhea and all McDonald's other foreign partners adopted the system's policy of improving the quality of locally produced food supplies and restaurant equipment instead of importing goods. Design engineers from McDonald's and from its U.S. equipment suppliers began meeting with equipment manufacturers around the world to assist them in building kitchen equipment to the chain's specifications. The system's U.S. food suppliers provided similar technical assistance to foreign processors selected to supply McDonald's abroad. To provide foreign suppliers with an incentive to upgrade their operations, McDonald's even covered the capital cost of the new production equipment, allowing the suppliers to pay for the improvements over the long term from the profits they generated on McDonald's business.

When local suppliers could not be found or when they resisted McDonald's suggestions to improve their facilities and products, the chain turned to its established U.S. suppliers to build facilities in foreign countries. Occasionally, McDonald's itself became a partner in such operations. When Jack Simplot put in a french fry line in Germany to supply stores in Europe, McDonald's spent $2 million to build Europe's largest and most sophisticated potato-storage facility. And after months of trying unsuccessfully to persuade its English baker to overhaul his plant to produce a more consistent hamburger bun, McDonald's U.K. went into the bun business itself, building a plant in Great Britain in a joint venture with an English operating partner and Dick West, who operates two bakeries serving McDonald's in the United States. When his local syrup supplier failed to address quality-control issues he raised, Rhea added a syrup manufacturing operation next to the bun plant. McDonald's U.K. even went into the distribution business as an answer to unreliable deliveries from local distributors. "The vertical integration of McDonald's U.K. was the direct result of the British food industry's refusal to give us what we wanted," Rhea says. "They could have had all of our business, but they lacked the willingness to take an investment risk."

While its purchasing specialists searched worldwide for food processors willing to upgrade local plants, McDonald's food researchers began working closely with foreign growers in an attempt to develop raw materials more consistent with those in the United States. The company, for example, succeeded in growing Idaho Russets in Spain and Australia, and it is testing them in Poland. It experimented with different blends of grasses in Europe in an attempt to develop beef similar to the grain-fed product it uses in the United States. It has even added grain-finishing pens in Australia.

If relying on foreign partners and suppliers involved time-consuming work and enormous risks, it also offered some significant rewards. In less developed countries with weak trading positions, McDonald's could gain access to the market only by relying on local suppliers who were protected by prohibitive tariffs on imported agricultural products. McDonald's also benefited by marketing its menu abroad as a "home-grown" product. "To be accepted in a foreign country, we have to be recognized as someone who is not exploiting the country's economy," Barnes says. "All we want to export is our technology."

As things turned out, however, the local connections in foreign markets yielded much more than marketing gains. They defended McDonald's from the pervasive anti-Americanism that existed during and after the Vietnam War. As it successfully expanded internationally, McDonald's became a prime symbol of American business—and the prime target of foreign attacks against it. Were it not for its local partners, the chain might never have been able to weather the storm.

Nowhere was McDonald's more threatened by anti-Americanism than in Sweden. During the mid-1970s, two of Lederhausen's units were hit with smoke bombs, and Lederhausen himself became the target of hate mail. Newspaper stories criticized McDonald's for exploiting Sweden and corrupting its youth by introducing an American lifestyle that was broadly perceived as damaging to the more "wholesome" traditions of the Swedish culture. As one Swedish journalist put it, "Do we need bulk food in plastic environments?"

Lederhausen was determined to fight back. He started a one-man letter-writing campaign to respond to each negative newspaper story on McDonald's. He made speeches before groups to defend his position. He even appeared on television news shows. His message was always the same: "We are a locally owned business. We are supplied by a Swedish bakery, by a Swedish meat company, and by Swedish distributors. We employ six hundred Swedish kids, and our wages meet the standards of the unions. We have nothing to hide."

Anti-American fervor was also exploited by powerful unions, particularly in Ireland and Australia, which were attempting to organize McDonald's stores, not by appealing to McDonald's crews, but by pressuring its managers. The unions threatened to unleash a barrage of anti-American attacks on the chain if its managers refused to enroll their employees in the unions. But the chain's local operators concluded that that was blackmail, and they refused to cooperate.

Still, they were stunned by the intensity of the union opposition. In Australia, the Shop Assistants Union did battle with McDonald's for three years. It worked with other trade unions to cut off food deliveries and block electrical hook-ups to new stores. It challenged the chain in Industrial Court to reverse its policy of hiring teenaged crew members. The Australian unions also mounted a fierce anti-McDonald's media campaign in union newspapers and in the general press, invariably taking on the McDonald's operation where it was most vulnerable—its connection with an American company. "They said we were exploiting the youth of the country," recalls Australian President Peter Ritchie. "They called on Australians to 'stop these Americans from shoving rotten plastic food down our throats.'" In fact, anti-American fervor against McDonald's ran so high that when Ritchie offered to sponsor a Ronald McDonald House at the Royal Children's Hospital in Melbourne, the offer was rebuffed as "crass commercialism."

When similar union tactics were used in Ireland, McDonald's successfully countered them by developing a new marketing slogan reflecting the local ownership and control of their chain's Dublin stores: "Our name may be American, but we're all Irish." (In fact, the name was Irish, too. Dick and Mac McDonald were second-generation descendants of Irish immigrants.) Now, Ritchie decided to use the same local control argument to deflect the much sharper union challenge in Australia. But he delivered that message more forcefully than anyone else. He sued the union leaders and two members of Parliament for defamation relating to their comments on McDonald's, and he personally took his case to the public with appeals in the press, on radio, and on television talk shows. Yet, his arguments against compulsory unionism in Australia were effective only because he made them as an Australian, not as a manager of an American company.

By the end of the 1970s, Ritchie's public visibility and his depiction of McDonald's as a local retailer had countered the union challenge. The negative treatment in the press ended. Television talk show audiences were openly supportive of Ritchie's arguments. McDonald's continued to employ mostly nonunion teenagers at its stores. And in 1981, a Ronald McDonald House opened at the Alexandria Hospital for Children in Sydney. In fact, it received such favorable public support that a year later Ritchie was approached by officials of Melbourne's Royal Children's Hospital. They now wanted a Ronald McDonald House, too.

Ritchie's response to the union challenge even helped improve sales by supporting the marketing message that McDonald's in Australia was essentially an Australian experience, not a mere import of an American fast-food product. Thus, as the union battle raged, McDonald's in Australia began turning a profit for the first time. Yet, as Ritchie was publicly projecting an Australian image, he was quietly shifting away from his Australianized menu. His customers had not only acquired the taste for the American menu but had adopted it as their own. Ritchie recalls a letter he received from an Australian woman who had just gotten back from a three-week trip to the Soviet Union. "I had a terrible time trying to get used to the food there," she wrote, "but when we pulled into Frankfurt on our way back, we saw a McDonald's. It was just like being at home."

McDonald's has never lacked for patience in its attempt to export its food system. Other fast-food competitors have pulled out of foreign markets after being discouraged by the initial losses, but McDonald's has yet to retreat from any market. In The Netherlands— where the international marketing effort began—it took twelve years for McDonald's to make a profit. And on the average, the chain has waited nine years for each new international venture to make money. It has hung on in some markets even after disastrous setbacks. After the Gibson-Goldstein partnership collapsed in the Caribbean, McDonald's returned to those markets, working with existing and new local franchisees, who now operate profitable units in Puerto Rico, Costa Rica, and Panama.

In fact, McDonald's supreme confidence that foreign markets will eventually accept its American menu has taken its own international partners by surprise. When McDonald's U.K. rolled up big losses at the start, Bob Rhea realized that he stood to lose the $1.7 million he had made on the sale of his five units in Ohio. If he died, Rhea thought, his family would be flat broke. But when he voiced the concern to former Vice Chairman Ed Schmitt, he got immediate support: a $2 million life insurance policy paid for by McDonald's. Similarly, after building forty restaurants in Australia and having nothing to show for it but $6 million in losses, even Ritchie was having serious doubts about the future of the venture. In fact, he suggested that McDonald's sell half of it to spread the risk to other investors, but Turner would not hear of it. Instead, he flew Australia's top managers to Canada to meet with Cohon's executives just so that they could hear about the early losing years of McDonald's Canada. Turner's message: McDonald's is in the market for the long term, and if the Australian operators just stick to the QSC&V basics, the volume will come in time. "They didn't panic," Ritchie says. "They just said I had to have the guts to keep going."

That patience is paying huge dividends now. McDonald's Australia, in 1994, had sales of $1.105 billion (Australian dollars) and an operating profit (pre-tax) of $82.6 million from its 455 units. Overall, the system now makes a profit in most of the seventy-nine countries in which it operates outside the U.S. Furthermore, in each new foreign market, the initial resistance to McDonald's menu is less, perhaps because its fast-food system is now recognized as an international phenomenon, not an American creation. Whatever the reason, the profits from new foreign markets are coming sooner—sometimes with the first restaurant. After five years of attempting to find the right partner and gain government approvals, McDonald's entered Taiwan in 1984 with a flourish. Sales at its first restaurant there hit $3.7 million in the first year, ranking it among the ten highest-volume McDonald's around the globe. Today, Taiwan is one of McDonald's fastest-growing markets, with 82 restaurants opened after just ten years.

Yet, it is obvious that McDonald's has only scratched the surface of the international market. In fact, It appears now to be entering a second phase of international development, not unlike the expansive stage it went through in the United States after Turner took over the presidency. After adding few new foreign markets in the early 1980s, McDonald's is now exploding from its initial international base into a host of new markets.

In 1992 and 1993, new stores were opened for the first time in the Czech Republic, Brunei, Guadeloupe, Iceland, Israel, Poland, Morocco, Monaco, Saipan, Saudi Arabia, and Slovenia. And in 1994, Oman, Kuwait, New Caledonia, Trinidad, Bulgaria, Latvia, Bahrain, United Arab Emirates, and Egypt are slated for addition to the company's international roster.

Turner predicts that by the turn of the century, McDonald's international sales will exceed its domestic sales. Meeting that goal will almost certainly require in the next five years the same missionary zeal for the fast-food business and the same commitment to the basics that have been McDonald's trademark for the last forty years. In some respects, the task will get harder, not easier. To be sure, McDonald's began its era of global market development from a much stronger base than it had when Kroc was trying to exploit the domestic market. Still, the McDonald's founder was an inspired entrepreneur. His operations staffers were young tigers, fiercely loyal to Kroc and dedicated to his mission. His franchisees were innovative operators. They were pioneers, and Kroc gave them an enormous incentive to take pioneering risks because his franchising system—more than any other before or since—was fair and generous. What was true about Kroc's relationship with his franchisees was also true about his relationships with his suppliers, all of whom were entrepreneurial vendors who took on established and powerful suppliers—and outsmarted them.

How can McDonald's maintain that fine cutting edge? Turner believes the answer is not to be found by discovering a new business but by reaffirming the essence of McDonald's existing business—its entrepreneurship. McDonald's has already taken some steps in that direction. With its now formidable corporate size, McDonald's necessarily has had to introduce some measure of bureaucracy, but it does so begrudgingly. Corporate reporting forms are used sparingly, and managers are still encouraged to cross over into one another's decision-making territories. McDonald's even named former personnel executive Jim Kuhn to a management post that may have been one of a kind

in corporate America—vice president of individuality—and charged
him with developing incentives and other programs designed to foster
individual initiative and discourage those things that stifle it.

Similarly, expansion abroad is stimulating the system not only by
adding a varied new group of franchisees but by creating an exciting
and challenging list of new markets to conquer. In fact, its pioneering
in foreign markets is already producing innovations that McDonald's
can apply around the world. In the early years of international development, McDonald's foreign partners lifted ideas from the States, but now
some domestic managers are benefiting from a reverse flow of innovation.

Still, Turner concedes that to stave off boredom McDonald's may
have to look even deeper within itself to find the regenerative power it
needs to maintain its aggressiveness in fast food through the rest of this
century and beyond.

His answer is bold yet simple: to convert McDonald's into a company owned primarily by all the participants of the system—its managers, its franchisees, and its suppliers. The one way to ensure that
McDonald's remains an entrepreneurial company, he reasons, is by
ensuring that the entrepreneurs of McDonald's *own* McDonald's. It
would be a massive undertaking. McDonald's is one of Wall Street's
most active and most cherished stocks. Its 363 million shares by early
1992 had a market value of about $17 billion.

It is not a plan; it is a dream, no more or less achievable than Ray
Kroc's dream of building the world's largest hamburger chain. But it is
entirely consistent with Ray Kroc's principles of sharing the rewards of
success with those people—*all* of those people—who made success
possible. Long ago, that philosophy converted McDonald's owner/op-
erators into the wealthiest group the franchising business has ever
known. Long ago, the same principle propelled McDonald's suppliers
from tiny food processors and equipment vendors into some of the
largest and richest suppliers in the food service trade.

And since taking the helm of the company, Fred Turner has followed the same principle to make McDonald's managers—even those
on the middle and lower rungs of the corporate ladder—among the
best paid in all of American business. McDonald's has one of the most
generous profit-sharing programs of any company in the world. Most
full-time and some part-time employees—more than sixteen thousand
people—receive an annual payment from McDonald's (actually, from
the company and from profit-sharing funds forfeited by others leaving

the company) into their profit-sharing accounts equal to 14 percent of their salaries. In 1993 alone, that amount totaled $47.1 million. The company's stock option program is also the largest in the history of American business. Presently, about 6,700 employees—down to $28,000-per-year restaurant managers—qualify for annual stock options, from as few as fifty shares to as many as five hundred shares.

The stock options, of course, only grant an employee the right to buy McDonald's shares at the market price on the day the options are granted. Still, because that price is frozen for the seven-year life of the option and because McDonald's stock has consistently been one of the strongest performers on Wall Street, McDonald's managers have been enriched by the company's stock option program. Even those in middle management have been rewarded better than some companies reward their senior managers.

Consider the example of a thirty-six-year-old regional manager who is responsible for a market area of two hundred McDonald's stores: His 1985 annual compensation was $175,000. Ten years earlier, when he was an area supervisor in charge of five McDonald's, he was making $25,000 a year, and he entered the profit-sharing and stock option programs for the first time. In that decade, McDonald's contributions to his profit-sharing program totaled nearly $200,000. And the value of his stock options—the 1985 market price less the exercise price he would pay to buy them—was $1 million. At age thirty-six, this middle manager, holding the seemingly humble position of regional manager of McDonald's Corporation, would have become a millionaire.

It is McDonald's very generosity and fairness to its employees, suppliers, and franchisees that make Turner's dream of ownership of McDonald's by the entrepreneurs of McDonald's something more than fantasy. Turner believes there is enough potential wealth within the system for the partners of McDonald's to buy at least half of the company's stock by the end of this century, enough to control it. Indeed, at the 1986 McDonald's Operators Convention in Los Angeles, which brought together more than six thousand McDonald's franchisees, suppliers, and managers, Senior Chairman Turner kicked off the first phase of the buy-back process. His goal is increasing ownership of McDonald's by the three major participants in the system from 10 to 20 percent in a few years. "I own some of your store," he told the convention. "Now, I want you to own some of mine."

It is premature to speculate whether McDonald's will achieve its senior chairman's goals on ownership, but Turner's motivation for setting them is clear. With ownership of McDonald's in the hands of those who have always made the system work, he knows McDonald's will remain devoted to the food service business that transformed the American culture. He also realizes that ownership by entrepreneurs is the only way to guarantee that McDonald's will sustain for the long term the spirit of enterprise, the enthusiasm for taking risks, and the creative energy that have brought the system this far. And, in the end, he knows that his dream of ownership is the one way to permanently cement the partnerships between independent franchisees, suppliers, and managers that Ray Kroc put together to form the world's most successful franchising system.

"It's my dream, my ambition," Turner says. "What is more appropriate than for the licensees, suppliers, and employees of the system to make a go of owning it? That strikes me as the essence of entrepreneurship, of hands-on management, of owner on the premises. That is what McDonald's is all about. If we could make it happen, it would make it perfect."

Epilogue

When Mike Quinlan addressed the McDonald's biennial Worldwide Convention in Las Vegas on April 14, 1994, he was able to call the turn on the company's quiet revolution. "Two years ago, we were suffering from a very un-McDonald's case of self-doubt, but rather than let it eat us up, we went to work on it," Quinlan said to the more than ten thousand members of the extended-family gathering of franchisees, suppliers, and employees at the Thomas & Mack Arena. "Together, we're changing our focus and looking at the business through the eyes of the customer. This is a one hundred and eighty degree change from where we were before, and to embrace that kind of change for a company this size amounts to turning on a dime."

At forty-nine, Quinlan was just the third man to serve as chairman as McDonald's approached its fortieth anniversary, and his rise to the top after starting as a part-time mailroom employee was a quintessential McDonald's success story. He had been named CEO in March of 1987 and took over the full reins of leadership from Fred Turner on March 31, 1990, when Turner became senior chairman and a self-described "company nudge." Since that time, Quinlan had presided over an uncharacteristically rocky economic period in McDonald's history, particularly by the company's own high expectations.

And what the young executive had accomplished was that most rare corporate commodity—change, a process of sweeping, fundamental, and meaningful change for the entire business in response to the rapidly changing world around them. At the convention, Quinlan could point to an event that *didn't* happen as evidence of the new McDonald's.

"We passed a major milestone when we sold our one hundred billionth hamburger a few weeks ago," Quinlan said. "But when it happened, this milestone went practically unnoticed, and that's good. A few years ago, when we were focused on ourselves instead of the customer, we would have been running commercials and hanging banners and calling for a national holiday and breaking our arms patting ourselves on the back.

"But you know what? The customer doesn't care. One hundred billion hamburgers doesn't mean a thing to the customer standing in line waiting to buy number one hundred billion and one. Today, we're focused on the customer—the next one, not the hundred billion that came before. The operation of our restaurants is the key to customer satisfaction and the key to our success."

To the external world, the trauma facing the McDonald's system was not all that evident; indeed, many companies that had been forced into painful restructurings in the late 1980s and early 1990s would have loved to have McDonald's "problems." From 1986 through 1994, systemwide sales increased almost 110 percent from $12.4 to $25.9 billion, total revenues more than doubled from $4.1 to $8.3 billion, and net income increased 50 percent from $480 million to more than $1.2 billion. However, for several of those years, these results were being driven strongly by the growing influence of McDonald's international network, which represented 42 percent of sales in 1994 compared with just 23 percent of sales eight years earlier. Customer transactions per restaurant in the United States were declining in the late 1980s—a worrisome trend that has now been reversed—and competitors were growing faster than McDonald's.

McDonald's had quietly begun a behind-the-scenes painstaking evaluation of itself in 1990 that was resulting in changes to the very structure of the corporation that Ray Kroc founded and Fred Turner built. And yet, the flexibility of the system Kroc and Turner had nurtured provided a framework that allowed fundamental changes to take place at a speed rare among large corporations. "As big as McDonald's is today, we obviously can't change directions as quickly as we could in the beginning years," says Al Golin, head of Golin-Harris Communications and Ray Kroc's original public relations counsel. "But it is still a very flexible company for its size."

In essence, McDonald's had successfully reinvented itself while no one was looking.

To understand the dilemma that McDonald's faced on the home front, it's necessary to look at the U.S. quick-service restaurant environment in which it was operating during the late 1980s. From an industry-wide perspective, the traditional assumption that real estate growth fostered market share growth was no longer valid. During the 1980s, the reality was that quick-service restaurants continued to add units, but no longer took any market share away from midscale and upscale restaurants. McDonald's itself grew from about seventy-three hundred domestic restaurants in 1986 to some eighty-six hundred outlets in 1990, yet found competitors—particularly PepsiCo's Taco Bell and Pizza Hut—taking visit shares away.

The cost of growth was increasing rapidly as well. The average cost of opening a new McDonald's restaurant in the United States in 1986 was $1.21 million, and that increased by 28 percent to $1.55 million in 1990. "In retrospect, we invested too much into the business, which drove the need to increase prices and caused our value structure to get out of whack," says Bob Thurston, a board member since 1974. The company's supply system was also feeling the stress of leveraged buyouts and acquisitions that were affecting the rest of American industry. The increased debt loads of the surviving supplier companies also found their way to McDonald's in the form of increased costs of ingredients and materials.

McDonald's paid these higher bills by increasing prices, which made the company particularly vulnerable to the economic downturn that began in the 1990s. Between 1985 and 1990, for example, McDonald's domestic prices increased significantly faster than the rest of the eating-out industry and the Consumer Price Index. These price increases helped McDonald's achieve a compound annual growth rate in sales of 12 percent during the 1980s, while masking the underlying problems.

These weaknesses did not capture the full attention of the McDonald's System until the recession hit full force in the 1990s. It was a different recession than the country had been accustomed to because of its impact on service and white-collar workers, the downsizing of many American industries, and the heavy cost of debt on the economy. Also, the recession was led by consumers to an extent rarely seen before, and consumer spending is perhaps *the* key indicator for McDonald's.

For example, during the 1980s, the United States enjoyed average annual retail sales growth of 6.6 percent. In 1990, retail sales growth was 3.4 percent, and in 1991, it grew only 0.7 percent. That, coupled with continued growth in quick-service units, resulted in more restaurants fighting for a stagnant number of customer dollars. "We had relied on our QSC&V standards to carry us through in the past, and that was fine when you didn't have a recession and you didn't have all this competition," said board member David Wallerstein, a director of long standing who died in 1993. "But when we saw our comparable sales declining, it was suddenly clear that it was necessary to change."

So what might have been viewed as subtle problems in the system suddenly emerged as very clear challenges to address and overcome. "Whatever arrogance there was in the company ranks was humbled and wrung out of the system," says Quinlan. "These big changes had been emerging for the past fifteen years, but it became abundantly clear that our U.S. value perceptions were seriously out of alignment and we were paying the price of customer defections."

If anyone were aware of the need for change, it would be Fred Turner, who had guided McDonald's through a period of remarkable growth. And Turner's decision to turn over the reins of the company while still a relatively young man himself indicated his understanding that a new management team could better bring about the sweeping changes necessary to carry McDonald's to a new plateau. "Fred Turner always called this a young person's company, and he very aggressively pushed to have Mike Quinlan elevated to the CEO position," says Thurston. "Turner was really the architect of the modern McDonald's and the board was incredulous that he would want to pass along the CEO responsibilities at such a relatively young age. But it's an enormous credit to him that he saw the need—and he was right!"

Turner knew that he was giving the leadership over to a strong management team because, in fact, he had been working with them for a long time. He also knew that holding on to power for another decade would only restrain that team's potential. With courage and foresight rare in corporate America, Turner paved the way for the next round of change by insisting that he step aside for the new team. "No one suggested, and no one would have suggested, that a change was desirable," recalls board member Don Lubin. "But Fred rightly saw that bringing in a younger management team, a vigorous team with a fresh look, would be beneficial to the company, and that was an absolutely

brilliant decision on his part. People usually don't voluntarily relinquish the reins of a large company, and you have to give credit to Fred
for doing it in such a way that it was clear that Mike Quinlan was in
charge, even though Fred remains a presence in the company."

The process began on March 1, 1987, when the board of directors
elected Quinlan president and chief executive officer, while Turner
continued as board chairman and chairman of a newly formed executive committee. Three years later, Quinlan became chairman of the
board as well. Ed Rensi continued as president and CEO of McDonald's USA and Jim Cantalupo as president and CEO of McDonald's
International. In 1992, Jack Greenberg—a ten-year McDonald's veteran
who, like Cantalupo, came to the company from its accounting firm of
Ernst & Young—joined this senior management group as vice chairman, while continuing his duties as chief financial officer of the company.

The fact is, Turner had been effectively running the entire company for the previous twenty years, with all the attendant stress which
that entailed. Since the late 1960s, Ray Kroc had not been interested in
managing the day-to-day operations or overall administration of the
company. So, from the day Turner became president, all the responsibilities and all the pressure of running a worldwide organization with
hundreds of thousands of employees, franchisees, and suppliers fell
under his wing, and he compiled an astonishing track record. His latest
accomplishment was to set the stage for change at a time when the
system needed it most.

"We've done fabulously well by any measure except our own,"
says Greenberg. "There's so much pride here that even a hiccup like a
couple of years being below our expectations created a whole lot of
ferment for change within the system."

Quinlan says that the onset of the recession at the beginning of his
term as chairman was simply a coincidence, but that it certainly provided the impetus for change. In fact, he candidly describes the budding renaissance of McDonald's as "a work in progress," which will
continue to unfold in years to come.

"Frankly, our value perceptions had gotten out of sync in the late
1980s, and we probably were a little too arrogant to think that there was
anything wrong with our system," says Quinlan. "But when everyone
saw the bad implications of rising costs, lower sales and customer
counts, and shrunken profits for owner/operators and the company,

we were able to commission a series of changes to reverse those negative trends—without the need for restructuring or write-offs. There's a real energy surging through the company again."

If there were a signal that change was coming to the U.S. organization, it might have been a letter from Ed Rensi, president and CEO of McDonald's USA, to the entire McDonald's family on June 21, 1990. Noting that the company had gone through several periods of renewal and redefinition already, Rensi wrote, "I believe it is time to renew ourselves again. Internally and externally. A continued evolution. Our challenge . . . is to affirm that our system will continue to work as we grow and expand in the future. There's an adage that says, 'If it ain't broke, don't fix it.' Here's a modern adaptation—'If you wait till it's broke, it's too late to fix it.' "

Rensi's letter—sent directly to the homes of several thousand people in the McDonald's system, including operators, suppliers, and company personnel (a group Rensi and others fondly call "the McFamily") —began a steady stream of correspondence that challenged the system to do better in every aspect of the company's operations.

The environment and nutrition were issues McDonald's perceived as major threats to its sales in the 1980s. McDonald's discovered during the decade that part of the price of its extraordinary success was its very high visibility, a two-edged sword that was a tremendous asset when opening a new restaurant, but not so good when the company found itself at the center of controversial issues. "McDonald's has become a lightning rod for anything and everything," says Golin. "That's the price of leadership."

Increased public interest and concern over the environment was resulting in McDonald's becoming identified as the symbol of the throw-away society. "We got ourselves into a bad position by being on the defensive," says Lubin. "Because of our high visibility, the environment was becoming a monumental problem for us." The company was not only a good target for environmental activists because it was large, but the fact that it had outlets in virtually every U.S. community of any size made McDonald's accessible to picketers and protesters everywhere, in some cases for issues that the company was not remotely involved in.

Most of the protest against McDonald's focused on the company's use of polystyrene foam as a packaging product, particularly the clamshell packages developed specially for its large sandwiches. Ironically, the company had turned to the experts at the Stanford Research Institute in the 1970s to study how different packaging options affected the environment, and it was their findings that led to McDonald's adoption of polystyrene foam as an efficient, effective, and environmentally sound food package. In the 1980s, when scientists determined that fully halogenated chlorofluorocarbons could harm the ozone layer, the company directed its foam packaging suppliers to eliminate those elements from the manufacturing process—and McDonald's clout prompted the rest of the industry to change.

Nevertheless, foam packaging had become a symbol of the waste problem in the United States, and McDonald's was identified as the major proponent of foam packaging. "That one thing was hurting all the other wonderful things we were doing in the environmental area," says Greenberg. Despite initiating waste reduction, material reuse, and recycling efforts throughout its system—including the creation of the largest polystyrene foam recycling program in the nation—McDonald's continued to be on the defensive on environmental issues.

Then, in a dramatic move, Rensi announced on October 25, 1990, that McDonald's was phasing out of foam packaging in the United States. The suddenness and gut-wrenching nature of that decision, announced on a Thursday, was illustrated by the fact that the company had planned a major press conference the following Monday, which was to have announced a national recycling plan for foam packaging. It was a tough decision—but there was little doubt as to its effectiveness in the public's mind.

What was ultimately persuasive to McDonald's was the fact that many of its customers just weren't comfortable with foam packaging, despite the technical arguments in its favor, and being right was beginning to hurt sales. "We were spending more time on that issue than we were on our hamburger business," recalls Quinlan. "Making the decision to switch from foam packaging was like taking a huge millstone off our backs." Moreover, changing to paper packaging would eventually save each restaurant about $2,000 per year.

McDonald's also disarmed the opposition through a daring, full-fledged partnership with the Environmental Defense Fund (EDF), launched in August 1990. That relationship produced a very strong environmental policy statement and a comprehensive solid waste reduction action plan, with forty-two initiatives, pilot projects, and tests in the areas of source reduction, reuse, recycling, and composting. Collectively, these initiatives—blessed by the EDF—could ultimately reduce as much as 80 percent of McDonald's solid waste.

Virtually overnight, McDonald's turned from one of the environmental bad guys to a nationally recognized green company. For example, a Cambridge Reports/Research International study showing how consumers rate the environmental performance of twenty-three leading U.S. companies ranked McDonald's number one in 1991 —a 28 percent improvement over the previous year's rating. McDonald's led the industry in the development of 100 percent recycled brown bags for carryout orders, and by 1994, the company had spent more than $1 billion purchasing products made—frequently at McDonald's urging—from recycled materials.

The second major public issue that McDonald's confronted hit much closer to home: the nutritional value of its food. Again, as the industry leader, the company found itself as the most visible target of food advocates of every stripe, despite its own high-quality standards, despite its early (and voluntary) publication of nutritional values for each of its food items, and despite extensive public education efforts.

The issue erupted across the country in April 1990 when a small businessman named Phil Sokolof bought full-page advertisements in the twenty largest newspapers in the country with the bold headline: "The Poisoning of America: McDonald's—Your Hamburgers Have Too Much Fat." The company immediately fought back.

Issuing a press release the afternoon before the ads appeared, the company conducted interviews with the Associated Press, *The Wall Street Journal,* and *USA Today* to ensure that its side of the story was told in the same editions that the ad appeared. Senior Vice President Dick Starmann then pressed the company's case by appearing with Phil Sokolof on all three network TV morning shows to rebut the charges and tell McDonald's positive nutrition story. He noted that the advertisements not only used scare tactics but were grossly inaccurate in describing the content of McDonald's food. The company's response also included a stern warning letter to the newspapers from former Health, Education, and Welfare Secretary Joseph Califano, now a consulting attorney for the company, that put them on notice that their ads were incorrect to the point of libel.

In fact, when McDonald's announced later that year that it was changing the formulation of its deep fry oil to a vegetable oil recipe after extensive research and development efforts, Sokolof gave his endorsement in a subsequent advertisement. And like the decision to abandon foam packaging, this turn of events highlighted many of the other nutritional menu choices that McDonald's had developed over the previous three to four years. "We can, and do, make some mistakes in fighting these issues," says Lubin. "But in most of these situations, McDonald's has had the ability to admit that there's another side, to change, and then to move forward."

With these issues of public perception under relative control by mid-1991, McDonald's still had to focus on the major underlying problem it faced—defections of its mainstream heavy users. Indeed, the concentrated focus on the environment and nutrition issues in the late 1980s took attention away from many of the real problems, according to Thurston, who says, "As a prominent company, we obviously had to respond to public criticism. But while they were the front burner issues for the company, they were not front burner issues for heavy consumers of our products. If we had paid more attention to our research, we would have realized that our number one problem was value." And it became abundantly clear as the recession set in during 1990 that the price of McDonald's food was increasingly a barrier, especially with Taco Bell leading an onslaught of discounting throughout the fast food industry.

Discounting prices had traditionally been viewed as a local market tactic at McDonald's, rather than a recommended national marketing strategy. But clearly, with every single market embroiled in fierce competition for local customers, it was time to develop a national strategy. "We finally learned that you have to discount smart," said Wallerstein. "It took this very competitive period to convince us that we had to change our tactics in the marketplace."

The first glimpse of what was to come was a national $1.99 hamburger Happy Meal offer. The results were eye-opening to the system— transaction increases ranging from 40 to 50 percent when the Happy Meal was priced under $2. Meanwhile, the system's local entrepreneurs were tinkering with efforts to give advertising support for low-price promotions in particular regions—most notably Kansas City and Houston—as part of the process of determining what would work best at the national level.

Before long, the elements of the program were ready to be put before the owner/operators, whose independent participation would be crucial for McDonald's to be able to promote prices meaningfully across the country. "One of the great things about our franchising system is that it's very unlikely that we'll be able to convince our owner/operators to do something stupid," says Greenberg. "It may take us longer to do things, but we avoid the big mistakes. And when we do move, we're able to execute better than anyone else because our franchisees have their own money at stake."

The McDonald's value strategy included low-priced menu leaders: 59-cent hamburgers; 69-cent cheeseburgers; 79-cent sausage biscuits; the continuation of the $1.99 hamburger Happy Meals; and several value combinations—called Extra Value Meals—made up of a sandwich, fries, and a drink. To support its recommended strategy, McDonald's put up $47 million in 1991 to subsidize the effort, and later introduced the first national "price advertising" to support the program. The ads refer to McDonald's recommended price and the independent owner/operator's ultimate decision to participate or vary the price. And almost all of McDonald's U.S. restaurants decided to participate. "It took a bold move to provide the financial impetus that would help the franchisees get this value effort off the ground as soon as it did," says Lubin. "We might have started a little slowly, but once we committed to value pricing, we moved decisively." Quinlan admits advancing the $47 million was a gamble, but it would have been a bigger gamble to do nothing. "Very simply, we had to get a value program initiated," says Quinlan, "This incentive put our money where our mouth was."

This dramatic pricing attack definitely took the company back to its roots, when Ray Kroc built the business on the back of a 15-cent hamburger. As Ed Rensi pointed out to security analysts in the fall of 1991, the 59-cent hamburger, discounted for inflation, would have sold for 13 cents in 1955. "Value is how Ray started the system, and we've recaptured our roots on value by lowering our prices in real dollars," says Greenberg.

Value has become a key plank in McDonald's efforts to satisfy its customers. The company expanded its Extra Value Meal program in 1994 to three tiers, adding a smaller and less expensive All America Meal and a Super Sizing option to upgrade a regular Extra Value Meal with large fries and drinks. And in the summer of 1994, the company used new McDonald's Communications Network (MCN) video satellite technology to gain approval for a national advertising campaign in unprecedented time. MCN allowed management to televise its marketing and business plan live to all forty U.S. regions on June 29 for same-day approval, so that the actual ad campaign was able to start within a week. Management views MCN and other innovative new communications technology—which allows the system to move fast and effectively in the marketplace—as its own lane on the communications super-highway.

But the company also recognized that there is much more to value than simply price. As competitors joined the value bandwagon, low prices became the "greens fee" to get in the game, but McDonald's believes that the total experience of what customers receive for what they pay is the true value equation. And the one area where the company is confident it can differentiate itself from its competitors is through customer satisfaction—outstanding service enhancing the total McDonald's experience.

This required a loosening of the traditional operational standards which dictated that customers, to get fast service, would have to accept the food the way McDonald's made it. Quinlan appeared on the cover of the March 1991 issue of the internal *Management News* in a seemingly innocuous picture with a Filet-O-Fish sandwich in one hand and lettuce in the other. But the message was driven home loud and clear throughout the system: If the customer wants the sandwich with lettuce, that's the way we'll serve it. "The single biggest change we're making is that we're now willing to challenge everything we do as it's seen through the eyes of the customer," says Quinlan. "This allows us to cut through the bureaucracy and think more strategically."

McDonald's moved quickly to instill its Customer Care Culture throughout the system. The change was not without some internal stress, however. The whole foundation of McDonald's quick-service concept was standardized operations that did not allow for exceptions in the composition of the products. Even as special customer requests were accommodated, the price was longer waits for the special order to be prepared and increased confusion behind the counter.

To make the system work at the counter, the company created a new method for preparing its food, based on innovative technology, such as clamshell grills that cook the meat on both sides at the same time, improved fryers, faster toasters, and high-technology holding cabinets that control both heat and humidity. The cabinets allow restaurant crews to keep product components ready for final assembly when the customer actually orders it. Thus the food is not only served hotter and faster, but special orders can be accommodated without upsetting the procedural routines. "Talk about a revolution," says Greenberg. "Who would have ever thought five years ago that we'd change the way we produce our food? And we made that change in our operating system just to give our customers a better product."

The new food production operation was introduced for use during the breakfast part of the day, where McDonald's already maintained an impressive 36 percent of the quick-service market. The results showed impressive gains in service, particularly in the drive-thru, where the number of customers asked to "pull ahead" and wait for their order declined significantly. In 1992, the new production method was expanded to the regular menu throughout the U.S. system, giving restaurants the ability to handle significant menu changes, even during the dinner hours, without sacrificing speed or product quality.

The new technology was important to McDonald's efforts to provide total satisfaction to its customers, but even more critical was the need to change its employees' attitude toward service. Market research showed that the love affair McDonald's had enjoyed with its customers during its growth years had faded, and in some cases, competitors were ahead and gaining. "There's been a significant change of emphasis from when McDonald's graded itself on how well it was doing, to asking the public how it was doing and making changes to deal with that," says Lubin.

The company began its Service Enhancement program to look at its business from the customers' point of view on a restaurant-by-restaurant basis and empower local managers and crew to do whatever it takes to satisfy their own customers. "We have the opportunity to redefine what a quick-service restaurant experience is," says Greenberg. "We have a vision of how to differentiate the customer experience at McDonald's, and we have the techniques to get us there." Service Enhancement was supported by new job descriptions and new training, which rewarded employees for putting the customer first. In some cases, it was as simple as giving the crew member at the counter the ability to settle disputes without having to call for the manager. In others, it was a matter of putting store managers in the lobby, where the customers were. "I think Ray Kroc would be thrilled to see us making all these changes," Wallerstein said. "He always said to be different, to be daring, and he always liked to see managers out in the store, finding out what customers wanted."

By the time Quinlan addressed the 1994 Worldwide Convention, there were already ample signs that the company's moves were beginning to pay dividends. Transaction counts in the United States reversed their decline early in 1991, largely because of the company's value strategy, despite the fact that the recession's effect was lingering throughout the economy. U.S. sales were up 6 percent in 1992 and 7 percent in 1993, and U.S. operating income increased 4 percent both years. Furthermore, McDonald's found it could live with low prices, and still profit, by using its size to squeeze costs out of the system. "For thirty-five years, we solved problems at McDonald's by building sales," says Greenberg. "That's still the best way, but a corollary is to focus an enormous amount of attention on lowering operating costs. That's a cultural change for us, and cost-cutting is a much more focused enterprise at McDonald's than it's ever been. We're on a continuous improvement track and we will continue to pass those savings along to our customers."

In a penny-profit business, it doesn't take long for small savings to add up. For example, when the company began using a new filter powder to extend the life of shortening used to cook its french fries, it saved each restaurant $2,800 annually. Shifting from a company-sponsored insurance program to eight approved insurance companies to give restaurant operators the flexibility to control costs through competitive bidding saved the average restaurant $4,000 in property and casualty insurance annually. Just those two programs, combined with the savings from shifting to paper packaging, amounts to more than $80 million per year when applied across more than ninety-three hundred U.S. restaurants. "We can't be the low-cost producer because our quality standards are higher than most," says Greenberg. "But we'll continue to focus on lowering operating costs so we can be the most efficient producer for the quality we're delivering."

More significant for the future, McDonald's slashed the cost of building new restaurants by creating more sophisticated techniques to determine optimum sizing for individual markets, by using more cost-effective construction methods and alternate materials, and by redesigning building features. "We built beautiful restaurants and we're proud of them because they wear well," says Greenberg. "But we got to a point where the costs made it harder and harder to find places to put them because we needed such a high volume of sales to make a profit." Cost-cutting efforts caused the total average development cost of a U.S. restaurant to decline by more than 27 percent from 1990 through 1993.

In addition, the company created the new Series 2000 building, which is half the size of a traditional McDonald's but has a kitchen engineered to do nearly as much volume as a standard kitchen. These "mini-McDonald's" cost about 30 percent less than the average restaurant built in 1991, yet they can handle the same volume as 96 percent of the existing "full-sized" restaurants. Low cost building designs comprised nearly 80 percent of 1993 U.S. restaurant openings, compared with 60 percent in 1992. One of the significant advantages of these smaller units is that their lower costs make new market niches feasible to develop—small towns and market seams between existing restaurants that were not economically viable before. "There's a tremendous strategic significance in being able to put our restaurants into so many more places because lower development costs mean lower sales break-even points," says Greenberg. "And when we put our restaurants in more traditional locations, we'll just make more money."

In addition, McDonald's began expanding aggressively into even smaller nontraditional sites in 1993 with satellite locations served by carts, kiosks, mobile units, and snack bars supported by an existing restaurant. From a standing start, for example, McDonald's opened more than eighty satellite locations in Wal-Mart stores in less than a full year as part of an alliance forged with its fellow American retailing giant. Other targeted satellite locations include gas stations, shopping malls, schools, hospitals, businesses, recreation sites, and major sporting events—emphasizing what McDonald's executives call a "faces, not places" strategy to bring their food to where the people are.

Meanwhile, McDonald's International, which had been carried by the U.S. system while the company learned how to export its restaurants, began to play a significant role in producing sales and profits on its own. "We've seen the vindication of a number of key decisions Fred Turner made early on—the decision to go overseas, to partner with individuals rather than corporations, and to be prepared to invest money even though we knew we wouldn't be profitable right away," says Lubin. Turner's early confidence in international expansion has turned into a major strength. International sales increased from $2.9 billion in 1986 to $11.0 billion in 1994, an annual growth rate of 35 percent. International's contribution to McDonald's total revenues grew from just 27 to 50 percent over the same time period.

"Over the past five years, we've recognized and acted upon the potential of international—a conscious decision made possible by the evolution of our infrastructure," says Cantalupo. "Our infrastructure can now support faster growth in existing markets as well as handle new markets much more efficiently." From 2,138 restaurants in forty-five countries at the end of 1986, McDonald's International operations grew to incorporate 5,461 units in seventy-nine countries at the end of

1994. And the "Big Six"—Australia, Canada, the United Kingdom, France, Germany, and Japan—currently provide about 80 percent of international's operating income. Significantly, France was able to turn its operations around after McDonald's had to go to court in 1982 to oust its initial franchisee. "Today, France is coming pretty close to Germany and the U.K., which is a remarkable turnaround considering we had to stop and start over," says Cantalupo.

"Our international potential is boundless," adds Quinlan. "We are light-years ahead of where we were five years ago—we're operating with increased efficiency and much quicker profitability." Thurston maintains that there is no other retailer in the world that has the commitment to international growth that McDonald's has. "There is a feeling throughout the company that we can figure out how to do business in almost any country or culture—and it keeps being reinforced," he says. McDonald's plans to open from eight hundred to a thousand new restaurants in international markets for the balance of the decade. "To the extent that we can open restaurants profitably in existing markets, we're going to accelerate our growth," says Cantalupo. "We'll continue to do it in a patient, methodical way to make sure the infrastructure keeps pace, but we are going to accelerate growth."

Indeed, in spite of tremendous growth in its major markets, punctuated by such world news events as the first McDonald's in Moscow, Beijing, Warsaw, and Cairo, the real story of international's success is the patient, methodical approach behind the scenes—and that's what Cantalupo is most proud of. The company has learned that building a solid infrastructure—a network of local partners, franchise operators, and suppliers—is the critical first step to support rapid growth.

The McDonald's calling card—the second most recognized brand name in the world—is an impressive credential. "The McDonald's name and what we stand for opens a tremendous number of doors," says Cantalupo. "Governments we call on are one hundred percent supportive because they understand that we're selling a system and not a trademark, and that we have a history of taking the long-term perspective in all the countries where we've established operations. And our partners will tell you that we've always exceeded their expectations in the area of support."

In Eastern Europe, for example, negotiations that led to the first McDonald's in Moscow began in 1976, long before glasnost. McDonald's Development Company of Central Europe, based in Vienna, Austria, had been quietly laying the groundwork for expansion for several years, leading to the Golden Arches rising in Hungary and the former Yugoslavia, even before the fall of the Berlin Wall. "It was amazing to discover that forty-two percent of the people in [the former] Czechoslovakia already recognized the McDonald's logo before we went into that country," says Cantalupo.

Nowhere is McDonald's long-term view being tested more thoroughly than in Russia. George Cohon, president and CEO at the time and now senior chairman of McDonald's Restaurants of Canada, first broached the subject to then-Soviet officials during the Montreal Olympics. Years of talks with a multitude of Soviet agencies ultimately led to a 1988 agreement to construct up to twenty McDonald's restaurants in Moscow. And finally, the entire world watched in awe as more than thirty thousand people lined up on a cold winter day—many of them arriving hours early—to visit the 23,681-square-foot McDonald's on Pushkin Square when it opened on January 31, 1990, the most customers a restaurant had ever served in a single day. The crew of eleven hundred was soon serving between forty and fifty thousand people each day. The Moscow restaurant served fifteen million people in its first year of operation—a number the average U.S. restaurant takes thirty years to achieve. To put that level of business in perspective, consider that in a typical month, the restaurant serves 487,000 orders of fries, 477,000 soft drinks, 390,000 milk shakes, 330,000 Big Macs, and 227,000 apple pies.

Nobody knew when the Moscow restaurant opened that the Communist system would soon collapse, that the Soviet Union would break up, or that severe food shortages would sweep the country. Through all of that, the Moscow McDonald's continued to serve its customers, even as the world watched Boris Yeltsin defy the abortive coup attempt that ultimately led to the fall of the Soviet government. As a "rubles only" restaurant, McDonald's was one of the few foreign businesses in Moscow that accepted local currency, which greatly increased the value to customers of the food it sold. "The primary fact is that it doesn't matter how long the line is, the people know there will be hamburgers and fries and shakes for them when they get to the counter," says Marc Winer, general director of the Moscow McDonald's joint venture between McDonald's Restaurants of Canada Limited and Mosrestaurantservice, the Food Service Administration of the Moscow City Council. "I don't think people wonder about where we get our food. They know that's the way McDonald's operates, and I think it gives them hope and confidence that they can someday achieve the same kind of reliability themselves."

But securing a reliable supply of food to make sure there is always food available at the counter is a major challenge. To meet the unrelenting demand, McDonald's built a $45 million food-processing facility in the Solntsevo region of Moscow, one of the most modern food-processing facilities in Europe and the only McDonald's-owned food-processing plant in the world (the rest of the system still purchases from independent suppliers). Raw ingredients are purchased from more than forty-five Russian Federation suppliers throughout several of the republics. McDonald's also imported seeds and agricultural equipment so that the necessary crops—such as the Russet Burbank potatoes needed for McDonald's fries—could be locally grown and harvested. And while the economic and political turmoil in Russia itself has delayed McDonald's plans for rapid expansion throughout the federation, the company has few second thoughts about the decision. Greenberg looks at it almost like a research-and-development effort. "We're making an investment in a marketplace of three hundred million people, and we know the pay-off is a long way off," says Greenberg. "But it's an investment in our future."

"No one thought it was going to be easy when we went into Moscow, and it turned out that it wasn't," adds Cantalupo. "Our entry into the market was a very opportunistic move, and considering all we've had to deal with, it has been a remarkable accomplishment. We are in there for the long term, it's a large potential market, and our position is only enhanced because we're already there. We see the same kind of potential in China. Today, perhaps there might only be one hundred and fifty million Chinese who can afford us, but by the time we reach all of them, there will be another hundred and fifty million who will be able to."

McDonald's opening in Beijing on April 23, 1991 shattered the opening day record that had been set in Moscow, attracting some forty thousand customers to the twenty-eight-thousand-square-foot restaurant which featured twenty-nine cash registers to handle the flow. Located on the corner of Wangfujing and Changanjie in the city's busiest shopping district, the restaurant has about eight hundred thousand pedestrians passing by daily.

The joint venture partnership between McDonald's and the General Corporation of Beijing Agriculture, Industry, and Commerce

(BAIC) had been working for five years to establish a network of local farmers, manufacturers, and other suppliers to support not only the Beijing restaurant but the new units opening in other Chinese cities. When Beijing opened, 95 percent of the products were supplied locally, including beef, chicken, fish, potatoes, lettuce, and various beverages. The potential in a market of 1.2 billion people is unlimited; indeed, to give the same coverage to China as McDonald's has in the United States, assuming the Chinese market develops effectively, would require an estimated twenty-four thousand restaurants.

Cantalupo points out that it is a great advantage to McDonald's that it can test the waters in a new country with a relatively modest investment. "We can go in with just one restaurant to test a market from a cultural standpoint, to judge local acceptance, and to determine growth rates," he says, quickly adding that today, most new country restaurants begin making profits in the first year. "The point is, long past the turn of the century, countries like China, Russia, and Indonesia are going to be providing great growth opportunities for incremental sales and earnings," he says.

While these headline events punctuated McDonald's international growth, the development of its infrastructure throughout the world promises even more dramatic results in the future. "We've become much more global in the way we operate," says Cantalupo. "We're acting more and more concertedly as a worldwide system, which we never used to do when each country was responsible for setting up their own supply lines." The purchasing power of McDonald's fourteen thousand-plus store system and the economies of scale it has now achieved have allowed the system to leverage its resources as never before in what Cantalupo terms "global purchasing." This worldwide leveraging saved the McDonald's system $20 million in 1992 and $70 million in 1993.

Today, for example, new restaurants throughout Europe feature tabletops from Belgium; chairs and floor and wall tiles from Italy; doors from Austria; lighting systems from The Netherlands; and heating, ventilation, and air-conditioning systems from the United States—all utilizing low-cost, quality suppliers. As a result, the total cost of building and opening a new McDonald's restaurant in Europe has been cut significantly.

In addition, while most restaurants will continue to be supplied locally, McDonald's is increasingly taking advantage of its worldwide scope to purchase supplies more effectively. "We look for quality suppliers to meet our specifications at the least cost, whether they are in the United States or Kuala Lumpur," says Cantalupo. Today, New Zealand cheese is flown to South America, while beef from Uruguay is distributed in Malaysia, and Malaysian packaging is shipped throughout Asia. The United States supplies potatoes for Hong Kong and Japan, all the sesame seeds in McDonald's buns are produced in Mexico, Australia ships beef products to Japan, and all the pie mix and crust materials used by the system are produced by a single supplier in the United States. And the company is able to get around currency problems by barter arrangements, such as Russia shipping pies to Germany in return for packaging, lobby trays, and cleaning materials.

"Our biggest challenge in most of the countries we go into is to have menu prices that can tap the broad population," says Cantalupo. "So as we develop a truly global purchasing infrastructure, we can ensure ourselves a position as the low-cost producer in all of the countries we operate in. The next couple of decades are going to be extremely exciting as we see our global system grow and mature." Near term, he sees countries like Taiwan, Spain, Italy, and Hong Kong (combined with China) with the potential to become major contributors to the system, while Western Europe, with only seventeen hundred restaurants serving some 330 million people continues to have great potential. Brazil, Mexico, Indonesia, and the Eastern European countries are beginning to develop the infrastructure needed to support good long-term growth. And Cantalupo looks longingly at virtually untapped markets like India, Africa, and the Middle East as targets for the next century.

"We really have no limit," he says. "By the turn of the century, I hope to have a Big Fifteen established, with another Big Fifteen coming in right behind—and we certainly have the potential to be opening fifteen hundred new restaurants a year one of these days."

Despite the rapid changes in the way it does business, one principle has remained constant at McDonald's over the years: its commitment to good corporate citizenship. "People didn't realize that what we do in community relations in the United States could also be effective in our new international markets," says Golin. "But the fact that Ronald McDonald Houses are opening around the world and more and more people want to get involved says a lot about the importance of these programs."

The company's philosophy of giving something back to the com-

munities in which it does business has been highlighted by the growth
of Ronald McDonald's Children Charities (RMCC)—founded in memory of Ray Kroc in 1984—and by the continued expansion of the
Ronald McDonald House program. "RMCC is just now emerging as a
major organization—one of largest organizations financially devoted
to the welfare of children—and it will only get bigger and bigger," says
Lubin. "No one else has the tremendous fund-raising abilities and the
ability to do things for the benefit of children." RMCC has issued seventeen hundred grants totaling more than $100 million to hundreds of
organizations serving children to develop and support programs in the
areas of health care and medical research, specially designed rehabili-
tation facilities, and special youth education programs. And there are
162 Ronald McDonald Houses in the U.S. and eleven other countries
throughout the world.

Lubin points out that RMCC has reached the point where it no
longer has to rely on reacting to requests, "but can actively seek out
constructive projects it can take on." Looking forward, Quinlan thinks
that the RMCC efforts to date have merely scratched the surface of what
can be accomplished. "It's a great program, carried out in Ray's memory, and we're getting better at it," says Quinlan. "But as our efforts
become more integrated, the RMCC effort will only get bigger—in fact,
I hope to see the day when the foundation is actually endowed. It may
be a pipe dream, but we would need one hundred twenty to one
hundred forty million dollars to support the twelve to fifteen million
dollars in annual grants that we are awarding today."

McDonald's continued to set the pace for large corporations
through its McJobs employment program to assist mentally and physically challenged individuals; the McMasters program for recruiting,
training, and retaining of people aged fifty-five and over; and through
its Diversity Development programs, which apply not only to corporate
employees but to franchisees as well. Rensi notes that McDonald's has
become the primary entry-level job trainer in the United States, a role
that used to be filled by the armed forces. "McDonald's today is a
reflection of America," says Rensi.

The company's franchisees represent the largest group of minority
entrepreneurs in the country, and 60 percent of those in training to be
new franchisees are minorities and women. Lubin, pointing out that
the company's involvement in litigation within its family has shrunk
dramatically compared with the contentious 1970s, says the focus has
always been on trying to do what's fair from the very beginning. "The

company has been willing to stand up for its policies when principles are at stake because it's made the effort to be fair from the first," says Lubin. "In most franchising communities, there's more tension, but McDonald's has managed to preserve more of the family feeling."

As one of the largest employers of young people, McDonald's continues to be active in education issues at both the national and local levels, believing that education is the number one priority for its student employees. In addition to supporting the development of educational curriculum and support programs on a national level, its franchisees and managers work with schools to address critical issues such as literacy, drop-out prevention, and substance abuse through local mentoring, incentive, and tutorial programs.

And the corporate commitment to good citizenship continues to be reflected on the local level by owner/operators who support their business efforts by being active, contributing members of their local communities. One of the most visible demonstrations of how much the company cares for the communities in which it does business comes in times of emergencies and natural disasters, like the Florida and Hawaii hurricanes of 1992, the Midwest floods of 1993, and the Los Angeles earthquakes of 1994. Through its partnership with the American Red Cross, McDonald's not only provides assistance to victims but also supplies food and other resources to the professionals and volunteers who help communities recover from natural disasters. And just being there, open for business as usual, is reassuring. As Red Cross worker Harvey Oswald said after the L.A. earthquakes, "Children are disoriented during a major crisis, and seeing McDonald's helps them begin to feel that things are getting back to normal."

The effectiveness of this commitment was borne out dramatically during the Los Angeles riots in April 1992, when McDonald's was barely affected by the looting, arson, and vandalism that caused an estimated $2 billion in damage to the other businesses in the area. McDonald's restaurants were back open for business shortly after the curfew was lifted, serving both emergency personnel and citizens of the burned out areas. Here's how *Time* magazine described it: "When the smoke cleared after mobs burned through South Central Los Angeles, hundreds of businesses, many of them black owned, had been destroyed. Yet not a single McDonald's restaurant had been torched. . . . The Los Angeles experience was vindication of enlightened social policies begun more than three decades ago. . . . As a result, McDonald's stands out not only as one of the more socially responsible companies in America, but also as one of the nation's truly effective social engineers." Rensi added that good policies had to be implemented by the company and its owner-operators. "To the rest of the world, it was nothing short of a miracle," he says. "But this miracle wasn't magic—it was manufactured by years and years of commitment to our communities and service to our customers."

Having turned McDonald's ship of state around, Quinlan looks to the future with unbridled optimism, chuckling at the idea of any near-term limitations on McDonald's. "Those of us who have grown up with the company through the years have been through a number of cycles," he says, noting that the magnitude of change might have been the major surprise in this particular cycle.

"We'd been riding a horse that had won a lot of races, so a lot of people were upset that we had to get off that particular horse," Quinlan says. "But I'm glad it happened sooner rather than later, because it gave us the chance to stop and effect true, significant change in all aspects of our business. Now we have a whole stable of new horses that we're riding."

Quinlan downplays significant diversification so long as there continues to be so much potential for McDonald's in its existing business. "There's more than enough to keep us busy as we explore McDonald's to the best of our ability," says Quinlan. "Our international potential is obvious, but we have a tremendous opportunity for incremental sales and profit growth in the United States as well, through one hundred percent customer satisfaction, continued menu development, emphasis on specific parts of the day, and utilization of new and creative locations where we can deliver the McDonald's experience to our customers."

Lubin notes that the implications of McDonald's International's potential for continued growth are just beginning to be realized. "We are a major global player," he says. "This provides not only continued growth opportunities for the company but new growth opportunities for individuals within the company as well."

Quinlan sees the future in terms of executing the company's value and customer care strategies so well that the system opens a gap between itself and the competition that is impossible to overtake. "My goal for the year 2000 is for us to be able to look at McDonald's and see that we are firmly entrenched as the leader in all facets of our business and that our prospects for the new century are just as bright and promising as they are today. I want us to be able to say that in the quick-service restaurant business, there's McDonald's and then there's everyone else. If we can stand apart as the class act of the industry in satisfying our customers, we'll reach all our financial goals automatically.

"In that sense, I don't think this serves as the conclusion of the McDonald's story, not by any means—because our best years are still ahead of us," Quinlan adds. "This is not an epilogue, it's really just the prologue."

Index